OPEN SOURCE DEVELOPMENT, COMMUNITIES AND QUALITY

IFIP – The International Federation for Information Processing

IFIP was founded in 1960 under the auspices of UNESCO, following the First World Computer Congress held in Paris the previous year. An umbrella organization for societies working in information processing, IFIP's aim is two-fold: to support information processing within its member countries and to encourage technology transfer to developing nations. As its mission statement clearly states,

> *IFIP's mission is to be the leading, truly international, apolitical organization which encourages and assists in the development, exploitation and application of information technology for the benefit of all people.*

IFIP is a non-profitmaking organization, run almost solely by 2500 volunteers. It operates through a number of technical committees, which organize events and publications. IFIP's events range from an international congress to local seminars, but the most important are:

- The IFIP World Computer Congress, held every second year;
- Open conferences;
- Working conferences.

The flagship event is the IFIP World Computer Congress, at which both invited and contributed papers are presented. Contributed papers are rigorously refereed and the rejection rate is high.

As with the Congress, participation in the open conferences is open to all and papers may be invited or submitted. Again, submitted papers are stringently refereed.

The working conferences are structured differently. They are usually run by a working group and attendance is small and by invitation only. Their purpose is to create an atmosphere conducive to innovation and development. Refereeing is less rigorous and papers are subjected to extensive group discussion.

Publications arising from IFIP events vary. The papers presented at the IFIP World Computer Congress and at open conferences are published as conference proceedings, while the results of the working conferences are often published as collections of selected and edited papers.

Any national society whose primary activity is in information may apply to become a full member of IFIP, although full membership is restricted to one society per country. Full members are entitled to vote at the annual General Assembly, National societies preferring a less committed involvement may apply for associate or corresponding membership. Associate members enjoy the same benefits as full members, but without voting rights. Corresponding members are not represented in IFIP bodies. Affiliated membership is open to non-national societies, and individual and honorary membership schemes are also offered.

OPEN SOURCE DEVELOPMENT, COMMUNITIES AND QUALITY

IFIP 20th World Computer Congress,
Working Group 2.3 on Open Source Software,
September 7-10, 2008, Milano, Italy

Edited by

Barbara Russo
Free University of Bolzano-Bozen
Italy

Ernesto Damiani
University of Milano-Bicocca
Italy

Scott Hissam
Carnegie Mellon Software
Engineering Institute
USA

Björn Lundell
University of Skövde
Sweden

Giancarlo Succi
Free University of Bolzano-Bozen
Italy

Springer

Open Source Development, Communities and Quality

Edited by Barbara Russo, Ernesto Damiani, Scott Hissam, Björn Lundell and Giancarlo Succi

p. cm. (IFIP International Federation for Information Processing, a Springer Series in Computer Science)

ISSN: 1571-5736 / 1861-2288 (Internet)

ISBN 978-1-4419-3516-8 ISBN 978-0-387-09684-1 (eBook)

Printed on acid-free paper

9 8 7 6 5 4 3 2 1

springer.com

IFIP 2008 World Computer Congress (WCC'08)

Message from the Chairs

Every two years, the International Federation for Information Processing hosts a major event which showcases the scientific endeavours of its over one hundred Technical Committees and Working Groups. 2008 sees the 20th World Computer Congress (WCC 2008) take place for the first time in Italy, in Milan from 7-10 September 2008, at the MIC - Milano Convention Centre. The Congress is hosted by the Italian Computer Society, AICA, under the chairmanship of Giulio Occhini.

The Congress runs as a federation of co-located conferences offered by the different IFIP bodies, under the chairmanship of the scientific chair, Judith Bishop. For this Congress, we have a larger than usual number of thirteen conferences, ranging from Theoretical Computer Science, to Open Source Systems, to Entertainment Computing. Some of these are established conferences that run each year and some represent new, breaking areas of computing. Each conference had a call for papers, an International Programme Committee of experts and a thorough peer reviewed process. The Congress received 661 papers for the thirteen conferences, and selected 375 from those representing an acceptance rate of 56% (averaged over all conferences).

An innovative feature of WCC 2008 is the setting aside of two hours each day for cross-sessions relating to the integration of business and research, featuring the use of IT in Italian industry, sport, fashion and so on. This part is organized by Ivo De Lotto. The Congress will be opened by representatives from government bodies and Societies associated with IT in Italy.

This volume is one of fourteen volumes associated with the scientific conferences and the industry sessions. Each covers a specific topic and separately or together they form a valuable record of the state of computing research in the world in 2008. Each volume was prepared for publication in the Springer IFIP Series by the conference's volume editors. The overall Chair for all the volumes published for the Congress is John Impagliazzo.

For full details on the Congress, refer to the webpage http://www.wcc2008.org.

Judith Bishop, South Africa, Co-Chair, International Program Committee
Ivo De Lotto, Italy, Co-Chair, International Program Committee
Giulio Occhini, Italy, Chair, Organizing Committee
John Impagliazzo, United States, Publications Chair

WCC 2008 Scientific Conferences

TC12	AI	Artificial Intelligence 2008
TC10	BICC	Biologically Inspired Cooperative Computing
WG 5.4	CAI	Computer-Aided Innovation (Topical Session)
WG 10.2	DIPES	Distributed and Parallel Embedded Systems
TC14	ECS	Entertainment Computing Symposium
TC3	ED_L2L	Learning to Live in the Knowledge Society
WG 9.7 TC3	HCE3	History of Computing and Education 3
TC13	HCI	Human Computer Interaction
TC8	ISREP	Information Systems Research, Education and Practice
WG 12.6	KMIA	Knowledge Management in Action
TC2 WG 2.13	OSS	Open Source Systems
TC11	IFIP SEC	Information Security Conference
TC1	TCS	Theoretical Computer Science

IFIP

- is the leading multinational, apolitical organization in Information and Communications Technologies and Sciences
- is recognized by United Nations and other world bodies
- represents IT Societies from 56 countries or regions, covering all 5 continents with a total membership of over half a million
- links more than 3500 scientists from Academia and Industry, organized in more than 101 Working Groups reporting to 13 Technical Committees
- sponsors 100 conferences yearly providing unparalleled coverage from theoretical informatics to the relationship between informatics and society including hardware and software technologies, and networked information systems

Details of the IFIP Technical Committees and Working Groups can be found on the website at http://www.ifip.org.

Contents

Part I Full Papers

Part II Short Papers

Part IV Posters and Demonstrations

Preface

We are very pleased to introduce *Open Source Development, Communities and Quality.* The *International Conference on Open Source Systems* has come to its fourth edition – OSS 2008. Now, Free, Libre, and Open Source software is by all means now one of the most relevant subjects of study in several disciplines, ranging from information technology to social sciences and including also law, business, and political sciences. There are several conference tracks devoted to open source software with several publications appearing in high quality journals and magazines.

OSS 2008 has been organized with the purpose of being **the** reference venue for those working in this area, being the most prominent conference in this area. For this reason OSS 2008 has been located within the frameworks of the 20th World Computer Congress, WCC 2008, in Milan, the largest event of IFIP in 2008.

We believe that this conference series, and the IFIP working group it represents, can play an important role in meeting these challenges, and hope that this book will become a valuable contribution to the open source body of research.

The response of the research community has exceeded our expectations. A significant number of high-quality submission from all parts of the world were carefully peer-reviewed; in the end, 19 papers are published here as full papers (Part I) and 20 published in a condensed form as short papers (Part II). Additionally, 3 submissions presented their work in posters and demonstrations form for discussion at the conference (Part IV). Complementing the paper program, we are pleased to include the description of a panel (Part III) as an engaging and important part of the conference event. In addition to this there are three outstanding keynotes tackling three orthogonal perspectives: the use of Open Source to build a successful business; its adoption in public administration to promote savings, transparency and inclusion; the research done in this area by large public-private consortiums.

Altogether, we believe that this work is an essential milestone in the understanding of OSS and we are confident that the readers of this volume will find it useful and also enjoyable.

About IFIP WG 2.13

The OSS2008 Conference is the fourth conference in this very successful series of conferences on the open source topic. The IFIP Working Group 2.13 on Open Source Software was founded to further consolidate the discipline and to ensure a continuing and professional conference series with an established publisher, and to establish a conference series that would move around the world over time. Proposals for a number of conferences for the next few years have already been received, and anyone who would like to propose a conference theme and venue should come to the next conference and present a formal proposal.

The Working Group has 27 founding members from Europe, North America, Middle East, Asia /Pacific and Africa. The main objective of the Working Group is to enable the diverse community of free, libre and open source software (OSS) researchers and practitioners to rigorously investigate the technology, work practices, development processes, community dynamics within OSS systems, complementing appropriately other IFIP Working Groups where OSS is increasingly relevant. The scope of the Working Group is detailed on the website[1] which is being maintained by Kevin Crowston. Last, becoming a member of the Working Group is open to anyone attending at least two IFIP WG 2.13 meetings. We hope you will join us.

Since the group has been founded, the have been several exciting developments in which group members have been centrally involved. Ongoing projects in which the Working Group's members are central include the following:

- *COSI*[2] focusing on transferring the lessons of open source and agile methods to traditional in-house development;
- *FOSSRRI*[3] designing a global research infrastructure for FLOSS researchers and developers for access to data, artifacts, analyses, and published studies drawn from multi-project FLOSS repositories such as FLOSSmole[4], the SourceForge Research Data Archive at Notre Dame[5], and Google Code[6];
- *OPAALS* (www.opaals.org) seeking to build a sustainable interdisciplinary research community in the area of digital ecosystems;
- *QualiPSo*[7] studying the quality and trust aspects of Open Source Software and its adoption in the main stream industrial process - in the framework of QualiPSo several competence centers on Open Source are being created around the world;
- *Open Code, Content and Commerce (O3C) Business models*, a three-year investigation of open innovation and value-creation strategies

[1] http://www.ifipwg213.org
[2] www.itea-cosi.org
[3] fossrri.rotterdam.ics.uci.edu
[4] ossmole.sourceforge.net
[5] zerlot.cse.nd.edu
[6] google.com/code
[7] www.qualipso.org

IFIP WG 2.13 OFFICERS

General Chair:	Brian Fitzgerald, Lero, University of Limerick, Ireland
Vice-Chair:	Walt Scacchi, University of California atIrvine, US
Vice-Chair:	Giancarlo Succi, Free University of Bolzano-Bozen, Italy
Secretary:	Ernesto Damiani, University of Milan, Italy

Acknowledgements

We gratefully acknowledge the contributions made by the other OSS 2008 Conference officials: Stefano De Panfilis (Workshop Chair), Alberto Colombo (Workshop Co-Chair and Web Master), and Fulvio Frati (Workshop Co-Chair and Web Master). Special thanks go to Arie Gurfinkel as LaTeX wizard for his aid in preparing this volume. We would like to thank the OSS 2008 international program committee and all the local volunteer organizers and supporters, without whom this conference could not take place. Finally, we thank all the authors, panelists, and workshop organizers who provided this years conference with such an excellent program.

Barbara Russo (Track Chair)[8]
Ernesto Damiani (General Co-Chair)[9]
Scott Hissam (Track Chair)[10]
Björn Lundell (Track-Chair)[11]
Giancarlo Succi (General Co-Chair)[12]

Milan, Italy
September 2008

[8] Free University of Bolzano-Bozen, Italy
[9] University of Milan, Italy
[10] Carnegie Mellon Software Engineering Institute, Pittsburgh, USA
[11] University of Skövde, Sweden
[12] Free University of Bolzano-Bozen, Italy

OSS 2008 Conference Organization

Conference Officials

General Chairs:	Ernesto Damiani	University of Milan, Italy
	Giancarlo Succi	Free University of Bolzano-Bozen, Italy
Track Chairs:	Barbara Russo	Free University of Bolzano-Bozen, Italy
	Scott A. Hissam	Carnegie Mellon Software Engineering Institute, Pittsburgh, USA
	Björn Lundell	University of Skövde, Sweden
Workshop Chair:	Stefano De Panfilis	Engineering Ingeneria Informatica, Italy
Workshop co-Chairs and Web Masters:	Alberto Colombo	University of Milan, Italy
	Fulvio Frati	University of Milan, Italy

Program Committee

Pär J. Ågerfalk
Uppsala University, Sweden

Olivier Berger
Dept. INF - Institut National des Télécommunications, France

Gerry Coleman
Dundalk Institute of Technology, Ireland

Kieran Conboy
National University of Ireland, Galway, Ireland

Kevin Crowston
Syracuse University, USA

Jean-Michel Dalle
University Pierre-et-Marie-Curie, Paris, France

Paul A. David
Stanford/Oxford University, USA/UK

Stefano De Panfilis
Engineering Ingegneria Informatica S.p.a, Italy

Gregory Lopez
Thales, France

Paul Malone
Waterford Institute of Technology, Ireland

Pentti Marttin
Nokia Siemens Networks, Finland

Catharina Melian
Stockholm School of Economics, Sweden

Martin Michlmayr
HP, Austria

Sandro Morasca
Università degli Studi dell'Insubria, Varese, Italy

John Noll
Santa Clara University, USA

Bülent Özel
Instanbul Bilgi University, Turkey

Francesco Di Cerbo
Free University of Bolzano-Bozen, Italy

Gabriella Dodero
Free University of Bolzano-Bozen, Italy

Mahmoud Elish
King Fahd University, Saudi Arabia

Joseph Feller
UCC, Ireland

Pat Finnegan
UCC, Ireland

Brian Fitzgerald
Lero, University of Limerick, Ireland

Rishab Aiyer Ghosh
MERIT Netherlands

Jesus Gonzalez-Barahona
Universidad Rey Juan Carlos, Spain

Jeremy Hayes
University College Cork, Ireland

Joseph Kiniry
University College Dublin, Ireland

Stefan Koch
University of Economics and BA, Austria

Derrick Kourie
University of Pretoria, South Africa

Jean Pierre Laisne
ObjectWeb, France

Stéphane Laurière
Mandriva, France

Witold Pedrycz
University of Alberta, Canada

Paolo Pumilia
EST, Italy

Walt Scacchi
University of California, Irvine, USA

Marco Scotto
Free University of Bolzano-Bozen, Italy

Barbara Scozzi
Politecnico di Bari, Italy

Alberto Sillitti
Free University of Bolzano-Bozen, Italy

Gregory Simmons
University of Ballarat, Australia

Sandra A. Slaughter
Georgia Institute of Technology, USA

Diomidis Spinellis
Athens University of Economics and Business, Greece

Frank van der Linden
Philips, The Netherlands

Tony Wasserman
Carnegie-Mellon West, USA

Charles Weinstock
Software Engineering Institute, USA

Hongbo Xu
South China University Of Technology, China

Board of Reviewers

Morkel Theunissen — University of Pretoria, South Africa

List of Contributors

Giovanni Acampora
University of Salerno, IT
gacampora@unisa.it

Paul Adams
Sirius Corporation Ltd., UK
paul.adams@siriusit.co.uk

Claudio Agostino Ardagna
University of Milan, IT
ardagna@dti.unimi.it

Marco Antonio Balieiro
Faculdade de Computação –
Universidade Federal do Pará BR
ma.balieiro@gmail.com

Massimo Banzi
Telecom italy, IT
massimo.banzi@telecomitalia.it

Andrea Bosin
Università degli Studi di Cagliari, IT
andrea.bosin@dsf.unica.it

Guido Bruno
Telecom italy, IT
guido.bruno@telecomitalia.it

Giovanni Caire
Telecom italy, IT
giovanni.caire@telecomitalia.it

Andrea Capiluppi
University of Lincoln, UK
acapiluppi@lincoln.ac.uk

Eugenio Capra
Politecnico di Milano, IT
eugenio.capra@polimi.it

Davide Dalle Carbonare
Engineering Ingegneria Informatica
S.p.A., IT
davide.dallecarbonare@eng.it

Alberto Colombo
University of Milan, IT
colombo@dti.unimi.it

Reidar Conradi
Norwegian University of Science and
Technology, NO
reidar.conradi@idi.ntnu.no

Alain Corbière
Le Mans University, FR
alain.corbiere@univ-lemans.fr

Kevin Crowston
Syracuse University, US
crowston@syr.edu

Jean-Michel Dalle
Université Pierre et Marie Curie, FR
jean-michel.dalle@upmc.fr

Ernesto Damiani
University of Milan, IT
damiani@dti.unimi.it

Vincenzo D'Andrea
University of Trento, IT
vincenzo.dandrea@dit.unitn.it

Adriaan de Groot
Sirius Corporation Ltd., UK
groot@kde.org

Stefano De Panfilis
Engineering Ingegneria Informatica, IT
stefano.depanfilis@eng.it

Stefano De Paoli
University of Trento, IT
stefano.depaoli@soc.unitn.it

Samuel De Sousa Júnior
Faculdade de Computaȩ –
Universidade Federal do ParąBR
sfelixjr@gmail.com

Cleidson De Souza
Faculdade de Computaȩ –
Universidade Federal do ParąBR
cdesouza@ufpa.br

Vieri del Bianco
University of Insubria, IT
vieri.delbianco@uninsubria.it

Matthijs den Besten
University of Oxford, UK
matthijs.denbesten@oerc.ox.ac.uk

Amit Deshpande
SAP Labs LLC, US
amit@amit-deshpande.com

Nicoletta Dessì
Universitàdegli Studi di Cagliari, IT
dessi@unica.it

Francesco Di Cerbo
Free University of Bolzano-Bozen, IT
francesco.dicerbo@unibz.it

Leonhard Dobusch
Free University of Berlin, DE
leonhard.dobusch@wiwiss.fu-berlin.de

Gabriella Dodero
Free University of Bolzano-Bozen, IT
gabriella.dodero@unibz.it

Nabil El Ioini
Free University of Bolzano-Bozen, IT
Nabil.ElIoini@stud-inf.unibz.it

Robert Feldt
Blekinge Institute of Technology, SE
rfd@bth.se

Joseph Feller
University College Cork, IE
JFeller@afis.ucc.ie

Rafael Fernández
Universidad Politénica de Madrid, ES

Brian Fitzgerald
University of Limerick, IE
Brian.Fitzgerald@ul.ie

Chiara Francalanci
Politecnico di Milano, IT
francala@elet.polimi.it

Fulvio Frati
University of Milan, IT
frati@dti.unimi.it

Maria Grazia Fugini
Politecnico di Milano, IT
fugini@elet.polimi.it

Loris Gaio
Universitàdi Trento, IT
lgaio@cs.unitn.it

Les Gasser
University of Illinois, US
gasser@uiuc.edu

Jaco Geldenhuys
Stellenbosch University, ZA
jacogeld@gmail.com

Pietro Giovannini
Free University of Bolzano-Bozen, IT
Pietro.Giovannini@stud-inf.unibz.it

Jesus M Gonzalez-Barahona
Universidad Rey Juan Carlos, ES
jgb@gsyc.escet.urjc.es

Tony Gorschek
Blekinge Institute of Technology, SE
tgo@bth.se

Georgios Gousios
Athens University of Economics and Business, GR
gousiosg@aueb.gr

Imed Hammouda
Tampere University of Technology, FI
imed.hammouda@tut.fi

Øyvind Hauge
Norwegian University of Science and Technology, NO
oyvind.hauge@idi.ntnu.no

Henrik Hedberg
University of Oulu, FI
henrik.hedberg@oulu.fi

Juan José Hierro
Telefóica Investigació y Desarrollo, ES
jhierro@tid.es

Scott Hissam
Carnegie Mellon
Software Engineering Institute, US
shissam@sei.cmu.edu

James Howison
Syracuse University, US
jhowison@syr.edu

Netta Iivari
University of Oulu, FI
netta.iivari@oulu.fi

Juha Järvensivu
Tampere University of Technology, FI
juha.jarvensivu@tut.fi

Yasutaka Kamei
Nara Institute of Science and Technology, JP
yasuta-k@is.naist.jp

Tanja Kirves
University of Oulu, FI
tanjakir@mail.student.oulu.fi

Stefan Koch
Vienna University of Economics and BA, AT
stefan.koch@wu-wien.ac.at

Luigi Lavazza
University of Insubria, IT
luigi.lavazza@uninsubria.it

Diego Liberati
IEIIT CNR c/o Politecnico di Milano, IT
liberati@elet.polimi.it

Juho Lindman
Helsinki School of Economics, FI
juho.lindman@hse.fi

Vincenzo Loia
University of Salerno, IT
loia@unisa.it

Crista Lopes
University of California, US
lopes@ics.uci.edu

Dario Lorenzi
Politecnico di Milano, IT
dario.lorenzi@polimi.it

Max Loubser
Oxford Internet Institute, UK
max.loubser@magd.ox.ac.uk

Björn Lundell
University of Skövde, SE
bjorn.lundell@his.se

Hirotaka Maeshima
Nara Institute of Science and Technology, JP
hirotaka-m@is.naist.jp

Magnus Mähring
Stockholm School of Economics, SE
magnus.mahring@hhs.se

Andrés Martínez
Universidad Rey Juan Carlos, ES
aleonar@gsyc.escet.urjc.es

Juan Martinez-Romo
E.T.S.I. Informatica (UNED), ES
juaner@lsi.uned.es

Pentti Marttiin
Nokia Siemens Networks, FI
pentti.marttiin@nsn.com

Héla Masmoudi
UniversitéPierre et Marie Curie, FR
masmoudi_hela@yahoo.fr

Ken-ichi Matsumoto
Nara Institute of Science and Technology, JP
matumoto@is.naist.jp

Shinsuke Matsumoto
Nara Institute of Science and Technology, JP
shinsuke-m@is.naist.jp

Aurelien Mayoue
TELECOM &Management SudParis, FR
aurelien.mayoue@int-edu.eu

Catharina Melian
Stockholm School of Economics, SE
catharina.melian@hhs.se

Francesco Merlo
Politecnico di Milano, IT
merlo@elet.polimi.it

Tommi Mikkonen
Tampere University of Technology, FI
tommi.mikkonen@tut.fi

Sandro Morasca
University of Insubria, IT
sandro.morasca@uninsubria.it

John Noll
Santa Clara University, US
jhnoll@gmail.com

Masao Ohira
Nara Institute of Science and Technology, JP
masao@is.naist.jp

Yoji Onishi
Nara Institute of Science and Technology, JP
yoji-o@is.naist.jp

Heikki Orsila
Tampere University of Technology, FI
heikki.orsila@tut.fi

Miguel A. Ortuño-Perez
Universidad Rey Juan Carlos, ES
mortuno@gsyc.escet.urjc.es

Barbara Pes
Università degli Studi di Cagliari, IT
pes@unica.it

Etiel Petrinja
University of Bolzano, IT
etiel.petrinja@unibz.it

Dijana Petrovska-Delacretaz
TELECOM & Management SudParis, FR
dijana.petrovska@int-edu.eu

Alvaro Polo
Universidad Rey Juan Carlos, ES
apoloval@gsyc.escet.urjc.es

Pascal Ravesteyn
University of Applied Science Utrecht, NL
pascal.ravesteijn@hu.nl

Marcos Reyes
Telefónica Investigación y Desarrollo, ES
mru@tid.es

Dirk Riehle
SAP Labs LLC, US
dirk@riehle.org

Gregorio Robles
Universidad Rey Juan Carlos, ES
grex@gsyc.escet.urjc.es

Alessandro Rossi
Università di Trento, IT
arossi@cs.unitn.it

Cristina Rossi
Politecnico di Milano, IT
cristina1.rossi@polimi.it

Matti Rossi
Helsinki School of Economics, FI
matti.rossi@hse.fi

Anna Ruokonen
Tampere University of Technology, FI
anna.ruokonen@tut.fi

Barbara Russo
Free University of Bolzano-Bozen, IT
Barbara.Russo@unibz.it

Ioannis Samoladas
Aristotle University of Thessaloniki, GR
ioansam@csd.auth.gr

Walt Scacchi
University of California, US
wscacchi@uci.edu

Nico Schellingerhout
Philips Medical Systems, NL
nico.schellingerhout@philips.com

Alberto Sillitti
University of Bolzano, IT
alberto.sillitti@unibz.it

Gilbert Silvius
University of Applied Science Utrecht, NL
gilbert.silvius@hu.nl

Susan Elliott Sim
University of California, US
ses@ics.uci.edu

Carl-Fredrik Sørensen
Norwegian University of Science and Technology, NO
carl.fredrik.sorensen@idi.ntnu.no

Javier Soriano
Universidad Politénica de Madrid, ES

Sulayman K. Sowe
Aristotle University of Thessaloniki, GR
sksowe@csd.auth.gr

Diomidis Spinellis
Athens University of Economics and Business, GR
dds@aueb.gr

Ioannis Stamelos
Aristotle University of Thessaloniki, GR
stamelos@csd.auth.gr

Volker Stix
Vienna University of Economics and BA, AT
volker.stix@wu-wien.ac.at

Giancarlo Succi
Free University of Bolzano-Bozen, IT
giancarlo.succi@unibz.it

Davide Taibi
University of Insubria, IT
davide.taibi@uninsubria.it

Romaric Tchokpon
Institut de Mathématiques et de Sciences Physiques, BJ
ricotchfr@yahoo.fr

Maurizio Teli
University of Trento, IT
maurizio.teli@soc.unitn.it

Richard Torkar
Blekinge Institute of Technology, SE
rto@bth.se

Medha Umarji
University of Maryland Baltimore County, US
medha1@umbc.edu

Anthony I. Wasserman
Carnegie Mellon West, US
tonyw@west.cmu.edu

Andrea Wiggins
Syracuse University, US
awiggins@syr.edu

A Framework for Evaluating Managerial Styles in Open Source Projects

Eugenio Capra[1] and Anthony I. Wasserman[2]
[1] Department of Electronics and Information, Politecnico di Milano, Piazza Leonardo da Vinci 32, 20133 Milano, Italy, eugenio.capra@polimi.it
[2] Center for Open Source Investigation, Carnegie Mellon West, Mountain View, CA 94035 USA, tonyw@west.cmu.edu

Abstract. This paper presents the Software Project Governance Framework (SPGF) for characterizing management of software projects, based on mechanisms used for communication and collaboration, the organizational structure of projects, and testing and quality assurance procedures. The framework was developed and validated from interviews and surveys with leaders of more than 70 commercial and community-based software projects, including both closed and open source projects.

Keywords: Management of OSS development; Working practices; Industry contribution; Community contribution

1 Introduction

Open source software and accompanying "open" development practices have had a major impact on the software industry. "Open" software development processes involve new managerial styles, governance and social models, working practices and communication techniques (cf. [1], [4], [5], [9], and [10]).

Open source products fall into two major categories, which we term "community" and "commercial". Community Open Source projects are led by a community of developers or stakeholders and are distributed under an approved open source license, e.g., GPL, BSD, or Apache. Companies or institutions may have a significant role in the governance of the project, and may contribute many of the resources needed for the ongoing development of the project, but there are few, if any, limitations on who may participate in the various aspects of the project. Development is done "in the open" so that anyone may have complete, no-cost access to the current state of the project. These projects, such as those sponsored by the Apache Software Foundation, have established policies for granting "commit rights" that allow individuals to modify the code base.

Commercial Open Source projects are led by a company, which has usually developed most or all of the code, and then sells subscriptions and services for the developed product. Commercial Open Source applications are very often distributed with a dual license scheme, one offering unrestricted use of the software (community version) and one intended for commercial use of the software. In some cases, the two

---

Please use the following format when citing this chapter:

Capra, E. and Wasserman, A.I., 2008, in IFIP International Federation for Information Processing, Volume 275; *Open Source Development, Communities and Quality*; Barbara Russo, Ernesto Damiani, Scott Hissam, Björn Lundell, Giancarlo Succi; (Boston: Springer), pp. 1–14.

versions of the software differ, with the commercial version including features that are not present in the unrestricted version. In that situation, the commercial version of the software typically includes some closed source code. Also, the license for the community version may not be an "approved", i.e., an OSI-listed, open source license.

These approaches are beginning to blend with traditional closed-source software development. Numerous companies offer both closed and open source products, and also participate in non-commercial open source projects. In many cases, companies have completely different policies for each type of project.

While open source is technically a licensing model, its impact on software development processes goes well beyond licensing. The open source phenomenon has had a global impact on the way organizations and individuals create, distribute, and use software, and has challenged the conventional wisdom of the software engineering and software business communities. For this reason, we have focused on managerial and governance approaches to open source projects with the primary goal of creating a framework to characterize these different managerial styles and to evaluate the "openness" of a software project (as opposed to the software itself). The resulting framework allows potential users of the project to identify well-managed projects and allows potential contributors to see if there is a good opportunity to participate in the project.

Governance theory has been applied to software development in a number of different approaches [6], and is defined as the complex process that is responsible for the control of project scope, progress, and continuous commitment of developers [8]. It would be very difficult to elaborate a framework able to encompass all the possible governance dimensions of a software project. We propose a governance framework that allows one to position a software project along the continuum between "fully open" and "fully closed" approach.

This paper is organized as follows: Section 2 gives a brief overview of the study we conducted to define the framework. Section 3 presents the framework with some quantitative and qualitative metrics to evaluate software projects along several dimensions. Section 4 describes some existing open source projects and discusses how they can be classified according to our framework as an example. Section 5 briefly discusses how the framework was applied to our sample. Finally, Section 6 gives preliminary conclusions and topics for further study.

2 Methodology

Our framework aims at positioning a software project along the continuum between fully open and fully closed governance practices. It was developed through preliminary empirical analysis based on individual face-to-face interviews with 25 project managers of major software projects along the continuum, including traditional closed source development projects (packaged software and software as a service), Commercial Open Source and Community Open Source projects. Project managers were asked which governance dimensions were most significant to measure the degree of openness of a software project. We identified four fundamental governance dimensions: contribution, project leadership, working practices, and testing. These dimensions were chosen since they were widely cited by the project managers, and since they had the highest ranking of all of the cited dimensions.

Subsequently, we refined and validated our framework through a continuing study of more than 70 software projects. We included projects from SourceForge.org, Apache.org, Tigris and Java.net that met the following criteria:

- Mature status (according to the classification provided by the repositories, when available, or to common sense for major projects);
- At least 2 administrators (committers);
- At least 2 developers or contributors.

We have focused on large and well-known projects, rather than those developed by small teams, because these projects had developed and evolved their managerial and governance approaches. Our goal was to identify the dimensions that best illustrate the continuum between open and closed governance approaches. Our research approach has been informal, aimed at identifying the key dimensions and differentiators among projects of varying age, size, diffusion and domain. Table 1 describes how these parameters vary across the sample.

Table 1 – Description of age, size and diffusion of the projects analyzed.

Variable	Minimum value	Average value	Maximum value
Age [year]	<1	8	30
Size [core developers]	10	100	1,000
Size [kSLOC]	40	1,000	6,000
Diffusion [downloads or users]	2	25,000	200,000

Data was collected through interviews with and surveys of key project personnel, namely community managers, QA managers, VPs of engineering, committers, and project leaders, with follow-up calls made as needed for clarification and consistency.

The interviews focused on the following topics:

- *Governance and organization:* Is the project more similar to a "benevolent dictatorship" or to a democracy? Is it self-organizing or centrally controlled?

What is the role of the internal community versus the external community? How many developers are paid?

- *Work practices and tools*: How is the right to commit code granted? How is code reviewed? How important is automated testing? How many management tasks and non-code-developing tasks are shared in the community?
- *Communication and social culture:* Which tools (cvs, bug tracking, IRC, wiki, etc.) are used? How frequent is face-to-face communication? How open are discussions? How is consensus reached?
- *Comparison between open and traditional projects:* How do closed and open projects differ in management practice? What are the relative advantages of open source development compared with traditional closed development?

The results of these interviews formed the basis for our framework, which we call the Software Project Governance Framework (SPGF). The methodology we adopted to formalize the evidence we gathered is based on three major steps. First, we identified and characterized two hypothetical projects representing the two extremes of the spectrum, i.e. a completely traditional closed software project and a completely open source community-based project (see also [3]). Second, we defined dimensions along which these projects can be evaluated, eventually selecting four dimensions that gave the most accurate picture of governance. Third, we scored each dimension of each project from 1 to 4, where 1 indicates a closed-style approach and 4 signifies an open-style approach. We show the detail of the scoring for each dimension below. Note that neither licensing nor the distribution model are part of the framework.

The SPGF framework provides a qualitative assessment of the degree of openness and, accordingly, scales are ordinal. Assessing governance by means of ratio variables not only is difficult, but may also be misleading [5], [11]. The SPGF framework is intended for comparing projects rather than providing absolute assessments. Moreover, the output of our framework may be employed within quantitative methodology according to the approach discussed by Briand et al. in [1].

We would also note that the interviews covered a wide range of topics, and our dimensions have been extracted as the most important factors to distinguish different approaches to project governance. Some of the interviews ranged beyond the specific issues of the framework and helped us to validate the overall approach.

3 The Framework

This section presents our framework. First, we characterize the properties of a completely closed and a completely open project. Then we describe the four dimensions at the base of the framework and provide a graphical representation methodology.

3.1 A traditional closed source project

A "traditional" software project is led by a company or an organization which strictly controls the development process. The proprietary code is closed and is developed by paid staff, possibly including contractors or outsourced teams. Most projects have a well-defined organizational structure following a development process aimed at producing a high quality product (or service) on a predictable schedule. Members of the team "meet" regularly, and report their progress through their organization's management structure.

Many companies have user groups, advisory boards, forums, and other ways for users to interact with the development team, but the final decisions are all made by the company, which has responsibility for all of the code and documentation. In general, the development team has its own communication mechanism, which is not open to outsiders.

The company does most of its own testing and fixes problems even before releasing a beta version to users. Many make their beta versions available to a broad community of users, providing mechanisms for reporting issues and problems in functionality, performance, installation, usability, stability, and/or security.

3.2 A completely open software project

At the opposite end of the spectrum are the thousands of Community Open Source projects, each with its own community, open to anyone who is interested in the project. The work is done entirely in the open, and is typically hosted in such repositories as SourceForge, Tigris.org, Apache Software Foundation, and Java.net. The software can be acquired and used by anyone, subject to the terms of the project's license agreement.

In an open source project, a project lead (or leadership group) is responsible for overall project management, such as determining when a version of the software is ready (stable version), selecting the license to be used with the software release, and deciding who can have "commit rights" to the code.

Some projects are very informal, without formal organization and governance bodies. Decisions are usually made by informally discussing issues within forums, mailing lists or IRC channels. Some communities may have a voting mechanism for resolving issues.

Project participation is open to all, independent of organizational affiliation. Many projects include both volunteers, who have another job and work on the project in their spare time, as well as people who are paid by companies to work on the project.

Since project participation is often a volunteer activity, the project leadership cannot easily compel someone to work on a specific task or to adhere to a schedule, as is the case in a commercial software project. Participants in these community-based projects rarely meet in person. Instead, they communicate by mechanisms such as forums, mailing lists, IRC channels, instant messaging systems, wikis, blogs, online shared task lists or similar devices. Each community relies on one or more of these tools according to its tradition and habits.

A Community Open Source project doesn't have formal testing or quality assurance processes, but instead relies upon individual developers to test their own code, and for community members to test the software and post issues (and possibly fixes) using the project's issue tracking system. Well-managed projects respond quickly to posted bugs, relying on individual committers to make any needed changes or enhancements to their code. While commercial projects control the number of releases and offer customer support for those releases, no comparable support mechanism is in place for community-based open source projects.

3.3 Dimensions of the SPGF

Using these typical approaches for project management, we defined the following dimensions along which software projects can be evaluated.

3.3.1 Contributions

This dimension measures the relative amount of voluntary code development. Most Commercial Open Source companies resemble proprietary software companies in their reliance on paid development.

In a community-based open source project, code is usually developed on a voluntary basis. However, contributors may be employed or hired by a company or an organization that wants to lead the project or to accomplish specific tasks (e.g., to implement a new feature or to fix a specific bug).

A significant difference between hired and voluntary developers is that the former have to follow the guidelines and deadlines imposed by their employers, whereas the latter are really free to work according to their will and inclination.

Table 2 provides a quantitative metric for this dimension.

Please note that we use the term *hired developer* rather than *employee* as a way to distinguish volunteers from people who receive regular compensation for their contributions to a software project. Whoever is the employer and whatever the form of contract, a person who is paid to develop an application will behave differently from a person who writes code in his spare time just for personal satisfaction. Some companies pay a nominal "bounty" to individuals for small contributions; we do not consider them to be hired developers.

We used 80% as a threshold since the percentage of code committed by volunteers on commercial projects is typically below 10%. In community-based projects, less than 50% of the code is developed by hired employees.

Table 2 – Evaluation of *contributions* dimension.

Value	Description
1	100% of the code is developed by hired developers
2	>80% of the code is developed by hired developers
3	>50% of the code is developed by hired developers
4	Most of the code is developed by volunteers

3.3.2 Project leadership

This dimension indicates the degree to which the leadership of a project is hierarchical. Commercial Open Source projects are led by a company, which usually defines a roadmap and sets schedules. Companies might also play a significant role in guiding and managing community projects. Some Community Open Source projects are indirectly governed by a predominant company, which defines the roadmap of the project and leverages the community to reach its goals. Communities may be led not only by a company, but also by a foundation or by an independent committee. Some projects are managed by a "benevolent dictator": participation and discussion are fostered, but final decisions are made by the project leader or an entrusted committee. The Linux Kernel project is an example this style of governance. On the other hand, fully open communities often lack a formal organization. Decisions are made by voting or by governance bodies which are directly elected by active contributors. Less formal communities adopt the *lazy consensus* approach, i.e., issues are discussed within forums and mailing lists and decisions are made when nobody has anything more to add.

It is very difficult to provide a quantitative metric to evaluate this dimension. For the cases we analyzed, we developed a qualitative scale, shown in Table 3.

Table 3 – Evaluation of *Project leadership* dimension.

Value	Description
1	Roadmap and development process are led by one company or organization which has a predominant leadership role, makes decisions and sets schedules.
2	Roadmap and development process are led by one company or organization. However, free discussion and participation to the governance of the project is fostered.
3	The community is ruled by some formal rules and principles. Decisions are made mainly by voting or by governance bodies directly elected by contributors.
4	The community completely lacks a formal organization and governance bodies. Decisions are made by informally discussing issues.

3.3.3 Working practices

This dimension indicates the degree to which the working and communication practices of a project are geographically distributed and virtual.

Proprietary software projects and many Commercial Open Source projects rely primarily on a closed community working for a single employer, often in close physical proximity. A Community Open Source project, by contrast, often has a geographically dispersed membership. With little funding to support physical meetings of the project team, these projects rely heavily on collaborative tools. Note that such tools may also be used by those in close proximity to each other.

Table 4 presents a qualitative scale for this dimension.

Table 4 – Evaluation of *working practices* dimension.

Value	Description
1	Developers work on the same site, communicate in traditional ways and have regular physical meetings.
2	Most developers work on the same site and have regular physical meetings, with some remote participants
3	The community is dispersed and most developers are remote. Some subsets of developers, however, work at the same location and meet regularly.
4	The community is widely dispersed and all the developers communicate through virtual tools. Physical meetings are totally absent or very rare (1-2 per year).

3.3.4 Testing

This dimension aims at describing the testing process, as well as the presence and role of a Quality Assurance department (or resources) within the project.

As noted in Section 3.1, commercial software development organizations typically have Quality Assurance departments that define formal test processes and are responsible for the quality of the application. A Quality Assurance department also defines quality standards, including those for contributions submitted for inclusion in the code base.

By contrast, Community Open Source projects rely on their own developers and their user community for testing, with relatively few formal processes or tools. In general, open source projects tend not to have specific QA roles, even though some open source projects have very strict pair reviewing rules that determine when new code or patches can be committed to the code base.

Table 5 provides a qualitative scale for this dimension. Please note that by "internally" we also mean testing done by the committers or the core developers of a project. The word "community" in this context refers to users or casual contributors.

Table 5 – Evaluation of *testing* dimension.

Value	Description
1	All the testing is controlled internally by specific QA roles. New versions of the application are released only after being thoroughly tested.
2	Most testing (>50%) is performed internally before new versions of the application are released. The user community is leveraged as a broader testing platform, for example by releasing beta versions and then collecting feedback and bug notifications.
3	Some testing (<=50%) is performed internally, but most of it is left to the community of users.
4	Testing is completely left to the community of users.

3.3.5 Graphical representation

We use a diamond graph to show where projects fall on the spectrum for each dimension. Figure 1 shows the extreme cases of a traditional closed source and a completely open software projects.

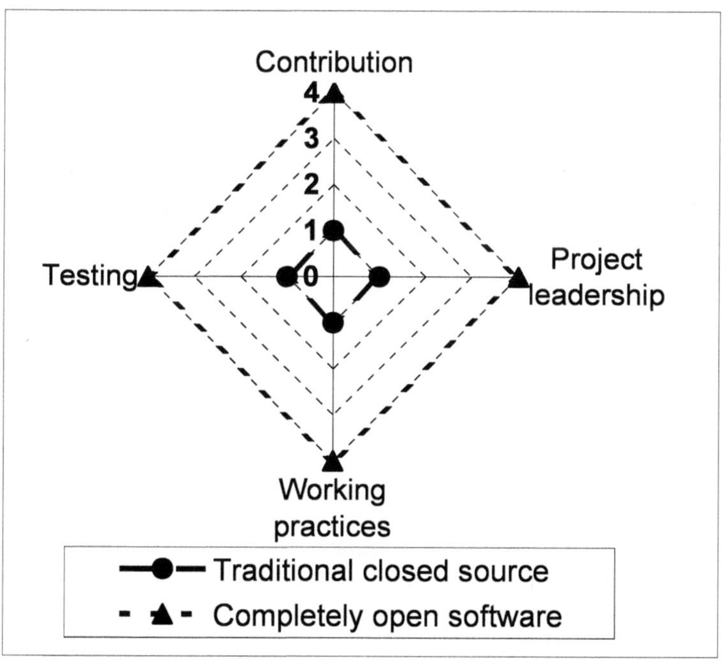

Fig. 1 – Graphical representation of project management dimensions.

4 Case Studies

In this section we provide some examples on how the SPGF may be applied to real projects. We apply the SPGF to three open source projects: OpenOffice.org, MySQL and SugarCRM. We chose these since they are well known applications, and show differences among the dimensions of the framework.

Figure 2 presents a graphical representation of the positioning of these projects. A first glance at the picture shows that OpenOffice.org and MySQL are closer to the completely open source approach, while SugarCRM is closer to closed software projects.

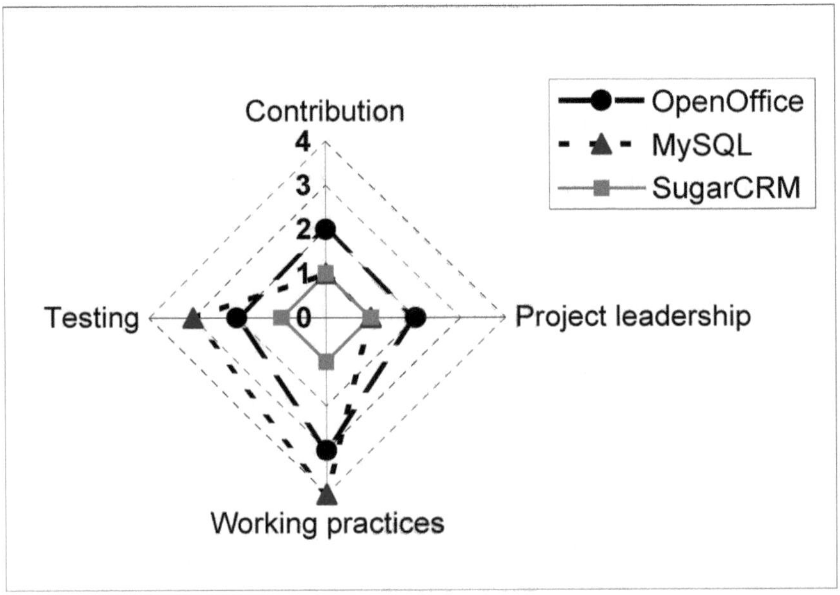

Fig. 2 – Graphical representation of the assessment of a project according to the framework.

4.1 OpenOffice

OpenOffice (OpenOffice.org) is a widely used open source office suite with more than 100 million downloads.

OpenOffice is quite a monolithic project. Although everybody can contribute to the project and can earn commit right, Sun Microsystems and IBM have historically contributed almost 90% of the code, paying more than 90 developers for their work. Other companies, such as RedHat and Novell, also contribute to the code. This accounts for the score 2 on *contribution* dimension.

The community has a very structured governance model, based on a Community Council and an Engineering Steering Committee. The Community Council is constituted by members of the community but is deeply influenced by Sun and IBM. The project has a clear and shared roadmap, which probably could not exist without a corporate structure in the background. All these factors lead to score 2 on the *project leadership* dimension.

Communication within the community mainly takes place on mailing lists and on IRC channels. However, most of Sun's developers work in Hamburg and meet daily. As a result, issues are often discussed in person and then conclusions are posted on mailing lists, so that remote community members can be informed. Moreover, occasional cross-corporation meetings are held several times a year. Consequently, *working practices* score 3.

OpenOffice began as StarOffice with Sun, and the QA team that worked on StarOffice now works on OpenOffice. There are currently about 550 QA members with *canconfirm* privilege, i.e. the ability to approve some feature before it is issued. In this particular aspect, OpenOffice is very similar to a traditional software house. Testing is also managed in a very structured way. Specific test suites have been written, integration and system testing are carried out regularly, daily smoke tests, regression testing and code coverage tools are adopted on a regular basis. Every developer is responsible for testing his code, but pair review is applied, too, and the QA team has to confirm the validity of new code. Feedback and bug notifications from users are also accepted and encouraged. This behavior accounts for score 2 on *testing* dimension.

4.2 MySQL

MySQL (www.MySQL.com) is distributed by MySQL, AB (now part of Sun Microsystems). Even though the code is open, it is mainly developed (99%) by employees of the company. The community is invited to submit new code, which is reviewed according to strict and documented internal standards before it is accepted. However, this is quite rare, given the size and complexity of the code base. This accounts for the score 1 on *contribution* dimension.

MySQL (the company) controls governance of the project. The corporate culture is very open to discussion, which is fostered by means of online communication tools, such as blogs, wikis, and forums, but MySQL, as a traditional software house, makes the final decisions. Thus, we assign a score of 1 to *project leadership* dimension.

The real value of the community is mainly to create a broad marketing platform and to provide extensive testing that augments the internal MySQL QA department. Functional tests and cross-platform tests are usually done by the internal development team, then QA tests the alpha versionusing their own scripts. Once the code is released, more than 50% of testing is left to the community, which also performs most of the integration tests. This combination of internal QA and external testing explains the scores 3 on the *testing* dimension.

Although MySQL is managed as a traditional company, many of its working practices resemble those of community projects. Developers are located in 26 countries around the world, and work from home, meeting only once or twice a year. They mainly communicate through asynchronous tools, such as highly specific internal IRC channels, shared task lists and e-mails, to overcome time zone differences. Telephone conference calls and video chats are also organized, but they are always combined with e-mails or forum posts. This accounts for the score of 4 on the *working practices* dimension.

4.3 SugarCRM

SugarCRM (www.SugarCRM.com) is another Commercial Open Source project. Similarly to MySQL, most of the code is open, but it is developed by internal employees only. The core application is centrally controlled by the company, while the community is involved in the creation of new projects, such as extensions and plug-ins, which are hosted on the SugarForge website. Consequently, the score for *contribution* and *project leadership* dimensions is the same as MySQL.

On the other hand, most of the developers work in the same location and have regular meetings. Forums and mailing lists are used, but by external community members rather than internal developers. VoIP phone conferences are frequent, but this happens even in very traditional closed source projects. Consequently, it scores 1 on the *working practices* dimension.

Most quality assurance and testing is performed by the internal QA department, which is also responsible for bug fixing. This accounts for score 1 on the *testing* dimension.

SugarCRM governance and managerial styles are actually very similar to those of a traditional closed software project, with the only exceptions that most of the code is open and that external people can contribute code.

5 Application of the Framework to the Sample

After defining the framework, we applied it to our sample of Community Open Source projects. Table 6 shows the distribution of the scoring of the projects in the sample along the four dimensions of the framework.

Table 6 – Distribution of SPGF scores across the sample.

Dimension x	x<3	3<=x<4	x=4
Contribution	43%	10%	47%
Project Leadership	30%	48%	22%
Working Practice	7%	37%	57%
Testing	33%	44%	15%

Most of the communities have some kind of organization and governance bodies, which control new contributions and part of the testing. In particular, the survey showed that approximately 50% of the code of the applications in the sample is developed by hired developers and that physical meeting are held in 35% of projects.

6 Conclusions and Future Work

The Software Project Governance Framework provides a consistent way to analyze projects based on their governance and managerial styles. The central idea behind the framework is that open source has a deep impact on the governance of a software project and, consequently, may impact its quality and costs. The empirical analyses we conducted allowed us to study and embrace a wide range of different software projects. The SPGF provides a structured methodology to analyze managerial and governance models, and to categorize these projects according to the dimensions that are regarded as the most significant by the project leaders. We think that the SPGF may enable a deeper comprehension of software projects and may be useful to a wide range of users.

First, it may be used by researchers to quickly assess and cluster projects. This allows one to select a homogenous sample of projects from a governance point of view before performing further surveys and analysis. We are working on a research project that seeks correlations between the SPGF dimensions and quality of design and development effort of a software project. Second, this framework is valuable to end users seeking information about the structure of various open source projects. For example, a company which is evaluating the adoption of an open source application may want to know and classify the governance approach behind the development of that application. Third, this framework may be used as a reference by developers and project leaders who want to position their products among the different typologies of open source projects and clearly present their managerial style to the public.

In the future, we are planning to further validate and potentially extend this framework. We will expand our sample through additional interviews and surveys, and also seek correlations between these dimensions and project success.

Acknowledgments

We are grateful to the project managers who provided data to us. For the projects identified in this paper, we specifically acknowledge the participation of Louis Suarez-Potts (OpenOffice), Kaj Arnö and Omer BarNir (MySQL), and Jacob Taylor (SugarCRM). We also thank Professor Chiara Francalanci and Francesco Merlo (Politecnico di Milano) for their support and advice.

References

[1] L.C. Briand, K. El Emam, and S. Morasca, "On the application of measurement theory in software engineering", Journal of Empirical Software Engineering, vol. 1, no. 1, pp. 61-88, 1996

[2] B. Fitzgerald, "The Transformation of Open Source Software, *MIS Quarterly,* vol. 30, no. 3, 2006.

[3] K. Fogel, "Producing Open Source Software", O'Reilly, Sebastopol (CA), 2006.

[4] G. Goth, "Open Source Business Models: Ready for Prime Tim", *IEEE Software,* Nov/Dec 2005, pp. 99-100.

[5] M. Griffiths. (2006, Oct. 5). Most software development metrics are misleading and counterproductive [Online]. Agile Journal, Available: http://www.agilejournal.com/content/view/107

[6] L.J. Kirsch, "The management of complex tasks in organizations: controlling the systems development process", *Organization Science,* vol. 7, no. 1, pp. 1-21, 1996.

[7] A. MacCormack, J. Rusnak, and C.Y. Baldwin, "Exploring the Structure of Complex Software Designs: An Empirical Study of Open Source and Proprietary Code", *Management Science* (forthcoming).

[8] P.S. Renz, *Project governance: implementing corporate governance and business ethics in nonprofit organizations,* Heidelber, Physica-Verl, 2007.

[9] S. Slaughter, J. Roberts, and I. Hann, "Communication Networks in an Open Source Software Project", *Proc. of 2nd Conference on Open Source Systems,* Italy, Jun 2006.

[10] S. Slaughter, J. Roberts, and I. Hann, "Motivations, Participation and Performance in Open Source Software Development", *Management Science*, (forthcoming).

[11] J. Sonnenfeld, "Good governance and the misleading myths of bad metrics", Academy of Management Executives, vol. 18, no. 1, pp. 108-113, 2004.

Forging A Community – Not: Experiences On Establishing An Open Source Project

Juha Järvensivu[1] and Tommi Mikkonen[1]
[1] Institute of Software Systems, Tampere University of Technology
Korkeakoulunkatu 1, FI-33720 Tampere, Finland
{juha.jarvensivu, tommi.mikkonen}@tut.fi

Abstract. Open source has recently become a practical and advocated fashion to develop, integrate, and license software. As a consequence, open source communities that commonly perform the development work are becoming important in the practice of software engineering. A community that is lively can often produce high-quality systems that continuously grow in terms of features, whereas communities that do not gain interest will inevitably perish. Despite their newly established central role, creation, organization, and management of such communities have not yet been widely studied from the viewpoint of software engineering practices. In this paper, we discuss experiences gained in the scope of Laika, an open source project established to develop an integrated software development environment for developing applications that run in Linux based mobile devices.

Keywords: Software engineering, open source community establishment

1 Introduction

Open source development has recently become a practical fashion to develop different types of software systems. This also affects commercial systems, where open source code can be used in tools, platforms, and general-purpose libraries, for instance. Also commercial systems that are largely based on open source components exist, as contrary to the common misbelief these are not contradicting concepts. A good example of such a system is Nokia 770 Internet Tablet, which is based on popular open source components.

Open source software development takes place in communities that developers participate to compose, maintain and further develop associated software. Then, the fashion such communities operate and how they are composed of becomes an important aspect for the future of the system as well as for its users.

Some the differences of open source and proprietary software have already been addressed (e.g. [6], [14]). However, there are little practical research results on several key questions related to communities as software developing entities. Such include

---

Please use the following format when citing this chapter:

Järvensivu, G. and Mikkonen, T., 2008, in IFIP International Federation for Information Processing, Volume 275; *Open Source Development, Communities and Quality*; Barbara Russo, Ernesto Damiani, Scott Hissam, Björn Lundell, Giancarlo Succi; (Boston: Springer), pp. 15–27.

how to organize a community in a meaningful and long-lasting fashion,

how to identify a community that is the most promising from others developing similar systems,

how to ensure that the results that a community has produced will be maintained and remain readily available in the future, even if it seems that like software development in general, also communities can be very person-dependent [1].

Moreover, life cycles of open source systems and communities maintaining them are rarely documented explicitly, although a lot of practical knowledge definitely exists among practitioners and the history of high-profile communities is definitely widely and well known.

The first step towards understanding community driven software development practices is to document and share experiences from establishing and maintaining an open source community. In this paper, we provide an overview to project Laika, which has developed an integrated development environment (IDE) based on Eclipse for Nokia Internet Tablet type of devices (N770, N800) running Linux. In the beginning, we were counting on the interest among developers working with the platform, as facilities that readily existed in this environment were not too sophisticated. At first, things looked promising. We were able to compose a fully functional version of the system, and gained a lot of outside interest and publicity. At present, we however face difficulties in supporting the new versions of both the platform and other programs that act as components in our system. The community has simply not been attractive enough for other developers to join, something we took for granted for long time during the project.

The rest of this paper presents our experiences structured as follows. Section 2 discusses our motivation and the target environment we had in mind when we started the project. Section 3 discusses the history of the project, and describes the phases that we have been able to identify in the progress. Section 4 forms the core of the paper by describing our experiences on the creation and maintenance of an open source community. Section 5 draws some final conclusions.

2 Target Environment

The open source project addressed in this paper, Laika, aims at the creation of an integrated development environment (IDE) for developing applications for embedded Linux devices. The particular devices we had in mind, Nokia N770 and N800 Internet Tablets, are based on the Maemo platform [15], and provide Internet browsing capabilities with a relatively large high-resolution touch screen.

The goal of our project was to integrate the work of several open source development projects into a single tool that is sophisticated enough for industry scale software development. When doing so, we planned to implement the necessary glue code ourselves, but rely on the effort of other communities for everything else.

In the beginning, we could readily find several open source projects whose output was valuable for Laika. Most importantly, we decided to build our project on

Maemo [15], Scratchbox [18], and Eclipse [4], which will be addressed in more detail in the following. In addition, we have used other components as well, although their role can be considered less important than that of the above projects. All open source components that are currently included in Laika are listed in Table 1.

Table 1. Component communities of Laika

Component	Description
CDT	C/C++ development environment for Eclipse, which served as a starting point for our development effort.
Eclipse	Vendor-neutral open development platform, whose plugin Laika is.
Glade/Gazpacho	Graphical user interface builder for GTK+.
Maemo	Development platform to create applications for the Nokia 770.
PyDev	Python development environment for the Eclipse platform.
Scratchbox	A cross-compilation toolkit used by the Maemo platform.

Maemo. Maemo, which acts as the software platform for Nokia's N770 and N800 Internet Tablet, is composed of a set of popular open source software components that are widely deployed in today's leading desktop Linux distributions [15]. Maemo consists of precompiled Linux kernel, platform libraries, and Hildon user interface framework. The Hildon UI framework in turn is based on GTK+, and as a whole the platform is binary compatible with GTK+ binaries [7]. The structure of the system is illustrated in Fig. 1, and illustrated components are introduced in more detail in Table 2.

Scratchbox. Currently available mobile devices based on Maemo run on ARM processor, whereas most developers prefer using an Intel-based computer like a PC as their development environment. The creation of ARM binaries with such development setup requires cross-compilation, where a host computer is used to compile software for a target that uses a different instruction set. In our case, we have performed cross-compilation using a PC running Scratchbox, which is a toolkit designed to ease embedded Linux application development [18]. The target platform is ARM, the hardware environment of our devices.

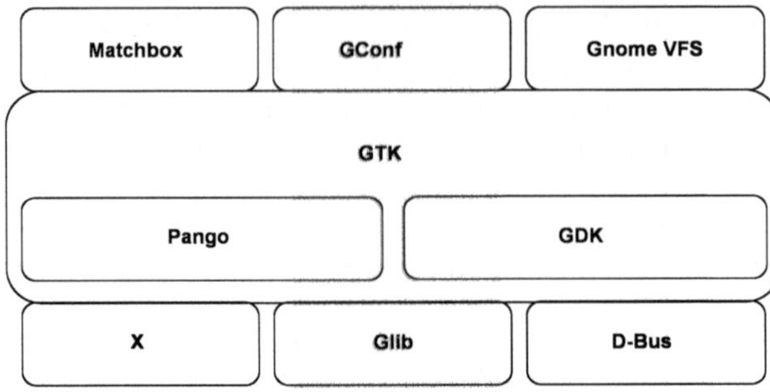

Fig. 1. Maemo's main software components

Table 2. Maemo's main software components

Component	Description
Matchbox	A light-weight window manager that is responsible for managing X11 client window geometry, stacking, and decorations in our target device.
GConf	A generic system for storing application preferences.
Gnome VFS	Gnome virtual file system, provides an abstraction layer for accessing files in both local file systems and the web.
GTK+	The Gimp toolkit, a toolkit for creating windowing applications. The kit also provides an extensive set of readily available widgets.
Pango	A library for text layout, rendering, and internationalization.
GDK	Gimp drawing kit, a graphics library that wraps routines providing low-level access to a display.
X	X Window System, a networking and display protocol for building windowing systems.
Glib	A low-level library that contains commonly needed generic routines for wrappers and runtime routines including event handling, dynamic loading, and threading.
D-Bux	Light-weight inter-process communication system.

Eclipse. The Eclipse platform is a vendor-neutral open development platform that provides tools for managing workspaces and building, debugging, and launching applications for building integrated development environments (IDEs) [4]. In essence, the Eclipse platform is a framework and toolkit that provides a foundation for running third-party development tools. The basic mechanism of extensibility in Eclipse is adding new plugins, which can also add new processing elements to plugins that already exist. In accordance to this architecture, the Laika plugin is based on the C/C++ development tools (CDT) plugin [3], which in turn is a subproject of the Eclipse community [4].

3 Short History of Project Laika

In this section, we describe the history of project Laika. The goal is to give an overview to the main events that the project has experienced, and how we have ended up in the current situation.

3.1 Becoming of Age

The origins of Laika are in meetings between Institute of Software Systems at Tampere University of Technology (TUT) and Nokia Multimedia (Nokia) during the Fall 2004, when the first Maemo based device was nearing completion. A common goal was set by both parties to aim at the development of an industry-strength integrated development environment that would encapsulate facilities necessary for Maemo development. The plan was that in the first phase, we would only implement minimal functionality, which could later be extended. The extensions would be made by either the original developers that were responsible for the first release, or by other parties that we would be able to attract to participate in the community. A related plan was that the experiment would also give the university first-hand information on how open source communities work.

As already documented in [9], the development was initiated by establishing a co-located team of students working as summer-time trainees within the premises provided by the university. Moreover, university already had existing server infrastructure that could be used for hosting the community and enabling download of Laika software. Thus, the initial investment was small, and the actual work could be started within a short period of time from the actual decision.

At the university, the project was supervised by a graduate student and a professor who had participated in meetings with Nokia. As a practical starting point, some code was provided to the community by Nokia Research Center, which had already investigated an opportunity to develop such an IDE [19]. This code then formed the baseline for further development that was carried out by the Laika community.

The first actual release of Laika was made towards the end of the summer of 2005, with the majority, if not all, the work performed by the summer trainees. At this point, the system simply comprised Eclipse, CDT, and Scratchbox, as well as some compilation and debugging capabilities that we felt were important for the project. The system is illustrated in Fig. 2.

The 1st release proved that there indeed was a need for an IDE for Maemo, and that Laika was really something that people found useful, at least based on the number of download and the feedback received from people installing and using the system. A total of 603 downloads were made during the time version 1.0 (and bug fix version 1.1 that was released a week later) was available for download. A number of downloads were from private companies that were doing industrial-scale development in Maemo environment.

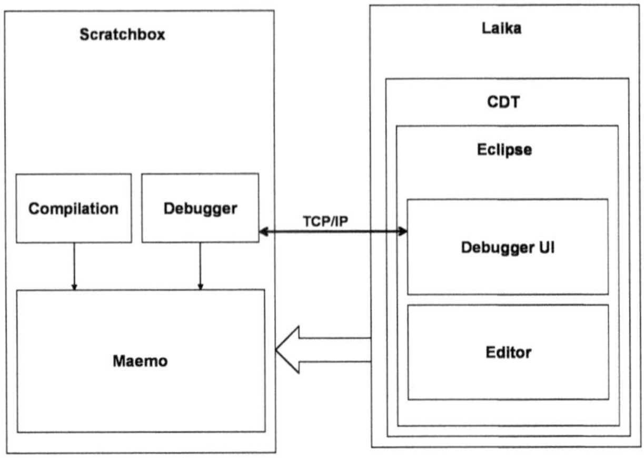

Fig. 2. Laika Release 1 components

During this development period, the main challenge of the project was to be able to create the first running version of the system, because the component systems originating from different communities were not straightforward to integrate. A part of the success is due to the technical skills of people who had already started the development work at Nokia. However, the effort invested in the development by the students should not be underestimated.

3.2 Peak of Fame

Upon completing the first public release of Laika, further interested stakeholders were identified. To begin with, a local company wanted to participate in the development of the system, and they agreed to integrate a user interface editor to the system, a task that the community happily welcomed them to perform. Secondly, project funding was provided to the community both from companies and by the university hosting the project in exchange for using the project as a guinea pig for open source related research. Funding from both sources was gladly accepted by the project, and used for further development of the system. In practice, the three students who had already worked on the system were now all hired to maintain and further develop the system by the university.

The additional funding and support described above kept the project running from September 2005 to January 2007. During this time period, a number of improvements were added to the system, including the above-mentioned UI editor, which was added by the company, as well as support for Python, a dynamic scripting language with which it is easy to compose small applications. The resulting system, illustrated in Fig. 3, required some changes in the tool architecture, as available open source components were based on different designs. In addition, a number of smaller enhancements were made, that in general eased application development.

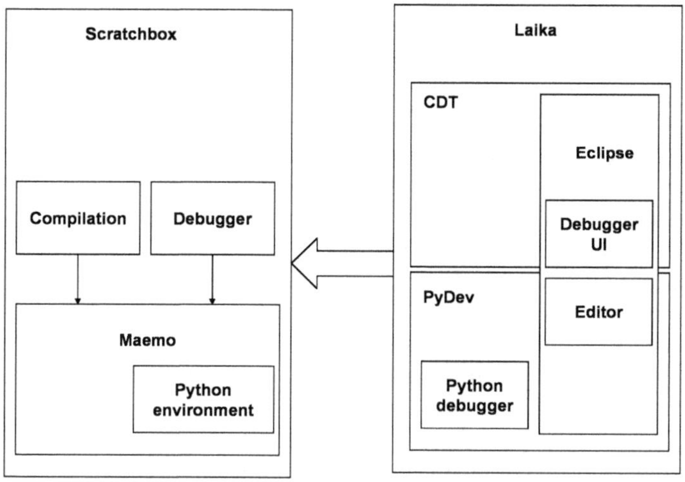

Fig. 3. Laika Release 3 components

At this point of the development, the downside of using a collection of existing components started to manifest. Creating a new configuration where some versions of component subsystems were supported often required additional coding and testing, which seemed to offer little reward for developers.

In general, a lot of external interest was paid to the community at this point, including a number of accepted papers [9][10] as well as a presentation regarding the project at one of the collocated sessions at GNOME User and Developer European Conference (GUADEC) 2006 [16].

In this phase, the main challenge of the community was to cope with ever-increasing number of updates in subsystems that comprise Laika. As already described in [10], new releases of other systems forced the community to perform regression testing of Laika repeatedly. Another issue that can be considered important is user support, which was found a difficult task to perform well. The reason is that most of the issues were related to component subsystems, not Laika as such, and we felt that to some extent this task was beyond our community's scope. In fact, in some occasions, the community ended up supporting people in installing and using Eclipse for instance in order to allow them to use Laika.

3.3 Decline

By January 2007, project Laika and the related community started running out of steam. To begin with, one of the three students that were originally participating in the development had left the project, and the other two were just about to complete their thesis about the experiences with Laika [11]. Generous funding from different sources was terminating. Moreover, also the project manager and the responsible professor had assumed other tasks and responsibilities, and it was not an option for them to take a leading role in code-level activities in Laika. A lead developer, on the other hand, was considered a necessity for the project to remain vital.

Despite the fact that the future of the community started looking weary, a number of positive things was happening. The community still gained a lot of interest, and there have been active negotiations on receiving support from involved companies, either in the form of funding or developers. Recently, Laika's code base was moved from university's server to a new location in Maemo Garage [12], a high-visibility web site hosting Maemo related material.

The essential question was how to continue with the development and to establish a real community instead of simply maintaining the project as long as continuous funding exists, and terminate it when the funding ends. At present, there still is interest in Laika, and attracting companies or institutions to participate in development is a reasonable goal. It may even be possible to integrate our system with another similar system, like Esbox [5] for instance, which builds on the same main components as Laika, which in turn would strengthen development. Even more importantly, we need to find a suitable long-term lead for the community – preferably one of the people who have already participated in the development. Motivating the lead, however, might require external attention or in the best case secured funding over some period of time.

3.4 Epilogue

Around the same time the first complete version of this paper was composed, we decided that due to resource restrictions joining forces with Esbox would be best for the Maemo developers. As a result, a new project was established in Maemo Garage under the name Esbox, which in the end will hopefully put together the best parts of Laika and Esbox. At present, however, core developers of Laika are yet to participate in this activity, and no major role has been assumed by us.

4 Lessons Learned

Obviously, there are numerous issues that could have been implemented differently in the course of our project. However, we trust that the reasons why we were unable to attract other people onboard – the real reason for not becoming a lively community – are few. Matters related to this creation of an active developer community are addressed in the following.

Focused mission which remained undocumented. One of the particularities of open source development is the mission of the community. In our case the mission was to "implement an industry-scale integrated toolset for composing Maemo applications", which also sets the scope for the community. For instance, it overrules extending the community to systems other than Maemo. In addition, we decided to base our work to existing, readily available open source subsystems. With this as the starting point, we were able to establish the first running system relatively rapidly, which in turn gave us instant credibility. Not documenting the mission can be considered a mistake, however. Without manifesting the mission, it has been difficult for other developers to grasp what Laika really is about.

Too much a debugging, integration, and testing project and too little a real development project. Another mistake regarding the mission is that we defined it in terms of what the community would provide, not what the community would implement in the technical sense. This led to two-fold development focus. One part was about developing support in terms of code that was composed by us, whereas another part was selecting and integrating suitable components that readily existed. To satisfy the latter, it was necessary to perform a lot of straightforward debugging and bug fixing when new versions were released. After a while, constant debugging, integration, and testing started to overrule the project. In an ideal world, we could have geared our own implementation into a direction where maintenance and building new releases would have been eased. This never happened, though.

Developers interested in SDK development, not that much in Maemo programming. Almost from the beginning of the project it became obvious that all developers were focused to developing SDK, and that developing Maemo applications was not an important issue. As a result, the development effort started from SDK and features that would be interesting from SDK point of view, not from the development of Maemo applications and easing it except indirectly. The effect of this lack of "eating our own dogfood", advocated by Spolsky in [20], to the community is hard to estimate. However, as we had another team, working in a neighboring office that was performing development using also our tools, we feel that this shortcoming is not too severe.

Relying on agile principles that are not necessarily ideal for community building. We organized our development following the spirit and principles of agile software development and extreme programming, like pair programming, collective code ownership, and a common development room [2][13]. In addition, the mindset we adopted was to go for a development mode, where code would be the main artifact, and other items would only be written when absolutely necessary. While the approach has worked well in our own development, there were some problematic issues. In particular, as we were busy developing the system ourselves, we were not too open for other potential participants. This resulted in entry barriers for new contributors, which in turn made our community closed. As the main activity of the community was focused in a single office, where all the developers and the project manager were co-located, this office quickly became the mental home of the community. Therefore, in order for others to participate, barriers existed already in the physical environment. A better alternative, at least from the viewpoint of community creation, would have been to rely on practices and processes that have already been documented explicitly in the scope of open source software [17].

Steep allocation of responsibilities but minimal staffing. The allocation of responsibilities in the community can also be considered. Led by a professor and a project manager, a number of students were performing the actual tasks. This unfortunate setting has resulted in a situation where the students had the real technical control, while the professor and the project manager were mainly focused to obtaining funding, users, and partners. When the students had their theses completed and they moved to different positions around the same time, the project was left without a lead who singlehandedly could manage both technical aspects and external relations.

Subcontracting for money instead of community building for free. While in general considered positive – and probably a major reason for the possibility to establish a community in the first place – the generous funding we obtained also has some downsides. As our plan was to create a self-sustaining community, the development was soon driven by feature requests associated with funding, not with our own plans. This in turn strengthened an attitude that we are actually performing feature-based subcontracting, not establishing a community.

Lack of active marketing, user support, and other related supporting facilities. As pointed out in [8], open source systems require marketing, similarly to any other software whose use is being advocated. Corresponding arguments can be made for other supporting facilities, including user support for instance. This aspect of the community building remained overlooked in Laika. As a consequence, only people that we were able to relate to had the potential to become participants in the community. Moreover, even using the system built in the community required considerable technical skills.

Single client community. In many cases, open source projects can be taken as common solutions for recurring problems encountered by several organizations. In our case, however, we were only aiming at easing the development of Maemo applications, something that only associates with one other actor. While there were several companies that had interest in developing applications, in practice what we believed was the best for Maemo community was something that we in practice had to obey to a great extent.

No experience on establishing an open source project. An issue that we did not consider important when we started was experience on community work. Looking back now, it would have been essential to involve someone with experience on ramping up an open source project in the community. However, while simple on paper, achieving this in practice might have been difficult.

5 Discussion

Considering Laika now, we feel that we got the development technology right, although one can argue that for instance versioning support could be drastically improved. In addition, we were able to create pull from users of our system. They accepted our system as their development environment and in fact approached us with future development ideas. Moreover, we were able to compose a system that did satisfy – and in many cases exceeded – the requirements we initially set to it. Obviously, we owe a great deal of our success to other open source communities, as without using existing components this would have been impossible. However, we were still unable to attract more developers to help us with our effort, which in the end has led to a decline.

During the development of Laika, we encountered a number of properties that have larger significance for community-based development. Our main observations are listed in the following:

- Community-based development worked well when developing new features. In contrast it was hard to motivate developers volunteering in the project when tasks like integration and testing was repeatedly requested. Building a toolset that would have eased the latter would have been an essential element for the continuation of the community.
- Distributing responsibilities in a fashion that resembled a small project, where managers were focusing on funding rather than coding, led to a community where no lead developer existed. As a result, there is no single actor that could (or would) singlehandedly continue maintaining the project.
- Agile practices that emphasize the importance of collocated development teams were harmful when trying to attract new developers to join the community. Instead, we should have embraced new developers by offering easy ways to practically participate in the development.
- Using the system ourselves might have helped in solving some of the problems associated with our development effort, especially when considering the priorities of different features. As a result, people using the system might have benefited more.
- Allowing supporters – especially those who provide funding – to overly control a community was fruitful in the beginning, as it gave us confidence on our mission. In the long run, however, this led to subcontracting mode, where funding was associated with individual features instead of supporting the community in general.
- It is easy to overextend the development effort, as the number of readily available open source components that can be integrated in the system is so large. However, in order to keep the system manageable in the long run, it is essential to focus on a relatively small number of key features at least in the initial phases when the community is small.

Still, to our knowledge there was no single community at the time aiming at supporting industrial IDE in Maemo environment that would be considerably stronger than our attempt. Moreover, we have received frequent requests for new features and updates, but have been unable to comply with the requests due to resource constraints in community personnel. This exhaustion of resources, more than anything else, can be taken as an indication that we have failed in forging a lively community.

Acknowledgments

The authors are grateful to the whole Laika community as well as all the partners who have participated in our work. In addition, we wish to thank also the users of Laika for their choice of a development system.

References

[1] Aaltonen, Timo, Järvensivu, J., and Mikkonen, T. OSS architecture and implications. 67-77, Empirical Insights on Open Source Software Business (Eds. Nina Helander and Maria Mäntymäki), *eBRC Research Reports 34*, Tampere, Finland, 2006.

[2] Beck, K. *Extreme Programming Explained – Embrace Change*. Addison-Wesley, 1999.

[3] CDT homepage. *Available on the Internet at http://www.eclipse.org/cdt/.*

[4] Eclipse homepage. *Available on the Internet at http://www.eclipse.org.*

[5] Esbox homepage. *Available on the Internet at http://wiki.embeddedacademy.org/index.php/ ESbox_Plug-in.*

[6] Feller, J., Fitzgerald, B., Hissam, S., Lakhani, K. *Perspectives on Free and Open Source Software Development*. MIT Press, Cambridge, MA, USA. 2005.

[7] GTK+ homepage. *Available on the Internet at http://www.gtk.org.*

[8] Henttonen, K. *Stylebase for Eclipse. An Open Source Tool to Support the Modeling of Quality-Driven Software Architecture.* VTT Research Notes 2387, Espoo, Finland, 2007.

[9] Järvensivu, J., Helander, N. and Mikkonen, T. Dependencies, Networks, and Priorities in an Open Source Project. 116-125, *Handbook of Research on Open Source Software: Technological, Economic and Social Perspectives* (Eds. Kirk St.Amant and Brian Still), IGI Global, 2007.

[10] Järvensivu, J., Kosola, M., Kuusipalo, M., Reijula, P. and Mikkonen, T. Developing an Open Source Integrated Development Environment for a Mobile Device. *International Conference on Software Engineering Advances*, Tahiti, French Polynesia, Oct. 29.-Nov.3., 2006.

[11] Kuusipalo, M. and Reijula, P. *Implementing a Visual Development Environment for Maemo Compatible Devices*. MSc. thesis, Tampere University of Technology, 2007. In Finnish.

[12] Laika homepage. Available on the Internet at *http://garage.maemo.org/projects/laika.*

[13] Larman, G. *Agile and Iterative Development.* Addison-Wesley, 2003.

[14] MacCormack, A., Rusnak, J., Baldwin, C. Exploring the structure of complex software designs: An empirical study of open source and proprietary code. 1015-1030, *Management Science*. Vol. 52, No. 7, July 2006.

[15] Maemo homepage. *Available on the Internet at http://www.maemo.org.*

[16] Reijula, P. Integrating Maemo Development Environment with Eclipse. *GNOME User and Developer European Conference (Guadec) 2006 warmup weekend*, Barcelona, Spain, Jun 24, 2006.

[17] Scacchi, W., Feller, J., Fitzgerald. B., Hissam, S., and Lakhani, K. Understanding free/open source software development processes. *Software Process Improvement and Practice*, 92-105, No. 11, 2006.

[18] Scratchbox homepage. *Available on the Internet at http://www.scratchbox.org/.*

[19] Sillanpää, M. Extending Eclipse and CDT for embedded systems development. *EclipseCon 2006*, Santa Clara Convention Center, Santa Clara, CA, USA. March 20-23, 2006.

[20] Spolsky, J. *Joel on Software: And on Diverse and Occasionally Related Matters That Will Prove of Interest to Software Developers, Designers, and Managers, and to Those Who, Whether by Good Fortune or Ill Luck, Work with Them in Some Capacity.* Apress, 2004.

Mapping Linux Security Targets to Existing Test Suites

C.A. Ardagna[1], E. Damiani[1], N. El Ioini[2], F. Frati[1], P. Giovannini[2] and R. Tchokpon[3]
[1] Department of Information Technology - University of Milan
via Bramante, 65 – 26013 Crema (CR) - Italy
{ardagna,damiani,frati}@dti.unimi.it
[2] Free University of Bozen-Bolzano
{Pietro.Giovannini,Nabil.ElIoini}@stud-inf.unibz.it
[3] Institut de Mathématiques et de Sciences Physiques – Benin
ricotchfr@yahoo.fr

Abstract. The Common Criteria standard provides an infrastructure for evaluating security functions of IT products and for certifying that security policies claimed by product suppliers are correctly enforced by the security functions themselves. Certifying Open Source software (OSS) can pave the way to OSS adoption in a number of security-conscious application environments. Recent experiences in certifying Linux distributions has pointed out the problem of finding a mapping between descriptions of OSS security functions and existing test suites developed independently, such as the Linux Test Project. In this paper, we describe a mechanism, based on matching techniques, which semi-automatically associates security functions to existing test suite such as the ones developed by Open Source communities.

1 Introduction

Security software evaluation and certification have become an important technique for selecting IT products to be deployed in security-conscious environments. The main goal of software security evaluation is to certify that software products provide and correctly implement some required security functionalities. This means that a good evaluation criterion should give an assessment of system security revealing all the security problems and weaknesses of IT products, which could lead to any unexpected behaviour.
The first attempt (carried out in 1985) to create a standard for security certification was the Trusted Security Evaluation Criteria (TCSEC) by U.S Department of Defense, also known as *Orange Book*. The Orange book has been defined to assist the design and development of security requirements and to fill the communication gap between vendors, evaluators, and customers [16]. However, the Orange Book soon proved too rigid to adapt to the new changes.

Please use the following format when citing this chapter:

Ardagna, C.A., Damiani, E., El Ioini, N., Frati, F., Giovannini, P. and Tchokpon, R., 2008, in IFIP International Federation for Information Processing, Volume 275; *Open Source Development, Communities and Quality*; Barbara Russo, Ernesto Damiani, Scott Hissam, Björn Lundell, Giancarlo Succi; (Boston: Springer), pp. 29–45.

From 1990, a specific European standard known as *Information Technology Security Evaluation Criteria* (ITSEC) has been adopted in Europe [20]. A few years later, several countries like Germany, United Kingdom, France and Canada have introduced their own national standards for security evaluation. The diversity of certifications standards, however, made the process of certifying an IT product at an international level somewhat difficult and expensive.
More recently, the *Common Criteria* (CC) certification standard has been defined to fulfil the needs of an international standard for affordable software security certification. Common Criteria is now an ISO standard (ISO 15408); it provides an unified process and a flexible framework to specify, design, and evaluate the security properties of IT products [9]. The CC standard is the result of a joint effort of many international organizations that have worked for two decades to specify a common structure for evaluating security properties of IT products [9]. A major goal of the CC evaluation is to certify that the security policies claimed by the developer are correctly enforced by the security functions of the product under evaluation.
Today, many development communities and other organizations working on Open Source software (OSS) recognize that a standard way to obtain the security certification of an OSS product can pave the way to its adoption in a number of security-conscious application environments.
In this paper, we focus on CC certification testing, which is aimed at ensuring that security functions under evaluation are correctly implemented and work according to the specification. In this context, one of the main problems to be faced is to find an easy map between test suites and security functions. This is especially true in OSS scenario, where security functions developers are often different from test suites developers. Recent experiences in certifying Linux distributions [18,19] has pointed to the problem of finding a mapping between descriptions of OSS security functions and existing test suites developed independently, such as the Linux Test Project. Semi-automatic mapping allows, using existing test suites, to support certification and may be the only possibility when tests are developed and made available independently with respect to source code. In the fullness of time, our approach will support a mechanism based on semantics-aware test descriptions for automatically associating security functions to existing test suites.

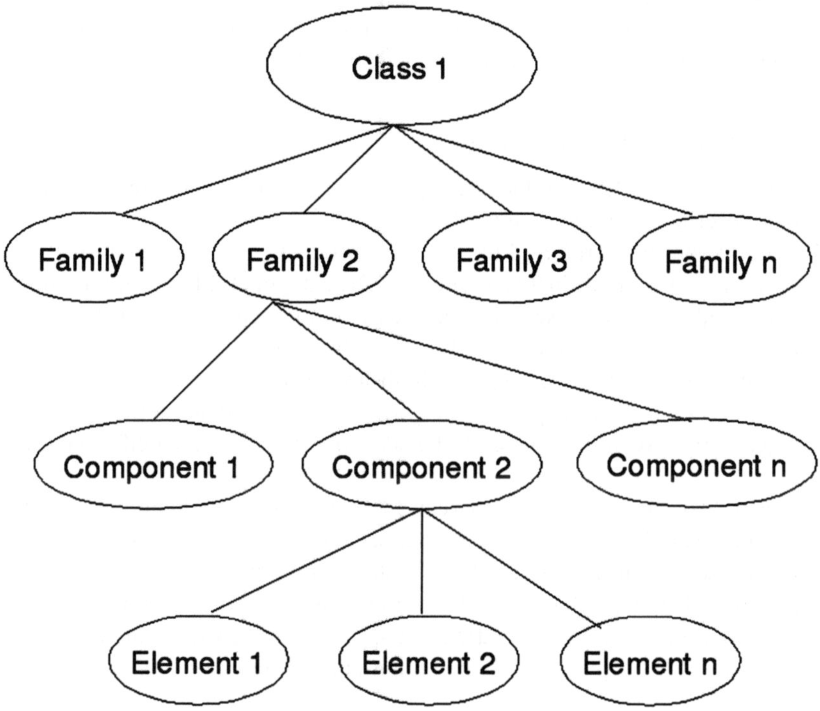

Fig. 2.1 The hierarchical structure of the SFRs.

2 Structure of Common Criteria Certification

The CC certification is based on different components that fall in the following categories [8].

Security Functional and Assurance Requirements.

The CC certification defines two types of security requirements: *Security Functional Requirements* (SFRs) and *Security Assurance Requirement* (SARs). SFRs define the requirements the security functions of the product under evaluation should satisfy [8].The CC standard includes a predefined extendable catalogue of security functional requirements "that are known and agreed to be of value by the CC part 2 authors" [6].

SFRs are organized in a hierarchical structure, as depicted in Fig. 2.1 [9].
SARs describe practical ways to check the effectiveness of the security functions of the product under evaluation [18]. The SARs catalogue includes many predefined requirements focusing on different phases of the product life cycle such as development, configuration management, testing and so forth.

Protection Profile and Security Target.

A Protection Profile (PP) is a document produced by consumers groups and communities that describes its authors' security needs.
A PP is not meant to be referred to a specific product (i.e., the Target of Evaluation (TOE)), but rather to a product type (i.e., a TOE category). PP defines an implementation-independent set of IT security requirements for a category of TOEs, to be used as a starting point for the evaluation of a particular IT product.
Users can create their PP based on their high-level security needs, without looking at any implementation detail [9]. A Security Target (ST) instead contains the security requirements of a given IT product, to be achieved by a set of specific security functions.
The ST is a basis for agreement between the developers, evaluators and, where appropriate, users on the TOE security properties and on the scope of the evaluation.
A ST can be derived from a given PP by instantiation; in general, the construction of a ST corresponds to a particular PP definition. A ST may then claim conformance to a PP by providing the implementation details concerning the security requirements defined by that PP [12]. Also, ST may augment the requirements derived from the PP.
There might be cases where there is no PP that matches the security properties of a specific product. In this case, the product developer can still create its own ST without claiming conformance to any PP [12].
An important aspect about ST requirements specification is the definition of the *threats* and *security objectives* of the TOE and its environment. In particular, threats identify situations that could compromise the system assets, while *security objectives* contain all the statements about the intents to counter identified threats and/or satisfy identified organization security policies and assumptions. Based on threats and security objectives, the ST defines the *security requirements* that the TOE security functions need to satisfy to achieve the security objectives.

Evaluation Assurance Levels.

The Common Criteria standard defines seven hierarchical Evaluation Assurance Levels (EAL), which balance the desired level of security and the cost of deploying the corresponding degree of assurance [3]. EALs identify different sets of security assurance requirements, which are shown in Table 2.1. In case the predefined requirements do not match the level of assurance required, the EAL might be augmented by adding additional assurance requirements.

Table 2.1 Evaluation Assurance Levels.

EAL	Description
EAL1	Functionally tested (black box testing)
EAL2	Structurally tested
EAL3	Methodologically tested and checked
EAL4	Methodologically designed, tested and reviewed
EAL5	Semiformally designed and tested
EAL6	Semiformally verified design and tested
EAL7	Formally verified design and tested

3 The Linux Security Target

As mentioned earlier, a PP defines a security target template directed to particular application domains, describing the security needs of consumers. This potentially results in different PPs listing different requirements for the same type of products. For instance, two groups of users of the same operating system may have different security needs. The first group could require the operating system to provide secure authentication and authorization mechanisms, while the second group could require the operating system to include a secure data transmission mechanism. These two groups of consumers would construct or cite two different PPs for the same product type, based on their expectations.

In this paper, we focus on the certification of Suse Linux Enterprise Server V8 distribution with service pack 3 (SLES8). The ST adopted for SLES8 claims conformance to the Controlled Access Protection Profile (CAPP), which has been released by the Information Systems Security Organization (ISSO) as part of its program to promote security standards for information systems [17]. According to the ISSO "CAPP-conformant products support access controls that are capable of enforcing access limitations on individual users and data objects CAPP-conformant products also provide an audit capability which records the security-relevant events which occur within the system" [17].

In the following of this section, we discuss the SLES8 ST, describing its main components and giving some examples as reported in the SLES8 ST.

Threats, Objectives, and Security Requirements.

The threats part of a ST identifies the threats that could compromise the system assets. In the case of SLES8, the assets to be protected include the information stored, processed or transmitted by the TOE (SLES8) [11]. The threats are generally divided in two categories: *i)* threats to be countered by the TOE, which exploit weaknesses in the TOE itself, and *ii)* threats to be countered by the TOE environment, which exploit the weaknesses of the TOE environment.

Examples of threats to be countered by the TOE and by its environment are, respectively [11]:

- an authorized user of the TOE may access information resources without having permission from the person who owns, or is responsible for the information resource for the type of access;
- an attacker with legitimate physical access to the hardware of the TOE may cause a hardware malfunction with the effect that a user is losing stored data due to this hardware malfunction.

Security objectives provide statements about the intents to address and counter the identified threats [9]. Based on the above examples, the following security objectives for the TOE and TOE environment, respectively, can be defined [11]:

- the TOE security function must control access to resources based on the identity of users, it must also allow the authorized users to specify which resources may be accessed by which users;
- those responsible for the TOE must ensure that those parts of the TOE critical to security policy are protected from physical attack.

Once the threats have been identified and the objectives to counter them have been set, the ST specifies how those objectives will be achieved by defining the security requirements. Security requirements section provides all the details concerning each of the SFRs selected to reach the security objectives. An example of a SFR provided by the SLES8 ST is: "the TOE security function shall be able to include or exclude auditable events from the set of audited events based on the following attributes [11]: *i)* User identity, *ii)* System call number, and *iii)* Directory or file name."
The SLES8 ST includes seven security functions to be evaluated with respect to SFRs: *identification and authentication, audit, discretionary access control, objective reuse, security management, security communication*, and *TOE security function protection* [11].

4 Associating Tests to Target

One of the main responsibilities of CC security evaluation teams is to ensure that the security functions claimed by developers have been implemented and are being correctly enforced. To this aim, security development and evaluation teams execute a set of tests to check each security function of the TOE. However, to be able to carry out this task successfully, security teams need to know in advance which tests will be used for which security functions. In other words, a mapping between security functions and test cases is necessary. When products are developed from scratch following the CC standard, developers can create a mapping between the security functions and their test cases during the test phase of the product life cycle. For existing products, however, security development and evaluation teams need to find out which existing tests match the desired security functions.

This problem is hard in general, as test documentation can be terse or entirely lacking, and is even harder in case of OSS evaluation. OSS development activities are not tracked, configuration management is skeletal and in many cases developers of the system functionalities do not write test cases. Therefore, finding the right mappings becomes a time-consuming task.

Our approach is aimed at providing a general automatic solution, based on matching techniques, for associating ST's security functions to tests. In the following, we show how our solution is used to map SLES8 security functions to Linux Test Project existing test suites. We relied on an extended set of test suites that has been used for SLES8 EAL3 certification [11].

4.1 The Linux Test Project

A fundamental aspect of CC certification is represented by extensive testing of the security functions of the TOE, using tests which cover all the range of security functions under evaluation.

The Linux Test Project (LTP) [15] defines a set of tests for Linux with a huge amount of security functions-related tests, which simplify the certification of Linux kernels.

LTP, which started in 2000 with one hundred test programs developed by Silicon Graphics Inc. (SGI), has been developed to improve the Linux kernel by providing automated testing of kernel functionalities [10]. LTP represented a "revolution" in Linux testing and assurance, since no formal testing environment was previously available to developers. The major advantage provided by the development of LTP was not the definition of batteries of tests, but the provisioning of a framework for systematic integration of testing activities. Furthermore, LTP includes an environment for defining new tests, integrating existing benchmarks and analyzing test results.

Nowadays, the latest version of LTP contains more than three thousands tests. In addition to the test suites, LTP also provides test results, a test tools matrix, technical papers and *HowTos* on Linux testing, and a code coverage analysis tool [15].

LTP tests cover a wide range of kernel functions, including system calls, networking and file system functionalities, and their results are restricted to *PASS* or *FAIL*. LTP provides a testing environment simple to install and use, which includes three scripts for executing three different suites of automatic tests [14]: *i) runalltests.sh, ii) network.sh, and iii) diskio.sh.* To give a clear understanding of a LTP test suite evaluation, in Table 4.1 we provide the summary report of the evaluation of Linux kernel 2.6 on a 64 bit Intel Itanium architecture (formerly called IA-64)[1].

[1] The complete evaluation is available at http://surfnet.dl.sourceforge.net/sourceforge/ltp/ltp-full-20071130_ia64_output.html.

Table 4.1 LTP summary report of Linux kernel evaluation.

Test Summary	Pan reported some tests FAIL
LTP Version	LTP-20071130
Start Time	Tue Dec 4 02:11:29 PST 2007
End Time	Tue Dec 4 03:11:52 PST 2007
Log Result	/root/subrata/ltp/ltp-full-20071130/results
Output/Failed Result	/root/subrata/ltp/ltp-full-20071130/output
Total Tests	849
Total Failures	0
Kernel Version	2.6.16.21-0.8-default
Machine Architecture	ia64
Hostname	elm3b159

In our context, LTP is used to evaluate the security related functionalities of Linux kernels with respect to CC certification.

As an example, starting from LTP, test suites for the CAPP/EAL3+ certification of SuSE Linux Enterprise Server 8 has been implemented [11]; test cases have been written by IBM, SuSE, and atsec, or taken directly from the LTP.

A detailed test plan has been produced to test the functions of SLES8 on each evaluated platform, and such plan includes an analysis of the test coverage, the functional interfaces tested, and the testing against the high level design.

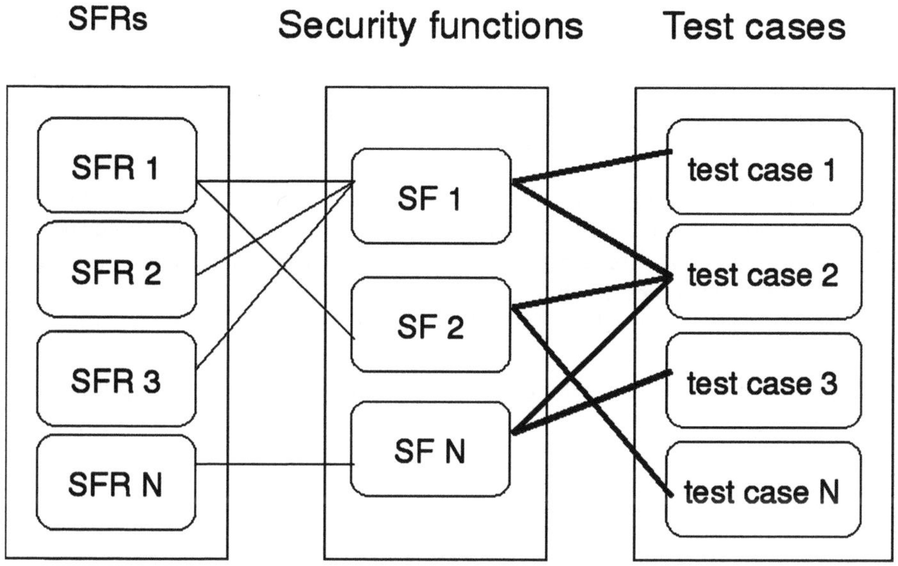

Fig. 4.1 Mapping between SFRs, security functions and testcases.

LTP has been used to test more than fifty kernel versions, where more than five hundreds vulnerabilities have been found. Nevertheless, LTP lacks of adaptability from a security certification point of view, that is, it lacks of an effective technique for associating batteries of tests to specific security functions to be evaluated. LTP, in fact, makes available only three pre-configured scripts for a general purpose testing, making difficult for developers to intuitively identify the batteries of tests that should be adopted for testing specific functions. In the remainder of this section, we discuss a possible solution to this problem.

4.2 Automatic Test Selection for Security Functions

Security functions testing, which is aimed at confirming that the functions operate according to their specification and satisfy the SFRs, is an important part of Common Criteria certification.

However, a major problem to be faced in security functions testing is that no framework for automatic linking between test suites and security functions is available. Developers and evaluators are then forced to associate tests to security functions basing on their experience only. To the best of our knowledge, in the past, this task has been done manually by creating two types of mappings. The first mapping connects each SFR with the security function or set of security functions that implement it. For instance, considering SLES8 security target, the security function *User Identity Changing (IA.4)* contributes to satisfy the SFR *User-Subject Binding (FIA_USB.1)* [11]. The second mapping is done between the security functions and available testcases. Figure 4.1 depicts the two mappings. Note that, whereas the first mapping is part of the TOE security specification section of the ST, the second one is not part of the ST [5].

Our solution focuses on the second mapping and consists of a generic framework for the automatic selection of test suites for the evaluation of security functions. Our framework, depicted in Figure 4.2, is composed of three main components:

- *Certification Test Suites*, which represents a hierarchical structure containing the set of test suites to be used in the certification process. Each node of the structure is assumed to be labelled using a self-explaining name and enriched of metadata describing its semantics. Each leaf-node represents a single test;
- *Security Functions*, which include the functions description of the TOE to be evaluated;
- *Matching Engine*, which is the component responsible for associating tests to security functions.

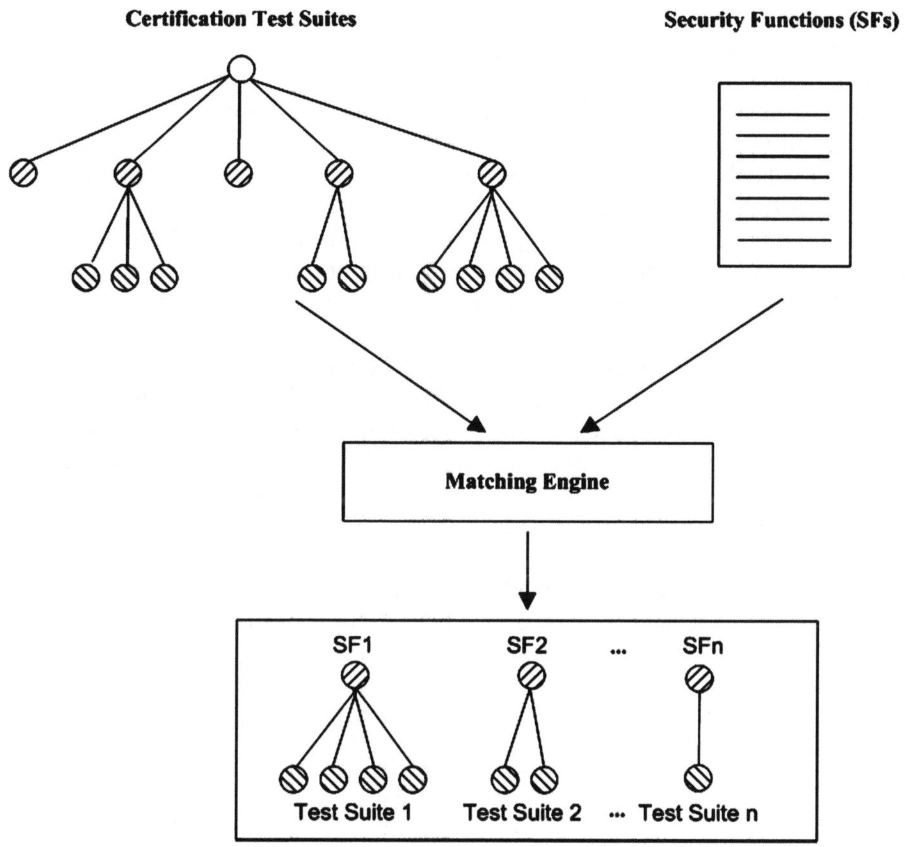

Fig. 4.2 Matching engine.

The first step towards the development of a matching engine for automatic test selection is the introduction of a common vocabulary. A vocabulary can be defined as a set of keywords $\{k_1,\ldots,k_n\}$ to be used in the definition of test suites metadata and name, and for the description of the security functions to be evaluated.

The vocabulary V allows to define both certification test suites and security functions descriptions based on a common grammar, which simplify the matching engine process. Our matching engine can be defined as a function f that takes in input the vocabulary *V*, the security functions *SF* and the test suites *TS*, and returns the association between the security functions *SF* and the test suites *TS*. The mapping process is composed of three phases: *keyword extraction*, *semantic expansion*, and *search/match.*

In the first phase, given a security function $sf \in SF$, the matching engine searches inside *sf* all keywords $\{k_1,\ldots,k_n\} \in V$ extracting a set $K \subseteq V$ of all the keywords used in *sf* description. Then, each keyword in $k_i \in K$ is expanded by means of a suitable thesaurus, and the expanded set of keywords is searched in the test suites paths and in each node metadata. All nodes that contain at least one matching, i.e., where at least one keyword is found, are selected and used by the matching engine as the roots of the subtrees to be considered. Finally, the matching engine returns all the selected subtrees, which are used to test security function *sf*.

Although general enough to be adopted in a generic scenario, our solution is used in the context of the SLES8 Linux distribution. In particular, our framework relies on an extended version of Linux Test Project, which has been used for SLES8 EAL3 certification [11], and on the security functions specification used for the definition of the security target of SLES8.

Since no formal metadata describing the test suites for SLES8 EAL3 certification are available and no agreement between security functions and test suites vocabulary is in place for this application, we assume that the vocabulary used by our matching engine is composed by the set of node names used in the hierarchical structure of the certification test suites, together with some predefined keywords. For instance, the certification test suites used in SLES8 EAL3 certification contains the node path *network/nsfv4/acl* that includes a large set of tests among which: *create_users*, *test_acl*, and many others. All the node names in the path and the test names are used as keywords for searching inside the security functions description and finding the association security functions/test suites.

In the following section, we present a worked-out example based on SLES8 test suites and security target. In particular, after selecting three security functions, we used our engine to select the set of tests to be used for the certification process.

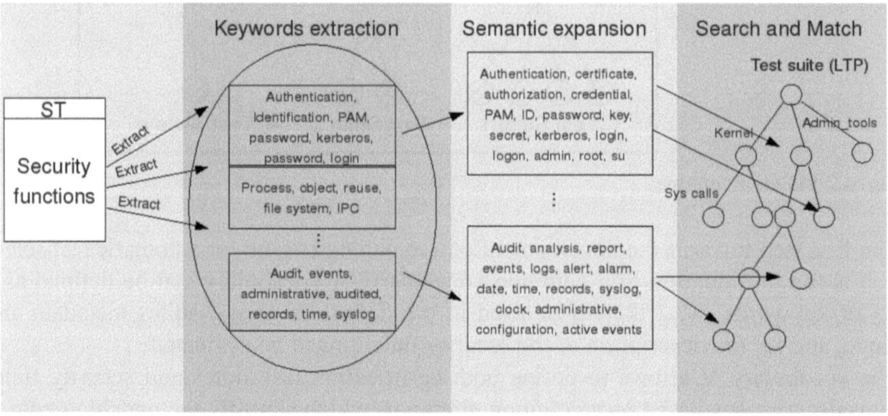

Fig. 4.3 The automated mapping approach between security functions and testcases.

4.3 Automatic Test Selection Example Based on SLES8 Security Functions

The SLES8-based example is summarized in Fig. 4.3 and the results are provided in Table 4.2. During the keyword extraction phase, all the security-related vocabulary keywords are extracted by security functions description (see underlined words in second column of Table 4.2. In the second phase, keywords are semantically expanded using an *ad-hoc* security related thesaurus, generating the column tree of Ta-

ble 4.2. Finally, in the search/match phase, the expanded set of keywords is searched in the LTP testcases directory hierarchy[2]. If a node matches at least one keyword, it will be automatically mapped to the security function to which that keyword belongs (see column four in Table 4.2).
In our approach, the search/match phase relies on the Linux command *grep*, which is applied to the extended LTP tree structure.
The *grep* command, developed within the GNU project, searches one or more input strings and returns any line containing a match to a specified pattern. Based on *grep* command, scripts are generated automatically starting from the keywords retrieved in the semantic expansion phase. These scripts search the keywords retrieved during the keyword extraction and semantic expansion phases, inside the directory structure of extended LTP tree and inside the comments in the testcases. Figure 4.4 presents a sample script, which is executed to retrieve the set of tests for the SC.1 security function described in Table 4.2[3].

```
grep -l -i -e 'tunneling' -e 'port 22'
            -e 'secure channel' -e 'secure socket layer'
            -e 'ssl' -e 'ssh'  -e 'secure shell'
            -r linux_security_test_suite_EAL3
```

Fig. 4.4 Example of search/match script applied to the SC.1 security function. The -l and -i options allow to print the list of matching files ignoring case distinctions.

Our experimental results prove the suitability of our solution, since our matching engine always returns all the relevant test cases selected manually by developers during SLES8 certification. Of course, our matching is not entirely precise, and some redundant tests are also selected.

Table 4.2 Automatic test selection results. For sake of conciseness, the table only reports a significant subpart of each security function and a partial list of tests. A complete description of the functions can be found in [11].

Security Function	Description	Semantic Expansion	Tests
Access Control Lists supported by SLES (DA.3)	SLES provides support for POSIX type ACLs for the ext3 file system allowing defining a fine grained access control on a user basis.	permission, allowed, entry, discretionary, DAC, etc.	access04.c, signal01.c, fcntl07B.c, readdir02.c, etc.
Kernel Modules (TP.3)	SLES supports dynamically loadable kernel modules that are loaded automatically on demand. Kernel modules are actually a part of the kernel that is not resi-	Kernel mode, loadable module, modules, trusted program, modprobe etc.	create_module01.c, create_module02.c, delete_module01.c, delete_module02.c, delete_module03.c,

[2] Search process considers also the comments inside the testcases files.

[3] The complete output produced by the execution of the *grep* command is summarized in Appendix A.

Security Function	Description	Semantic Expansion	Tests
	dent but loaded as part of the kernel when needed.		modules.conf01, modules.conf02, etc.
Secure Protocols (SC.1)	The TOE offers two protocols that applications can use to securely communicate with another trusted IT product (…). Those protocols are the Secure Shell Protocol Version 2 (SSH v2) and the Secure Socket Layer Protocol Version 3 SSL v3).	network, secure channel, data transmission, port 22, tunnelling, cryptographic protocol, secure communication, etc.	ssh01, ssh02, ssh03, ssh04, etc.

5 Conclusions and Outlook

In this paper, we outlined a framework aimed at supporting OSS security certifications including a matching engine for the automatic association of tests to security functions. Our solution is a first attempt to provide such an automatic infrastructure, and much additional work remains to be done. In particular, the proposed methodology has the main disadvantage of selecting a redundant set of tests. Our engine in fact chooses all the subtrees of the nodes whose names and/or description match with at least one of the keywords contained in the security functions under evaluation. This results in a situation where unnecessary tests are executed. To overcome this problem, we plan to provide two major improvements in our future work: *i)* the definition of a complete and formal vocabulary, and *ii)* the definition of a formal ontology used to reason about metadata describing the elements to be chosen (i.e., the nodes of the certification test suites hierarchy) and the correlations among them. Such an approach will allow us to exploit automatic reasoning techniques. Also, the combination of a complete vocabulary and a detailed ontology will lead to the development of an engine able to select only the suites of tests that effectively match the specified security functions, thus limiting unnecessary tests executions.

Another important issue is the actual testing environment to be used. It is well known that the development and running of intensive tests, especially for networking applications/devices, could affect the overall consistence of the system under evaluation and of the network that hosts the system. Furthermore, network tests need the participation of at least two physical machines, making them more expensive and demanding more implementation efforts. Also the risk of compromising the integrity of the real system becomes considerable. To eliminate the risk and to reduce the efforts introduced by such an extensive testing, a possible solution consists in setting up a *Virtual Test Environment* (VTE) that accurately reproduces the real environment in which the target application should be evaluated.

Several VTEs have been already provided in literature in different contexts and aimed at several goals [1,2,4,7]. Among them, we have provided a multi-purpose virtual environments, which supplies Virtual Laboratories for the on-line degree courses on Information Systems and Network Security of University of Milan [1,2]. This infrastructure also allows the use of the virtual systems for general testing and, in particular, for network functions testing. More in details, the system in [1,2] consists of a virtual subnet composed of a three hosts acting as a firewall, an external generic host, and an internal host working under the firewall. In our future work, we plan to adapt such a virtual network to make it suitable for security testing of applications that should be evaluated to achieve security certification.

Acknowledgments This work was supported in part by the European Union within the PRIME Project in the FP6/IST Programme under contract IST-2002-507591, and within the SecureSCM project in the FP7-ICT Programme under contract n.AOR 213531 and by contract/grant sponsor FIRB research fund of MIUR, research project TEKNE (contract/grant n.RBNE05FKZ2).

6 References

1. Anisetti M, Bellandi V, Colombo A, Cremonini M, Damiani E, Frati F, Hounsou JT, Rebeccani D (2007) Learning computer networking on open paravirtual laboratories. IEEE Transactions on Education, 50(4):302-311
2. Anisetti M, Bellandi V, Damiani E, Frati F, Raimondi U, Rebeccani D (2006) The open source virtual lab: a case study. In Proc. the Workshop on Free and Open Source Learning Environments and Tools - FOSLET 2006, Como, Italy
3. Caplan K, Sanders JL (1999) Building an international security standard. IEEE Educational Activities Department, 22(3):29-34
4. Gambit Communications. Mimic virtual lab CCNA (2007) www.gambitcomm.com/site/products/vlab_ccna.shtml. Accessed December 2007.
5. The International Organization for Standardization and the International Electrotechnical Commission (2007) Common Criteria for Information Technology Security Evaluation, Evaluation methodology
6. The International Organization for Standardization and the International Electrotechnical Commission (2007) Common Criteria for Information Technology Security Evaluation, Part 2: Security functional components
7. Grigoriadou M, Kanidis E, Gogoulou A (2006) A web-based educational environment for teaching the computer cache memory. IEEE Transactions on Education, 49(1):147-156
8. R. Harland R (2007) The canadian common criteria scheme. http://strategis.ic.gc.ca/epic/site/ad-ad.nsf/vwapj/CSE_Harland.ppt
9. Herrmann DS (2002) Using the Common Criteria for IT security evaluation. Auerbach publications, London
10. Hinds N (2004) Kernel korner: The Linux test project. Linux Journal
11. IBM, SuSE, atsec (2007) SuSE Linux Enterprise Server 8 w/SP3 CAPP/EAL 3+ Certification Test Suite. http://ltp.sourceforge.net/EAL3.html. Accessed December 2007
12. ISO/IEC. Guide for the production of Protection Pro_les and Security Targets, 2004.
13. Katzke S (2007) The common criteria (cc) paradigm. ieeeia.org/iasw/Katzke-CC.ppt. Accessed December 2007
14. Larson P (2002) Testing linux with the linux test project. In Proc. of the Ottawa Linux Symposium, Ottawa, Ontario, Canada
15. Linux Test Project (2007) http://ltp.sourceforge.net. Accessed December 2007
16. Lipner S (1999) Twenty years of evaluation criteria and commercial technology. In Proc. of the 1999 IEEE Symposium on Security and Privacy
17. Information Systems Security Organization (1999). Controlled Access Protection Profile version 1.d

18. Shankar KS, Kirch O, Ratliff E (2004) Achieving capp/eal3+ security certification for Linux. In Proc. of the Linux Symposium, volume 2:18-30
19. Shankar KS, Kurth H (2004) Certifying open source - The linux experience. IEEE Security & Privacy, 2(6):28-33
20. Shi W, Sun Y (2001) An investigation of cc's contribution to confidence in security. In Proc. of the 2001 International Conference on Computer Networks and Mobile Computing, 333-338

Appendix A

An example of a grep-based search/match phase

In Fig. A.1 we provide the complete output produced by our matching engine when mapping between security function SC.1 and testcases is searched. Based on the following grep-based script, where Fig. A.2 shows the set of testcases to be used in the evaluation of security function SC.1.

```
grep -l -i -e 'tunneling' -e 'port 22' -e 'secure channel'
        -e 'secure socket layer' -e 'ssl' -e 'ssh'
        -e 'secure shell' -r linux_security_test_suite_EAL3
```

```
linux_security_test_suite_EAL3/ltp_EAL2/testcases/network/tcp_cmds/ssh/ssh04
linux_security_test_suite_EAL3/ltp_EAL2/testcases/network/tcp_cmds/ssh/ssh01_s1
linux_security_test_suite_EAL3/ltp_EAL2/testcases/network/tcp_cmds/ssh/ssh03
linux_security_test_suite_EAL3/ltp_EAL2/testcases/network/tcp_cmds/ssh/ssh03_s1
linux_security_test_suite_EAL3/ltp_EAL2/testcases/network/tcp_cmds/ssh/ssh02_s1
linux_security_test_suite_EAL3/ltp_EAL2/testcases/network/tcp_cmds/ssh/ssh02
linux_security_test_suite_EAL3/ltp_EAL2/testcases/network/tcp_cmds/ssh/ssh01
linux_security_test_suite_EAL3/ltp_EAL2/testcases/user_databases/lastlog01
linux_security_test_suite_EAL3/ltp_EAL2/testcases/user_databases/faillog01
linux_security_test_suite_EAL3/ltp_OpenSSL/testcases/openssl/test/send_new_rsa_key.sh
linux_security_test_suite_EAL3/ltp_OpenSSL/testcases/openssl/test/restore_date.sh
linux_security_test_suite_EAL3/ltp_OpenSSL/testcases/openssl/test/rsa_login.sh
linux_security_test_suite_EAL3/ltp_OpenSSL/testcases/openssl/test/rsa_test.c
linux_security_test_suite_EAL3/ltp_OpenSSL/testcases/openssl/test/dsatest.c
linux_security_test_suite_EAL3/ltp_OpenSSL/testcases/openssl/test/aestest.c
linux_security_test_suite_EAL3/ltp_OpenSSL/testcases/openssl/test/delete_accounts.sh
linux_security_test_suite_EAL3/ltp_OpenSSL/testcases/openssl/test/sha1test.c
linux_security_test_suite_EAL3/ltp_OpenSSL/testcases/openssl/test/setup_date.sh
linux_security_test_suite_EAL3/ltp_OpenSSL/testcases/openssl/test/rsa_auth.sh
linux_security_test_suite_EAL3/ltp_OpenSSL/testcases/openssl/test/server.c
linux_security_test_suite_EAL3/ltp_OpenSSL/testcases/openssl/test/setup_accounts.sh
linux_security_test_suite_EAL3/ltp_OpenSSL/testcases/openssl/test/rc4test.c
linux_security_test_suite_EAL3/ltp_OpenSSL/testcases/openssl/test/dsa_auth.sh
linux_security_test_suite_EAL3/ltp_OpenSSL/testcases/openssl/test/stunnel_dsa.sh
linux_security_test_suite_EAL3/ltp_OpenSSL/testcases/openssl/test/dhtest.c
linux_security_test_suite_EAL3/ltp_OpenSSL/testcases/openssl/test/password_auth.sh
linux_security_test_suite_EAL3/ltp_OpenSSL/testcases/openssl/test/send_new_dsa_key.sh
linux_security_test_suite_EAL3/ltp_OpenSSL/testcases/openssl/test/stunnel_rsa.sh
linux_security_test_suite_EAL3/ltp_OpenSSL/testcases/openssl/test/dsa_login.sh
linux_security_test_suite_EAL3/ltp_OpenSSL/testcases/openssl/test/client.c
linux_security_test_suite_EAL3/ltp_OpenSSL/testcases/openssl/test/destest.c
linux_security_test_suite_EAL3/ltp_OpenSSL/testcases/openssl/test/randtest.c
linux_security_test_suite_EAL3/ltp_OpenSSL/testcases/openssl/openssl01
linux_security_test_suite_EAL3/laus_test/audit_tools/ssh01_s1
linux_security_test_suite_EAL3/laus_test/audit_tools/au_login
linux_security_test_suite_EAL3/laus_test/audit_tools/ssh01
linux_security_test_suite_EAL3/laus_test/libpam/tests/test_sshd.c
linux_security_test_suite_EAL3/laus_test/libpam/libpam.c
linux_security_test_suite_EAL3/laus_test/pam_laus/pam_laus.c
linux_security_test_suite_EAL3/laus_test/pam_laus/tests/test_sshd.c
```

Fig. A.1 Grep-based script for keyword matching and set of testcases retrieved for SC.1 security function evaluation.

Overview on Trust in Large FLOSS Communities

Etiel Petrinja, Alberto Sillitti, and Giancarlo Succi
CASE – Center for Applied Software Engineering
Free University of Bolzano/Bozen
Piazza Domenicani, 3
I-39100 Bolzano-Bozen,
{Etiel.Petrinja|Alberto.Sillitti|Giancarlo.Succi}@unibz.it
WWW home page: http://www.unibz.it

Abstract. The paper presents a survey of mature Free/Libre Open Source Software communities. The main focus of the survey is the collection of data related to the practices of these communities related to trust elements in their products. The survey is carried out using a structured questionnaire about thoughts and practices followed by Free/Libre Open Source Software communities. The survey focuses on the analysis of the development processes adopted by such communities. The results of the survey confirms basic ideas related to Free/Libre Open Source Software and explains in more detail specific issues related to trust and trustworthiness of the Free/Libre Open Source Software development process.

Keywords: FLOSS Communities, Software Quality, FLOSS Development Process

1 Introduction

The survey presented in this paper analyses a set of Free/Libre Open Source Software (FLOSS) projects that are used by large communities. The survey focuses on issues related to the trust that users have in adopting FLOSS products. We are interested mainly in processes, tools, methods, and approaches adopted to develop FLOSS products. The survey is part of a four year EU funded project named QualiPSo (Quality Platform for Open Source Software) aiming at studying methodologies, technologies, and policies to leverage the Open Source Software development to sound, well recognised, and established industrial operations [8].

In the last decade, FLOSS products are increasingly being used. This increase is supported by several factors including the absence of direct license costs and the availability of the source code that allows users to adjust FLOSS products to their specific needs. An important drawback of FLOSS is the lack of quality assurance metrics that prove its validity. In commercial environments, the problem is addressed

Please use the following format when citing this chapter:

Petrinja, E., Sillitti, A. and Succi, G., 2008, in IFIP International Federation for Information Processing, Volume 275; *Open Source Development, Communities and Quality*; Barbara Russo, Ernesto Damiani, Scott Hissam, Björn Lundell, Giancarlo Succi; (Boston: Springer), pp. 47–56.

in a different way. The concept of quality is often related to the certification of the production process of the producer (e.g., CMMI). This approach can be extended also to the FLOSS production (in particular, for FLOSS developed supported by companies). The survey presented in this paper is trying to find out which elements contribute to the trustworthiness that people have in FLOSS products. Trust is linked to both characteristics of the final product and the overall development process followed. In particular, the process is an element that may vary considerably among different FLOSS projects. The survey collects information about different approaches and synthesises them to identify benefits and avoid pitfalls of FLOSS development.

2 Background

In the last decade, intensive research has been carried out on FLOSS. Benchmark results have provided a list of characteristics that are common in the FLOSS development process. The most important are the following [1]:

- it is parallel, rather than linear,
- it involves large communities of globally distributed developers,
- it utilizes truly independent peer review,
- it provides prompt feedback to user and developer contributions,
- it includes the participation of highly talented, highly motivated developers,
- it includes increased levels of user involvement, and
- it makes use of extremely rapid release schedules.

Moreover, the whole FLOSS life cycle differs from the classical software development processes. Mockus *at al.* [7] and Jorgensen [4] proposed similar models identifying phases that are present in FLOSS development projects. The Jorgensen's model [4] includes the following list of phases: code, review, pre-commit test, development release, parallel debugging, and production release.

FLOSS development is strongly influenced by software development tools used by both developers and contributors. In contrast to the diffusion of Computer Aided Software Development (CASE) tools used by traditional software development, FLOSS process adopted software tools as issue/bug trackers, mailing lists, forums, collaboration environments, etc. An important collaborative development environment – SourceForge [3] – provides an integrated environment where more than 100.000 FLOSS projects are being stored and developed (even if only a small portion of them are active projects involving several developers). FLOSS uses also traditional software engineering tools, however not all tools are available as FLOSS products. Therefore, in the near future these tools will eventually appear as FLOSS and will further improve the FLOSS process.

Many researchers have studied the quality and trustworthiness of FLOSS products and their development processes. Since quality is a fundamental ingredient of software and a relevant criterion for adopting FLOSS products, the research was oriented toward the evaluation of the current quality of FLOSS products and how to improve it. Lipner [5] explored the benefits and possible pitfalls of FLOSS development. McGraw [6] stated that "openish" products will not improve security of the software. Schneider [9] stated that source code inspections are just one of possible approaches to improve software's quality by discovering bugs. Witten [11] explored economics of FLOSS products, metrics used to assess it, and models available.

3 Research Design

The survey includes two parts: one related to FLOSS products and the other related to FLOSS processes. Results presented in this paper deal only with the second part of the questionnaire.

4 Scope

The survey includes seven well-known FLOSS projects: Apache HTTP Server, Eclipse, Emacs, Linux Kernel, Mozilla project, GNOME, and Debian.

5 Methodology

The survey uses the approach proposed by Silverman [10]. It requires the design of a structured and formal research involving two basic and partially correlated concepts:

- The methodology, that is, the specific technique for gathering data (survey, interview, questionnaire, case study, etc.).
- The method, that is, whether performing a quantitative or a qualitative investigation.

Such decisions are based on an evaluation of the goals of the research and the kind of information required.

Our study focuses on gathering opinions about the FLOSS process and products adopted in the surveyed communities. Therefore, we have to conduct a qualitative investigation that involves the analysis of data such as words and sentences instead of numbers [10]. Our research methodology is based on a semi-structured questionnaire filled in mainly by analysing projects' web sources such as web pages, CVS repositories, mailing lists, and forums. Moreover, some data comes from face-to-face or telephone interviews.

5.1.1 GQM

The overall structure of the research is based on the GQM approach [2], as follows.

- Goal: Evaluate the actual adoption of FLOSS in the software industry.
- Question: The questionnaire is composed of 53 questions with additional sub-questions.
- Metrics: Metrics about the level of adoption and the trust in FLOSS products.

5.1.2 Questionnaire

The questionnaire is organized in 16 sections dealing with different topics related to the FLOSS development processes. The 16 topics are the following:

1. Personal information
2. Company information
3. Role of the organization with respect to FLOSS
4. Issues that can be taken into account when deciding whether to adopt FLOSS
5. Trust
6. Quality assurance
7. General questions
8. Roles and responsibilities
9. Architecture definition
10. Development techniques and practices
11. Tools used
12. Features to implement
13. Documentation and bug management
14. Version control and people management
15. Business model
16. Workflows of the processes identified

The answers gathered through face-to-face interviews are collected following the following steps:

- The respondents are contacted to determine their general interest in the study.
- The questionnaire is sent to the respondents to verify the actual availability.
- Data is collected by personal or telephone interviews.
- The results of the interviews are sent to the interviewees for a final check.

Only upon a positive feedback from the interviewee, the questionnaire is considered accepted and the data is processed. Participants are guaranteed anonymity and the information reported is reviewed so that no individual person or company can be identified. The final questionnaire was designed iteratively; during the survey we added just a small number of new questions and in a few cases we have changed the order of questions to improve the focus on specific topics.

6 Results

In the following subsections we present four topics of the questionnaire: quality related issues, stakeholders related issues, technology related issues and business related issues.

6.1 Quality issues

6.1.1 Trust

Important elements to people surveyed are: openness of the whole development process, openness of the planning process, testing and integration builds, presence of intermediate milestones and visibility of the planed and the actual development process. Moreover, communities trust more common elements such as: the quality of the source code, the correct behaviour of the product, its performance, and often the security of the developed product. We have found out that communities try to fulfil classical trust-related criteria first and additionally they attempt to satisfy important FLOSS-related criteria as well. The same is true when they are testing external FLOSS products to be adopted by the community.

6.1.2 Quality assurance

Quality elements considered important by FLOSS communities vary considerably among different communities. The most important elements listed by communities are the following: the planning process used, the development process followed, the compatibility of the licenses used by specific subprojects, the bug/issue reporting and solving procedure, the availability of appropriate documentation, the simplicity of installation, and a proper integration of different subparts of the final product.

Answers related to testing processes of FLOSS products, either developed by the community or adopted by it, is quite homogeneous among the considered communities. The majority bases the testing process on users and developers that produce FLOSS products. Almost half of the communities have specific test teams that provide a defined quality level of the developed products. On the contrary, one quarter of the communities said explicitly that they do not use any specialized test team. Part of the communities employs beta testers selected from the group of their regular users that provide useful bug/issue reports before the product is largely distributed to the public (Fig. 1).

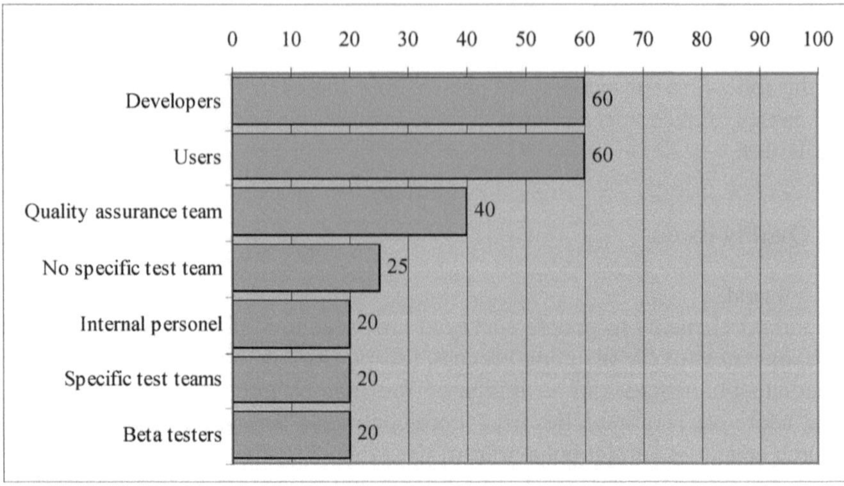

Fig. 1. Percentage of different stakeholders testing FLOSS products.

6.2 Stakeholders related issues

6.2.1 Roles and responsibilities

The number of developers involved in each surveyed FLOSS project varies from 25 core developers to more than 1000 developers. The roles represented in these communities are: simple users, developers, committers, and Project Management Committee (PMC) members. Communities have often an additional management body as can be a technical or a non-technical board that reviews the work done by the community and the progress of the project. Half of the communities surveyed are also supported by a foundation that manages the project and overviews the alignment of the project evolution with basic directives that the project has to satisfy. There is not a common hierarchy structure in different communities. Usually, FLOSS communities do not have many hierarchy levels and they tend to implement a democratic system where everybody has the possibility to express his opinion.

Roles are not always strictly fixed and users can obtain more privileges by providing good quality contributions, stay aligned with local policies and written and not-written rules. In some communities, users can become developers if they provide good quality code and can become committers if their contributions are significant. The role of a user depends on the definition of specific roles in different communities. Often the PMC is responsible for granting new roles and privileges.

6.2.2 Features to implement

New features to be implemented in FLOSS projects are usually proposed in mailing lists or in bug/issue management systems. Features are usually not ranked in the surveyed communities. Exceptions are some bug fixes and features related to impellent architecture modifications. In some communities, new features can be implemented immediately by developers and contributors, in others, more structured communities, these suggestions can be included in the future implementation plans and roadmaps. The majority of surveyed communities have a time plan for new features to be implemented in the following few months. Usually, plans are available also on web pages to allow everybody to see which features will be added in the near future. In this way, users can participate to the implementation process with source code or documentation contributions.

When changes are proposed, the PMC, the supporting foundation or the responsible person for a specific module decides which features will be implemented. Usually, in the more hierarchically structured communities surveyed there is a specialized development team that implements new features. This team is composed by developers and committers that are responsible to the PMC or to the owners of specific modules. In less hierarchical communities, developers and committers may decide which new features they would like to implement. The possibility to choose which features a developer will implement can be an important productivity advantage that FLOSS processes have in comparison to the proprietary ones.

6.3 Technology issues

6.3.1 The overall architecture

The architecture of the system is defined incrementally or, in few cases, it is planed from the beginning. This depends on the nature and on the size of the project. If projects are strongly centralized they usually have a well planed architecture; on contrary, if projects are a collection of smaller modules, the architecture of the system is defined by just few leading rules. In the majority of the surveyed communities, the architecture planning is often the combination of both approaches.

FLOSS projects are often based on very specific standards. It is the case of the Apache HTTP web server that implements the HTTP open standard. Standards implemented are in the majority of the cases open and sometimes also supported and proposed by FLOSS communities. Another important element present in the surveyed FLOSS communities is the interoperability of the software developed with other (FLOSS and commercial) products. Open standards and interoperability issues are usually interconnected.

6.3.2 Tools used

The operating system used to develop FLOSS projects by all the surveyed communities is either Linux or a Unix-like operating systems. Since the projects surveyed have started many years ago, the products have been adapted to several popular operating systems. More than half of them can run on Microsoft operating systems and many on MacOS.

The most frequently used programming language is not Java as we expected from the current mainstream FLOSS development, but C/C++. The main reason for this is the longevity of the projects surveyed that started in the '90s when Java was not yet so popular. However, the surveyed communities often use also other languages such as C#, Perl, Python, Lisp, and Java.

The number of different programming tools used by the surveyed communities is very large. One FLOSS community reported that they use 820 different tools and libraries for their development. However, the tools used by the majority of the communities are source code management tool such as CVS (but also GIT, Bit Keeper, LXR, etc.), bug/issue tracking tools such as Bugzilla, and mailing lists .

6.3.3 Development techniques and methodologies

Usually, the adopted development techniques are not well described by the surveyed communities. However, they often explicitly write guiding principles that are used inside the community. Such principles are for instance Quality Culture, Collective Reputation, Freedom, Autonomy, and Evolution. Another element present in the majority of communities is the development process divided into distinct phases that are clearly defined by the community. Transitions from one phase to another are open and there are public reviews. Common phases are: Pre-proposal, Proposal, Incubation, Mature, Top-Level, and Archived.

6.3.4 Documentation

A detailed documentation is a very important part of all the projects developed by the surveyed FLOSS communities. Usually, they start a subproject that is responsible of documentation. It can be produced in different forms, most often as user manuals (separate documents), documentation inserted inside the code (JavaDoc or similar), developer's and maintainer's manuals, and web pages. The creation and the maintenance of the documentation are open to everybody willing to contribute with some effort. Contributors can come also from persons that are not programmers. Documentation is usually protected by a FLOSS consistent license such as Creative Commons.

6.3.5 Bug/Issue management

All the communities surveyed have mailing lists focused on bugs. The majority of communities have also an automatic bug/issue tracking system that helps users and developers to report and manage bugs. More than half of the communities use Bugzilla as the FLOSS bug/issue-tracking solution.

The bug solving procedure depends on the severity of the bug reported, the size of the project, the specific community, and some other issues related to specific bug. The time needed to solve a bug inside communities varies considerably: from one day for 75% of the bugs, up to 140 days for 90% of the bugs in the Apache Server community. Other communities report longer response times for not critical bugs. However, the majority of communities try to provide some answer to critical bugs in one to three days from the notification.

6.4 Business related issues

The business model driving the FLOSS movement does not include revenues obtained from selling licenses for the products. However, there are many additional services, courses, publications, and adaptations that are offered to the market by companies that in many cases collaborate with FLOSS communities. Moreover, there are many indirect benefits that are offered to contributors. Some of them are: the improvement of the reputation of developers, the possibility to get better job positions, working with people that share the same ideas, advancing of FLOSS software in comparison with proprietary software, etc. Some FLOSS communities distribute also grants and prizes that are offered by supporting companies.

A very important aspect that has emerged from various researches done in the last decade on the FLOSS movement, and also from our survey, is the support offered by large software companies to the FLOSS movement. Key developers and leaders in FLOSS communities are often employees of world leading IT companies such as IBM, Hewlett-Packard, Intel, Red Hat, Sun Microsystems, etc. Developers are paid to work on the development of FLOSS products. Companies supporting FLOSS development receives benefits from other sources such as: publicity obtained by contributing to the community, a deep knowledge of FLOSS that can be sold along with proprietary products, attracting good young developers, etc.

7 Conclusions

The results of the survey confirm our expectations on the most important trustworthy elements perceived by FLOSS products developers and users as: the number of downloads, the longevity and the level of activity in the community. The survey revealed additionally more in details which characteristics are essential for FLOSS communities to trust external FLOSS products. The most important aspects of FLOSS development are, as expected, the openness of the whole development process and continuous testing of the product. FLOSS communities try to fulfil first important generic requirements that are guiding also proprietary software development, and additionally they try to accomplish also specific FLOSS related requirements.

Important elements that proof the quality of FLOSS products are: the license used, the quality and completeness of the documentation, and a thorough testing. FLOSS communities often base their testing on specific groups of developers but they rely especially on the large community of users that is an essential part of each FLOSS project. The survey has confirmed also a growing importance that have traditional world leading software companies in further growing of the FLOSS movement. Companies contribute intensively to FLOSS communities usually by paying developers that work for the community. Therefore, many trust related approaches and procedures are often migrated from companies to FLOSS communities.

Standard software development techniques combined with essential FLOSS principles form a higher quality and trustworthy hybrid software development approach. These changes will eventually improve the credibility of FLOSS products and increase their use in companies and public administrations.

8 Acknowledgment

The authors would like to thank the partners of the QualiPSo project that have been involved in the survey. In particular, Prof. Sandro Morasca of the Università dell'Insubria (Italy) who participated to the design of the questionnaire, Prof. Jesus M. Gonzalez-Barahona and Prof. Gregorio Robles of the University Rey Juan Carlos (Spain) who collected the data about the GNOME and Debian communities.

9 References

[1] The Leading Linux Resource in the World! http://linux.sys-con.com/, Last visit December 2007.

[2] V. R. Basilli: Software modeling and measurement: The Goal/Question/Metric paradigm. Department of Computer Science, University of Maryland, 1992.

[3] J. Howinson and K. Crowston: The Perils and Pitfalls of Mining SourceForge. University Academic Department.

[4] N. Jorgensen: Putting it All in the Trunk, Incremental Software Development in the FreeBSD Open Source Project. Information Systems Journal, (2001), 11, 321-336.

[5] S. B. Lipner: Security and source code access: Issues and realities. University Academic Department, 124-125.

[6] G. McGraw: Will openish source really improve security? University Academic Department, 128-129.

[7] A. Mockus, R. Fielding and J. Herbsleb: A Case Study of Open Source Software Development: The Apache Server. University Academic Department, 263-272.

[8] QualiPSo - Quality Platform for Open Source Software. http://www.qualipso.org/index.php, Last visit December 2007.

[9] F. B. Schneider: Open source in security: Visiting the bizarre. University Academic Department, 126-127.

[10] D. Silverman: Doing qualitative research. Sage Publications, 2000.

[11] B. Witten, C. Landwehr and M. Caloyannides: Will open source really improve security? University Academic Department.

PMLite: An Open Source Solution for Process Monitoring

Alberto Colombo, Ernesto Damiani, and Fulvio Frati
Department of Information Technology - University of Milan
via Bramante 65, 26013 Crema (CR) – Italy
{colombo, damiani, frati}@dti.unimi.it

Abstract. Process Monitoring represents a big challenge for organizations that aim to manage software projects adopting different development paradigms. In fact, across-process enterprise-level measurement campaigns can be difficult to enact since process attributes to retrieve are semantically diverse and may be difficult to integrate. In this paper, we present PMLite (Process Monitoring Lite) an open source solution to this problem. PMLite is based on an open metamodel and paves the way to the definition of ad-hoc open monitoring frameworks.

Keywords: open source, process monitoring, PMLite, open metamodel

1. Introduction

Adopting multiple development processes is becoming common in an increasing number of organizations and communities. Different commercial agreements, or different development scenarios, lead to the adoption of a paradigm rather than a different one; as for instance, a development community could use an agile process to develop an open source Enterprise Resource Planning application, where a commercial software house working for a government agency would most probably follow structured Uniform Process (UP) or a waterfall-like process, often formalized in the supply agreement itself.

Such a situation suggests a new vision about software process monitoring: managers need to have a global view of performance, although development activity may be based on different processes that, at a first sight, are incomparable and whose performance data are hard to integrate.

Many research works have attempted a formalization of the notion of software development process and of the associated measurement framework. Piattini *et al.* [7] describes the advantages of using MOF and XMI to represent development processes, giving an overview of MOF and XMI languages and an example of repository for software development process, while Ventura Martins *et al.* [5] presents the *ProjectIT Initiative*, that provides a complete software development workbench and shows an example of development process metamodel. All the approaches above are related to the SPEM (Software Process Engineering Metamodel) specification [4]

Please use the following format when citing this chapter:

Colombo, A., Damiani, E. and Frati, F., 2008, in IFIP International Federation for Information Processing, Volume 275; *Open Source Development, Communities and Quality*; Barbara Russo, Ernesto Damiani, Scott Hissam, Björn Lundell, Giancarlo Succi; (Boston: Springer), pp. 57–68.

proposed by Object Management Group (OMG), that describes a concrete software development process or a family of related software development processes.

Other existing standard frameworks, such as UML and CWM (Common Warehouse Model) have been used to generate metadata describing complex systems, and can be used for development process representation as well.

Starting from these standards and research works, our group has formalized and tested a metamodel [2] for measuring and assessing generic development process models (see Section 2). In this paper, we highlight the progress of our researches presenting the open source application PMLite (Process Monitoring Lite) [6], available on SourceForge, that fully embraces our methodology. The tool has been developed as a proof-of-concept of our approach, and could be adopted in small medium enterprises that need a lightweight across-process monitoring tool.

The paper is organized as follows. Section 2 provides an overview of the metamodel that defines the structure of the tool, whereas Section 3 describes in details PMLite implementation. Finally, Section 4 shows future extensions of our work and Section 5 draws our conclusions.

2. Defining a Metamodel for Process Monitoring

The first step to define a common environment, for measuring different development process, is to produce a general schema, a *metamodel*, that will describe the underlying structure of processes and the relative measuring framework. We start from the work of Piattini *et al.* in [7], that uses MOF and XMI to represent software processes. In particular, MOF (Meta-Object Facility) [3] is a standard supported by OMG [5] that defines a generic pattern for the construction of systems based on metadata. MOF can be described by its four levels structure: starting from the top there is *i)* the definition of all the concepts and attributes of the language itself, used to build a *ii)* metamodel, that defines the structure and semantic of the metadata related to a generic environment; then, this metamodel is used to create *iii)* models, that depict specific objects and describe the structure for *iv)* the user data.

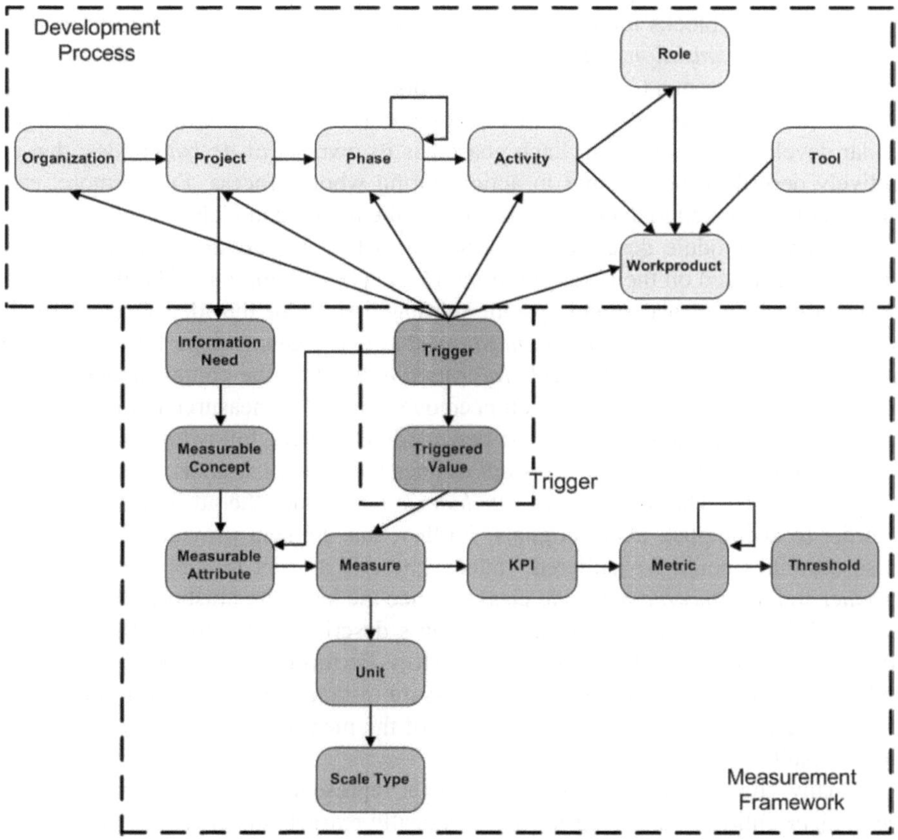

Fig. 2.1 Our modular meta-model. The yellow, green, and red colors correspond to Process, Measurement, and Trigger modules.

Following the MOF approach, we define the development process and the measurement framework metamodels that are used as basis to model specific development processes and measurement frameworks, and a simple trigger layer to connect the two metamodels. The whole metamodel is presented in Fig. 2.1 where the colors define the individual models.

A complete description of any elements of the metamodel could be found in [2]; for the sake of conciseness, in this paper we limit the description only to the elements that would be directly involved in PMLite development.

Metamodel description.

The three colors in Fig. 2.1 define the three parts of our modular metamodel. It is important to note how the process module is independent from the measurement one, thanks to decoupling via the trigger layer. Such decoupling allows to apply the same measurement framework to projects implementing different development processes, and, consequently, to elaborate across-process assessment.

The yellow blocks identify the development process module. The first node is the element *Organization*, that describe the overall organization and allows enterprise-level measurement campaigns. Each organization manages a set of *Project* classes, each one realized by its own set of *Phases*, that are characteristic of a particular development paradigm. Each phase has its own set of *Activity* nodes, that effectively describes the task put in action during whole process. Furthermore, each phase could be linked to another phase to describe iterative models.

The green module describes the structure of the measurement framework. The framework is based on the *Goal-Question-Metric* (GQM) approach [1], which drives the creation of a measurement system starting first, from the identification of the *goals* of the measures, then of the *questions* that will evaluate them through a set of specific *metrics*. The first element, *Information Need*, is the container node of the module and describes the information need over which the measurement is based and it is used as conceptual link for the two modules. Then, following the GQM approach, the entity *Measurable Concept* defines the areas, i.e. goals, over which the analysis is based. The *Measurable Attributes* node defines the attributes to measure in order to accomplish analysis goals. Further, this element provides the way how these attributes could be gathered; indeed, there is a strict relation between *Work Product* and *Measurable Attribute* classes, since the latter are attributes that could be extracted from the former. The *Measure* class describes the value of the measured attributes and it is strictly related to *KPI* (Key Performance Indicator) and *Metric* nodes, that define an elaboration of the measure instances in order to provide indicators that, respectively, lower the cardinality of the measures and qualitatively evaluate the results.

Finally, the red module isolates the trigger representation, which simply defines the *Trigger* entities, i.e. a plug-in, that physically extracts the attributes values from the work products, storing data in the *Triggered Value* class. As said above, triggers allow modules to be independent one from each other, since they know which attributes to extract and in which work product they have to be physically extracted and in which way.

Instance example: the Scrum agile process.

Our open metamodel has been designed as general as possible, in order to be able to model processes that embrace different paradigms. To demonstrate such property, in Fig. 2.2 we present an instance of the metamodel describing the agile process Scrum [2,8].

We choose an agile development process to show the flexibility of our approach; in fact, agile processes, and in particular Scrum, are intrinsically unpredictable, although a control mechanism is used to guarantee flexibility, responsiveness, and reliability of the results. These characteristics could make difficult the implementation of such a rigorous measurement framework. Thanks to the independence between process and measurement module, our metamodel could seamlessly superimposes a measurement framework to agile-based projects.

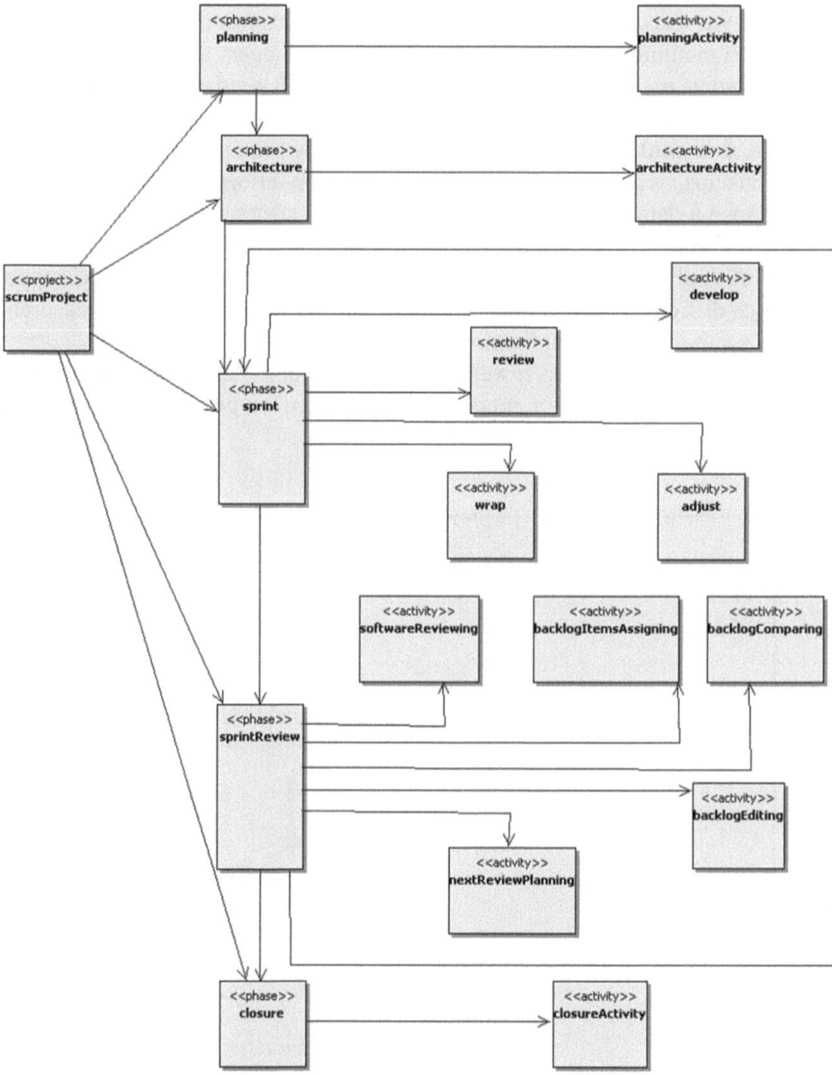

Fig. 2.2 Model of the agile development process Scrum.

3. PMLite: Process Monitoring Lite

The requirements that have driven the development of PMLite are essentially three.

First of all, we wanted to develop a web-based application that fully adopts and verifies our open metamodel representation, allowing managers to model any type of process and organize measurement campaigns to gather all needed attributes.

Secondly, we wanted PMLite to be essentially an easy-to-use tool, with a gentle learning curve, that could be adopted also in small software houses and open source development groups, without any particular installation effort. For this reason, we choose to propose a data collecting technique based on surveys instead of automatic probes, lowering installation problems and development effort. Furthermore, the huge number of applications used during software development and during support activities makes difficult to implement automatic probes that will extract measurable attribute from a suitable set of applications work products.

Finally, PMLite is a first step toward developing a complete process monitoring platform, which could exploit our metamodel approach for generic monitoring generic business processes.

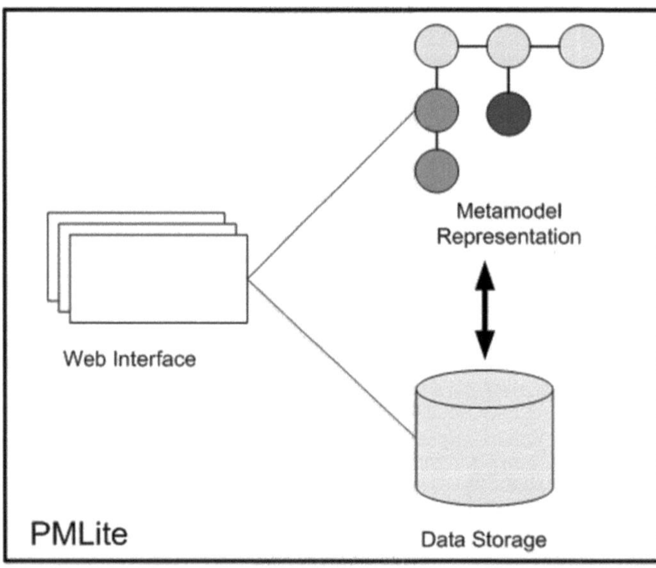

Fig. 2.1 Conceptual structure of PMLite.

3.1. PMLite Description

The conceptual structure of PMLite is depicted in Fig. 2.1. Both web pages and data storage have been designed basing on the metamodel structure and classes, and the supplied activities start from defining, for any project, activities and phases of the relative development process, the measurable attributes to be retrieved, and the questions that compose the surveys.

Fig. 3.2 PMLite homepage.

Fig. 3.3 Interface for the insertion of a new activity.

To better describe the structure of the tool, we concentrate on three key actions: *i)* definition of the process, *ii)* definition of the survey, and *iii)* execution of the survey.

Definition of the process.

The homepage of PMLite (Fig. 3.2) allows the access to specific functions of the application.

The first step is the definition of the specific development processes in terms of phases, activities (see Fig. 3.3), and relationships between phases and related activities. Further, the tool allows to define the transitions between the activities them selves. In this way, the process is well defined and projects can be linked to the specific process.

Then, managers have to define the attributes over which the analysis will be based. The tool makes simple the insertion of measurable attributes (see Fig. 3.4) but the procedure of specification of them is critical, since they will be the basis for the definition of questions, of surveys, and, consequently, of the whole measurement framework. At the time being, an attribute is only characterized by its name and description.

Definition of the survey.

In its full implementation, the metamodel requires attributes to be retrieved by automatic extractors (i.e. instances of trigger classes). However, for the reasons explained above, PMLite simulates the automatic triggers via specific question sets; users interact with PMLite by answering to the questions associated to the current activity.

PMLite gives specific interfaces to fulfil these actions. In particular, the interface in Fig. 3.5 presents a complete set of questions. Each question is characterized by a text and three possible types of answers (*clear text*, *single choice*, and *multiple choices*). Each question is then gathered in a specific *Question Set*, which, in turn, is associated to a specific process phase or activity. This allows the system presenting to developers the questions sets concerning the specific development action they are performing.

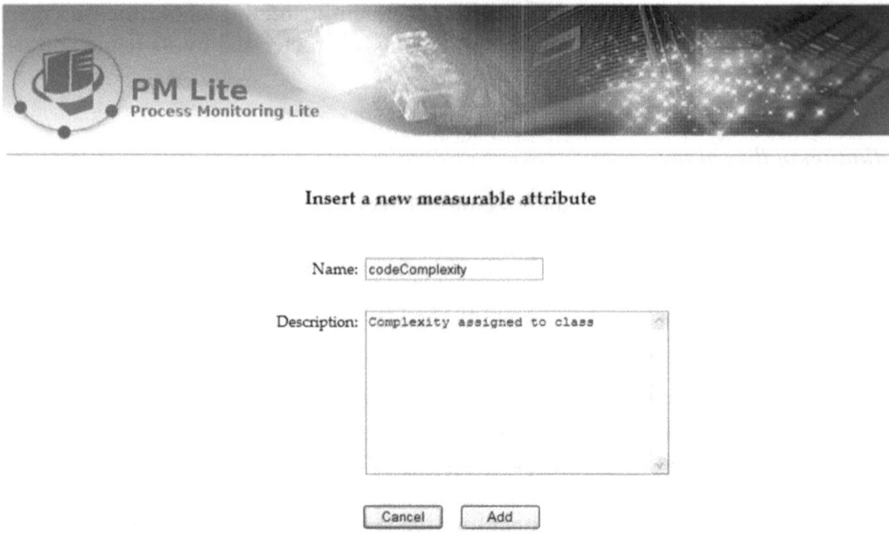

Fig. 3.4 Interface for the insertion of a new attribute.

Fig. 3.5 Interface for the management of questions.

Execution of the survey.

As said above, each questions set is relative to a specific phase or activity of a process, therefore it is important that the tool will presents to users the questions that are specific of the activity or the phase they are working on. In the interface in Fig. 3.6 first, developers choose the current activity or phase, then, PMLite presents to them the relative series of questions.

The approach followed in developing PMLite, at a first sight, could seem too intrusive, since developers have to manually interact with the survey interface any time they start a new activity or a new process. However, this allows adopting PMLite even in lightweight development environments where no configuration management or event tracking is available.

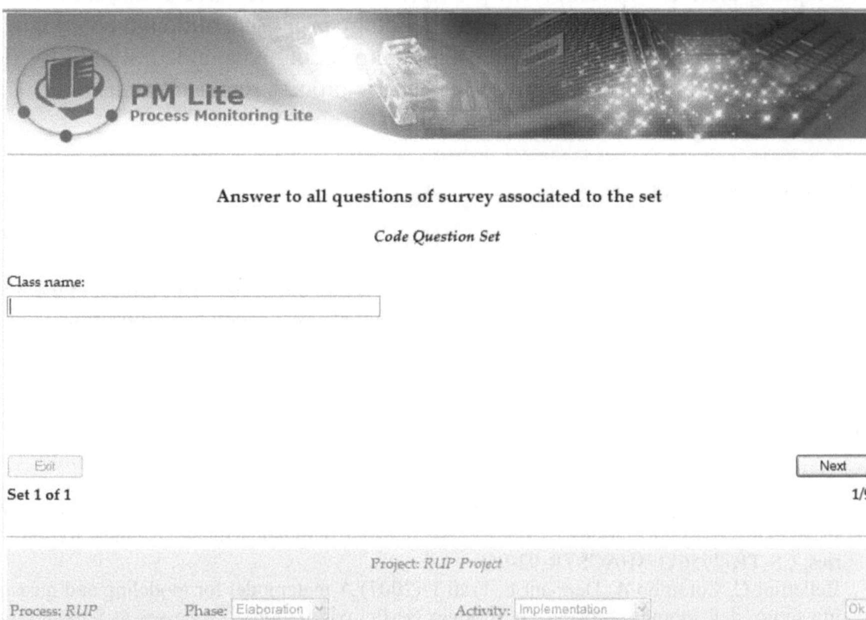

Fig. 3.6 Interface for the execution of the surveys.

4. Future Works

PMLite is only the first step in the development of a complete and automatic process monitoring environment, which will be fully transparent and non-intrusive for the developers, but allows us to test and proof our approach.

Our metamodel has been fully exploited for the designing of the structure of a more complete monitoring open source tool, Spago4Q [9].

We plan to exploit PMLite also for the definition and as proof-of-concept of specialized GQM, as for instance for the quality assessment of Open Source products and for the complexity evaluation of business process.

5. Conclusions

In this paper we presented our new open source tool, PMLite, which implements our study [2] of a metamodel to completely formalize an enterprise-level process monitoring framework. PMLite is directed to these organizations that manage projects adopting different development processes and want to have a snapshot of the global status of the current works. The methodology proposed, although could seems intrusive for developers, has the unique strength of being adaptable not only for development process monitoring, but also for generic process representations.

Acknowledgments

This work was supported in part by the European Union within the SecureSCM project in the FP7-ICT Programme under contract n. AO213531, and by contract/grant sponsor FIRB research fund of MIUR, research project TEKNE (contract/grant n.RBNE05FKZ2).

References

[1] Basili VR (1992) Software modeling and measurement: The goal question metric paradigm. In MD University of Maryland, College Park, editor, Computer Science Technical Report Series, CS-TR-2956 (UMIACSTR-92-96)

[2] Bellettini C, Colombo A, Damiani E, Frati F (2007) A metamodel for modeling and measuring scrum development process. In Springer Berlin, editor, Agile Processes in Software Engineering and Extreme Programming - Lecture Notes in Computer Science, 4536:74-83

[3] OMG Group (2008) Mof - metaobject facility. www.omg.org/mof/. Accessed January 2008.

[4] OMG Group (2008) Spem software process engineering metamodel. www.omg.org/technology/ documents/formal/spem.htm. Accessed January 2008

[5] Ventura Martins P, Rodrigues da Silva A (2005) Pit-p2m: Projectit process and project metamodel. In Proc. of OTM Workshops, Cyprus, 516-525

[6] PMLite (2007) Process monitoring lite. sourceforge.net/projects/ pm-lite/. Accessed January 2008.

[7] F. Ruìz, A. Vizcaìno, F. Garcìa, and M. Piattini (2003) Using xmi and mof for representation and interchange of software processes. In Proc. of 14th International Workshop on Database and Expert Systems Applications (DEXA'03), Prague, Czech Republic

[8] K. Schwaber (1995) Scrum development process. In Proc. of OOPSLA'95 Workshop on Business Object Design and Implementation, Austin, TX, US

[9] Spago Solutions (2007) Spago4q. www.spago.org/. Accessed January 2008

Requirements Acquisition in Open Source Development: Firefox 2.0

John Noll

Computer Engineering Department
Santa Clara University
500 El Camino Real, Santa Clara, CA 95053 USA
jhnoll@gmail.com

Abstract. Open Source Software Development appears to depart radically from conventional notions of software engineering. In particular, requirements for Open Source projects seem to be asserted rather than elicited.

This paper examines features of the latest major release of the Firefox web browser in attempt to understand how prevalent this phenomenon is. Using archives of mailing lists and issue tracking databases, these features were traced from first mention to release, to determine the process by which requirements are proposed, adopted, and implemented in Firefox. The results confirm the importance of user participation as developers of open source products.

Key words: Innovation, Open Source, Requirements Elicitation, Software Development

1 Introduction

Open source products have garnered significant interest in the popular as well as research literature. Banner projects like Linux, Mozilla, and Apache seem to represent a radical departure from conventional ideas of software engineering, harnessing the labor of numerous volunteers who are distributed throughout the world, contribute according to their desires and abilities, and are motivated apparently only by the joy of creating software, to produce high quality products that dominate their respective markets.

In his essay "The Cathedral and the Bazaar," Eric Raymond captured this popular conception of the differences between open source and conventional software development, arguing that open source project organization emerges from a marketplace of developers, who gradually take on increasing leadership responsibilities as their contributions to the project are recognised by their peers (the "Bazaar"). This is in contrast to the traditional top-down approach where managers set schedules and assign tasks (like priests in a "Cathedral") [43].

Research has shown that the perceived differences between open source and conventional software development projects are only partially true, at least for the highly visible projects. For example, the most successful open source software projects em-

---

Please use the following format when citing this chapter:

Noll, J., 2008, in IFIP International Federation for Information Processing, Volume 275; *Open Source Development, Communities and Quality*; Barbara Russo, Ernesto Damiani, Scott Hissam, Björn Lundell, Giancarlo Succi; (Boston: Springer), pp. 69–79.

ploy substantial numbers of paid programmers [25]. The Mozilla project has regular face-to-face meetings (augmented by teleconferencing) to review project status [35].

One area where open source software development does appear to differ is in requirements acquisition. Requirements for open source products are often asserted by developers, rather than elicited from users, in contrast to the conventional approach in which user needs are discovered through focus groups, interviews, and other means. This phenomenon has been observed by several researchers studying open source software development [13, 45].

How frequently are requirements asserted in an open source project? This paper presents results of a study of one open source product: the Firefox web browser produced by the Mozilla foundation [30]. The study attempted to determine how many features in the third major release (2.0) of Firefox were actually asserted by developers, rather than derived from user input or other sources.

Of fifteen new features in the Firefox 2 release, nine were determined to be asserted by developers, three were derived from user input, and two features had origins in "extensions" implemented by third parties using Firefox's extension mechanism.

The rest of this paper is organized as follows: the next section describes the method used to study the product's features; following that, the study results are presented. The paper concludes with a survey of related work, and conclusions.

2 Method

The Firefox project is interesting for a number of reasons. It has a large user community and is considered to be among the best web browsers available, with superior functionality and security [19]. The Firefox development organization is large and mature, so the processes used for the current release are well established and therefore represent a "typical" way of doing things for a project of this size.

As an open source project, Firefox is unusual in that it incorporates some aspects of more conventional software development organizations: regular (weekly) in-person status meetings are held (although remote participants can contribute via conference calling) [35]; a formal requirements document for Firefox 2 was written [33] and updated periodically [34]; project schedules are created and posted for review [32]. As such, one would expect to see elements of conventional software engineering practices in Firefox development processes, including requirements engineering.

The method employed for this research involved three steps:

1. Identify the set of features comprising the current (2.0) Firefox release.
2. Examine Internet resources related to Firefox, such as archives of discussion groups, web logs, issue databases, and other online forums, to discover when the feature was first proposed, and what role the person proposing the feature played (such as user or developer).
3. Determine the initial implementation of the feature (prototype by a developer, Firefox extension, or enhancement to the core codebase).
4. Categorize the requirement as asserted by a developer, either from his or her personal experience or knowledge of user needs; derived from user contribution, for

example by filing a bug report or "Request for Enhancement" in the Bugzilla issue database; or derived from competition.

The release notes for Firefox 2 (code named "Bon Echo") list fifteen new features, or enhancements to existing features, for this release:

1. "Visual Refresh" (enhancement).
2. Phishing protection (new).
3. "Enhanced search capabilities" (new).
4. "Improved" tabbed-browsing (enhancement).
5. Resumption of previous browsing session (new).
6. Web feed (RSS) preview and subscription (enhancement).
7. Spell checking (new).
8. "Live Titles" (new).
9. "Improved Add-ons manager" (enhancement).
10. Update to JavaScript version 1.7 (enhancement).
11. Search engine "plugins" in Sherlock or OpenSearch format (new).
12. Updated extension mechanism (enhancement).
13. Support for SVG text (bug fix).
14. New installer for Microsoft Windows©systems, based on the Nullsoft Scriptable Install System (enhancement) [31].

Some of these (phishing protection, session resumption, RSS subscription, spell checking, and "live titles") represent new features that were not present in previous releases. For these, the first expression of the need for the new feature was used to establish the source of the feature. Other features, such as tabbed-browsing improvements and updated extension mechanism, are modifications to existing features. In these cases, the first expression of need for enhancement (or fix) was used to establish the source of the requirement.

Some "features" listed in the release notes are really collections of enhancements to some category of Firefox behavior or appearance. For example, the "visual refresh" involves changes to icons, colors, and the shapes of buttons and panels. Likewise, the updated extension mechanism involves several changes to the way Firefox incorporates extensions developed by third parties (for example, MultiZilla [42] and Zotero [56]). In such cases, an attempt was made to establish whether the initial need was expressed as a collection, or whether separate needs were later collected under a single category.

3 Results

The results of the analysis are summarized in Table 3. The second column identifies the artifact where the first expression of the requirement was found. In two cases (Enhanced Search and JavaScript 1.7), no mention of the requirement appears before the Firefox Product Requirements Document was published; the source document for these is identified as 'PRD.'

Table 1: Source and classification of Firefox 2 Requirements

Feature	Requirement Source	Initial Implementation	Classification
Visual Re-fresh	discussion forum[8, 10]	core	asserted, from knowledge of user needs
Phishing Protection	Bugzilla[48], Internet Explorer[49]	extension (Google Safe Browsing[17])	asserted, from knowledge of user needs and competition
Enhanced Search	PRD[33]	extension (Google search toolbar[18])	derived from extension
Improved Tabbed Browsing	Mozilla Wiki[3, 16], Bugzilla[14]	prototype	asserted and formally validated
Session Resume	extensions (SessionSaver[4], Tabbedbrowser Extensions[21]), Opera	extensions	derived from extension; competition[12]
Web Feed Preview	Bugzilla[2, 28]	extensions (RSS Reader Panel[22], Sage[42])	asserted, from personal experience
Spell Checking	Bugzilla[5, 9]	extensions (SpellBound[51], Torisugari[53])	user contributed
Live Titles	discussion forum[26], developer web log[27]	prototype[26]	asserted, from personal experience
Improved Add-ons Manager	Mozilla wiki[15]	core	asserted, from personal experience
Javascript 1.7	PRD[33]	core	asserted, from personal experience[6]
Search Plugins	Safari[24], Mycroft[36], Sherlock[50], Opera[40]	core	competition
Updated Extension Mechanism	Bugzilla[39]	core	user contributed
SVG Text Support	Bugzilla[41]	core	user contributed (bug)
Windows Installer	Bugzilla[1, 38, 52]	prototype[7]	asserted, from knowledge of user needs

The third column identifies where the first implementation of the behavior appeared in Firefox; 'core' refers to the Firefox core codebase; 'extension(s)' to a package implemented using Firefox's extension mechanism that allows third parties to enhance Firefox's features with substantial functionality; and 'prototype' to a developer's prototype distributed for evaluation by the community.

The last column categorizes how the requirement was proposed; there are five categories:

1. asserted by a developer, from his or her own personal experience;
2. asserted by a developer, based on his or her personal knowledge of what users need;
3. contributed by a user who is not a developer, by posting a bug report or request for enhancement to the Bugzilla issue database;
4. derived from the success of an extension;
5. motivated by appearance of the feature in a competing product.

The majority of requirements (seven total) were asserted by developers, based on either their personal experience or knowledge of user needs.

Three features were influenced, at least in part, by competition from other browsers: Search Plugins are supported by Opera [40] and Safari [24], and are defined by the open-source search plugin efforts Mycroft [36] and Sherlock [50]; Phishing Protection was rumored to be part of an upcoming release of Internet Explorer [49]; and, Session Resume was implemented by Opera [12].

Two features (Phishing Protection and Enhanced Search) were derived directly from successful extension implementations (Google Safe Browsing [17] and Google Search toolbar [18], respectively).

Three features were derived from user contributed bug reports or requests for enhancement: Spell Checking [5, 9], Updated Extension Mechanism [39], and SVG Text Support [41].

The distinction between requirements asserted by developers, and requirements elicited from users in the textbook manner, is not as extreme as it might appear. In the case of Firefox, developers are users as well, so the difference is more one of how requirements are validated than from where they originate: in the Firefox project, requirements asserted by developers are rarely validated by a formal process; in only one case – Improved Tabbed Browsing – was any formal validation process undertaken to confirm that users did indeed need the feature [16].

Rather, requirements are typically posted to discussion forums for informal validation through feedback from other developers, and any dedicated users that participate in the forums. As a consequence, it appears that an open source project like Firefox must have a certain number of developers who are also users, in order to provide accurate requirements: since developers are the source of requirements, enough developers must be in touch with the larger user community to keep the feature set relevant to the bulk of users.

In a few cases, features were initially implemented as extensions, rather than as part of the Firefox core codebase; these extensions proved popular enough, by virtue of the number of people who installed and used them, to be considered for incorporation into the core. Similarly, some features are influenced by the same functionality being present in a competing product. Both cases, in effect, represent requirements that are implicitly validated by the market.

However, most other requirements, including those originating with user contributions, are informally validated by consensus of the core developers.

Since web browsers are a ubiquitous tool, one would expect that the majority of Firefox developers are also Firefox users with needs that are the same as the larger user community, and so this process of informal validation could be expected to work well. This may not be the case for other open source products with more focused user communities, such as ERP or health care applications.

4 Related Work

Studies of open source software development projects address a wide range of topics from economics [55] to maintainability [47].

A number of case studies have examined open source development processes, including those employed by Apache and Mozilla [29, 44, 46]. In particular, Reis and de Mattos Fortes, in their study of Mozilla development processes, report that high level requirements are specified by the Mozilla Foundation management, but all development on the Mozilla code base originates with a "bug" report, which might be submitted by another developer, tester, or end user [44]. These reports may document some product failure, or a request for enhancement.

Feller and Fitzgerald note that users are a "critical feature" [11, 10] of open source projects, as the source of new requirements. Scacchi has made several studies of requirements acquisition in open source software development; he observes that requirements "emerge" from on-line discussions which are usually open forums, rather than through traditional requirements elicitation processes, but that this emergent process, though less formal, is also effective [45, 46]. He also notes that requirements are "asserted" after the fact; other researchers have echoed this observation. In particular, German reports a similar situation in the Gnome project [13]. This seems to contradict conventional understanding that cites failure to understand requirements as a major source of software project failure.

But Trudelle observes, in his discussion of lessons learned from experience working on Mozilla, that this approach led to rework of some of the Mozilla implementation in response to user-submitted bug reports; his view is that this rework could have been avoided with traditional up-front requirements analysis and design activities [54]. Henderson echoes this view, claiming that open source projects do not employ "requirements elicitation," but that this could (and should) be easily added to open source processes [20]. Further, Nichols and Twidale observe that usability requirements are not captured well by open source projects, due to the mismatch between developers and users; their view is that the open source approach of "coding as early as possible" violates "good interface design [37]."

These observations run counter to the prevailing open source view that de-emphasizes formal design and requirements gathering, yet also hint at the possible evolution of mature projects like Firefox. One the one hand, Trudelle's view – that open source software projects need an overarching UI design and design function – seems to contradict the current success of Firefox, which is widely recognized as among the most innovative web browsers. In particular, Nichols and Twidale's assertion that "commercial software establishes the state of the art" [37] seems to be contradicted by Opera and Firefox, both of which included UI features (tabbed browsing, for example) well before Internet Explorer. Yet, the results of this study of Firefox 2 show that some formal user experience design is being undertaken; and, at least three features did follow the lead of competing commercial products.

5 Conclusions

Most Firefox requirements are asserted by developers. The Firefox project does, however, occasionally resort to more rigorous requirements validation, as in the case of the "Visual Refresh" where usability studies were conducted at Google on behalf of the Firefox effort. This confirms the views of Trudelle [54] and Henderson [20], that open source software projects could benefit from more formal requirements analysis.

Firefox is not a "pure" open source project in the spirit of Raymond's community of volunteers scratching an "itch [43]." The Firefox project incorporates some aspects of "traditional" software engineering such as requirements documents and usability studies; it also inherits face-to-face meetings, paid developers, and a formal corporate infrastructure from the Mozilla Foundation. At the same time, the Firefox project has the key aspects of an open source project that distinguish this kind of software development from conventional commercial development: transparency through publicly accessible documents and discussion forums, and direct participation by enthusiastic users.

This philosophy seems to be summed up nicely by the following comment to a usability issue in the Mozilla issue database:

> As an average user I would think: how many clicks does it need to get there?
> But there are many different average users :)
> What people really find convenient you can only know when you make a test browser with the new feature, let a thousand users use it for some weeks and then ask the right questions [23].

References

[1] alanjstr: Bug 231062 provide Firefox MSI package. `https://bugzilla.mozilla.org/show_bug.cgi?id=231062` (2004). Issue posted to Firefox issue database, accessed December 12, 2007.
[2] aldo-public: Comment on bug 270541. `https://bugzilla.mozilla.org/show_bug.cgi?id=270541c3` (2005). Comment on request for enhancement posted to Mozilla issue database, accessed October 29, 2007.

[3] Beltzner, M.: Firefox/feature brainstorming. http://wiki.mozilla.org/index.php?title=Firefox/Feature_Brainstorming&oldid=16495 (2006). Entry in Mozilla Wiki, accessed December 4, 2007.

[4] Burnett, G.: Firefox 1.5 session saver extension. http://www.yista.com/gburnett/firefox-15-session-saver-extension/ (2005). Entry posted to the *Yah, I Saw That Already* web log, accessed December 15, 2007.

[5] Cassin, R.: Bug 56301 (spellchecker) connect a spellchecker engine for Mozilla. https://bugzilla.mozilla.org/show_bug.cgi?id=56301 (2000). Issue posted to the Mozilla issue database describing a need for spell checking in Mozilla Composer, accessed December 14, 2007.

[6] Champeon, S.: JavaScript: How did we get here? http://www.oreillynet.com/pub/a/javascript/2001/04/06/js_history.html (2001). Web page, accessed December 18, 2007.

[7] Delahaye, S.: Firebird installer. http://seb.mozdev.org/firebird/ (2003). Web page, accessed December 12, 2007.

[8] Dotzler, A.: Reply to 'complete support of XP visual style?'. http://forums.mozillazine.org/viewtopic.php?p=2668 (2002). Reply to comment posted to Mozilla Themes Development forum, accessed October 3, 2007.

[9] Epperson, B.: Bug 16409 invoke spell check in browser window (multiple form fields). https://bugzilla.mozilla.org/show_bug.cgi?id=16409 (1999). Issue posted to the Mozilla issue database describing a need for spell checking in the Mozilla web browser, accessed December 14, 2007.

[10] ExNihilo: Complete support of XP visual style? http://forums.mozillazine.org/viewtopic.php?t=452 (2002). Comment posted to Mozilla Themes Development forum, accessed October 3, 2007.

[11] Feller, J., Fitzgerald, B.: A framework analysis of the open source software development paradigm. In: Proceedings of the International Conference on Information Systems, pp. 58–69. Association for Information Systems (2000)

[12] Ganesh, V.: Top 10 usability features I would like in a browser. http://geekswithblogs.net/vganesh/archive/2005/09/22/54669.aspx (2005). Web log entry, accessed December 18, 2007.

[13] German, D.M.: GNOME, a case of open source global software development. In: Proceedings of the 6th International Workshop on Global Software Development. Portland, OR USA (2003)

[14] Goodger, B.: Bug 308396 - UE fixes for tabbed browsing. https://bugzilla.mozilla.org/show_bug.cgi?id=308396 (2005). Issue posted to Firefox issue database, accessed December 5, 2007.

[15] Goodger, B.: Firefox:extension manager UI. http://wiki.mozilla.org/Firefox:Extension_Manager_UI (2005). Entry posted to Mozilla Wiki describing problems and possible solutions with the Firefox extension manager user interface, accessed November 20, 2007.

[16] Goodger, B.: Link targeting. http://wiki.mozilla.org/Link_Targeting (2006). Entry in Mozilla Wiki, accessed December 4, 2007.

[17] Goodger, B.: Phishing protection. http://wiki.mozilla.org/Phishing_Protection (2006). Mozilla wiki entry describing history and design of Firefox Phishing Protection feature.

[18] Google, Inc.: Google toolbar for Firefox. http://www.google.com/tools/firefox/toolbar/FT3/intl/en/ (2007). Web page for Google Toolbar, accessed December 12, 2007.

[19] Hamm, S.: A Firefox in IE's henhouse. Business Week (2004)

[20] Henderson, L.G.R.: Requirements elicitation in open-source programs. CrossTalk - The Journal of Defense Software Engineering **13**(7), 28–30 (2000). http://www.stsc.hill.af.mil/crosstalk/2000/07/henderson.html

[21] Hiroshi, H.: Tabbrowser extensions. http://piro.sakura.ne.jp/xul/tabextensions/old_index.html.en (2007). Web home page for (now obsolete) Tabbedbrowser Extensions, accessed December 15, 2007.

[22] jacob667: Using the RSS reader panel [tip 28]. http://jacob667.livejournal.com/9948.html (2004). Entry posted to "Jacob's Mozilla Tips" web log, accessed October 25, 2007.

[23] Klassen, R.: Comment on bug 335781. https://bugzilla.mozilla.org/show_bug.cgi?id=335781#c2 (2006). Comment to issue posted to Mozilla issue database, accessed November 19, 2007.

[24] Kottke, J.: Why are Safari and Sherlock two different applications? http://www.kottke.org/03/01/safari-sherlock-different (2003). Entry posted to *kottke.org* web log, accessed November 12, 2007.

[25] Lakhani, K.R., Wolf, R.G.: Perspectives on Free and Open Source Software, chap. Why Hackers Do What They Do: Understanding Motivation and Effort in Free/Open Source Software Projects. MIT Press (2005)

[26] Melez, M.: Microsummaries in Firefox 2.0. http://groups.google.com/group/mozilla.dev.apps.firefox/tree/browse_frm/thread/e6b47d5f7af7d77d/670a06e452b63b9d?rnum=1&_done=%2Fgroup%2Fmozilla.dev.apps.firefox%2Fbrowse_frm%2Fthread%2Fe6b47d5f7af7d77d%2F670a06e452b63b9d%3F#doc_670a06e452b63b9d (2006). Post to mozilla.dev.apps.firefox discussion group, accessed December 10, 2007.

[27] Melez, M.: son of live bookmarks. http://www.melez.com/mykzilla/2006/01/son-of-live-bookmarks.html (2006). Web log entry, accessed December 10, 2007.

[28] Milford, D.: Bug 270541 - support drag-and-drop of RSS feed (icon) from Firefox. https://bugzilla.mozilla.org/show_bug.cgi?id=270541 (2004). Request for enhancement posted to Mozilla issue database, accessed October 29, 2007.

[29] Mockus, A., Fielding, R.T., Herbsleb, J.: A case study of open source software development: The Apache server. In: Proceedings of the 22nd International Conference on Software Engineering, pp. 263–272. Limerick, Ireland (2000)

[30] Mozilla Corporation: Firefox 2. http://www.mozilla.com/en-US/firefox/ (2007). Web page about the Firefox web browser, accessed December 12, 2007.
[31] Mozilla Development Team: Firefox 2 release notes. http://en.www.mozilla.com/en/firefox/2.0/releasenotes/ (2007). Web page, accessed October 26, 2007.
[32] Mozilla Foundation: Firefox2/HistoricalSchedule. http://wiki.mozilla.org/Firefox2/HistoricalSchedule (2006). Web page describing the Firefox 2 release schedule, accessed December 12, 2007.
[33] Mozilla Foundation: Firefox2/PRD. http://wiki.mozilla.org/Firefox2/PRD (2006). Web page containing Mozilla Firefox 2 Product Requirements Document, accessed August 24, 2007
[34] Mozilla Foundation: Firefox2/Requirements. http://wiki.mozilla.org/Firefox2/Requirements (2006). Entry in Mozilla Wiki describing Firefox 2 requirements.
[35] Mozilla Foundation: Firefox2/StatusMeetings. http://wiki.mozilla.org/Firefox2/StatusMeetings (2006). Web page indexing Mozilla Firefox 2 status meeting notes, accessed October 2, 2007.
[36] Mycroft Project: Mycroft project: Sherlock & OpenSearch search engine plugins. http://mycroft.mozdev.org/index.html (2007). Web page describing the Mycroft search engine plugin collection project, accessed November 4, 2007. The "Mycroft" name comes from the name of Sherlock Holmes's brother, Mycroft, from the novels of Arthur Conan Doyle.
[37] Nichols, D.M., Twidale, M.B.: The usability of open source software. First Monday **8**(1) (2003)
[38] Nicholson, G.: Bug 238212 Firefox should have a net installer, like Seamonkey. https://bugzilla.mozilla.org/show_bug.cgi?id=238212 (2004). Issue posted to Firefox issue database, accessed December 11, 2007.
[39] Nicolas: Bug 285848 - extension manager should be able to manage the language of the extensions. https://bugzilla.mozilla.org/show_bug.cgi?id=285848 (2005). Request for enhancement posted to Firefox issue database, accessed November 21, 2007.
[40] Opera Software ASA: Changelog for Opera 6.1 beta 1 for Linux. http://www.opera.com/docs/changelogs/linux/610b1/index.dml (2001). Web page, accessed November 5, 2007.
[41] Ortyl, P.: Bug 282579 - implement <svg:textPath>. https://bugzilla.mozilla.org/show_bug.cgi?id=282579 (2005). Issue database entry describing Firefox deficiency handling <svg:textPath> tag.
[42] van Rantwijk, H.J.: MultiZilla's home page. http://multizilla.mozdev.org (2006). Home page for the MultiZilla project, cited September 6, 2006.
[43] Raymond, E.S.: The cathedral and the bazaar. In: The Cathedral and the Bazaar. O'Reilly and Associates (1999)

[44] Reis, C.R., de Mattos Fortes, R.P.: An overview of the software engineering process in the Mozilla project. In: Proceedings of the Open Source Software Development Workshop. Newcastle upon Tyne, UK (2002)

[45] Scacchi, W.: Understanding the requirements for developing open source software systems. IEE Proceedings – Software **149**(1), 24–39 (2002)

[46] Scacchi, W.: Free and open source development practices in the game community. IEEE Software pp. 59–66 (2004)

[47] Schach, S.R., Jin, B., Wright, D.R., Heller, G.Z., Offut, A.J.: Maintainability of the Linux kernel. IEE Proceedings – Software **149**(1) (2002)

[48] Schneider, F.: Bug 329292 - add SafeBrowsing anti-phishing extension to trunk for evaluation. `https://bugzilla.mozilla.org/show_bug.cgi?id=329292` (2006). Request for enhancement posted to Mozilla issue database, asserting need to integrate Safe Browsing into Firefox core.

[49] Schultz, K.: Comment on bug 329292. `https://bugzilla.mozilla.org/show_bug.cgi?id=329292#c9` (2006). Comment #9 posted to Mozilla issue database discussion of Bug 329292.

[50] Sellers, D.: Better searching with Sherlock 2. `http://www.computeruser.com/articles/1906,5,18,1,0601,00.html` (2000). Article posted to the Computer User web site, access November 12, 2007.

[51] Strong, R.: SpellBound - release notes. `http://spellbound.sourceforge.net/relnotes` (2005). Web page containing release history for the SpellBound extension to Firefox, accessed December 14, 2007.

[52] Strong, R.: Bug 326580 - Firefox 2.0 Windows installer. `https://bugzilla.mozilla.org/show_bug.cgi?id=326580` (2006). Issue posted to Firefox issue database, accessed December 11, 2007.

[53] Torisugari: Spell checker for Firebird. `http://forums.mozillazine.org/viewtopic.php?t=34799&postdays=0&postorder=asc&postsperpage=15&start=0` (2003). Entry in MozzillaZine "Extension Development" discussion forum describing initial port of Thunderbird spell checking mechanism to Firebird v. 0.7, accessed December 14, 2007.

[54] Trudelle, P.: Shall we dance? Ten lessons learned from Netscape's flirtation with open source UI development. Tech. rep., Mozilla.org (2002). URL `\url{http://www.iol.ie/\~calum/chi2002/peter_trudelle.txt}`. Presented at the Open Source Meets Usability Workshop, Conference on Human Factors in Computer Systems (CHI 2002), Minneapolis, MN. Accessed December 28, 2006.

[55] Wheeler, D.A.: Why open source software / free software (OSS/FS, FLOSS, or FOSS)? Look at the numbers! Technical report, dwheeler.com (2005). URL `http://www.dwheeler.com/oss_fs_why.html`

[56] Zotero Project: Zotero - the next generation research tool. `http://www.zotero.org/` (2007). Home page of the Zotero Project, accessed December 15, 2007.

Analysis of Coordination Between Developers and Users in the Apache Community

Yasutaka Kamei[1], Shinsuke Matsumoto[1], Hirotaka Maeshima[1],
Yoji Onishi[1], Masao Ohira[1], and Ken-ichi Matsumoto[1]
[1] Graduate School of Information Science, Nara Institute of Science and Technology 8916-5 Takayama, Ikoma, Nara 630-0192, Japan
{yasuta-k,shinsuke-m,hirotaka-m,yoji-o,masao,matumoto}@is.naist.jp

Abstract. Coordination is one of the keys for the success of open source software (OSS) communities because geographically distributed members need to collaborate on their work using communication tools (e.g., mailing lists, bulletin board systems, bug tracking systems, and so on). In this paper, we investigated the informal social structure among developers and users by analyzing two mailing lists of developers and users in the Apache community based on betweenness centrality, one centrality measure proposed by Freeman. From the analysis results, we found that (1) participants with high betweenness coordinated activities between developers and users and (2) some participants have been functioning as coordinators in the community for a long time.

1 Introduction

Today, open source software (OSS) is widely used by both individuals and users in administrative agencies and educational institutions, since many OSS products with high functionality and quality are free. Generally, OSS is developed in OSS communities on the WWW, where developers and users discuss, share, and realize diverse, innovative ideas on OSS products under development using such electronic media as mailing lists and bulletin board systems [3].

However, the community-based development process occasionally bogs down or remains stagnant due to such social factors as dissension among developers, downturns in user demand, emergence of a superior OSS, and so forth. The cessation of OSS development means end-users cannot obtain continual, sufficient support from the community for bug fixes and functional enhancement. Therefore, system administrators in an organization need to carefully decide whether they should adopt OSS as an alternative for existing commercial software.

As OSS systems become critical information infrastructure in our society, many researchers and practitioners are very interested in understanding *why OSS communities are sometimes very successful and vice versa, how participants in OSS communities can create sustainable communities, what can be done to anticipate whether OSS communities will maintain their activities in the future* and so forth. Recent studies

---

Please use the following format when citing this chapter:

Kamei, Y., Matsumoto, S., Maeshima, H., Onishi, Y., Ohira, M. and Matsumoto, K., 2008, in IFIP International Federation for Information Processing, Volume 275; *Open Source Development, Communities and Quality*; Barbara Russo, Ernesto Damiani, Scott Hissam, Björn Lundell, Giancarlo Succi; (Boston: Springer), pp. 81–92.

have tried to reveal the process of OSS development and success factors in OSS communities [7, 9].

For understanding the success factors of OSS communities, for instance, Howison et al. analyzed the informal social structure constructed from communication patterns among developers in OSS communities [6]. They found that a long-lived community does not dynamically change the structure of communications among developers [2, 6]. Raymond pointed out that user feedback to OSS products is also an important success factor [10]. Because such feedback from users as requests for new features and bug reports indicates the demand for their products, responding to such feedback allows developers to address social needs. That is, users play an important role in motivating developers to continuous OSS development.

As Raymond suggested, we also believe that feedback from users is a crucial success factor of OSS development. From this point of view, a prior study [6], which attempted to reveal the informal social structure in OSS communities, might be insufficient to understand the relationships among developers and users. In this paper, we investigate the informal social structure among developers and users, using the history data of communications in OSS communities (e.g., mailing lists).

The rest of our paper is organized as follows. Section 2 introduces related work. Section 3 explains the informal social structure in OSS communities, and Section 4 describes the details of our analysis method. Section 5 provides our case study, and Section 6 discusses the analysis results. Section 7 summarizes our paper and presents some future topics of research.

2 Related Work

Many studies on software development in OSS communities have been reported. Mockus et al. [9] investigated assumptions of OSS development using CVS logs and bug reports and revealed that a mere 4% of Apache developers contributed to 88% of the added lines of code and 66% of the fixed defects. [5] also reported similar results about community-driven OSS development. Although [5, 9] introduced the reality of OSS development from the perspective of software production by OSS developers, they did not suggest interactions among OSS developers (how they collaborate with each other and coordinate their activities). In contrast with these studies, Jensen et al. [7] illustrated role migration and advancement processes in OSS communities including the Apache community, based on qualitative and ethnographic methods. In this paper, we also analyze an aspect of OSS development processes in Apache communities by focusing on coordination processes in OSS development.

Studies have already reported the coordination process in OSS communities. Yamauchi et al. described how geographically distributed developers coordinated their activities and how electronic media were used in the coordination by analyzing the mailing lists of FreeBSD Newconfig and GNU GCC community [11]. Howison et al. analyzed the outdegree centrality of developers in five OSS communities based on bug report data in a bug tracking system [6]. [6] showed that most communities had a single core developer for long periods of time and that larger communities do not change core developers compared with smaller communities. Bird et al. examined the correlation between centralities and Apache developer contributions from developer mailing lists and the changed history of source code [1]. The analysis results indicated that developers communicating with many other developers contributed more to source code changes. The above three studies clarified the coordination and collaboration processes in OSS communities by focusing on developer activities. In this paper, we analyze the coordination between developers and users based on the above described reasons.

3 Informal Social Structure in OSS Communities

General OSS communities form a kind of online community in which participants are geographically distributed and communicate with each other through electronic media such as mailing lists and bulletin board systems (BBS). They can freely discuss ideas and exchange information on an equal footing without the influence of seniority or social position. OSS communities often provide participants with multiple mailing lists and/or BBS because diverse topics are discussed in the community, depending on the roles of participants. Most OSS communities have several subgroups (e.g., developers using the development mailing list) to encourage specific discussions.

The informal social structure with the above characteristics is represented as a communication network in Figure 1. Here the network is defined by regarding each node as a sender of a message and an edge as a sender-receiver relationship. For instance, if participant A sends message (M) to BBS and then participant B replies to M, A and B are the sender and receiver, respectively, creating a sender-receiver relationship. Based on the individual roles and purposes of the participants in OSS communities, each participant joins one or more subgroups to communicate with other participants. Below, we call participants who only join discussions in a developer group P_{dev}, participants who only have discussions in user group P_{user}, and participants who join discussions in both the developer and user groups $P_{d\cap u}$.

In OSS communities, discussions in the developer and user groups are independent of each other by nature. Therefore, the community requires people who moderately coordinate the activities to maintain their momentum in the OSS communities. We consider that the existence of a person who coordinates the activities between developers and users (e.g., center-black node in Figure 1) has important implications for OSS community activities as a whole.

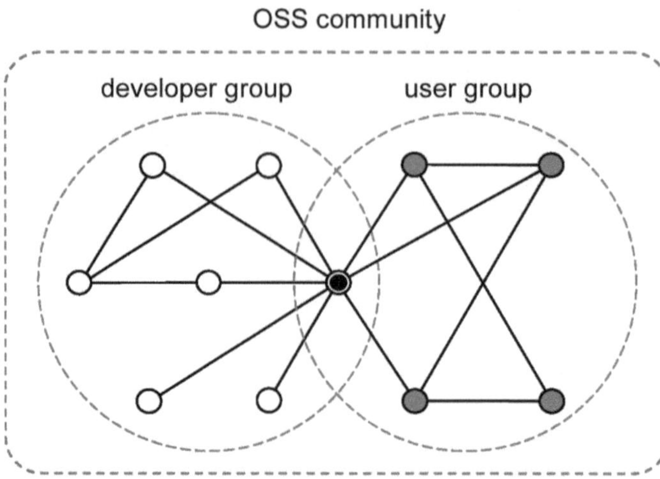

Fig. 1. Informal social structure of OSS community

4 Analysis

4.1 Analysis of coordinators

In this paper, we suppose $P_{d \cap u}$, which was discussed in both the developer and user groups, as a coordinator who arranges interactions between developers and users. We focus on a coordinator as a person who actively mediates between them. $P_{d \cap u}$ with a high degree of intermediation tightly connects developers and users and coordinates activities between developers and users. Howison et al. applied the outdegree centrality measure to the developer group in Apache to identify developers who provide a variety of information with other developers [6]. In this paper, we analyze and identify the developers who strongly connect developers and users in Apache. We use betweenness centrality, one of the centrality measures proposed by Freeman [4], as the degree of intermediation between both groups. Our analysis is composed of the following.

Visualizing the informal social structure
Visualizing the informal social structure to understand the whole picture of the structure.

Calculating the betweenness centrality
Identifying $P_{d \cap u}$ with a high degree of intermediation between developers and users by calculating the betweenness centrality for each actor in the network.

Reading contents of messages

Reading the contents of messages posted by $P_{d\cap u}$ that show high betweenness to confirm whether $P_{d\cap u}$ actually coordinates activities between both groups.

4.2 Betweenness centrality

The following describes the betweenness centrality measure proposed by Freeman [4]. Betweenness Centrality $C_{betweenness}(v_i)$ is formulated as below.

$$C_{betweenness}(v_i) = \frac{\sum^n \sum^n_{j<k} p_{jk}(v_i)}{\sum^n \sum^n_{j<k} p_{jk}}, \tag{1}$$

where n shows the number of nodes in the network, p_{jk} shows the shortest path from v_j to v_k, $\sum^n \sum^n_{j<k} p_{jk}$ shows the number of paths from v_j to v_k, and $\sum^n \sum^n_{j<k} p_{jk}(v_i)$ shows the number of paths from v_j to v_k including v_i.

$C_{betweenness}(v_i)$ takes a value from 0 to 1, and a node with a higher betweenness indicates a node that acts as an intermediator in the network. In OSS communities, we assume a node with high betweenness centrality is a participant who strongly connects other participants. Thus, if a participant with high betweenness centrality suddenly leaves the project, other participants might have trouble communicating with each other.

5 Case Study

This section describes our case study of the Apache HTTP Server community that has been developing a web server software product with the biggest market share.

5.1 Data source

In the case study, we used the following archival data sources.

Developer mailing lists

Anyone interested in working on Apache development can join this mailing list that has been archived monthly since March 1995. It is mainly used for discussions on the development of Apache, including technical topics and bug fixes.

User mailing lists

Anyone who needs support to use Apache can join this mailing list that has been archived monthly since November 2001. It is mainly used for user support, including questions and answers about Apache installation and reports about error comments.

We analyzed the above two mailing lists for three months before and after the release of the latest major version of Apache (2.2.0). We consider the person who only sends e-mails to the developer mailing lists as P_{dev}, the person who only sends emails to the user mailing lists only as P_{user} and the person who sends emails to both of them as $P_{d\cap u}$.

5.2 Data cleaning

Since some participants in the mailing lists may have several email addresses, we need to clean the data to identify such participants. We identified the same person in the mailing lists based on the following steps.

Step 1. *A sender of messages with the same email address and different "Name"*: If the same email addresses are used by different "Name" senders such as "Alice" and "Bobby," we consider them the same person.

Step 2. *A sender of messages with the same name at "From" and partially the same address before at mark (@)*: If two email addresses such as chris@domain1.com and chris@domain2.com are used by the same "Name" sender such as "Chris," we consider them the same person.

Step 3. *A sender of messages with the same name at "From" and different email addresses*: If two email addresses such as daniel@domain3.org and johnson@domain4.edu are used by the same "Name" sender such as "Daniel," we judge they are used by the same person after confirming the body of the messages (e.g., messages with the same signature).

In cleaning the data, we found 740 unique senders by applying step 1 to the data, 683 unique senders by applying step 2 to the data after step 1, and 678 unique senders by applying step 3 to the data after step 2.

5.3 Analysis results

Informal social structure We visualized the informal social structure in the Apache community based on the definition described in Section 3 to understand the whole picture of the community structure.

Figure 2 represents the network of the Apache community for the period when version 2.2.0 was released. In Figure 2, developers P_{dev}, users P_{user}, and $P_{d\cap u}$ are positioned respectively at the left, right, and center. There are $P_{d\cap u}$ with many edges between both users and developers.

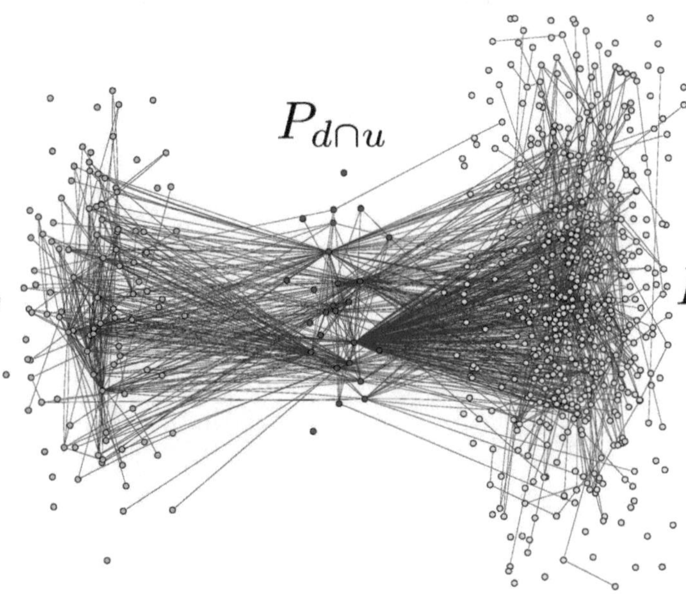

Fig. 2. Informal social structure in Apache community

Betweenness centrality We calculated the betweenness centrality of each $P_{d \cap u}$ in the network to identify the $P_{d \cap u}$ with high degree of intermediation between P_{dev} and P_{user}. Figure 3 shows the network of the top 5 $P_{d \cap u}$ of betweenness centrality. Comparing the two networks in Figures 2 and 3, we can see the top 5 $P_{d \cap u}$ intermediates between more than half of the users and developers. Counting the number of edges of the top 5 $P_{d \cap u}$, they communicated with 55 of 112 P_{dev} in the developer mailing list and with 249 of 540 P_{user} in the user mailing list.

Table 1. Statistics of top 5 $P_{d \cap u}$

	$P1_{d \cap u}$	$P2_{d \cap u}$	$P3_{d \cap u}$	$P4_{d \cap u}$	$P5_{d \cap u}$	median
Betweenness	0.179	0.044	0.043	0.022	0.019	0.001
Num. of emails	592	193	261	127	62	17
Num. of degrees with developers	15	29	33	18	11	2
Num. of degrees with users	189	31	28	19	21	1

Table 1 indicates the statistical values of the top 5 $P_{d \cap u}$. $P1_{d \cap u}$ with the highest betweenness has an extremely large number of degrees with developers (P_{dev}), compared with the left $P_{d \cap u}$. The betweenness centrality of the top 5 $P_{d \cap u}$ is 10 times higher than the median, meaning they act as intermediates between many developers and users.

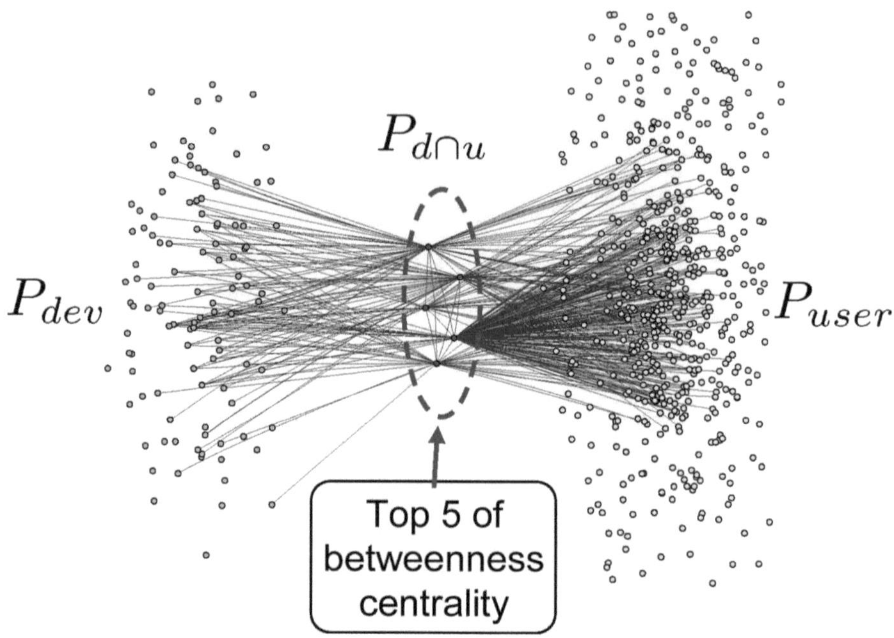

Fig. 3. Informal social structure of top 5 $P_{d\cap u}$

Content of messages We checked the contents of messages posted by the top 5 $P_{d\cap u}$ to confirm whether they actually coordinated activities between both P_{dev} and P_{user}. Five experimenters judged whether the messages related to the coordination actions of $P_{d\cap u}$. If more than three experimenters judged that a message implied coordination actions, we decided the message is related to coordination actions.

From experimenter reviews of the content of messages, we found that the top 5 $P_{d\cap u}$ with high betweenness centrality coordinated activities between developers and users. Due to space limitations in this paper, we can only show part of the reviews in Tables 2, 3, and 4.

Table 2 shows a kind of coordinative action, which is a guide of discussions (users→developers). If developer-related topics were discussed in a user group and $P_{d\cap u}$ guided them to be discussed in a developer group, we considered such action of $P_{d\cap u}$ coordination. For instance, as in Table 2, this should be discussed in a developer group, because the topic concerns implementation. In this situation, coordination is required to guide the discussions to an appropriate place (developer group).

Table 2. Guide of discussions: users→developers

sender	dialog	notes
user	*I implemented a module of Apache in a Windows environment. I want to run it on Linux.*	The user is asking a user group about the module development of Apache.
$P1_{d\frown u}$	*This should be discussed at developer ML because it is an implementation matter.*	$P1_{d\frown u}$ is guiding the user to the developer group.

Table 3 shows a kind of coordinative action, which is information transfer (users →developers). If $P_{d\frown u}$ transferred information to a developer group that only users had, we considered such action of $P_{d\frown u}$ coordination. For instance, as in Figure 3, requests for new features and product evaluations should be conveyed to developers for further development. In this situation, coordination is required to provide user feedback to a developer group.

Table 3. Information transfer: users→developers

sender	dialog	notes
developer	*Some versions do not seem very popular.*	The developer is suggesting in the developer group that some versions of Apache should be stopped from being made public because they are not popular.
$P3_{d\frown u}$	*Since I have personally received emails from users regarding their versions, I think the versions are still popular.*	$P3_{d\frown u}$ is telling the developers that the versions mentioned by the developers are still popular. He is motivating the developers to continue Apache development by describing its popularity among users.

Table 4 shows a kind of coordinative action, which is a request for participation (developers→users). The shortage of members in one group means that members not only in the group but also the developer group face bigger burdens. For instance, the shortage of testers, as in Table 4, imposes not only on current testers but also on developers because they have to develop and test the software. In this situation, coordination is required to ask users to participate in a group with few members.

Table 4. Request for participation: developers→users

sender	dialog	notes
$P3_{d\frown u}$	*It is short of testers for some minor OS. We need your contributions as testers.*	Due to the shortage of testers for some versions of Apache compiled for some minor OS, $P3_{d\frown u}$ asks the user group to participate in the tester group. Such coordination would contribute to the development by reducing the burden of developers.

6 Discussion

From the analysis results focusing on the betweenness centrality, we confirmed the existence of coordinators (the top 5 $P_{d\cap u}$ of the betweenness) who support the activities of developers and users. However, since the analysis target in Section 5.3 was only the data for the three months before and after the latest major version of Apache (2.2.0) was released, it remains unclear whether the top 5 $P_{d\cap u}$ only supported the activities of developers and users for the analysis period or also for other periods. In this section, we analyze the transition of the betweenness centrality of the top 5 $P_{d\cap u}$ from November 2001 to September 2006.

Figure 4 shows the change in the ranking of the top 5 $P_{d\cap u}$ over time. The x- and y-axes indicate the time and the betweenness centrality, respectively. We calculated the betweenness centrality using the sliding time method [8]. Here, centrality is calculated by sliding the three month analysis window month-by-month.

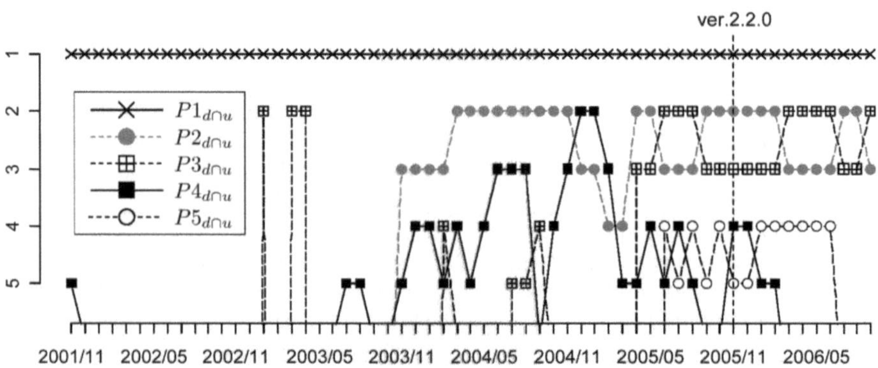

Fig. 3. Informal social structure of top 5 $P_{d\cap u}$

Figure 4 shows the existence of particular $P_{d\cap u}$ who have been intermediating between developers and users for a long time. The betweenness centrality of $P1_{d\cap u}$ was the highest for the whole period. Though we did not check all messages posted by $P1_{d\cap u}$, we believe that coordinators with consistently higher betweenness such as $P1_{d\cap u}$ continues coordinating activities between developers and users. In the Linux community, one of the most successful communities, Linus Torvalds, coordinator of the Linux Kernel community, has been contributing to its development since its start in 1991. One of the success factors of the OSS communities is the existence of coordinators who facilitate and coordinate activities among the members of OSS communities.

7 Conclusion and Future Work

In this paper, we investigated the informal social structure among developers and users using two mailing lists of developers and users in the Apache community. The following are the findings of our case study.

- participants with high betweenness coordinated activities between developers, and
- some participants have been functioning as coordinators in the community for a long time.

Here, note that our analysis results are applicable to the data from the mailing lists used in the Apache community. We need to investigate other datasets (e.g., history data in bug tracking systems) and other communities to increase the appropriateness of our results. Furthermore, the data cleaning described in Section might be imperfect because we did not find any message senders who used different names at "From" and different email addresses. We need to increase the sophistication of the data cleaning method in the near future.

Acknowledgments

This research was conducted as part of the EASE project in the Comprehensive Development of e-Society Foundation Software program, and the Stage Project, the Development of Next Generation IT Infrastructure, and Grant-in-aid for Scientific Research (B) 17300007, 2007 and for Young Scientists (B), 17700111, 2007, by the Ministry of Education, Culture, Sports, Science and Technology of Japan.

References

1. Christian Bird, Alex Gourley, Prem Devanbu, Michael Gertz, and Anand Swaminathan. Mining email social networks. In Proceedings of the 2006 International Workshop on Mining Software Repositories (MSR'06), pp. 137-143, 2006.
2. Kevin Crowston and James Howison. The social structure of free and open source software development. First Monday, Vol. 10, No. 2, 2005.
3. Joseph Feller and Brian Fitzgerald. Understanding Open Source Software Development. Addison-Wesley, 2002.
4. Linton C. Freeman. Centrality in social networks: Conceptual clarification. Social Networks, Vol. 1, No. 3, pp. 215-239, 1979.
5. Daniel German and Audris Mockus. Automating the measurement of open source projects. In Proceedings of the 3rd Workshop on Open Source Software Engineering, pp. 63-67, Portland, Oregon, 2003.

6. James Howison, Keisuke Inoue, and Kevin Crowston. Social dynamics of free and open source team communications. In Proceedings of the 2nd International Conference on Open Source Systems (OSS'06), pp. 319-330, 2006.
7. Chris Jensen and Walt Scacchi. Role migration and advancement processes in ossd projects: A comparative case study. In Proceedings of the 29th International Conference on Software Engineering (ICSE'07), pp. 364-374, 2007.
8. Takeshi Kakimoto, Yasutaka Kamei, Masao Ohira, and Kenichi Matsumoto. Social network analysis on communications for knowledge collaboration in oss communities. In Proceedings of the International Workshop on Supporting Knowledge Collaboration in Software Development (KCSD'06), pp. 35-41, September 2006.
9. Audris Mockus, Roy T Fielding, and James D Herbsleb. Two case studies of open source software development: Apache and mozilla. ACM Transactions on Software Engineering and Methodology, Vol. 11, No. 3, pp. 309-346, 2002.
10. Eric S. Raymond. The Cathedral and the Bazaar: Musings on Linux and Open Source by an Accidental Revolutionary. O'Reilly and Associates, 1999.
11. Yutaka Yamauchi, Makoto Yokozawa, Takeshi Shinohara, and Toru Ishida. Collaboration with lean media: How open-source software succeeds. In Proceedings of the 2000 Conference on Computer Supported Cooperative Work (CSCW'00), pp. 329-338, 2000.

Lost and Gained in Translation: Adoption of Open Source Software Development at Hewlett-Packard

Catharina Melian[1] and Magnus Mähring[2]
[1] Stockholm School of Economics, Center for Media and Economic Psychology, Box 6501, SE-11383 Stockholm, Sweden
catharina.melian@hhs.se
WWW home page: http://www.sse.edu
[2] Stockholm School of Economics, Department of Marketing and Strategy, Box 6501, SE-11383 Stockholm, Sweden
magnus.mahring@sse.se
WWW home page: http://www.sse.edu

Abstract. What happens when an organization form that has emerged in one context is brought into a different context? In this paper, a longitudinal field study approach is used to explore how Hewlett-Packard (HP) molded open source software development (OSSD) into a proprietary software development approach called "Progressive Open Source" (POS). With the help of actor-network theory, we understand this as a process of translation and find that some central characteristics of OSSD where lost in the translation into POS while other characteristics were gained.

1 Introduction

The advent of open source software development (OSSD) has spurred considerable interest not only amongst individual systems developers participating in voluntary and unpaid software development over the Internet, but also increasingly amongst software development organizations seeking to improve the quality and productivity of their products and services [23, 34]. In this paper, we explore what happens when OSSD is brought into a traditional, high-performing, software development organization? With the help of actor-network theory, we explore this process of *translation* [6] in Hewlett-Packard, where key actors shaped and constructed the idea of Progressive Open Source (POS) through interactions and through the meanings that they assigned to their work, interactions and experiences [18]. The purpose of the study is thus to explore the translation of an extra-organizational form of organizing, open source software development, into a corporate context.

Please use the following format when citing this chapter:

Melian, C. and Mähring, M., 2008, in IFIP International Federation for Information Processing, Volume 275; *Open Source Development, Communities and Quality*; Barbara Russo, Ernesto Damiani, Scott Hissam, Björn Lundell, Giancarlo Succi; (Boston: Springer), pp. 93–104.

2 Background

Typically, open source software development takes place in Internet-based communities of software developers who voluntarily collaborate to develop free software that they or their organizations need [26, 34]. OSSD can be seen as a new way of organizing—different from software development conducted according to the traditional paradigm [24, 28]. While there is a lot of interest in adoption and adaption of OSSD within a corporate context, and development platforms for OSSD are now offered in corporate versions [3], little research has so far been devoted to the emergence and anatomy of "hybrid" organizational forms that combine OSSD practices with corporate requirements and needs [29].

Actor-network theory (ANT) addresses how technology influences and is influenced by social elements in a setting over time [6, 7, 20]. According to ANT, the ideas, values and intentions of social actors become inscribed in a technology through interaction. As a result, intentions become immutable [1, 2, 18]. The process through which this occurs involves creation of networks of aligned interests: actors form alliances, enroll other actors and use non-human actors (artifacts, technologies) to secure their interests. The resulting actor-networks are made up of human and non-human actors [7, 19].

The creation of an actor-network, referred to as translation or "the methods by which an actor enrolls others" [5, p. xvii], results—if successful—in a stable actor-network that encompasses non-human actors. In our case, the focal non-human actor is the idea or technology of open source. ANT predicts that the translation of OSSD into a particular context includes some transformation of the idea/technology; the involved actors become aligned in interests, commitments and obligations and as part of this development the idea/technology is instantiated or situated [32].

In this paper, we employ two supplementing views of translation. Steiner [31] emphasizes the journey (or re-formation) of an idea, while Callon [6] emphasizes the formation of the network of actors that in an interactive process constructs itself and incorporates the idea/technology. With this combined view of translation, the process can be described as follows:

1. *Initial act of trust* [31] and *problematization* [6]: At the beginning of the process, a translator assumes that a particular model or idea (e.g., OSSD) makes sense and that it can be reproduced in a different context [31]. The translator opens up for new ways of thinking, and through social interaction the identities and interests of a set of relevant actors start to emerge [6].
2. *Incursion* and *extraction* [31] and *interessèment* [6]: The translator(s) raids the original idea for sense, and bring back that which makes particular sense for the organization. Relatedly, actors attempt to define "the problem" by manipulating and (re)negotiating relationships between concerned actors.
3. *Incorporation* [31] and *enrolment* [6]: In this stage, actors mold, or give particular form and body, to those aspects of an idea that fit into the organizational texture and the idea becomes incorporated. As this happens, actors come to accept

the designated roles attributed to them and the formation of an actor-network occurs.

4. *Appropriation* [31] and *mobilization* [6]: At this stage, the original idea is transformed and becomes intertwined with the organization. The idea is also appropriated—the new idea has taken over all relevant meaning from the old idea and the original idea has no separate identity anymore. Correspondingly, some actors come to represent others and mechanisms are put in place that stabilize the actor-network and keep actors behaving in accordance with interests. At this point, the actor-network and its ideas, technology, and artifacts have become institutionalized and are no longer seen as controversial.
5. *Reciprocation* [31]: While the actor-network is already at this point stable, the translated idea may at this point come to enhance the original idea. For example, the idea resulting from a translation may, if successfully institutionalized, contribute to enhancing the stature of the original idea.

The idea/technology in focus in this study is OSSD, and the translation studied is the re-formation of OSSD into POS within Hewlett-Packard. The challenge of adapting OSSD in a corporate context [29] can thus be seen as dependent on the molding of the idea of open source into a form that fits the context and the corresponding formation of a stable actor-network that performs the appropriation of the idea and sustains the idea and its use. On the basis of this argument and our brief exposé of ANT, we argue that ANT is well suited to advance our understanding of the challenge of corporate OSSD adoption. However, we have not found any studies of corporate OSSD adoption that employ ANT and only one study of OSSD using ANT outside of the corporate context [33]. This sets the stage for our study.

3 Methodology

In 2001, the first author established initial contact with Hewlett-Packard (HP). An agreement was reached to document HP's efforts to introduce the new software development paradigm within the organization. Access to contacts, data and other resources was provided and the field researcher was assigned an office cubicle at HP labs in Palo Alto, California.

The longitudinal field study [4, 25] encompassed nine months in the field at HP between October 2001 and April 2002, in August 2002, and in May 2003. Time spent in the field included direct observation of work, participation in meetings, participation in workplace conversations and dialogues, and extensive field note writing [8, 9]. The study also encompassed 52 formal interviews (semi-structured interviews averaging two hours that were taped and transcribed), corporate and external documents and other forms of secondary data [27]. The data was subsequently coded using NVivo software for qualitative data analysis.[1] For the purpose of this paper, an

[1] For more information on research methodology and case details, see Melian [22].

actor-network lens was selected to further deepen the emerging understanding of the transformation (or translation) of OSSD in the HP context. In particular, the translation model presented in the previous section was used to structure, present and analyze the case.

4 The Translation of Open Source at Hewlett-Packard

In this section we briefly summarize the chains of events that resulted in the widespread use of progressive open source (POS) within Hewlett-Packard Company in the period from 2001 to 2003. Then as now, HP was an engineering company where product development and hi-tech engineering were high-status activities seen as central to the organization's survival and success.

4.1 Initial Act of Trust and Problematization

At the end of the 1990s, actors in several units within HP were involved in discussions on challenges related to product development. The 1990s had seen extremely rapid development in IT products and services as well as a rapid increase in demand for such products and services. There were recurrent discussions within different software development units in HP on the need to reform the software development process and a number of possible remedies and aspirations were studied. In order to increase cost efficiency and shorten time to market, it was perceived necessary to increase use of third parties (for collaborative and outsourced development) and to conduct around the clock ("24/7") development. In addition, software modularization and extensive, systematic reuse of software components was seen as an approach to avoid "reinventing the wheel" and to increase component compatibility.

> *A discussion came up about how we need to find a way we can work better with third parties, and there was some bantering about how there is Open Source, but we have security needs that we have to make sure that we don't expose our IP[2] .... — HP Software developer.*

Many developers within HP were already tinkering with OSSD in their free time and examples of successful open source projects (Linux, Apache web server) were well-known within HP.

The idea of open source as an idea was thus met with an initial act of trust: actors within HP believed OSSD to offer an attractive approach and solution to perceived problems and challenges [31]. The descriptions and definitions of problems were, from an ANT perspective, not objective depictions of a "real" reality, but rather expressions of interests and interpretations by actors involved in the organizational discourse [7, 19]. The engineering community within HP was dominant in this initial identification of OSSD as a preferred idea for organizational betterment and object of trust.

[2] Intellectual property.

4.2 Incursion and Extraction, and Interessèment

The chief technology officer (CTO) of the Imaging and Printing business area, Lee Caldwell, initiated a project to address these issues, called CDP (for Collaborative Development Program). Robert (Rob) Miller, a senior scientist at HP, was appointed to lead the project.

> *Rob was just having the idea that this is just one of his jobs, and he kind of looking around and it was a combination of both Open Source and just the issue around collaboration and being able to tap into the expertise around the business and the company. — HP Software developer.*

Miller started to search for successful examples of collaboration between development teams in HP and found the Sirius Firmware Cooperative, a group that had developed new firmware architecture for multifunction peripherals in the early 1990s. Four geographically dispersed teams collaborated using a common work process with interconnected core teams and a well-defined peer review process. In order to learn more about Sirius, Miller contacted Cathy Ammirati, head of the Sirius co-op. Ammirati was subsequently invited to join the CDP effort, while Sirius continued to function as a separate entity. In parallel, people involved in the CDP effort read the open source literature and tapped into the discourse on the potential of corporate adoption of open source present in Silicon Valley at this time.

> *I started learning about open source, and did the typical thing most people do, read 'The Cathedral and the Bazaar',3 started reading up as much as I could about it and said its very fascinating to see how we could bring this into HP, and how it could work inside of HP in such a structured environment of Hewlett-Packard... — Software developer involved in setting up CDP.*

While the CDP effort was initiated by the CTO and had strong corporate backing, engineers also maintained and nurtured open source as "their thing". For example, the adoption of open source in the corporate setting was seen as a way to cope with the organizational "reality" shaped by the administrative/managerial community. In this way, different actors were able to selectively assign meaning to the new idea [31] and inscribe it with their intentions [1, 18].

4.3 Incorporation and Enrolment

By now the approach of CDP was to try to learn and evaluate what open source could mean to HP through experience with real software development tasks. By July 2000, the first tasks were set up in the CDP environment, which was still under development:

> *...we are driving the car down the road and we are improving it as we go. We're in there tinkering under the hood, somebody's hanging off the side fixing the door lock.... — Manager, CDP.*

[3] See Raymond [26].

Independent of the CDP effort, senior scientist Pankaj Garg at HP Labs had at this time initiated a software development environment, Corporate Source (CS), devised to function as an open source environment restricted to HP employees. Most of the development effort went into CDP as a development platform (including development, storage and communication tools) was purchased. CS was used separately and was continuously compared with CDP. In late 2000, the concept of progressive open source (POS) was put forward as a way to describe open source initiatives within HP. HP's increasing attention *to open source was also reflected in public speeches by HP's CEO:*

> *The open source movement is natural, inevitable and creates huge benefits. It's part of the next wave of computing, and that will involve participants and users within the industry in open source. — CEO Carly Fiorina, October 2000.*

Within CDP, a set of defined benefits were formulated that matched the previously identified challenges for HP software development. These included increased code reuse, improved code quality, faster development, faster debugging, and selected partner collaboration. In addition, rapid re-deployment of key developers between projects was seen as facilitated by the common platform and work process. Leading actors posted internal "tech reports" (later presented at public conference [10, 11]) that outlined the benefits of adopting open source within Hewlett-Packard.

The creation of the "POS" concept can be understood as creation of a vessel that facilitated the extraction of meaning from OSSD and the transfer of relevant meaning from the original to the new concept [31]. Also, this phase sees the introduction of an important non-human actor: the CDP development platform and the key attributes of the platform and related services (such as security, search and navigation, migration, and technical support).

4.4. Appropriation and Mobilization

In late 2001 and early 2002, POS was established as a new and paradigmatically different approach to software development within HP. The different breeds and varieties of "open source" initiatives within HP are now explicitly and systematically described as being part of POS, with the notable exception of Sirius. Over a period of 18 months from the original launch of the CDP development platform, there was considerable growth in the number of developers on the CDP platform. The pilot project had encompassed 600 developers. In April 2001, CDP moved to a production environment and by August there were over 2000 users, ten percent of which outside HP. By January 2002 there were 3500 users and over the next few years, the CDP environment would grow to over 10,000 users.

The diffusion of the CDP platform was supported through increasingly well-defined roles: executive champions (the chief technology officer and the chief information officer), sponsors, R&D change leaders, and information technology staff. The executive champions stressed the need for collaboration between development groups in the organization and applied pressure on software managers to transition to the CDP platform. The sponsors committed development resources and the R&D

change leaders were appointed to enable and support a dialogue of culture change and POS training. The IT staff provided the critical collaboration infrastructure on a 24x7 supported basis.

The standardization of development work through the CDP development platform was a painful process for many development teams, but in most cases teams decided to adopt and adapt to the platform and related work methods. The CDP platform thus constituted a mechanism—inscribed with intentions—that stabilized the actor-network and restricted actors to behave in accordance with inscribed interests [6]. POS and CDP had by this time become dominant concepts to describe activities within HP aiming at open, collaborative development. Open source was no longer an important or frequently used concept. In accordance with Steiner's [31] view of translation, the new idea had taken over all relevant meaning from the old idea and the original idea had no separate identity in this particular context anymore.

As more developers transition into the CDP development environment, the development platform becomes an increasingly important non-human actor: Because of the standardization on CDP, third-party developers collaborating with HP had to transition into CDP. Acceptance of the CDP environment and its rules and roles became a necessary prerequisite for continuing to do business with HP.

However, as the use of CDP increased quite rapidly, scalability problems appeared: there were several breakdowns of the development platform during the growth period during 2002. In spite of the breakdowns, the actor-network had become strong and stable enough to impose itself on a gradually larger percentage of HP developers who are faced with a "take it or leave it" offer of joining CDP. For individual developers, there was a risk that the change in development environment would manifest itself in loss of productivity and motivation.

More profound changes in the software development process also started to appear. The previous common practice of *working* "under the radar" was no longer a preferred or even allowed approach to development work. Instead, all development work needed to be out in the open on the CDP platform. Software developers perceived increased pressure as a result of the open and transparent process: In the POS/CDP environment, every contribution, absence of contribution, mistake, misunderstanding, and spontaneous comment was directly attributable to an identified individual. This was in direct contrast to OSSD, where contributing developers are normally anonymous. While POS technology facilitated openness it also besieged privacy and exposed the individual:

...the fishbowl aspect of feeling like you're being watched with every little thing you do. ... It does affect the way that I post to the forum. — Software developer.

In relation to this, HP managers started to comment to each other that a new "breed" of employee was needed—people that could cope with the "fish bowl" visibility of their actions and not let that hamper their openness or they way they interact with others.

4.5 Reciprocation

Through POS, HP managed to improve the efficiency, speed and quality of software development. Unlike the original idea of open source, the POS reincarnation also adhered to traditional criteria for software development in that development work was successfully conducted within time and budget. In this sense, POS can be seen as contributing to the status of OSSD [31] by demonstrating its superiority as development approach also in the (foreign) corporate context.

5 Discussion

We have followed the OSSD idea/technology as it traveled from its original, extra-organizational context and translated into POS; transformed, yet partly the same [17, 31]. Main differences between open source software development and progressive open source in Hewlett-Packard are found in

POS became different from OSSD in order to survive and prosper; that is, in order to become an integral part of a stable and growing actor-network [6, 18]. In particular, our analysis of the case shows that key elements of the HP organization were perceived to be at odds with OSSD *as organizing*. The formal hierarchy and related reporting and control structure—including financial and other goals per unit and area, individual evaluations and rewards—as well as the HP culture were also seen as dominant and immutable features of the HP organization.

Consequently, the incursion and extraction of meaning [31] from OSSD by HP actors focused on those elements of OSSD that were compatible with key organizational design elements of the existing HP organization. The translation of OSSD into POS was mainly intended to change work practices related to software development work, to extend those work practices to incorporate selected corporate partners in controlled ways, and to allow tinkering with open communities for software development.

In this respect, POS can be considered a success. The goals of 24/7 development, more effective reuse of technology and increased number of parallel development processes were achieved. The spread of POS within HP has also been considerable and the practices developed during the case period are still used. In other words, a stable and growing actor-network that formed by the originators of POS, over 10,000 developers, the idea of POS and the CDP development platform. It can also be argued that the success of POS within HP has enhanced the original idea of OSSD (i.e., reciprocation) by making OSSD a more credible idea/technology for organizational adaption [31].

Table 1. A Comparison of Open Source and Progressive Open Source

Open Source Software Development (OSSD) [Based on 12, 15, 16, 26, 30, 35, 36]	Progressive Open Source (POS)
No formal organization, rather a social phenomenon.	Formal organizational entity, sometimes involving 3rd party developers.
Gift system [21]. Underlying notion: abundance. Each gift is part of system of reciprocity. Every gift has to be returned in a perpetual cycle of exchanges.	Market system. Underlying notion: scarcity. Calculated gains and losses, utility maximization.
Very open and free flow of information.	Progressively more open – however controlled flow of information between trusted partners internal and sometimes external to the formal organization.
Voluntary teams working on projects.	Designated teams, i.e. employees and/or contractors working on defined projects loyal to a formal organization.
Meritocracy/benevolent dictatorship.	Traditional hierarchical organization.
Sociological phenomenon. Has the potential of bringing together software practitioners regardless of their prior record (employment, education, age, status, etc.). Only the validity of the contribution counts.	Organizational phenomenon. Technology in place that enables collaboration between software engineers employed and/or contracted by the organization and trusted partners.
No time and budget constraints.	Often strict time frames and budget restrictions.
Potentially limitless influx of knowledge and skills – infinite number of developers.	Controlled number of developers. Significantly smaller than Open Source community.
Public good: Non-rival (one person's consumption of the good does not reduce the amount available to another) and non-excludable (excluding others from consuming the public good is difficult or impossible)	Privately owned/controlled intellectual property rights.
Challenge: How to get people to contribute and avoid free riding. How to coordinate a large group of individuals that want to contribute.	Challenge: How to move from a control based organization to an organization based on empowerment and trust. How to reward collaborative behavior.
Motivation to contribute: Identity (honor, reputation, ego-boosting) Reciprocity Efficacy: individuals contribute because they have some impact on the system. Art and beauty of solving problems Work as vocation	Motivation to contribute: Monetary Patents Ranking system/reward-system

However, several interesting apparent paradoxes can be observed through comparison between OSSD and POS. POS has not only failed to fulfill some of the promises of the OSSD idea: in some aspects, POS produces the opposite of the original OSSD idea. While OSSD takes place in loosely coupled cyberspace communities [16] with weak ties [14] and without many of the restrictions and requirements of corporate contexts [16], the introduction of POS at HP increased the level of structure and standardization of development work. Standardization included forms of expression, language use, defined layers of openness, and the requirement to safeguard intellectual property also in controlled "open" source projects. In some ways, this was far from the corporate culture of "cowboy development", while in other ways it further enabled micro-managing by managers.

There were also considerable resemblances between OSSD and POS, such as transparency of the development process, constant up-to-date documentation, the large number of "eyeballs" involved in debugging, and 24/7 development. Together, these similarities suggest that central aspects of the open source development work process remained quite intact through the translation process. On the individual level, however, the differences were fundamental. Whereas OSSD enables flexible participation in development work with limited real life consequences, POS has created quite the opposite work environment. In the organizational context, with long-term social relationships and well-defined hierarchy, POS makes the quality and level of contribution of individual developers highly visible. This visibility shapes an environment where an underperforming employee can neither run, nor hide from scrutiny—a virtual panopticon in which every mistake is likely to get noticed [13]. In addition, the balance between openness and safeguarding of intellectual property places intellectual property decisions with individual developers and makes these decisions a part of daily practice.

6 Conclusions and Implications

Using actor-network theory, this research has studied the appropriation of open source practices in HP as a translation of an organization form from an extra-organizational context to a corporate context. The study shows that in the translation of open source into the corporate context, some fundamental aspects of OSSD are lost, while other fundamental aspects of the new hybrid form of software development—progressive open source—are shaped.

The study strongly suggests that a translation of OSSD into the corporate context may come to yield substantial and lasting benefits to efficiency, speed, quality, flexibility and reusability in software development. However, our study also reveals that while many of the characteristics of the work process may remain intact through the translation, the organizational characteristics of open source in the corporate context, particularly in terms of monitoring and control of the individual, may starkly contrast traditional open source environments. The implications of these findings for stakeholders in organizations considering OSSD adoption are far-reaching and will hopefully inspire further research.

Acknowledgments

We sincerely thank the people in Hewlett-Packard for generously giving of their time and thoughts, and for their enthusiasm—for their own work as well as for this study.

References

1. Akrich, M. The de-scription of technical objects, in W.E. Bijker and J. Law, ed., *Shaping technology/building society: Studies in sociotechnical change*, Cambridge, MA: MIT Press, 1992, 205-224.
2. Akrich, M., and Latour, B. A summary of a convenient vocabulary for the semiotics of human and nonhuman assemblies, in W.E. Bijker and J. Law, ed., *Shaping technology/building society: Studies in sociotechnical change*, Cambridge, MA: MIT press, 1992, 259-264.
3. Augustin, L.; Bressler, D.; and Smith, G. Accelerating software development through collaboration, in *Proceedings of The 24th International Conference on Software Engineering* Orlando, FL, 2002559-563.
4. Barley, N. *The innocent anthropologist: Notes from a mud hut.* Long Grove, IL: Waveland Press, 1983.
5. Callon, M. The sociology of an actor-network: The case of the electric vehicle, in M. Callon, J. Law, and A. Rip, ed., *Mapping the dynamics of science and technology*, London: Macmillan, 1986.
6. Callon, M. Some elements of a sociology of translation: Domestication of the scallops and the fishermen of st brieuc bay, in J. Law, ed., *Power, action and belief: A new sociology of knowledge?*, London: Routledge and Kegan Paul, 1986, 196-233.
7. Callon, M., and Latour, B. Unscrewing the big leviathan: How actors macro-structure reality and how sociologists help them to do so, in K. Knorr-Cetina and A.V. Cicourel, ed., *Advances in social theory and methodology: Toward an integration of micro-and macro-sociologies*, London: Routledge and Kegan Paul, 1981, 277-303.
8. Czarniawska, B. *Narrating the organization. Dramas of institutional identity.* Chicago and London: The University of Chicago Press, 1997.
9. Czarniawska, B. *Writing management.* Oxford University Press, 1999.
10. Dinkelacker, J., and Garg, P.K. Corporate Source: Applying open source concepts to a corporate environment, in *Proceedings of Proceedings of the First ICSE International Workshop on Open Source Software Engineering*, Toronto, Canada, 2001.
11. Dinkelacker, J.; Garg, P.K.; Miller, R.; and Nelson, D. Progressive open source, in *Proceedings of Proceedings of the 24th International Conference on Software Engineering (ICSE)*, Orlando, FL., 2002177-184.
12. Fitzgerald, B. The transformation of open source software. *MIS Quarterly*, 30, 3, 2006, 587-598.
13. Foucault, M. *Discipline and punish: The birth of the prison.* Harmondsworth: Penguin, 1977.

14. Granovetter, M.S. The strength of weak ties. *The American Journal of Sociology*, 78, 6, 1973, 1360-1380.
15. Kollock, P. The economies of online cooperation: Gifts and public goods in cyberspace, in M.A. Smith and P. Kollock, ed., *Communities in cyberspace*, London: Routledge, 1999, 220-242.
16. Kollock, P., and Smith, M.A. Communities in cyberspace, in M.A. Smith and P. Kollock, ed., *Communities in cyberspace*, London: Routledge, 1999, 3-28.
17. Latour, B. The powers of association, in John Law, ed., *Power, action and belief. A new sociology of knowledge?*, London: Routledge & Kegan Paul, 1986, 264-280.
18. Latour, B. Technology is society made durable, in J. Law, ed., *A sociology of monsters: Essays on power, technology and domination*, London: Routledge and Kegan Paul, 1991, 103-131.
19. Latour, B. *Aramis, or the love of technology*. Cambridge, MA: Harvard University Press, 1996.
20. Latour, B. *Pandora's hope: Essays on the reality of science studies*. Cambridge, MA: Harvard University Press, 1999.
21. Mauss, M. *The gift: The form and reason for exchange in archaic societies*. New York, NY: W.W. Norton, 1950.
22. Melian, C. *Progressive Open Source: The construction of a development project at Hewlett-Packard*, Dissertation, Stockholm School of Economics, 2007.
23. Nelson, M.L.; Sen, R.; and Subramaniam, C. Understanding open source software: A research classification framework. *Communications of the Association for Information Systems*, 2006, 17, 2006, 2-37.
24. O'Mahony, S., and Ferraro, F. The emergence of governance in an open source community. *Academy of Management Journal*, 50, 5, 2007, 1079-1106.
25. Pettigrew, A.M. Longitudinal field research on change: Theory and practice. *Organization Science*, 1, 3, 1990, 267-292.
26. Raymond, E.S. The cathedral and the bazaar. *FirstMonday*, 3, 3, 1997, Accessed: February 26, 2007, http://www.firstmonday.org/issues/issue3_3/raymond/.
27. Richards, L. *Handling qualitative data: A practical guide*. London: Sage Publications, 2005.
28. Roberts, J.A.; Il-Horn, H.; and Slaughter, S.A. Understanding the motivations, participation, and performance of open source software developers: A longitudinal study of the apache projects. *Management Science*, 52, 7, 2006, 984-999.
29. Shah, S.K. Motivation, governance, and the viability of hybrid forms in open source software development. *Management Science*, 52, 7, 2006, 1000-1014.
30. Smith, M.A. Invisible crowds in cyberspace: Mapping the social structure of the Usenet, in M.A. Smith and P. Kollock, ed., *Communities in cyberspace*, London: Routledge, 1999, 195-219.
31. Steiner, G. *After Babel: Aspects of language and translation*. Third ed., Oxford: Oxford University Press, 1998.
32. Suchman, L.A. *Plans and situated actions: The problem of human-machine communication*. Cambridge: Cambridge University Press, 1987.
33. Tuomi, I. Internet, innovation, and open source: Actors in the network. *FirstMonday*, 6, 1, 2001, Accessed: December 8, 2007, http://www.firstmonday.org/ISSUES/issue6_1/tuomi/index.html.
34. von Hippel, E., and von Krogh, G. Open source software and the 'private-collective' innovation model: Issues for organization science. *Organization Science*, 14, 2, 2003, 209-223.
35. von Krogh, G., and von Hippel, E. The promise of research on open source software. *Management Science*, 52, 7, 2006, 975-983.
36. Weber, S. *The success of open source*. Cambridge, MA: Harvard University Press, 2004.

Mining for Practices in Community Collections: Finds From Simple Wikipedia

Matthijs den Besten[1], Alessandro Rossi[2], Loris Gaio[2], Max Loubser[3], and Jean-Michel Dalle[4]
[1] University of Oxford, Oxford e-Research Centre, 7 Keble Road, OX13QG, Oxford, UK
matthijs.denbesten@oerc.ox.ac.uk,
WWW home page: http://users.ox.ac.uk/~ierc0002
[2] University of Trento, Department of Computer and Management Science, Via Inama 5, I-38100, Trento, Italy
{arossi,lgaio}@cs.unitn.it,
WWW home page: http://rock.cs.unitn.it/{arossi,lgaio}
[3] Oxford Internet Institute, 1 St Giles, OX13JS, Oxford, UK
max.loubser@magd.ox.ac.uk,
WWW home page: http://people.oii.ox.ac.uk/loubser
[4] Université Pierre et Marie Curie, c/o Agoranov, 3, rue Castex 75004, Paris, France
jean-michel.dalle@upmc.fr,
WWW home page: http://www.upmc.fr

Abstract. The challenges of commons based peer production are usually associated with the development of complex software projects such as Linux and Apache. But the case of open content production should not be treated as a trivial one. For instance, while the task of maintaining a collection of encyclopedic articles might seem negligible compared to the one of keeping together a software system with its many modules and interdependencies, it still poses quite demanding problems. In this paper, we describe the methods and practices adopted by Simple Wikipedia to keep its articles easy to read. Based on measurements of article readability and similarity, we conclude that while the mechanisms adopted by the community had some effect, in the long run more efforts and new practices might be necessary in order to maintain an acceptable level of readability in the Simple Wikipedia collection.

1 Introduction

Issues pertaining to how communities form, operate, and sustain themselves loom large in any project where voluntary participants gather to create something of value. There are growing concerns regarding which methods and practices within these communities account for their success. This is particularly important if one is interested in replicating successful models to other types of commons–based peer productions. This question is also fueled by quality concerns: if we are to employ a

Please use the following format when citing this chapter:

Besten, M., Rossi, A., Gaio, L., Loubser, M. and Dalle, J.-M., 2008, in IFIP International Federation for Information Processing, Volume 275; *Open Source Development, Communities and Quality*; Barbara Russo, Ernesto Damiani, Scott Hissam, Björn Lundell, Giancarlo Succi; (Boston: Springer), pp. 105–120.

peer produced collection, we would want to be reassured that what is made available is of sufficient quality and will remain so in the near future. The above considerations hold as much for open source communities developing systems like Linux and Apache as for open content communities creating collaborative repositories like Wikipedia.

Wikipedia is a large-scale collaborative project where voluntary contributors join forces to put together an encyclopaedia that is free for everyone to read and edit. The collaboration has produced, amongst others, an English version with over 2 million articles, a German version with over 600,000 articles and a Simple English version with over 20,000 articles. At the same time, Wikipedia has become extremely visible: for instance, its pages frequently appear high in the result list of search engines [2] and are nowadays commonly referenced by the media. In this paper we take a closer look at the organization of Wikipedia: we speculate on the problems it faces and on the way they are addressed, and, ultimately, we assess its potential for the future: will Wikipedia become an even more established source of information than it already is or will its efforts whither under the weight of vandalism and bureaucracy [7, 14]?

At first sight, Wikipedia is a clear success. On 15 December 2005, *Nature* published a special report comparing the quality of online encyclopaedias. Its findings highlighted that the upstart Wikipedia had a number of errors comparable to Encyclopaedia Britannica [9]. Britannica was compared to Wikipedia for quality by sampling 42 science articles that were sent to experts in the relative field for blind review. While the study was criticized by the Britannica organization for the way articles were selected and compared and clearly suffers from the weakness of a small sample from a large collection, it was influential in establishing that the distributed collaboration on Wikipedia can show performance approximately comparable to traditional methods of encyclopaedia production.[1]

In terms of gross production, Wikipedia seems healthy too: content grew exponentially from 2002 to 2005 [18]. However, this is only a rough approximation of performance and does not take into account the quality of the content and as Denning *et al.* [4] note, a proper assessment of the performance and quality of Wiki projects would require attention to many more factors.

With tremendous growth, performance is affected by how well maintenance and organizational work is carried out and how well this non-article related work can be scaled. Reagle [15] examines the way the Wikipedia community develops a neutral point of view in articles and the norms that govern meta-discussions, such as those that take place on article discussion pages. Kittur *et al.* [10] measure directly the impact of these meta-discussions on the performance of the project. They found that the proportion of work on non-article content (such as discussion and fixing

[1] It is worth to note also that while all Wikipedia's inaccuracies raised by the Nature's study has been fixed in a matter of few days (the last being corrected on 25 January, 2006). On the contrary, at least 8 errors (out of the 64 inaccuracies that were not contested by Britannica) still stand nowadays untouched into the current online version of the Encyclopaedia Britannica.

vandalism) is increasing in Wikipedia, showing that more overhead is required as the collection grows and casting doubt over its sustainability.

The increasing demand for maintenance work includes the need to undo the actions of those with malicious intent. In this regard Wikipedia appears to be performing satisfactorily. Even in the early stages of development, it was clear that malicious edits were removed quickly: Ciffolilli [1] argues that it is the nature of the Wiki that makes it easy for friendly contributors to "clean up" vandalism. Later work by Viegas *et al.* [17] showed that "obscene" edits from their sample had a median lifetime of only 1.7 minutes.

Doubts remain over the long-term viability of Wikipedia as a reliable source of information [6, 11]. From the outside, vandalism and well-meaning ignorance are a continuous threat to article quality and from the inside, the dominance of difficult people with lots of time on their hands could easily become a danger of equal if not larger size. In the end, all depends on how well Wikipedia as a community manages to address these threats.

In the paper we take some steps towards studying how organizational practices enable to increase the overall quality of the collection of articles belonging to Simple Wikipedia, a spinoff project of the larger Wikipedia. In order to do so, we have to take into account that communities like Simple Wikipedia might employ methods and practices very different from the ones used in other commons based peer communities. In this sense, our work is very sympathetic with the theory of information goods production developed by Mateos Garcia and Steinmueller [13]. These scholars identify four distinct roles in the production process – that of the author, the editor, the integrator and the conductor – and argue that what distinguishes the "vertical" production of systems like Linux from the "horizontal" production of collections like Wikipedia, is that the cumulative dependencies of components in vertical production make the task of editor and integrator far more valuable and rewarding than the complementary dependencies in horizontal production. What we set out to do for the study reported in this paper was to see if we could identify integration efforts in collections anyway despite the low payoff for volunteers.

In what follows, we report on our findings. We first describe how we selected Simple Wikipedia as a collection, and why it is a good case study to address issues regarding quality and level of integration of the collection. We then lay out what data we have retrieved and how we have mined those data. Finally, we present our findings, which suggest that in the case of Simple Wikipedia that the integration efforts that we were able to identify have some effect but seem insufficient in order to maintain the quality of the collection in the long run.

2 Simple Wikipedia

In order to test our approach, we did a pilot study on Simple Wikipedia. Simple Wikipedia is a spin-off of Wikipedia that was initiated in 2003 because people felt that many articles in Wikipedia were too hard to read, due to jargon, formality, or for other reasons – especially for children and non-native speakers of English. Simple Wikipedia, was the hope, would be the place where people go to look for an easily readable descriptions of topics. At the same time, contributors to Simple Wikipedia would commit to the ideals of this sub-project or at least adhere to an editorial policy that calls for greater readability when contributing descriptions of topics.

Simple Wikipedia is an ideal candidate to study the performance of commons based peer communities, since it is relatively easy to determine how well it adheres to its goals, zoom in on efforts that are made to address specific problems, and assess the result of these efforts. First of all, with less then 20,000 articles in its collection Simple Wikipedia is a relatively small encyclopedia project. Consequently, no extraordinary computational resources are needed to extract the project archive and analyze its contents. Besides, Simple Wikipedia is a project centered on a very specific goal: readability. What's more, readability is something that can be measured. So, here we have a project that we can assess on its own terms. Moreover, Simple Wikipedia, as a separate project, was able to experiment and implement with its own editorial policies and managerial policies specifically to help attain its goal of simplicity. Most importantly, Simple Wikipedia has come to rely on the tag "unsimple" – more recently called "complex" – to single out articles, which do not meet its standards and need to be improved.

3 Data

The archive of Simple Wikipedia is available from the web at http://downloads.wikimedia.org. Our analysis here is based on the archive of July 2007, which contains the revision history of over 25,000 articles and around 27,000 pages of a different type such as discussion pages and user-pages where regular contributors present themselves. For each edit on an article, the archive lists the IP address or user-name and user-id of the editor, the time of edit, comments made by the editor, and the actual text of resulting from the edit. The text is marked up with tags to identify structural elements like sections and sub-sections and tags of a different type to identify labels – also called templates – that are applied to the text. For instance, an article that is considered to be hard to read will contain the string "{{unsimple}}" in the raw text. The status of an editor is slightly harder to determine. We can easily distinguish between editors who are known to the system and editors who contribute anonymously as the latter are identified by their user-id while for the former only the IP address is listed. Bots, scripts that carry out small repetitive edits such as spell checks and interlinking of articles, usually have a user-name that ends with "bot". In addition, the user-id of these bots is listed as a user belonging to a special group in the auxiliary user-group table, as is the user-id of the users with special rights known as administrators.

3.1 Metrics

In the results that we outline further in this section, we make use of two classes of computational linguistics metrics as a way to characterize changes, made overtime in the Simple Wikipedia articles, resulting from the collaborative and iterative editing process. We are in particular interested in studying two different, albeit interconnected, evolving features of articles: first of all we what to assess how the readability of an article changes over time; subsequently we want to focus on change *tout court* by introducing measures of similarity, accounting for the degree of change/persistence of information in the various revisions of the articles.

The readability of an article is determined by computing the Flesch readability score of the article's text with help of the GNU Style package. This score is a function of the number of syllables per word and the number of words per sentence [8]. More precisely, the formula 'score = 206.835 – 84.6*syllables/words – 1.1015*words/sentences' yields a number that is usually between 0 and 100 and between 60 and 70 for standard English texts. This Flesch reading easy formula, which has been elaborated on the basis of school texts by Flesch in 1948, has been very popular, especially in the US, as a measure of plain English. Its popularity rests on the fact that the formula is easy to compute, yet often accurate. Even word processing applications, such as Microsoft Word, often provide the score as part of their statistics.

The second class of language metrics focuses more explicitly on characterizing the magnitude of persistence and variability of information over time.

The approach proposed here stems from the analysis of text similarities, which is used to compare documents in large text corpora, in order to assess the repetitions of patterns. In this respect, similarity is thus considered a measurable property assessing the degree of relation between two or more information artifacts.

There is a plethora of similarity measures (for an extensive review see [12]) to evaluate this feature; in this study we will take into account two particular vector-based metrics that have been selected for their particular properties.

A measure often used for comparing different documents is represented by the Jaccard coefficient (J), a distance metric defined as follows: given two documents A and B, let a and b the sets of terms occurring in A and B respectively. Define I as the intersection of a and b, and K as their union. Then the Jaccard similarity is the number of elements (cardinality) of I divided by the cardinality of K, thus

$$J = |I| \,/\, |K|. \tag{1}$$

Conversely, the Cosine similarity (C) is computed in the following way: let A_s and B_s be sets of terms occurring in A and B, as in the previous measure; define K as the union of A_s and B_s, and let k_i be the i-th element in K. Then the vector terms in A and B are:

$$\begin{aligned} a &= [nA(k_1), nA(k_2), \ldots, nA(k_n)]; \\ b &= [nB(k_1), nB(k_2), \ldots, nB(k_n)], \end{aligned} \tag{2}$$

where $nA(k_i)$ is the number of occurrences of term k_i in A, and $nB(k_i)$ is the same for B. In this respect, Cosine similarity between two original document sets is defined as

$$C = (a \cdot b) / \|a\| \, \|b\|, \tag{3}$$

that is the ratio between the scalar product of vectors a and b and their Euclidean norm.

Both measures are widely used for comparisons among documents on broad masses of text corpora, and broadly applied in information retrieval applications and tools [16, 5].

There is a significant difference between the Jaccard coefficient and the Cosine index: both enable to compare two texts, but the former gives more importance to non-overlapped information in the denominator: for this reason, the Jaccard index is much more sensitive to the relative size of documents. Thus, this metric allows to address size differences among documents, while the Cosine metric accounts for the preservation of the same sets of information in different texts. Consequently, when comparing changing versions of the same document in a time domain, the former metric can be used to measure the magnitude of total change, taking into account both the inclusion of new tokens/lemmas and increase/decrease in text size, while the latter signals how much of the former information has been preserved between two versions of a document.

Technically, while the Flesch readability score can be computed directly over the unwikified version of the article (a version cleaned from all wiki tags), further preprocessing of an article is needed before computing the Jaccard and Cosine coefficients: in particular the text needs to be cleaned from stop-words (such as, for instance, propositions and conjunctions) and all remaining words are then truncated into stems.

3.2 Trends

On the basis of the archive, it is possible to reconstruct the history of Simple Wikipedia. For each article in the archive we know when it was first introduced and for every month that Simple Wikipedia existed, we can find the versions of the articles in the archive that existed in that month and we can count their number and properties like their overall readability. Figure 1 in the appendix shows the result of such a reconstruction for Simple Wikipedia from January 2003 until December 2007. The figure shows an upward sloping line indicating the total number of articles in the collection for each month and a downward sloping line indicating the overall readability of the articles in the collection for each month. Note that the continuous growth in the number of articles in Simple Wikipedia is at least partially due to the fact that articles that have been removed from the collection and are not currently available anymore, do not appear in the most recent archive either. Even so, the growth in the number of articles over time is impressive. This rate of growth may be a factor explaining why the readability indicated by the Flesch readability score shows a gradual decline: as the size of articles in Simple Wikipedia grew, it became more unwieldy and editors faced an ever harder task to maintain the standards of readability, is one interpretation that suggests itself. Looking closely, we can distinguish a phase of substantial decline in readability in the first half of 2004 followed by a more stable phase in the second half of 2004. It was in the second half of 2004 that the practice of tagging articles with the label "unsimple" first appeared. It might be that the slow down in the decline in readability could be attributed to this. With a readability index of over 70, Simple Wikipedia still scores very well given that standard English falls between 60 and 70. Still, the fact that readability continues to decline should be taken seriously into account in the close future.

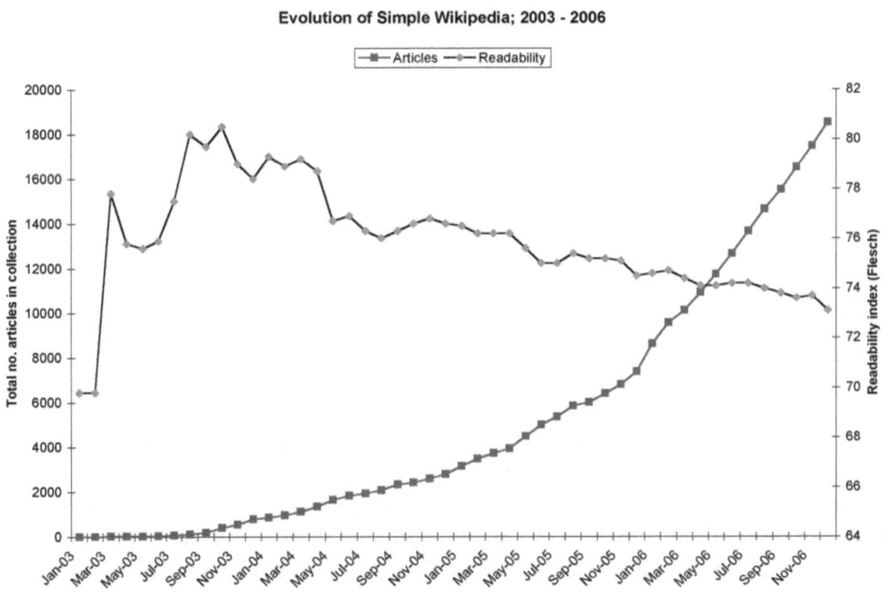

Fig. 1. Performance at Project Level – Simple Wikipedia: total number of articles per month and mean readability index per month.

Figure 2 shows how the similarity indexes change as the articles are revised. Similarity values are averaged for the various articles according to the same revision. Similarity of the *n*-th revision is computed, respectively, with reference to the first revision of the article (left side) and with respect to the previous revision (right side). Note here and for all subsequent graphical representations of similarity that the metrics are computed over the subset of all the articles which have been labeled as "unsimple" at least once and that the effects of vandal editing have been filtered out in order to improve readability.

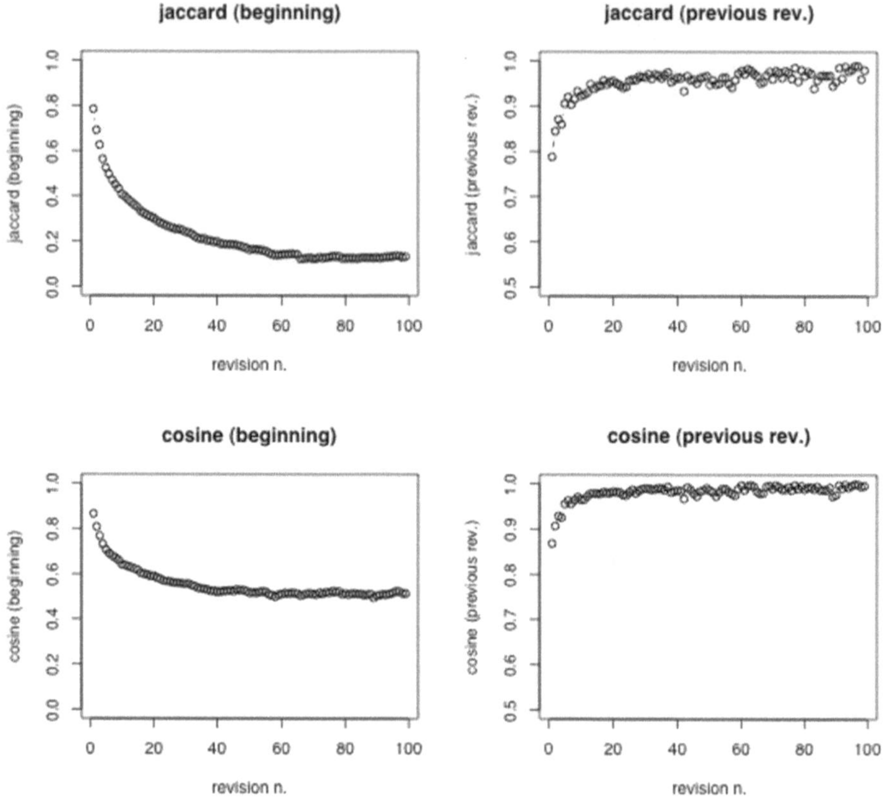

Fig. 2. Evolution of Cosine and Jaccard similarity indexes (vandalisms are filtered out).

The left side of Figure 2 shows that articles on average change considerably with respect to their initial stub and tend to converge to a stable similarity index after circa 40 revisions. Cosine similarity is higher than the Jaccard index, meaning that on average there is a relatively high persistence of initial words/lemmas compared to the high dissimilarity that is introduced overtime by introducing new words/lemmas and by increasing the text size.[2] The right side of Figure 2 confirms that, as the number of revisions increases, changes become more and more incremental, but since the similarity indexes oscillate at some degree near the lower bound of 1, the revision process still exhibits some, albeit minimal, degree of dissimilarity.[3]

[2] This claim takes into account that most articles start as short stub and are enlarged later on, but similar considerations holds also for those articles which are initially copied almost verbatim from en.wikipedia and that are later on simplified and shortened to comply with the Simple Wiki policies.

[3] It is maybe worth to note that findings on the left side of the figure are not in contrast with right side ones if one considers that some revisions are circular (as in the frequent case of edit

Figure 3 tries to shed a light on who has been editing articles in Simple Wikipedia from 2004 until 2006. Most dominantly, it shows the growing importance of bots – indicating that automated and semi-automated scripts are relied upon more and more to keep the articles consistent. At the same time, the proportion of edits done by people who do not identify themselves to the system decreases and the proportion of edits do by people who are registered increases relative to them. Whatever causes the gradual decline in readability, it is probably not the hordes of outsiders in the case of Simple Wikipedia.

A final issue is the number of articles that have been identified as "unsimple". This turns out to be a relatively small number: Less than 200 between 2004 and 2006. We do find however that there is a clear improvement in readability on average following the appearance of the label. Another interesting finding is that the act of tagging seems to be carried out by users with a special administrator status most of the time and hardly by anonymous outsiders (cfr. [3]).

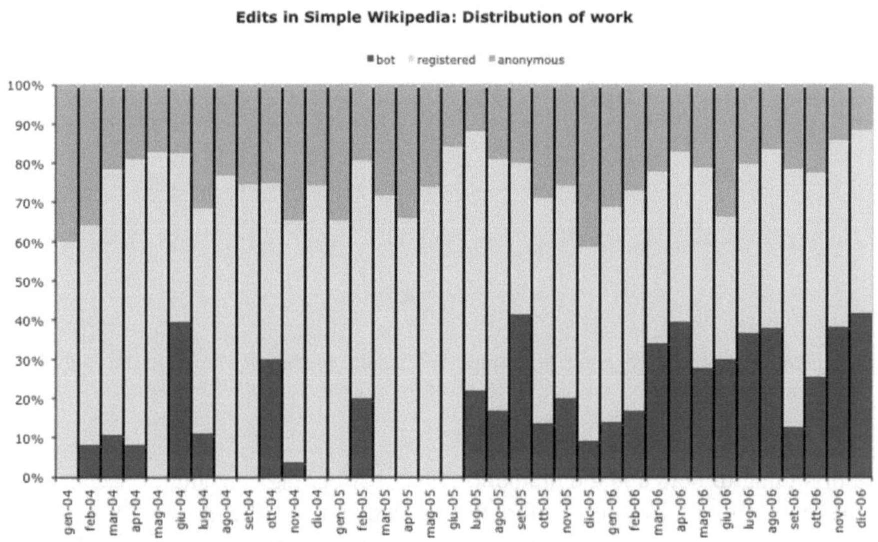

Fig. 3. Variation in editor background over time.

3.3 Triage

Despite the overall trend towards a decline in readability and the limited number of articles that have been labeled with "unsimple", applying such a label does seem to have the desired effect in several cases. Take for instance the article on propaganda.

---

warring) and that in the other cases two subsequent revisions, while still presenting some degree of dissimilarity between them, might be relatively equally dissimilar to the initial revision of the article.

Figure 4 depicts the evolution of the readability over time of this page. Readability is based on the Flesch reading easy score and time is given as the number of days relative to the first occurrence of the tag "unsimple" on the page. In addition, the dotted vertical lines indicate the period during which the page was labeled with the tag "unsimple" and the shapes of the points correspond to the different contributors to the page.

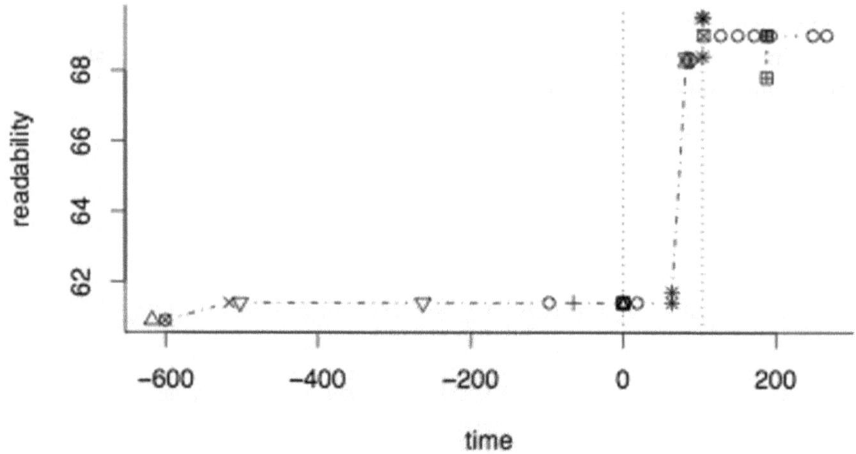

Fig. 4. Treatment of "Propaganda" in Simple Wikipedia: readability index in the "simple" and in the "unsimple" regimes.

The first thing to notice is the dramatic effect that the tag "unsimple" seems to have on the readability of the page. Before the tag first appears, the readability score of the page hovers around the border between a standard and a fairly difficult level of readability. When the tag is removed, 100 days later, the readability has jumped to the other side of the spectrum, now bordering between a standard and a fairly easy level of readability. Looking at the shapes of the points, a history emerges in which someone wrote the initial page to which others then added a bit without changing much in terms of readability. At some point, day 0, a new guy comes along and points out that the page is too difficult to read for an article in the Simple Wikipedia collection. The tag "unsimple" then attracts the attention of someone else who actively starts working to improve the readability of the page. As soon as the problem has been remedied, the tag "unsimple" is removed and regular maintenance is resumed. More specifically the history that this figure represents is as follows (http://simple.wikipedia.org/w/index.php?title=Propaganda&action=history): the first version of the article on propaganda appeared on 1 March 2004 and was written by

Randywombat. In the year that followed we see edits by five edits by non-identified users and two by identified users. There are also three edits by bots, but these do nothing more than adding so-called inter-wiki links to similar pages in other languages. In November 2005, the user Heroismic, a high-school junior (according to his/her user-page) who has not edited the page before, comes along and labels the article "unsimple". In the following months, we see a concerted effort by the users Eptalon, according to his/her user-page a Simple Wiki administrator from Central Europe, and AmanitaMuscaria to improve the page. On 22 February 2006 Eptalon decides that the page has become readable enough and removes the label "unsimple".

Figure 5 shows the development of readability for few more selected articles. In this figure, the readability of the articles is represented by a 'o' while the article has the label "unsimple" and a '+' otherwise. Sometimes readability increases but no one bothers to remove the "unsimple" label. In other cases, the label leads to some improvement in readability initially but contributors fall back on bad habits later. And, sometimes, the label seems to be ignored altogether. The interesting question here is not just how likely it is that this kind of "treatment" by labeling succeeds sometimes, but more why it succeeds in some cases and not in others (for more on this topic see also below in the final section).

Similarly to what we did for readability, we can apply the similarity metrics to selected articles in order to single out different editing processes at work in "simple" *vs.* "unsimple" regimes. Figure 6 shows the similarity indexes for the article on the year 2001 ("2001"): here for any given revision similarity is computed with respect to the first revision of the ongoing regime. Both Cosine and Jaccard similarity indexes drop abruptly at the beginning; this is largely due to the fact that the article starts as a very short stub on 5/7/04 and it is subsequently substituted at its third revision (on 5/15/04) with a verbatim copy from en.wikipedia. The article remains in the "simple" regime for a total of 37 revisions in the period 5/7/04 – 5/7/06, at the end of which C=0.32166 and J=0.00179. The unsimple tag is placed by an admin and remains in its place for the subsequent 22 revisions until the article status switches back to "simple" on 12/4/06 for all the remaining available observations (21 revisions up to 6/11/07). If one look closely to the figure, there is a considerable difference in end of regime measures of similarity. At the end of the unsimple regime C=0.97457 and J=0.92732, while at the end of the second simple regime C=0.62334 and J=0.88344.

These large differences seem to suggest the existence of rather different patterns of article revision during the "unsimple" regime compared to the "simple" one. In particular, what seems to be particularly counterintuitive is the realizing that the troublesome "unsimple" regime seems to be characterized by a sensibly slower pace of change. While this finding doesn't hold in principle for all the articles (and calls for more accurate analysis at the single article level), it seems to be confirmed, on average, at the aggregate level.

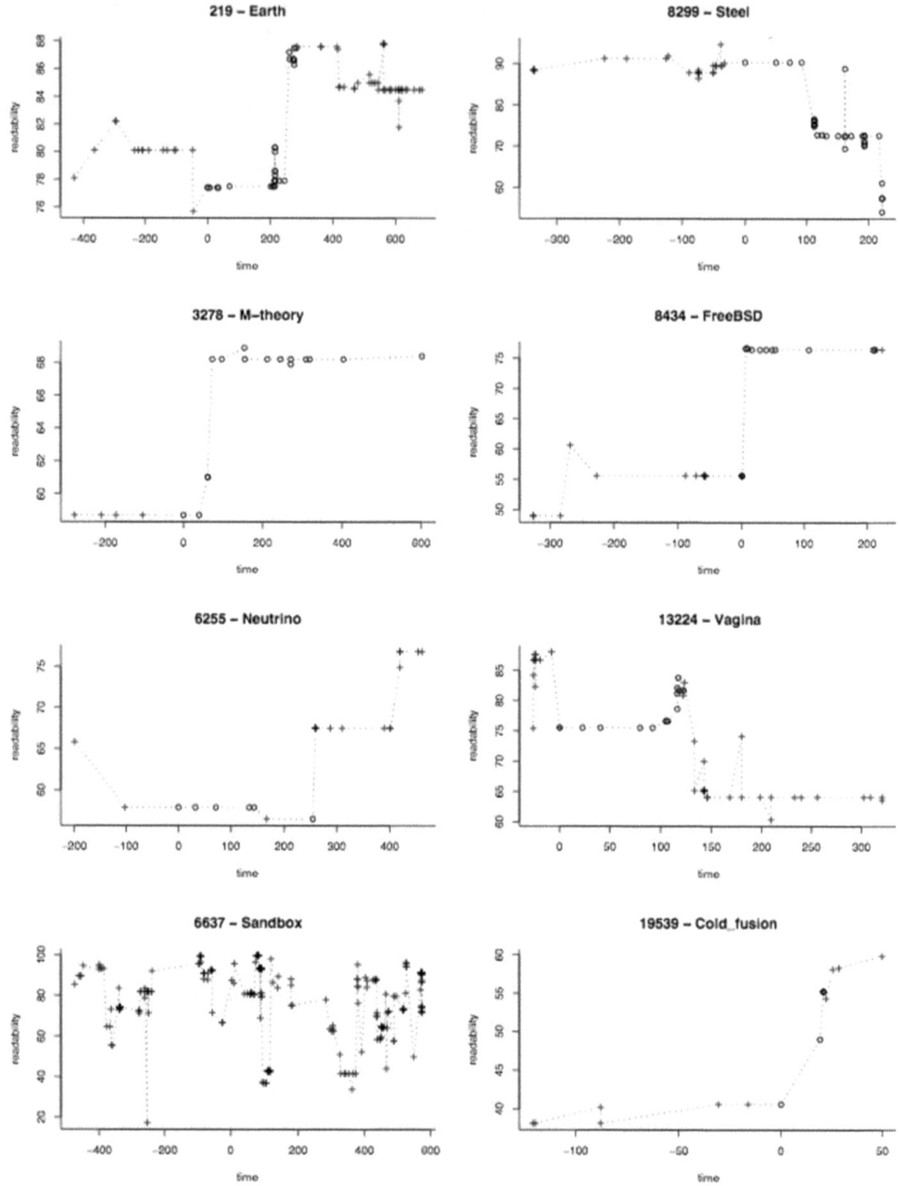

Fig. 5. Development of Readability in Selected Articles.

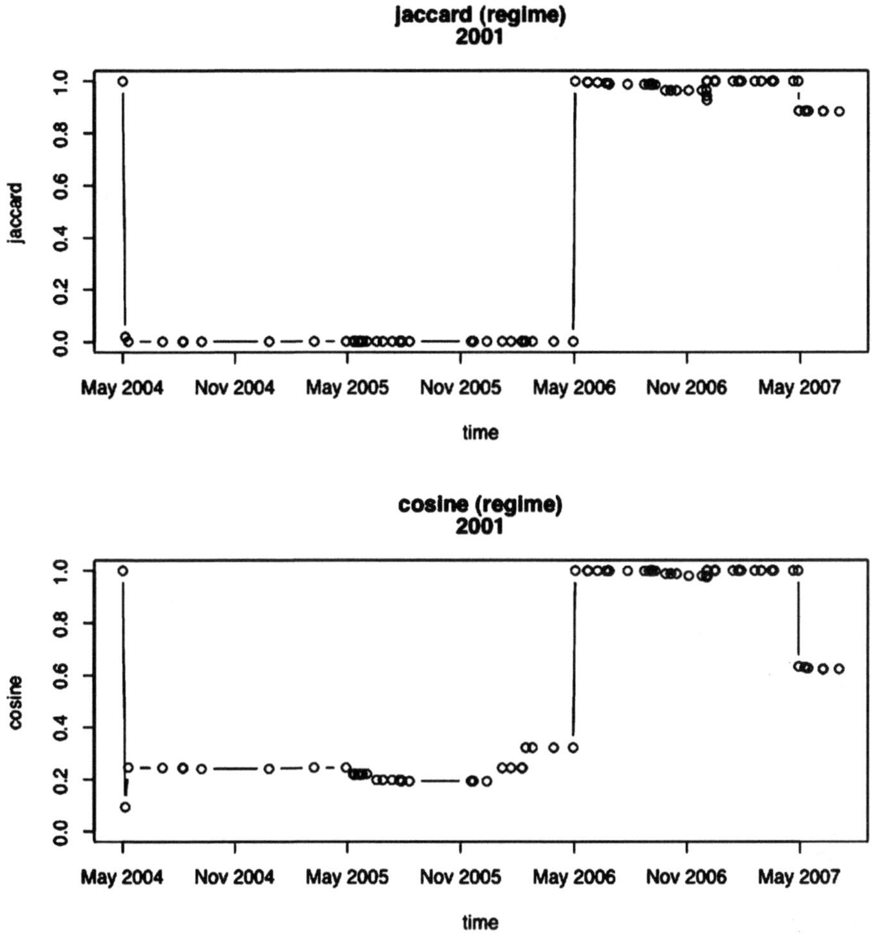

Fig. 6. Treatment of "2001" in Simple Wikipedia: similarity indexes in the simple/unsimple regimes (metrics are computed for any revision with respect to the first revision of the outstanding regime).

Figure 7 shows the distributions of C and J indexes (computed according to the method described for Figure 6) for the first 3 regimes., where regime 1 corresponds to the initial period of editing, regime 2 starts at the first time the article is tagged as "unsimple" and regime 3 starts when the tag is removed (and lasts, eventually, until the "unsimple" tag is placed again). The figure seems clearly to suggest the existence of a two-speed process according to which in the first "simple" regime dissimilarity increase at a very fast pace (mean values: J=0.549, C=0.726) while revisions in the "unsimple" regime 2 are more incremental (mean values: J=0.764, C=0.9), and dissimilarity increases again in the subsequent "simple" regime 3 (mean values: J=0.703, C=0.834). All these differences between two subsequent regimes are statistically significant (Wilcoxon signed rank test, one sided, α=5% or lower). Overall, this finding suggests that during non–pathological periods, the editing style seems to favor large revisions making the article progressively more complicated. On the contrary, when the article is tagged as "unsimple", efforts towards regaining simplicity goes into the direction of more careful and incremental revisions.

We claim that these findings call for further inspection, in particular we find promising to cross readability and similarity analysis looking for a more articulated explanation of the above mentioned differences between "simple" and "unsimple" regimes.

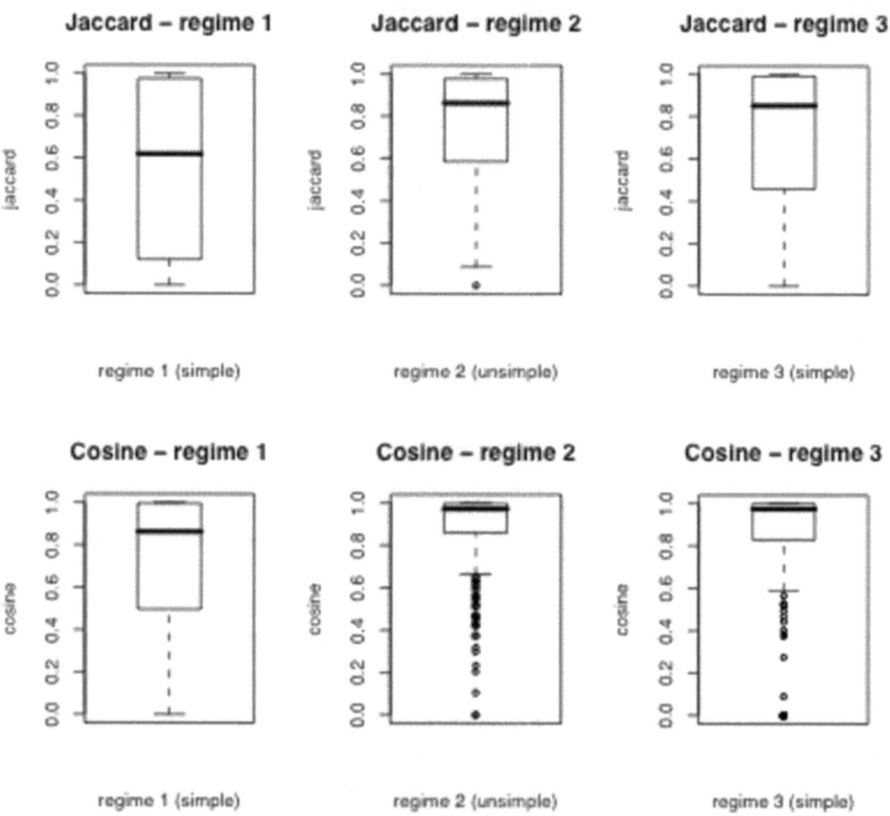

Fig. 7. Box-and-whisker plots of J and C similarity in "unsimple" and "simple" regimes in Simple Wikipedia.

4 Conclusions

The quality and sustainability of Wikipedia is a topic in which scholars of all kinds are getting more and more interested. In this paper, we have provided a review of recent studies of Wikipedia and we have proposed a new approach to study its performance that takes advantage of the way in which this encyclopedia project is organized. In particular, we propose to look for signs within the Wikipedia archive that specific shortcomings of articles are identified and then assess how well these shortcomings are addressed. We have illustrated our approach with a pilot study of Simple Wikipedia, a spin-off of the main Wikipedia that focuses on articles that are easy to read. We found that while the editors of this collection have a difficult time in keeping articles simple, the label "unsimple" that they employ to single out articles that are particularly problematic still provides a good entry-point in studying how this particular community manages to keep its encyclopaedia readable.

With the Simple Wikipedia study as a "proof of concept", the time is now ripe to move to other, larger, Wikipedia projects and extend the study to indicators of shortcomings like "controversial" and "stub". In particular, we find promising to carry out a survival analysis on several variables describing the articles' state at the point of triage and subsequent edits during the treatment to study the effectiveness of labeling as an organizational practice.

References

1. A. Ciffolilli, Phantom authority, self-selective recruitment and retention of members in virtual communities: The case of Wikipedia, *First Monday*, Vol. 8 (2003) No. 12.

2. J. Čuhalev, Ranking of Wikipedia articles on search engines for searches about its own articles, 2007, http://www.kiberpipa.org/~gandalf/blog-files/wikistatus/wikistatus.pdf (last retrieval November 30, 2007).

3. M. den Besten, J.-M. Dalle, Collaborative maintenance of collections – keep it simple: a companion for Simple Wikipedia?, Industry and Innovation, Vol. 15 (2008) No.2, pp.169–178.

4. P. Denning, J. Horning, D. Parnas, L. Weinstein, Wikipedia risks, *Communications of the ACM*, Vol. 48 (2005) No. 12, pp. 152–152.

5. I.S. Dhillon, D. Modha, Concept decompositions for large sparse text data using clustering, *Machine Learning*, Vol. 42 (2001) No. 1, pp. 143–175.

6. P. Duguid, Limits of self-organization: Peer production and laws of quality, *First Monday*, Vol. 11 (2006) No. 10.

7. S. Finkelstein, Read me first: Inside, Wikipedia is more like a sweatshop than Santa's workshop, *The Guardian*, December 6, 2007.

8. R. Flesch, How to Write Plain English, Harper and Row, New York, 1979.

9. J. Giles, Internet encyclopaedias go head to head, *Nature*, Vol. 438 (2005) No. 7070, pp. 900–901.

10. A. Kittur, B. Suh, B.A. Pendleton, E.H. Chi, He says, she says: conflict and coordination in Wikipedia, CHI '07: Proceedings of the SIGCHI conference on Human factors in computing systems, New York, ACM Press, 2007, pp. 453–462.

11. J. Lanier, Digital Maoism: The Hazards of the New Online Collectivism, *Edge*, May 30, 2006.

12. L. Lee, Measures of distributional similarity, Proceedings of the 37th conference on Association for Computational Linguistics, Montreal, Association for Computational Linguistics, Morristown, 1998, pp. 25–32.

13. J. Mateos Garcia, W.E. Steinmueller, Applying the open source development model to knowledge work, INK Open Source Research Working Paper 2, SPRU – Science and Technology Policy Research, University of Sussex, 2003.

14. A. Orlowski, Farewell, Wikipedia? *The Register*, March 6, 2007.

15. J. Reagle, A Case of Mutual Aid: Wikipedia, Politeness, and Perspective Taking, 2004, http://reagle.org/joseph/2004/agree/wikip-agree.html (last retrieval May 10, 2007).

16. G. Salton, M. McGill, Introduction to Modern Information Retrieval, McGraw-Hill, New York, 1983.

17. F. Viégas, M. Wattenberg, K. Dave, Studying cooperation and conflict between authors with history flow visualizations, Proceedings of the SIGCHI conference on Human factors in computing systems, 2004, ACM Press, New York, pp. 575–582.

18. J. Voß, Measuring Wikipedia, in: P. Ingwersen, B. Larsen (eds): Proceedings of the 10th International Conference of the International Society for Scientometrics and Informetrics, Karolinska University Press, Stockholm, 2005.

Open to Grok. How do Hackers' Practices Produce Hackers?

Vincenzo D'Andrea[1], Stefano De Paoli, and Maurizio Teli[2]
[1] Department of Information and Communication Technology
vincenzo.dandrea@dit.unitn.it
[2] Department of Sociology and Social Research, University of Trento, Italy
{name.surname}@soc.unitn.it

Abstract. How do hackers' practices produce hackers' identities? In this paper we argue that the association between science fiction and software programs is rooted in hackers' practices, defining how hackers' knowledge' emerge. The mediation is the one of the Heinlein verb "to grok", part of the Jargon file and of the name of a code browser, OpenGrok, the technology mediating the relationship between OpenSolaris developers and the code base. Starting with a description of the peculiarity of the verb "to grok", and its connection with a non-Cartesian view of knowledge, we discuss how the history of OpenGrok and its use by developers make this knowledge part of hackers' practices and identities, as someone involved in a true, deep understanding of software.

1 Introduction[1]

In this article we explore the importance of Science Fiction (SF) in organizing hackers' practices of software development and identities. SF is often part of hackers' everyday life and this claim can be verifiable thanks to several stories and technologies [2],[11].

Nevertheless, research focusing on the role of SF in terms of influencing hacker practices and identities has not been carried out. We maintain that, in hackers' practices, SF has an active role which goes beyond any metaphoric use of it.

Before entering into our contribution we account for two domains of description: identities in FLOSS and the role of SF within organizational studies. The interest of organizational studies for SF is not new, nevertheless in many cases this interest has limited SF to the role of a source of concepts and metaphors, used in the interpretation of concrete cases [1].

For example Srinivas [13] used the concept of Android, inspired by Philip K. Dick's novels. This concept represents the situation of a human being that is no longer entirely human, since he/she finds him or herself caged in a process of commodification. In such sense the contribution provided by Srinivas is that Dick's android becomes a literary resource that can encourage the organizational subjects to withstand the process of "androidization" which subjugate them.

[1] We want to thank Camilla Rossi and the anonymous reviewer.

Please use the following format when citing this chapter:

D'Andrea, V., Paoli, S. and Teli, M., 2008, in IFIP International Federation for Information Processing, Volume 275; *Open Source Development, Communities and Quality*; Barbara Russo, Ernesto Damiani, Scott Hissam, Björn Lundell, Giancarlo Succi; (Boston: Springer), pp. 121–129.

Even though SF has been found in hackers' story-telling, it has not been studied as a domain for the production of hackers' identities. Trying to understand "who is an hacker?", we found a rational approach to hackerdom, simplified by motivational research ("why do they do that?"), that forgets to consider how hackers' practices produce hackers, focusing only on why they are motivated to participate [12].

Against these uses we claim that the explanatory role of the SF results diminished in the above accounts, because SF is not only a source of interpretative concepts, but it can also be an active part of the organizational processes, contributing to the production of hackers identities. To deepen this claim we focus our analysis on the Martian concept of "Grok", described in the novel "Stranger in a Strange Land" by Robert Heinlein [6]. In order to understand in which ways the concept of Grok participates in software development and use, we studied a software development project known as OpenGrok, paying particular attention to the practices that surround and constitute it.

2 Stranger in a strange land

The novel "Stranger in a Strange Land" narrates the story of Valentine Michael Smith (Mike), a human being raised by Martians on the planet Mars. The novel describes Mike's interactions with the terrestrial culture after its return on Earth after his adolescence. Mike is the child of two members of the first earthling mission on Mars. Because of the death of his parents Mike grew up as a Martian. Mike can then be considered a "man of Mars", in other words he is a human being in his physical structure but a Martian in his mental structure: "He's a man by ancestry, a Martian by environment." [6, p. 20].

The second mission on Mars brought Mike on Earth so that he could be submitted to careful studies. Once arrived on Earth, the condition of Mike is that of a "Stranger in a Strange Land", a Martian man among the humans that observes with Martian eyes the events of which he is protagonist. The novel is focused on the story of Mike, from his initial contact with the human beings, to his understanding of their culture, to the impact of his actions to the human society.

At the same time, in Heinlein's novel emerges that the human beings attempt to understand the knowledge activity of Mike and especially how this activity is mediated by the Martian language. The Martian dictionary articulates around a fundamental verb that is "to grok". This verb, according to the Martian tongue, assumes a multiple meaning: to drink, to understand, to love or "to be one with" a person. To grok means therefore to know a thing or a person in his/her completeness, in the totality of his/her being and at the same time to become part of this thing or person; if we want to express this with a sentence: to grok a thing means "to be one" with that thing.

"'Grok' means to understand so thoroughly that the observer becomes a part of the process being observed [...] and it means as little to us as colour means to a blind man." [6, p.266]. Grok separates human beings from Martians, defining different identities and knowledge practices.

2.1 Knowledge and Grok

Why it is interesting to investigate the concept of grok? Firstly, this verb connotes a knowledge that is superior to that perceived or realized by an external observer. The relationship between the observer and the object of investigation is essential here: the knowledge realized by the man of Mars seems to be able to revert the perspective, typical of western modernity, of the separation among who observes and the object that is investigated.

Secondly, the knowledge realized in "grokking" does not seem to have a place in the breast of the Cartesian dualism between subject and object [3]: in grokking activities the observer and observed object become one single thing, which is not part of any of dualism. We can remember that the meaning of grok is to drink and it means to become one with the water that is drunk. Comparing the knowledge realized in grokking - in which a unity is realized between the person and the water - with that of the observer that investigates the water as external object, we can locate the verb to grok in a place at the opposite of the Cartesian perspective.

2.2 Grokking the code

The description provided by Heinlein is a point of departure to show the knowledge dynamics linked with the concept of grok. This task requires an empirical investigation and a discussion of how grok is articulated in practice.

For many aspects, a breakup in the relationship among the observer and an observed object can be found in those practices defined as hacking practices and in the relationship between hackers and calculators. According to the description offered by many [16],[14] this relationship doesn't seem to be instrumental, as that of an external observer towards an object.

Weizenbaum for example describes the differences between "professional programmers", which think of the calculator as an instrument that is separated from its user, and hackers, that only exist through and for computers [16]. The same rhetoric is presented in Turkle, for whom hackers see computers as "things in themselves", as opposed to the programmers idea of computers as instruments [14].

Given the consideration above, the verb "to grok" could provide an interesting way to describe hacking practices. Our goal is not to use the verb "to grok" for interpreting hacking practices, on the contrary we would like to observe how this verb is both active part of such practices and how our understanding of such practices would profit from an empirical inquiry.

According to the Jargon File, to grok "Connotes intimate and exhaustive knowledge. When you claim to 'grok' some knowledge or technique, you are asserting that you have not merely learned it in a detached instrumental way but that it has become part of you, part of your identity. For example, to say that you "know" LISP is simply to assert that you can code in it if necessary — but to say you "grok" LISP is to claim that you have deeply entered the world-view and spirit of the language, with the implication that it has transformed your view of programming."[2]. Thus, a person that groks a certain technology (e.g. LISP) becomes "one with" that technology in a way that this act of grokking has changed radically his/her own personality. Hackers define themselves as involved in grokking software, and grokking involves hackers' identities.

3 OpenGrok: grok in practice

What said so far is not enough to justify our point of view on SF. To understand how the concept of grok participates to software development activities, we studied a development project called OpenGrok, focusing on the practices surrounding and constituting it. OpenGrok is the tool to surf the OpenSolaris operating system code base and, in this way, it participates to the developers' understanding of the OpenSolaris source code. In relation to these practices, the name OpenGrok reminds the association between surfing the code of a FLOSS project and the knowledge translated with the reference to Heinlein's novel. In the following part, we show how this association implies a definition/redefinition of the identities of actors involved, which are allowed by technological mediation to participate to this kind of knowledge; on the other side, we show how the same association between intimate knowledge and this program, is embedded in pre-existing practices and participates to their modification.

In order to study the OpenGrok case we chose to base our theoretical framework on the perspective of the Sociology of associations [7], [8], [9].

We follow the concept of "translation" considered as the interpretation given by technology builders "of their interest and that of the people they enroll" [7, p. 108]. This concept underlines how technological projects are built in attempt to involve more and more people in the projects.

In addition we must consider these practices as "practices of association" where developers build technology mixing together (associating) human and non-human elements.

These acts of enrolling and associating elements is possible thanks to technological mediation. In Latour [8] terms, mediators are entities that "transform, translate, distort, and modify the meaning of the elements that they are supposed to carry" (p.39). Following a mediator helps to understand the definition/redefinition of the elements involved into a translation.

From sociology of associations, we also assume the ethnomethodological perspective. Ethnomethodology [4] is a sociological discipline that aims at understanding the ways people make sense of their world and the ways they produce a shared social order. While other sociologies provide accounts of the social order

2 http://www.catb.org/~esr/jargon/html/G/grok.html

which competes with that of the people who are members of the society, ethnomethodology aims at describing the practices these people use in their actual descriptions of the social order.

As such, the socio-technical order can be considered as an effect caused by the association between them, and sociology of translation aims at describing the practices that technology builders use in their actual construction of technology.

Finally, we assume that these practices of association are part of an ensemble of pre-existing practices, materials, and textual elements [9], that technologies are not built starting from scratch but they are embedded in pre-existing practices and participate to the modification of such practices.

Methodologically, we observed the discussions taking place in the mailing lists osol-discuss@opensolaris.org and opengrok-discuss@opensolaris.org, hosted at the OpenSolaris website, we analyzed the blog entries related to OpenGrok, and conducted three email interviews with three OpenGrok developers, the two main developers (CH, TR) and another one (KN). The interview outline has been constructed after the analysis of documents and mailing lists, according to a grounded theory approach [5]. Interviews and observation have been conducted during a two – years long cyberethnography [15] of the OpenSolaris project.

3.1 Toward OpenGrok: a security sentry problems

Initially, we have tried to understand how the association between OpenGrok and to grok emerged, and how it translated the meaning of the Heinlein's verb in practices different from the SF genre. OpenGrok has been developed by CH, a security sentry at Sun Microsystems. In his blog, telling the story of OpenGrok, CH writes: "I keep a watch on reports of newly discovered security holes and then check if any Sun software is affected by them". The relationship between subject (developer) and object (software) involved practices of view and control; these practices involved the participation of another program, cscope, allowing a series of searches about the relationship between different functions of a program written in C language. Two elements of cscope were considered a limitation in the relationship between programmer and software: first, Solaris is a "Wad of Stuff", with the presence of source files and binary ones; second, some of the programs observed didn't allow access to cscope indexes. These boundaries for the reproduction of the sentry status have been the input to create new relationships with the software, new kinds of relationship that brought to OpenGrok.

3.2 Toward OpenGrok: from collecting information to understand them

As shown, OpenGrok (formerly rob.pl) has been developed with the aim of enlarging the number of information available for programmers, particularly collecting text strings from binary files; information able to shorten the distance between what a program does (cscope) and what a sentry search. Obtaining this kind of information is not the unique element of "grokking the code": the practice of control about the presence of security bugs is improved by a search engine able to order the information disposable. CH choice was to use Lucene, "The good thing about Lucene, is that it does not understand document content. You will have to write analyzers for your own content. So you have the control and freedom to interpret different kinds of files the way you want. Lucene does a good job storing your interpretation and searching it." . The relationship between programmers and the code is mediated by the file interpretation that the same programmer considers relevant. The construction of information useful to reproduce the CH practices is not built as independent from the programmer, but the same programming practices participate to that. The boundary between the object and the knowing subject has been canceled through the mediation of a program which is rooted in and strengthens the unity between subject and object. It seems clear how the association between grok and this program has been sustained by a pre-existing practice, that has defined the need for it and has been redefined by this definition. What has brought to the stabilization of this association in the name "OpenGrok"?

3.3 Toward OpenGrok: relishing the code

It's the same CH, in an email interview, who describes the choice of the name: "We wanted a short, Google unique name [...]. A colleague suggested to use the word 'grok' as it means to fully understand something." (emphasis added). In this statement, we find another practice, the use of the Google search engine to do web searches, pushing for a short name and an unambiguous recognition of the project. This practice is embedded in the developer field of action, the offices of Sun Microsystems, and the cooperative practices around projects, which are able to associate rob.pl+Lucene to a kind of full understanding, which is summarized by the word "grok". The analogy with Heinlein story goes on when grok had to be declined to become an unambiguous name; it's still CH telling: "We had initially thought of 'Groktose' to rhyme with Fructose and Glucose. After some discussions with Marketing it became OpenGrok.". When we asked: "which was the aim of this "sweet" flavour you wanted for your program?", the answer was "You could through your source code in a tar ball and hope that public will catch it, or you can 'serve' it with OpenGrok and hope people will relish it :-)". Other two elements emerge in connection with OpenGrok and the relationship between programmers and code: first, involving competences and people of the marketing area, the practices to spread OpenSolaris connect the project name with the same operating system, through the use of the prefix "Open", used also in other Sun's projects; and second, the programmers conceptualization strengthen the idea of physical relationships, like Heinlein's "to drink", that in this case become "to relish".

3.4 Beyond Grok: OpenGrok redefines the concept

Something differentiates the SF concept from its practical and discursive actualization: if, according to Heinlein, to grok is a concept humans can't understand, constructing a boundary between Mike and human beings; according to CH, OpenSolaris developer, and the Sun marketing area, OpenGrok, and the possibility to relish the code, can be interpreted as a way to enlarge the number of participants to OpenSolaris, allowing a more direct relationship with the code. They put the full understanding of the system as basic requirement for participation and as a way to overcome boundaries between participants and not-participants, as the references to "public" and "people" make clear. At the same time, the public able to be attracted is not indistinguishable and undetermined, as another OpenGrok developer (KN) underlined in an interview: "Having a name that just says what the product does is too dull, so you try to find a name which both tells something about the product and gives some other associations". The access to OpenGrok and OpenSolaris by the public is mediated by other elements: first, the capacity to interpret the name meaning, as connecting "to grok" to a full understanding; second, other practices can allow the contact between developers and the program, postponing the activity of attribution of meaning to the name. For example, in the KN case, being a Sun employee in Norway, engaged in the development of Apache Derby, as another OpenGrok developer, allowed KN to begin using OpenGrok without knowing the meaning of "to grok": "In fact, I was not familiar with the word "grok" when I started using OpenGrok, so I needed to search for it to find out what it really meant. The exact meaning is still not entirely clear to me, but I think I've understood enough of it to say that it's probably a suitable name. :)". We are able to evaluate another element which makes relevant the study of SF as an active discursive resource: the association between a program and a SF expression constitutes one of the ways through which the same meaning of what hackers are and do is redefined, and put developers in a learning process about "what it really meant".

We can summarize the different ways through which the association "rob.pl + Lucene + grok" participates to hacking practices: a form of full understanding of code is part of the requirement of development practices, like the sentry ones. This knowledge translates in having programs that reduce the distance between programmer and source code, as the choice of Lucene shows; the association of this understanding with the word grok, on one side strengthen the physical relationship between programmer and code, like the suggestion of Groktose shows, on the other side it constructs boundaries around the practices that can produce subjects (hackers) able to participate to this knowledge, practices that do not require to interpret the name OpenGrok. In conclusion, grok associated to a program, translates a meaning rooted in pre-existing programming practices, it gives them new meanings connected with the relationship programmer/code, it also participates to establish how is it possible to access to the practices translated by the same "to grok", and what an hacker is.

4 Conclusions

Our aim with this paper, has been to inquiry in which way SF is an active part of hacking practices, and how its translation as a discursive resource helps defining what an hacker is. We started from the consideration that previous studies looked at SF as a source of interpretative concepts in organization studies, without considering how this can be considered also an active part in organizing processes; and how those studies have considered identities as expressed in motivations, and not as a result of practices.

To empirically strengthen our argument, we have investigated the concept of "grok" as described in Heinlein's novel "Stranger in a Strange Land", observing how this represents a knowledge practice though which the observer gets blurred and becomes one with the observed object. The shift to an empirical field brought us to consider this kind of knowledge as part of the hacking practices, as described in the Jargon File, a discursive – conceptual resource for the hacker social world. In the following part, we have described an empirical case, the program OpenGrok: its birth; its lexical association with Heinlein's word; and its relationship of anchorage to a translation of hacking practices.

With this empirical analysis, we have shown how "to grok", taken as an example of the SF imaginary, participates to hacking practices by defining modalities of relationships between the source code of a program and developers, and being itself translated by the participation to the same practices: the hackers' grok allows humans to become Martians, that is to become hackers. Coming back to Heinlein's novel: «the words in English are a mere tautology, empty. In Martian they are a complete set of working instructions.» [6, p.490].

5 References

[1] A.A. V.V. (1999), Special Issue on Science Fiction, *Organization* 6(4), pp. 579-692.

[2] Crispin, M. (1978). Software Wars, http://panda.com/tops-20/software-wars.txt [13/12/2007]

[3] Descartes, R. (1637). *Discourse on the Method*, It. Trans. Il discorso sul metodo, 3rd edizione, Paravia.

[4] Garfinkel, H. (1967). *Studies in Ethnomethodology*. Englewood Cliffs. Prentice-Hall, NJ.

[5] Glaser, B. G & Strauss, A. L. (1967). *Discovery of Grounded Theory: strategies for qualitative research*, Aldine Transaction, Chicago

[6] Heinlein, R. (1961). *Stranger in a strange land* – Original uncut version, Penguin, New York, 1991.

[7] Latour B. (1987). *Science in Action: How to Follow Scientists and Engineers* Through Society, Milton Keynes, Open University Press.

[8] Latour B.(2005). *Reassembling the Social*, Oxford Univ. Press, Oxford, NY.

[9] Law J. (2004). *After Method:: Mess in social science research.* London: Routledge.
[10] Raymond, E. S. (ed.) (2003). The Jargon File. Version 4.4.7, http://www.catb.org/~esr/jargon/ [13/12/2007]
[11] Raymond, E. S. (1998). Unix Wars (version 1.1), http://www.catb.org/~esr/writings/unixwars.html [13/12/2007]
[12] Risan, L.. "Hackers produce more than software, they produce hackers," Version 2.1 http://folk.uio.no/lr isan/Linux/Identity_games/ [13/12/2007]
[13] Srinivas, N. (1999). Managers as Androids: Reading Moral Agency in Philip Dick, in *Organization* 6(4), pp. 609-624.
[14] Turkle, S. (1984). *The Second Self: Computers and the Human Spirit*, Simon, New York.
[15] Ward, K. (1999). Cyber-ethnography and the emergence of the virtually new community. *Journal of Information Technology*, 14, 95-105.
[16] Weizenbaum, J. (1976). *Computer Power and Human Reason*, San Francisco, W.H. Freeman.

Social Dynamics of FLOSS Team Communication Across Channels

Andrea Wiggins, James Howison, and Kevin Crowston
Syracuse University School of Information Studies
Hinds Hall, Syracuse, NY, 13244 USA
(awiggins|jhowison|crowston)@syr.edu
WWW home page: http://floss.syr.edu

Abstract. This paper extends prior investigation into the social dynamics of free and open source (FLOSS) teams by examining the methodological questions arising from research using social network analysis on open source projects. We evaluate the validity of data sampling by examining dynamics of communication centralization, which vary across multiple communication channels. We also introduce a method for intensity-based smoothing in dynamic social network analysis.

1 Introduction and Literature Review

Increasing use of social network analysis (SNA) techniques in the research of FLOSS development projects raises concern about the validity of the measured constructs. Centralization is a measure of particular interest for describing the organization of FLOSS teams through the structure of social interactions, as FLOSS team structure has often been claimed by practitioners to exhibit decentralization, while researchers have argued that communication centralization may indicate the kind of strong leadership that enables success in an otherwise decentralized organizational context. However, centralization can vary widely within teams over time and venues [1-5], so an aggregate network structure may provide an overly simplified representation of the interactions in FLOSS teams. In this paper, we present a dynamic approach to assessing project network centralization. To motivate our proposed approach, we first discuss problems with current approaches, namely inappropriate use of measures, non-dynamic analyses, failure to consider intensity of relationships and a focus on a single forum. We then introduce an alternative approach and illustrate its utility in a study of two FLOSS teams.

Research that applies SNA techniques to studies of FLOSS team communication networks (as opposed to team membership networks [3]), typically constructs a social network by using the reply structure of the public threads in a venue as a proxy for direct communication between individuals. This approach defines a link as the interaction between a replier and the immediately previous poster in a threaded

---

Please use the following format when citing this chapter:

Wiggins, A., Howison, J. and Crowston, K., 2008, in IFIP International Federation for Information Processing, Volume 275; *Open Source Development, Communities and Quality*; Barbara Russo, Ernesto Damiani, Scott Hissam, Björn Lundell, Giancarlo Succi; (Boston: Springer), pp. 131–142.

discussion. Studies of the information flow characteristics of social networks assume that information flows point-to-point, but depending on the mailing list structure, actual message recipients may include all project participants or all previous posters to the thread, not just the immediately previous poster. The broadcast structure of most of these communication channels therefore restricts the choice of SNA measures that are meaningful, as the potentially public nature of the messages clearly violates the assumptions of information brokerage measures such as betweenness centralization [6], among others. Following [2], we therefore use outdegree centralization [7] as a whole-network measure of inequality of communicative contributions in the network. High values indicate that a few individuals respond to more participants; lower values indicate more equal sharing of communicative work.

Time also presents several challenges for working with these data; all communication networks are sensitive to validity problems from collapsing events over a long period of time. While aggregating events over time is more analytically tractable, it often masks meaningful dynamics and typically fails to retain information about the intensity of relationships [1, 3]. We therefore develop a dynamic analysis of the network. Dynamic analysis requires sampling a time series of snapshots of the networks, based on the time-stamp assigned to the message upon receipt by the message server.

In the projects we studied, periods without any communications were surprisingly common, and this presents a further analytical challenge, as a lack of observations does not necessarily equate to a lack of network structure in the community; people may still have on-going relationships even if they haven't spoken in a particular month. This problem is typically addressed in time-series analysis through smoothing, in which data are divided into overlapping snapshots and sampled in windows (e.g., of 90 days) moving the window forward by a fixed unit (e.g., by 30 days) for each observation [1]. Using a 90-day sliding window, however, means that a single dyad may be reflected in up to three consecutive snapshots; window size is selected to assure that enough observations are present for most forums to generate analysis data for each time period.

A comparison of the effects of smoothing on communication network centralizations is shown in Figure 1; effective smoothing reduces the standard deviation of the network centralizations, but is problematic in that it tends to inflate the mean value. In addition, it tends to "shift" the observations of dynamics forward in time, so that a peak observed in February 2005 with the 30-day window, in Figure 1, only becomes evident in March 2005 with 60-day smoothing, and does not appear until April 2005 when 90-day smoothing is applied.

Intensity of relationships introduces another challenge for SNA in communication networks, for which it has long been known that the strength of ties affects the interactions between individuals [8]. Like most SNA measures, the standard interpretation of outdegree centralization evaluates the centralization of a dichotomous network, those in which ties are either present or absent between any pair of dyads. The measures assume binary relationships because they are designed to evaluate abstract relationships as opposed to the individual communications that researchers use as a proxy for relationships. In a communication network, a dichotomous representation is a reduction of the available source data.

Most approaches that preserve the information about intensity of interactions in networks employ edge weightings based on unit weighting. Unit weighting increases the weight of each edge by incrementing the edge value by a fixed unit for each

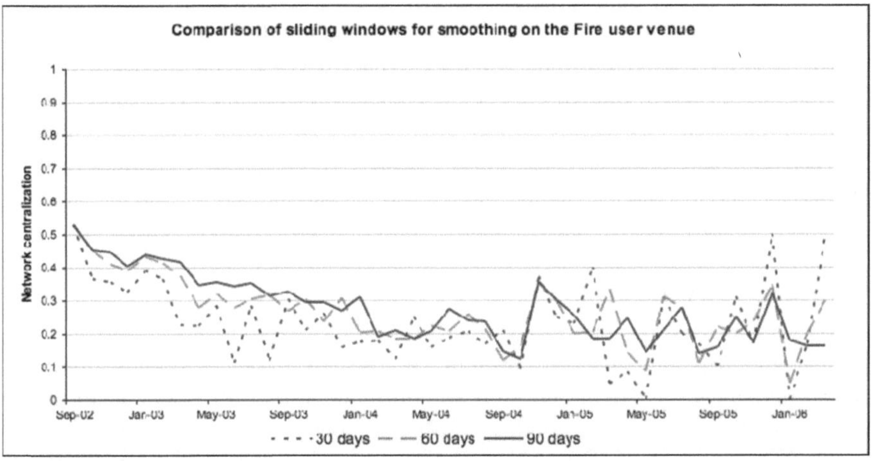

Fig. 1. Comparing the network centralizations observed with different smoothing windows demonstrates the noise reduction from smoothing, such as the period between May and September of 2003. The effect of smoothing also evident for months when no data were available, such as in May 2005, or were very sparse, as in February through April of 2005. For these data, using 90-day periods instead of non-overlapping 30-day periods reduced the standard deviation of the centralizations from 0.14 to 0.12, and increased the mean value from 0.22 to 0.26.

message between a pair in the network sample. Node strength is another option for evaluating centrality with this edge weighting method [9], which indicates the volume of activity in dyadic pairs but assumes a fixed value to each interaction. As few robust measures utilize edge weights, the usual compromise dichotomizes networks based on threshold criteria. This approach allows the analysis of weighted networks using measures that assume dichotomous relationships, but further complicates interpretation by the necessity of selecting threshold criteria, which can be sensitive to such factors as the size of the data sample.

Finally, there are validity considerations inherent in the selection of venues for data sampling. Bug trackers, email lists, and forums have all been used individually for studies of communication networks, but these venues have important differences in function and audience that may affect their interaction dynamics. Many analyses of FLOSS networks analyze only one communication channel to represent the activity of the entire project community. Howison et al. [2] explored the potential for identifying leadership through patterns of contribution to communications, but noted that development contribution is also considered a strong leadership indicator in

FLOSS project teams. Despite theoretical reasons for sampling in particular channels, such as bug trackers or developer email lists, examining the social dynamics of project groups from the perspective of only one communication channel presents an incomplete view of project participation [10]. For example, if we take contribution as a proxy for leadership behavior, we still cannot assume that leadership will be evident in only one of several channels of communication. Participation in bug-fixing, for example, may represent a different form of leadership than participation on a developer or core email list, as seen in analysis of the negotiation processes of bug-fixing [11]. It is therefore reasonable to expect variance in the communication dynamics of user-oriented and developer-oriented venues, and in discussion-oriented versus bug-fixing venues, which poses a potential threat to convergent validity in FLOSS studies that use SNA methods.

2 Data and Methods

In this section of the paper, we present an intensity-based smoothing method to address challenges with dynamic SNA in communication networks and to mitigate the effects of the overlapping window of observations. In our method the recency of a message affects its salience in an ongoing dynamic structure. From this perspective, a more recent interaction has more impact on the current state of the network in each snapshot than an interaction from the very beginning of the time window selected for analysis.

We then examine the validity of venue selection in the following section by comparing the dynamics of communication in multiple venues within projects to determine whether the centralizations of these communication channels show correlated, comparable patterns of change over the course of the project lifespan. Finally we cautiously interpret these measurements for substantive findings in a comparison between two FLOSS projects.

2.1 Sample Selection and Raw Data

Our analysis focuses on the communication patterns in two projects, Fire and Gaim. These projects are similar in that they are both community initiated multi-protocol instant messaging (IM) clients but differ in their ability to sustain project success. Gaim was founded in 1999 as a Linux AOL messenger client and has continued to grow, eventually being ported to Windows and Mac OS X. In early 2006, Gaim changed its project name to Pidgin; our data is selected from the period from the founding of the project in November 1999 until the name change in April 2006. Fire was founded in 2001 on Mac OS X and was initially quite successful, but eventually faced difficulties and made its final release in 2006. Our analysis uses the entire range of Fire's active development lifespan, from 2001 through March 2006.

For each of these projects, communications in the form of email lists, forums, and trackers were obtained from the FLOSSmole [12] and Notre Dame Sourceforge repositories[1], which collected them from SourceForge. These data were imported into a database (now available through FLOSSmole) to allow automated analysis. We note that FLOSS developers are widely recognized as users of their own products, so we can expect that as developers of IM clients conduct a portion of their communications via IM, and these data are not available for analysis. The observed communication patterns in these projects may therefore differ from the trends that might be seen in projects that are not developing IM clients due to the nature of the product that they develop; analysis to explore this possibility remains for future work. For the Fire project, the communication channels included two trackers, two developer email lists and one user-oriented email list; for Gaim, the channels included four trackers, a user forum, and two developer email lists. For the purposes of comparison, we aggregate individual communications channels into audience-based communication venues because these venues support different types of activities (e.g., discussing programming questions versus user support [10]), making it reasonable to expect that the communication patterns will differ for these groupings of venues.

2.2 Operationalization

To implement intensity-based smoothing for communication dynamics, we developed an original exponential decay function that assigns a weight to each interaction based on its recency and then sums the individual interaction weights to find the edge weight for each dyad. The edge weight decay function shown below is calculated using three dates for each event; the beginning (t_1) and end dates (t_n) for the period, and the date of the event (t_e). The function uses a rate parameter r, determined by the recency of the message event within the total time period t, to scale the value of the message weight w: Let $t = t_n - t_1 + 1$ and $t_{elapsed} = t_e - t_1 + 1$ such that $r = (t - t_{elapsed})/t$. Interaction weights w are given by $w = e^{(-ln(t)*r)}$ and the interaction weights for each dyad are summed for the edge weight. This assigns the oldest messages in the period a weight that approaches zero, and messages sent on the final day in the period receive a weight of one.

The exponentially decayed weighting is intended to reduce the effects of overlapping windows for data smoothing. To maintain the analytic value of the outdegree centralization measure, the edge weights were subject to a dichotomization threshold so that only edges with values at or above the 0.8 quantile were used to calculate centralization. This threshold selection was made based on sensitivity analysis on a subset of the data and likely affects the effectiveness of the weighting function; an exhaustive comparison of threshold options is a task for future research. Tests comparing the exponentially decayed weighting compared to unit weighting at this threshold saw no effects when applied to a very large data set, such as the Gaim data. Applied to the Fire venues, however, the exponentially decayed weighting

1 http://www.nd.edu/~oss/Data/data.html; access to the Notre Dame repository requires an academic license agreement. FLOSSmole data is publicly available.

showed some variations from the unit weighting, particularly in the less active developer venues, where the correlation between unit and exponentially decayed edge weightings was only 0.86.

The value of exponential edge weighting is best demonstrated on sparse data, for which it provides better smoothing than absolute dichotomization; the venue that showed greatest effect from the use of exponential weighting was also the least active overall. In addition, the exponential weighting better reflects sudden changes in levels of activity from period to period which might otherwise be masked by the use of a unit-weighted smoothing window. Preserving this type of dynamic is beneficial when evaluating the changes to network centralizations. Figure 2 shows the differences between this method and the absolute unit dichotomization method for one email list.

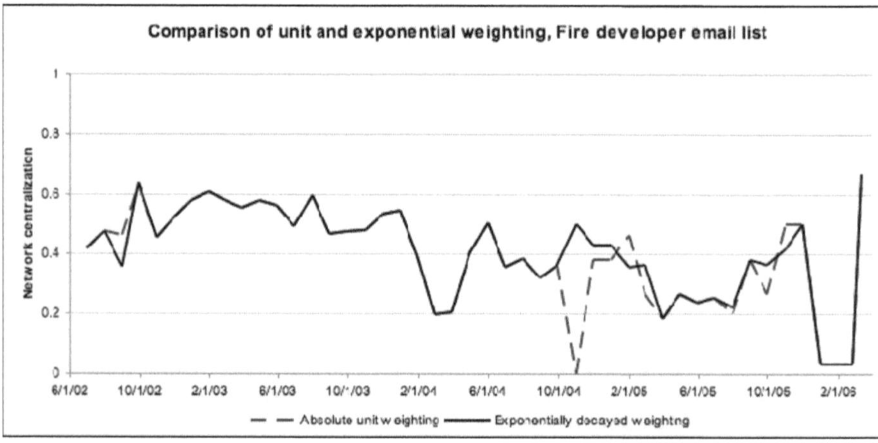

Fig. 2. Comparing network centralizations with absolute unit weighting and exponentially decayed weighting shows no differences for periods of time with higher activity levels, but the exponentially decayed weighting provides better smoothing during periods when there is very little activity.

The dynamic network analysis was performed using a scientific workflow tool, Taverna Workbench, which enabled the development of data analysis workflows that take advantage of modular design and utilize built-in iteration strategies to accomplish a series of data processing tasks over a number of project forum data sets. The workflow used in this analysis was designed to parse mailing list messages into graphs of network centralization over time, depicted in Figure 3[2]. While a brief series of virus messages in one of the venues, identified during content analysis for a separate study, could not be excluded from the current analysis and causes a small effect on one channel, this automated method enabled repeatable analysis of large

[2] The workflows and XML records of the workflow runs used to produce the analysis are available at http://ossmole.svn.sourceforge.net/viewvc/ossmole/taverna-workflows/sna/.

data sets. For example, the Gaim data set included over 41,000 events in the user forum, over 30,000 events in the developer venues, and about 20,000 events in the trackers.

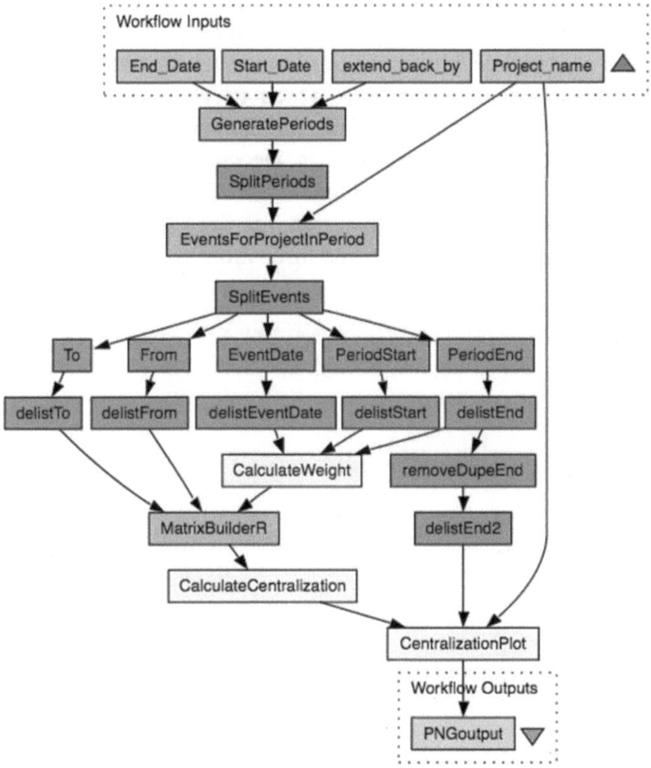

Fig. 3. Taverna Workbench analysis workflow to extract FLOSS message data based on user-provided project name and data sampling time frame for analysis and return an irregular time-series plot of network centralizations. The workflow is explained in further detail in a companion paper for the demonstration of the Taverna tool; see [13] for details.

3 Communication Venues

To examine communication centralization trends across the venues within each project, and between projects, we compare time series analyses for the two projects. Exponentially decayed smoothing was applied to monthly periods with a 90-day overlapping sliding window for the user, developer and tracker venues in both projects. Each project shows different dynamics in each venue; while both projects tend toward greater decentralization in communications over time, they display varying patterns of interaction. This variation is evident in the correlations between the communication venues within each project.

In three venues for the Fire project (Figure 4) there are comparable mean values for network centralization of trackers and developer email lists (Figure 5). The user email list had a lower average centralization, which reflects the larger and more diverse group of message respondents. The standard deviations of the centralizations are similar for the user and developer venues but higher for trackers due to a spike in centralization values in December of 2005, which affects the values for the following two months due to the sliding window. The sudden change from a very decentralized structure to a highly centralized structure in December of 2005 originates in the feature requests tracker, when one individual closed 279 bugs in a very short period of time. This was most likely in preparation for the end of project development activity, as the final release of Fire followed three months later.

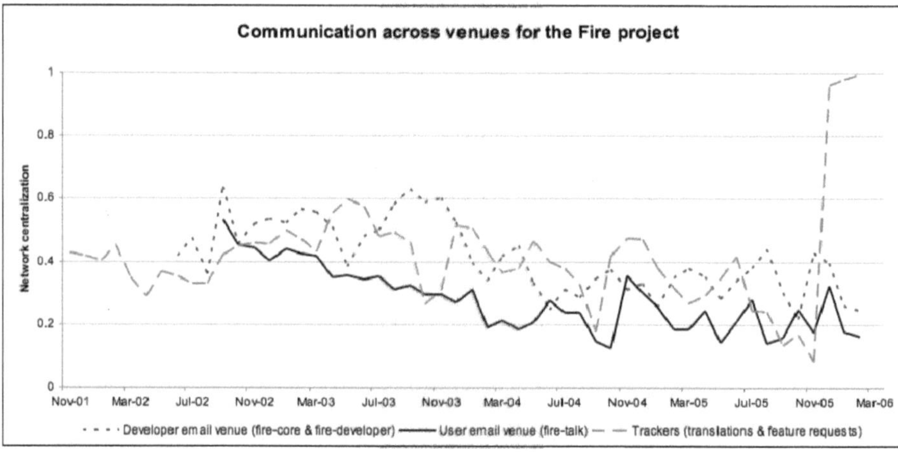

Fig. 4. Communication networks in different venues for the Fire project showed different dynamics over time, although all of the venues show a trend toward increasingly decentralized communications. The tracker shows an interesting exception to this trend just prior to the end of the project activity.

Excluding this period of unusually high centralizations, the mean and standard deviations of the tracker centralizations are comparable to those for the email lists, shown in Figure 5. This may imply some level of regularity across these different venues, and there is an overall downward trend in each venue as communications become increasingly decentralized. Despite these similarities, the three Fire communication venues clearly display different dynamics over time; the correlations in Table 1 show that the developer and user venues are most similar, while the developer venue and the trackers were negatively correlated.

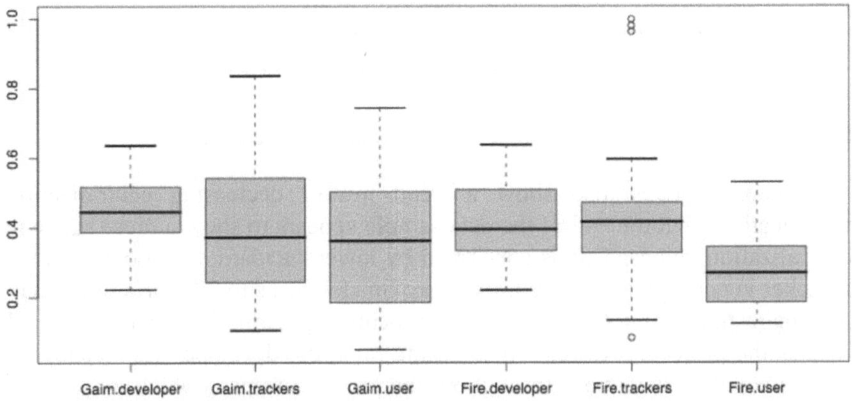

Fig. 5. The distributions for the Gaim and Fire network centralizations show similarity in the summary statistics for the trackers and user venue in Gaim that do not appear in Fire. For each project the user venues have lower centralizations than the developer venues.

Gaim also shows different communication dynamics in different venues (Figure 6); the average centralizations are lowest for the user forum and highest for the developer list, which has a smaller number of participants. The standard deviations of the centralizations for the user forum and the tracker are comparable, while the standard deviation for the developer list was much lower. Visual inspection of the centralization trends reflects a more varied participation dynamic in the user forum and trackers. Periodic spikes in tracker activity appear to indicate project "housecleaning", much like the phenomenon observed at the end of the Fire project, as there were several periods during which a large number of bugs were closed. These large batches of bug closing were conducted by one (or very few) individuals, generating the observed highly centralized network structures.

Gaim's user and developer venues both bear greater similarity to the trackers than to one another (Table 1). This result is very different from the correlations for Fire, where the user and developer venues are most alike, and may indicate different uses of these venues by the project participants. One possible explanation for this difference between the projects is that both the user and developer venues were email lists for the Fire project, while the user venue in Gaim was a forum. However, this usage would not explain the very different correlations between activity in developer venues and trackers, or the similarity of the Gaim trackers to the user and developer venues.

Table 1. Correlations of centralizations between communication venues in Fire and Gaim highlight differences in the project communication dynamics.

Project	User-Developer	Developer-Trackers	User-Trackers
Fire	0.62	-0.03	0.21
Gaim	0.17	0.57	0.57

The Gaim venues also show a trend toward decreasing centralization of communications, but the end of the data sample appears to show a more stable range of centralization values. This is confirmed by lower standard deviations for the user and tracker venues, both shifting from approximately 0.18 to 0.9 during the final two years, suggesting that more stable communication patterns have emerged in these venues as the projects matured. At the same time, the developer venue shows little change to standard deviations throughout the project lifespan, which may indicate a different strategy for moderation of development activities over time.

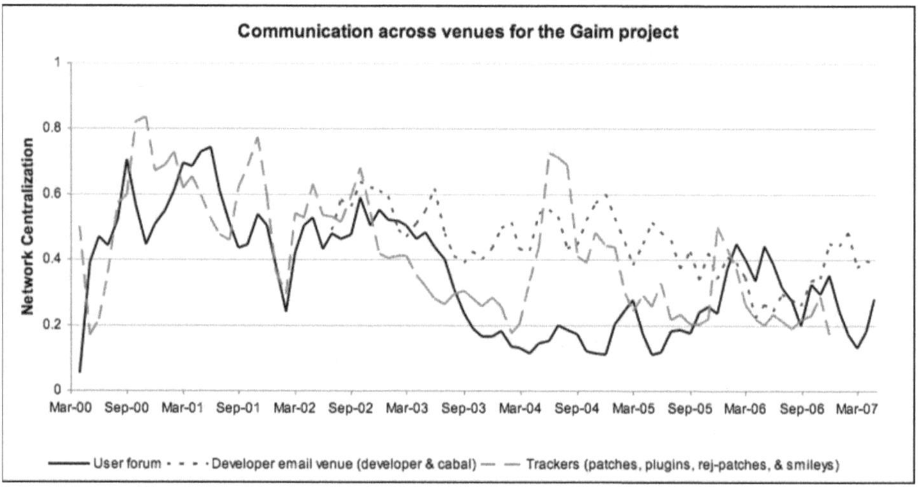

Fig. 6. Communication networks in different venues for the Gaim project also display different dynamics over time; the centralizations for both the user and developer venues were more strongly correlated with the trackers than with one another.

4 Discussion

The use of an intensity-based smoothing assists most with sparse data but the necessity for dichotomization introduces another complication with respect to sensitivity to threshold values, and loses information on the strength of relationships. The selection of smoothing window length may also play a role in the effectiveness of the exponentially decayed weighting, and is another topic for future research.

Analysis of the dynamics across venues shows different levels of correlation between venues for each project, suggesting that these different communication channels may be proxies for different types of relationships. In both projects, the user venue is more decentralized than the developer venue, reflecting the greater number of participants. Another common feature for all venues in both projects was the overall trend toward decentralization over time, although this could be the result of different influences in each case. In the Fire project, decentralization may be the result of loss of project leadership, while in the successful Gaim project it appears to reflect growth in user participation. Overall, variation in communication dynamics suggests that convergent validity is an important consideration for studies of FLOSS communication networks, and care should be taken in the selection of venues for data sampling, as observations in different venues will generate different results.

In addition, an interesting phenomenon was observed in each of the projects' trackers, where periodic mass bug closings by very few individuals caused sudden, isolated spikes in centralization values. This apparent "housekeeping" behavior, occurring several years into both of these projects, may be a common practice in managing resources for a long-term FLOSS project. We hope to continue the analysis with a larger number of projects to determine whether this phenomenon is common to other projects, which would pose additional challenges to validity for using bug trackers as a data source for analysis of communication dynamics, but which would also point to rhythms in group work, believed to be important to success in distributed environments [14].

5 Conclusion

The dynamic analysis of FLOSS team communications across channels has provided these findings:

- Communication centralization dynamics vary in different venues, suggesting that communication in these venues may be proxies for different kinds of relationships. Researchers should therefore be cautious in using single venues to characterize projects.
- Periodic project management activities in the trackers were evident in both projects, as batch bug closings by a few individuals caused a sudden, temporary shift to a highly centralized network structure. This is both an interesting behavioral phenomenon and a potential confound to analysis of bug trackers.
- All venues in both projects tended toward decentralization over time, a pattern we expect to observe in future analysis of additional projects. Periods in which centralization bucks this trend and rises might be particularly interesting for further study.

This paper also contributes an original method for computing exponentially decayed edge weightings in a dynamic network and makes it available to the research community via a downloadable workflow. Future research could extend this work by examining alternate measures of centrality, and by comparing the individual centralities of developers in multiple channels for each project over time, examining both the dynamics of the individual and aggregated communication channels.

References

1. López-Fernández, L., et al., *Applying Social Network Analysis Techniques to Community-Driven Libre Software Projects.* International Journal of Information Technology and Web Engineering, 2006. **1**(3).
2. Howison, J., K. Inoue, and K. Crowston. *Social dynamics of free and open source team communications.* in *IFIP 2nd International Conference on Open Source Software.* 2006. Lake Como, Italy: Springer.
3. Gao, Y. and G. Madey, *Network Analysis of the SourceForge.net Community*, in *The Third International Conference on Open Source Systems (OSS 2007), IFIP WG 2.13.* 2007: Limerick, Ireland.
4. Braha, D. and Y. Bar-Yam, *From Centrality to Temporary Fame: Dynamic Centrality in Complex Networks.* Complexity, 2006. **12**: p. 59-63.
5. Crowston, K. and J. Howison, *The Social Structure of Free and Open Source Software Development.* First Monday, 2005. **10**(2).
6. Wasserman, S. and K. Faust, *Social network analysis: methods and applications.* Structural analysis in the social sciences ; 8. 1994, Cambridge: Cambridge University Press. xxxi, 825 p.
7. Freeman, L., D. Roeder, and R. Mullholland, *Centrality in Social Networks: Ii. experimental results.* Social Networks, 1980. **2**: p. 119-141.
8. Granovetter, M.S., *The Strength of Weak Ties.* The American Journal of Sociology, 1973. **78**(6): p. 1360-1380.
9. Valverde, S., et al., *Self-organization patterns in wasp and open source communities.* IEEE Intelligent Systems, 2006. **21**(2): p. 36-40.
10. Sowe, S.K., I. Stamelos, and A. Lefteris, *Identifying knowledge brokers that yield software engineering knowledge.* Information and Software Technology, 2006. **48**(11): p. 1025-1033.
11. Sandusky, R.J. and L. Gasser. *Negotiation and the coordination of information and activity in distributed software problem management.* in *International ACM SIGGROUP Conference on Supporting Group Work.* 2005. Sanibel Island, Florida, USA: ACM.
12. Howison, J., M. Conklin, and K. Crowston, *Flossmole: A collaborative repository for FLOSS research data and analysis.* International Journal of Information Technology and Web Engineering, 2006. **1**(3): p. 17-26.
13. Howison, J., A. Wiggins, and K. Crowston, *eResearch workflows for studying free and open source software development*, in *Proceedings of Fourth International Conference on Open Source Software (IFIP 2.13).* Milan, Italy. September 2008.
14. Maznevski, M.L. and K.M. Chudoba, *Bridging space over time: Global virtual team dynamics and effectiveness.* Organization Science, 2000. **11**(5): p. 473-492.

Towards a Global Research Infrastructure for Multidisciplinary Study of Free/Open Source Software Development

Les Gasser[1,2] and Walt Scacchi[2]
[1]Graduate School of Library and Information Science, University of Illinois at Urbana/Champaign,
[2]Institute for Software Research
University of California Irvine,
Irvine, CA 92697-3455 USA
+1-949-824-4130, +1-949-824-1715 (fax)
gasser@uiuc.edu, wscacchi@uci.edu

Abstract. The Free/Open Source Software (F/OSS) research community is growing across and within multiple disciplines. This community faces a new and unusual situation. The traditional difficulties of gathering enough empirical data have been replaced by issues of dealing with enormous amounts of freely available public data from many disparate sources (online discussion forums, source code directories, bug reports, OSS Web portals, etc.). Consequently, these data are being discovered, gathered, analyzed, and used to support multidisciplinary research. However at present, no means exist for assembling these data under common access points and frameworks for comparative, longitudinal, and collaborative research across disciplines. Gathering and maintaining large F/OSS data collections reliably and making them usable present several research challenges. For example, current projects usually rely on direct access to, and mining of raw data from groups that generate it, and both of these methods require unique effort for each new corpus, or even for updating existing corpora. In this paper, we identify several needs and critical factors in F/OSS empirical research across disciplines, and suggest recommendations for design of a global research infrastructure for multi-disciplinary research into F/OSS development.

1 Introduction

A significant group of software researchers is beginning to investigate large software projects empirically, using freely available data from F/OSS projects. A body of recent work point out the need for community-wide data collections and research infrastructure to expand the depth and breadth of empirical F/OSS research, and several initial proposals have been made [6, 16, 17, 24, 28]. Most importantly, these data collections and proposed infrastructure are intended to support an active and

Please use the following format when citing this chapter:

Gasser, L. and Scacchi, W., 2008, in IFIP International Federation for Information Processing, Volume 275; *Open Source Development, Communities and Quality*; Barbara Russo, Ernesto Damiani, Scott Hissam, Björn Lundell, Giancarlo Succi; (Boston: Springer), pp. 143–158.

growing community F/OSS scholars addressing contemporary issues and theoretical foundations in disciplines that include anthropology, economics, informatics (computer-supported cooperative work), information systems, library and information science, management of technology and innovation, law, organization science, policy science, and software engineering. Approximately 200 published studies can be found at the MIT Free/Open Source research community Web site (http://opensource.mit.edu/). Furthermore, this research community has researchers based in Asia, Europe, North America, South America, and the South Pacific, thus denoting its international and global membership. Consequently, the research community engaged in empirical studies of F/OSS can be recognized as another member in the growing movement for interdisciplinary software engineering research.

This report attempts to justify and clarify the need for community-wide, sharable research infrastructure and collections of F/OSS data. We review the general case for empirical research on software repositories, articulate some specific current barriers to this empirical research approach, and sketch several community-wide options with the potential to address some of the most critical barriers. First, we review the range of research and research questions that could benefit from a research infrastructure and data collections. Second, we expose critical requirements of such a project. We then suggest a set of components that address these requirements, and put forth several specific recommendations.

2 Objects of Study and Research Questions

As an organizing framework, we identify five main *objects of study*--that is, things whose characteristics researchers are trying to describe and explain--in F/OSS-based empirical software research: *software artifacts and source code*, *software processes*, *development projects and communities*, and *participants' knowledge*. In Table 1 we provide a rough map of some representative characteristics that have been investigated for each of these objects of study, and show some critical factors that researchers have begun linking to these characteristics as explanations. It is important to point out that these objects of study are by no means independent from one another. They should be considered as interdependent elements of F/OSS (e.g., knowledge and processes affect artifacts, communities affect processes, etc.) Also, each of the outcomes shown in Table 1 may play a role as a critical factor in the other categories.

3 Current Research Approaches

We have identified at least four alternative approaches in empirical research on the objects and factors in Table 1 [cf. 50,51]:

- *Very large, population-scale studies* examining common objects selected and extracted from hundreds to tens-of-thousands of F/OSS projects [14, 24, 29, 32, 37] or surveys of comparable numbers of F/OSS developers [21, 25].
- *Large-scale cross-analyses of project and artifact characteristics*, such as code size and code change evolution, development group size, composition and organization, or development processes [7, 18, 23, 39].
- *Medium-scale comparative studies* across multiple kinds of F/OSS projects within different communities or software system types [2, 31, 49, 53].
- *Smaller-scale in-depth case studies* of specific F/OSS practices and processes, for concept/hypothesis development and exposing mechanism details [10, 30, 40, 44, 48, 50, 59].

Table 1: Characteristics of empirical F/OSS studies.

Objects	**Success Measures**	**Critical Driving Factors**
Source Code and Artifacts	Quality, downloads, reliability, usability, durability, fit, structure, growth, diversity, localization	Size, complexity, bugs and features, software architecture (structure, substrates, modularity, versions, infrastructure), information architecture, artifact types, and document genres
Processes	Efficiency, ease of improvement, adaptability, effectiveness, complexity, manageability, predictability	Size, distribution, collaboration, knowledge/information management, artifact structure, configuration, agility, innovativeness
Projects	Type, size, duration, number of participants, number of software versions released	Development platforms, tools supporting development and project coordination, software imported from elsewhere, social networks, roles and role migration paths, leadership and core developers, socio-technical vision
Communities	Ease of creation, sustainability, trust, increased social capital, lower rate of participant turnover	Size, economic setting, organizational architecture, behaviors, incentive structures, institutional forms, motivation, participation, core values, common-pool resources, public goods
Knowledge	Creation, codification, use, need, management	Tools, conventions, norms, social structures, technical content, acquisition, representations, reproduction, application

These four alternatives are separated less by fundamental differences in objectives than by technical limitations in existing tools and methods, or by the socio-technical research constraints associated with qualitative ethnographic research methods versus quantitative survey research. For example, qualitative analyses are hard to implement on a large scale, and quantitative methods have to rely on uniform, easily processed data. We believe these distinctions are becoming increasingly blurred as researchers develop and use more sophisticated analysis and modeling tools [e.g., 30, 36, 45, 47], leading to finer gradations in empirical data needs.

4 Available Empirical Data

Increasingly, F/OSS researchers have access to very large quantities and varieties of data, as most of the activity of F/OSS groups is carried on through persistent electronic media whose contents are open and freely available. The variety of data is manifested in several ways.

First, data vary in *content*, with types such as communications (threaded discussions, chats, digests, Web pages, Wikis/Blogs), documentation (user and developer documentation, HOWTO tutorials, FAQs), development data (source code, bug reports, design documents, attributed file directory structures, CVS check-in logs) [48, 51], and programming languages [7].

Second, data originates from different *types of repository* sources [8, 14, 24, 27, 40]. These include shared file systems, communication systems, version control systems, issue tracking systems, content management systems, multi-project FOSS portals (SourceForge.net, Freshmeat.net, Savannah.org, Advogato.org, Tigris.org, etc.), collaborative development or project management environments, FOSS code indexes or link servers (free-soft.org, LinuxLinks.com), search engines (Google.com/code, krugle.org), and others. Each type and instance of such a data repository may differ in the storage data model (relational, object-oriented, hierarchical, network), application data model (data definition schemas), data formats, data type semantics, and conflicts in data model namespaces (due to synonyms and homonyms), modeled, or derived data dependencies. Consequently, data from FOSS repositories is typically heterogeneous and difficult to integrate beyond semantic hypertext linking [41], rather than homogeneous and comparatively easy to integrate.

Third, data can be found from various spatial and temporal *locations*, such as community Web sites, software repositories and indexes, and individual FOSS project Web sites. Data may also be located within secondary sources appearing in research papers or paper collections (e.g., MIT FOSS research paper repository at http://opensource.mit.edu), where researchers have published some form of their data set within a publication [40, 52, 60].

Fourth, different *types of data extraction tools and interfaces* (query languages, application program interfaces, Open Data Base Connectors, command shells, embedded scripting languages, or object request brokers) are needed to select, extract, categorize, and other activities that mine, gather, and prepare data from one or more sources for further analysis [15, 18, 30, 32, 45, 47].

Last, most FOSS project data is available as *artifacts or byproducts* of development, usage, or maintenance activities in FOSS communities. These artifacts/byproducts are a critical part of the FOSS innovation process [61]. However, very little data is directly available in forms specifically intended for research use. This artifact/byproduct origin has several implications for the needs expressed above [16, 49, 51].

5 Addressing Issues with Empirical Data

The main objective of a research infrastructure that collects, aggregates, organizes, and offer data analysis services is to address community-wide resource issues in community-specific way [1, 58]. For F/OSS research, the objective is to improve the collective productivity of software research by lowering the access cost and effort for data that will address the critical questions of software development research. In this section we offer some possible approaches to such an infrastructure, by first briefly describing each "component", and then considering its benefits and drawbacks.

5.1 Metadata and Meta-models

One of the broadest approaches to common infrastructure is the use of representation standards [1, 59] as meta-data. Such standards would move some issues of cross-source data normalization forward in the process that produces F/OSS projects' information. The use of metadata permits researchers to identify relevant characteristics of specific data collections. Metadata can serve numerous roles in the organization and access of scientific data and documents, including roles in location, identification, security/access control, preservation, and collocation [54]. Standardization of metadata and addition of metadata to F/OSS information repositories, especially at the point of creation, would let the research community identify much more easily the data used in each study, understand and compare data formats, and would also simplify the selection process, by making visible critical selection information [13]. Fortunately, some metadata creation can be automated; unfortunately, representation standards are also an issue for metadata.

Meta-models [38] are ontological schemes that characterize how families of different model sub-types or kinds are interrelated. Meta-models thus provide a critical framework for how to associate and integrate heterogeneous data or metadata sets into a common inter-model substrate. F/OSS tools like Protégé-2000 [43] act as meta-models editors for constructing domain-independent or domain-specific ontologies, which in turn can produce/output metadata definitions that conceptually unify different data source into common shareable views [30].

5.2 Extracting, Analyzing, Modeling, Visualizing, Simulating, Reenacting, and More with the Available Data

Tools could potentially be developed to address each of the issues reviewed in the previous section. Some such tools already partially exist in a generic form or are developed as needed by research groups. Tools such as web-scrapers that gather data, entity extractors that mine for specific entities like people and dates, or cross-references that link multiple information sources of a single project are commonly developed from scratch in each research effort. These tools are part of the basic toolbox of almost every empirical F/OSS researcher and could easily be provided as such. In fact, several efforts are already underway to produce such tools (e.g.[27, 47]).

Another contribution of a research infrastructure could be to place research data access and manipulation tools upstream, directly within software development tools used by the F/OSS community (e.g., CVS, Subversion, Bugzilla), instead of requiring sometimes-tedious and potentially risky post processing. For example, in most cases, F/OSS tools rely on databases for data storage and manipulation. These databases contain valuable information that is often lost during the translation to a web-visible front-end. (Usually the front-ends rely on web interfaces that display information in a user-friendly fashion but drop important structure in the process). Access to the underlying database can be much more valuable (and in many cases easier) than the current techniques of web-scraping that must recreate such missing relations post-hoc, and may not be successful.

5.3 Integrated Data-to-Literature Environments: Digital libraries and new electronic journal/publishing archives featuring open content and open data.

Putting all the previous components together would lead to a set of normalized, processed and integrated collections of F/OSS data made available to the research community through either federated or centralized mechanisms. These research collections need to be curated and organized as digital libraries that organize and preserve different data sets, meta-data, derived views, analyses, and provenance that span multiple data sets/bases as well as views that span multi-disciplinary models and studies that can be accessed anytime and from anywhere [13, 54]. Furthermore, it should be both possible and desirable to offer subscription and publication services to those who want to be notified when data in the library are changed or updated [3, 12], so that they can re-analyze existing models or derived views.

Finally, an advanced contemporary approach would be an attempt to connect both data sources and research literature in a seamless and interlocking web, so that research findings can be traced back to sources, and so that basic source data can be linked directly to inferences made from it. Such arrangements provide powerful intrinsic means of discovering connections among research themes and ideas, as they are linked through both citation, through common or related uses of underlying data, and through associations among concepts. Similar efforts are underway in many other sciences (e.g., [1, 58]). Networks of literature and data created in this way, with automated support, can reduce cognitive complexity, establish collocation of concepts and findings, and establish/maintain social organization within and across F/OSS projects. The DSpace repository developed at MIT and Fedora repository [57] are among the leading research candidates that could serve as the storage and archiving facility through which F/OSS data sets, models, views, and analyses can be accessed, published, updated, and redistributed to interested researchers, in an open source, open science manner [cf. 6]. Alternatively, it may be desirable to utilize large, globally accessible repositories, index, and search services as might be provide by a commercial service provider such as Google.

6 Discussion

In our view, the multi-discipline F/OSS research community seeks to establish a *scholarly commons* that provides for communicating, sharing, and building on the ideas, artifacts, tools, and facilities of community participants in an open, globally accessible, and public way [cf. 26, 35]. A shared infrastructure, or in our case, a shared information infrastructure, is a key component and operational facility of such a commons [1, 9, 44]. Such an infrastructure provides a medium for sharing resources of common interest (e.g., F/OSS data sets, domain models, tools for processing data in F/OSS repositories, research pre-prints and publications), common-pool resources (F/OSS portals like SourceForge [55]), and public goods (scientific knowledge, Internet access and connectivity). However, a globally shared information infrastructure supporting F/OSS research may not just emerge spontaneously, though it could emerge in an *ad hoc* manner whose design and operation does not provide for a reasonably equitable distribution of access, costs, or benefits for community participants.

We want to avoid or minimize conditions that make such an infrastructure a venue for conflict (e.g., across disciplines, over data formats, making free riders pay, or rules that limit unconditional access). Consequently, community participants must allocation some attention and effort to address the infrastructure's design and operation. This in turn needs to support and embrace a diverse set of multidisciplinary research interests, but with limited resources. Unsurprisingly, this leads us to a design strategy that is not only iterative, incremental, and continuous, as many F/OSS researchers have agreed [17], but also one that embraces and builds on the practice of F/OSS development practices, processes, artifacts, and tools that are also the subject of our collective research interests. This in part seems inevitable as a way to address the concomitant need for administratively lightweight governance structures, modest and sustainable financial strategies, and national and international research partnerships among collaborators in different institutions, as well as enabling educational and community growth efforts [9, 26].

7 Recommendations

In accord with the rationales outlined above and the strong sense of the F/OSS community [17, 44], as well as from results developed at the 2008 F/OSS Repositories and Research Infrastructures Workshop (see http://fossrri.rotterdam.ics.uci.edu), we recommend that F/OSS researchers begin collective efforts to create sharable infrastructure for collaborative empirical research. This infrastructure should be assembled incrementally, with activity in many of the recommendations defined below.

This paper has provided a sketch of some ideas toward robust and useful infrastructure that can support research within and across the multiple disciplines already investing scholarly effort into the area of F/OSS. The ideas and motivations presented here however need more development, thus collaborative interdisciplinary efforts are encouraged.

Many standards for sharable scientific data exist for other communities, as do many repositories of data conforming to those standards. We should do further research on what other communities have done to organize research data. For example, many collections of social science data are maintained around the world[1]. We should use the experiences of these projects as a basis for the F/OSS research infrastructure. The success of these archives in the social science community is also a partial answer to questions of "why bother?" Beyond this, we and others recommend consideration of the following actions that may benefit the global F/OSS research community.

7.1 Instrument Existing Tools and Repositories

We should work with existing F/OSS community development tool projects to design plug-ins to instrument widely used F/OSS tools (such as Bugzilla, CVS/Subversion, etc.) to make the content of those tools available via APIs in standardized formats, administratively controllable by original tool/data owners. Such an effort could also benefit the community of F/OSS developers itself; this sort of instrumentation could help interfacing multiple tools, projects, and communities, and might increase willingness to participate. Further, finding F/OSS projects or multi-project portals that are willing to add support for wide-area event notification

[1] See for example http://www.iue.it/LIB/EResources/E-data/online_archive.shtml for a list of such collections.

services [3] that can publish data set updates to remote research subscribers is real challenge that has been demonstrated to have multiple practical payoffs.

7.2 Continuously Develop Self-Managing F/OSS Research Infrastructure Prototypes

As a proof of concept, we should mock up a complete F/OSS research infrastructure model embodying as many of the desired characteristics as feasible. We should gather data sets, models, analyses, simulations, published studies and more from the many disciplines that are engaged in empirical studies of F/OSS. Such a partial implementation might use, for example, a complete cross section of sharable information from a single project, including chat, news, CVS, bug reporting, and so on. Initial efforts of this kind have produced encouraging results [15, 28, 33]. We and others have already instigated some local efforts in a few of these areas, such as generalized bug report schemas, semi-automated extraction of social processes, preliminary data taxonomies, and automated analysis tools [e.g.,14, 18, 20, 30, 32, 37, 45, 46, 47]. However, there is still a basic need to codify and capture the scientific workflow that FOSS scholars engage in when they analyze FOSS data across many repositories [22].

7.3 Federate FOSS Data Repositories

The European FOSS research community may have more resources (provided by the EC IS&T Programme) already dedicated to development of public FOSS data repositories, data analysis tools, and to the cross-sectional analysis of FOSS data, compared to the U.S. FOSS research community. At a minimum, it would benefit the U.S. FOSS research community to be able to partner with its EU and other international research counterparts to help establish a global FOSS research infrastructure and network of federated FOSS data repositories. Beyond this, it would be of greater research value if the U.S., European, and Asian FOSS research data repositories were collectively federated within a global FOSS research data and community support infrastructure, providing resources to researchers looking to use or host repository data and for FOSS practitioners interested in providing research data.

7.4 Offer Guidance and Incentives for Contributions to a Global Census of FOSS Project Repositories

The diversity and population of FOSS project repositories is unclear and unknown. There is great interest in the research community for a baseline and ongoing census of FOSS project repositories. As FOSS projects choose to collect, organize, and share the raw data of software development as an activity in their self-interest, then it behooves us within the research community to offer some guidance or incentives for these independent FOSS projects to contribute to such a census. Similarly, we need to articulate what benefits (e.g., socio-economic impacts or intellectual contributions) the research community might offer in return to the FOSS projects that contribute to such a census.

7.5 Identify Research Questions that can Best be Answered through FOSS Data Repositories

The open and public accessibility of raw data from FOSS project repositories and multi-project repositories (e.g., SourceForge.net, FLOSSmole, Google Code [cf. 14, 15, 16, 23]) is providing a new, empirically grounded view of software technology and software development practice—a view that enables comparative, cross-sectional, and ecosystem level studies. This in turn means news kinds of research questions can be posed and new knowledge can be discovered, derived, or created. For example, repository-based studies of successful FOSS projects (of which there are now at least a few thousand such projects) indicate that their software code base, functionality, development artifacts, and developer contributions, and user base can undergo sustained exponential growth, apparently in contradiction to long-standing "laws of software evolution" which traditionally predict sub-linear, inverse square growth rates [cf. 2, 8, 34, 50]. As such, the kind of research questions that follow may ask what model or theory accounts for the super-linear evolution of FOSS systems?

Another example: are there software patterns that constitute a kind of "software genome" that characterize the evolutionary mechanisms of different families of independently developed FOSS systems? Similarly, are the critical software components or functions that lie at the heart of different software families, and does such software represent a critical evolutionary or security vulnerability (e.g., the `glibc` library is commonly bound with FOSS coded in the C programming language)? Also, what development processes best characterize FOSS projects that demonstrate sustained exponential growth of their code and functionality base, as well as the growth of the number of contributors, but with comparable growth/decline of software quality? Last, what can we learn about the evolution of FOSS systems across multiple releases, across multiple platforms, and across different independently developed variants? Exploring any questions like these all require data drawn from multiple FOSS projects or project repositories, and this data is now available. As such, we are on the verge of possible discontinuous advance in our knowledge about software, once again based on empirical studies of FOSS.

7.6 Develop and Share Practices for Curating and Archiving FOSS Project Data

Articulating new knowledge of software products, processes, practices, and organizational forms depends in part on careful and systematic empirical study of FOSS project data. However, this data is not trivial to collect, use, or analyze. As such, there is need to articulate practices for the curation of FOSS project data in forms that increase the likelihood for the data use, reuse, and (re)analysis by people in different disciplines and settings. There is also need to help capture data provenance as well as data annotation and data analysis workflow tools & techniques. Other science disciplines have recognized similar needs, so there is an opportunity for current investments in such areas to be structured to both discipline-specific and cross-discipline research efforts. At present, the FOSS research community has little practice and access to these tools and techniques, and as a result, has little incentive to take on their application or reinvention.

7.7 Identify How Commercial Software Companies can Benefit from Studies Employing FOSS Data Repositories

The commercial software products and service industry in the U.S. is in an awkward strategic position regarding whether or how to take advantage of FOSS, or the results arising from studies of FOSS development data. Software product companies like Microsoft seem hesitant about what to do about FOSS, while software service companies like Google seem to embrace FOSS (as do computer vendors like IBM and SUN). But it appears that all software companies can benefit from empirical studies of FOSS products, processes, practices, and organizational forms that are comparative or cross-sectional, for different competitive reasons.

7.8 Encourage Corporate Sponsors of FOSS Projects to Share their Data with the Research Community

Last, companies like Google, SUN, IBM, and Microsoft Research have established a community of OSS development projects under their corporate sponsorship. These projects are sponsored as a way for these companies to help increase the pool of future software developers who might then transition into the commercial software workforce. These projects also serve to provide a situated, real-world experiment in informal software engineering education, that often takes place outside of the traditional higher education environment. However, “data” from these informal educational experiences is generally not open, nor publicly available, as it is sometimes said to be sensitive, confidential, and proprietary. Thus it is unclear how well these informal experiments work, or whether/how they can be improved both from a corporate perspective as well as from an academic perspective. Perhaps there is an opportunity to bring together the academic software research and software engineering education community together with the commercial software industry through a government sponsored or coordinated forum so as to articulate how to best advance U.S. socio-economic and scholarly interests for mutual benefit and growth of the software community.

In the end, we believe efforts in these directions identified in these recommendations will pay off in the form of deeper collaborations within and across the empirical software research community, wider awareness of important research issues and means of addressing them, and ultimately in more systematic, grounded knowledge and theory-driven practice in software development.

Acknowledgements: Preparation of this report was supported in part through research grants from the National Science Foundation #0083705, #0205679, #0205724, #0350754, #0534771 and #0749353. No endorsement implied. Collaborators on these projects include Mark Ackerman at University of Michigan, Ann-Arbor, John Noll at Santa Clara University, Margaret Elliott, Chris Jensen, and others at the Institute for Software Research. Megan Conklin, Kevin Crowston, Greg Madey, and others also helped in organizing and contributing recommendations from the *2008 NSF Workshop of Free/Open Source Software Repositories and Research Infrastructures*, (see http://fossrri.rotterdam,ics.uci.edu) on which some of the results here are based.

References

1. Bowker G, Baker K, Millerand F. and Ribes D, (2007). Towards Information Infrastructure Studies: Ways of Knowing in a Networked Environment, in J. Hunsinger, M. Allen, and L. Klasrup (eds.), *International Handbook of Internet Research.*
2. Capiluppi A, Morisio M, and Lago, P, (2004). Evolution of Understandability in OSSProjects, *Proc. Eighth European Conf. Software Maintenance and Reengineering* (CSMR'04).
3. Carzaniga A, Rosenblum D, and Wolf A, (2001). Design and Evaluation of a Wide-Area Event Notification Service, *ACM Trans. Computer Systems*, 19(3), 332-383.
4. Choi SC, Scacchi W, (1990). Extracting and Restructuring the Design of Large Software Systems, *IEEE Software*, 7(1), 66-71, January/February.
5. Conklin M, (2007). Project Entity Matching in FLOSS Repositories, in Feller, J, Fitzgerald, B, Scacchi, W, and Sillitti, A. (Eds.), *Open Source Development, Adoption, and Innovation,* IFIP Vol. 234, Springer, 45-58.
6. David P, Spence M, (2003).*Towards an Institutional Infrastructure for E-Science: The Scope and Challenge,* Oxford Internet Institute Report, September.

7. Delorey D, Knutson C, and Chun S, (2007). Do Programming Languages Affect Productivity? A Case Study using Data from Open Source Projects, *Proc. First International Workshop on Emerging Trends in FLOSS Research and Development* (*FLOSS'07*), ACM Press, Minneapolis, MN, May.
8. Deshpande A, Riehle D, (2008). The Total Growth of Open Source, *Proc. Fourth IFIP International Conference on Open Source Systems (OSS2008)*, Milan, IT (to appear, September 2008).
9. Dietz T, Ostrom E, and Stern PC, (2003). The Struggle to Govern the Commons, *Science*, 302, 1907-1912, 12 December.
10. Elliott M, Scacchi W, (2005). Free software development: Cooperation and conflict in a virtual organizational culture. In S Koch, (Ed.), *Free/Open Source Software Development*, Idea Group Publishing, Hershey, PA, 152-173.
11. English R, Schweik, C, (2007). Identifying Success and Tragedy of FLOSS Commons: A Preliminary Classification of SourceForge.net Projects, *Proc. First Intern. Workshop on Emerging Trends in FLOSS Research and Development*, Minneapolis, MN, May 2007.
12. Eugster PT, Felber PA, Guerraoui R, and Kermarrec A-M, (2003). The Many Faces of Publish/Subscribe, *ACM Computing Surveys*, 35(2), 114-131.
13. Evans, G.E, *Developing library and information center collections*. Libraries Unlimited, Englewood, CO, 4th Edition, 2000.
14. Gao Y, Madey G, (2007) Network Analysis of the SourceForge Community, in Feller, J, Fitzgerald, B, Scacchi, W, and Sillitti, A. (Eds.), *Open Source Development, Adoption, and Innovation,* IFIP Vol. 234, Springer, 187-200.
15. Garg PK, Gschwind T, and Inoue K, (2004). Multi-Project Software Engineering: An Example, *Proc. Intern Workshop on Mining Software Repositories*, Edinburgh, Scotland, May.
16. Gasser L, Ripoche G, and Sandusky R, (2004). Research Infrastructure for Empirical Science of F/OSS, Proc. Intern. Workshop on Mining Software Repositories, Edinburgh, Scotland, May.
17. Gasser L, Scacchi W, (2003). *Continuous design of free/open source software: Workshop report and research agenda*, October. http://www.isr.uci.edu/events/ContinuousDesign/Continuous-Design-OSS-report.pdf
18. German D, Mockus A, (2003). Automating the Measurement of Open Source Projects. In Proc. 3rd. Workshop Open Source Software Engineering, Portland, OR, 63-68, May.
19. GForge, (2008). Gforge Project: A Collaborative Software Development Environment, http://gforge.org. Accessed March 2008.
20. Ghosh RA, (2003). Clustering and Dependencies in Free/Open Source Software Development: Methodology and Tools, *First Monday*, 8(4), April.
21. Ghosh RA, and Prakash V, (2000). The Orbiten Free Software Survey, *First Monday,* 5(7).

22. Gil Y, Deelman E, Ellisman M, *et al*, (2007). Examining the Challenges of Scientific Workflows, *Computer*, 40(12), 24-32, December.
23. Gonzalez-Barahona JM, Lopez L, and Robles G, Community Structure of Modules in the Apache Project, Proc. 4th Intern. Workshop on Open Source Software Engineering, *44-48,* Edinburgh, Scotland, 2004.
24. Hahsler M. and Koch S, (2005). Discussion of a Large-Scale Open Source Data Collection Methodology, *Proc. 38th Hawaii Intern. Conf. Systems Sciences*, Kailua-Kona, HI, January.
25. Hertel G, Neidner S, and Hermann S, (2003). Motivation of software developers in Open Source projects: an Internet-based survey of contributors to the Linux kernel, *Research Policy*, 32(7), 1159-1177, July.
26. Hess C, Ostrom E, (2004). A Framework for Analyzing Scholarly Communication as a Commons, Presented at the *Workshop on Scholarly Communication as a Commons, Workshop in Political Theory and Policy Analysis*, Indiana University, Bloomington, IN, March 31-April 24.
27. Howison, J, Conklin M, and Crowston K, (2006). FLOSSmole: A collaborative repository for FLOSS research data and analysis. *Intern. J. Information Technology and Web Engineering*, 1(3), 17-26.
28. Huang Y, Xiang X, and Madey G, (2004). A Self Manageable Infrastructure for Supporting Web-based Simulations, *37th Annual Simulation Symposium at the Advanced Simulation Technologies Conference 2004 (ASTC'04)*, Arlington, VA, April.
29. Hunt F. and Johnson P, (2002). On the Pareto Distribution of SourceForge Projects, in C Gacekand B. Eds.), Proc. Open Source Software Development Workshop, 122-129, Newcastle, UK, February.
30. Jensen C, Scacchi W, (2006). Experiences in Discovering, Modeling, and Reenacting Open Source Software Development Processes, in M Li, BE Boehm, and LJ Osterweil (eds.), *Unifying the Software Process Spectrum: Proc. Software Process Workshop*, Beijing, China, May 2005, 442-469, Springer.
31. Jensen C, Scacchi, W, (2007). Role migration and advancement processes in OSSD projects: A comparative case study, in *Proc. 29th Intern. Conf. Soft. Eng,* ACM, Minneapolis, MN, 364-374.
32. Kawaguchi S, Garg PK. Inoue, K, (2003). On Automatic Categorization of Open Source Software, in Proc. 3rd Workshop OSS Engineering, Portland, OR, 63-68, May.
33. Kim S, Pan K, and Whitehead EJ, (2004). WebDAV: Open Source Collaborative Development Environment, Proc. 4th *Intern. Workshop on Open Source Software Engineering,* 44-48.
34. Koch S. (2005). Evolution of Open Source Software Systems—A Large-Scale Investigation, in *Proc. 1st Intern, Conf. Open Source Systems (OSS2005)*, Genoa, Italy.
35. Kranich N, (2004). The Role of Research Libraries in Conceptualizing and Fostering Scholarly Commons, Presented at the *Workshop on Scholarly*

Communication as a Commons, Workshop in Political Theory and Policy Analysis, Indiana University, Bloomington, IN, March 31-April 2.

36. Lopez-Fernandez L, Robles G, and Gonzalez-Barahona JM, (2004). Applying Social Network Analysis to the Information in CVS Repositories, Proc. Intern Workshop on Mining Software Repositories, Edinburgh, May..
37. Madey G, Freeh V, and Tynan R, (2005). Modeling the F/OSS Community: A Quantitative Investigation, in Koch, S. (ed.), *Free/Open Source Software Development*, 203-221, Idea Group Publishing, Hershey, PA.
38. Mi P, Scacchi W (1996). A Meta-Model for Formulating Knowledge-Based Models of Software Development, *Decision Support Systems*, 17(4), 313-330.
39. Mockus A, (2007). Large-Scale Code Reuse in Open Source Software, *Proc. First International Workshop on Emerging Trends in FLOSS Research and Development* (*FLOSS'07*), ACM Press, Minneapolis, MN, May.
40. Mockus A, Fielding RT, and Herbsleb J, (2002). Two case studies of open source software development: Apache and Mozilla. *ACM Transactions on Software Engineering and Methodology*, 11(3):1-38, July.
41. Noll J, Scacchi W, (1991). Integrating Diverse Information Repositories: A Distributed Hypertext Approach, *Computer*, 24(12), 38-45, December.
42. Noll J, Scacchi W, (1999). Supporting Software Development in Virtual Enterprises, Journal of Digital Information, 1(4), February.
43. Noy NF, Sintek M, Decker S, Crubezy M, Fergerson RW, and Musen MA, (2001). Creating Semantic Web Contents with Protégé-2000, *IEEE Intelligent Systems*, 16(2), 60-71, March/April.
44. O'Mahony S, (2003). Guarding the Commons: How community managed software projects protect their work, *Research Policy*, 32(7), 1179-1198, July.
45. Ripoche G, Gasser L, (2003). Scalable automatic extraction of process models for understanding F/OSS bug repair. In *Proc. Intern. Conf. Software & Systems Engineering and their Applications (CSSEA'03)*, December.
46. Robles G, Gonzalez-Barahona JM, Centeno-Gonzalez J, Matellan-Olivera V, and Rodero-Merino L, (2003). Studying the evolution of libre software projects using publicly available data, in Proc. 3rd Workshop on OSS Engineering, Portland, OR, 63-68, May.
47. Robles G, Gonzalez-Barahona JM, Ghosh R, (2004). GluTheos: Automating the Retrieval and Analysis of Data from Publicly Available Software Repositories, Proc. Intern Workshop on Mining Software Repositories, Edinburgh, Scotland, May.
48. Sandusky R, Gasser L, and Ripoche G, (2004). Bug report networks: Varieties, strategies, and impacts in an OSS development community. Proc. Intern Workshop on Mining Software Repositories, Edinburgh, Scotland, May.
49. Scacchi W, (2002). Understanding the Requirements for Developing Open Source Software Systems, *IEE Proceedings--Software*, 149(1), 24-39.

50. Scacchi W, (2006). Understanding Free/Open Source Software Evolution, in N.H. Madhavji, J.F. Ramil and D. Perry (Eds.), *Software Evolution and Feedback: Theory and Practice*, John Wiley and Sons Inc, New York, 181-206.
51. Scacchi W, (2007). Free/Open Source Software Development: Recent Research Results and Methods, in M. Zelkowitz (Ed.), *Advances in Computers*, 69, 243-295.
52. Scacchi W, Jensen C, Noll J, and Elliott M, (2006). Multi-Modal Modeling, Analysis and Validation of Open Source Software Development Processes, *Intern. J. Information Technology and Web Engineering*, 1(3), 49-63, 2006.
53. Smith N, Ramil JF, Capiluppi A, (2004). Qualitative Analysis and Simulation of Open Source Software Evolution, *Proc. 5th Intern. Workshop Software Process Simulation and Modeling*, Edinburgh, Scotland, UK, 25-26 May.
54. Smith TR, (1996). The Meta-Information Environment of Digital Libraries. *D-Lib Magazine*, July/August.
55. SourceForge, (2008). http://www.sourceforge.net Accessed March 2008.
56. Sowe SK, Angelis L, Stamelos I, and Manopoulos Y, (2007). Using Repository of Repositories (RoRs) to Study the Growth of F/OSS Projects: A Meta-Analysis Research Approach, in Feller, J, Fitzgerald, B, Scacchi, W, and Sillitti, A. (Eds.), *Open Source Development, Adoption, and Innovation,* IFIP Vol. 234, Springer, 147-160.
57. Staples T, Wayland R, and Payette S, (2003). The Fedora Project: An Open-source Digital Object Repository System, *D-Lib Magazine*, April. http://www.dlib.org/dlib/april03/staples/04staples.html
58. Star SL, Ruhleder K, (1996). Steps Toward an Ecology of Infrastructure: Design and access for large information spaces. *Information Systems Research*, 7(1):111-134.
59. von Krogh G, Spaeth S, and Lakhani K, (2003). Community, joining, and specialization in open source software innovation: a case study, *Research Policy*, 32(7), 1217-1241, July.
60. Wasserman A, Capra E, (2007). Evaluating Software Engineering Processes in Commercial and Community Open Source Projects, *Proc. First Intern. Workshop on Emerging Trends in FLOSS Research and Development*, Minneapolis, MN, May.
61. West J, Gallagher S, (2006). Patterns of Open Innovation in Open Source Software, Chapter 5 in H. Chesbrough, W. Vanhaverbeke and J. West, (Eds.), *Open Innovation: Researching a New Paradigm*, Oxford, UK, Oxford University Press.

Update Propagation Practices in Highly Reusable Open Source Components

Heikki Orsila[1], Jaco Geldenhuys[2], Anna Ruokonen[3], and Imed Hammouda[3]

[1] Department of Computer Systems, Tampere University of Technology, PO Box 553, FI-33101 Tampere, Finland, heikki.orsila@tut.fi
[2] Department of Computer Science, Stellenbosch University, Private Bag X1, 7602 Matieland, South Africa, jaco@cs.sun.ac.za
[3] Department of Software Systems, Tampere University of Technology, PO Box 553, FI-33101 Tampere, Finland, firstname.lastname@tut.fi

Abstract. In today's business and software arena, more and more companies are adopting open source software. An example of this rising phenomenon is to base software products on highly reusable open source components. In this scenario, the evolution of the software product is coupled with the evolution of the open source component. A common assumption is that component updates are immediately and regularly propagated to the project. This paper investigates this assumption empirically by studying update propagation practices in two popular open source libraries, `zlib` and `FFmpeg`. For each library, we analyze various repository sources with information such as bug reports, revision history, and source code. The results of the case studies suggest that update propagation is subject to several technical and non-technical factors including the way the open source library is used, the extent to which updates are documented, and the degree of community involvement. Based on these findings, we propose a set of recommendations that would allow better follow-up of updates and smoother update propagation.

1 Introduction

Driven by various business and technical motives such as shorter development cycles, lower development costs, improved product quality, and access to source code, more and more software developers and companies are basing their software products on open source components (i.e., libraries, platforms, etc.) [1, 2]. Adopting open source software is sometimes considered a risky business strategy, mainly because of a lack of trust in community-driven software. The main concerns are that many quality attributes such as reliability, security, and safety are hidden properties that have to be carefully checked, and that fixing software defects pertaining to such quality attributes can never be guaranteed. Furthermore, empirical research shows that many advocated hypotheses made about open source software are not always true [3].

Please use the following format when citing this chapter:

Orsila, H., Geldenhuys, J., Ruokonen, A. and Hammouda, I., 2008, in IFIP International Federation for Information Processing, Volume 275; *Open Source Development, Communities and Quality*; Barbara Russo, Ernesto Damiani, Scott Hissam, Björn Lundell, Giancarlo Succi; (Boston: Springer), pp. 159–170.

A basic practice to overcome part of the challenges sketched above is to regularly update to newer versions of the used open source components, which leads to faster incorporation of community contributions such as bug fixes and new component features. Thus, in the case of highly reusable components, one expects the following basic usage pattern: whenever a new version of a component is released, users of that component immediately switch to the new release. At the other end, one might hypothesize that most practices will eventually deviate from this basic principle due to various influential factors.

Based on the observations above, our research problem can be formulated as analyzing update propagation practices in the case of highly reusable open source components. In particular, we are interested in issues like the frequency of update propagations, the kind of interactions between the components and the projects using them, and the influential factors shaping these interactions. Our goal is ultimately to identify a set of guidelines that would promote better follow-up of updates and smoother update propagation. The good news is that open source projects come with a rich repository of models, source code, resource files, defect reports, change logs, etc., which makes it possible to mine such information.

To investigate our research problem, we focused on two popular software libraries: `FFmpeg` [5] and `zlib` [4]. We carried out our study empirically by analyzing the software repositories of these two libraries for update propagation. The updates concern bug fixes or new features contributed by the community. As expected, mining the information needed was not an easy task as we had to consider various repository sources such as bug reports, revision history and the source code itself. The results of the study show that practices vary from one case to another. In most of the cases, however, we were able to find answers to our research questions and make "educated guesses" for the reasons of the results. Our findings suggest that there are several technical and non-technical factors that have a direct effect on update propagation. These include the way the open source library is being used, the extent of documenting updates, and the degree of involvement in the community.

The rest of the paper is organized as follows. Section 2 presents the background of this work and discusses related studies. Sections 3 and 4 introduce the case studies and empirically explore our research questions. In Section 5 we present a set of recommendations supporting update propagation, and in Section 6 we conclude the paper.

2 Background

The repository sources most relevant to our empirical study are bug reports and revision logs. Most open source projects include an open bug repository, to which users of the software have full access. It is used to report and track bugs and potential enhancements. An open bug repository might potentially increase the number of problems identified in the system and enable more efficient fixing of problems. Bug reporting, resolving bug reports, and improving bug management have been discussed before [6, 7]. Although many open source software developers interact with the bug repository on a regular basis, there is little data available to characterize their interactions. Similarly, revision logs are useful sources in the sense that they record the evolution of an open source project, but they often come with challenges such as insufficient and unreliable data.

In open source projects, code contribution and bug fixing can be regarded as alternating phases in a continuous, cyclical process. Maintainability has been identified as the core quality issue in open source development [7]: developing an OSS system implies a series of frequent maintenance efforts mainly for debugging existing functionality and adding new features to the system. Maintenance activities can be categorized into four classes: adaptive (e.g., supporting new platforms), corrective (e.g., fixing bugs), perfective (e.g., improving quality attributes), and preventive (e.g., code cleanup and refactoring) [8]. According to this view, open source maintenance is mainly adaptive and corrective. However, in this paper we are more interested in how rapidly the user community reacts to maintenance updates, and in what motivates their reactions.

Reuse of open source software has been the subject of many studies. For example, Capiluppi et al. propose guidelines to identify highly reusable components and to improve the reusability of open source components [9]. Large-scale reuse involving open source repositories has also been studied by Mockus [10]. He identifies widely reused code blocks, typically a component, and common patterns of reuse. In this empircal study the focus is mainly on the immediacy, frequency, usage patterns, and underlying motivation of updates.

In the case of open source components, reuse can be divided (roughly) into the following practices:

A. Always part of source: the component is incorporated during development time (e.g., the Linux kernel)
B. Added when released: the component is incorporated during release time (e.g., `xvidcap` project)
C. User must provide source: the component source code is incorporated by the user when the project is recompiled (e.g., eCos tool chain [11])
D. User must provide binary: the component binary is provided by the user when the project is linked (e.g., OpenSSH [12])

In special cases, the reuse may even be a combination of two or more of the above (e.g., AbiWord [13]). Reuse of binary distribution makes use of either static or dynamic linking. In static linking the component binary is included in a local, stand-alone copy of the project at compile-time. Dynamic linking means that the component binary is loaded at runtime, and can therefore be updated independently of the project that is using it. In this respect dynamic linking is not relevant to the questions addressed in this paper.

Our research methodology can be summarized in five main steps: we 1) formulate the research questions, 2) select suitable component candidates 3) extract the relevant data by exploring the component repositories, 4) analyze the data with respect to the questions raised, and 5) make recommendations. The research questions we explore include the following:

- What reuse mechanisms are adopted most often when reusing open source components?
- What kind of update propagation patterns are practiced?
- How fast/often does the user community react to new releases of highly reusable open source components?
- What technical and non-technical criteria influence the community response (e.g., reuse mechanism, product domain, product development phase, etc.)?
- What best practices can be identified to promote better follow-up of updates and smoother update propagation?

As candidate components, we have selected two highly reusable libraries, `zlib` and `FFmpeg`. The former is a lossless compression library which implements a standard coding system [14, 15, 16]; it is used in many file formats and protocols, and in many popular systems such as Linux and Python. The latter is a collection of utilities for processing audio and video files and streams. It includes tools to play and record different media, and a server for distributing media over the internet, for example, for live broadcasts. The library has been incorporated in more than 90 projects.

3 Case Study: `zlib`

3.1 Analysis

The `zlib` source code is included in numerous projects. We looked at three security-related bugs that were found in the `zlib` source code, and analyzed the time it took the bug fix to propagate into 8 projects: `AbiWord`, `BZFlag`, `CVS`, `Linux`, `ppp`, `Python`, `RPM`, and `zlib`.

There are only two core authors for the `zlib` project, but 42 authors have contributed code to the library. Of the 628 documented changes, 89% come from the top 5 out of 42 contributors. This information comes from the credits in the library's `ChangeLog` file. We studied the latest `zlib`, version 1.2.3 released on 2005-07-18. The `Changelog` entries are dated 1995-04-11 to 2005-07-18, a period of approximately 10 years.

We investigated fixes for the following bugs:

1. *A double free bug* reported on 2002-03-11
2. *A DoS/crash bug* reported on 2004-08-25
3. *A buffer overrun/DoS/crash bug* reported on 2005-06-30

For each of the projects that use `zlib`, the bug status was classified as follows:

- **Does not apply**: The bug doesn't have an effect on the project, because the vulnerable code never existed inside the project (e.g., Linux kernel)
- **Known**: The time (in days) to fix a bug is known from version history (e.g., CVS)
- **Not fixed**: The bug is still not fixed (e.g., AbiWord for Windows)
- **Unknown**: Status of the fix is unknown due to unavailability of version history (e.g., Python)

The results are shown in Table 1. The mean and median times for fixing a bug, computed over all the projects in the table, are 97 and 19 days, respectively.

Table 1. Number of days to fix 3 different `zlib` bugs

Project	Bug 1	Bug 2	Bug 3
`AbiWord`	1	Not fixed	Not fixed
`BZFlag`	Does not apply	Does not apply	583
`CVS`	1	63	87
`Linux`	8	Does not apply	Does not apply
`ppp`	21	Does not apply	Does not apply
`Python`	Unknown	Unknown	90
`RPM`	432	25	16
`zlib`	0	15	11
Min	0	15	11
Mean	77	34	157
Median	5	25	87
Max	432	63	583

3.2 Discussion

We noticed two issues from the `zlib` results:

Bug Fix Delay Varies Significantly The time to fix bugs varies a lot from project to project, which means that the median and mean times to fix bugs are far apart. In one case (`AbiWord`) the project is still vulnerable for bugs that were discovered years ago.

We did not find any project, apart from one operating system distributor, with an explicit system for checking for updates in other projects. Such an automatic mechanism is a necessity for scalable code reuse. Possible reasons for this lapse may be weak virtual organization, lack of explicit task lists, and lack of command hierarchy. Another possible reason that stabilized products fail to incorporate `zlib` updates is that their maintainers do not have the resources for testing a new `zlib` version and/or backporting necessary fixes.

Investigated projects seem to fall into three update propagation patterns: random updates, negligence, and systematic. We address these issues further in the guidelines in Section 5.

Microsoft Windows Programs Are Biased Towards Binary And Source Duplication Table 2 shows each project and its reuse category. Almost all GNU/Linux projects use `zlib` as a dynamic library, which can be updated through a common packet manager for all applications. Unfortunately the Microsoft Windows operating system lacks a common packet manager for non-Microsoft products. This suggests that there could be a general bias in Microsoft Windows to use source duplication (category A and B) instead of dynamic libraries (category D), because it is so much harder to update those systems.

Table 2. Projects and their reuse categories

Project	Reuse categories
`AbiWord`	A, D
`BZFlag`	A, D
`CVS`	A, D
`Linux`	A
`ppp`	A
`Python`	A
`RPM`	A, D
`zlib`	A

For example, `AbiWord` and `Python` 1.6-2.4 can be run on both GNU/Linux and Microsoft Windows, but the Windows versions are more vulnerable to bugs because the GNU/Linux versions use a dynamic library. `Python` 2.5 and later are in category A, and therefore they are vulnerable on both GNU/Linux and Microsoft Windows. Bug 3 is one manifestation of this problem.

4 Case Study: `FFmpeg`

4.1 Analysis

`FFmpeg` has a core library called `libavcodec` that contains encoders and decoders for a wide range of multimedia formats. The `FFmpeg` project web page lists some 90 other projects that incorporate parts or all of `FFmpeg`. We focused our attention on `libavcodec` and, in particular, the libary interface specification in the header file `avcodec.h`.

Material related to this case study is available at [17].

Figure 1 shows the development of `avcodec.h`. Each dot represents one change, and its color identifies the responsible user. During the period 2001-07 to 2007-06, 38 different users made a total of 617 changes and the file grew from 177 (5.1 kbytes) to 2940 (90 kbytes) lines of code. Only the most active users are listed in the figure.

As a first approximation we studied the revision history of `avcodec.h` in the following projects:

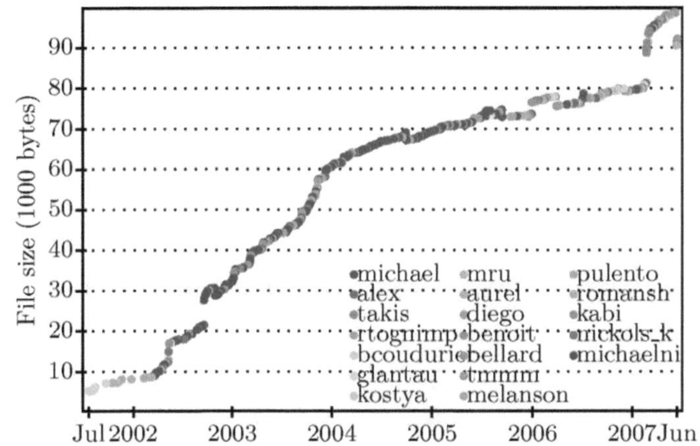

Fig. 1. The evolution of `avcodec.h`

- `avidemux` is a video editing suite
- `avifile` is a multimedia player for Linux systems
- `ffdshow` is a media decoder and encoder for Microsoft Windows systems
- `gstreamer` is a server for streaming audio/video over the internet
- `mythtv` is a software-based personal video recorder for Linux and Mac OS X
- `xbmc` is a multimedia player for Microsoft's Xbox

Unfortunately, it soon became clear that the revision history by itself is not sufficient. Log entries such as "`libavcodec resync`" do not identify the exact revision of `libavcodec` that was used for the update. Even when such information is given, there is no guarantee that the comment is accurate, and in several cases it proved not to be. To overcome this problem, different revisions of `avcodec.h` were downloaded and compared one by one to find matching versions. Together with the information in the revision logs, this produced the kind of information shown in Figure 2. The upper and lower horizontal lines represent the `avifile` and `FFmpeg` projects, respectively. Arrows indicate updates from the latter to the former on the dates shown above and below the project lines, and the small vertical lines on the `FFmpeg` line indicate different revisions of `avcodec.h`.

Table 3. Summary of update data

Project	Period	Nr. of updates	Delay (days) Min	Max	Ave
`avidemux`	2004-01–2007-01	10	1.8	26.8	5.7
`avifile`	2002-05–2007-05	163	<hour	14.6	2.1
`gstreamer`	2004-03–2006-09	9	1.1	18.0	5.2
`mythtv`	2002-08–2007-06	82	<hour	60.6	3.7
`xbmc`	2004-04–2007-04	7	2.9	118.7	29.8

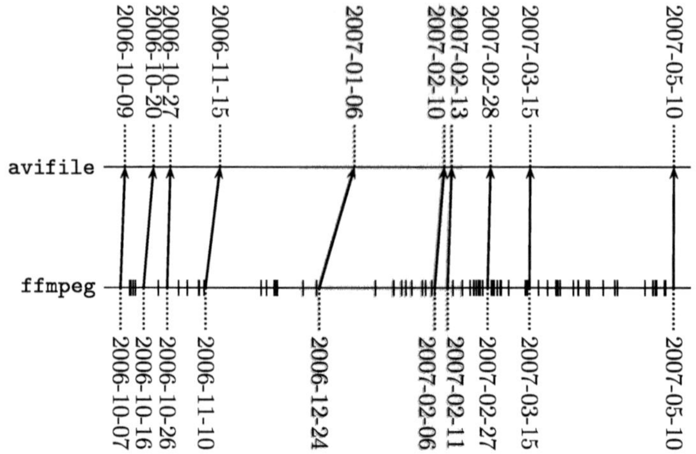

Fig. 2. The 10 most recent updates (from 2006-10-09 to 2007-05-10) of `avcodec.h` in `avifile`

The results are summarized in Table 3. In the three rightmost columns, *Delay* refers to the number of elapsed days between the production of a revision and its use in an update, in other words, how "fresh" it is. In many cases, the update delay is less than a week. `avifile` and `mythtv` were clearly updated much more frequently than the others, even when the longer time frames are taken into account. Still, on at least one occasion the `mythtv` project was not updated for about two months. One fact not shown in this table is that these two projects are updated less and less frequently over time, possibly because `libavcodec` has reached a level of stability where fewer bugs are reported.

4.2 Discussion

We noticed some issues from the `FFmpeg` results:

Shared Interests, Features and Developers New features in the `avifile` project were introduced first in child projects and later introduced into the parent project. This is the result of common developers and interests between the projects. For example, one active developer is a member of both the `FFmpeg` and `avifile` projects.

Feature propagation to and from the parent project supports the theory of OSS development model. If new features are only added in the central project, it would cast serious doubt on the OSS model, and distributed models in general. Bugs are often fixed through inter-project co-operation by users and developers directly communicating with each other. We argue that code reuse in some OSS projects comes close to sharing developers, not just sharing features (code).

Update Propagation Entails Significant Effort In the case of `mythtv` the mismatches were more numerous and more substantial. The requirements of this software include specialized features such as closed captioning and support for multilingual soundtracks, which are not provided by the `libavcodec` library. In at least one case, a feature was first introduced in the `mythtv` project and only later in `FFmpeg`, but, as far as we can tell, the later implementation was not derived from the earlier one. In all events, `mythtv` is one example of an unforeseen pattern: code reuse takes place, but the code undergoes non-trivial modifications within the new setting, requiring significant effort in update propagation. This happens either because the new setting is significantly different from the original, or because there are new feature requirements.

On Update Propagation Patterns All the projects mentioned above include a complete copy of the `libavcodec` code and fall into category A. Sometimes, as in the case of `mythtv`, this is unavoidable if the code needs modification before use.

One example of a project that belongs to category B is `xvidcap`, a screen capture program for recording user activity, to create video tutorials and other material. Whenever this project is released, the developers include the latest version of `libavcodec`. This may appear safer, since the library is not as tightly integrated in the source code. However, category A reuse allows users to download a more recent, albeit less stable, development version of the software. In theory, users could themselves replace the copy of `libavcodec` in `xvidcap` with the latest release in order incorporate the latest bug fixes, but it is not realistic that this would occur widely in practice.

In the case of `ffdshow`, we failed to trace updates accurately, because the project modifies `avcodec.h` too dramatically, but we observed that at least some bugs were reported back to the `FFmpeg` project.

Comparison of `zlib` and FFmpeg Bug fix delays in the `zlib` project were relatively long compared to those in `FFmpeg`. The main difference in these projects is that functionality of `zlib` is fixed; it just implements a specific functionality. In constrast, new features are continuously added to `FFmpeg`. This suggests that that shared interests in developing the same features, as well as shared developers, can decrease the update propagation delay.

5 Guidelines for Managing Bug Fixes

Based on our experience of tracking bug fixes we argue for some guidelines for managing bug fixing inside and between open source projects.

5.1 Avoid Source and Binary Code Duplication

Use dynamic libraries instead of static libraries or source code inclusion. Source code inclusion means that reused code has to be constantly maintained and monitored. In general, dynamic libraries avoid redundant information in the system. This is by far the best practice for code reuse, because it also allows other parties, mostly operating system distributors, to help you.

5.2 Document Important Changes in Version Control History

Maintain a special `SECURITY` file that lists the specific corrective maintenance operations in version control history that fix a security issue. This helps operating system maintainers and other interested parties to track important updates. Also, backporting the security fixes to older and stable versions is easier when the specific commit is known. This is important for production systems that operate for several years. This approach is not limited to security fixes. It can also be used to document other bugs, properties, or interesting factors.

5.3 Tag Important Changes in Version Control History

A special tag (e.g., "`[SECURITY]`") should be added to each commit message that fixes a security issue in the version control system. This makes searching for security fixes easier.

5.4 Maintain a Global Notification System for Changes

Fast updates between projects is important if new features are needed or security matters. Achieving this demands easy updates. We propose that each project create a global notification system for important changes (e.g., a mailing list), that alerts interested parties of specific fixes and features. The system should not flood interested parties about small changes, only the important ones. Also, notifications should be archived so that users can access older changes.

5.5 Facilitate Follow-up of Component Updates

To address the issue of weak command hierarchy, we propose that each project creates a list of reused software components, annotated with a timestamp and an unique identifier (such as the version number or a commit identifier) about the last update.

Also, if possible, a responsible person should be assigned to particpate actively in the project community of the reused component. This will decrease update propagation time and may help to promote a project's interests. This happens when companies contribute to projects like Linux, `gcc` and Samba.

5.6 Write a Procedure for the Update Process

Virtual organization and distributed development means that any developer should be able to replace another developer — at least in theory — but unfortunately experience and knowledge is not easily transfered. A detailed set of guidelines to raise awareness about maintenance operations should help new developers to be more productive. Such guidelines could, for example, spell out how to cross-check for important updates, such as security fixes.

Guidelines should cover issues relating to project maintenance and releases, including managing updates (notification of changes to and from other projects), managing new releases, and the preferred communication style between developers (IRC channels, mailing lists, etc.).

6 Conclusions

Many software companies and software developers are adopting open source components. These components often undergo constant maintenance actions. This paper studied the causes of maintenance in open source components and what controls the user community reaction to maintenance updates. We studied update propagation delay. In particular, we analyzed the effect of the following factors on update propagation delay: reuse category, documentation of changes, and the update process itself.

To find answers we explored updates and bug fix delays in the `zlib` and `FFmpeg` software repositories. We found that update propagation delay varies significantly among projects. Based on this information, we formulated the following guidelines for reusing open source components:

1. Avoid source and binary code duplication.
2. Document important changes in version control history.
3. Tag important changes in version control history.
4. Maintain a global notification system for changes.
5. Facilitate follow-up of component updates.
6. Write a procedure for update process.

Since we have only studied update propagation in the context of two libraries, we cannot claim that the results are generalizable. For further investigation, more case studies should be considered. In our case studies we used custom-built scripts and analysis by hand; a full record of our experiments is available at the website [17]. Although the details are specific to the libraries we looked at, the approach is applicable to other cases, and scalable to larger projects. If the guidelines we have suggested are followed, our approach would be even easier and faster. In order to validate the relevance of the proposed guidelines, a questionnaire to the open source community could be planned and carried out.

References

1. Bolado, M., Castillo, J., Posadas, H., Sanchez, P., Villar, E., Sanchez, C., Blasco, P., Fouren, H.: Using open source cores in real applications. In: DCIS 2003. (2003), 683–688
2. Madanmoha, T., Deapos, R.: Open source reuse in commercial firms. Comm. ACM (2004), 62–69

3. Paulson, J.W., Succi, G., Eberlein, A.: An empirical study of open-source and closed-source software products. IEEE Trans. on Softw. Eng. (2004), 246–256
4. zlib web site: `http://zlib.net`
5. FFmpeg web site: `http://ffmpeg.mplayerhq.hu`
6. Anvik, J., Hiew, L., Murphy, G.C.: Coping with an open bug repository. In: eclipse '05: Proceedings of the 2005 OOPSLA workshop on Eclipse technology eXchange, ACM Press (2005), 35–39
7. Samoladas, I., Stamelos, I., Angelis, L., Oikonomou, A.: Open source software development should strive for even greater code maintainability. Comm. ACM (2004), 83–87
8. Lientz, B.P., Swanson, E.B.: Software Maintenance Management. Addison-Wesley (1980)
9. Capiluppi, A., Boldyreff, C.: Coupling patterns in the effective reuse of open source software. In Proceedings of the 1st International Workshop on Emerging Trends in FLOSS Research and Development (FLOSS'07), IEEE Computer Society (2007)
10. Mockus, A.: Large-scale code reuse in open source software. In Proceedings of the 1st International Workshop on Emerging Trends in FLOSS Research and Development (FLOSS'07), IEEE Computer Society (2007)
11. eCos tool chain: `http://ecos.sourceware.org/build-toolchain.html`
12. OpenSSH web site: `http://www.openssh.com`
13. AbiWord web site: `http://www.abisource.com`
14. Internet Society RFC 1950: ZLIB Compressed Data Format Specification version 3.3, `http://tools.ietf.org/html/rfc1950`
15. Internet Society RFC 1951: DEFLATE Compressed Data Format Specification version 1.3 `http://tools.ietf.org/html/rfc1951`
16. Internet Society RFC 1952: GZIP File Format Specification version 4.3 `http://tools.ietf.org/html/rfc1952`
17. `http://www.iki.fi/shd/publications/oss2008/`, and a full dump of the web site: `http://www.iki.fi/shd/publications/oss2008.tar.gz`

Using Social Network Analysis Techniques to Study Collaboration between a FLOSS Community and a Company

Juan Martinez-Romo[1], Gregorio Robles[2], Jesus M. Gonzalez-Barahona[2], and Miguel Ortuño-Perez[2]

[1] Dpto. Lenguajes y Sistemas Informaticos, E.T.S.I. Informatica (UNED)
juaner@lsi.uned.es
[2] Grupo de Sistemas y Comunicaciones, Universidad Rey Juan Carlos
{grex,jgb,mortuno}@gsyc.escet.urjc.es

Abstract. Because of the sheer volume of information available in FLOSS repositories, simple analysis have to face the problems of filtering the relevant information. Hence, it is essential to apply methodologies that highlight that information for a given aspect of the project. In this paper, some techniques from the social sciences have been used on data from version control systems to extract information about the development process of FLOSS projects with the aim of highlighting several processes that occur in FLOSS projects and that are difficult to obtain by other means. In particular, the collaboration between the FLOSS community and a company has been studied by selecting two projects as case studies. The results highlight aspects such as efficiency in the development process, release management and leadership turnover.

1 Introduction

Software projects are usually the collective work of many developers. In most cases, and especially in the case of large projects, those developers are formally organised in a well defined (usually hierarchical) structure, with clear guidelines about how to interact with each other, and the procedures and channels to use. Each team of developers is assigned to certain modules of the system, and only in rare cases they work outside their *territory*. However, this is usually not the case in FLOSS projects, where only loose (if any) formal structures can be recognised. On the contrary, FLOSS developers usually have access to any part of the software, and even in the case of large projects they can *move* more or less freely from one module to another with only some restrictions imposed by the common uses in the project, and the rules on which developers themselves have agreed. A large mount of spontaneous interaction structures arise, evolve and disappear without the intervention of a central control, yielding complex networks.

Among complex networks, social network analysis (SNA) appear as a method for analysing the structure and interactions of people and groups of

Please use the following format when citing this chapter:

Martinez-Romo, J., Robles, G., Gonzalez-Barahona, M. and Ortuño-Perez, M., 2008, in IFIP International Federation for Information Processing, Volume 275; *Open Source Development, Communities and Quality*; Barbara Russo, Ernesto Damiani, Scott Hissam, Björn Lundell, Giancarlo Succi; (Boston: Springer), pp. 171–186.

people within extensive organisations. A vast amount of scientific works show applications of these techniques in fields that go from the social sciences to physics and computer networks [20, 10].

The goal of this paper is to apply classical social network concepts to data extracted from FLOSS projects, in particular to FLOSS projects that show a tight collaboration between a company and the FLOSS community. As, even in the presence of a company, FLOSS projects have a loose management style and are based heavily on third-party contributions, social network analyses may provide with some insight into the underlying processes that are responsible for the development. In this way, we have an ad-hoc network of interpersonal dependencies that come from the interactions between the nodes that integrate it. Therefore, this work is mainly descriptive and has the purpose of showing how the application of techniques of social networks can be useful in scopes beyond the original ones.

The rest of this paper is organised as follows. The next section describes related research on this topic. Next, the methodology designed to extract data from source code management systems and a series of technical aspects on which we have based our study is presented. Afterwards, a brief historical review of the main events within the projects will be given and then the results are shown and discussed. A final section with some conclusions and hints about further research closes the paper.

2 Related Research

Much attention in the area of research on FLOSS projects has been focused on the organisational structure of the projects [9, 17, 15], but little attention to the dynamics of the group of developers. A noteworthy contribution in this sense, although not directly addressing the evolution of developer communities, is the *onion model* [5], which shows how developers and users are positioned in communities. This model differentiates among core developers (those who have a high involvement in the project), codevelopers (with specific but frequent contributions), active users (contributing only occasionally) and passive users [18, 7, 13].

The onion model provides only a static picture of a project, lacking the time dimension that is required for studying processes, among these the ones of joining and leaving a project. A more theoretical identification and description of the roles, including also some dynamics [26], has helped to fill the gap. According to this refinement, a core developer is supposed to go through all the outlying roles, starting as a user, until she eventually reaches the core team. Some research has tried to measure how long this process takes for a volunteer participant (i.e. somebody who is not hired by a company to work on the project), obtaining that the time that passes from the first e-mails to the mailing lists (considered as the first participation) to the first commit (considered as the developer becoming part of the core group) is in the mean of around 30 months [11]. An alternative approach has been proposed [12] after studying and modelling the processes of role migration for some FLOSS communities, focusing on end-users who become developers. This has lead to the identification of various paths for the joining process, concluding that the organisational structure of the studied projects is highly dynamic in comparison to traditional software development organisations. The attraction of human resources to FLOSS projects has also been analysed [6, 24], with different models proposed about how developers enter new projects.

With respect to abandonment, the number of Debian developers leaving the project has been studied [22], and how this affects its evolution (i.e. what happens to software packages that become unmaintained because of the abandonment). The authors propose a half-life parameter, defined as the time required for a certain group of contributors to fall to half of its initial population, which is of 7.5 years for the Debian project.

3 Methodology

3.1 Construction of the Developers Network

The methodology used in this study is based on retrieving data about the activity of developers from the source code management repository of the project [19, 27]. In the case of FLOSS projects, this usually means either a CVS or a Subversion repository, which is mined using CVSAnalY [23]. This tool retrieves the information about every commit to the repository, and inserts it into a database where it can be conveniently analysed. This information includes, for each commit (modification in a file in the repository): the date, the username of the developer (commiter), and the number of lines involved.

Once the information has been stored in the database, we proceed to construct the developer network. Each vertex represents a particular developer and two vertices will be linked by an edge when both they have contributed, at least, one common software artifact[1]. Edges may be weighted by means of a *weight of the relationship*, defined for instance, as the total number of commits performed by both developers on artifacts to which both have contributed. Therefore, a relation between two developers (vertices) exist when both have worked in the same artifact, and a link will exist between them (edge) whether both have made, at least, a *commit* in the same artifact.

3.2 Indexes

When the networks are constructed based on the previous definitions, and the degrees and costs of relationship have been calculated for linked nodes, we

[1] We will consider in this paper software artifacts at the file level, although others could be chosen, such as directories.

can apply standard SNA concepts to define a wide range of parameters of the network that can help characterising the network and its nodes [21]. Beyond classical parameters, others more sophisticated can be used to extract more specific information. This paper makes use of these parameters, calculated by means of Conan [14], which are introduced next:

- **Distance centrality** [25]: The distance centrality of a vertex, D_c, is a measurement of its proximity to the rest. It is sometimes called *closeness centrality* as the higher its value the closer that vertex is (on average) to the others. The distance centrality can be interpreted as a measurement of the influence of a vertex in a graph because the higher its value, the easier for that vertex to spread information through that network. Observe that when a given vertex is *far* from the others, it has a low degree of relationship (i.e. a high cost of relationship) with the rest.
  Research has shown that employees who are central in networks learn faster, perform better and are more committed to the organisation. These employees are also less likely to turn over. Besides, from the point of view of information propagation, vertices with high centrality are like *hills* on the plain, in the sense that any knowledge is put on them is rapidly seen by the rest and spreads easily to the rest of the organisation.
- **Betweenness centrality** [8, 2]: The betweenness centrality of a vertex, B_c, is a measurement of the number of shortest paths traversing that particular vertex.
  The betweenness centrality of a vertex can be interpreted as a measurement of the information control that it can perform on a graph, in the sense that vertices with a high value are intermediate nodes for the communication of the rest. In our context, given that we have weighted networks, multiple shortest paths between any pair of vertices are highly improbable. The betweenness centrality is just a measurement of the number of shortest paths traversing a given vertex.
  In the SNA literature vertices with high betweenness centrality are known to cover *structural holes*. That is, those vertices glue together parts of the organisation that would be otherwise far away from each other. They receive a diverse combination of information available to no one else in the network and have therefore a higher probability of being involved in the knowledge generation processes.
- **Coordination degree** [1, 16]: The coordination degree of a vertex, measures the ability of this vertex in a graph to interchange information. The coordination degree of a vertex, has a great importance inside our study, since it shows the ability of a certain node to receive information of the network and capture the activity in a project precisely.
  There are several manners to model this magnitude, but one of the easiest ways is to consider the coordination degree to be exponentially related to the distance between the vertices [16]. In this way, we define the coordination degree γ_{ij} between two vertices i and j as $\gamma_{ij} = e^{-\xi d_{ij}}$, where d_{ij} is the

distance between the two vertices and ξ is a real positive constant, measuring the strength of the relationship which we call the coordination strength.
Thus, we can define the total coordination degree of a vertex i in a graph as the sum of all the coordination degrees between that particular vertex and the rest. Namely, $\Gamma_i = \sum_{j=1}^{N} \gamma_{ij}$, where N is the order of the graph (the total number of vertices in that particular graph). The total coordination degree of a vertex is a measure of the amount of information that the vertex is able to receive belonging to that particular network.

- **Centrality Eigenvector** [4, 3]: Eigenvector centrality is a measure of the importance of a node in a network. It assigns relative scores to all nodes in the network based on the principle that connections to high-scoring nodes contribute more to the score of the node in question than equal connections to low-scoring nodes.
  Eigenvector centrality is defined as the principal eigenvector of the adjacency matrix defining the network. The defining equation of an eigenvector is $\lambda v = Av$ where A is the adjacency matrix of the graph, *lambda* is a constant (the eigenvalue) and V is the eigenvector. The equation lends itself to the interpretation that a node that has a high eigenvector score is one that is adjacent to nodes that are themselves high scorers.
  The idea is that even if a node influences just one other node, who subsequently influences many other nodes, then the first node in that chain is highly influential. Hence, the eigenvector centrality may give good advice about leadership in the project under study.

4 Case studies: Evolution and Mono

We have selected two FLOSS projects in order to apply the social network analysis techniques on them and to show what kind of information we can extract with such a type of analysis. In both projects, there is a high involvement of a company (Ximian) that has assigned several employees to the development of the project and there is a surrounding FLOSS community whose contributions are always welcome.

4.1 Evolution

Evolution is the official personal information manager and work group information management tool for GNOME. It combines e-mail, calendar, address book, and task list management functions.

The origin of the project goes back to 1998, when it was started by some GNOME volunteers. But it is not until a company called Helix Code identified it as a strategic project that it did not win in importance. In October 1999, Helix Code became Ximian Inc. due to trademark problems. Evolution, then, was mainly developed by Ximian employees although in strong collaboration with the GNOME community for several years. Finally, Ximian was acquired by Novell in September 2004 and the maintenance of the then-mature Evolution tool was "outsourced" to Novell employees in India. Since then, contributions by the GNOME community are much lower, also in part because of the mature state of the tool.

There are other noteworthy events in the history of Evolution summarised in table 1.

Table 1. Most important events in the history of Evolution.

Event	Date
First commits	early 1998
Ximian takeover	October 1999
Version 0.0	July 2000
Version 1.0	February 2001
Takeover by Novell	October 2003
Death of main developer	January 2004
Version 2.0	October 2004
Version 2.2	April 2005
Version 2.4	October 2005
Version 2.6	April 2006
Version 2.8	October 2006

4.2 Mono

Mono is a project led by Novell (formerly by Ximian) to create an ECMA standard compliant .NET compatible set of tools, including among others a C# compiler and a Common Language Runtime. Mono can be run on Linux, FreeBSD, UNIX, Mac OS X, Solaris and Windows operating systems.

The dates of some of the most important events for Mono appear summarised in table 2.

5 Results

We have applied the SNA indexes to the two projects; results will be shown in this section. The samples have been taken from the first activity in each versioning system of the projects up to January 2007. Time slots of three months have been taken and two developers who have made at least one *commit* to any file within the same directory will be linked. This link will be weighted by the number of *commits* that both have in that time slot in the given directory. The interpretation of the following figures (each figure corresponds to a different measurement) is the following one: the horizontal axis is time, whereas the vertical z axis represents the result for a given measure. Therefore, each line in

Table 2. Most important events in the history of Mono.

Event	**Date**
First commits	mid-2001
First version of Gtk# checked into CVS	September 2001
Version 0.7	September 2001
Version 0.9	February 2002
GTK+ 2.2	December 2002
.NET Framework 1.1	April 2003
Version 1.0	June 2004
GNOME 2.10	March 2005
GTK+ 2.8	August 2005
.NET Framework 2.0	November 2005
Version 1.2	November 2006

the figure corresponds to the evolution over time of the values of a developer. We had to filter out less active developers as graphs that include all of them are hard to read. Hence, only the top 40 developers will be displayed.

5.1 Analysis of Evolution

If we analyse figure 1(a) representing the *coordination degree*, four phases can be clearly identified. An initial stage, until the takeover by *Ximian*, with a weak activity typical of a project in its early days. A second stage, until the *1.0 release*, where the work shows the highest gain in the history of the project, typical of the effort for developing a first stable version. Since then and until the takeover by *Novell*, a significant stagnation is originated due to a maintenance and debugging period. Finally, and because of the fact that a periodic release policy is introduced, peaks of work of two different dimensions can be observed alternating in time. The highest peaks correspond to new releases, with a high number of commits corresponding to new developments, translations and documentation. Meanwhile, the lows are due to stages of development and maintenance in which the kind of activity is different, being reflected in a smaller number of commits. It is therefore significant that time-based release management (i.e. a new version will be released every 6 months) seems to boost the development in general terms in comparison to feature-based release management (a new version will be made public when all features to be included are finished).

In addition to the own activity of a project, the *average coordination degree* of a network provides a measurement of the efficiency if we compare it with other values, such as the number of commits or the number of active developers. Figure 1(b) provides this comparison.

If we pay attention to the curves of the *average coordination degree* (cd mean) and the number of active developers (nodes), we can notice different moments at which one is over the other. The interpretation of these relative positions is the following: when the average coordination degree of the network is over the number of developers, the network structure is efficient. However, when the curve of the number of developers is over the average coordination degree, the social structure of the network is not efficient. In this way we can observe two stages with low efficiency in the network, one of them from the beginning of the project until the takeover by *Ximian*, the other one from the time when periodic releases where introduced (2004) until today. In between, since the takeover by *Ximian* in 1999 and up to the release of version *2.0* (in 2004), the network has an efficient structure. This evidences that a corporate involvement in the development of a FLOSS project may result in a more efficient development, but that both the involved company and the community have to find ways to allow the other party to participate properly. The first phase, where there was no involvement of the company, or the last one, where it seems that the company has chosen to move away from community have lead to an inefficient structure.

Figure 2(a) gives the evolution over time of the *betweenness centrality* for each developer. This figure is useful to identify who is the leader of the project at any given time, but also allows to predict who could be the following leader. If we attend the leadership curve in a particular moment, we can look for the curve just underneath. Usually, as the leader succession takes place gradually, we could figure out who is going to be the next leader of the project if the current one reduces his activity substantially.

Figure 2(b) is a bar chart with the main leaders of the project for every time period. The measure that has been used is the *weighted betweenness* (the same as in Figure 2(a)). For the computation of this measure, we have to count the shortest paths that cross a vertex, so this measure is dependant on the number of developers in the network. For this reason, although the maximum values evolve at the same pace as the number of developers grows, it is an efficient measurement. From these results, three different stages can be observed. The two first stages in which "unammx" and "ettore" lead the project during several years, and one third stage since mid-2003 in which different leaders succeed themselves in short periods of time (all of them less than one year).

As noted before, the *eigenvalue* can be interpreted like a numerical assignment of the relevance of a node in the network. According to this interpretation, the higher the value of a given node, the higher its relevance. In figure 3(a) we can observe the evolution over time of this measure for each developer. At every moment, we can identify the main leader(s) of the project. If we compare the outline of the curve with the *coordination degree* or with the values of *betweenness*, it is possible to notice that the values of this measure do not depend on the number of developers, and therefore, the activity of the project is not reflected in the outline of the curves.

If we attend to the figure 3(b), we can find again the main leaders in every time slot, this time using the *eigenvalue*. If we compare these results with the ones obtained for the betweenness, we will see high similarities as expected. However, we must emphasise the differences in some time slots in which the

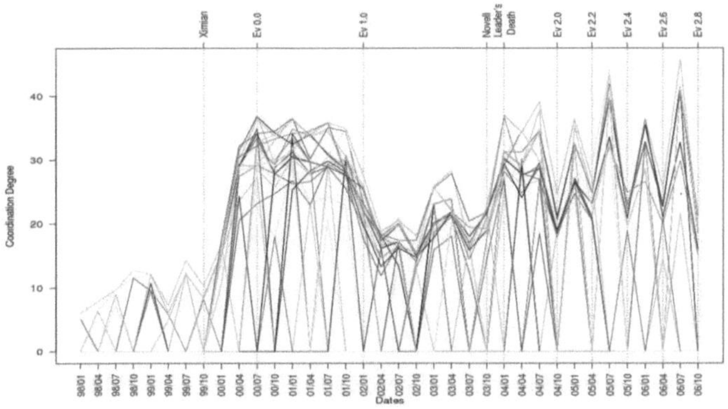

(a) Evolution of the Coordination Degree for Evolution

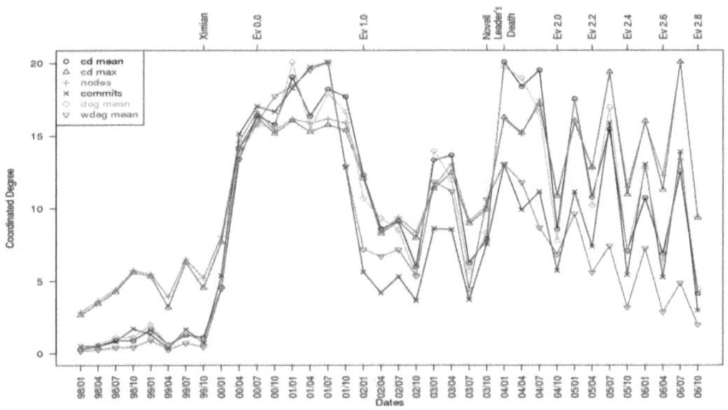

(b) Coordination Degree comparative for Evolution

Fig. 1. Coordination Degree values and a comparative for top 40 commiters in Evolution.

identified leader differs. This is because the *betweenness* focuses on the control of the information flows whereas the *eigenvalue* provides a node valuation from the point of view of centrality. Thus, the periods where leaders remain the main contributors to a project are smaller for the second value, because a greater effort has to be carried out to keep this privileged position. In the same way, the number of different persons who achieve the leadership is higher using *eigenvalues*. So, we can see that gaining control over information flows in the project is an easier task than obtaining a high influence on the network.

5.2 Analysis of Mono

The activity of Mono is marked clearly by five events that can be appreciated in Figure 4(a). The first one is the *Mono 0.7* release (first unstable version) that additionally happens at the same time as the initial check-in of the *GTK#*

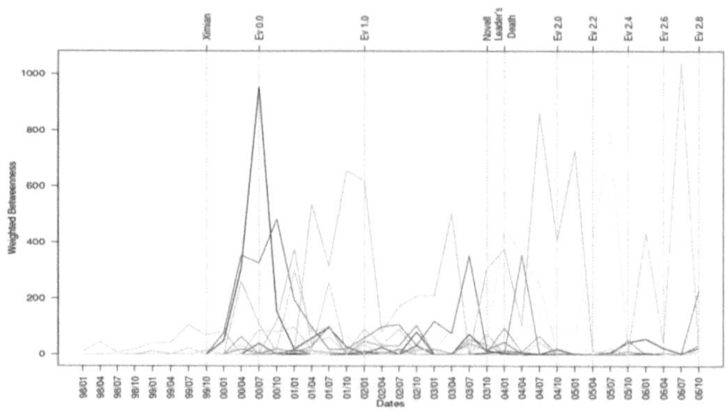

(a) Evolution of the Weighted Betweenness for Evolution

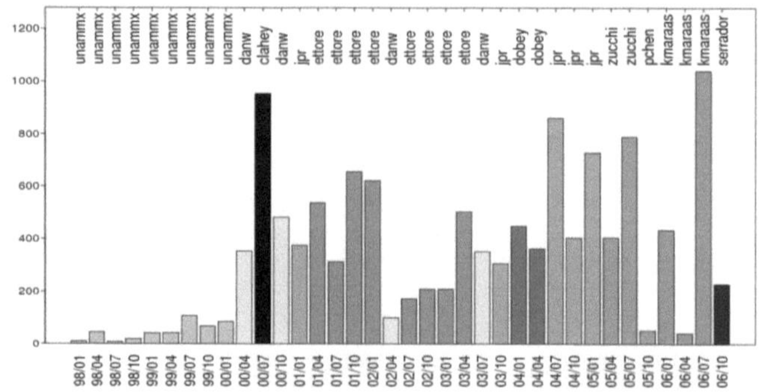

(b) Weighted Betweenness comparative for Evolution

Fig. 2. Weighted Betweenness values and a comparative for top 40 commiters in Evolution.

module in the repository. Then a progressive increase of the activity took place, reaching its highest peak in the middle of 2003. An external fact caused an extraordinary activity: the *.NET1.1* release, which Mono had to react to be able to support this specification in its next version. This adaptation was completed in *Mono 1.0* in 2004. In 2005 another noteworthy moment took place, when the Mono team started to adapt the *.NET 2.0* specifications.

The development of Mono does not have a continuous growth, but it shows momentary efforts to achieve the *.NET* functionality. This kind of development is reflected in its social structure as it is not efficient most of the time. As it can be observed from Figure 4(b) while the number of developers grows smoothly, their activity has several peaks. In any case, compared to the previous case study, we can conclude that in this case Ximian has not achieved such a high community involvement in Mono as in Evolution.

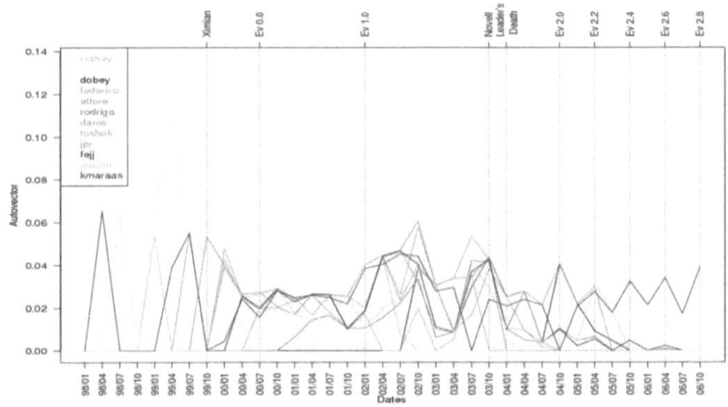

(a) Evolution of the Eigenvalue for Evolution

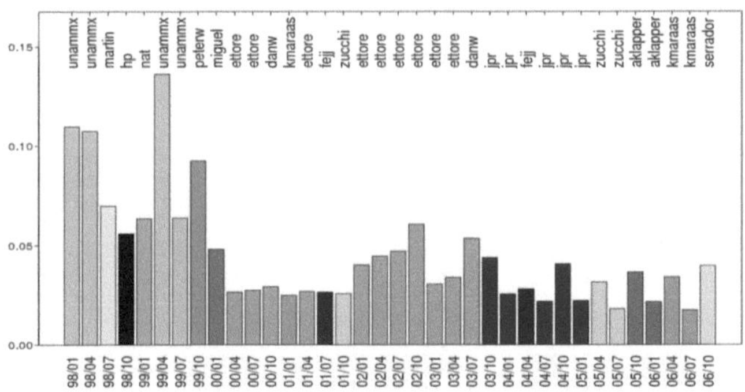

(b) Eigenvalue comparative for Evolution

Fig. 3. Eigenvalue values and a comparative for top 40 commiters in Evolution.

The Mono project is composed currently of over 80 developers. As it can be seen from Figure 5(a), and a large difference between the values of the main leader and the ones for the rest of developers exist. The yellow line belongs to Miguel de Icaza, the founder of the project, while the red one to Gonzalo Paniagua, a Novell-hired developer, and the green lines correspond to Raja R. Harinath and Ben Maurer, also Novell employees. Miguel de Icaza is clearly the main leader in Mono as he has the maximum value in 16 quarters, in the early stages and also recently. Gonzalo Paniagua had a more prominent role in the first half of the project as well as in the last phases.

If we use *eigenvalues* (see Figure 6(a)), the difference between the project leaders and the rest of developers are not that high as found using *betweenness*. In any case, if we compare Figure 6(b) with figure 5(b) the main leaders continue being the same. Even though, eigenvalue helps us obtaining additional information on the development community as it allows to rank developers by their activity and their position in the network.

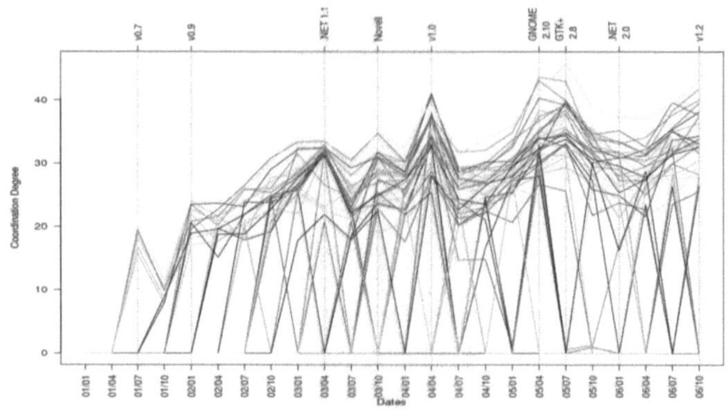

(a) Evolution of the Coordination Degree for Mono

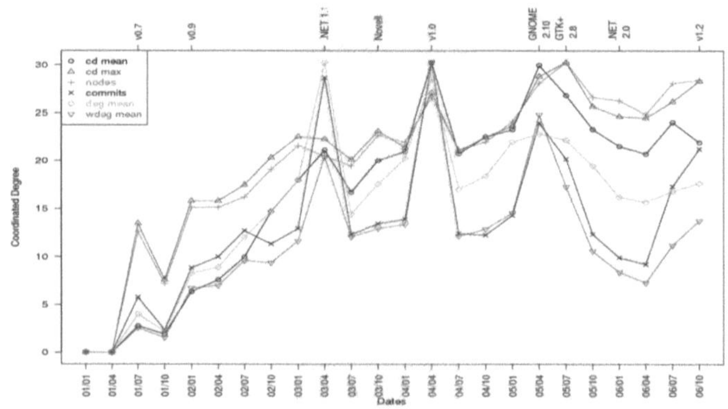

(b) Coordination Degree comparative for Mono

Fig. 4. Coordination Degree values and a comparative for top 40 commiters in Mono.

6 Conclusions and Further work

In this paper a descriptive study of several social networks of FLOSS projects where a company and the community collaborate has been presented. We have seen that although there is access to the interactions that developers have in the source code management system, the amount of information is that high that we require additional methods to properly analyse the community and extract facts and information from it.

Thanks to the use of social networks analysis techniques we have been able to obtain some information on these projects, in particular, that time-based release management seems to animate the development of projects or that the collaboration between the company and the community can, if properly handled, drive a more efficient development. Future research should be devoted to analyse the differences between the studied projects to try to find out the aspects that drive one of the case studies (Evolution) to have at least for some

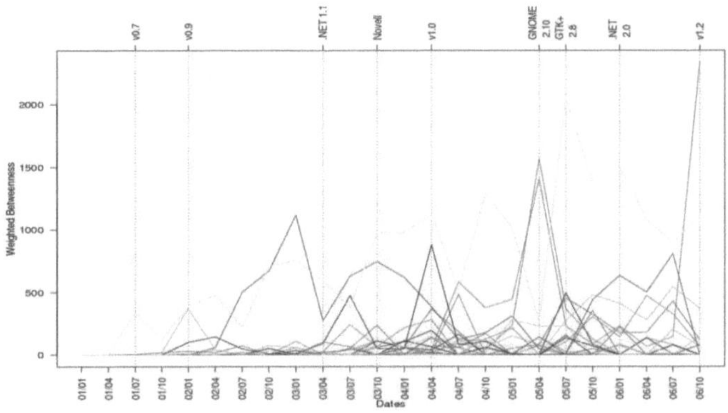

(a) Evolution of the Weighted Betweenness for Mono

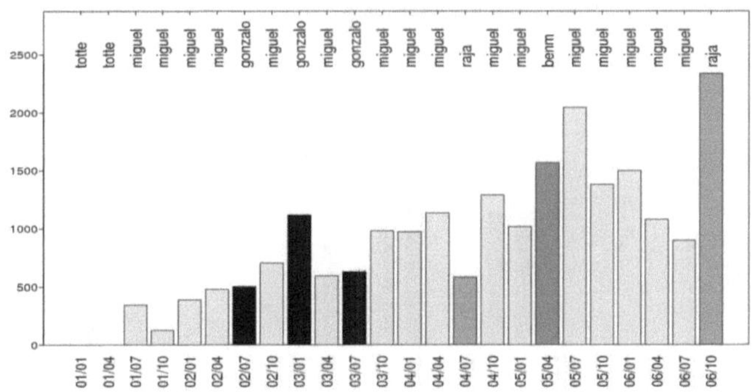

(b) Weighted Betweenness comparative for Mono

Fig. 5. Weighted Betweenness values and a comparative for top 40 commiters in Mono.

time an efficient development, while this is an exception for the other project (Mono) under study.

In addition, we have identified the most important nodes (developers) in the project and have observed them from from several points of view (leadership, information control flows, etc.) and how they evolve over time. In both case studies, the most prominent positions where held by company employees, showing a low turnover over the years. Future work could be devoted to find out if this behaviour is similar in community-led projects.

All in all, this paper demonstrates that the techniques from the social networks analysis field can be of great interest for the study and characterisation of any kind of network and with particular interest in the study of how the software industry can interact with the FLOSS community entering the development of projects.

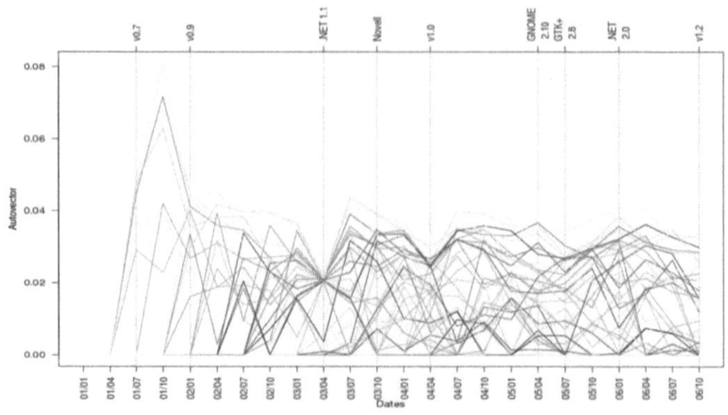

(a) Evolution of the Eigenvalue for Mono

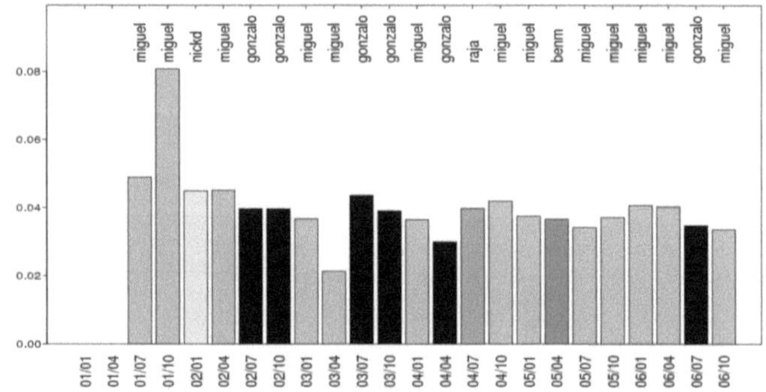

(b) Eigenvalue comparative for Mono

Fig. 6. Eigenvalue values and a comparative for top 40 commiters in Mono.

7 Acknowledgements

This work has been funded in part by the European Commission, under the QUALIPSO (FP6-IST-034763), FLOSSMETRICS (FP6-IST-5-033547) and QUALOSS (FP6-IST-5-033547) projects, and by the Spanish CICyT, project SobreSalto (TIN2007-66172).

We would like to thank the QualiPSo Activity 6 partners for comments and suggestions on this research.

References

1. J. A. Almendral, L. Lopez, and M. A. F. Sanjuan. Information flow in generalized hierarchical networks. *Physica A Statistical Mechanics and its Applications*, 324:424–429, June 2003.

2. Jac M. Anthonisse. The rush in a directed graph. Technical report, Stichting Mathemastisch Centrum, Amsterdam, The Netherlands, 1971.
3. Phillip Bonacich. Factoring and weighting approaches to status scores and clique identification. *Journal of Mathematical Sociology*, 2:113–120, 1972.
4. Stephen P. Borgatti. Centrality and network flow. *Social Networks*, 27(1):55–71, January 2005.
5. Kevin Crowston and James Howison. The social structure of free and open source software development. *First Monday*, 10(2), February 2005.
6. Jean-Michel Dalle and Paul A. David. The allocation of software development resources in open source production mode. Technical Report SIEPR Discussion Paper No. 02-27, Stanford Institute for Economic Policy Research, February 2003.
7. Trung T. Dinh-Trong and James M. Bieman. The FreeBSD project: A replication case study of Open Source development. *IEEE Transactions on Software Engineering*, 31(6):481–494, June 2005.
8. Linton C. Freeman. A set of measures of centrality based on betweenness. *Sociometry 40, 35-41*, 1977.
9. Daniel M. German. The GNOME project: a case study of open source, global software development. *Journal of Software Process: Improvement and Practice*, 8(4):201–215, 2004.
10. Roger Guimera, Albert Diaz-Guilera, F. Vega-Redondo, A. Cabrales, and Alex Arenas. Optimal network topologies for local search with congestion. *Physical Review Let. 89, 248701*, 2002.
11. Israel Herraiz, Gregorio Robles, Juan JosÉ Amor, Teófilo Romera, and Jesús M. Gonzâlez Barahona. The processes of joining in global distributed software projects. In *GSD '06: Proceedings of the 2006 international workshop on Global software development for the practitioner*, pages 27–33, New York, NY, USA, 2006. ACM Press.
12. Chris Jensen and Walter Scacchi. Modeling recruitment and role migration processes in OSSD projects. In *Proceedings of 6th International Workshop on Software Process Simulation and Modeling*, St. Louis, May 2005.
13. Stefan Koch and Georg Schneider. Effort, cooperation and coordination in an open source software project: GNOME. *Information Systems Journal*, 12(1):27–42, 2002.
14. Luis Lopez and Juan Martinez-Romo. Conan: Generating social network analysis. `http://tools.libresoft.es/conan`.
15. Luis Lopez, Gregorio Robles, Jesus M. Gonzalez Barahona, and Israel Herraiz. Applying social network analysis techniques to community-driven libre software projects. *International Journal of Information Technology and Web Engineering*, 1(3):27–48, July-September 2006.
16. Luis Lopez and Miguel A. F. Sanjuan. Relation between structure and size in social networks. *Phys. Rev. E*, 65(3):036107, Feb 2002.
17. Gregory Madey, Vincent Freeh, and Renee Tynan. Modeling the Free/Open Source software community: A quantitative investigation. In Stefan Koch and Stefan Koch, editors, *Free/Open Source Software Development*, pages 203–221. Idea Group Publishing, Hershey, Pennsylvania, USA, 2004.
18. Audris Mockus, Roy T. Fielding, and James D. Herbsleb. Two case studies of Open Source software development: Apache and Mozilla. *ACM Transactions on Software Engineering and Methodology*, 11(3):309–346, 2002.

19. Audris Mockus and Lawrence G. Votta. Identifying reasons for software changes using historic databases. In *Proceedings of the International Conference on Software Maintenance*, pages 120–130, October 2000.
20. Mark E. J. Newman. Scientific collaboration networks: I. network construction and fundamental results. *Phys. Rev. E 64, 016131*, 2001.
21. Gregorio Robles. *Empirical Software Engineering Research on Libre Software: Data Sources, Methodologies and Results.* PhD thesis, Escuela Superior de Ciencias Experimentales y Tecnologia, Universidad Rey Juan Carlos, 2006.
22. Gregorio Robles, Jesus M. Gonzalez-Barahona, and Martin Michlmayr. Evolution of volunteer participation in libre software projects: evidence from Debian. In *Proceedings of the 1st International Conference on Open Source Systems*, pages 100–107, Genoa, Italy, July 2005.
23. Gregorio Robles, Stefan Koch, and Jesus M. Gonzalez-Barahona. Remote analysis and measurement of libre software systems by means of the CVSAnalY tool. In *Proceedings of the 2nd ICSE Workshop on Remote Analysis and Measurement of Software Systems (RAMSS)*, pages 51–56, Edinburgh, Scotland, UK, 2004.
24. Gregorio Robles, Juan Julian Merelo, and Jesus M. Gonzalez-Barahona. Self-organized development in libre software: a model based on the stigmergy concept. In *Proceedings of the 6th International Workshop on Software Process Simulation and Modeling (ProSim 2005)*, St.Louis, Missouri, USA, May 2005.
25. Gert Sabidussi. The centrality index of a graph. *Psychometirka 31, 581-606*, 1996.
26. Yuwan Ye, Kumiyo Nakakoji, Yasuhiro Yamamoto, and Kouichi Kishida. The co-evolution of systems and communities in Free and Open Source software development. In Stefan Koch and Stefan Koch, editors, *Free/Open Source Software Development*, pages 59–82. Idea Group Publishing, Hershey, Pennsylvania, USA, 2004.
27. Thomas Zimmermann, Peter Weissgerber, Stephan Diehl, and Andreas Zeller. Mining version histories to guide software changes. *IEEE Transactions on Software Engineering*, 31(6):429–445, June 2005.

Empirical Analysis of the Bug Fixing Process in Open Source Projects

Chiara Francalanci and Francesco Merlo
Dipartimento di Elettronica ed Informazione, Politecnico di Milano
via Ponzio 34/5, I-20133 Milano, Italy
{francala | merlo}@elet.polimi.it

Abstract. Monitoring the performance of processes is often considered critical in classic engineering fields. However, in the area of software engineering (and especially in the Open Source context) it seems that the literature has not yet taken into consideration the problem of identifying the process characteristics and performance of debugging. The aim of this paper is the identification of the performance characteristics of the bug fixing process of Open Source applications, focusing on continuity and efficiency indicators. The importance of such indicators is even more relevant today, since Open Source software is now adopted also in many business contexts. We have analyzed the debugging process of 9 active and popular Open Source projects, collecting a dataset comprising more than 65,000 closed bugs. Results have highlighted four types of bug fixing processes that can be distinguished by considering temporal continuity and efficiency dimensions.

Key Words: Open Source Software debugging process quality

1 Introduction

Debugging is defined in [9] as "the activity of locating and correcting errors" in software programs. It is an important part of the software development and maintenance process, since a lot of time is spent by developers in activities related to the location and resolution of bugs. As pointed out by a NIST research [21], software bugs are so prevalent and so detrimental that they cost the U.S. economy an estimated $59.5 billion annually, or about 0.6 percent of the gross domestic product.

In the literature, many studies have focused on debugging. Relevant results have been achieved in the field of software testing, with the aim of detecting the presence of errors in programs. An overview of software testing can be found in [16, 2, 13, 9]. However, as noted by [9], debugging is "one of the least understood activities in software development and is practiced with the least amount of discipline; it is often approached with much hope and little planning". In particular, one of the most difficult problems is bug localization, that is, finding where bugs are located in the

Please use the following format when citing this chapter:

Francalanci, C. and Merlo, F., 2008, in IFIP International Federation for Information Processing, Volume 275; *Open Source Development, Communities and Quality*; Barbara Russo, Ernesto Damiani, Scott Hissam, Björn Lundell, Giancarlo Succi; (Boston: Springer), pp. 187–196.

source code (as opposed to testing, which is concerned with the identification of the presence of bugs). Consequently, bug localization is one of the most widely addressed problems. Techniques such as statistical debugging [20, 12, 25, 17, 1] try to identify bug predictors (e.g., software quality metrics like CK object-oriented metrics [5]) that may refer to the actual bug location.

Although some studies have already been published [15, 6, 19, 14, 7], it seems that the problem of identifying the process characteristics and performance of debugging has not been taken into account yet.

For other "classic" engineering processes, performance indicators are considered critical. The importance of such indicators is even more relevant today since Open Source software is now adopted also in many business contexts. As noted by Wasserman and Capra [24], Goldman [10], Goth [11] and Riehle [18], when evaluating an Open Source product for business adoption a number of variables different from those considered for the classical proprietary software should be taken into account. For example, the quality of the support provided by the community, or the quality of the bug fixing process itself are cited as new software selection variables to be taken into account in the Open Source context.

The aim of this paper is the identification of the performance characteristics of the bug fixing process of Open Source applications that can be used as indicators to assess the quality of the process itself. In particular, our goal is to focus on variables related to the continuity and efficiency of the bug fixing process, since these characteristics are among the most relevant when assessing debugging performance, especially in a business context.

The paper is structured as follows: Section 2 describes the data sample we have used for the analysis of bug fixing processes, Section 3 presents the analysis and the related empirical results, while Section 4 discusses the main findings and presents some concluding remarks on this work.

2 Data Sample

The dataset used for this study is composed by 9 active and popular Open Source projects: Table 1 shows the summary descriptive statistics of the dataset. Each application is identified by a mnemonic code.

A tool developed *ad-hoc* has been used to collect data. In particular, the tool has been used to parse the information provided by the bug tracker of each project. In order to guarantee the homogeneity of the collected dataset, we have used the same parameters to query each bug tracker. That is, we have focused on bugs with closed status related only to Microsoft Windows and Linux operating systems. Moreover, we have excluded all external components or additional plugins, analyzing only bugs located in the core components of each project (the project sizes reported in Table 1 are however related to the whole applications).

Table 1. Dataset summary statistics.

Mnemonic Code	Domain	Size (KSLOC)	Collected Bugs	Time span (months)	Bug tracking Tool
A	IDE	2,063	51,485	65.4	Apache's JIRA
B	IDE	152	2,529	76.6	SF Tracker Tool
C	DBMS	713	8,478	48.5	bugs.php.net Bugs Sys
D	DBMS	810	997	26.2	Apache's JIRA
E	DBMS	660	577	78.8	SF Tracker Tool
F	DBMS	159	737	65.9	SF Tracker Tool
G	DBMS	392	515	34.0	SF Tracker Tool
H	DBMS	522	270	65.8	Apache's JIRA
I	DBMS	153	713	8.0	Apache's JIRA
Total		5,624	66,301	ns	
Average		624	7,367	52.1	

The selection of bugs related to the core components of each application has been performed by manually specifying the correct parameters when querying the bug tracking systems. After the data collection phase, a manual data preprocessing has been carried out to ensure data cleaning and normalization. For each bug, we have collected information about its status (either *opened* or *closed*), the opening and closing dates, the affected project component, the level of priority/severity, the textual description, the application version affected and the operating system.

3 Empirical Analyses and Results

This section presents the analyses that we have performed on our dataset and related empirical results. In particular, we have focused our analyses on the time required to close bugs (referred to as MTTR - Mean Time To Repair, by analogy with hardware systems), defined for a generic bug *b* as follows:

$$MTTR(b) = date_{closed}(b) - date_{opened}(b),$$

where $date_{closed}(b)$ and $date_{opened}(b)$ refer to the change of bug status (*closed* and *open*, respectively) registered by the project bug tracker tool. As a consequence, we have focused our analyses only on *closed bugs*.

The influence of the release train mechanism on the bug fixing process. The first analysis that we have carried out on the dataset has been a qualitative evaluation of the MTTR values for each project. To accomplish this task, we have considered for each application in our dataset the scatter plot of the MTTR values of each bug collected by the bug tracker. Figure 1 shows an example for project C. Each data point in the plot identifies a closed bug; the X axis reports the bug's opening date, while the Y axis reports the MTTR value.

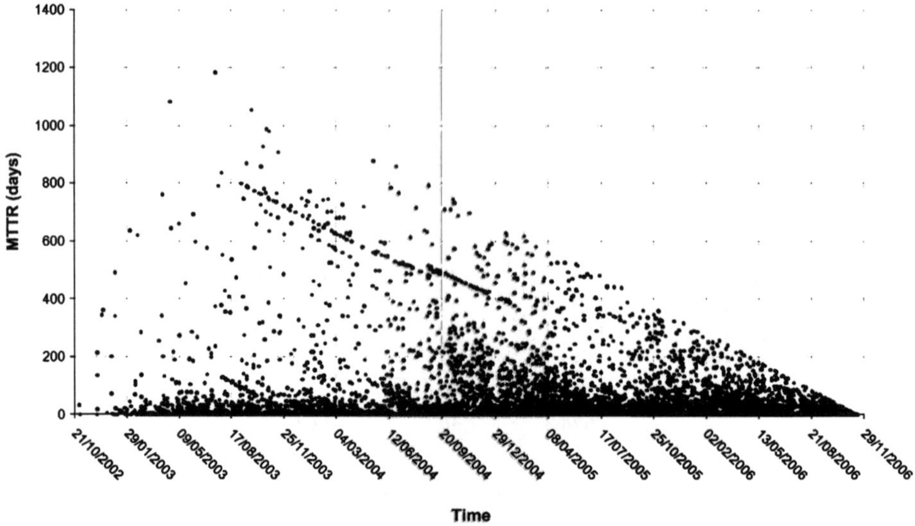

Fig. 1. Scatter plot of MTTR values of project C.

It is worth noting that Figure 2 (the scatter plot of MTTR values of project F) shows a set of oblique lines: these lines can be interpreted as an effect of the release train mechanism, since each line includes the bugs that have been closed in the proximity of a release date. The intuitive meaning of this phenomenon is that when a release date approaches, developers hasten to correct bugs with the aim of including corrections in the forthcoming release. In fact, if changes are verified and committed before the scheduled deadline, they can be included in the release; otherwise, they would shift to the next release. Figure 2 shows how each line can be traced back to the release date of a version of the application. By checking the dates identified on the plots against the official release dates taken from the website of each project, we have verified that more than 90% of official release dates could be correctly identified in this way.

From the bug fixing quality point of view, this phenomenon is certainly relevant. If bug corrections are made too close to the release date, the overall quality of the bug fixing process can be worse, due to the possible inaccuracy of interventions and scarce documentation of changes. As noted by Capra et al. [4], these are some of the most relevant causes that contribute to increase software entropy, which is proved to negatively affect overall software quality and increase maintenance costs.

The bug fixing process quality continuum. A fundamental point that has to be taken into account when considering the quality of the bug fixing process is the analysis of the bug opening and closing trends.

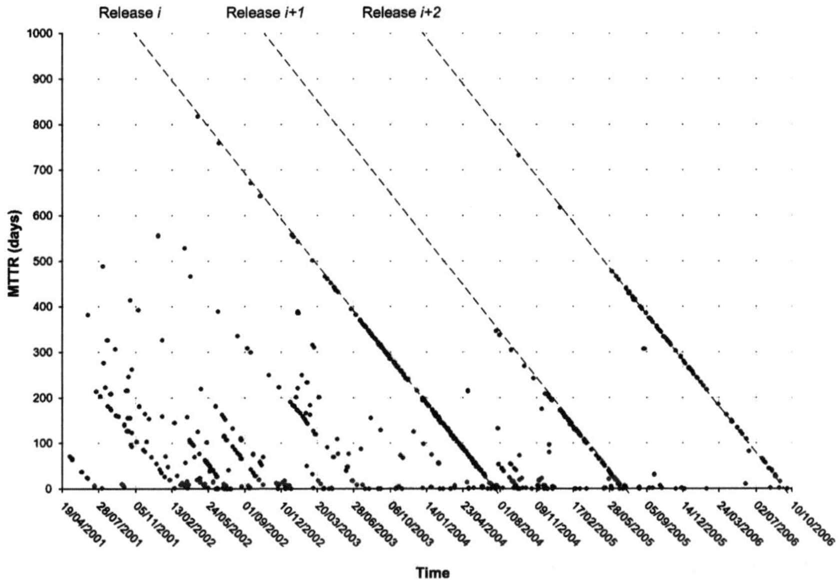

Fig. 2. Influence of the release train mechanism on bug fixing process of project F.

The bug opening trend is related to the process of submission and acceptance of new bugs by considering the cumulated number of opened and verified bugs over time. The bug closing trend is the cumulated number of bugs that are resolved and closed over time. Figure 3 shows an example of bug opening and closing trend curves. As it can be noted, the distance between the two curves at a given point in time represents the number of bugs simultaneously open at that time. The closing trend curve can be directly derived from the distribution of MTTR values: for each time interval (typically on a daily basis), the increment of the closing trend curve is equal to the number of closed bugs in that time interval.

A high quality debugging process is generally considered to be continuous over time [23]. That is, there should not be any discontinuity in the debugging process and the number of closed bugs should grow at least as fast as the number of opened bugs to avoid the uncontrolled growth of unresolved bugs.

The characteristics of the ideal bug fixing process can be translated into visual properties of the bug opening and closing trend curves:

- Process continuity - trend smoothness: if the bug fixing process is continuous, then the closing trend curve is smooth and without peaks or steps.
- Process efficiency - number of open bugs: if the debugging process is efficient (i.e., bugs are closed at least at the same rate with which they are opened), the closing trend curve stays near to the opening trend curve, without increasing the overall number of open bugs.

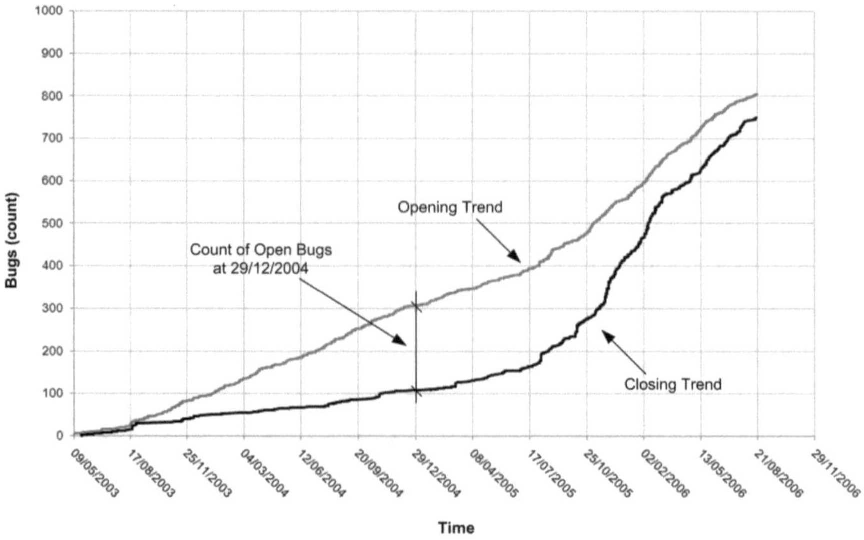

Fig. 3. Bug opening and closing trends.

Based on these considerations, it is possible to assess different quality levels of the bug fixing process by analyzing the bug opening and closing trend curves. It is worth noting that, at this point, evaluations are qualitative. Figure 4 shows four examples of trend curves for projects in our dataset, ordered by the quality level of the bug fixing process. As it can be noted, a high variance of the quality level of the bug fixing process can be identified among the projects in our dataset.

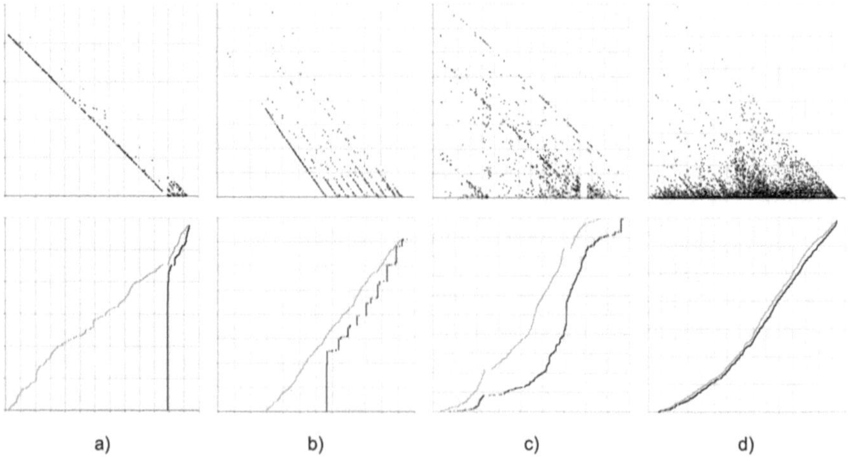

Fig. 4. Sample bug fixing processes: a) project E; b) project I; c) project D; d) project B.

Case *a)* of Figure 4 denotes a low quality bug fixing process since the closing trend shows a step, corresponding to a mass correction of bugs. At the opposite end, case *d)* can be considered as a high quality bug fixing process: the closing trend curve is smooth and very close to the opening trend curve. Cases *b)* and *c)* are positioned along the quality continuum between these two extremes: case *b)* represents a discontinuous process since the closing curve shows numerous steps, while case *c)* is a more continuous but not efficient process, since the closing trend curve is quite far from the opening trend curve. Please note that these considerations are not influenced by the fact that in practice there might be some bugs that are never fixed, as noted for example by [7]: since this seems to be a very common problem [14, 7, 22], it can be considered a common bias uniformly spread across projects.

The projects in our dataset can thus be divided into four categories on the basis of the visual properties of the opening and closing curves:

a) Inefficient and discontinuous;
b) Inefficient and continuous;
c) Efficient and discontinuous;
d) Efficient and continuous.

Distinctive properties of the bug fixing process. The distinction between different levels of quality of the debugging process should be quantified. Along with the scatter plot we have considered also the distribution of MTTR values. Figure 5 shows two examples related to projects B and E. This kind of graph shows the number of bugs that have been closed with the same MTTR value. By analyzing the distribution of the MTTR values of a project, two statistical indexes can be considered to quantify the quality level of the debugging process: skewness and kurtosis. The values of such indexes can provide significant information to compare different bug fixing processes, given that the MTTR values are comparable.

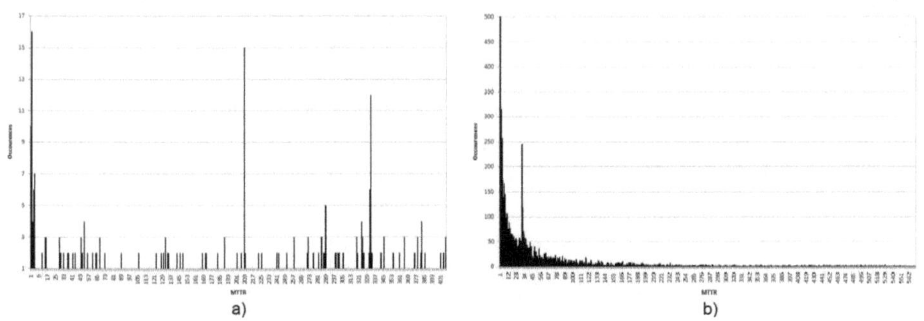

Fig. 5. Distribution of MTTR values for *a)* project E and *b)* project B.

The skewness index γ is a measure of the asymmetry of the distribution of the MTTR. That is, the distribution shows different tail shapes on the two sides of the average value. Considering the debugging process, the skew is typically positive, since it is more frequent that the MTTR distribution is right-tailed: in fact, the mean value of MTTR is typically influenced by a number of bugs whose closing times are much higher than the average one (i.e., a high value of skewness can be considered as indicator of the presence of "superbugs", see [7]).

The kurtosis index κ is a measure of the *peakedness* of the distribution of the MTTR. Higher kurtosis values indicate that most of the variance is due to a few very high deviations, as opposed to frequent small deviations from the mean value of MTTR. From the bug fixing process point of view, a high kurtosis means that the variance of the MTTR distribution can be explained by a few bugs that have required extremely long closing times. As a consequence, high kurtosis values are desirable, since they can be considered as an index of efficiency. For instance, by considering case *a)* of Figure 5, it is clear that many bugs show a closing time much higher than the average MTTR value, while in case *b)* the number of bugs with very high MTTR is considerably lower and negligible with respect to case *a)*.

4 Conclusions

Results indicate that the release train mechanism, widely adopted in the Open Source context, affects the debugging process. In particular, there is empirical evidence that a great number of bugs tends to be resolved close to scheduled releases. From a project management point of view, this phenomenon should be taken into account when scheduling releases, since if they are too frequent the quality of interventions for bug resolution could be lowered. Consequently, software entropy could be increased, leading to higher maintenance costs/effort. From the user point of view, a project with a debugging process that is too affected by the release train mechanism could be less dependable due to inaccurate bug corrections.

Another relevant empirical result is that even in the Open Source context, which is commonly addressed to as a high quality software development practice [8, 3], the quality of the bug fixing process is extremely variable. The projects in our dataset showed different quality levels, which can be positioned along a continuum depending on the performance of the bug fixing process.

The quantitative distinction between different bug fixing quality levels can be measured by means of two statistical indexes of the MTTR distribution, namely skewness and kurtosis. These indexes measure two relevant characteristics of the debugging process, temporal continuity and efficiency.

Future work is focused at extending the empirical data set of applications to provide better statistical significance and at better understanding the skewness and kurtosis indexes from a software development process point of view.

Acknowledgements

We would like to thank Marco Balzarini for his support in the data collection and analysis phases.

References

1. The cooperative bug isolation project. http://www.cs.wisc.edu/cbi.
2. B. Beizer. Software Testing Techniques. John Wiley and Sons, New York, 1983.
3. Boulanger. Open source versus proprietary software: is one more reliable and secure that the other? IBM Systems Journal, vol. 44, no.2:p. 239, 2005.
4. E. Capra, C. Francalanci, and F. Merlo. The economics of open source software: An empirical analysis of maintenance costs. In Proc. Int'l Conf. Software Maintenance, pages 395-404, 2007.
5. S. Chidamber and C. Kemerer. A metrics suite for object-oriented design. IEEE Trans. Software Eng., vol.20, no. 6:pp. 476-493, 1994.
6. K. Crowston and B. Scozzi. Coordination practices for bug fixing within FLOSS development teams. In Proceedings of CSAC, 2004.
7. J. M. Dalle and M. den Besten. Different bug fixing regimes? a preliminary case for superbugs. In Proceedings of OSS Systems Conference, pages 247-252, 2007.
8. Fitzgerald. A critical look at open source. IEEE Computer, vol. 37, no. 7:pp.92-94, 2004.
9. Ghezzi, M. Jazayeri, and D. Mandrioli. Fundamentals of Software Engineering. Prentice Hall, New Jersey, 2003.
10. R. Goldman and R. Gabriel. Innovation happens elsewhere: Open Source as business strategy. Morgan Kauffmann, 2005.
11. G. Goth. Open source business models: ready for prime time. IEEE Software, vol. 22, no. 3:pp. 99-100, 2005.
12. T. Gyimothy, R. Ferenc, and I. Siket. Empirical validation of object-oriented metrics on open source software for fault prediction. IEEE Trans. Software Eng., vol. 31, no. 10:pp. 897-910, 2005.
13. W. E. Howden. Functional program testing. McGraw Hill, New York, 1987.
14. M. Michlmayr and A. Senyard. The Economics of Open Source Software Development, chapter A Statistical analysis of defects in Debian and strategies for improving quality in free software projects, pages 131-148. Elsevier B. V., 2006.
15. Mockus, R. T. Fielding, and J. D. Herbsleb. Two case studies of open source software development. ACM Transactions on Software Engineering Methodology, vol. 11:pp. 309-346, 2002.
16. G. J. Myers. The Art of Software Testing. John Wiley and Sons, New York, 1979.
17. P. A. Nainar, T. Chen, J. Rosin, and B. Liblit. Statistical debugging using compound boolean predicates. In Proc. Int'l Symp. Software Testing and Analysis, 2007.
18. Riehle. The economic motivation of open source software: stakeholder perspective. IEEE Computer, vol.40, no. 4:pp. 25-32, 2007.
19. R. J. Sandusky, L. Gasser, and G. Ripoche. Bug report networks. In Proceedings of ICSE MSR, 2004.
20. R. Subramanyam and M. S. Krishnan. Empirical analysis of CK metrics for object-oriented design complexity: implications for software defects. IEEE Trans. Software Eng., vol. 29, no. 4:pp. 297-310, 2003.
21. G. Tassey. The economic impacts of inadequate infrastructure for software testing. Technical Report 7007.011, National Institute of Standards and Technology, Acquisition and Assistance Division, May 2002.
22. L. Villa. Large free software projects and Bugzilla: Lessons from GNOME project QA. In Proceedings of the Linux Symposium, 2003.

23. H. Wang and C. Wang. Open source software adoption: a status report. IEEE Software, vol. 18; no. 2:pp. 90-95, 2001.
24. I. Wasserman and E. Capra. Evaluating software engineering processes in commercial and community open source. In Int'l Workshop Emerging Trends in FLOSS Research and Development, 2007.
25. Y. Zhou and H. Leung. Empirical analysis of object-oriented design metrics for predicting high and low severity faults. IEEE Trans. Software Eng., vol. 32, no. 10:pp. 771-789, 2006.

The Total Growth of Open Source

Amit Deshpande
SAP Research, SAP Labs LLC
3475 Deer Creek Rd
Palo Alto, CA, 94304 U.S.A.
amit@amit-deshpande.com

Dirk Riehle
SAP Research, SAP Labs LLC
3475 Deer Creek Rd
Palo Alto, CA, 94304 U.S.A.
dirk@riehle.org

Abstract. Software development is undergoing a major change away from a fully closed software process towards a process that incorporates open source software in products and services. Just how significant is that change? To answer this question we need to look at the overall growth of open source as well as its growth rate. In this paper, we quantitatively analyze the growth of more than 5000 active and popular open source software projects. We show that the total amount of source code as well as the total number of open source projects is growing at an exponential rate. Previous research showed linear and quadratic growth in lines of source code of individual open source projects. Our work shows that open source is expanding into new domains and applications at an exponential rate.

1 Introduction

Software development is undergoing a major change from being a fully closed software development process towards a more community driven open source software development process. Successful open source projects like Linux, Apache, PostgreSQL and many others are growing super-linearly. Previous research showed that linear and quadratic growth is the dominant growth pattern of open source software projects [5] [8] [15] [16] [18] [22].

In this paper, we analyze the combined growth of open source software in terms of lines of source code as well as number of projects. Our database contains more than 5000 active and popular open source projects. The database provides fine granular data of developer actions over the last 17 years from 1990 to 2006. We analyze the average amount of source code added per month for the time frame of January 1995 to December 2006 as well as the number of projects added over time.

We find that both the growth rate as well as the absolute amount of source code is best explained using an exponential model. Given that previous research showed that most open source projects grow at a polynomial rate, we suggest and then verify that the number of open source projects is growing at an exponential rate.

This paper is organized as follows. Section 2 discusses our motivation, the hypothesis, and its implications. Section 3 discusses our database and approach. Section 4 presents the results of the analysis. Section 5 discusses some limitations of the analysis and Section 6 discusses related work. Section 7 concludes the paper.

Please use the following format when citing this chapter:

Deshpande, A. and Riehle, D., 2008, in IFIP International Federation for Information Processing, Volume 275; *Open Source Development, Communities and Quality*; Barbara Russo, Ernesto Damiani, Scott Hissam, Björn Lundell, Giancarlo Succi; (Boston: Springer), pp. 197–209.

2 The Growth of Open Source

Open source software is having a major impact on the software industry and its production processes. Many software products today contain at least some open source software components. Some commercial products are completely open source software [9]. In some markets, for example, web servers, open source software holds a dominant market share [10].

Open source software today has a strong presence in industry and government. Walli *et al.* observe [19]: "Organizations are saving millions of dollars on IT by using open source software. In 2004, open source software saved large companies (with annual revenue of over $1 billion) an average of $3.3 million. Medium-sized companies (between $50 million and $1 billion in annual revenue) saved an average $1.1 million. Firms with revenues under $50 million saved an average $520,000."

Commercially, the significance and growth of open source is measured in terms of revenue generated from it. Lawton and Notarfonzo state that packaged open source applications generated revenues of $1.8 billion in 2006 [9]. The software division of the Software & Information Industry Association estimates that total packaged software revenues were $235 billion in 2006 [4]. Thus, open source revenue, while still small compared to the overall market (~0.7%) is not trivial any longer.

However, open source software today is part of many proprietary (closed) source products, and measuring its growth solely by packaged software revenue is likely to underestimate its size and growth by a wide margin. To measure the growth of open source we need to look at the total growth of open source projects and their source code.

Several studies have been undertaken to measure the growth and evolution of individual open source software projects [5] [15] [16] [18]. Most of these studies are exemplary, focusing on a few selected projects only. The exception is Koch's work, which uses a large sample (>4000 projects) to determine overall growth patterns in open source projects, concluding that polynomial growth patterns provide good models for these projects [8] [20]. Such work is mostly motivated by trying to understand how individual open source projects grow and evolve.

The work presented in this paper, in contrast, analyzes the overall growth of open source, aggregating data from more than 5000 active and popular open source projects to determine the total growth of source code and number of projects. Assuming a positive correlation between work spent on open source, its total growth in terms of code and number of projects, and the revenue generated from it, understanding the overall growth of open source will give us a better indication of how significant a role open source will play in the future.

Understanding overall open source growth helps more easily answer questions about, for example, future product structures (how much code of an application is likely to be open source code?), labor economics (how much and which open source skills does a company need?), and revenue (what percentage of the software market's revenue will come from open source?).

The work presented in this paper shows that the total amount of open source code and the total number of projects is growing exponentially. Assuming a base of 0.7% of the market's revenue, exponential growth is a strong indicator that open source will be of significantly increasing commercial importance. The remainder of this paper discusses our study and validates the hypothesis of exponential growth of open source.

3 Data Source and Approach

On SourceForge, the dominant open source project hosting service, there are more than 150,000 projects registered, most of which are considered inactive [1] [17]. Daffara estimates that as of today there are only about 18,000 active open source projects in the world [3].

For our analysis, we use the database of the open source analytics firm Ohloh.net, which has been crawling open source software code repositories since 2005 [11]. Our database snapshot contains 5122 active and popular open source projects written in 30 different programming languages covering 103 open source licenses. All data is updated on at least a weekly basis.

The database contains the most popular open source projects as measured by the number of in-links to their website. The in-links are provided by the Yahoo! search engine. The database contains data from January 1990 until May 2007. Of this time horizon, we analyze the time frame from January 1995 to December 2006. We omit data before 1995 because it is too sparse to be useful.

Ohloh.net provides high-level data like project structures and developer information, but also data that goes down to the level of individual developer actions. Specifically, Ohloh provides each individual commit action of all projects over their entire history to the extent that they are publicly available.

A commit is the action with which a developer contributes a piece of code to the project's repository. A developer's workweek typically consists of a stream of commit actions by which he or she shares the results of their work with the team, contributing to the product or project under way.

We use the amount of source code added to a project (or removed) as an approximation of the work contributed. We count code in source lines of code (SLoC), omitting empty or commented lines of code. Each commit action stored in the database lists the number of lines of code added and removed in the commit. The number of lines added or removed is calculated using the Unix diff command applied to two consecutive versions. Empty or commented lines of code are ignored. Using this data, we calculate the change in the size of a source code file by adding or subtracting the number of lines of code added to or removed from its existing size.

This data collection method gracefully handles file and directory renaming. Such renaming is modeled as if the file or directory was removed and then re-added under a new name. Both code added and code removed will have equal (large) values, so the net change is zero. This avoids any undue bias in the analysis.

Libraries are typically used across many projects. For instance, the GIMP project and the GNOME project have many libraries in common. If the lines of code for both projects were added up independently we would be double-counting the libraries, leading to skewed results. We make sure that we are not double-counting code by considering each change to the original library.

However, we cannot unambiguously identify situations where a developer adds redundant source code to the code base. Copy and paste is a common practice in software development, independently of whether it is internal, external, planned or opportunistic. To deal with this issue, we adopt two approaches.

1. In the first approach we ignore the copy and paste problem and analyze the source lines of code added. The argument is that copy and paste is a reality of software development and that the copied code is part of the project. Hence, copy and paste simply needs to be accepted.
2. In the second approach we find the average and the standard deviation for the code added over time. We ignore all commits where lines of code added is greater than average code added per commit plus three times the standard deviation. The heuristic's assumption is that by not considering such large commits we ignore all commits based on copy and paste.

An analysis of average code contribution size in commits provides a cut-off value of 3060 SLoC that we use for the heuristic. This second approach is conservative in that we ignore not only copy and paste but also commits containing new code added. So we err on the lower side of total open source contributions.

We employ these two approaches to get an upper and a lower bound for the growth in source lines of code and number of projects. We can therefore say that properties like the exponential growth observed in both the upper and lower bound curve apply to the real curve as well.

4 Analysis and Results

We first analyze growth rate and total growth in open source software code and then analyze growth rate and total growth in open source software projects.

4.1 Growth in source code

Figures 1 and 2 show plots that represent the growth in source lines of code added using Approach 1 and 2 respectively. The Y-axis shows the number of lines of code added each month and the X-axis shows the time. Each data point on the plot represents the total number of lines of code added during that month. The time frame is 1995 through 2006 for all projects. We can see an upward trend in the amount of code added over time. Both Approach 1 and 2 show a similar pattern of growth.

Table 1 shows models for the two plots. In both cases, the best fitting model is an exponential curve with an R-square value of about 0.9, giving us confidence in the validity of the claim that the amount of code added is growing exponentially.

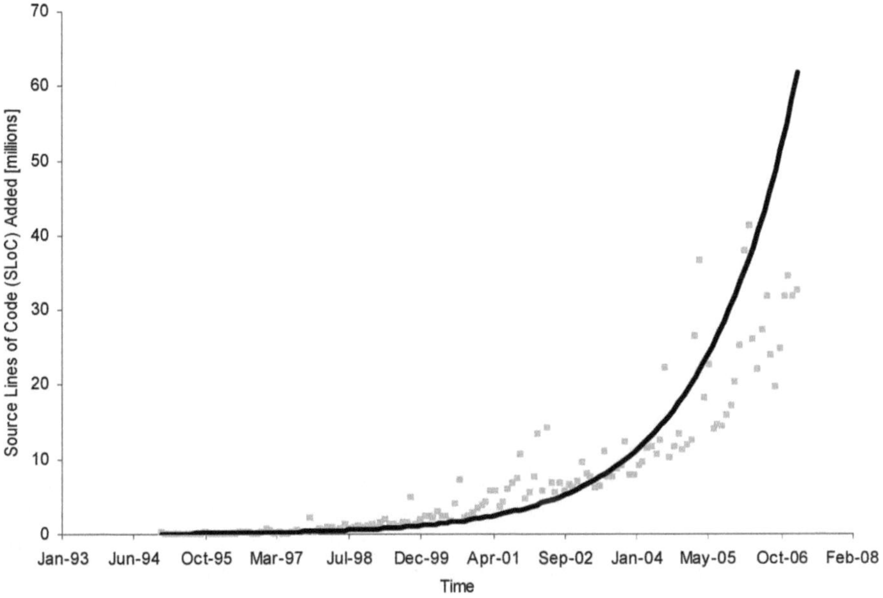

Fig. 1. Graph of source lines of code added [millions] (Approach 1)

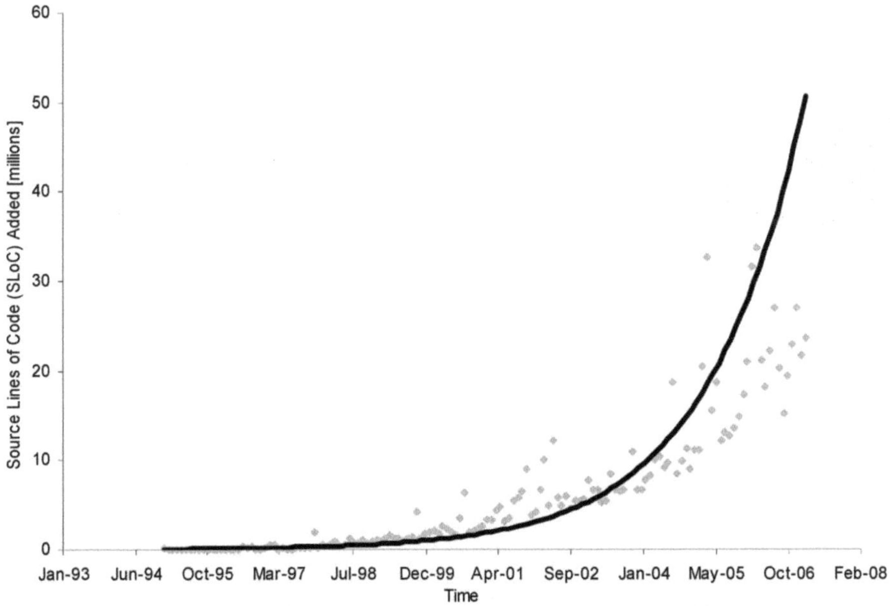

Fig. 2. Graph of source lines of code added [millions] (Approach 2)

Table 1. Model of source lines of code added

Approach	Model	R-square value
1	$y = 70833*e^{0.0464x}$	0.901
2	$y = 64004*e^{0.046x}$	0.897
where, y: Source lines of open source code added x: Time from Jan 1995 to Dec 2006 in months		

Figure 3 shows the total number of lines of open source code over time. Table 2 shows the statistical models for the two approaches. The doubling time for Approach 1 is 12.5 months, and the doubling time for Approach 2 is 14.9 months. We observe that the total code in Approach 2 is lower than in Approach 1 but follows a similar trend. This behavior is expected as we eliminated all large commits in the second approach to exclude copy and paste contributions.

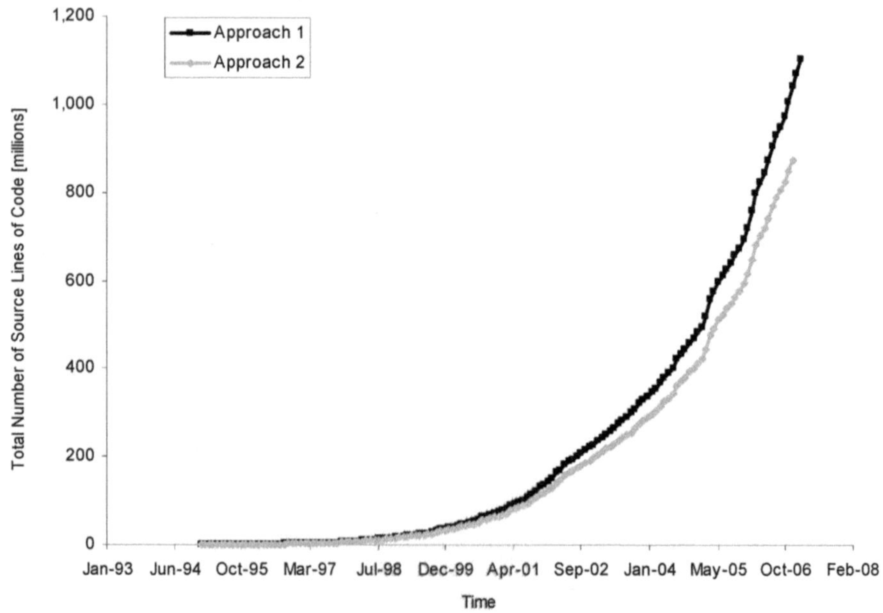

Fig. 3. Graph of total source lines of code [millions] (both approaches)

Table 2. Model of total source lines of code

Approach	Model	R-square value
1	$y = 784098*e^{0.0555x}$	0.961
2	$y = 2E+06*e^{0.0464x}$	0.964
where, y: Total open source lines of code x: Time from Jan 1995 to Dec 2006 in months		

4.2 Growth in projects

Figure 4 shows the number of projects added over time and Table 3 shows the model and its fit with the data. For each project, there is a first occurrence of a project action (for example, the initial commit action), and that point of time is considered the birth date of the project. This is the point of time when the project is counted as added to the overall set of projects.

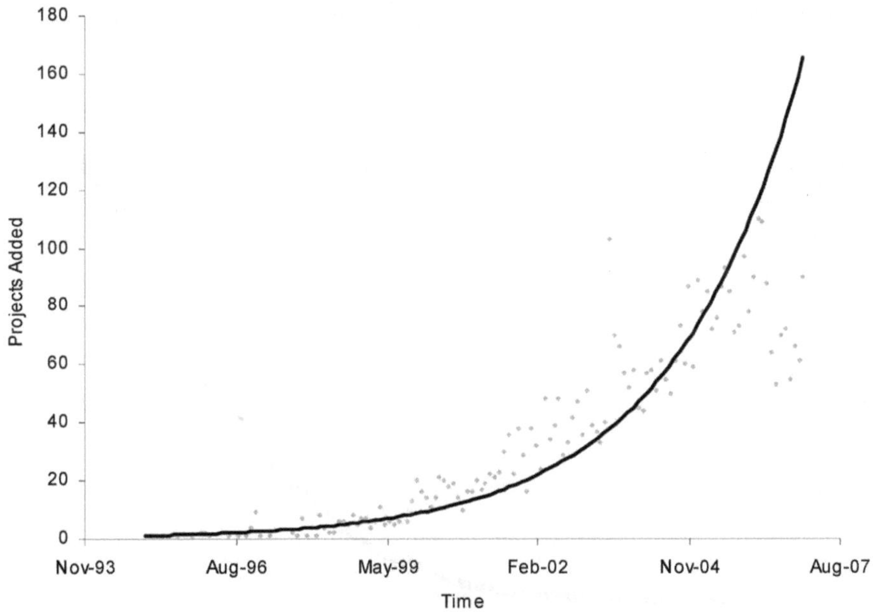

Fig. 4. Graph of number of open source projects added

Large distributions like Debian are counted as one project. Popular projects such as GNU Emacs are counted as projects of their own, little known or obsolete packages such as the Zoo archive utility are ignored. Many of the projects that were included in a Debian distribution around 1998 are not popular enough today (as stand-alone projects) to be included in our copy of the Ohloh database.

And again, we get the best fit for the resulting curve for an exponential model with an R-square value of 0.88.

Table 3. Model of number of open source projects added

Model	R-square value
$y = 1.0641e^{0.035x}$	0.884
where, y: Total number of open source projects x: Time from Jan 1995 to Dec 2006 in months	

Figure 5 then shows the total number of projects and Table 4 shows the corresponding model and its fit with the data. Again, we get the best fit for an exponential model with an R-square value of 0.96. The doubling time is 13.9 months.

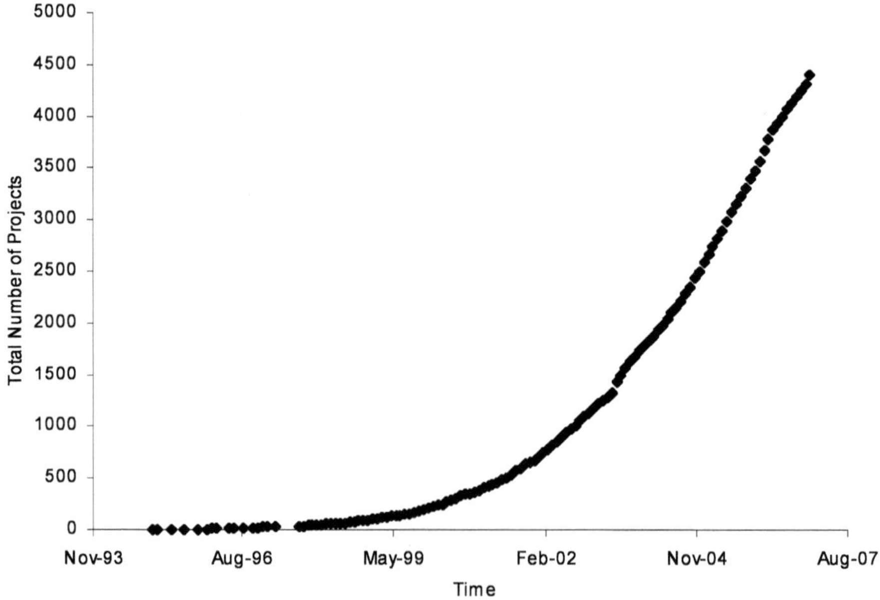

Fig. 5. Graph of total number of open source projects

Table 4. Model of total number of open source projects

Model	R-square value
$y = 7.1511e^{0.0499x}$	0.956
where, y: Total number of open source projects x: Time from Jan 1995 to Dec 2006 in months	

4.3 Review of findings

This section shows the growth of source code in open source projects as well as the growth of open source projects itself. We consistently get the best fit for the data using exponential models. The doubling time based on the exponential models is about 14 months for both the total amount of source code and the total number of projects. It should be noted that if we were to break up the data sets into separate time periods, we might find better fits for other models than the exponential model. In future work we will analyze the overall growth in distinct phases, each of which is best explained by a separate growth model.

In [13] we discuss the size and frequency of code contributions to open source projects. We can use those results to further increase our confidence in the results presented above. Specifically, the lines of code added can be assumed equal to the product of the average size of a commit in terms of source lines of code and the commit frequency. Our analysis shows that the average commit size is almost constant while the commit frequency (number of commits per week) increases exponentially between Jan 1995 to Dec 2006. This verifies our findings about the exponential growth in open source.

5 Limitations of Analysis

The quantitative analysis and the conclusions we draw have the following shortcomings and limitations.

- *Sample size.* We considered 5122 active and popular open source projects. The total number of open source projects in the world is much larger. However, Daffara estimates that of the total number only 18,000 projects (lower bound) are actually active [3]. So we believe that the sample we are using is relevant for analyzing trends and patterns in open source growth.
- *Data incompleteness.* Some amount of revision control information in open source projects has already been lost forever, as projects have moved on from no configuration management (CM) to CM with CVS and on to other CM tools, frequently dropping the history with each move. Thus, the project

history for each project is not always complete. However, for a current project, we have the most recent history, which is what is most relevant for our analysis. Thus, the lack of some of the early histories of some of the open source projects has little effect on the validity of our conclusions.

- *Project source.* A current limitation of Ohloh is that it only connects to CVS, Subversion and Git source code repositories. We believe that this limitation is not a big issue for our purposes because almost all open source projects are maintained in one of these repositories and our sample size can be considered representative.
- *Copy and paste.* Our approach to eliminating copy and paste issues (Approach 2) is limited in its effectiveness: The filter excludes a lot of good values while still allowing minor copy and paste to pass. For the purposes of our analysis, however, it is not a major issue, because we are interested in the overall trend, and even the conservative Approach 2 still validates our hypothesis of exponential growth.

We are continuing our work to iron out possible pitfalls based on these limitations. However, we believe that while the respective critiques can be made, the effects are rather limited, as argued above in each case.

6 Related Work

Several studies of the evolution of open source projects have been undertaken.

- González-Barahona *et al.* estimated the lines of code in the Debian 2.0 release and concluded that the system represents an effort of more than 14,000 person-years, which translates to about 2 billion USD [6].
- Succi *et al.* showed a linear growth rate for the GCC and Apache projects. They also showed that Linux has super linear growth [18]. They found that Linux (in 2000) violates Lehman's fourth law of software evolution.
- In contrast to this, Roy and Cordy examined the evolution of the Barcode Library and the zlib project and showed that these two smaller projects follow Lehman's laws of software evolution [16].
- Godfrey and Tu showed a super-linear increase in source lines of code over time in the Linux kernel and the VIM text editor [5].
- Robles *et al.* confirmed that the Linux kernel is growing super-linearly [15]. The NetBSD, FreeBSD, OpenBSD (until 2001) and 18 other projects showed an almost linear growth pattern.
- Koch's study of 4047 open source projects on SourceForge indicates that a quadratic growth model fits the growth of an individual project better than a linear growth model [8] [20].

- Scacchi reviews prior results on open source evolution, suggesting that the growth patterns for large open source projects are not representative for all of open source [22]. His discussion of the evolution of open source software suggests that Lehman's laws of software evolution based on closed-source systems do not apply to open source, and that further study is needed.

Most of the research listed above explores the evolution of individual projects. The growth models of projects are typically linear or quadratic. None of the related work quantitatively analyzes the total growth of open source software.

Our analysis does not focus on any particular project but on the general trend in open source software. The projects considered are independent of any particular license, language, topic or size.

7 Conclusion

The significance of open source has been continuously increasing over time. Our research validates this claim by looking at the total growth of open source. Our work shows that the additions to open source projects, the total project size (measured in source lines of code), the number of new open source projects, and the total number of open source projects are growing at an exponential rate. The total amount of source code and the total number of projects double about every 14 months.

Our results open gates for further research around the growth of open source and the acceptance of open source in industry and government. Future research should explore questions like what factors are influencing this exponential growth, how source code growth relates to the number of engaged software developers, and whether or how long open source can sustain this exponential growth.

Acknowledgments

We would like to thank Prem Devanbu and Gregorio Robles for their feedback on earlier versions of the paper as well as their encouragement for the work presented. We also would like to thank Oliver Arafat and Mario Fernandez for proofreading the paper.

References

[1] Comino, S, Manenti, F.M., Parisi, M. L. *From Planning to Mature: On the Determinants of Open Source Take Off.* Department of Economics Working Papers 0517, Department of Economics, University of Trento, Italia. 2005.

[2] Crowston, K. and Scozzi, B. Open Source Software Projects as Virtual Organizations: Competency Rallying for Software Development. *IEE Proceedings---Software Engineering,* vol. 149, no. 1, 2002: 3-17.

[3] Daffara, C. How Many Stable and Active Libre Software Projects? Retrieved on Sept 13, 2007, from http://flossmetrics.org/news/11.
[4] Software & Information Industry Association. *Packaged Software Industry Revenue and Growth, 2006.* Available from http://siia.net/software/
[5] Godfrey, M., Tu, M. Growth, Evolution, and Structural Change in Open Source Software. In *Proceedings of the 4th International Workshop on Principles of Software Evolution.* ACM Press, 2001: 103-106.
[6] González-Barahona, J., Ortuño Pérez, M., de las Heras Quirós, P., Centeno González, J., Matellán Olivera, V. Counting potatoes: The Size of Debian 2.2. Retrieved on Sept 13, 2007, from http://people.debian.org/~jgb/debian-counting/counting-potatoes/.
[7] Haruvy, E., Wu F. and Chakravarty S. Incentives for Developers' Contributions and Product Performance Metric in Open Source Development: An Empirical Exploration. University of Texas Working Paper.
[8] Koch, S. Evolution of Open Source Software Systems---A Large-Scale Investigation. In *Proceedings of the 1st International Conference on Open Source Systems* (OSS 2005).
[9] Lawton, M., Notarfonzo, R. Worldwide Open Source Software Business Models 2007–2011 Forecast: A Preliminary View. IDC Inc.
[10] Netcraft. Netcraft Web Server Survey. Netcraft, 2007. Retrieved on Sept 13, 2007, from http://survey.netcraft.com/Reports/200708/byserver/.
[11] Ohloh Corporation. See http://www.ohloh.net.
[12] Raymond, E. S. The Cathedral and the Bazaar. O'Reilly & Associates, 1999.
[13] Deshpande, A. Riehle, D. Continuous Integration in Open Source Software Projects. Submitted to the *4th International Conference on Open Source Systems* (OSS 2008).
[14] Robles, G., Gonzalez-Barahona, J. M., Michlmayr, M., and Amor, J. J. Mining Large Software Compilations Over Time: Another Perspective of Software Evolution. In *Proceedings of the 2006 International Workshop on Mining Software Repositories* (MSR 2006). ACM Press, 2006: 3-9.
[15] Robles, G., Amor, J. J., Gonzalez-Barahona, J. M., and Herraiz, I. Evolution and Growth in Large Libre Software Projects. In *Proceedings of the Eighth International Workshop on Principles of Software Evolution* (IWPSE 2005). IEEE Computer Society, 2005: 165-174.
[16] Roy, C. K. and Cordy, J. R. Evaluating the Evolution of Small Scale Open Source Software Systems. See http://citeseer.ist.psu.edu/761885.html.
[17] SourceForge. See http://www.sourceforge.net.
[18] Succi, G., Paulson, J., Eberlein, A. Preliminary Results From an Empirical Study on the Growth of Open Source and Commercial Software Products. In *EDSER-3 Workshop* (2001): 14-15.
[19] Walli, S., Gynn, D., Rotz, B. V. The Growth of Open Source Software in Organizations: A Report. Retrieved on Sept 13, 2007, from http://optaros.com/en/publications/white_papers_reports/the_growth_of_open_source_software_in_organizations.

[20] Koch, S. Software Evolution in Open Source Projects–A Large-Scale Investigation. In *Journal of Software Maintenance and Evolution: Research and Practice* 2007; 19: 361-382.

[21] Karim, R., Lakhani, R.G. Wolf. Why Hackers Do What They Do: Understanding Motivation and Effort in Free/Open Source Software Projects. In *Perspectives on Free and Open Source Software.* MIT Press, 2005: 3-22.

[22] Walt Scacchi. Understanding Open Source Software Evolution. In *Software Evolution and Feedback.* John Wiley & Sons, 2006.

Adoption of Open Source in the Software Industry

Øyvind Hauge, Carl-Fredrik Sørensen, and Reidar Conradi
Norwegian University of Science and Technology
{oyvind.hauge|carl.fredrik.sorensen|reidar.conradi}@idi.ntnu.no

Abstract. Is Open Source Software (OSS) undergoing a transformation to a more commercially viable form? We have performed a survey to investigate the adoption of OSS in the Norwegian software industry. The survey was based on an extensive screening of software companies, with more than 700 responses. The survey results support the transformation predicted by Fitzgerald [4]. Close to 50% of the software industry integrate OSS components into vertical solutions serving all major business sectors. In addition, more than 30% of the 95 respondents in our survey have more than 40% of their income from OSS related services or software. The extensive adoption of OSS in the software industry may be a precursor of the OSS adoption in other business sectors.

1 Introduction

Open source software (OSS) is predicted to transform "into a more mainstream and commercially viable form" [4], where companies play an increasingly more important role. A premise for this transformation is increased commercial participation in the development of OSS products and increased use of OSS in vertical domains. However, only a few surveys provide empirical findings which support this assumed transformation, and most of these focus on the use of desktop tools and horizontal infrastructures like the LAMP stack. Is really OSS undergoing a transformation?

To answer this question we have performed a large scale survey in the Norwegian software industry. Our analysis shows that close to 50% of the software industry integrate OSS components into vertical solutions targeting customers from all major business sectors. In addition, more than 30% of the respondents in our survey have more than 40% of their income from OSS related services or software.

Our results show that the adoption of OSS in the Norwegian software industry is significant. The industry's contribution to the OSS community is however limited. Nevertheless, it is reason to believe that OSS is actually undergoing a transformation into a more commercially viable form. The use of OSS in the software industry may eventually influence the rest of the market when software companies integrate OSS into their products. However, a lack of software companies adopting OSS may hamper the adoption of OSS in other sectors [15].

Please use the following format when citing this chapter:

Hauge, Ø., Sørensen, C.-F. and Conradi, R., 2008, in IFIP International Federation for Information Processing, Volume 275; *Open Source Development, Communities and Quality*; Barbara Russo, Ernesto Damiani, Scott Hissam, Björn Lundell, Giancarlo Succi; (Boston: Springer), pp. 211–221.

2 Related Work

Estimating the market share of OSS is a comprehensive task. Nevertheless, several attempts have been made e.g. [5, 6, and 18]. Common to most of these is their focus on a few products like the LAMP stack and end-user applications like mail or office tools. One example is the Netcraft[1] survey of web servers on the Internet. While several consultancy companies have attempted to estimate the adoption of OSS, we rather focus on research published through academic channels.

Without providing any numbers, Glynn et al. conclude that OSS has had significant penetration in the software/consultancy and service/communication sector, but that it is more limited in the government/public sector [7]. Studies from the UK [17], Finland [15], and the U.S. [16] report only limited OSS adoption in the public sector with Linux as the only exception. Linux was used by more than 50% of the respondents in both the study from Finland and the U.S. Together with the other elements of the LAMP stack, Linux is quite frequently used in other sectors as well [6]. How-ever, this adoption varies from country to country, on company size, and between sectors. For a mixed sample from industry and public sector, the use or planned use is reported to be as low as 17.7% in Sweden and as high as 43.7% in Germany [6]. Furthermore, numbers vary between about 10% and 75% for different strata [6]. A survey on Australia's top companies reports that 26% of the respondents used a varied spectrum of OSS products [8]. With the exception of Linux, Apache HTTP Server and perhaps a few others, most surveys report that less than 30% of the respondents have adopted OSS. Yet, little is known about the extent of the internal adoption of OSS in these companies.

In studies focusing on the software sector, 44% of the companies in a Finnish sample use OSS in their business [13] and in a study on Off-the-Shelf development, 44 or 38.3% of the 115 projects use OSS components [11]. Without being able to provide any numbers representative for the whole population, an Italian study found that software companies using OSS commonly adapt or build on top of these OSS products [1].

The transformation predicted by Fitzgerald involves company participation in the development of OSS products [4]. Companies are already known to be contributing by allowing employees spend their time at work participating in OSS projects [10]. Companies are among others involved in 97 of the 300 most active SourceForge projects [2]. However, this is most likely not representative for all of SourceForge's more than 170 000 projects. A Swedish survey also found that several companies actively contribute to OSS projects [12].

We see that companies and organizations have adopted OSS and that they are involved in the development of OSS. There are however only a limited number of empirical findings which show the extent of this adoption and the demography of these companies. This paper will provide results which quantifies the adoption of OSS components in the Norwegian software industry.

[1] http://news.netcraft.com/

3 Survey Method

The purpose of the study was to investigate to what extent the Norwegian software industry approaches OSS development. As an expansion of [9], we carried out a nationwide survey to investigate this matter.

3.1 Population: The Norwegian Software Industry

Legal entities in Norway are registered in The Norwegian Central Coordinating Register for Legal Entities[2] (CCRLE) with a Nomenclature Generale des Activites Economiques dans L'Union Europee (NACE) code. Based on 2005 data from CCRLE and other registers, Statistics Norway[3] (SSB) reports that about 70 000 employees, or 4.7 % of all employees in Norway, are employed in the whole ICT sector [14]. In addition, the sector has a turnover of about €22 billion [14].

Table 1. The Norwegian 72.xx sector based on data from CCRLE 2007

Sub sector	NACE	Entities
Computer and related activities	72.00	26105
Hardware consultancy	72.10	251
Software consultancy and supply	72.20	21559
- Publishing of software (software houses: resale)	72.21	1295
- Other software consultancy and supply (single sale)	72.22	20264
Data processing	72.30	489
Database activities	72.40	2916
Maintenance & repair: office, accounting and comp. machinery	72.50	733
Other computer related activities	72.60	163

The ICT sector in Norway includes telecommunication (64.20), ICT manufacture industry (32.xx), ICT wholesale and retail trade (51.8x), and the soft- and hardware sector (72.xx). Based on CCRLE data from 2007, we found that approximately 26 000 legal entities and 38 500 employees constitute the soft- and hardware sector, see Table 1. This gives an average company size of about 1.5 employees. According to SSB only about 13 000 of these legal entities are active companies. More than 70% of these have less than one full time employee and about 1300 have five or more employees [14]. We will in this paper focus on the software sector (72.2x).

[2] http://www.brreg.no/

[3] The Norwegian counterpart to the U.S. Census Bureau http://www.ssb.no/

3.2 The Sampling Process

Data from CCRLE helped us constructing a close-to representative sample of software companies [3], with a focus on software (72.21) and consultancy (72.22) companies with more than five employees. However, the sample also included companies from the other 72.xx sub-sectors and companies with fewer than five employees. The purpose of the sampling process illustrated in Fig. 1 was twofold. First, estimate the share of companies integrating OSS components into their products. Second, create a sample for our survey consisting of companies using OSS components.

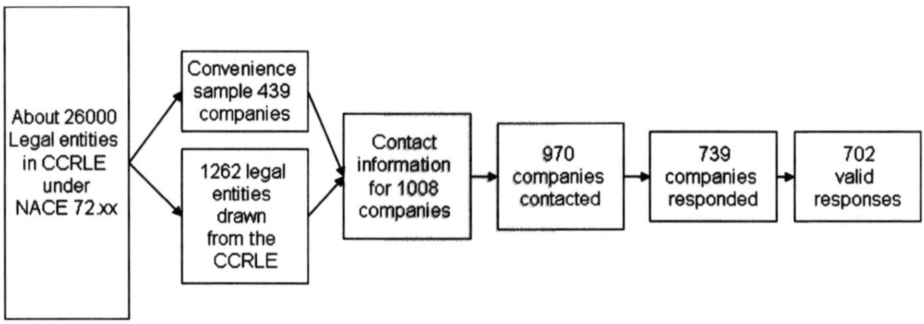

Fig. 1. The sampling process

Step 1: The sample was constructed based on a convenience sample of 439 companies and a stratified random sample of 1262 legal entities from CCRLE. The convenience sample was based on stratified random samples two from earlier studies and supplemented with companies from our knowledge and companies appearing in the media. The strata were defined according to the business organization form, the 72.xx sub-sectors, and the number of employees.

Step 2: Then, the two lists were merged. 300 duplicates entries were removed during this merger. Several companies occurred in both samples and some companies were registered with more than one legal entity, typically larger companies. We used data from CCRLE and the Internet to find web-sites and email addresses for the companies. Another 395 or 31.3 % of the 1262 randomly selected legal entities were removed from the list because no contact information could be found. Knowing that only about 50% of the companies in the sector were active, this was not a surprise. The vast majority of these companies were small and most likely inactive companies. The final list contained contact information for 1008 companies from the Norwegian software industry.

Step 3: The screening process was carried out by sending the companies a brief request on email containing the questions stated below. About 200 of the companies from the convenience sample were contacted in March 2007 and the rest in June/July. One reminder was sent by email in September. The 200 companies contacted in March were only asked the first three questions while the remaining companies were asked all four questions.

1. How many employees do you have in Norway?
2. Are you doing software development in Norway?
3. Do you use open source components in your products or services (other than Linux, Apache HTTP Server, Eclipse, PHP/Perl, MySQL etc.)?
4. Do you participate in or run any open source projects?

38 of the 1008 email addresses did not work, leaving 970 companies. 201 of these companies came from the convenience sample, 555 from the stratified random sample, and 236 companies were included in both samples. 739 companies replied which give us a response rate of 73.3%. 32 companies responded that their company was inactive or about to be dissolved, one company did not want to participate, and another four duplicate legal entities were found, leaving 702 or 69.6% valid responses. The response rates were similar across most of the different strata (size and sector). The names of the respondents and their email addresses were stored together with the other contact information.

Step 4: 569 or 81.1% of the 702 companies in our screening process confirmed that they perform software development. These companies make the basis for further analysis. The percentage of companies involved in software development is similar across different size and business types. However, when looking at sectors, the percentage varies from 73.6% (72.40 Database activities) to 90.2% (72.20 Publishing of software).

3.3 The Survey Process

Close to 50% of the 569 companies constituting our sample integrate OSS components into their products. 204 of these companies were invited to participate in a web survey. The survey contained three parts focusing on (1) development of a commercial OSS product, (2) integration of OSS components into a software product, and (3) demographic information. The respondents should answer based on their experiences with the development of a typical software product containing OSS components. This product was selected by respondents and we had no control over this selection. To learn more about the companies and to increase the response rates, every second company ordered by size was contacted by phone. The companies were asked if they could participate and were sent an email with instructions if they accepted our invitation. The other half was invited to participate through email. One reminder was sent by email about a month later. 12 or 5.9% of the 204 companies could not or did not want to participate. Nevertheless, 95 of the 204 companies or 46.6% completed the survey. Of these 95, 21 were only involved in software development without directly developing software products, for instance consultancy companies providing developers to external customers. This left 74 or 36.3% valid responses for the two main parts.

4 Results

This section presents results from both the screening process and from the survey.

4.1 Selection and Integration of OSS Components

Out of the 569 companies constituting our sample, 266 or 46.9% integrate OSS components into their software solutions. This use goes beyond merely using OSS operating systems, databases, infrastructure, development tools, and programming languages. The companies actually find, evaluate, and integrate OSS components into their software solutions. The integration of OSS components happens less frequently in software houses. Only 34.1% of the companies registered in sector 72.21, use OSS components in their products, see Table 2.

Table 2. Adoption of OSS components distributed over sectors

Sector	Sample Size	OSS Adoption
72.21 Publishing of software	129	34.1%
72.22 Other software consultancy and supply	328	51.5%
72.30 Data processing	18	38.9%
72.40 Database activities	39	53.8%
Other	55	47.3%

From Table 3 we see that large companies integrate OSS components more often into their products than smaller companies. 56.9% of the companies with more than 100 employees use OSS and 50.0% of the companies with 25 to 99 employees integrate OSS components into their products compared to around 43% of the companies with between 2 and 24 employees. Companies with one or less than one full time employee, use OSS components somewhat more frequently.

Table 3. Adoption of OSS components distributed over the number of employees

Number of employees	Sample Size	OSS Adoption
0 to 1	33	48.5%
2 to 4	61	42.6%
5 to 9	80	43.8%
10 to 24	189	43.9%
25 to 99	146	50.0%
More than 100	58	56.9%

66 companies completed the second part of the survey based on their experiences from the development of a software product containing OSS component. The products delivered by these companies serve all main business sectors with a small

emphasis on the public and health sector. The functionality of these products was directed mainly towards web/portals and enterprise solutions. The respondents classified 40.9% of the products as domain specific and 36.4% as differentiating end-user products.

Even though OSS components can reduce the development effort substantially, they are in most cases integrated as part of a larger solution. In 72.7% of the products, OSS components provide less than 40% of the functionality of the end product. The number of OSS components is also kept low. 68.2% of the products contain less than six OSS components and 83.3% contain less than eleven OSS components. The effort spent developing these products during the last year, range from less than one (1) person-month to between 101 and 500 person-months.

4.2 OSS Related Activities

During the last year, 75.8% of the companies have developed between one and three software products containing OSS components. In one extreme case, one company had developed more than 50 products containing OSS components. In Part 3 of the survey, we requested the respondent to estimate how much of the company's income is generated by OSS related services or software development, see Table 4. Even though 41 of the 95 respondents answered less than 20% and 22 answered "don't know", 29 or 30.5% answered that more than 40% of their income comes from OSS related services or software.

Table 4. Income from OSS related services and software development

Income from OSS	Number of companies
NA/Don't know	22
0%	8
1-20%	33
21-40%	3
41-60%	7
61-80%	9
81-99%	6
100 %	7

4.3 Participation in OSS Projects

In total 368 of the 569 companies developing software responded to the fourth screening question. 60 or 16.3% of the respondents said that employees in their company participated in OSS projects. This participation was in some cases part of their job and in other more a hobby. Another 18 or 4.9% of the 368 companies said they have their own OSS project. However, through the researchers' previous experience with some of these companies we would say that the OSS projects are only an important part of the business for a few of them.

30 of the 66 companies completing Part 2 of the survey answered that they interacted with or participated in OSS projects during the development of their product. This interaction and participation was in all but three cases not organized through the company but rather left up to the individual developer.

5 Discussion

The use of OSS in Norwegian software industry is significant. Close to 50% of the companies developing software have integrated OSS components into one or more of their products and more than 30% of the respondents to our survey get over 40% of their income from OSS related services or software. The use of OSS in software houses (72.21) living of the sales of software licenses is somewhat lower than in other software sectors. This could be caused by reciprocal OSS licenses (e.g. GPL) which requires derivate products to be released under the same license, thus removing the software houses profits from sales of licenses. Another conceivable explanation is that companies focusing on development of their own software products are involved in the development of fewer products per year than consulting companies serving several different customers.

The products developed by the respondents served all major business sectors and 77.3% of them were classified as domain specific or differentiating end-user products. Thus, we can conclude that OSS is used in vertical products targeting all business sectors.

We observed increasing OSS use in relation to increasing company size. However, Lundell et al. observed that companies with more than 250 employees seemed more conservative towards OSS adoption [12], Bonaccorsi et al. found that size does not favor OSS adoption [1], and Ghosh et al. found variations in the adoption of OSS over company size, countries, and sectors [6]. The relation between size and OSS adoption needs to be investigated in future research. However, we see two possible explanations for this increased use of OSS. First, small companies commonly focus on a limited number of customers and specialize on a small set of different technologies. Several such companies replied that they were not using OSS because they focused only on one not-OSS-compatible technology. While large companies, often serve many customers using several different technologies, including OSS. Second, large companies hire more people. Because they hire more people it is more likely that they employ people with prior experiences with OSS.

Comparing the results from this survey with other results is a bit complicated. First, the number of related studies is fairly limited. Second, while we focused on integration of OSS components, most studies include all kinds of OSS products. Third, other studies focus on other sectors than the software sector. The 46.9% adoption of OSS components in the software sector is therefore lower than some of the extreme results in [5, 6]. If our survey had included all kinds of OSS, we suspect the percent-age of OSS users to be significantly higher. On the other hand, our results are in line with the results from [13] where 44% of the software companies used OSS in their business.

Generalization to other countries is made somewhat more difficult because of the variations found in other studies [6]. There are also factors which influence the adoption of OSS in the Norwegian software sector. While the effects of these factors must be further examined, we believe the size of the companies, influence the OSS adoption. Most software companies in Norway are small or medium sized. Many have relatively few and mostly domestic customers, and they have also chosen to focus on a limited set of technologies. In addition, the Norwegian government has the last years increased its focus on open standards and OSS through public reports and the establishment of a national centre of expertise of OSS. Furthermore, there seems to be a push in Norway towards increased use of agile methods. While using such methods it is important to get something up and running as fast as possible. This and the fact that the cost of personnel in Norway is quite high may encourage higher re-use of code and components, including OSS.

Industrial participation in OSS projects seems limited and managed on an individual level. Only 16% of the software companies confirm that they do participate in the development of one or more external OSS products. This number has however some uncertainty. First, 200 of the companies in the screening process were not asked whether they participated in any OSS projects. Second, there is some confusion about what participation is. Some companies answered "we do not participate but we report bugs and share occasional bug fixes" while others answered "we do participate with some bug reports and bug fixes". However, we interpreted both these statements as participation. Third, participation in OSS projects is in most cases managed on a personal level. Knowing what all other employees are doing is difficult if not impossible for the respondents in our screening process and the number of companies participating in OSS projects could therefore be higher.

The sample has an intentional bias towards companies with more than five employees. This bias was reinforced by the fact that we were unable to find contact in-formation for several small and probably inactive companies. The majority of companies without a web site are most likely inactive since nowadays the Web is considered the most important communication channel. To aid the sampling we benefited from CCRLE and the NACE sector codes. While this classification was of great help, the software industry is an industry with rapid and frequent changes. As a consequence of these changes, central registers such as CCREL are not up-to-date at all times. For example, only about 90% of the companies under 72.20 "Publishing of software" actually develop software.

Response rates of 73.3% for the screening process and 36.3% valid responses in the main survey is decent compared to many other studies but low response rates is one of the challenges with survey research. Even though there is room for improvement, we have been able to get responses from a large and close to representative sample of the Norwegian software industry. The research design is well documented and replicating the survey in another setting should be easy, though labor-intensive.

6 Conclusion

Results from our study show limited company involvement in the development of OSS products but widespread use of OSS components. By integrating OSS into vertical products serving all major business sectors, the software industry will contribute to wider adoption of OSS. The software industry has clearly started to adopt OSS products and contribute to the transformation of OSS into a commercially viable form. However, this transformation is far from completed.

The results presented here are currently followed up in several ways. In parallel to this survey, we have also approached OSS adoption through qualitative studies. Data from both the survey and these qualitative studies is currently being analyzed. Findings from these analyses will provide a basis for further research. This survey focuses on the Norwegian software sector, which is dominated by small and medium sized companies. The adoption of OSS may be different in other sectors and in other countries. We are therefore looking at the possibilities of conducting similar surveys in both other sectors and European countries. To understand the trend of OSS adoption, we are also considering a replication of the survey in Norway. Furthermore, the survey identified a few companies developing their own OSS products. We plan to follow up on these companies to try to understand if they manage to attract and sustain communities and how they interact with these communities.

References

1. Andrea Bonaccorsi, Silvia Giannangeli, and Cristina Rossi. Entry Strategies under Competing Standards: Hybrid Business Models in the Open Source Software Industry. Management Sci-ence, 52(7):1085-1098, July 2006.
2. Andrea Bonaccorsi, Dario Lorenzi, Monica Merito, and Cristina Rossi. Business Firms' Engage-ment in Community Projects. Empirical Evidence and Further Developments of the Research. In Proceedings of the First International Workshop on Emerging Trends in FLOSS Research and Development FLOSS'07, page 13, Minneapolis, US, 2007. IEEE Computer Society.
3. Reidar Conradi, Jingyue Li, Odd Petter N. Slyngstad, Vigdis By Kampenes, Christian Bunse, Maurizio Morisio, and Marco Torchiano. Reflections on Conducting an International Survey of Software Engineering. In June Verner and Guilherme H. Travassos, editors, Proceedings on In-ternational Symposium on Empirical Software Engineering ISESE'05, pages 214-223, Brisbane, Australia, 2005.
4. Brian Fitzgerald. The Transformation of Open Source Software. MIS Quarterly, 30(3), 2006.

5. Rishab Aiyer Ghosh. Study on the Economic Impact of Open Source Software on Innovation and the Competiveness of the Information and Communication Technologies (ICT) Sector in the EU. Technical report, UNU-MERIT, 2006.
6. Rishab Aiyer Ghosh, Gregorio Robles, and Ruediger Glott. Free Libre and Open Source Soft-ware: Survey and Study. Technical report, International Institute of Infonomics, University of Maastricht, 2002.
7. Eugene Glynn, Brian Fitzgerald, and Chris Exton. Commercial Adoption of Open Source Soft-ware: An Empirical Study. In Proceedings of International Conference on Empirical Software Engineering, pages 225-234, Noosa Heads, Australia, 2005.
8. Sigi Goode. Something for Nothing: Management Rejection of Open Source Software in Austra-lia's Top Firms. Information & Management, 42(5):669-681, 2005.
9. Ø¬yvind Hauge, Carl-Fredrik Sørensen, and Andreas Røsdal. Surveying Industrial Roles in Open Source Software Development. In Joseph Feller, Brian Fitzgerald, Walt Scacchi, and Alberto Sillitti, editors, Proceedings on the Third International Conference on Open Source Systems, pages 259-264, Limerick, Ireland, 2007. Springer.
10. Karim R. Lakhani and Robert G. Wolf. Why Hackers Do What They Do: Understanding Moti-vations and Effort in Free/Open Source Software Projects. In Joseph Feller, Brian Fitzgerald, Scott A. Hissam, and Karim R. Lakhani, editors, Perspectives on Free and Open Source Soft-ware, pages 3-23. MIT Press, 2005.
11. Jingyue Li, Reidar Conradi, Odd Petter N. Slyngstad, Christian Bunse, Umair Khan, Marco Torchiano, and Maurizio Morisio. An Empirical Study on Off-the-Shelf Component Usage in Industrial Projects. In Frank Bomarius and Seija Komi-Sirvio, editors, Proceedings of the 6th In-ternational Conference on Product Focused Software Process Improvement PROFES'2005, pages 54-68. Springer, 2005.
12. Björn Lundell, Brian Lings, and Edvin Lindqvist. Perceptions and Uptake of Open Source in Swedish Organisations. In Ernesto Damiani, Brian Fitzgerald, Walt Scacchi, Marco Scotto, and Giancarlo Succi, editors, Proceedings of The Second International Conference on Open Source Systems, pages 155-163, Como, Italy, 2006. Springer.
13. Uolevi Nikula and Sami Jantunen. Quantifying the Interest in Open Source System: Case South-East Finland. In Marco Scotto and Giancarlo Succi, editors, OSS 2005: Proceedings of the First International Conference on Open Source Systems, 11-15 July 2005, Genova, Italy, pages 192-195, 2005.
14. SSB. StatBank Norway, 2007. http://statbank.ssb.no/statistikkbanken/, accessed 2007-08-01.
15. Mikko Välimäki, Ville Oksanen, and Juha Laine. An Empirical Look at the Problems of Open Source Adoption in Finnish Municipalities. In Proceedings of the 7th International Conference on Electronic Commerce ICEC'05, pages 514-520, Xi'an, China, 2005. ACM.
16. Shahron van Rooij. Open Source software in US higher education: Reality or illusion? Educa-tion and Information Technologies, 12(4):191-209, December 2007.
17. Teresa Waring and Philip Maddocks. Open Source Software implementation in the UK public sector: Evidence from the field and implications for the future. International Journal of Informa-tion Management, 25(5):411-428, October 2005.
18. David A. Wheeler. Why Open Source Software / Free Software (OSS/FS, FLOSS, or FOSS)? Look at the Numbers!. http://www.dwheeler.com/oss_fs_why.html, accessed 2007-12-09.

[illegible]

Migration Discourse Structures: Escaping Microsoft's Desktop Path

Leonhard Dobusch
Free University Berlin – School for Business & Economics,
Garystr. 21, 14195 Berlin,
leonhard.dobusch@wiwiss.fu-berlin.de
WWW home page: http://www.pfadkolleg.de

Abstract. Most studies of FOSS organizational migration projects focus solely on technological and economical aspects, neglecting the importance of organizational discourse structures for migration decisions as well as success. In looking at the case of the municipality of Munich this paper uses structuration theory in combination with discourse analysis to explain why and how in this case actors were able to overcome strong barriers to migration in the field of desktop software.

Keywords: Open Source Software; Path Dependency; Technology Adoption; Structuration Theory; Discourse Analysis

1 Introduction

Of all recent examples of organizations switching their software environment to Free/Open Source Software (FOSS) the municipality of Munich in Germany received significant attention, at least in the media. The reasons for this are the following:

- Munich decided to migrate the whole desktop software environment including operating system and office suite to FOSS – not only server software or office suits as had done many organizations before.
- With approximately 14.000 desktops the municipality in Munich is by far larger than other municipal predecessors such as for example Schwäbisch-Hall with about 225 desktop PCs [19].
- Only few weeks before the migration decision in May 2003 Microsoft's CEO Steven Ballmer met with Munich's mayor Ude to convince him not to do so and failed.

But aside these aspects the migration decision and process in Munich is also a critical case [34] for studying why and how organizations take the lead in adopting a minority system in markets with strong network effects, often referred to as "path

Please use the following format when citing this chapter:

Dobusch, L., 2008, in IFIP International Federation for Information Processing, Volume 275; *Open Source Development, Communities and Quality*; Barbara Russo, Ernesto Damiani, Scott Hissam, Björn Lundell, Giancarlo Succi; (Boston: Springer), pp. 223–235.

dependent" [6, 3][1] . Whereas many studies of FOSS adoption, especially in the domain of information systems, focus on technical implementation and migration issues (e.g. [22]) and do not distinguish between desktop and server usage (e.g. [1]), the organizational processes associated with these migrations are often overlooked or underrated.

In combining structuration theory [12, 20, 21, 24] with concepts of discourse analysis [14, 4, 5] this paper tries to conceptualize why and how organizations take the lead in escaping Microsoft's desktop software path.

2 FOSS Adoption as a Case of Path Breaking

2.1 Path dependency in software markets

Following Shapiro and Varian [23] as well as Varian et al. [29] there are several mechanisms in software markets such as network effects, investment and learning spirals or complementarity (see Table 1) that differentiate them from "classic markets". All these mechanisms are recursively self-reinforcing and thus increase switching costs of individual adopters over time, making a migration to FOSS an expensive and laborious task. Following David's [6, 7] notion of path dependency, Microsoft's monopoly position in the market for desktop operating systems and office suites doesn't prevail because of the superiority of its products but because of their customer's lock-in on them.

Table 1. Selection of mechanisms leading to switching costs in desktop software markets

Mechanism	Example
Direct and indirect network effects	The larger the installed base of a piece of software, the greater the benefits (also for the individual actor) of adopting it. [10]
Investment and learning spirals	Investments into a specific piece of software lead to even more investments into the same, creating a growing stock of idiosyncratic assets. [33]
Complementarity	Two (or more) in principle autonomous mechanisms – e.g. software diversity and organizational decentralization – reinforce one another. [26]

However, the logic that leads to path dependency of (in particular: organizational) actors in software markets results from mutual and recursive interdependencies between technological and social structures. Orlikowski [20, 21] calls this the "duality of technology":

1 Shapiro and Varian [23] even call the market for desktop software „everyone's favourite example" for concepts like "lock-in" or "increasing returns".

The duality of technology identifies prior views of technology – as either objective force or as socially constructed product – as a false dichotomy. Technology is the product of human action, while it also assumes structural properties. That is, technology is physically constructed by actors working in a given social context, and technology is socially constructed by actors through the different meanings they attach to it and the various features they emphasize and use. [20:496]

In an organizational context the mechanisms described in Table 1 do not effect software adoption directly but are mediated through intra-organizational dynamics and structures. Stones' [24] "quadripartite" notion of structuration [12] was originally developed for the individual actor but seems to be applicable on the organizational level, as well (see Figure 1). The main point of structuration theory is to ac-knowledge the "duality at work in which agents and structures are not kept apart but in which they are mutually constitutive of one another" [24:21].

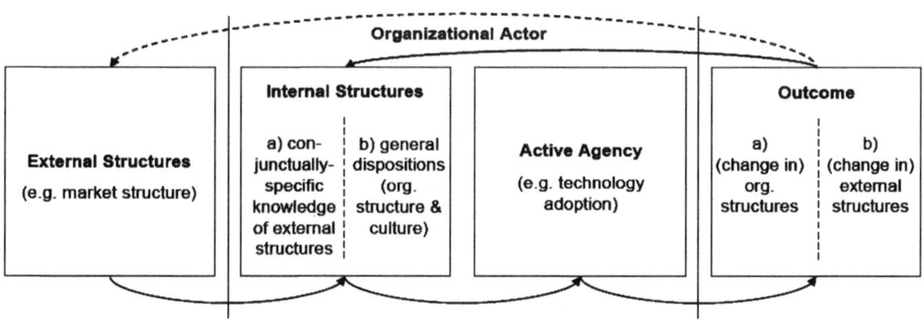

Fig. 1. Structuration model of technology adoption

2.2 Path breaking FOSS?

The reasons why there is still competition in the market for desktop PC operating systems lie in the idiosyncratic characteristics of recently developed FOSS alternatives such as GNU/Linux which differ in development process [31], license fees, access to source code, and strong competition among several suppliers in a way that is impossible to imitate for Microsoft if it wants to prolong its business model.[2] Nevertheless, the barriers to migration especially in the market for desktop operating systems – contrary to the server market – still seem to prevent Microsoft from serious competition in this field [13]. Especially large organizations hesitate to

[2] For an overview of the differences between Free/Open Source and proprietary software, see the anthology by [11].

switch their desktop software environment to alternatives provided by open source software competitors ([32], see Table 2), and still little is known why and how they do so.

Table 2. FOSS desktop usage in organizations in three countries (taken from Wichmann [32])

Size*	UK	Sweden	Germany
Small	7,6%	3,4%	13,7%
Large	2,0%	3,2%	6,5%

* < 500 employees = small; > 500 employees = large

What we do know, however, is that technological and economic reasons may not play a decisive role in the question whether to adopt FOSS or stay on the Microsoft path, as Varian and Shapiro ([30:12]; italics by L.D.) summarize their review of TCO comparisons in the literature:

> There have been several attempts to compare the TCO of Windows and of Linux in various computing environments. In most of the studies the difference in TCO is on the order of 10 or 15 percent. This difference is not large; a 10 percent difference in TCO could easily be swamped by local conditions, random events, and other considerations. To a first approximation, it seems reasonable to suppose that neither of these two platforms has a striking advantage over the other in terms of conventional measures of TCO.

So the question remains why and how do organizations then decide to migrate their desktop software environment to FOSS alternatives in spite of strong network effects? This paper suggests taking a look at the organizational migration discourse.

3 Method Section

3.1 Data collection

Following Yin [34:8], the unique strength of a case study is "its ability to deal with a full variety of evidence", including documents, artifacts, interviews, and observations. To live up to this potential and for triangulation reasons, over a two year period from 2006 to 2007 data was collected in form of open-ended interviews with actors on different organisational levels, transcripts of talks given at practitioner conferences, archival documents including the "Client Study" of Unilog Integrata (consulting firm, [28]) and media coverage. All data was integrated into a case study database (see Table 3) but only transcripts were included in the discourse analysis.

Table 3. Case Study database

transcripts	
interviews / persons	7 / 7
talks / persons	3 / 3
Σ transcripts / persons	10 / 9
per functional area (transcripts / persons):	
political administration	2 / 2
central IT	5 / 3
decentral IT	2 / 2
external*	2 / 2
media coverage (2001-2007)**	
articles (online / print)	68 / 34
archival documents	
sets of slides	11
agenda papers	31
miscellaneous	7

* "external" includes service provider and consultants
** articles from the following sources from 2002-2007 : Heise.de, Computerwoche, Frankfurter Allgemeine Zeitung, Frankfurter Rundschau, Süddeutsche Zeitung

3.2 Discourse analysis

In adopting the cyclical ideal of qualitative research [25], the data analysis was divided into three parts that were not undertaken in strict consecutiveness: Inductive generation of theoretical categories of both mechanisms enforcing and weakening path dependency is complemented with chronological process descriptions. These two parts are connected in a final theoretical integration, using archival documents and media coverage to cross-check interview data and for the right temporal ordering.

For categorization, the literally transcribed interviews and talks were reduced to 692 paraphrases as the basis for coding the data. Then, in multiple, consecutive rounds a system of coding categories was developed with focus on the meta-category "barriers and drivers for the adoption of an alternative (i.e. non-Microsoft) desktop operating system" [16, 18]. These inductively generated categories were then classified as predominantly covering "Framing" or "Program" aspects of the migration discourse – a dichotomy taken from Campbell's [4, 5:94] typology of ideas, which differentiates between the two as follows:

- Programs are "ideas as elite prescriptions that enable [...] the charting of a clear and specific course of action"
- Frames are "ideas as symbols and concepts that enable decision makers to legitimise programs to their constituents".

In integrating these categories in an organizational structuration model as it is presented in Figure 2, the translation of discourse into organizational technology adoption can be conceptualized.

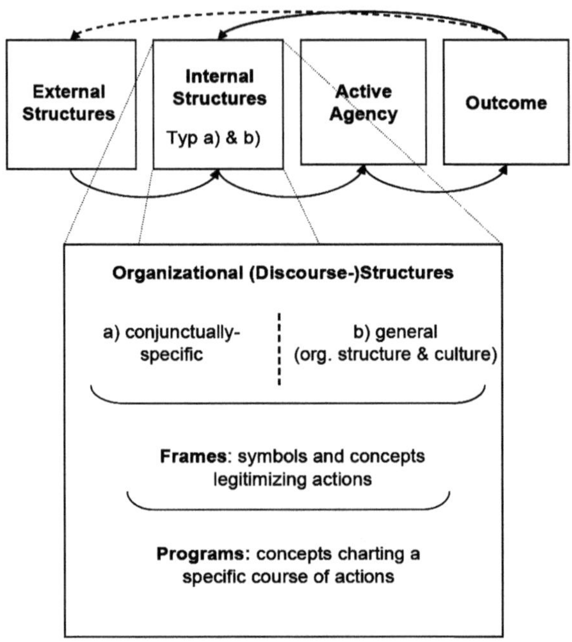

Fig. 2. Organizational discourse structures

4 Munich's Migration Process and Discourse

The following description of the FOSS migration process in Munich is a radically condensed version of a much more detailed narration provided in [8].

4.1 The process: emergence of radical change

One core concept of path dependency theory in a narrow sense[3] is that of "small events": A series of small, partially unrelated or even stochastic events sets in motion a self-reinforcing process that eventually leads from a contingent state at the

[3] "Narrow" is meant in the tradition of David [6] and Arthur [3] and compared to scholars using "path" and "path dependency" only as a metaphor for the truism that "history matters". For an extensive discussion, see Dobusch and Schüßler [9].

beginning to a state of ex-ante unpredictable lock-in [7, 26,].The case of Munich demonstrates that small events can also play a decisive role in the early stages of a path breaking process.

The politician – a private user of the proprietary "Ami Pro" – who set the ball rolling by suggesting the search for alternatives to Microsoft (MS) Office was only a backbencher ("Hinterbänkler") in the city council, which he left soon after his motion. The first reaction of the IT officials was an attempt to turn the whole issue done by a simple product comparison between MS Office and several alternatives (see Table 4).

Table 4. Product comparison prepared by the central IT department for the responsible council committee's meeting in Nov. 2001

Advantages	Disadvantages
StarOffice is Open Source Software	Re-working in existing documents necessary because of - partial lack of import/export - different macro languages - different object models
Lower purchase costs	New product line needs requires more training and, therefore, leads to higher training costs
End of dependence on Microsoft	There is no in-house training personnel
Cross platform applicability (StarOffice)	Insufficent online-help (StarOffice)
	StarOffice/SmartSuite data formats are mostly not suitable for data exchange. Documents would have to be handed on in MS Office or RTF format.
	The already deployed – and paid for – MS Office products would have to be replaced all over although they are often not even amortised (to ensure readability in internal data exchange)
	No mail-client (SmartSuite)

Dissatisfied with their IT official's analysis, the political members of the committee demanded a second, more in-depth evaluation with special focus on economic efficiency, also taking into consideration the desktop operating system, as Microsoft had already cancelled its support for the Windows version in use. The following expert's advice [28] then convinced the IT staff of the viability of a FOSS solution. When this result was presented to the council committee, the situation surprisingly was the opposite way round compared to autumn 2001, as one of the officials describes:

> "When, for the first time, we proposed Linux on the basis of the external study in autumn 2002 in the IT committee [...] we got a lot of stick ((laughs)) [...] and I thought we don't even need to continue, we slunk off with our tails between our legs."

At the same time, the results of the "Client Study" and its recommendation to migrate alerted Microsoft – up to the CEO level: In April 2003, Microsoft CEO Steven

Ballmer interrupted his holidays in Switzerland to visit Munich's mayor. But, again, an attempt to turn down the migration plan even strengthened the momentum behind it: The amount of media coverage skyrocketed, thus increasing pressure on politicians to resist to the monopolist's power. As another consequence of the increased public interest, many firms and other municipalities encouraged Munich's officials and politicians to stay on their way and offered knowledge exchange. Additionally, Microsoft's move also motivated its competitors IBM and NovellSuse to upgrade their offers of assistance during a potential migration process. In May 2003, after weeks of heated seesaw changes in the calculation of the different alternatives, the council made the principle decision in favour of a migration to FOSS and authorised its IT department to work out a detailed draft for the project.

Consciousness of the actual costs, complexity and efforts connected with this decision only rose incrementally along the following migration process. What had started as a search for an alternative office software suite in 2001 had ended as a complete restructuring of the municipality's IT organization and processes:

- After the migration, only one standardized and centrally developed operating system version replaced the several different Windows versions.
- As a consequence of the standardized client, many prior decentralised tasks and routines (e.g. operating system set up[4], administration and configuration) were going to be fulfilled by a central client team.
- In introducing a new standardized tool to manage office forms and master documents called "Wollmux"[5], the city's corporate design guidelines were to be reinforced and – for the first time in history – to be implemented uniformly in the whole municipality.
- The change of the operating system gave reason for a general consolidation of the municipality's diverse software landscape, reducing the variety of applications in use.

Summing up this short description, there are at least three remarkable aspects of Munich's odyssey from Windows to FOSS (see also Figure 3): First, technology adoption and organisational change – especially concerning different degrees of organisational (de)centrality – are deeply intertwined and reciprocally enforcing. Second, roles and preferences of individual actors change during the process, converting some of them from opponents into proponents and vice-versa. It is, therefore, impossible – or at least, misleading – to simply reduce individual attitudes towards the adoption of Free and Open Source Software to their job functions as it is tried by Alexy and Henkel [1], and underlines the importance of applying a process perspective in researching adoption decisions. Third, external advice and

[4] Although all departments had adopted the same operating system (Windows NT), its set up in terms of administration tools, settings, and support software varied.

[5] "Wollmux" is a neologism combining the German "eierlegende Wollmilchsau" (colloquial for "all-in-one device suitable for every purpose") and the name of the Linux mascot "Tux".

interventions play an important catalytic role in the process, but at the same time are only "perturbations" [17] of overall internal organizational dynamics.

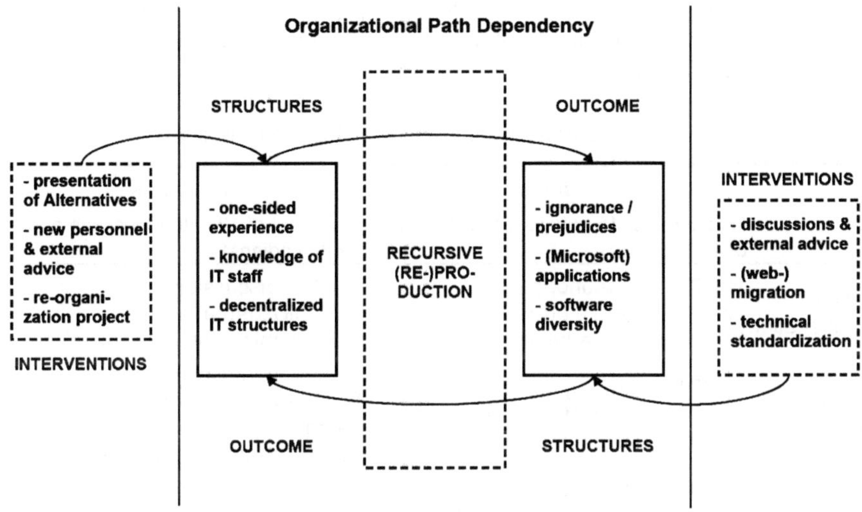

Fig. 3. Recursive re-production of organizational software paths and respective interventions

4.2 The discourse: coalitions of actors and issues

Table 5 depicts relative frequencies of dominant issues raised by actors in different organizational subsystems – political administration, central and decentral IT departments – on the basis of inductively generated coding categories [18]. It distinguishes thereby between legitimizing frames and programs charting a specific course of action [4, 5] both of which were – depending on the respective context – predominantly coded as either pro- or anti-migration[6].

In Munich, two different organizational camps applied different frames to legitimize the same FOSS migration project and thus build what Hajer [14] calls a "discourse coalition". On the one hand, politicians stressed frames referring to a diffuse "anti-monopoly" ideology and the particular responsibility as a public administration. The central IT officials, on the other hand, framed the introduction of FOSS above all as the (looked-for) opportunity to re-centralize the municipality's organizational IT structure; for them – as the only subgroup – switching gains exceed switching efforts. Together, these two camps generate enough momentum [15] to

[6] Except for some unidimensional coding categories, most categories aggregate two antithetic codes that cover statements referring either to barriers and downsides or drivers and advantages of a migration to FOSS. A category was classified as "predominantly pro- or anti-migration" if there was a difference larger than unity between the two.

overcome the strong innovation barriers of the desktop software markets. Together, these two camps generate enough momentum to overcome the strong barriers to FOSS introduction that materialized also in resistance in decentralized IT departments. Those opposed the migration as their expert's knowledge – gained over years of "learning by doing" [2] – depreciated rapidly under a new operating system because of the „creative destruction" of skills and knowledge in every technological innovation process [27].

Table 5. Dominant Frames and Programs in Munich's Migration Discourse

	Frames (Top 3 out of 15 categories with a total of 439 codings)	Programs (Top 3 out of 12 categories with a total of 486 codings)
Political administration	18,68 % anti-monopoly(***) 17,58 % (overall) profitability 14,29 % public administration issues	27,14 % discussions 15,71 % external advice 12,86 % migration complexity(*)
Central IT department	25,98 % switching gains & efforts 18,63 % organisational structures(*) 15,20 % (overall) profitability	27,52 % migration strategy 24,03 % applications (incl. macros)(**) 9,30 % organisational know-how(*)
Decentral IT departments	26,39 % organisational structures(*) 22,92 % switching gains & efforts(*) 14,58 % expectations & uncertainty	17,09 % organisational know-how(*) 16,46 % migration strategy 15,19 % migration complexity(*)

(*) predominantly coded anti-migration
(**) unidimensional anti-migration code
(***) unidimensional pro-migration code

Looking at the categories that predominantly cover program aspects in the migration discourse (see right column in Table 5) one can see several facets more clearly: First, migration to FOSS is hard work and requires a lot of effort, in particular in cases of large-scale, rather complete migration projects like the one in Munich: Especially in both IT-departments categories that are predominantly coded anti-migration prevail and reflect the efforts necessary to migrate hundreds of special purpose applications and thousands of macros, forms and templates. Second, the program categories mirror the interventions depicted in Figure 3 and hence give an impression of the great variety of tasks necessary in such a migration project. Third, the again anti-migration position of the officials in the decentralized IT departments corresponds with the fact that they have to carry most of the migration burdens. Many of the migration tasks such as for example altering macros or forms means work, which at least in parts is additional to day-to-day routines.

Compared to other prominent and large-scale FOSS migration examples like the French car manufacturer PSA Peugeot[7] or police forces in France and

[7] http://ec.europa.eu/idabc/en/document/6674/469, accessed 27 February 2008.

Niedersachsen/Germany[8], Munich's migration enterprise is illuminative for at least two reasons: First, migration complexity and efforts seem to grow disproportionately if not only significant parts as in the case of PSA Peugeot but the complete software environment is to be changed in a rather short period of time. Second, migration complexity and efforts seem to grow disproportionately with functional and hence software diversity in an organization. As opposed to police force cases in France and Germany where only few special purpose applications have to be migrated and the functional diversity is relatively low, in large municipal administrations the situation is the other way round. This in turn led at least in Munich to the need for organizational re-structuring which complicated the migration process and vice-versa.

5 Conclusions

Not only because of a municipality being a (at least: partially) political organization, the decision to (not) adopt FOSS in organizational contexts is always a political one: In organizations there will be winners and losers of migration processes as switching one's desktop software environment affects (complementary) organizational variables such as degree of decentralization or individual and organizational know-how. As a consequence, future research of FOSS adoption processes should include both looking at the (changes in the) migration discourse and at its organizational contextualisation. This study can only be a first step into this direction.

Acknowledgments

I wish to thank Jörg Sydow, Sigrid Quack, Jochen Koch, Arndt Sorge and Elke Schüßler as well as all other members of the doctoral program "Research on Organizational Paths" at Freie Universitaet Berlin and the participants at the First Graz Schumpeter Summer School 2007 for their valuable comments.

References

[1] Alexy, O. and J. Henkel (2007). Promoting the Penguin: Who is Advocating Open Source Software in Commercial Settings? Working Paper. http://papers.ssrn.com/sol3/papers.cfm?abstract_id=988363. Accessed 16 October 2007.

[2] Arrow, K.J. (1962). The Economic Implications of Learning By Doing. The Review of Economic Studies, 29(3), 155-173

[8] http://ec.europa.eu/idabc/en/document/7343/528, accessed 27 February 2008 and http://www.heise.de/newsticker/meldung/40374/ accessed 14 December 2008.

[3] Arthur, B. (1989). Competing Technologies, Increasing Returns, and Lock-In by Historical Events. The Economic Journal, 99, 116-131

[4] Campbell, J.L. (1998). Institutional analysis and the role of ideas in the political economy. Theory and Society, 27, 377-409

[5] Campbell, J.L. (2004). Institutional Change and Globalization. Princeton: Princeton University Press.

[6] David, P.A. (1985). Clio and the economics of QWERTY. American Economic Review, 75 (2), 332-337

[7] David, P.A. (2000). Path Dependence, its critics and the quest for historical economics. Stanford Working Paper Series. http://www-econ.stanford.edu/faculty/workp/swp00011.pdf. Accessed 16 April 2007.

[8] Dobusch, L. (2007). Adopter Innovation in Network Markets: The Case of Linux in Munich. Paper presented at the SASE Annual Meeting, Kopenhagen 28-30 June 2007, Network on Knowledge, Technology and Innovation.

[9] Dobusch, L. and E.S. Schuessler (2007). From Storytelling to Theory: Unlocking Path Dependency from Metaphorical Usage. Paper presented at 23rd EGOS Colloquium, Vienna 5-7 July 2007, Sub-theme 14: Path dependencies and beyond.

[10] Farrell, J. and G. Saloner (1986). Installed Base and Compatibility: Innovation, Product Preannouncements, and Predation. The American Economic Review, 76 (5): 940-955

[11] Feller, J., B. Fitzgerald, S.A. Hissam, and E.R. Lakhani (Eds./2007). Perspectives on Free and Open Source Software. MIT Press. http://mitpress.mit.edu/books/chapters/0262562278.pdf. Accessed 28 March 2007.

[12] Giddens, A. (1984). The Constitution of Society: Outline of the Theory of Structuration. Cam-bridge: Polity Press.

[13] Gosh, R.A., B. Krieger, R. Glott and G. Robles (2002). Free/Libre and Open Source Software: Survey and Study. Part 2B: Open Source Software in the Public Sector: Policy within the European Union. International Institute of Infonomics, University of Maastricht. http://www.flossproject.org/report/FLOSSFinal_2b.pdf. Accessed 15 October 2007.

[14] Hajer, M.A. (1993). Discourse Coalitions and the Institutionalization of Practice: The Case of Acid Rain in Great Britain. In Fischer, F. and J. Forester (Eds.): The Argumentative Turn in Policy Analysis and Planning (pp. 43-76). Durham and London: Duke University Press.

[15] Hughes, T.P. (1983). Networks of Power: Electrification in Western Society 1880-1930. Baltimore: Johns Hopkins University Press.

[16] Mayring, P. (2003). Qualitative Inhaltsanalyse: Grundlagen und Techniken.: Weinheim and Basel: Beltz

[17] Maturana, H.R. and F.J. Varela (1987). The Tree of Knowledge: The Biological Roots of Human Understanding. Boston: Shambhala.

[18] Miles, M.B./Huberman, A.M. (1994). Qualitative Data Analysis: An expanded Sourcebook. Second Edition. Thousand Oaks: Sage

[19] Nagler, M. (2005). Migration of the German City of Schwäbisch Hall. http://ec.europa.eu/idabc/servlets/Doc?id=19734. Accessed 12 December 2007.

[20] Orlikowski, W.J. (1992). The Duality of Technology: Rethinking the Concept of Technology in Organizations. Organization Science, 3 (3), 398-427

[21] Orlikowski, W.J. (2000). Using Technology and Constituting Structures: A Practice Lens for Studying Technology in Organizations. Organization Science, 11 (4), 404-428

[22] Rossi, B., B. Russo and G. Succi, G. (2007). Open Source Software and Open Data Standards as a form of Technology Adoption: a Case Study. In Feller, J., B. Fitzgerald, W.

Scacchi and A. Sillitti (Eds.): IFIP International Federation for Information Processing, Volume 234, Open Source Development, Adoption and Innovation, 325-330

[23] Shapiro, C. and H.R. Varian (1999). Information Rules: a strategic guide to the network economy. Cambridge (MA): Harvard Business School Press

[24] Stones, R. (2005). Structuration Theory. Houndmills et al.: Palgrave Macmillan:

[25] Strauss, A.L. and J. Corbin (1990). Basics of Qualitative Research: Grounded Theory Procedures and Techniques. Newbury Park (CA): Sage

[26] Sydow, J., G. Schreyögg, G. and J. Koch (2005). Organizational Paths: Path Dependency and Beyond. Paper presented at the 21st EGOS Colloquium, June 30 - July 2, 2005, Berlin, Germany

[27] Tushman, M.L. and P. Anderson (1986). Technological Discontinuities and Organizational En-vironments. Administrative Science Quarterly, 31, 439-465

[28] Unilog Integrata (2003). Client Studie der Landeshauptstadt München: Kurzfassung des Abschlussbereichts inklusive Nachtrag. Stand 02.07.2003. http://www.muenchen.de/limux. Accessed 26 February 2008.

[29] Varian, H.R., J. Farell, and C. Shapiro (2004). The Economics of Information Technology: An Introduction. Cambridge (UK): Cambridge University Press.

[30] Varian, Hal R. and Carl Shapiro (2003), Linux Adoption in the Public Sector: An Economic Analysis, http://www.sims.berkeley.edu/~hal/Papers/2004/linux-adoption-in-the-public-sector.pdf. Accessed 28 October 2005.

[31] von Hippel, E. and G. von Krogh (2003). Open Source Software and the „Private-Collective“ Innovation Model: Issues for Organization Science. Organization Science,14(2), 209-223

[32] Wichmann, T. (2002). FLOSS Final Report – Part 1: Use of Open Source Software in Firms and Public Institutions – Evidence from Germany, Sweden and UK. Berlin: Berlecon Research.

[33] Williamson, O.F. (1985). The Economic Institutions of Capitalism. New York: The Free Press.

[34] Yin, R.K. (1994). Case Study Research. Design and Methods. Thousand Oaks: Sage.

The SQO-OSS Quality Model: Measurement Based Open Source Software Evaluation

Ioannis Samoladas[1], Georgios Gousios[2],
Diomidis Spinellis[2], and Ioannis Stamelos[1]
[1] Department of Informatics, Aristotle University of Thessaloniki,
541 24, Thessaloniki, Greece
{ioansam, stamelos}@csd.auth.gr
[2] Department of Management Science and Technology,
Athens University of Economics and Business, 104 34, Athens, Greece
{gousiosg, dds}@aueb.gr

Abstract. Software quality evaluation has always been an important part of software business. The quality evaluation process is usually based on hierarchical quality models that measure various aspects of software quality and deduce a characterization of the product quality being evaluated. The particular nature of open source software has rendered existing models inappropriate for detailed quality evaluations. In this paper, we present a hierarchical quality model that evaluates source code and community processes, based on automatic calculation of metric values and their correlation to a set of predefined quality profiles.[1]

Keywords: Quality models, automated measurement, software metrics

1 Introduction

One of the main concerns of software engineering is the production of high quality software systems and thus software quality evaluation has always been a critical task for software professionals. IT managers often face the problem of evaluating software in order to decide whether it is suitable for their needs. Additionally, software houses perform evaluations on the software they develop to decide whether it has matured enough to be deployed. Evaluations are based on software models that define and measure software quality, usually by combining software metrics and experts' opinions. The advent of free, libre and open source software (OSS) has rendered the traditional quality evaluation models non applicable to some extent, as

[1] This work was partially supported by the European Community's Sixth Framework Programme under the contract IST-2005-033331 "Software Quality Observatory for Open Source Software (SQO-OSS)".

Please use the following format when citing this chapter:

Samoladas, I., Gousios, G., Spinellis, D. and Stamelos, I., 2008, in IFIP International Federation for Information Processing, Volume 275; *Open Source Development, Communities and Quality*; Barbara Russo, Ernesto Damiani, Scott Hissam, Björn Lundell, Giancarlo Succi; (Boston: Springer), pp. 237–248.

they cannot be tuned to reflect OSS development practices and therefore cannot be used to evaluate both the software and the community as a whole.

In this paper, we present a novel software quality evaluation model, specifically targeted to OSS. The SQO-OSS model was constructed to support an automated software evaluation system; its variables are mainly metric-oriented while human intervention is minimal. Additionally, our model evaluates all aspects of OSS development, both the product (code) and the community. The evaluation weights and criteria can be tuned by the evaluator, while a set of predefined profiles that cover basic evaluation cases are offered.

The remainder of the paper is organized as follows: In Section 2, we present related work in the area of both traditional and open source software quality evaluation; in Section 3, we present the SQO-OSS quality model definition and the evaluation process. Section 4 presents an application of a part of the model on three example open source projects. The paper concludes with a description of the Alitheia system, the host system for software metric calculations, as well as our plans for future work.

2 Related Work

Since researchers started investigating the issue of quality in software systems, they employed specific models to express it. Models usually decompose quality into an hierarchy of criteria and attributes[2]. These hierarchical models lead to metrics at their lowest level. Metrics are directly measurable attributes of software and they are used to express certain aspects of the product that affect quality [1]. Examples of traditional software quality models are the McCall and Boehm's models [1], the more widely accepted ISO/IEC 9126 model [2], and its more recent implementation by SQuaRE, the ISO 25000:2005 [3].

The adoption of OSS in many organizations has raised the issue of OSS quality evaluation. Due to the nature of OSS development where standard practices include open access to the source code, shared artifact repositories, peer review of committed code, asynchronous global development and lack of formal support, traditional software quality models may not be sufficient. An array of quality models specifically targeted to OSS development can be found in the literature, but most of them are either purpose specific or require significant human intervention,.

The OSMM [4] model assumes that the quality of an open source project proportional to its maturity. The latter is decomposed into six constituents (*Product software, Support, Documentation, Training, Product integrations* and *Professional services*), each one having some weight. The evaluator assigns a score to each element and the final evaluation mark is the weighted sum of the scores. Although

[2] Throughout the paper the terms criterion and attribute (sub-criterion and sub-attribute) are used interchangeably.

OSMM is simple and thus easy to apply, it is often criticized for not taking into account some important software artifacts, such as the source code itself.

The Open Business Readiness Rating (OpenBRR) [5] defines a model and a process for evaluating OSS, with particular emphasis on attributes interesting to businesses. OpenBRR uses a variety of high-level criteria for evaluation, such as functionality, operational software characteristics, support and service and adoption and development process. The assessment process involves defining a reference application and through it identifying a set of characteristics (and weights for them) that are desirable in the evaluated applications. The evaluation result is extracted by assigning grades to each characteristic and averaging the results from the evaluators. While the OpenBRR method is a step forward from OSMM through the inclusion of the community process in the evaluation, the notion of the reference application has been criticized as a major drawback. Furthermore, the evaluation itself is highly subjective, while the overall process seems complicated, offering very little prospect for automation.

The Qualification and Selection of Open Source Software (QSOS) [6] is another open source evaluation model. The evaluation process is done in four iterative phases. Phase one is the definition of the evaluation factors. The second phase involves the collection of information from the open source community and the construction of an identity card for the evaluated software. The quality criteria are then scored in a range from zero to two according to specific guidelines provided by the methodology. Phase three is the definition of the selection criteria according to user's needs and constraints. The last phase is the identification of the software that fulfills user requirements and more generally compares software from the same family. Like OpenBRR, QSOS offers a tool that supports the evaluation process. Although QSOS scoring guidelines allow for objective results among users, the whole process is not flexible enough and difficult to handle.

The SQO-OSS quality model distinguishes from existing open source quality models in various ways:

1. The SQO-OSS model was constructed with a focus to automation, while the rest of the models require heavy user interference and lack automation of metrics collection.

2. The SQO-OSS model is the core of a continuous quality monitoring system and automatic metrics collection guarantee that assessments are made with relatively recent data.

3. The SQO-OSS model does not evaluate functionality. Functionality assessment requires the evaluator to play an important role in the assessment process and thus introduces subjectivity. The SQO-OSS model focuses on fundamental aspects of OSS quality, namely OSS project maintainability, reliability and security.

4. The SQO-OSS model focuses on source code. Source code is the single most important product of a software development project and its quality must play a significant role in determining the final assessment of the product.

5. The SQO-OSS model also considers the open source community. However, it takes into account only those community factors that can be measured automatically.

6. As the evaluation must necessarily take into account the evaluator's point of view, we allow the user to intervene in the measurement-based evaluation process by modifying category profiles.

3 The SQO-OSS Quality Model

We can generally assume that an evaluation process can be divided into two phases, the definition of the evaluation model and the definition of the measurement process. In our case, each phase includes two distinct steps:

Phase One: *Definition of the evaluation model*

1. Definition of the model criteria (attributes and sub-attributes).
2. Definition of metrics.

Phase Two: *Definition of the aggregation method*

1. Definition of the evaluation categories
2. Definition of the profiles of those categories

Phase one represents the work done in order to define the evaluation framework, applying our notion of quality, the definition of the quality criteria and the metrics that measure these criteria. The second phase represents the data collection part and the aggregation of the measurement results in order to reach an outcome for the quality of the artifact under evaluation. At this point we have to lay more emphasis on the fact that throughout this process, automation was the main concern. We wanted a model that can be applied automatically and on a fair amount of projects, fed continuously with data from the SQO-OSS observatory. Thus we tried to focus on quality attributes that can be measured with minimum human interference. For example usability involves extensive human interaction so it was not chosen as a quality attribute for our model. The same approach was followed for metrics selection.

3.1 Model definition

Prior to starting the construction of our model, we took into account that the quality and the health of an OSS project depends on the quality of its source code base and that of the community built around it. In order to measure these two aspects of quality and construct the SQO-OSS quality model we used a simplified version of the Goal-Question-Metric (GQM) process [7].

For the first part, we formulated our first goal, "*analyze the source code of an open source project*". This analysis has to be done in order to characterize code quality with respect to its maintainability, reliability and security. So, for this goal we formulated the question *"How is source code quality measured?"*. We then formulated the question as *"How is maintainability, reliability and security measures?"* In turn, each one of these aspects of source code quality is a small goal itself with its own questions. We kept on formulating questions iteratively until we reached a level where an attribute can be measured using straightforward metrics, i.e. without any usage of compound metrics.

For example, in order to measure *Maintainability*, we chose to follow its definition in the ISO/IEC 9126 quality model: *Analyzability*, *Changeability*, *Stability*, *Testability*. To measure each one of these sub-attributes we used direct source code metrics. In order to differentiate between structured and object oriented programming we used different definitions of *Maintainability* attribute for these two programming paradigms. Metrics selection was a difficult part, since software engineering metrics research is a very active topic and many researchers express their concerns on various metrics. For our own model we chose to select only widely acceptable metrics and metrics that have been validated extensively [8]. For an extensive review on metrics please refer to [9] and [1].

In a similar fashion, we constructed a hierarchical view of our quality model as a tree. The root represents the overall quality model, the next two nodes the source code and community quality, while the leaves represent the metrics. After constructing the initial model, we uploaded the model on the wiki page of our project asking from our consortium partners to review it and comment on it. Our partners come from the OSS community (developers, users), academia and companies specializing on OSS development and support. Additionally, we also asked them to change the model (both model leaves and respective metrics) and justify their opinion. The only thing stressed to the partners was the importance of automatic metric collection. The history facility of the wiki allowed us to review the changes, discuss them with the partners and finalize the model. A tree view of the model is presented in Figure 1, while the metrics selected for the evaluation of the selected criteria (the leaves on the tree view) can be seen in Table 1. At this point, we should mention that our system allows partial evaluation of a product, i.e. evaluation of a single attribute like *Testability*. Thus, we have used the same metrics in more than one attribute.

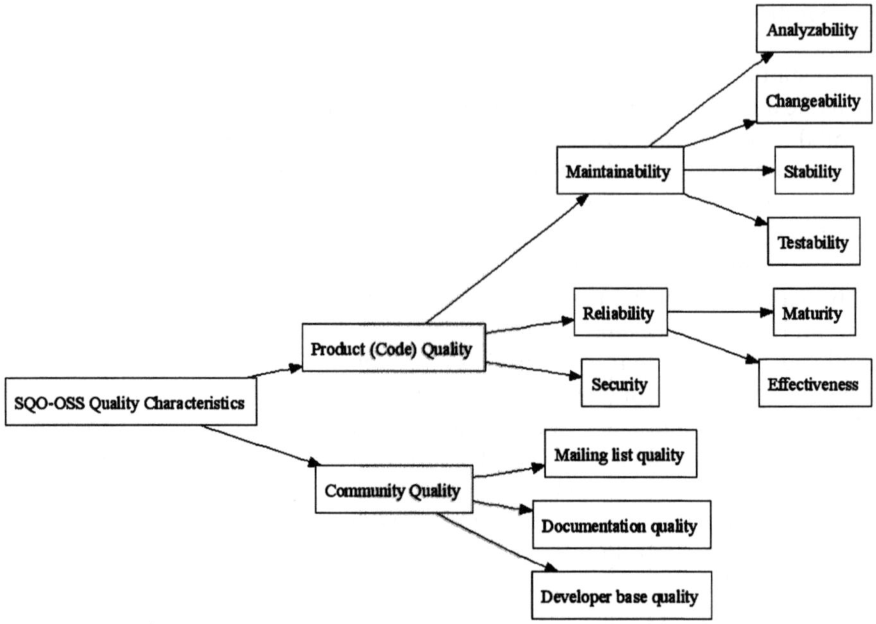

Fig. 1. The SQO-OSS quality model.

Table 1. Metrics for criteria of Product (Code) Quality and Community Quality

Attribute	Metric
Analyzability	Cyclomatic Number
	Number of statements
	Comments frequency
	Average size of statements
	Weighted methods per class (WMC)
	Number of base classes
	Class comments frequency
Changeability	Average size of statements
	Vocabulary frequency
	Number of unconditional jumps
	Number of nested levels
	Coupling between objects (CBO)
	Lack of cohesion (LCOM)
	Depth of inheritance tree (DIT)
Stability	Number of unconditional jumps
	Number of entry nodes
	Number of exit nodes

	Directly called components
	Number of children (NOC)
	Coupling between objects (CBO)
	Depth of inheritance tree (DIT)
Testability	Number of exits of conditional structs
	Cyclomatic number
	Number of nested levels
	Number of unconditional jumps
	Response for a class (RFC)
	Average cyclomatic complexity per method
	Number of children (NOC)
Maturity	Number of open critical bugs in the last 6 months
	Number of open bugs in the last six months
Effectiveness	Number of critical bugs fixed in the last 6 Months
	Number of bugs fixed in the last 6 months
Security	Null dereferences
	Undefined values
Mailing list	Number of unique subscribers
	Number of messages in user/support list per month
	Number of messages in developers list per month
	Average thread depth
Documentation	Available documentation documents
	Update frequency
Developer base	Rate of developer intake
	Rate of developer turnover
	Growth in active developers

3.2 Evaluation Process

In order to evaluate the quality of an open source project, we have to combine all these measurements in one single view to obtain an evaluation result, i.e. we have to aggregate the measurements. For this, we used the profile-based evaluation method described in detail in reference [10]. Most evaluation methods presented in the literature use a weighted average sum function as their aggregation method. A drawback for applying this aggregation method on our model is that it uses measures with interval scales, while our goal was to provide results in an ordinal scale (such as *good*, *fair* or *poor*). The method we selected allows us to combine all kind of measurements, based on either ordinal or interval scales.

In order to apply an ordinal scaling aggregation method, we must first decide how many categories of evaluation ranking are required. In reference [10], Morisio et al. discuss that the ideal number of evaluation categories is between three and five. Based on that, for our model, we used four categories: **Excellent** (*E*), **Good** (*G*), **Fair** (*F*) and **Poor** (*P*) (or as an ordinal scale $E>G>F>P$). Having four categories, the aggregation method requires the definition of three profiles, each one for the first three categories (*E, G* and *F*). If an artifact cannot be fitted into one of these three categories, then it is automatically categorized as poor. The profiles represent the least measurement values required for each category and they are defined separately for each composed criterion of the model. Then each criterion is further decomposed into its sub-criteria (hierarchically, according to the quality model) and each decomposed criterion has its own profile. For the quality model leaves, which consist of an array metrics used to assess their parent criterion, we use a vector of numbers that is constructed by the application of each specific metric to the assessed artifact. We used the thresholds indicated by the literature [11, 12, 13] to correlate the measurement value vectors to the profiles we had developed (see Table 2).

Decomposing root attributes of our quality model into more fine-grained criteria and then down to metrics entails that profiles correspond to each decomposed criterion. Thus, in order to characterize the product quality of a product as "Excellent", Maintainability, Reliability and Security must be also characterized as "Excellent". Table 2 shows that a software component that scores "*Excellent*" in Maintainability must score *"Excellent"* in the Analyzability sub-attribute, too. This, in turn, means that the corresponding metrics applied to the evaluated component must return values equivalent to or higher than the vector [4,10,0.5,2]. Similar profiles correlating metric values to profiles can be applied to the rest of the criteria. Due to space limitations, Table 2 shows only the metrics values for Analyzability and Changeability; however, similar thresholds exist for the rest of criteria. Users of the model can modify the profiles according to their needs, e.g. a security aware user may define higher default values for each of the profiles. Additionally, the method allows usage of weights on the various metrics, but such practice is not recommended, as we assume that all metrics are of equal importance.

The aggregation process is done with the use of specific outranking relations iteratively with all the given profiles. The outranking relations express our decision of comparing the artifact with the profiles. Thus, an artifact *x* is considered to be *at least as good as* the *y* profile if and only if the "weighted" majority of the criteria agree so. If a set of tests agree, which represent the strength to be reached in order for an artifact to be categorized in a category *A* then *x* is assigned to *A*. The method also allows for two kinds of assignments in categories. The first is the pessimistic assignment representing the *at least as good as* relation (project *x* is *at least as good as* profile *y*). The second is the optimistic assignment, which identifies the profile which is surely worse than *x* and assigns *x* to the previous one (for example if *x* is strictly worse than *E* then it is assigned to *G*). If the two assignments coincide, then we are sure about our decision, otherwise it is the evaluator's decision which of the two assignments will be adopted. The mathematical foundations and the actual procedure of the aggregation process is presented in reference [10]. The method used here is different than Analytic Hierarchy Process, a widely used aggregation method, which requires ratio scales on all measures, a requirement that is not fulfilled in our case. Moreover, as already mentioned earlier, having a weighted average sum function as an aggregation method forces us to use measures with interval scales; our goal was to provide results on an ordinal scale, a feature that is provided with the method presented.

An example of the aggregation process is presented in the next section.

Table 2. Profiles for criteria Analyzability, Changeability, Stability and Testability

Composed Criterion	Criterion	Profile E	Profile G	Profile F	Scale
Analyzability	Cyclomatic number	4	6	8	Less is better
	Number of statements	10	25	50	Less is better
	Comments frequency	0.5	0.3	0.1	More is better
	Average size of statements	2	3	4	Less is better
Changeability	Average size of statements	2	3	4	Less is better
	Vocabulary frequency	4	7	10	Less is better
	Number of unconditional jumps	0	0	1	Less is better
	Number of nested levels	1	3	5	Less is better
Stability	Number of unconditional jumps	0	0	1	Less is better
	Number of entry nodes	1	2	3	Less is better
	Number of exit nodes	1	1	1	One is better
	Directly called components	2	5	7	Less is better
Testability	Number of exits of conditional structs	0	1	4	Less is better
	Cyclomatic Number	4	6	8	Less is better
	Number of nested levels	1	3	5	Less is better
	Number of unconditional jumps	0	0	1	Less is better

4 Evaluation Example

In this section, we present an example of application of the SQO-OSS quality model. For our example, we evaluated the source code of the CVS versioning system, the interpreter of the Perl programming language and the C files of the FreeBSD operating system. Table 5 shows the performance of these projects according to the various measurements. All measurements were performed using the metrics extracted from the application of the CScout refactoring browser [14] on the evaluated projects. According to the measurements, two out of our three projects scored well in the maintainability criterion. A direct interpretation of these results according to the proposed model is that CVS and FreeBSD are *at least as good as* the metrics thresholds for the **Good** profile, while Perl is *at least as good as* the thresholds for **Fair**.

A careful examination of the results reveals details of the performance of these projects in various sub-attributes of maintainability. All three projects achieve high marks in the changeability metrics and a good level of analyzability, perhaps due to their development model. Stability and testability are fair, but close to the metric thresholds we set for each respective criterion. Taking into consideration that the thresholds used in our example are relatively strict, the results are encouraging even for these two factors. Apart from providing predefined thresholds, our method has the benefit of presenting the results in a way that enables the developer to focus on measurements that are really interesting to him and also to receive both coarse and fine grained information.

Table 5. Example measurements of projects CVS, Perl and FreeBSD

Composed Criterion	**Project evaluation**		
	CVS	**Perl**	**FreeBSD**
Analyzability	[5.63, 37.8, 0.34, 1.89]	[3.0, 36.17, 0.08, 1.02]	[3.82, 29.99, 0.12, 1.99]
Evaluation	*Good*	*Fair*	*Excellent*
Changeability	[1.89, 2.91, 0.24, 1.13]	[1.02, 2.42, 0.28, 0.53]	[1.99, 2.87, 0.51, 0.86]
Evaluation	*Good*	*Excellent*	*Excellent*
Stability	[0.24, 3.28, 1.08, 4.49]	[0.08, 3.21, 0.78, 4.75]	[0.25, 3.99, 1.23, 4.10]
Evaluation	*Poor*	*Fair*	*Poor*
Testability	[0.57, 5.62, 1.13, 0.24]	[0.46, 3.0, 0.53, 0.08]	[0.55, 3.82, 0.86, 0.25]
Evaluation	*Good*	*Good*	*Good*
Maintainability	**Good**	**Fair**	**Good**

5 The Alitheia System

The quality model presented above serves as an automated decision support tool, integrated into the SQO-OSS system [15]. The SQO-OSS project aims to build a software quality observatory for OSS. For that purpose, we have developed Alitheia, a quality evaluation tool, and a web site with the results of the tool application on various OSS projects. The user is able to browse the product and process quality characteristics of the evaluated projects. The SQO-OSS quality model assists the user by incorporating the individual measurements in a comprehensive set of predefined quality profiles.

The Alitheia platform is an OSGi-based tool, targeted to the evaluation of software quality. It consists of a set of core services, such as accessors to project artifacts, job managers and relational data storage, and it is extensible through the use of plug-ins. Plug-ins can either implement basic software metrics or combine the results from other plug-ins arbitrarily. In fact, the quality model is a compound plug-in in Alitheia. The system allows full automation of the quality evaluation process after the initial project registration. The core communicates to the world through a web services interface. Clients being developed include the aforementioned web site and an Eclipse plug-in.

6 Conclusion and Future Work

In this paper we presented a new open source software quality evaluation model. The model was constructed for use in the Alitheia system, as a measurement-based decision support system, therefore automation was one of the first priorities while constructing the model. Previous models developed for OSS evaluation require a substantial effort from the user regarding the rating of the software under evaluation, while the model presented here asks for limited user interaction. Apart from the model itself, the evaluation process facilitates a profile based evaluation algorithm that is different from the traditional weighted aggregation that most of the models use. The profiles used for evaluation can be altered by the evaluator if he decides it is needed so.

Our immediate plans are to empirically validate our model. In order to test our model we are collecting measurements from an array of OSS projects. To meet our goal, we are going to perform a user based validation. Our project consortium includes members of a large OSS project, namely KDE Desktop Environment. Partners from the KDE project will evaluate software against our model and their opinions will be tested against the results or our evaluation process. In addition we want to evaluate its predictability and accuracy regarding its ability to classify software according to its quality. These tests will also allow us to calibrate the threshold values of our profiles. Moreover, we will work towards testing the relationships between metrics and categories and try to identify trends between aspects of quality and metrics.

References

1. Norman Fenton and Shari Lawrence Pfleeger. *Software Metrics - A Rigorous Approach.* International Thomson Publishing, London, 1997.
2. ISO. Software engineering - Product quality - Part 1: Quality model, ISO/IEC 9126-1:2001. ISO Geneva, 2001.
3. ISO. Software engineering Software product Quality Requirements and Evaluation (SQuaRE) Guide to SQuaRE. ISO Geneva, 2005.
4. Bernard Golden. *Making Open Source Ready for the Enterprise, The Open Source Maturity Model.* Extracted From Succeeding with Open Source, Addison-Wesley Publishing Company, 2005.
5. Business Readiness Rating. Business readiness rating for open source. http://www.openbrr.org.
6. QSOS. Method for qualification and selection of open source software (qsos) version 1.6. http://www.qsos.org.

7. R. Van Solingen. The goal/question/metric approach. *Encyclopedia of Software Engineering*, 2:578-583, 2002.
8. Tibor Gyimothy, Rudolf Ferenc, and Istvan Siket. Empirical validation of object-oriented metrics on open source software for fault prediction. *IEEE Transactions on Software Engineering*, 31(10):897-910, 2005.
9. Stephen H. Kan. Metrics and Models in Software Quality Engineering, 2nd Edition. Addison-Wesley Publishing Company, 2003.
10. Maurizio Morisio, Ioannis Stamelos, and Alexis Tsoukias. Software product and process assessment through profile-based evaluation. International Journal of *Software Engineering and Knowledge Engineering*, 13(5):495-512, 2003.
11. NASA and SATC. Recommended thresholds for non-oo languages. http://satc.gsfc.nasa.gov/metrics/codemetrics/non_oo/thresholds/index.html.
12. NASA and SATC. Recommended thresholds for oo languages. http://satc.gsfc.nasa.gov/metrics/codemetrics/oo/thresholds/index.html.
13. Saida Benlarbi, Khaled El Emam, Nishith Goel, and Shesh Rai. Thresholds for object-oriented measures. In *Proceedings of the 11th International Symposium on Software Reliability Engineering (ISSRE)*. IEEE Computer Society, 2000.
14. Diomidis Spinellis. Global analysis and transformations in preprocessed languages. *IEEE Transactions on Software Engineering*, 29(11):1019-1030, November 2003.
15. Georgios Gousios, Vassilios Karakoidas, Konstantinos Stroggylos, Panagiotis Louridas, Vasileios Vlachos, and Diomidis Spinellis. Software quality assesment of open source software. In *Proceedings of the 11th Panhellenic Conference on Informatics*, May 2007.

An Open Integrated Environment for Transparent Fuzzy Agents Design

Giovanni Acampora and Vincenzo Loia
Department of Mathematics and Computer Science, University of Salerno
via Ponte don Melillo, 84084 Fisciano, Salerno, Italy
{gacampora,loia}@unisa.it

Abstract. Recently, computational agents received significant attention in computer science research community. In fact, intelligent agents is a powerful artificial intelligence technology showing considerable promise as a new paradigm for mainstream software development and able to offer new ways of abstraction, decomposition, and organization that fit well with our natural view of the world. However, despite their promise, intelligent agents are still scarce in the market place. A key reason for this is that developing intelligent agent software requires significant training and skill. Artificial Intelligence methodologies and computer networking tools represent the necessary basic knowledge to design and implement advanced agents oriented systems. This papers introduces an integrated development environment supporting the agents developers to design fuzzy-based agents in a simple and fast way. Proposed framework has been realized by integration of theoretical methodologies as fuzzy logic and labeled tree, together with OSS tools as JaxMe2.

1 Introduction

Multi-Agent systems (MASs) consist of a large number of computational agents, interconnected by communication devices, that seamlessly work together in order to achieve prefixed common goals. Different methodologies and techniques have to be exploited in order to design advanced multi-agent systems, ranging from social science, business models, network architectures, up to human interaction design. This methodologies integration allows to design and implement agents-based environment characterized by many features [1]. However, in spite of hard exploitation of computational agents in several domains of computer applications, MAS developers need of significant training, skills and experiences to design and develop advanced MAS-based frameworks. In fact, as previously depicted, MAS can be considered as a composition of different computer science backgrounds, mainly, Artificial Intelligence and Computer Networking. This paper introduces a novel design framework (FuzzyIDE), based on transparent fuzzy agents[2], which allows the system designers to express their ideas in fast and simple way achieving the properties of MAS without additional effort. In particular, this paper introduces a novel tree-based representation for fuzzy controllers allowing the designer to draw their ideas in a natural way and, at the same time, to split the whole controller in

---

Please use the following format when citing this chapter:

Acampora, G. and Loia, V., 2008, in IFIP International Federation for Information Processing, Volume 275; *Open Source Development, Communities and Quality*; Barbara Russo, Ernesto Damiani, Scott Hissam, Björn Lundell, Giancarlo Succi; (Boston: Springer), pp. 249–255.

several subcontrollers by exploiting the subtree concept. Proposed framework has been realized by integration of theoretical and applicative methodologies as labeled tree and fuzzy control theory.

2 Transparent Fuzzy Control

Fuzzy control theory [3] can be considered as the most widely used application of fuzzy logic [4] [5] From a high level point of view, a Fuzzy Logic Controller (FLC) is an adequate methodology for designing and developing controllers capable of supplying high quality performance in environments characterized by high level of uncertainty and imprecision. However, in spite of these unquestionable advantages, the real design of FLCs is strongly depends upon hardware architecture which will implements the running version of designed controller.

2.1 FLC Labeled Tree

In this section we discuss the labeled tree structure[6] which will be exploited to define the FLC Labeled Tree, the tree-oriented data structure modeling FLCs and representing the core element of *Transparent Fuzzy Control*. A labeled tree is a tree where each node is associated with a label. More formally: Let Σ_V be finite alphabets of vertex labels and edge labels, respectively. Let V be a finite nonempty set of vertices, l a total function $l: V \rightarrow$, E a set of unordered distinct vertices called edges, and a a total function $a: E \rightarrow$. Then $G = (V, l, E, a)$ is a *labeled graph*. A *labeled tree* is a connected, acyclic labeled graph. Labeled tree labels may be constants, node variables (corresponding to any node value), or path variables (corresponding to any path). Constants corresponds to element, attribute and text values populating XML models. In details, nodes labeled with text values are called text nodes and they are always leaf nodes. Attribute nodes can have only one child node, a text node. Also, any two attributes of a given element cannot have the same label. Element nodes can have zero or more child nodes that can be elements, attributes, or text nodes. Usually, the labels related to element nodes, attribute nodes and text nodes are denoted, respectively, with n_i, a_i and *pcdata*. Then, in the case of XML document modeling: $\Sigma_V = \cup_i \{n_i\} \cup \cup_i \{a_i\} \cup pcd$ and $\Sigma_E =$. In order to represent an FLC through labeled tree structures, it is necessary to individuate the different components of a FLC, to map them on appropriate values for the labels n_i, a_i and *pcdata* and, at the same time, to establish the opportune father-child relationships among different tree nodes. This analysis will result in an acyclic labeled graph, i.e, in a labeled tree. From a bottom-up point of view, a FLC can be view as a collection of fuzzy concepts and fuzzy rules composing, respectively, the fuzzy knowledge base and fuzzy rule base. Classic samples of fuzzy concepts are: temperature, pressure, speed, etc.. Each concept is defined, mainly, by means of: a *name*, a *universe of discourse* and a collection of fuzzy terms. Each fuzzy term can be represented through a pair *(Fuzzy Set, Linguistic Expression)*. By considering the a typical temperature fuzzy concept the following labels can be found:

$n_{FC_1} = FuzzyVariable, n_{FC_2} = n_{FC_3} = n_{FC_4} = FuzzyTe \quad n_{FC_5} = TriangularSh$

$a_{FC_1} = a_{FC_5} = name, a_{FC_2} = domainL$

$a_{FC_3} = domainRight, a_{FC_4} = scale, a_{FC_6} = not, a_{FC_7} = param1, a_{FC_8} = param2, a_{FC_9} = param3$

...

with:

$$\Sigma_{Var} = \{n_{FC_1}, n_{FC_2}, n_{FC_3}, n_{FC_4}, n_{FC_5}, a_{FC_1}, a_{FC_2}, a_{FC_3}, a_{FC_3}, a_{FC_4}, a_{FC_5}, a_{FC_7}, a_{FC_8}, a_{FC_9}, \ldots\}$$

and

$$E_{FC} = \{(n_{FC_1}, a_{FC_1}), (n_{FC_1}, a_{FC_2}), (n_{FC_1}, a_{FC_3}), (n_{FC_1}, a_{FC_4}), (n_{FC_1}, n_{FC_2}) \\ (n_{FC_2}, n_{FC_5}), (n_{FC_2}, a_{FC_1}), (n_{FC_2}, a_{FC_6}), (n_{FC_5}, a_{FC_7}), (n_{FC_5}, a_{FC_8}), (n_{FC_5}, a_{FC_9})$$

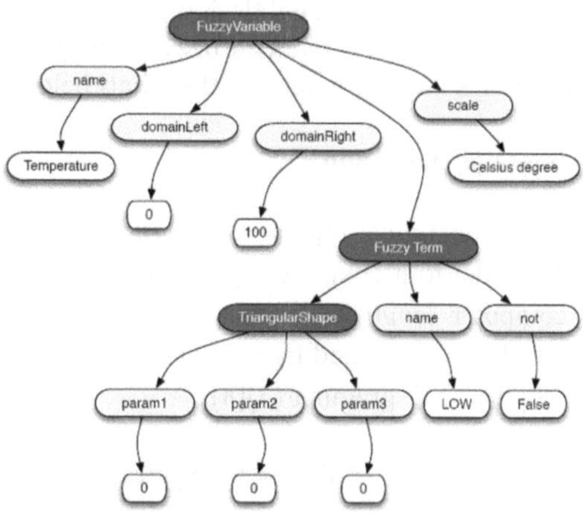

Fig. 1. Fuzzy Variable labeled tree

The *pcdata* information identifies the leaves of XML tree (white tree nodes), i.e., they are strongly depending upon real controller and, for this reason, they are not considered in previous analysis. Figure 1 shows the complete labeled tree derived from previous definitions. Finally, a fuzzy knowledge base can be modeled through a labeled tree whose labels are: $\Sigma_{KB} = \cup_i \Sigma_{Var_i} \cup$ with the following father-child relationships: $E_{KB} = \cup_i E_{FC_i} \cup \{(n_{KB}, n_{FC_1}), (n_{KB}, n_{FC_2}),$ where i is the label collection modeling i^{th} fuzzy concept and n_{KB} is a dummy root label joining together the different fuzzy concepts sub trees. At same way, focusing on fuzzy rule base, a fuzzy rule is a composition of fuzzy antecedent and consequent parts and, recursively, the antecedents and consequents can be characterized by a sequence of fuzzy clauses, where, each fuzzy clause, is represented through a pair *(FuzzyV ariable, FuzzyTerm)* (in Mamdani case). In short, the labeled tree modeling the fuzzy rule base is: $\Sigma_{RB} = \cup_i E_{FR_i} \cup \{(n_{RB}, n_{FR_1}), (n_{RB}, n_{FR_2})$, with the following father-child relationships: $E_{RB} = \cup_i E_{RB_i} \cup \{(n_{RB}, n_{RB_1}), (n_{RB}, n_{RB_2})$, where I is the label collection modeling i^{th} fuzzy rule and n_{RB} is a dummy root label joining together the different fuzzy rule sub trees. At the end each fuzzy controller can be modeled by means of a labeled tree populating by following labels: $\Sigma_{FLC} = \Sigma_{RB} \cup \Sigma_{KB} \cup \{n_I$ and $E_{FLC} = E_{KB} \cup E_{RB} \cup \{(n_{FLC}, n_{RB}), (n_{FLC}, n_K$, where n_{FLC} is a dummy node joining the fuzzy rule base and knowledge base.

3 A Novel Abstract Representation for Transparent Fuzzy Agent Design

The XML representation of FLC allows to model the controller in a human-readable and hardware independent way, i.e., through XML is possible to implement the same FLC on different hardware without additional design and implementation steps. The XML-based language modeling FLCs is named Fuzzy Markup Language(FML) and its fundamentals items, the tags and attributes, are the labels belonging to Σ set.

3.1 Fuzzy Markup Language Definition

The FLC labeled tree is an theoretical representation of a fuzzy logic controller. In order to move FLC tree model to a computer application context, it is necessary to define an opportune computer language grammar mapping the set of labels and relationships defined into the FLC labeled tree. *Document Type Definition* and *XML Schema* are used to define the FML grammar[7][8].

3.2 FLC Labeled Tree and FML in Multi-Agent Systems

The distribution of tasks and resources is both one of the major domains of multi-agent systems. In the FLC design could be very interesting and useful to distribute the fuzzy inference on different computing resources in order to speed up fuzzy computation and to localize rule subset 'near' their data sources. In order to allow this fuzzy distribution, FLC has to be considered as a set of distributed disjoint rule set evaluated in parallel fashion by software agents, hosted on different computing devices, and able to compute appropriate fuzzy operators. In order to fix our transparent FLC view in a multi-agent environment it is necessary to show how FLC tree can be broken in different subtasks, each one representing a portion of initial fuzzy rule base. Let $\Sigma_{RB} = \cup_i E_{FR_i} \cup \{(n_{RB}. n_{FR.}), (r_{RB}, r_{FR_2})$ be the rule base of our fuzzy controller and n the number of rules. For instance, this rule set can be simply splitted into two different rule base as follows:

$$\Sigma_{RB}^{1} = | \; | E_{FR_i} \cup \{ (n_{RB}, n_{FR_1}), (n_{RB}, n_{FR_3}), \ldots \}$$

$$\Sigma_{RB}^{2} = | \; | \; E_{FR_i} \cup \{ (n_{RB}, n_{FR_{\lceil n \rceil}}), (n_{RB}, n_{FR_{\lceil n \rceil \ldots}}), \ldots \}$$

This splitting produces two different controllers each one dealing with half of rules contained into . The proposed schema allows to create a fuzzy agency characterized by following agents categories: Splitter agents and Fuzzy agents. The *Splitter agent* is devoted to create a collection of disjoint rule set by following the previous schema; the *Fuzzy agent* is a software entity able to compute the fuzzy inference operator on a rule partition coming from Splitter agent. More in details, if n is the cardinality of initial rule base and m is the number of fuzzy agents populating the agency then the splitter agent move at most $\lceil n/m \rceil$ rules on each of fuzzy agents.

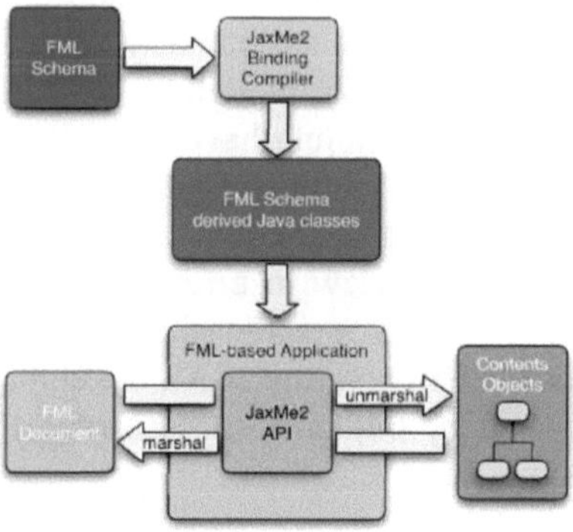

Fig. 3. JaxMe2/FML/Java binding

3.3 Implementing the FML Fuzzy Agents

The FML codes represent only an human-oriented and hardware-independent representation of a fuzzy controller, i.e., the FML programs cannot be computed in a direct way. JaxMe2 represents a direct way to compile and compute the FML services. In fact, the JaxMe2 allows to translate the XML tree structure (in our case, the FOM) into a Java classes hierarchy in direct and simple way through the JaxMe2 compiler. Specifically, JaxMe2 can generate Java classes from XML schemas by means of a JaxMe2 binding compiler. The JaxMe2 binding compiler takes XML schemas as input, and then generates a package of Java classes and interfaces, which reflect the rules defined in the source schema. The JaxMe2 binding framework provides methods for unmarshalling XML instance documents into Java content trees, a hierarchy of Java data objects that represent the source XML data, and for marshalling Java content trees back into XML instance documents. The

JaxMe2/FML/Java binding is depicted in figure 3. In order to complete the Java representation of FML fuzzy controllers, a fuzzy wrapper class, named FML-Controller has been coded. In particular, FMLController class exhibits a set of methods able to apply the appropriate fuzzy operators to the information derived from JaxMe2 objects. In particular, FMLController constructors allow to create a new fuzzy controller by using the unmarshall method of JaxMe2-API independently from FML file location (file system or network).

4 Integrated Development Environment for Transparent Fuzzy Agent Design

The tree representation of a FLC and, consequently, its mapping in FML language offers an additional important benefit: it allows to design and implement a fuzzy controller by means of simple visual steps. In other words, the FLC tree nature allow the designer to draw a controller through drag and drop actions, i.e., at the same way of visual programming languages allow to write computer programs only making use of the mouse device. By exploiting this benefit an advanced integrated development environment for FLC design and implementation has been realized Its main features are: 1) Fuzzy controller drawing; 2) FML modeling, 3) FML controller synthesis. Fuzzy controller drawing and FML modeling have been discussed previously. FML controller synthesis is a further benefit coming from XML nature of Fuzzy Markup Language. In fact, proposed application exploits the JaxMe2 tools in order to translate the FML abstract controller view in a real implementation based on Java computer languages. Figure 5 shows a screenshot of realized IDE application (FuzzyIDE). Through proposed approach, the MAS developer can define the agent intelligence simply drawing a fuzzy tree and, successively, they can 'compile' this tree obtaining an computable object.

5 Conclusion

In this paper, several principles for structuring systems support for smart multi-agent environments have been presented. Precisely, a novel model for fuzzy controller has been realized; this new representation, based on labeled tree structure, allows to design transparent fuzzy controller, i.e., control systems able to be reprogrammed on different hardware without repeating the design and implementation steps. Moreover, the recursive nature of labeled tree allows to embed the transparent fuzzy controllers in a distributed environment (multi-agent system) in a direct way. The joint use of labeled tree and multi-agent environment has allowed the implementation of an advanced graphical environment allowing the fuzzy designers to draw their ideas by means of distributed fuzzy controllers achieving a drastic decrease of control systems development time.

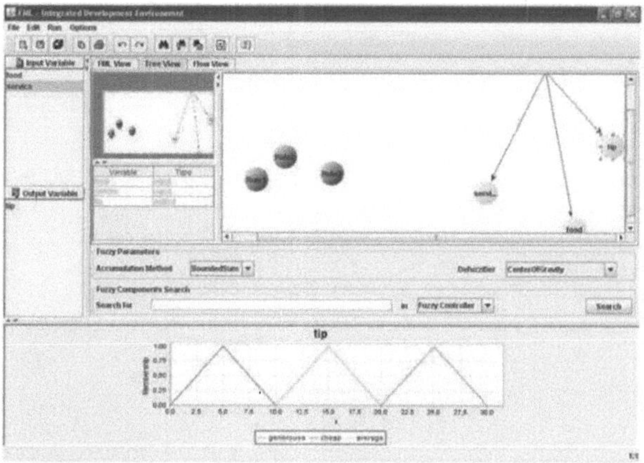

Fig. 4. FML IDE Screenshot

References

1. Ferber J (1999), Multi-Agent Systems: An Introduction to Distributed Artificial Intelligence, Addison Wesley.

2. Acampora G, Loia V (2005) Fuzzy control interoperability and scalability for adaptive domotic framework, *IEEE Transactions on Industrial Informatics*, Vol. 1, No. 2, pp. 97–111.

3. Mamdani EH (1974) Applications of fuzzy algorithms for simple dynamic plants, in *Proc. IEE*, vol. 121, pp. 1585–1588.

4. Zadeh LA (1965) Fuzzy set, *Inform. Control* vol. 8, pp. 338–353, 1965.

5. Hagras H (2007) Type-2 FLCs: A New Generation of Fuzzy Controllers, *IEEE Computational Intelligence Magazine*, Vol. 2, pp. 30–44.

6. Wang YL, Chen HC, Liu WK (1996) A Parallel Algorithm for Constructing a Labeled Tree, *IEEE Transactions on Parallel and Distributed Systems*, Vol. 8, pp. 1236–1240.

7. Acampora G, Loia V (2004) Fuzzy control interoperability for adaptive domotic framework, *IEEE International Conference on Industrial Informatics*, pp. 184–189

8. Acampora G, Loia V (2006) Ubiquitous Fuzzy Computing in Open Ambient Intelligence Environments, *IEEE International Conference on Fuzzy Systems*, Vancouver, Canada, pp. 465–470

Archetypal Internet-Scale Source Code Searching

Medha Umarji[1], Susan Elliott Sim[2], and Crista Lopes[2]
[1] University of Maryland Baltimore County,
Department of Information Systems
Baltimore, Maryland, USA
medha1@umbc.edu,
WWW home page: http://userpages.umbc.edu/~medha1/
[2] University of California, Irvine, Department of Informatics,
Irvine, California, USA
{ses, lopes}@ics.uci.edu,
WWW home page: http:// www.ics.uci.edu/~ses/
WWW home page: http:// www.ics.uci.edu/~lopes/

Abstract. Programmers often search for Open Source code to use in their projects. To understand how and why programmers search for source code, we conducted a web-based survey and collected data from 69 respondents, including 58 specific examples of searches. Analyzing these anecdotes, we found that they could be categorized along two orthogonal dimensions: motivation (reuse vs. reference example) and size of search target. The targets of these searches could range in size from a block (a few lines of code) to a subsystem (e.g. library or API), to an entire system. Within these six combinations of motivations and target sizes, nine repeating motifs, or archetypes, were created to characterize Internet-scale source code searching. Tools used for searching and the criteria for selecting a component are also discussed. We conclude with guidance on how these archetypes can inform better evaluation of Internet-scale code search engines, as well as the design of new features for these tools.

Keywords: *Source code, search engine, empirical study, Open Source*

1 Introduction

The growth of Open Source has made a "rich base of reusable software" available on the Internet that programmers leverage in their own software development projects [1]. As this opportunistic software development becomes increasingly prevalent, finding the right snippet, component or application to reuse becomes a common activity for developers. However, little is known about how they go about these searches. To this end, we conducted an online survey of programmers and asked them to give us specific examples of how they searched for source code, the tools they used, and criteria for making a final selection.

Please use the following format when citing this chapter:

Umarji, M., Sim, S.E. and Lopes, C., 2008, in IFIP International Federation for Information Processing, Volume 275; *Open Source Development, Communities and Quality*; Barbara Russo, Ernesto Damiani, Scott Hissam, Björn Lundell, Giancarlo Succi; (Boston: Springer), pp. 257–263.

A total of 69 participants responded to our survey and contributed 58 anecdotes about how they searched. By analyzing the anecdotes qualitatively and inductively, a number of patterns or "archetypes" were identified. These anecdotes could be categorized along two orthogonal dimensions: motivation and size of search target. With respect to motivation, participants tended to be looking for code that could be reused with little or no modification, or they were looking for code to use as a reference example. Often a search began by looking for code to reuse without modification, but when one was not found, a close match was used as a reference example. Within these categories, we identified nine different archetypes.

The remainder of this paper is organized as follows. We describe our research method in Section 2. In Section 3, we present our categorization and archetypes. In Section 4, we discuss how our participants conducted their searches. We explore how these archetypes can be applied in Section 5 and we make some concluding remarks in Section 6.

2 Online Survey

Surveys have become an established empirical method, especially for Internet usage [2][3]. We designed an online survey with 13 closed-ended questions and two open-ended questions. The survey also had questions about the different tools used during search, programmer background, and criteria for finally selecting a component. In this paper, we will be focusing on the data from one of the open-ended questions, which asked:

Please describe one or two scenarios when you were looking for source code on the Internet.
(Please address details such as: What were you trying to find? How did you formulate your queries? What information sources did you use to find the source code? Which implementation language were you working with? What criteria did you use to decide on the best match?)

We solicited responses using convenience sampling by sending invitations to participate in the survey to the following newsgroups and mailing lists: Javaworld mailing list, the CGI beginner's list on perl.org, comp.software-eng, comp.lang.c, and comp.lang.java. While our responses give us a broad overview of how software developers search for source code, there is no way to determine whether we obtained a representative, random sample. Consequently, we present our results as qualitative archetypes rather than quantitative statistics.

An archetype is a concept from literary theory. It serves to unify recurring images across literary works with a similar structure. In the context of source code searching, an archetype is a theory to unify and integrate typical or recurring searches. The archetypes were produced by analyzing the anecdotes for recurring patterns using open coding [4] and a grounded theory approach [5].

3 Archetypes

In this section, we present the archetypes that we found in our study. Each theme or archetype was a combination of a search motivation and size of search target with additional details about the context.

Detailed analysis of scenarios showed that respondents were either searching for *reusable code* (34) or *reference examples* (17). A key difference between the two motivations is how much modification was expected to reuse the code. Reusable code is source code that they could just drop into their program and use right away, such as a component implementing a quick sort algorithm. A reference example is a piece of code that illustrates a particular solution but needs to be re-implemented or significantly modified; for instance, the syntax of a particular method call in Java.

Across both types of searches, the size of the search target varied in a similar fashion. The size was a continuous variable ranging from a few lines to an entire system, but we defined three broad categories in our analysis. The sizes of the search targets were classified as a block (11), a subsystem (32), or a system (8).

Table 1: Motivation by Target Size

	Description	Code for Reuse	Reference Example	Row Total
Block	Wrappers, parsers, code excerpts	7	4	11
Subsystem	Code of algorithms and data structures, GUI widgets, Library, APIs	21	11	32
System	Stand-alone Applications	6	2	8
Column Total		34	17	51

3.1 Motivation: Reuse

As can be seen in Table 1, there were 34 searches that were motivated by reuse without modification. Upon performing a thematic appraisal, we were able to identify four archetypes or themes of searches within the reuse motivation. The archetypes are presented in increasing order of target size.

Looking for code snippets, wrappers or parsers: The seven searches where developers were looking for a block of code to reuse included searches for a "Java wrapper code for the native pcap library" and an "RSS feed parser." Also included were searches that performed some small functionality, like "encode/decode a URL" and "convert uploaded images of all types to jpeg". At this level of granularity we included searches for source code components that solved a small problem, or for code snippets to add functionality (with little or no modification).

Reusable data structures, algorithms and GUI widgets to be incorporated into an implementation: Participants were looking for subsystems such as algorithms and data structures; "two-way hash tables," "B+ trees," "trie trees," and "binary search algorithm" were some of the eight searches included in this archetype. These searches are popular, as there is a close match between the vocabulary in the code and the vocabulary for describing the search. There were also seven searches for graphical user interface (GUI) widgets in our data, for example "inserting a browser in a Java Swing frame." GUI widgets are easy to reuse, and provided the widget was written using the same GUI framework as the project being developed, there could be relatively few compatibility problems.

A reusable library to be incorporated into an implementation: There were six searches for a reusable package or API. Some examples of the searches were for "speech processing toolkits", "library for date manipulation in Perl" and "Java implementations of statistical techniques."

A reusable system to be used as a starting point for an implementation: In six searches, developers were looking for "stand-alone tools" or a "backbone for an upcoming project" or just a "big piece of code that does more or less what I want." Examples of search targets included an application server, an ERP package or a database management system. We conjecture that this type of search is common, because a system does not need to be de-contextualized before it is used in a new project. Also, systems are easy to find because they typically have web sites or project pages that contain text descriptions of the software.

3.2 Motivation: Reference Examples

There were 17 searches for reference examples, as shown in Table 1. We also used thematic appraisal on these searches, and coincidentally found four archetypes.

A block of code to be used as an example: Programmers were not looking for reusable components, but their goal was to learn through examples, such as "examples of thread implementation in python." Respondents reported that "reference examples of language syntax and idioms" were helpful when working with an unfamiliar programming language, and "…mostly I look for code for syntax, I don't always like to refer to books for syntax if it is readily available on my desktop."

Example of how to implement a data structure, algorithm or GUI widget: In three instances, developers looked for source code snippets to verify their solution or to aid in re-implementation, e.g. "to verify the implementation of a well-known algorithm." An implementation is more informative than a description or pseudocode, and a running program has a lot of credibility. There were also two searches for examples of how to use GUI widgets. These included searches for code samples on how to use a particular component from Swing and Microsoft Foundation Classes.

Example of how to use a library: Developers looked for examples of how to use a library in six instances, such as, "Sometimes; I did a source code searching when I don't know how to use a class or a library." Libraries and APIs can be complex to use, and a reference example is easier to understand than documentation, because it gives the programmer a starting point that can then be tweaked to suit the situation.

Looking at similar systems for ideas: While developing or modifying a system programmers look at existing similar systems for ideas. Two searches were for systems from which the logic/principles can be borrowed to construct new systems. This technique was mainly used when it was easier to construct a new system rather than adopt an existing one, or on a proprietary Closed Source project that could not be contaminated with Open Source code.

3.3 Information about Defects

There were five searches that did not fit the above motivations and search target matrix. These were searches for information on resolving defects.

Confirmation and resolution of defects: Developers prefer to search for a patch or quick-fix by forming natural language queries with the keywords from an error message or keywords based on the functionality deviation caused by a bug or defect. There were five searches that were looking for solutions to a defect. Sometimes the solution was in the form of a report or post to a forum that confirmed the presence of a bug. At other times, there was a patch that repaired the defect. Three of the searches led developers to find relevant information in mailing lists and forums.

4 Search Tools

A majority of the developers that responded to our survey were programmers in Java (54), C++ (58) and Perl (32). More than half of the respondents (37) had contributed to an Open Source project. Most of the respondents (41) had experience working on small teams with 1 to 5 people.

Sixty of the participants reported turning to a general-purpose search engine, such as Google or Yahoo! to search for source code. Project hosting sites came next, with 34 of the respondents using them for source code search. Only 11 out of 69 respondents reported using a code-specific search engine. Others were highly skeptical, with one participant writing, "In short, I would never rely on a 'code search engine'. This idea is just plan silly...sort of ivory tower. If you want to find something usable you have to look for people already using it." Some did just this, by using social tagging sites, such as (del.icio.us) to find code

While selecting which component to reuse, the most important single criterion was functionality. The type of software license came in second. Help from a local expert, an electronic forum, a mailing list archive, or active users, were other major considerations while choosing Open Source software. One respondent said he looked for "… issues which are then found by people, solved and posted on mailing lists of discussion forums." Overall, social characteristics of the project, such as the level of activity, seem to have precedence over characteristics of the source code, such as whether the code is peer reviewed and tested.

5 Applications of Archetypes

The search archetypes described here are a succinct representation of a developer's search for source code. We intend our results to inform further enhancement and design of these source code search engines, such as Koders, Google Code Search, and Krugle.

Inform the evaluation of code search engines: The archetypes can be instantiated into "scenarios" that closely represent the user's situation and are easily understandable by users. These scenarios can then be used to compare and evaluate the effectiveness of different search engines. For example, a generic archetype is a "Search for a reusable data structure." Now this can be instantiated into a scenario such as "Consider that you are looking for the Trie tree data structure written in C to use in your project". Such a scenario will provide the necessary contextual information for users to judge whether the results returned by search engine A are better or worse than those from search engine B.

Inform the design of additional features for these search engines: Our archetypes also point the way to possible new features in Internet-scale code search engines. For example, we found that users search for *information about a particular bug* within an open source project. This kind of search is currently not well supported by code search sites. Although a bug may not be resolved completely, people on forums and mailing lists may have discussed it, and users have to perform a text-based search to find this information. Another possible feature is *providing usage examples* for a library or package. In case a user searches for a particular library, package or API, his search experience will be enhanced if results also contain links to usage examples. Finally, based on our survey findings we observe that a *user rating or recommendation for each item returned* by a search engine will be helpful to a developer trying to choose between available options.

6 Conclusions

The main contribution of this work is insight into the varieties of Internet-scale source code searches that programmers perform. Until now, there has been little research about what types of source code programmers look for and how they find and use it. We conducted a web-based survey of how people look for code on the Internet. We identified a categorization for searches along two dimensions (motivation and size) and presented nine archetypes of searches within these categories.

The results of this study are applied to the design of tool features, and in the formation of scenarios for evaluating the existing search tools. Tools for locating source code would be complemented by recommender systems and reviews; more like Amazon.com and less like a library catalog. One of the future directions for this line of research is the use of scenarios to evaluate different search engines. We are continuing with experiments in this vein and hope to continue making contributions to Internet-scale source code searching.

References

[1] D. Spinellis and C. Szyperski, "Guest editors' introduction: How is open source affecting software development?" *IEEE Software* vol. 21 pp. 28-33 2004

[2] V. M. Sue and L. A. Ritter, *Conducting online surveys*: Sage Publications, 2007.

[3] S. E. Sim, C. L. A. Clarke, and R. C. Holt, "Archetypal source code searches: A survey of software developers and maintainers " in *Proceedings of the 6th International Workshop on Program Comprehension* IEEE Computer Society, 1998 pp. 180

[4] M. B. Miles and A. M. Huberman, *Qualitative data analysis*: Sage Publication, 1994.

[5] A. Strauss and J. Corbin, *Basics of qualitative research: Grounded theory procedures and technique*. Thousand Oaks: Sage Publications, 1990.

[6] S. Bajracharya, T. Ngo, E. Linstead, Y. Dou, P. Rigor, P. Baldi, C. Lopes. *Sourcerer: A Search Engine for Open Source Code Supporting Structure-based Search.* October 2006. Companion to the 21st ACM SIGPLAN conference on Object-oriented programming languages, systems, and applications OOPSLA '06. ACM Press.

Channeling Firefox Developers: Mom and Dad Aren't Happy Yet*

Jean-Michel Dalle[1], Matthijs den Besten[2], and Héla Masmoudi[1]

[1] Université Pierre et Marie Curie, Paris, France;
jean-michel.dalle@upmc.fr,masmoudi_hela@yahoo.fr
[2] University of Oxford, Oxford, UK; matthijs.denbesten@oerc.ox.ac.uk

Summary. Firefox, a browser targeted at mainstream users, has been one of the big successes of open source development in recent years. That Firefox succeeded where earlier attempts failed is undoubtedly due to the particular choices that were made in the process of development. In this paper, we look at this process in more detail. Mining bug reports and feature requests related to Firefox in Mozilla's Bugzilla bug tracker system, we find that the attention developers devoted to reports and requests was influenced by several factors. Most importantly, other things being equal, reports and requests from outsiders increasingly tend to be ignored. While such behavior may have helped to shield Firefox from the "alpha-geek power user" in the early stages of development, it also makes it difficult for "mom and dad" to let their voice be heard even after they have adopted Firefox.

1 Introduction

In June 2006, Blake Ross, one of the initiators of Firefox, gave an interview to Olivia Ryan. At some point, the conversation turned to the issue of project management [5]:

> Olivia Ryan: And so was it difficult sometimes to strike that balance between working on an open project and trying to keep end-users in mind? Blake Ross: Yes. Yes. Everybody hated us for a long time.

Everybody may have hated Blake Ross and his companions, but they succeeded: In 2004 Firefox appeared and it quickly became, as an article in Wired put it, "the hot new browser rocking the software world." What we would like to know now is how they succeeded.

Understanding the processes that helped shape Firefox is important for a variety of people. First of all, as more and more users adopt Firefox as their default browser, they need to be reassured that Firefox remains a stable and secure alternative that is geared towards their needs. But also the stakeholders

* The work presented here has benefited from discussions with Paul A. David and others in the context of the OII/MTI project on Distributed Problem Solving Networks.

Please use the following format when citing this chapter:

Dalle, J.-M., den Besten, M. and Masmoudi, H., 2008, in IFIP International Federation for Information Processing, Volume 275; *Open Source Development, Communities and Quality*; Barbara Russo, Ernesto Damiani, Scott Hissam, Björn Lundell, Giancarlo Succi; (Boston: Springer), pp. 265–271.

of companies that have invested in Firefox, or that consider participation in similar projects, need to ascertain whether the Firefox approach to open source development works. Ultimately, even the developers themselves, who may not always be aware of the processes that channel their behavior, could benefit from our exercise in data mining.

Methodologically, we subscribe to the suggestions of Scacchi and Sack and others [7, 6] that the processes of open source software development can be discovered by studying the patterns of interactions between the developers and the resulting code. Our recurring obsession, in this study and in previous studies, is to identify what one could call *stigmergic* features in the interactions [1]. Like pheromone guiding ants from the nest to the food source, we consider that, lacking strict managerial control, there must be elements in the code and documentation that nudge developers to devote their attention in specific directions. Previous results of ours suggest that developers do indeed react to signals like the complexity of the code and address *complex* tasks in teams [3]. Further, we found that *contextual* elements, be it the level of detail in the specification of the task or linkage with related tasks, affect the speed with which tasks are dealt with and we also found that a lack of contextual elements may make it necessary to revisit the task several times [2]. In the study here, we focus at the attraction of ownership: Does it make a difference whether the task stems from the project *core* or from its *periphery*? In particular, does it make a difference for the resolution of a bug, whether the bug was reported by an insider or by an outsider? Short answer: yes. The long-term research agenda to which this study contributes is to derive an ontology of distributed process management from the structured, semi-structured, and unstructured data that document open source software development. Our hope for our ontology is that it could help assess the sustainability and evolution of projects like Firefox.

"We're making a product for mom and dad." Blake Ross said of Firefox [4]. That is probably not the case for our research. Nevertheless, in what follows, we will make a valiant attempt to share our preliminary findings. First, we describe in greater detail the bug-report data that we collected and how we connected them with information on bug-histories and code-patches. Next, we will present our preliminary results which suggest that the same process that helped make Firefox a product for mom and dad in the first place now threaten to lead to a neglect of mom and dad's needs in the future.

2 Data

Sack and others note that developers coordinate their activity almost exclusively in three information spaces: "the implementation space, the documentation space, and the discussion space" [6]. Our collection covers each of these spaces, at least partially. It covers the implementation space in so far as we only consider bugs that are mentioned in commits to the official code base that were kept by the Mozilla concurrent versions system (CVS). For those bugs, in so far as they are associated with a file of which at least one revision is part of a Firefox release, we retrieve the bug-reports and the logs of changes to those bug reports kept by the bug tracker system Bugzilla. Thus, we are covering the documentation space as well. We also cover the discussion space since mailing-list style comments relating to the bugs are included in the reports. However, if Blake Ross is right in his assessment that Internet Relay Chat "was a big means of communication and especially with Firefox early on" [5], then we might have a problem, because, too our knowledge, archives of those chats have not been kept.

On the other hand, so far, we haven't done the text mining to which the chat archives and bug comments lend themselves. Instead, for now we have focused on a range of more readily quantifiable indicators. From the CVS, we retrieved for each bug the number of different authors referring to the bug in their commit-comments; the number of files touched by these commits; the number of distinct comments and the number of commit; and, finally, the number of lines of code added and deleted through the commits. From the bug-reports, we retrieved the number of persons copied in the bug resolution discussion; the number of other bugs the bug depends on or blocks; the numbers of attachments, patches and comments and the number of distinct contributors to the discussion; and, besides, the number of bugs that were identified as a duplicate of the bug reported. In addition, we retrieved the priority assigned and the severity estimated for each bug. With help of the change-log of the bug-reports, we also retrieved the time that passed between the opening of the report and the assignment of someone in charge of the resolution process; we retrieved the number of times the bug was (re-)assigned whether its priority was incremented or decremented or had been changed more than once; whether its severity increased or decreased or changed more than once — where the importance was judged to be in order of trivial, enhancement, minor, normal, major, critical, blocker. We determined whether the initial status of the bug report was New or Unconfirmed; whether the bug was reopened at least once; the number of report edits by the bug-reporter, and the number of report edits by the last person in charge of its resolution.

We drew two samples of bugs from the 40 000 or so that have resulted in a change to the Firefox code base. The first from the early stages of the project, when Firefox was still called Phoenix, in between release 0.1 and 0.5; the second from a later, more mature, phase between release 1.5 and release 2.0. For the moment, we ignore bugs where the severity was judged to be enhancement as we want to focus on bug reports rather than feature requests.

3 Results

Blake Ross described the Firefox development philosophy thus [4]:

> We're making a product for mom and dad. You still have a voice here, but some of the features that you think we should add may not be the

> ones that they want tot use. So you have to take our word for it that, even though 500 of you want something right now, you may actually be in the minority of a much larger group that we're pursuing that's going to be silent during this phase of development.

Bug reports provide an invaluable window where we should be able to see this philosophy in action. It is there that we can witness the interaction between users and developers and it is also there that we can see how developers manage to balance the demands from the early adopters, the "alpha-geek power user" against those from those targeted, mom and dad. Take for instance bug 213186[2]. This bug report is a request to alter the text in the preference pane and in particular to replace the geek-humour of "Cookies are delicious delicacies" with a more appropriate explanation for concerned users without prior knowledge of the concept. Blake Ross himself was responsible for the "delicious delicacies" joke in the first place and his mom and dad might well have approved. Many other users however might be put off by the lack of information provided by people who seriously want to consider whether want to accept cookies or not. And the eventual resolution of bug 213186 shows that the concerns of these people were eventually recognized as "delicious delicacies" was replaced by "pieces of information stored by web pages on your computer[. . .]." Table 1 gives a few indicators for the extent and the duration of the bug-report. From these indicators, it is already clear that considerable effort was required to resolve this bug — effort that was mainly devoted to the construction of consensus between the geeks who like this humour and the advocates of mom and dad who did not.

Table 1. Characterization of bug 213186–*Please remove 'Cookies are delicious delicacies' from Options→Privacy→Cookies* and bug 171349–*Mozilla Firefox Icon is Windowing System's Standard Icon.*

Parameter Description	Bug 213186	Bug 171349
Reported	2003-07-19	2002-09-28
Fixed	2004-12-03	2005-05-30
Initial Status	Unconfirmed	New
Severity	trivial	normal
Time to First Assignment(*hrs*)	314	576
Number of Comments	55	206
Number of Authors of Comments	18	89
Number of Duplicates	1	31
Number of Patches	9	11

Bug 171349[3] is the other bug that is characterized in the table. The subject matter is less exciting — a lot of the attention for bug 213186 could be because

[2] `https://bugzilla.mozilla.org/show_bug.cgi?id=213186`

[3] `https://bugzilla.mozilla.org/show_bug.cgi?id=171349`

it is a bike shed like discussion in which it is easy to have an opinion[4] — but that does not make this bug less important *per se*. What is interesting about this bug is why it took so long to resolve. As one commenter remarks:

> > This bug was first discovered about 2 1/2 years ago and is still listed as "NEW"?
> Mozilla, like all the other big projects, has a LOT of bureuacracy [sic] going on. Ireported this so long ago I forgot all about it, and probably would've submitted it again if it weren't for the recent activity of my report being marked as a dupe... But even if it requires 5 people to check it and give it their OK,surely adding a .ico to the package can't be /that/ hard, can it? (Shish, 16/03/2005, comment #165)

As bug 171349 is the kind of bug that typically matters more to mom and dad than to a power user, the question is relevant whether the difficulty of the resolution of this bug was typical in Firefox development or the exception.

In order to get an impression of the general patterns of bug resolution in Firefox, we performed a survival analysis of a variety of samples of bug-reports related to Firefox. Table 2 presents the results. We carried out regressions on six samples: A sample of bugs related to Firefox in the early phases of its development; a sample of bugs related to Firefox in a later phase of its development; and for both of these samples a sub-sample of bugs started their life as New and another sub-sample for those bugs that started their life as Unconfirmed.

The difference between New and Unconfirmed is due to the fact that only a subset of the members of the Firefox community have the so-called CanConfirm privilege, according to which their bugs start as New and do not need confirmation — which is precisely needed otherwise to move from Unconfirmed to New. This privilege is granted by cooptation, based on the past track record of developers asking for it, and we therefore consider for the sake of the analysis here that it characterizes members of the core of the community, as compared to more peripheral members without this privilege.

What emerges from the table is that bug treatment in the early phases of Firefox was different from treatment at a later stage. More in particular, the difference between the treatment of bugs that stem from outsiders in contrast to the treatment of bugs in general seems more pronounced in the more recent samples. Besides, issues like the complexity of the problem and effort devoted to the contextualisation of the problem still play a role in determining the speed with which a bug is typically resolved.

4 Conclusion

Firefox is an open source project that so far has enjoyed a wide appeal among mainstream users as well as developers. In this paper, we argued that a study

[4] see `http://www.bikeshed.org`

Table 2. Significance and impact of variables controlling for bug fixing regimes (Survival analysis; Weibull fit).

Sample:	Phoenix (< 0.5)			Firefox (> 1.5)		
Parameter Description	All	New	Unconf'ed	All	New	Unconf.
# Bugs	7596	6200	1366	4721	3465	1256
Intercept	+***	+*	+**	+***	+*	+**
Number Of Different Committers	+***	+***	+***	+***	+***	
Number Of Files Touched in Codebase	+***	+***	+***	+***	+**	+•
Number Of Different Comments in Commits				+***	+***	
Number Of Commits	−*		−***	−***	−*	
Number Of Lines Of Code Added	−***	−***	+***			
Number Of Lines Of Code Deleted			+*			
Number Of Persons Copied	−**	−**			+*	−***
Number Of Attachments	+*		+*			
Number Of Patches				+•		
Depends On How Many Other Bugs	+**	+*	+*			+•
Blocks How Many Other Bugs	+*	+**				
Number Of Comments			•			+**
Number Of Authors Of Comments	+***	+***	+***	+***	+***	+***
Severity Trivial	+***	+***	+***	+***	+***	
Severity Minor	+***	+***	+***	+***	+***	
Severity Normal	+***	+***	+***	+***	+***	
Severity Major	+***	+***	+***		+*	
Severity Critical	+***	+***	+***		+**	−*
No Priority	−*	−*				
Priority 1	−**	−*	−*			
Priority 2	−*					+*
Priority 3	−*	−*				+•
Priority 4						
Log Time To First Assignment	+***	+***	+***	+***	+***	+***
Number Of Times Bug Was Assigned	+***	+***	+***	+***	+***	+***
Priority Was Increased	+*	•				
Priority Was Decreased	+**	+*	•	+**	+**	
Priority Was Changed More Than Once	•	•				+•
Severity Was Increased				+**	+***	
Severity Was Decreased				+*		+*
Severity Was Changed More Than Once						
Initial Status Was New				−**		
Bug Was Reopened At Least Once	•					−•
Number Of Edits By Bug Reporter			•	−**	−**	−**
Number Of Edits By Last Assignee		+***	•		+*	
Number Of Duplicates		−*	−*	−***	−***	

of the Firefox bug resolution processes is crucial to an understanding of the dynamics of its development. We described bug-reports and their association with code-commits. We described two bugs in detail and we discusses our preliminary efforts to detects patterns in the survival of bugs in general. Our findings suggest that Firefox developers tend to ignore the concerns that are voiced by outsiders, especially so in the later stages of its development. Does this mean that mom and dad, for whom Firefox was meant, are increasingly ignored as well — that remains to be seen. If this were true, however, it wouldn't bode well for Firefox' future.

The research described here constitutes just the first steps of a more ambitious research agenda in which the ultimate goal is to derive an ontology of distributed project management. What we have done here is to investigate the interaction between core and periphery in one project. For now, all we have is a suggestion that the current situation might not be optimal. But as our understanding grows and as our ontology expands, we could imagine a future in which the ontology itself would be used to optimize the development processes of open source software by accounting for the management of attention. And that could be a further step in making mom and dad happier.

References

1. J.-M. Dalle and P. David. Simulating code growth in libre (open-source) mode. In N. Curien and E. Brousseau, editors, *The Economics of the Internet.* Cambridge University Press, Cambridge, UK, 2007.
2. J.-M. Dalle and M. den Besten. Different bug fixing regimes? A preliminary case for superbugs. In *Proceedings of the Third International Conference on Open Source Systems*, Limerick, Ireland, June 2007. To appear.
3. M. den Besten, J.-M. Dalle, and F. Galia. Collaborative maintenance in large open-source projects. In E. Damiani, B. Fitzgerald, W. Scacchi, M. Scotto, and G. Succi, editors, *Open Source Systems*, volume 203 of *IFIP International Federation for Information Processing*, pages 233–244, Boston, 2006. Springer. Received best paper award.
4. J. Livingston. Blake Ross; creator, Firefox. In *Founders at Work: Stories of Startups' Early Days.* Apress, 2007.
5. O. Ryan. Interview with Blake Ross. Archived at http://mozillamemory.org, June 2006.
6. W. Sack, F. Détienne, N. Duchenaut, J.-M. Burkhardt, D. Mahedran, and F. Barcellini. A methodological framework for socio-cognitive analyses of collaborative design of open source software. *Computer Supported Cooperative Work*, 15(2-3):229–250, 2006.
7. W. Scacchi. Socio-technical interaction networks in free/open source software development processes. In S. T. Acuna and N. Juristo, editors, *Software Process Modeling*, pages 1–27. Springer, New York, NY, 2005.

Continuous Integration in Open Source Software Development

Amit Deshpande,

TechSolve, Inc.
6705 Steger Drive
45237 Cincinnati, OH, U.S.A.

amit@amit-deshpande.com

Dirk Riehle

SAP Research, SAP Labs LLC
3475 Deer Creek Rd
94304 Palo Alto, CA, U.S.A.

dirk@riehle.org

Abstract. Commercial software firms are increasingly using and contributing to open source software. Thus, they need to understand and work with open source software development processes. This paper investigates whether the practice of continuous integration of agile software development methods has had an impact on open source software projects. Using fine-granular data from more than 5000 active open source software projects we analyze the size of code contributions over a project's life-span. Code contribution size has stayed flat. We interpret this to mean that open source software development has not changed its code integration practices. In particular, within the limits of this study, we claim that the practice of continuous integration has not yet significantly influenced the behavior of open source software developers.

1 Introduction

Open source software is having a major impact on software and its production processes. Many software products today contain at least some open source software components. Some commercial products are completely open source software. For commercial software firms it is therefore important to understand open source software development processes and ensure that employed developers are capable of participating in them [13].

Open source software development processes are different from commercial software development processes like the spiral model [5] or agile methods [4]. Open source processes can vary from project to project. With no single well-defined open source process, it is unclear for hiring managers what skills to look for when hiring people for open source software projects.

One common hypothesis is that open source software processes are similar to agile development processes and hence that agile method skills could serve as a proxy for open source software development skills [12] [14]. However, this hypothesis has never been validated. Indeed, it is impossible to prove as long as open source processes remain as vaguely defined as they are today.

This paper analyses the use of continuous integration within open source software projects. Continuous integration is a practice where software developers work

---

Please use the following format when citing this chapter:

Deshpande, A. and Riehle, D., 2008, in IFIP International Federation for Information Processing, Volume 275; *Open Source Development, Communities and Quality*; Barbara Russo, Ernesto Damiani, Scott Hissam, Björn Lundell, Giancarlo Succi; (Boston: Springer), pp. 273–280.

in small increments, contributing code to the project frequently, and ensuring that the project compiles and passes its test suites at any time [11].

Continuous integration is a core agile methods practice. If it is also an important open source development practice, managers can hire more confidently developers for open source projects who have been educated in agile methods and who have appropriate experience with continuous integration.

To answer the question "Have open source projects increasingly been using continuous integration?" we looked at the individual actions of developers from 5122 active open source software projects. Specifically, we looked at the size (in source lines of code) of code contributions and their frequency.

The paper is organized as follows. Section 2 frames our hypothesis. Section 3 discusses our database and the details of the validation approach. Section 4 presents the results of the analysis. Section 5 discusses the shortcomings and limitations of the analysis. Section 6 discusses related work. Section 7 concludes the paper.

2 Is Open Source Using Continuous Integration?

Agile software development methods like Extreme Programming "embrace change": There is no insistence on following a master-plan, but the willingness to respond to (requirements) change quickly [3]. This is in stark contrast to traditional approaches to software development with their insistence on detailed planning ahead.

It is not obvious how open source projects relate to agile methods. According to Fugetta, "[Agile methods] can be equally applied to proprietary and open source software" [1]. Thus, with the advent of agile methods around 1997/1998, one might expect to see an adoption of agile methods practices in open source software development over the last ten years.

Thus, we are asking: *What is the impact of (the arrival of) agile methods on open source software development processes?* And then, more specifically: *Is continuous integration a widely used practice in open source software projects?* The answer to this question is important to software firms who engage with open source software projects, because they need to hire, cultivate, and maintain the appropriate skill sets of their employees to work with open source projects.

We chose continuous integration as a representative practice of agile methods like Extreme Programming [3] or SCRUM [6]. "Continuous integration is the practice of making small well-defined changes to a project's code base and getting immediate feedback to see whether the test suites still pass" [11].

If continuous integration had not been employed in open source projects before its first formulations around 1997 but has been increasingly employed since then, we would expect to see a statistically significant behavioral change in how open source software developers contribute code to open source projects. Specifically: *We would expect to see that the average size of code contributions, the individual check-in into a source code repository, would have gone down over the last ten years, and we would expect to see that the average frequency of such check-ins has gone up.*

To investigate this hypothesis, we analyzed more than 5000 active open source software projects, as discussed in the following sections.

3 Data Source and Approach

For the analysis, we use the database of the open source analytics firm Ohloh.net [10]. The database contains 5122 current and active open source projects from 1990 until May 2007.

We analyze the last 16 years from January 1990 to December 2006. The database contains the most popular open source projects as measured by the number of in-links to their website. The in-links are provided by the Yahoo! search engine.

Ohloh.net goes down to the level of the individual developer action. Specifically, Ohloh.net provides each individual commit action of all the projects over their entire history. A commit is the action with which a developer contributes a piece of code to the project's repository.

3.1 The Commit Action

A commit action is the atomic contribution of source code to a code repository. We measure the amount of work that went into a commit in Source Lines of Code (SLoC) added, changed, and removed, ignoring empty lines and comments. SLoC is based on applying the Unix diff command to two consecutive source file versions.

Unfortunately, Ohloh.net counts a changed line as an old line removed and a new line added. One line of code edited will be tracked as one line added and one line removed. Table 1 represents the resulting three cases. From this data alone we cannot determine the exact number of lines of code affected. Thus, in Section 3.3 we will take two approaches representing the upper and the lower bound respectively.

3.2 Commit Action Filtering

We want to study the size of a commit over time. In order to perform a valid analysis we impose four filters to exclude special and undesired events:

1. The initial commit (creation) of a file
2. The final commit (deletion) of a file
3. Commits of a size larger than three standard deviations above the average
4. Commits of a size smaller than three standard deviations below the average

Filter 3 eliminates the cases where a developer adds a large amount of external code to an existing file and Filter 4 eliminates commits where a large amount of code is removed, like in a major refactoring. None of these events helps us understand changes in commit size patterns.

Table 1: Data semantics (SLoC = Line of Source Code)

Case	Commit Action	SLoC Added	SLoC Removed
1	One line of code added	1	0
2	One line of code removed	0	1
3	One line of code edited	1	1

3.3 Analysis of Commit Size

Approach 1 adds the number of lines of code added in one commit to the number of lines of code removed in the same commit. Following the discussion of Section 3.1, editing a single line will be counted as one line added plus one line removed. Thus, the size calculated by Approach 1 represents the upper bound for the commit size.

Figure 1 shows the average size of a commit (as defined by Approach 1) per week from 1990 to 2006. The size is shown on the Y-axis and time is shown on the X-axis. To smooth out fluctuations and to highlight the longer-term trends or cycles we fit a moving average (period = 10) curve on the plot. The commit size is nearly constant and shows no significant trend or pattern over time.

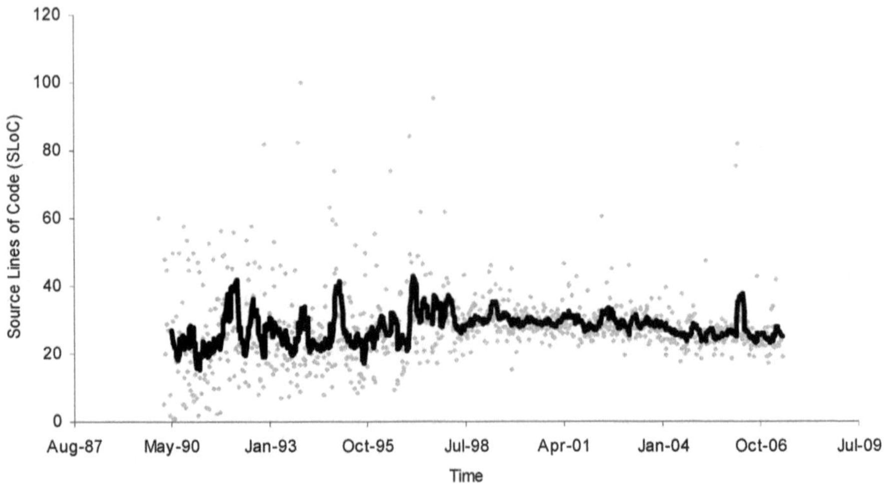

Figure 1: Upper bound of commit size in SLoC over time (Approach 1)

Approach 2 subtracts the number of lines of code removed from the number of lines of code added. Thus, an edited line will not be counted, and the value reflects the net change to the size of a file only. Thus, the commit size as calculated by Approach 2 represents the lower bound for the actual size of the commit.

Figure 2 shows the average size of a commit (as defined by Approach 2) per week using the same axes labeling and moving average curve. The commit size is nearly constant and shows no significant trend or pattern over time.

We tested the validity of our results using hypothesis testing. The null hypothesis is: The average commit size in any year is equal to the average size during the next year. The research hypothesis is: The average commit size in any year is greater than the average commit size during the next year.

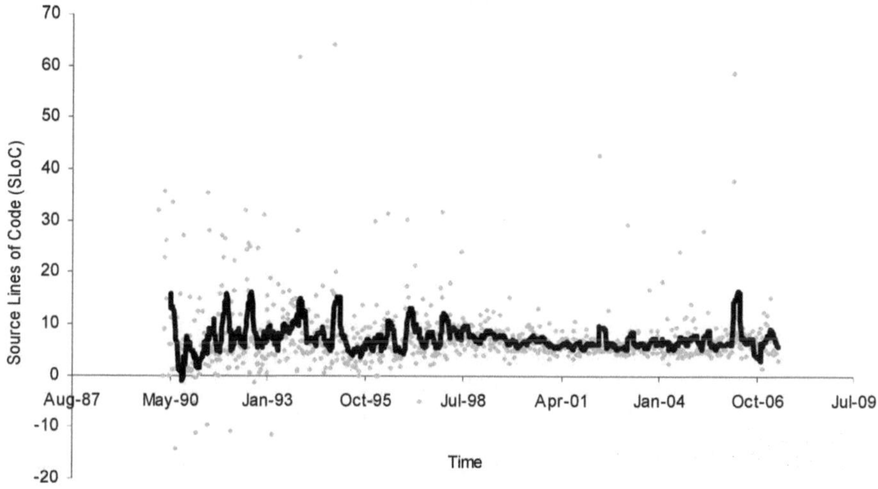

Figure 2: Lower bound of commit size in SLoC (Approach 2)

No clear picture resulted at the 95% confidence level. In a few cases, we could reject the null hypothesis, in most we could not. Within the limits of the study we conclude that the commit size remained constant with no significant trend or pattern over time.

4 Results of Analysis

Our analysis does not validate the hypothesis that open source software developers are practicing continuous integration. Our indicator, the average size of a commit, remained almost constant over the years with no significant trend or pattern. We applied a similar analysis (not given in this short paper) which showed that the commit frequency has remained stable over time as well.

One explanation is that open source projects have not adopted continuous integration on any significant scale. An alternative interpretation is that open source software development has always practiced continuous integration. In that case, the advent of agile methods did not lead to any changes, simply because it had long arrived in open source software development before.

5 Limitations of Analysis

The analysis and the conclusions we draw have at least the following limitations.

- *Sample size.* We considered 5122 open source projects. The total number of open source projects is much larger. However, our data source focuses on active projects of significant popularity. So we believe the sample we are using is relevant for analyzing agile methods practices in open source.
- *Data quality.* We couldn't calculate exact numbers of commit size due to the way Ohloh.net tracks changes to source code files. (See Section 3.1.) We believe that working with a lower/upper bound does not restrict the validity of our results as we care about the trend and not the actual values.
- *Data incompleteness.* Some amount of revision control information in open source projects has been lost forever, as projects have moved from one code repository to another. However, this is old data, and we believe the lack of some of the early histories do not affect the validity of our conclusions.
- *Improper summation across different programming languages.* One may argue that commit size depends on the programming language. We analyzed variation across languages and found that the programming language does not have a significant impact on the results presented in this paper.
- *Improper summation across different project sizes.* Some open source projects are small, some are large. Barry Boehm argues that agile methods don't scale well beyond a certain size limit [2]. Our data confirms within the given limitations that the practice of continuous integration has not found increasing adoption in open source projects over the last ten years.

We are working to remove these and other limitations. However, we believe that while the respective critiques can be made, the effects are limited, as argued above.

6 Related Work

Angioni et al. describe MADD, a "Methodology for Agile Distributed Development" and compare the similarity, differences and applicability of agile practices in open source development [9]. Less than 73% of the developers were knowledgeable about agile development practices. Less than 10% of the developers used core agile practices like pair programming or small iterations.

Turnu et al. studied the effect of applying agile methodology in the open source development environment [8]. Specifically, they studied the effects of applying Test Driven Development on open source development by using a simulation model developed from the Apache HTTP server project data. They concluded that use of agile methods in open source development can yield better results in terms of code quality.

7 Conclusions

Software firms seeking to work with open source software need to understand open source software development processes. Our analysis of the size of code contributions by open source software developers indicates that the core agile methods' practice of continuous integration has not had a significant impact on open source development practices. Hence, we conclude within the limits of our study that agile method skills are not a good proxy for open source software development skills.

Acknowledgements

We would like to thank Prem Devanbu and Gregorio Robles for their feedback on earlier versions of the paper as well as their encouragement for the work presented. We also would like to thank Oliver Arafat and Mario Fernandez for proofreading the paper. Finally, Amit Deshpande performed parts of this work while being employed at SAP Labs, LLC.

References

[1] Fugetta, A.: Open Source Software—An Evaluation. The Journal of Systems and Software (66) 77-90.
[2] Boehm, B.: Get Ready for Agile Methods, with Care. IEEE Computer (January 2002) 64-69.
[3] Beck, K.: Extreme Programming Explained: Embrace Change. Addison Wesley, 1999.
[4] Cockburn, A.: Agile Software Development. Addison-Wesley, 2001.
[5] Boehm, B.: A Spiral Model of Software Development and Enhancement. IEEE Computer (May 1988) 61-72.
[6] Schwaber, K.: Agile Software Development with SCRUM. Prentice-Hall, 2001.
[7] Lawton, M.: Open Source Business Models. IDC, 2007. Retrieved on Sept 13, 2007, from http://www.idc.com/getdoc.jsp?containerId=IDC_P13018
[8] Turnu, I., Melis, M., Cau, A., Setzu, A., Concas, G., and Mannaro, K. Modeling and Simulation of Open Source Development using an Agile Practice. J. Syst. Archit. 52, 11 (Nov. 2006) 610-618.
[9] Angioni, M., Sanna, R., Soro, A.: Defining a Distributed Agile Methodology for an Open Source Scenario. In Scotto, M., Succi, G. (eds.): Proceedings of the First International Conference on Open Source Systems. Springer Verlag (2005) 209-214.
[10] Ohloh Corporation, see http://www.ohloh.net.
[11] Duvall, P.: Continuous Integration: Improving Software Quality and Reducing Reducing Risk. Addison-Wesley, 2007.

[12] Koch, S.: Agile Principles and Open Source Software Development: A Theoretical and Empirical Discussion. In: Extreme Programming and Agile Processes in Software Engineering. Springer-Verlag (2004) 85–93.

[13] Morkel Theunissen, WH, Boake, A. Kourie, DG. In Search of the Sweet Spot: Agile Open Collaborative Corporate Software Development. In Proceedings of the 2005 SAISCIT: 268-277.

[14] Warsta, J. and Abrahamsson, P. Is Open Source Software Development Essentially an Agile Method? In: 3rd Workshop on Open Source Software Engineering, Portland, Oregon, USA.

Extracting Generally Applicable Patterns from Object-Oriented Programs for the Purpose of Test Case Creation

Richard Torkar, Robert Feldt, and Tony Gorschek
Blekinge Institute of Technology,
School of Engineering,
372 25 Ronneby, Sweden
{rto|rfd|tgo}@bth.se

Abstract. This paper presents an experiment performed on three large open source applications. The applications were instrumented automatically with a total of 10,494 instrumentation points. The purpose of the instrumentation was to collect and store data during the execution of each application that later could be analyzed off-line. Data analysis, on the collected data, allowed for the creation of test cases (test data, test fixtures and test evaluators) in addition to finding object message patterns for object-oriented software.

1 Introduction

In order to automate software quality assurance to a high(er) extent, one needs to look at techniques that are suitable for this purpose. In this respect random testing is a likely candidate for automation due to its nature where a minimum of human intervention is needed [1]. Unfortunately, random testing of object-oriented software has not been researched widely (for an overview please see [2]). One of the reasons for this is surely the fact that random testing traditionally compares well to other techniques when it comes to dealing with scalar (pre-defined or primitive) types, while usually is seen to have weaknesses dealing with compound (programmer-defined or higher-level) types. Another reason might be that random testing, again traditionally, has been used on small and delimited example.

This paper aims to:

1. Show how object message pattern analysis, from automatically instrumented applications, can be used to automatically create test cases. (Test cases in this context equal test data, evaluators and fixtures.)
2. Point to how random testing can be performed on these test cases.
3. Examine the possible existence of object message patterns in object-oriented software in addition to the question of general applicability of said patterns.
4. Point out current possibilities for using instrumentation of software items as an underlying foundation to automated software testing.

Please use the following format when citing this chapter:

Torkar, R., Feldt, R. and Gorschek, T., 2008, in IFIP International Federation for Information Processing, Volume 275; *Open Source Development, Communities and Quality*; Barbara Russo, Ernesto Damiani, Scott Hissam, Björn Lundell, Giancarlo Succi; (Boston: Springer), pp. 281–287.

Throughout this paper an empirically descriptive model is used, i.e. explaining a phenomenon sufficiently on 'real-life' software. Next, related work is presented. Following that, the setup of the experiment is presented (Sect. 2) while the results are covered in Sect. 3. Finally, this paper ends with conclusions and future work (Sect. 4).

1.1 Related Work

Related work for this paper can be divided mainly into four categories: random testing, type invariants, dynamic analysis and patterns in object-oriented software.

First, random testing [1], which acts a basis for our approach, is a fairly old research area which has seen several new contributions lately which directly or indirectly affect this paper.

Second, likely invariants has gained considerable attention following the work of Pacheco et al. [3] in addition to Yang et al. [4]. The concept of likely invariants is built upon the assumption that one can find *different* input values, for testing a software item, by looking at the *actual* values the software uses during a test run. Our approach does not focus on likely invariants per see but rather class interactions (not component interfaces [5]), which in its turn provides the order of the methods being executed as well as method signatures and actual input and return values and types.

Third, the concept of dynamic analysis, i.e. analysis of the software based on its execution, can in our approach best be described as a see-all-hear-all strategy. This way it resembles the omniscient debugger [6] that takes snapshots of every change in the state of the running application thus allowing the developer to move backwards and forwards when debugging the application. The difference in our approach is that every important piece of information during execution, is stored for later off-line analysis.

Finally, an overview of object-oriented software testing, and especially patterns in this area, can be found in e.g. [7]. Important to note, in this circumstance, is that the word pattern (as used by almost all of the references) has in many ways a different meaning compared to how it is used in this paper.

In order to clarify the concept of patterns, we use the name *Object Message Patterns* for our purposes. *Object* stands for the fact that the focus is set on object-oriented software. *Message* is short for the message-driven perspective as employed by object-oriented software and finally, *patterns* stands for the execution traces as found when analyzing software.

2 Experimental Setup

In this experiment the focus is set around testing intermediate representations of source code from open source software. Today, in industry, many would say that the centre of attention is mostly around the Java Virtual Machine and the Common

Language Infrastructure (CLI) with its Common Language Runtime (both inheriting from the original ideas brought forward by the UCSD P-System's developers in the late 70's [8]).

The experiment was performed on three different open source software items: Banshee (an open source media player), Beagle (an open source search tool) and the Mono C# compiler, Mcs (an open source implementation of the ECMA-334/335 standard). The selection of the software items was performed with the following in mind:

- The application should be written in a language, which can be compiled to an intermediate representation (in this case the Common Intermediate Language).
- The application should be sufficiently large and thus provide a large amount of data for later analysis.
- Separate development teams should have developed the applications.

In the end, Banshee, Beagle and Mcs, were considered to fit the profile for the case study. For each application, one use case was selected which would be executed after the application had been instrumented:

- *Banshee:* Start application, select media file, play media file, stop playback, shut down application.
- *Beagle:* Start search daemon in console (background process), perform query in console, close the GUI which presents the search results, stop search daemon.
- *Mcs:* Compile a traditional 'Hello World' application.

Table 1. An overview of the experiment showing the number of LOC (lines including comments, white spaces, declarations and macro calls), the size of the assemblies (in KB), the number of classes that were instrumented and the number of instrumentation points (IP), for each application. In addition the time to instrument (TTI) and execute (TTE) with and without instrumentation for each application is presented (in seconds).

App.	LOC	IL (KB)	#Classes	#IP	TTI	TTE w. instr.	TTE w/o instr.
Banshee	53,038	609	414	2,770	28	424	63
Beagle	146,021	1,268	1,045	5,084	71	74	6
Msc	56,196	816	585	2,640	166	34	0.8

After the selection of the candidate applications was accomplished the actual instrumentation took place (see Table 1 for some descriptive statistics). To begin with, each valid class in the Software Under Test (SUT), disregarding abstract, extern and interface annotated signatures, in every assembly (exe and dlls), had instructions inserted in each method which would collect runtime input and return value(s) and type(s), as well as the caller (i.e. what invoked the method). All this data, together with a time stamp, was then stored during runtime in an object database while the SUT was executed following one of the before mentioned use cases. That is to say, each time a method was executed, during the execution of a use case, an object containing all the values necessary to recreate that state (with its connections), was stored in the object database (i.e. a form of deep copy was saved). Having to serialize the data beforehand would be too resource intensive for obvious reasons not to mention posing some difficulties from a technical perspective.

Next, the content of the object database was analyzed looking for patterns and discovering likely critical regions. The selected paths could then be used for creating a test case (using the actual runtime values as test data and test evaluators). The execution of the use cases, as well as the instrumentation of the assemblies, was performed on Linux 2.6.15, Mac OS X 10.4.4 and Windows XP SP2 using Cecil 0.3 (open source assembly manipulator), AspectDNG 0.47 (open source tool to support aspect oriented programming) and the open source (in-memory) object database engine db4o 5.2.

3 Results

The intention of performing Object Message Pattern Analysis (OMPA) on data in this experiment was to find and generalize patterns that later could be used for testing the SUT. In addition to this the hypothesis is that patterns, if found, could be generally applicable to most, if not all, object-oriented software. Since the analysis was performed manually a limitation on the number of analyzed objects was needed. Thus, 300 objects (in a call sequence) from each application were analyzed from an arbitrary point in the object database (selected by a pseudo-random generator as found on pp. 283–284 in [9]). In the end, eight object message patterns were found during the analysis of the data stored in the object database (Tables 2–3, respectively).

The patterns found are of two different categories. Four patterns belong to, what has by us been defined as object unit patterns. Object unit patterns constitute of a sequence of method invocations on *one* object, i.e. methods in an object has been executed in a certain order. Object trace patterns, on the other hand, are slightly different. They cover the path of execution through *more than* one object.

Object Unit Patterns. Four object unit patterns were found during the OMPA (Table 2); these patterns exercised only one object consistently over time and were found in all three applications (needless to say, the names of the objects and classes differed in all three applications, but the pattern can nevertheless generally be applied on all three applications).

The first pattern, the Vault pattern (Table 2), is a straightforward pattern which is executed by first invoking a constructor then invoking a setter and, finally, multiple times, a getter (before a destructor is invoked). This can be seen as a very rudimentary pattern for storing data in an object which then is fetched by one or many objects, and as such is suitable to always execute in a testing scenario, i.e. data is stored in a simple vault. During the analysis the intermediate representation was used for examining if a method was defined as a getter or setter (property) by searching for the keyword `.property`. There is of course a possibility that a method is *acting* as getter or setter while not being defined as such, but in this analysis these types of methods are disregarded and an emphasize is put on the proper definition of a getter or setter according to the CIL.

Next, the Storage pattern is an evolved Vault pattern and the combinations of setter and getter invocations can be many (Table 2). Hence, the Storage pattern can be constructed in different ways and a combinatorial approach might be suitable in a testing scenario (compared to the Vault pattern which is very straightforward), i.e. data is stored in storage and the storage has (many) different ways of adding or offering content. The reason for distinguishing between Vault and Storage is that a Vault was common during OMPA and as such should always be used when testing object-oriented software, while Storage, on the other hand, is a more complex pattern (more steps performed) and as such needs additional analysis.

The Worker pattern at first glance looks like bad design. An object gets instantiated, and immediately filled with data. A method is next invoked which manipulates the data, returns the manipulated data and, finally, a destructor is invoked. The reason for this design might be to make sure that the method's implementation is accessible by different objects (extended) since it is declared `public`. If one had opted for a method declared as `private` or even `protected`, which could be invoked when the getter is invoked, then there would be no simple way to reuse the implementation.

Finally, the Cohesion pattern is a pattern that executes one or more methods in one object. It does this without *a priori* setting any values and the order of executing the methods is not always important, i.e. each and every method was found to be (by analyzing objects in the object database) an atomic unit with no dependency on other methods in the class and as such the word cohesion (united whole) was found to be appropriate to use.

Table 2. Different object unit patterns found in all three applications. The first column shows the name selected for the pattern and the second column the actual pattern. Abbreviations used: ctor and ~ctor is short for constructor and destructor respectively, while setter and getter is a method which sets or gets data stored in the object.

Name	Pattern
Vault	ctor → setter → 1...*n* getter → □ctor
Storage	ctor → setter → 1...*n* getter → 1...*n* setter → ... → □ctor
Worker	ctor → setter → method invocation → □ctor
Cohesion	ctor → 1...*n* method invocation → □ctor

Object Trace Patterns. Looking at the object trace patterns, one can see four patterns that can be generally applicable (see Table 3 on next page); these patterns exercise several objects and constitutes sequences of object:method invocations.

A fairly common pattern that seems to come up on a regular basis is the Cascading pattern. This pattern instantiates object after object, which all can be of different or same types. The approach seems to be quite common when object-oriented applications are starting up, but in addition shows up in several phases of an application's lifetime (from start up to shutdown).

Next, the Storing pattern and the Fetching pattern showed up many times as well. These patterns are directly connected to the object unit Storage and Vault patterns, and as such can be combined in many ways.

The final pattern is the Dispatch pattern. The Dispatch pattern simply invokes one method after another (not a constructor though). In most cases the Dispatch patterns ends up with executing the Storing or Fetching pattern as a final step.

Table 3. Different object trace patterns found in all three applications. Abbreviations used: ctor and ~ctor is short for constructor and destructor respectively, while setter and getter is a method which sets or gets data stored in the object. An alphabetical character in front of the abbreviation, i.e. A:ctor, indicates that a type A object's constructor is invoked.

Name	Pattern
Cascading	A:ctor → B:ctor → C:ctor → …
Storing	A:ctor → B:ctor; A:method → B:setter
Fetching	A:method → B:getter
Dispatch	A:method → B:method → C:method → …

3.1 Test Case Creation

Applying test case creation on the example (and on data in the experiment) is fairly straightforward when all entities needed can be found in the object database, i.e. the following data is available: methods' name, input type and values, and return type(s) and value(s).

In addition, information regarding the caller can be extracted from the object database by simply examining the caller value in the current method being executed (a value stored in the database) or by examining the time stamp for each stored entity in the database.

The above information provides us with an opportunity to automatically create test cases and, in the end, have a simple smoke test or regression test mechanism, depending on the aim of our testing efforts. In short, the software item is executed, test cases are created from the database, patterns are extracted from the database and the SUT is validated. Obviously, the end goal is to make this a fully automatic process.

4 Conclusions and Future Work

This paper presented eight software object message patterns, for testing object-oriented software. As such it indicates in our opinion that the first steps have been taken on the road to extract generally applicable object message patterns for the purpose of testing object-oriented software. In this case study, the patterns are accompanied with automatically generated test cases whose entities (test data, test fixture and test oracle) are retrieved from a database which stores runtime values that are collected when executing a use case on the SUT. These test cases are then stored and used as a simple regression testing mechanism, hence avoiding manual, error-prone and tedious test case creation.

In the future a replication of this study should be made were the focus would be put on large applications and extensive data collection (i.e. collecting more or all use cases during the system testing phase). In addition, a number of issues with respect to optimization must be solved and the analysis must be performed fully automatically for this approach to be beneficial.

References

1. Hamlet, D.: Random testing. In: Marciniak, J.J. (ed.): Encyclopedia of software engineering. John Wiley & Sons, New York (1994) 970-978
2. Binder, R.V.: Testing object-oriented systems: models, patterns, and tools. Addison-Wesley Longman Publishing Co., Inc. (1999)
3. Pacheco, C., Lahiri, S.K., Ernst, M.D., Ball, T.: Feedback-Directed Random Test Generation. Proceedings of the 29th International Conference on Software Engineering. IEEE Computer Society (2007)
4. Yang, J., Evans, D.: Dynamically inferring temporal properties. Proceedings of the 5th ACM SIGPLAN-SIGSOFT workshop on Program analysis for software tools and engineering. ACM, Washington DC, USA (2004)
5. Whaley, J., Martin, M.C., Lam, M.S.: Automatic extraction of object-oriented component interfaces. SIGSOFT Softw. Eng. Notes **27** (2002) 218-228
6. Lewis, B., Ducasse, M.: Using events to debug Java programs backwards in time. Companion of the 18th annual ACM SIGPLAN conference on Object-oriented programming, systems, languages, and applications. ACM, Anaheim, CA, USA (2003)
7. Lange, M.: It's Testing Time! Proceedings of the 6th European Conference on Pattern Languages of Programming and Computing, Irsee, Germany, UVK Universitatsverlag Konstanz GmbH (2001)
8. Institute for Information Systems, UCSD, University of California: UCSD PASCAL System II.0 User's Manual. (1979)
9. Press, W.H., Flannery, B.P., Teukolsky, S.A., Vetterling, W.T.: Numerical recipes in C: the art of scientific computing. Cambridge University Press (1988)

Social Networking Technologies for Free-Open Source E-Learning Systems

Francesco Di Cerbo, Gabriella Dodero, and Giancarlo Succi
CASE – Center for Applied Software Engineering
Free University of Bolzano/Bozen
Piazza Domenicani, 3
I-39100 Bolzano-Bozen,
{name.surname}@unibz.it
WWW home page: http://www.unibz.it

Abstract. In this paper, we illustrate our methodology for academic teaching, based on cooperative learning paradigm, which also relies on cutting edge e-learning techniques. We use Web 2.0 resources to fulfill requirements for an interactive-constructivistic "learning space", where blended-teaching paradigm may be proficiently applied. We extend an existing Free/Open Source Software Learning Management System, to create a cooperative and community-based learning space adherent to our proposal.

1 Introduction

Much emphasis has been put in the importance of a constructivistic approach to achieve effective learning at all levels, including the academic one. The so-called "Dublin descriptors" adopted in many European universities as common educational indicators stress the importance of coupling the "knowledge" with the "applied knowledge" within reference environments, and across Europe, academic teaching methodologies are now promoting deep restructuring of curricula. In facts, the development of the so-called "soft-skills" has become an indispensable complement to any discipline, be it technology oriented or in the humanities. Pedagogues have already identified methodologies which may be applied in order to achieve such results; they are collectively called "active learning". Examples are "problem-based learning" ([1]), "troubleshooting" ([2]) or "case-based teaching" ([3]).

Several pilot experiences already support this claim (see [4] and [5]), even if an exhaustive experimentation involving e-learning specialists and students at various levels and disciplines is not yet completed.

The development of a suitable technological infrastructure to support such activities has been mostly concentrated on the possibility to pass from the learning environment concept (the status-quo of the market) to that of "dynamical learning space" (DLS). In a DLS, people involved in learning are identified by their specificities, and meet each other to collaborate to the negotiation and construction of knowledge. The implementation of a DLS, giving importance and attention to the individuals inside a distributed process of learning, is our main goal.

Please use the following format when citing this chapter:

Di Cerbo, F., Dodero, G. and Succi, G., 2008, in IFIP International Federation for Information Processing, Volume 275; *Open Source Development, Communities and Quality*; Barbara Russo, Ernesto Damiani, Scott Hissam, Björn Lundell, Giancarlo Succi; (Boston: Springer), pp. 289–297.

The concept of "dynamical learning space" is not originating in the virtual environment by itself. Indeed, in a real (not virtual) learning space, both teacher and his/her class participate to the creation of a shared knowledge; they build up meanings and concepts where every individual has own importance inside the process. Teachers have the lead of the community, steering global effort towards learning targets, and every student may/must contribute.

Such a process requires very skillful teachers, able to involve learners' community, letting everyone get his/her own role inside the teamwork. In case of a virtual teaching, such as in e-learning scenarios, a teacher should rely on a set of software tools, letting him involve his/her class, like during lessons in presence. Our software helps the teachers to coordinate such virtual communities, specifically at interaction level, in order to form a social network.

We developed our software in order to make possible this co-construction of learning materials and concepts by means of virtual experiences. We find that such approach can be useful not only in virtual (e-learning) classes, but when lessons are given both in presence and in virtual systems (blended learning). Such software also gives a precise and "automatic" track of activities conducted, without the distractive effect caused by recording them by hand. In this way, students and teachers may concentrate on learning process, without caring too much about activities tracking. A more detailed description of the pedagogical design is available in [6].

In Section **Error! Reference source not found.** we describe the choice of tools, and interfacing functionalities to augment them according to the "DLS" paradigm. In Section **Error! Reference source not found.** the underlying technologies are briefly described. Conclusive remarks are presented in Section **Error! Reference source not found.**.

2 Tools

Inside an e-learning scenario, the concept of DLS naturally translates into that of a virtual environment, where interactions are welcomed and eased, and where every community service, like wikis and forums, contributes to the creation of a common knowledge as part of a structured learning process. Here, students and teachers are free to operate and move in a sort of virtual reality: a place, coherently with new Web 2.0[7] issues, where to put opinions or contents, to meet the class, even to find amusement, without a fixed interaction stereotype.

To this aim, previous research in Human-Computer Interaction (for instance, the work of Gräther and Prinz [8]) on community and presence awareness, and especially the concept of *social translucence* ([9]), were exploited. Functional interaction metaphors and schemes of services oriented to social networks were analyzed, where theories of cooperative learning and social constructivism can be put into practice.

But should such a new concept like the DLS be implemented from scratch, or can it be superimposed on top of some existing LMS? Existing infrastructures and services were evaluated with respect to suitability to social constructivism. Free/Open Source Software solutions were especially considered because of the availability of particular license agreements, which allow users to legally and easily extend software, under certain conditions (see [10],[11]).

What is important to remark, here, is the freedom of use that such software license gives to licensee; a user is entitled to use, to study, to modify, and to redistribute a derivative work made upon original one. Our analysis included both a technical evaluation and a qualitative-strategic one, with the aim to understand the extensibility, the quality of the implementation, size, and support provided by the international community. As a result, we chose the Learning Management System Moodle [12] as our privileged software environment.

For Moodle, as well as for any other LMS, the introduction of a DLS implements a new social networking model. since every user is associated to an avatar, free to move in a web page, interacting with other users and with resources (for instance, opening course material or a real time chat). Logical proximity of activities is naturally mapped into physical proximity of the avatars in the virtual space. The possibility of using a spatial metaphor has proven succesful in the past (e.g. [13]).

Fig. 1 Example of an interaction between an avatar and course material

A number of services of interest, like forums and wikis, are already found in Moodle. We added a videoconferencing system based only on Java (applets and services) in a client/server architecture, and an AJAX ([14]) whiteboard, shared among the community. Both are browser independent and do not require additional software installations at client side.

Figure 1 shows an example of an interaction between an avatar and a course material, for instance a book available to students. The avatar moves close to the icon representing materials, and a pop-up menu appears, showing next possible actions. This happens also in case of interactions between avatars, in order to open a private chat session. The software development process we followed includes strong involvement of pedagogues in the choices taken by developers. Early feedbacks from them guarantees the highest quality and usability for the customers of the final product.

3 Implementation

Our software consists on two main subsystems: one implements all the operations at client side, while the other is responsible for managing all the interactions between all the users and the system. We defined a set of system behaviors, called *actions*, regarding possible interactions between clients and server. Then, we also defined a set of widgets and utility objects to be used at client-side. Each object is associated to a number of actions that are needed to perform its own tasks. These definitions have been formalized in XML documents, in order to be independent from any programming language (neither client- nor server-side). We refer to these elements as “XML Interfaces”. A representation of the two subsystems as well as XML interfaces is available in Figure 2.

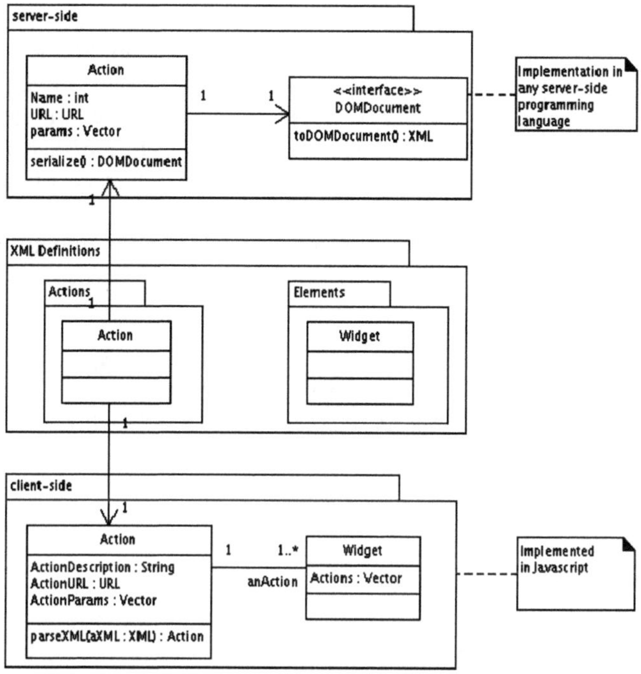

Fig. 2 Subsystems design

The development of objects for both sides was based on such XML interfaces; in fact, we designed and developed class definitions that are able to cope with specified exchange messages in XML format, if they can parse XML interfaces to produce accordingly XML requests. In this way, we are not bound to any programming language or software package.

Two special entities are responsible for communications between client and server: Status Manager and Status Monitor. Both of them embed the concept of "status"; as we aim at realizing a tool focused on live social interactions, we require that all the users share the same experience. Every user is cooperating with others, for instance by moving an avatar in response to another movement. As a consequence all users also have to share the very same status; we implemented this requirement keeping the state of the whole application server-side, and exchanging periodic updates with clients. Once an action has been performed by one of the clients, all the others are being notified within 1-2 seconds. This mechanism is based on the mentioned Status Monitor and Status Manager. Status Monitor is an object managing all the client side tasks and operations. In fact, it is responsible for creating the initial environment (avatars, rooms, widgets and so on), and to track any modification to its internal status (i.e., movement of the user's avatar, insertion of a new message in the real-time chat and so on). Once a modification happens, Status Monitor sends an update message to its server-side counterpart, Status Manager.

There are as many instances of Status Monitor as there are clients, while the system has one and only Status Manager, as we need a central coordination point for the whole system. Then, Status Manager sends an update message at predefined intervals; this message is created considering the past history of all the Status Monitors since the last update message.

Figure 3 provides a sequence diagram showing interactions among subsystems.

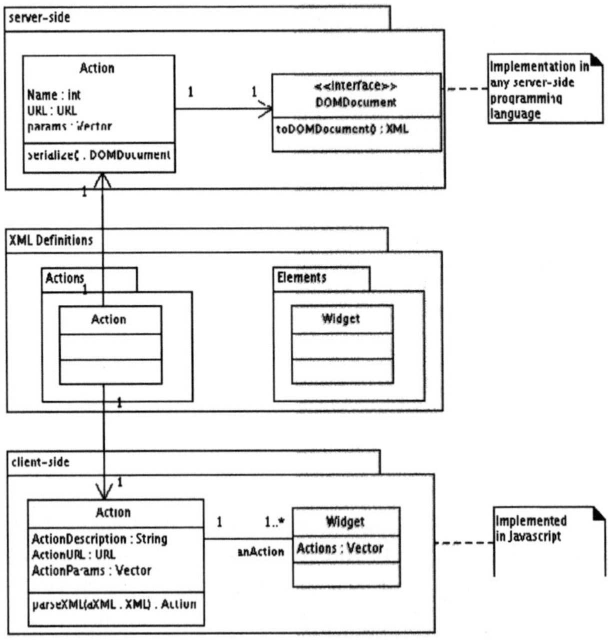

Fig. 3 Sequence Diagram for main objects: Status_Monitor and Status_Manager

XML Interfaces

In our system, interfaces are defined as XML Schema documents; they can be used to verify if a document is well-formed. We adopted XML Schema in order to enable verification of messages in our system, and to keep interfaces independent from actual language used in system implementation. Table 1 shows a sample action request.

Table 1: An example of XML Action message

```
<?xml ... ?>
<action name="aName">
 <param name="1"/ value=2>
 <param name="2"/ value=2>
  <url>

 </url>
</action>
```

Client-side implementation

Required objects and graphical widgets have been implemented in Javascript, the programming language we chose at client-side. Our main issue was delivering browser-independent code. In fact, different browsers often yield different behaviors for Javascript code, both in the graphical part, and in the invocations to asynchronous methods, that are the base of AJAX paradigm. For these reasons, we adopted a Javascript framework to encapsulate and provide us portable solutions for all the issues mentioned: the Dojo toolkit

Dojo (available from www.dojotoolkit.net) is an Open Source DHTML toolkit written in JavaScript. It supports asynchronous calls (i.e., all AJAX interactions), as well as unit testing and layering, with a very small core which provides the package system. The Dojo toolkit enables our software to be browser-independent, as it detects the type of browser where it is executed, and automatically adapts the actions it is required to perform to the actual environment.

Server-side implementation

We implemented our server-side subsystem using PHP, due to the choice of Moodle as our base LMS. PHP version 5 allowed us to exploit a number of services, including reflection and full support for Object-Oriented programming, that we needed. Moreover, as Moodle uses PHP, this simplifies the deployment process, without requiring to set up an heterogeneous system to use our software.

4 Conclusions

We have described the pedagogical approach, tools chosen, and implementation technologies that we have been employing in order to support social networking inside a new generation LMS. The system extends the well-known Moodle Free/Open Source software with a "dynamical learning space" concept, providing a novel interaction model, especially suited to support blended learning. At present, the system has been deployed on Moodle 1.8.3, and we are starting to extensively experience it with users (university teachers and students).

To evaluate our solution, we have started to use automatic tools for collecting process metrics ([15]) already available and developed at the Free University of Bolzano Bozen ([16],[17]). This will allow us to discover usability patterns inside users' experience in an objective way. It is possible, for instance, to understand what services are the most used, for how much time, and the "productivity", in terms of outcomes deriving from user's experience with that specific tool. This would provide a base of evidence useful on two different scenarios: a technical one, to analyze introduced improvements and eventually refine them, and the pedagogical one, to bring quantitative confirmations for qualitative considerations.

Using both feedbacks coming from educational specialists and quantitative measures, it shall be possible to formulate a complete report of our experience, that in conjunction with a new Learning Management System platform would result in a complete educational proposal, a framework able to coordinate and to combine both in-presence and virtual lessons.

Bibliography

[1] Ward, J.D. and Lee, C.L., A Review of Problem-based Learning, Journal of Family and Consumer Sciences Education, Vol. 20 , n. 1, 2002,

[2] Jonassen, D.H., Hung, W., Learning to Troubleshoot: A New Theory-Based Design Architecture, Educational Psychology Review, Vol. 18, n. 1 , 2006, DOI: 10.1007/s10648-006-9001-8

[3] Jonassen, D.H., Hernandez-Serrano, J., Case-based reasoning and instructional design: Using stories to support problem solving, Educational Technology Research and Development, Vol. 50 , n. 2 , 2002, DOI: 10.1007/BF02504994

[4] Stefanova E., Sendova E., Nikolova I., Nikolova N., When I*Teach means I*Learn: developing and implementing an innovative methodology for building ICT-enhanced skills., 2007, Proceedings of the IFIP Conference Informatics, Mathematics, and ICT: a 'golden triangle' IMICT 2007, pg., Northeastern University, Boston, MA,

[5] Dodero G., Ratcheva D., Stefanova E., Miranowicz M., Vertan C., Musankoviene V., The virtual training center: a support tool for teachers community, 2007, Proceedings of Balkan Conference in Informatics (BCI 2007), pg. , Demetra Ltd,

[6] Di Cerbo, F., Succi, G., A proposal for interactive-constructivistic teaching methods supported by Web 2.0 technologies and environments, 2007, Proc. of 18th International Conference on Database and Expert Systems Applications, 2007 (DEXA '07), pg. 648-652, ,

[7]O'Reilly, T., What Is Web 2.0, 2005, http://www.oreillynet.com/pub/a/oreilly/tim/news/2005/09/30/what-is-web-20.html

[8] Gräther, W. and Prinz, W., Supporting the Social Side of Large Scale Software Development, 2006, Supporting the Social Side of Large ScaleSoftware Development, pg. , Microsoft Research,

[9] Erickson, T. and Kellogg, W.A., Social translucence: An approach to designing systemsthat mesh with social processes., Trans. Computer-Human Interaction, Vol., n. 7, 1 , 2002,

[10]: Stallman, R.M., Free Software, Free Society: Selected Essays of Richard M. Stallman, 2002

[11] Raymond, E., Cathedral and Bazaar, 1999

[12] Dougiamas, M., Taylor, P.C., Moodle: Using Learning Communities to Create an Open Source Course Management System, 2003, roceedings of the EDMEDIA 2003 Conference.

[13] Pfister, H.-R., Wessner, M., Beck-Wilson, J., Miao, Y., & Steinmetz, R. (1998). Rooms, protocols, and nets: Metaphors for computer supported cooperative learning of distributed groups. In: Proceedings of the ICLS'98 - International Conference of the Learning Sciences (pp. 242-248). Charlottesville, VA: AACE Association for the Advancement of Computing in Education.

[14] Garrett, J., Ajax: A New Approach to Web Applications, , www.adaptivepath.com/publications/essays

[15] Humprey, W., Introduction to the Personal Software Process, 1997

[16] Sillitti A., Janes A., Succi G., Vernazza T., Collecting, Integrating and Analyzing Software Metrics and Personal Software Process Data, 2003, Proceedings of EUROMICRO 2003, pg. 336-342,

[17] Scotto M.,Vernazza T.,Sillitti A., Succi G., Managing Web-Based Information, 2004, Proceedings of ICEIS Conference, pg. 575-578.

The Networked Forge: New Environments for Libre Software Development[1]

Jesus M. Gonzalez-Barahona[1], Andrés Martínez[2], Alvaro Polo[2], Juan José Hierro[2], Marcos Reyes[2], Javier Soriano[3], and Rafael Fernández[3]
[1] GSyC/LibreSoft, Universidad Rey Juan Carlos
jgb@gsyc.escet.urjc.es
[2] Telefónica Investigación y Desarrollo
[3] Universidad Politécnica de Madrid

Abstract. Libre (free, open source) software forges (sites hosting the development infrastructure for a collection of projects) have been stable in architecture, services and concept since they become popular during the late 1990s. During this time several problems that cannot be solved without dramatic design changes have become evident. To overcome them, we propose a new concept, the "networked forge", focused on addressing the core characteristics of libre software development and the needs of developers. The key of this proposal is to re-engineer forges as a net of distributed components which can be composed and configured according to the needs of users, using a combination of web 2.0, semantic web and mashup technologies. This approach is flexible enough to accommodate different development processes, while at the same time interoperates with current facilities.

1 Introduction

The libre (free, open source) software[2] development community, considered as a whole, is one of the largest cases of informal, globally distributed, virtual organization oriented to the production of goods. Hundreds of thousands of developers (working for companies or as volunteers) share a large base of source code (hundreds of millions of lines of code) and knowledge which they use to produce and improve software products. This collaboration has been possible only thanks to the intensive use of Internet-based tools, currently offered mainly by development forges such as SourceForge.

1 2This work has been funded in part by the European Commission, through projects FLOSSMetrics, FP6-IST-5-033982, and Qualipso, FP6-IST-034763, and by the Spanish Ministry of Industry, through projects Morfeo, FIT-350400-2006-20, and Vulcano, FIT-340503-2006-3

2 In this paper the term "libre software" is used to refer both to "free software" (as defined by the Free Software Foundation) and "open source software" (as defined by the Open Source Initiative).

Please use the following format when citing this chapter:

Gonzalez-Barahona, J.M., Martínez, A., Polo, A., Hierro, J.J., Reyes, M., Soriano, J. and Fernández, R., 2008, in IFIP International Federation for Information Processing, Volume 275; *Open Source Development, Communities and Quality*; Barbara Russo, Ernesto Damiani, Scott Hissam, Björn Lundell, Giancarlo Succi; (Boston: Springer), pp. 299–306.

In fact, the dawn of libre software development communities is linked to the spread of the Internet. Since their startup, many development teams used Internet-based tools for collaboration, and dissemination of the produced software. With the spread of the web they were integrated in 'project sites' which provided the infrastructure used for collaboration [7]. Around 1995 those sites provided mailing lists, download areas, issue tracking, source code management (usually CVS), and static HTML pages with information and documentation about the project.

During late 1990s and early 2000s some organizations started to offer those facilities to large collections of projects. The most known, and by far the largest of them, is SourceForge, established in 1999, but many others do exist. Many of them run different forks of the original SourceForge software, of which the most popular (specially for small sites) is GForge. In addition, large projects (GNOME, KDE, Apache, Eclipse, OpenOffice.org, Mozilla, etc.) maintain their own forges, usually with ad-hoc software, and similar systems are used as well in corporate environments for the development of non-libre software [3].

The basic architecture and services of all these forges have evolved only slightly during the last decade, meeting many of the needs of development teams, and proving to scale well to the tens of thousands of projects, hundreds of thousands of developers, and hundred of millions of lines of code. However, they also show several problems, rooted in their incomplete adaption to the extremely distributed, interrelated and flexible nature of the libre software community. To fix them, we decided to rethink the concept of forge.

2 Current forges and their problems

The architecture of current forges is similar [8, 1], with the needed considerations for scale, which may lead to the use of computer farms in large cases. Their main components are a web server (as front-end), a web application (e.g., GForge, providing the specific services of the forge), an SQL database (persistent storage for non-massive elements) and some specific components (such as source control or mailing lists management).

The web application provides services such as: information about projects and developers (including authentication), issue tracking, news and forums, wikis, scheduling services, and a common web interface to most of the functionality (including downloads of code). In addition, specific components usually found accompanying this application are: a download manager, a source control management system (CVS, Subversion, etc.), and a mailing lists management system with archiving facilities.

About one decade of intense use of these forges have uncovered several problems:

- They are project-centric instead of developer- or user-centric. The service "unit" is the project, but both libre software developers and users are usually interested in many projects, hosted in several forges.
- Monolithic approach. Each forge offers a fixed set of services, each implemented by a specific system, which impedes that each project chose the software they prefer for every service, and slows down innovation (only administrators can add new modules).
- Isolation. For most practical purposes, each forge is isolated from others (even with federation facilities).
- Poor integration. Each separate component offer its own user interface.
- Lack of fine-grained coordination. Related elements in different subsystems are difficult to relate to each other (e.g., patch to fix a bug and its revision in source code management repository).
- Lack of support for views. A given project, or collection of projects, cannot offer multiple views to users.
- Little attention to collaborative knowledge sharing. Collaborative tagging, bookmarking and cataloguing, for instance, are missing.

There are also some concerns related to the extreme concentration in the most popular forges. Some of them are becoming single points of failure and potential control for libre software development as a whole [4, 5]. Therefore, they become a critical infrastructure that has to be maintained and defended something which is intensive in human resources, and difficult to scale.

A number of solutions to some of these problems have been proposed, either as improvements to existing forges, or as new systems (such as Launchpad), but they still remain open issues needing a comprehensive approach. In some reviews of future developments in the field [9], several scenarios that would address some of these problems are also described, but they do not propose detailed designs or implementations.

3 The networked forge

Given this situation, we found it reasonable to re-engineer the fundamentals of forges, under the following main lines: aggressive distribution (services located in different sites); easy relocation (backup and restores interfaces that allow for quick recovering of a service at another location); user-centric scenarios (which allow developers and users to access easily all the services they need, despite the project to which they are related); fine-grained links between different services (so that developers can access related information easily); federation and presence in different forges (so that a project can be supported by several sites); relationship with upstream and related projects (even when residing in different forges); composability of independent elements; and fostering the development and sharing of innovative component. As an important side-target, we also wanted to maintain a high level of interoperability with legacy services, to easy the transition.

Our proposal, the networked forge, is based on the idea of considering forges not as single sites providing a monolithic set of services to host projects as isolated silos of knowledge, but as a collection of distributed components providing services, among which knowledge is shared. Each project decides on its own customized set of services, and users can configure their own working environment. This idea matches that of mashups [6] or semantic web 2.0 applications [2].

The main components of the architecture are (see figure 1**Error! Reference source not found.**):

- Integrated services, specifically built to feed into the proposed framework.
- Legacy systems, that have to be integrated in the networked forge.
- Client components provide the user interfaces.
- Connectors and adapters, connecting legacy components to the rest of the system (connectors are used with those components providing a semantic, RDF-like interface, adapters with non-semantic components).
- Aggregators, collecting RDF channels and processing them in several ways.
- Locators, used as name services, allowing for the registration of specific components.
- Catalogues, in which components available for a certain community are registered.

Several connectors or adapters can work with the same legacy service, providing different interfaces to it. Conversely, a given connector or adapter can work with several instances of the same kind of legacy service, providing the same interface to several sites. Client components can interact directly with the integrated services, with some semantic legacy services, and with connectors, adapters and aggregators. Aggregators can interact as well with all these components.

The architecture imposes little limitations to where the different components may reside. Usually, legacy services will be hosted in different sites in the Internet. Integrated services will also run somewhere in the Internet, but they could even be located in some cases in the user workstation. Client components will usually be hosted in some web server in the Internet, but will run in the user browser. However, other combinations are possible: they could also run in servers and be visualized in web browsers, or reside in the client side, for instance as modules for an IDE.

The communication between all the non-legacy components is performed with HTTP and WebDAV, with all the components providing RDF channels via REST interfaces. The architecture uses semantic web technologies for the exchange, handling and querying of the data between the different components of a forge network.

All connecting components feature a common REST interface, which simplifies composition. The information provided by the component is always an RDF channel, including semantic labeling, which is obtained via HTTP. Aggregators act as filters, also accepting RDF channels as information.

Components provide RDF channels, but no other interface intended for end users (such as HTML pages). Therefore, the user interface is usually provided in the client side. When the client application is a web browser, AJAX techniques are used to display the data in useful ways. In fact, the most natural way of producing an application interface for a networked forge will be via a mashup (including those implemented using Google Gadgets or Yahoo Pipes). But it is important to notice that any kind of application could interface to the system from the desktop, including for instance RDF client-side aggregators, or components for an IDE such as Eclipse plugins.

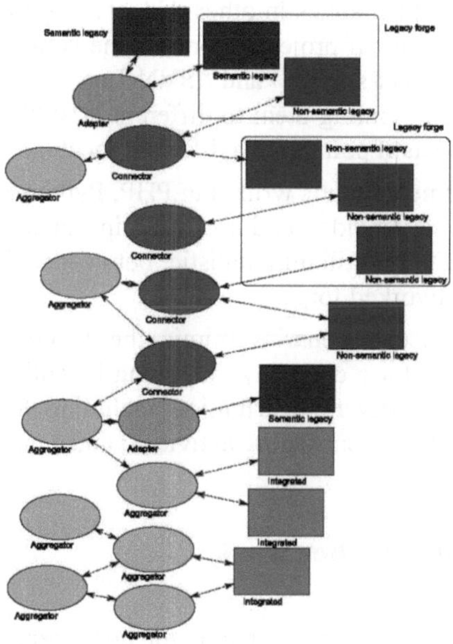

Fig. 1: General architecture. Clients, locators and catalogues are not shown to improve visibility.

Locators and catalogues are optional but important components. Both accept, at configuration or run time, information about the location of the different components (that is, their url), and provide upon request that information (either for all the components registered, or for a certain subset of them fulfilling some property).

Catalogues maintain information about available components to compose forges, while locators are configured to 'build' a networked forge: the components of the forge will be those registered with the locator. Therefore, components will be a part of several networked forges just by being registered with different locators.

To be functional, the services offered by the components of the networked forge are integrated in flexible and diverse ways. This integration can be accomplished either in the server side (using aggregators) or in the client side (using mashups, standalone RDF aggregators, or plugins in an IDE).

4 Implementing the concept

We have implemented a first version of the networked forge. A proof-of-concept setup using it is composed of several connectors and adapters to integrate legacy components (GForge, Trac, Subversion, etc.), several widgets (using Google Gadgets technology) to implement a client-side application to access the networked forge, and several locators. Figure 2**Error! Reference source not found.** shows a screenshot of this implementation.

Each widget reacts to changes in other widgets. For instance, the "My Vulcano" gadget (which shows a list of projects) controls the content of the "Project Details", "Project Tickets", "Project's Wiki" and "SVN Log" widgets. Widgets can also be configured by the user, pointing them to different urls: "My Vulcano" widget shows a different list of projects if pointed to a different locator.

The current implementation is written in PHP, Python and Java (standalone adapters or connectors on server side), and in JavaScript (client side adapters and connectors and gadgets logic). It is still minimalistic, but even so it shows the great potential of the concept of a networked forge.

Other proof-of-concept scenarios mimic the functionality of a legacy multi-project forge; the forge for a company, including its collaborations in libre software projects; the forge for a software distribution, including the development of upstream (original) products and their packaging activities; and a personal forge.

5 Conclusions and further work

Forges are an increasingly important tool for collaborative software development. However, the traditional model for implementing them has some shortcomings that we address with a new design: the networked forge. Networked forges allow for the easy integration of components residing in many different sites and administrative realms, while at the same time provide a great deal of flexibility.

Given a networked forge infrastructure, users, developers, projects, companies and other actors can configure the forges they need, share their configurations, and select the exact services they prefer. Interoperability with legacy systems is a part of the model, as well as a seamless integration with many different client-side environments, from web-based mashups to traditional IDE applications. The proposed architecture has been tested in proof-of-concept implementations.

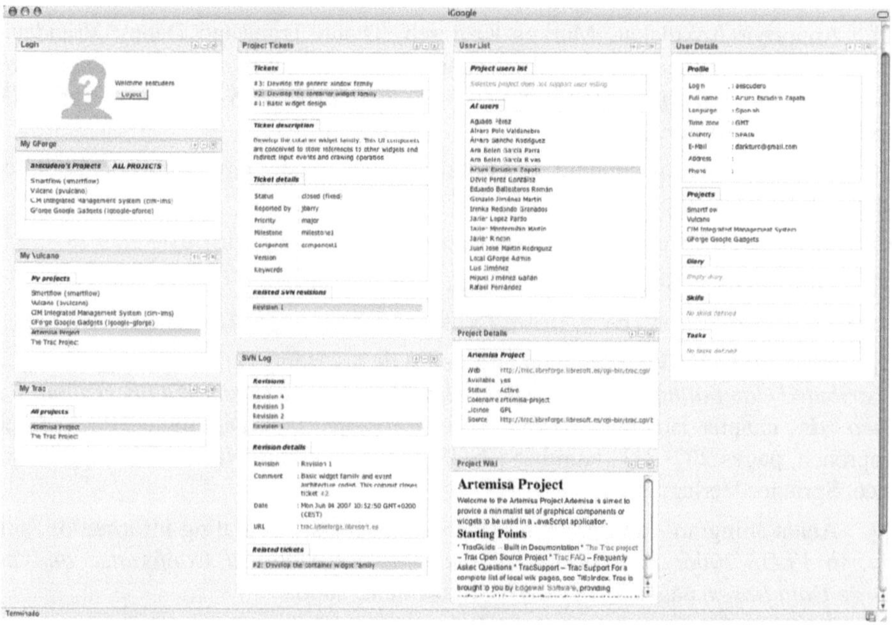

Fig. 2: Proof-of-concept networked forge. User interface implemented with Google Gadgets.

Some aspects of the design still remain open, while we explore several options for them. Security and authentication, for which we are studying single sign-on or common authentication infrastructure technologies, are two of them. Selection of ontologies for the exchange of information, and formats for specifying connections between components are also an open field. We are also developing more complete implementations in the context of the Vulcano and Qualipso projects.

In summary, the networked forge is a concept that suits well the practices of the libre software development community, and can also be applied in other more traditional environments.

Acknowledgements This work has benefited from many discussions in the context of the Vulcano, Morfeo, OSOR, FLOSSMetrics and Qualipso projects. We thank all the persons who contributed with ideas, comments and criticisms.

References

[1] Olivier Abdoun, Bernard Lange, Stéphane Laurière, Irenka Redondo, and Christian Rémy. Collaborative development environment: A state of the art. Technical report, Qualipso Project, 2007 (to be published).

[2] Anupriya Ankolekar, Markus Krötzsch, Thanh Tran, and Denny Vrandecic. The two cultures: mashing up web 2.0 and the semantic web. In *Proceedings of the 16th international conference on World Wide Web*, pages 825–834, New York, NY, USA, 2007. ACM Press.

[3] Grady Booch. Introducing collaborative development environments. Technical report, IBM, December 2006.

`http://www.alphaworks.ibm.com/contentnr/cdepaper.`

[4] Loïc Dachary. SourceForge drifting, 2001.

`http://fsfeurope.org/news/article2001-10-20-01.en.html.`

[5] Jesus M. Gonzalez-Barahona and Pedro de las Heras Quirós. *Future Trends in Distributed Computing. Andre Schiper, Alex Shvartsman, Hakim Weatherspoon, Ben Zhao eds.*, chapter Hosting of Libre Software Projects: A Distributed Peer-to-Peer Approach, pages 207–211. Number LNCS 2584 in Lecture Notes in Computer Science. Springer Verlag, 2003.

[6] Anant Jhingran. Enterprise information mashups: integrating information, simply. In *VLDB'2006: Proceedings of the 32nd international Conference on Very Large Data Bases*, pages 3–4. VLDB Endowment, 2006.

[7] Tim O'Reilly. Lessons from open-source software development. *Commun. ACM*, 42(4):32–37, 1999.

[8] Patrice-Emmanuel Schmitz, Abdelkrim Boujraf, Rishab Aiyer Ghosh, Emidio Stani, Juan José Amor Iglesias, Julia Anaya González, and Álvaro del Castillo San Félix. Feasibility study. Technical report, Open Source Observatory and Repository, IDABC, 2007 (to be published).

[9] Jim Whitehead. Collaboration in software engineering: A roadmap. In *Future of Software Engineering (FOSE '07)*, pages 214–225, 2007.

To What Extent Does It Pay to Approach Open Source Software for a Big Telco Player?

Massimo Banzi[1], Guido Bruno[2], and Giovanni Caire[3]
[1] Telecom Italia - Technology & Operations,
Innovation Architecture and Quality dep.,
Via Zambra 1, 38100 Trento Italy
Free Univerisity of Bolzano-Boozen Italy
massimo.banzi@telecomitalia.it
[2] Telecom Italia - Technology & Operations,
Innovation Architecture and Quality dep.,
Via Reiss Romoli 274, 10148 Torino Italy
guido.bruno@telecomitalia.it
[3] Telecom Italia - Technology & Operations,
Innovation Architecture and Quality dep.,
Via Reiss Romoli 274, 10148 Torino Italy
giovanni.caire@telecomitalia.it

Abstract. In this paper we describe the strategy under adoption in Telecom Italia (TI) Technology Department toward open source software. This stems from trying to create synergy among big Telco Player to increase knowledge and influence over strategic communities to the evaluation of the creation of new communities over internally developed applications. In particular here the approach and the expectations in starting the community on WADE (Workflow and Agent Development Environment) is described. This is a platform used to develop mission critical applications and is the main evolution of JADE a popular Open Source framework for the development of interoperable intelligent multi-agent systems. It adds to JADE the support for the execution of tasks defined according to the workflow metaphor as well as a number of mechanisms that help managing the complexity of the distribution both in terms of administration and fault tolerance. The idea is to use WADE as a mean to gather critical information on the opportunity of approaching OS as a strategic mean toward the development of always more important application in Operating Support System for TI, possibly also involving other great Telco Players For this reason great care is being paid in setting up the Community environment and in deciding which metrics are to be extracted from it, since the result will be the input for a strategic decision in TI.

Please use the following format when citing this chapter:

Banzi, M., Bruno, G. and Caire, G., 2008, in IFIP International Federation for Information Processing, Volume 275; *Open Source Development, Communities and Quality*; Barbara Russo, Ernesto Damiani, Scott Hissam, Björn Lundell, Giancarlo Succi; (Boston: Springer), pp. 307–315.

1 Introduction

What is the value in OS for a Big Telco Player such as TelecomItalia?

With 7.3 million broadband connections (retail and wholesale) 0, Telecom Italia is currently the leading operator in the national TLC market. It has one of the most penetrating and advanced network in Europe, with an extension of over 107 million Km in copper lines (access) and 3.8 million km of optical fibers (transport and access).

This is a question that is intriguing OSS Software Factory Management in TI Technology Department. Nowadays the constant search for reduction of Total Cost of Ownership (TCO) is forcing more and more to find solutions effective, but suitable to fulfill all OSS processes in a modern big Telco Company (Service Delivery, Network Creation and Inventory, Workforce Management, etc.). The analysis toward Open Source Software ha been obviously anticipated by initiatives such as the Service Rationalization and the Application Rationalization, to reduce redundancy of services and tools, but the obvious consequence has been the thought whether we could substitute Commercial tools with OS ones without loosing confidence and efficiency.

The first approach toward OS has been driven by a set of indicators that have been formalized as follows 0:

- The product has to fulfil a need and provide a well defined and understood service so that it can become a commodity.
- It ha to be a leader on the market in its context
- There should be a high number of "customers" that are also "contributors" for the product
- It has to be modular
- It must have a robust and well designed core
- The community needs to be large and talented.

This was the theory.

What actually happened was that, also according to several surveys 0, the core of ***use of OS in both mission-critical and non-mission-critical IT environments in TI rate higher for infrastructure than application software***, and infrastructure software uses OS components in conjunction with proprietary software.

More, in TI the use of OS applications in OSS vertical solutions is almost absent.

The ***reason stands mostly in the opportunistic adoption of OS*** in every single case, not driven by a real strategy.

In other words, in using OS software, an "opportunistic" approach (simply just use it) can be adopted or "a strategic one".

In the first case OS can be selected eventually also just as a proof of concept (using it simply as a leverage against COTS vendors). Or it can be simply used, directly, without even leaning on the community: it is downloaded, embedded in proprietary software and fully managed as an integral part of the solution.

Clearly in this case the community is used simply as a source of information for solving possible problems that can arise. No contribution is given.

In the second case two situations can arise

- if a community and a suitable OS solution considered as important does exist, it is necessary
  - the exploitation of community as a way to reduce development costs, accelerate the availability of new features, keep the product more robust trough the high number of users and contributors
  - since the product is probably to become an integral part in the player products portfolio, strong Competence Centres participating the communities are a necessity to be able to influence selected strategic communities and the roadmap of the products.
  - to keep a strong link between the innovation of the product in the community and the Telco production itself (basically an internal development branch has to be kept to validate every new added feature in the context the OS product is used by the company).

  Clearly all these can be achieved only by actively participating the community, injecting it with resources and competences..
- If a community and a suitable OS solution does not exist, it is possible to evaluate the possibility of "open" software solution internally developed or to create a new community from scratch, joining several stakeholders needs.

Up to now TI just used the opportunistic approach. But now things are changing. The main reason are the arising consciousness that OS ensure best-of-breed solutions, improved ROI, and vendor independence and flexibility.

Moreover OS solutions reached a quality comparable with that of proprietary Software, and the possibility to lean upon third companies providing support on OS solutions thus reducing risk in OS adoption are removing the remaining doubts.

2 Different approaches

According to the above consideration, TI Technology department decided to approach OS with a real strategy, without also rejecting the possibility of an opportunistic approach for non strategic solutions.

2.1 Synergy among big Telco players on existing communities

As said, in case the community exist, the Player typically uses the OS product directly or mediated by a broker upon which it unloads part of the risks.

Sometimes it also acquires from vendor or even brokers customized OS software.
For whatever choice of OS adoption strategy, needs in OSS for most Telco operators are similar, and the competition among Big Players is on services not on software solutions.
So a question arose: why not to coordinate the interaction with OS communities?
This can result in several benefits, first of all the influence on the community can be stronger but also if brokers are used, these can be shared; contributions can be distributed as well as competences and the weight on board of the community can be stronger.
Finally a common action on the communities, on brokers, but also on vendors can result in the possibility of defining standards instead of undergoing them.
Hence the idea of proposing a working-table among Telco Players to promote and manage the creation of community specific Working Groups that homogeneously interact with the community, eventually enforcing and promoting single player initiatives on OSS.

2.2 Creation of a new community

If a suitable community does not exist, maybe it can result profitable to share an internally developed solution to extend the test base or also the development one if enough interest can be excited on the solution. This is the case of WADE where a solution based upon an existing Open Source platform (JADE 0) used to develop internal critical application has been chosen as a laboratory to verify the opportunity of such an approach.
The model that we decided to adopt is depicted in 0 .

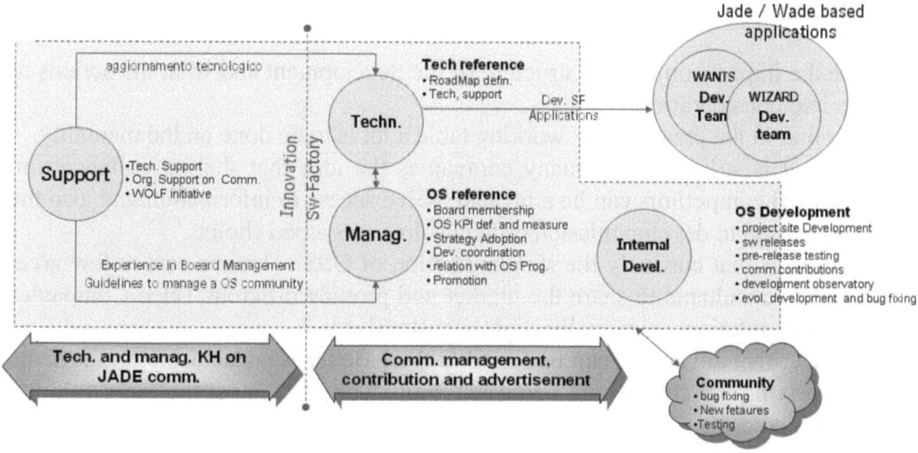

Organizational scenario

There, a Support Group has been identified, which is the original development team of WADE that clearly owns the major skill on the solution. It is engaged also in other activities and so it is expected to provide only a high level support to the initiative. A Technical manager for the specific solution has been identified within the Factory (the department in TI that actually develops or integrates software solutions). He currently is the responsible for all the applications developed on the top of WADE. He will also be responsible for deciding on the roadmap of the product within the arising community.

There is also a management role which is not just for the community created on WADE, but that is expected to manage all the solutions that will be opened. He will be responsible for the shared environment, the collection of metrics on it, its promotion, the coordination of the resources allocated on the community that will have to deal with internal builds, but also with releases, with the validation of community contributions, bug fixing, main evolution, etc.

The expectation is that we will be able to engage other companies in the initiative so that, others join the structure described in 0. Another technical reference is expected to be identified in the "other" company to create a "WADE working group" as well as "other" developers to contribute and a Manager to be the only reference in the "other" company for the sharing of OS solutions between the two. The two managers will be also members of the Working-table described above.

2.3 Impacts

What are the impacts on overall structure of the development and what the actions to be taken into consideration?
It is clear that in the creation of a working table a lot is to be done on the mentality.
Apparently it is still rooted in many companies the idea that sharing collaboration with historical competitors can be a mistake. Give access to information and also the source code used to develop mission critical solution is a bad choice.
But the truth is that currently the standardization of OSS solutions causes few great vendors and consultants to share the market and provide different Telco Companies with the same solutions, eventually slightly customized.
What competitive advantage can be found in this? Better is consciously do the same thing but driving the choose, not being led individually to almost the same solution with multiplied costs.
What we are currently doing is the exploitation of already existing channels (TMF Operator Committee) to promote the initiative among big Telco Players and verify the interest on it.
In crating the new WADE community instead we have to face other problems. As said we want to be able to measure the impact that introducing OS can have either in the organization or in the quality of the software.
As clearly stated by 0, opening up a project can add whole new sets of complexities, and cost *more* in the short term than simply keeping it in-house. Opening up means arranging the code to be comprehensible to complete strangers, so ***documentation*** needs to be clear where sometimes it is almost absent.
Moreover ***packaging*** is a topic that is underestimated when the development is internal, but in distributing it, it is necessary to create easy installable packages.
More if interest arise on the community, there is the added burden of answering developers' questions for a while before seeing any benefit from their presence.
This activity is much closer to promotion than to software development, but sometimes it is the first impact on the environment, on the care devoted to users, on the possibility of having support to ensure a success to the project, more than the embedded idea that can be successful.
Also ***management aspects*** are very different from those necessary in in-house development.
There are several developers, notoriously independent, who do not accept easily the idea that behind the product stands a big company. Even if the community will be done of just resources provided by different companies (and this is undoubtedly limiting) there is a coordinating activity far more complex than the one required for a homogenous group of co-located developers.
There should be a management conducting an activity closer to that of a psychologist that have to keep different people together giving them the consciousness that working together is more productive than working individually.
An Open Source community has to be treated more as a social network then as a developers team. This is also the reason of the importance of the development envi-

ronment that must provide the easiest tools for communicating, sharing experiences and problems. In other words it has to be a place developers want to keep coming back to.

Finally ***legal aspect*** have to be carefully treated since one of the most diffused license for instance, the GNU Public License, as discussed in 0 , appears to have the ability to expose proprietary software developers to substantial risk if used improperly.

2.4 Metrics

The purpose of the initiative is that of "measuring" the opportunity of using OS as a resource for TI. This means that all possible measures, translated into "savings" has to be collected.

What saving means is clear, not as much how indirect saving can be collected and then monetized.

And in using OS there are not just savings, as repeatedly stated above, there are extra costs: the cost of setting up an environment to be accessed from outside, the cost of the restructuring the product to be open effectively. The cost of a parallel internal environment to reproduce the build before delivering the solution to internal projects, the cost of internal development and management, etc.

Clearly an expense has been activated to charge the effort to be devoted to such activities that are clearly identified, and this can rate the direct cost of the initiative.

Similarly we are collecting the effort spent in past years for maintaining WADE, for a comparison of the values.

But obviously we want also to measure the contribution given by the community, that cannot be measured in man/hours.

So the usual environmental metrics are collected 0:

- The number and growth of "core" members divided by dominion
- The number and growth of downloads
- The number and growth of contributions either to the source code repository or to the mailing list (divided in developers and users, this measures the "vitality" of the community)
- The mean time to respond to an issue (again full and cleaned by our direct contributions)
- The fixing rate (internal, but more important form external contributors)
- The main fixing time from external contributors ("Reaction Rate")

As well as quality metrics:

- Delta times to manage the introduction of new features with respect to insourcing criteria
- Debugging times and quality
- Cohesion - change in cohesion - structural 0

- Bugs (normalized on LOC, bug fixing mean time) mainly on critical components (the more changed ones)

Also organizational metrics are to be collected:

- Measure the level of control and influence on the community: how many internally proposed new features have been accepted by the community and implemented by others than internal contributors

Clearly all these need to be translated into a real value for Telecom Italia and so apart form translating the indicators into objective numbers, it is necessary to find conversion parameters to turn these into saved effort.

We are still working on all this.

3 Conclusions

As widely described TI is trying the approach to OS as a possible way for further reduce the TCO of its OSS.

The strategic relevance of WADE and its choose as trial for such an initiative demonstrates the interest of TI to approach Open Source as a real resource for its business.

The process has just started: a plan for the initiative is ready and starting from March 2008 WADE will have its own environment, mailing list, forum , etc. and a web site from which it will be downloadable.

A document describing the full set of metrics that will be collected is under development in collaboration with the University of Milano and these metrics will be systematically collected to measure the effectiveness of the initiative and to refine the environment according to result as well as on feedback from the community.

Every three months these metrics will be published to the management who has great interest in the initiative.

Concurrently ha thread with TMF has been started with the goal of starting a catalyst project on OS to give the initiative all the strength of an organization that has also tha aim of proposing standards within Telco community.

It's a bet we expect to win.

References

The individual shareholder Guide Oct. 2007 http://ticlub.telecomitalia.com/pdf/Guida_1H_2007_ottobre_EN.pdf

Solari A. , Le opportunità del modello Open Source; un percorso in Telecom Italia - Technical Information Services verso il SW Open Source, OSBAIT Nov. 2006

Laurie Wurster, User Survey Analysis: Open-Source Software Summits, North America and Europe, 2006, Gartner

Rishab Aiyer Ghosh, Study on the:Economic impact of open source software on innovation and the competitiveness of the Information and Communication Technologies(ICT) sector in the EU, MERIT 2006,

Karl Fogel, Producing Open Source Software How to Run a Successful Free Software Project, http://producingoss.com/

JADE - Java Agent Development framework. http://jade.tilab.com.

Frost J., Some Economic & Legal Aspects of Open Source Software, 2005, http://students.washington.edu/jjfrost/

Ardagna C., Damiani E., Frati F. FOCSE an OWA-based Evaluation Framework for OS adoption in Critical Environment, in Open Source Development, Adoption and Innovation, Springer 2007

Misic V., Measuring the Coherence of Software Product Line Architectures, Tech. report TR 06/03 – Univ. of Manitoba

A Framework to Abstract The Design Practices of e-Learning System Projects

Alain Corbiere
LIUM-IUT, Le Mans University,
52, Route des Docteurs Calmette et Guérin,
53020 Laval Cedex 9, France

Abstract. The use of ALT (Advanced Learning Technologies) creates dynamic sharing and exchanging between open source communities that diffuse e-learning systems. In our opinion, the designer practices define new perspectives on e-learning design which are not structured and highlighted enough. This article shows the capabilities of a generic framework to analyse the design practices on a open source project and to explicit these practices. We describe how the semantics for architectural specifications proposed by RM-ODP (Reference Model-Open Distributed Process) framework were applied on an e-learning system project to analyse the principles of invariants, structural and functional.

1 Introduction

The current practices using ALT define new perspectives on e-learning design. First, the open source project applies a component-based software engineering [1] which makes it easier to specify and to reuse the software artefacts in design processes. Then, the e-learning designers are required to choose, understand and use the informational models provided by the IMS Global Learning Consortium to specify their decisions. The design intentions of an e-learning system are increasingly explicit.

These facts bring us to search for an abstract framework for the engineering and the re-engineering of software system and to apply on an e-learning system. This framework must define a set of terms to explicit the observations on the practice of the open source communities that design e-learning platforms. This framework must be sufficiently precise to analyse and to describe the code and the architecture, and sufficiently open to allow its own interpretation.

In this article, we propose the RM-ODP (Reference Model-Open Distributed Process) framework which was adopted as an ISO (International Organization for Standardization) standard. This framework combines the logic of a formal description to specify the architecture and to consider the distributed information technology evolution [2]. Moreover, the objective of the design of e-learning systems is described as "a collaboration between the disciplines of educational science and computer science" [12].

Please use the following format when citing this chapter:

Corbiere, A., 2008, in IFIP International Federation for Information Processing, Volume 275; *Open Source Development, Communities and Quality*; Barbara Russo, Ernesto Damiani, Scott Hissam, Björn Lundell, Giancarlo Succi; (Boston: Springer), pp. 317–323.

This article illustrates the use of the framework by describing one interpretation of a four step specification on an open source project. We abstract the design practices of the e-learning system project and explicit the new perspectives based on the information model diffused by IMS Global Learning Consortium.

2 RM-ODP framework

This framework is defined as a meta-standard on the distributed system [3]. It is domain independent and supports a specification process. This tool allows us to describe the different design practices observed while respecting the vocabulary and to structure it according to its architecture. This framework provides two abstraction levels and it represents describes the transformations corresponding to the acts of specification, structuring and modelling.

The first abstraction level is defined by five viewpoints "each with an associated viewpoint language which expresses concepts and rules relevant to a particular area of concern in terms of which of a system can be described from that viewpoint" ([3] item 6.2.1).

- The enterprise viewpoint: which defines communities, actors, roles, activities and tools focused on rationales, opportunities and strategies.
- The information viewpoint: which defines the information handled by the various system resources and how it is dealt with by the various components.
- The computational viewpoint: which defines the software mechanisms that allow component diffusion and execution on software platforms.
- The engineering viewpoint: which focuses on the component mechanisms and functions.
- The technology viewpoint: which defines the material and software technologies.

The second abstraction level defined terms that allow us to specify the coherence between viewpoints. Four abstract concepts are used to specify our interpretation of e-learning platform project design practice:

- Decomposition: "To specify objects and behaviours which constitute an object or a behaviour" ([4], item 9.3) ;
- Template: "The specification of the common features of a collection of entities in sufficient detail that an entity can be instantiated using it" ([4], item 9.11) ;
- Behavioural compatibility: "An object is behaviourally compatible with a second object with respect to a set of criteria" ([4], item 9.4) ;
- Trace: "A record of an object's interactions, from its initial state to some other state" ([4], item 9.6).

These concepts help us to describe four specification tasks. These consist of the analysis the source code, the design framework and the technical specification models applied in an e-learning system project.

3 Instance of RM-ODP framework on an e-learning system project: OpenUSS

By using the two abstraction levels proposed by RM-ODP framework, we explicit the design practices of OpenUSS[1] (Open University Support System). This open source community manages a web site which allows access to the e-learning system and diffuses the source code be installed, executed, copied, distributed, analysed and modified. The stability and the continuity of this community, the variety of roles and the number of the users (10,000 users: students, professors and assistants) justify our choice.

We create an instance of RM-ODP framework on this project:

- To abstract the design practices on EJB (Enterprise JavaBeans) component technology in e-learning ;
- To relate the informational models provided by the IMS consortium with an implementing entity ;
- To identify new perspectives of the ALT engineering.

3.1 Step 1 : Using the decomposition concept to specify the computational entities

This first step consists of specifying the platform's software architecture and describing the complex links between its components. We identify the first model published[2] on the OpenUSS web site. The dependence links use the UML (Unified Modelling Language) notation system describes the central position of the "foundation" component. This diagram corresponds to the first step of the abstraction process. However, this UML class diagram used describes the computational decomposition and the interactions between interfaces of different objects. This diagram corresponds to the computational viewpoint of RM-ODP framework. The analysis process must continue to transform the first specification into a more detailed specification.

The technical system, on which these components are deployed, is a platform compatibility with the EJB component technology of Sun Microsystems. Each component is specified by the deployment models provided by OpenUSS community.

In addition, the decomposition logic applied by the technical framework of this platform identifies the object type "workflow" as being central. Its associated model describes the states of the computational interfaces. This allows us to observe the behaviour by tracking the methods invoked on the object interfaces, and the operations of the container object in which it functions. Focused on this viewpoint, the analysis is limited.

---

[1] See, http://openuss.sourceforge.net/

[2] See, http://openuss.cvs.sourceforge.net/openuss/openuss/design-general/model/src/

This only communicates the production information to the technical administrator of platform. This information needs to be related to other aspects specified in the other viewpoints of the RM-ODP framework.

3.2 Step 2 : Using the template concept to specify the engineering choices

The decomposition of objects associated with the "foundation" component provided by OpenUSS community gives a list of objects from a computational viewpoint. The identification of the relations between two viewpoints allow us to transform a specification into a more detailed specification.
In this example, we look to model the relation which exists between the objects by specifying the computational objects from the engineering viewpoint.
The project OpenUSS designers apply a design process described in the technical framework EJOSA[3] (Enterprise Java Open Source Application). It defines an easy to understand structure to be followed by the development with EJB components. This framework integrates a template which requires the naming rules for the source code files, and a structure in which to organize them.
Any designer who wants to collaborate with the OpenUSS community must respect this pattern when submitting a new component. The designer must save the structure of class in the "specification" file directory, produced by the analysis process. The UML class diagram used corresponds to the class saved in the "specification" file directory[4] of "foundation" component. This UML diagram is the result of activity specification from an engineering viewpoint.

3.3 Step 3 : Using the behavioural compatibility concept to specify the conformance points

In addition, the RM-ODP framework defines itself as a guide to specify the conformance points between the ODP standard and a new specification. The act of specifying a compatibility between two objects bring us to define the relations between the specification selected and implementation the corresponding.
The conformance points depend on the terms of specification selected with observable behaviour in the e-learning platform. Moreover, for this framework the conformance points need to be identified and tests defined to satisfy in these points ([4], chapter 15). One of the four given conformance points classes defines "the behaviour of some physical medium so that information can be recorded on one system and

[3] See, http://www.enhydra.org/ejosa/

[4] See, http://openuss.cvs.sourceforge.net/openuss/openuss/dev-foundation/specification/src/

then physically transferred, directly or indirectly, to be used on another system" ([4], item 15.3.4).
The IMS Learning Design informational model [5] is the physical medium chosen. It is produced by a normalization process which aims to propose models that answer to the interoperability needs between e-learning systems. In addition, this model is used in the design practice of e-learning platform for discussion on the pedagogical practices [7] and on the learning scenarios [8].

3.4 Step 4 : Using the trace concept to specify the conformance tests

This last step seeks to validate the behavioural compatibility specification. Our choice used the IMS Learning Design informational model to represent the trace generated by the method invocation of "foundation" component.
Three schemas provided by RM-ODP framework guide the specification activities from the informational viewpoint: the static schema, the dynamic schema and the invariable schema ([3], chapter 6).
By taking the static aspect of the XML (eXtensible Markup Language) schema of IMS Learning Design informational model as the invariable schema, our interpretation is to consider that the behaviour of the "role" entity is linked to the behaviour of "activity structure" entity and "environment" entity.
In addition, the dynamic aspect identifies new informational objects : "method", "play", "act", "role part", "condition" and "property". As specified in the IMS Learning Design specification document [5], these entities allow the description of the dynamic aspect of the scenario and correspond to the static schema from informational viewpoint.

4 Assessment of this analysis: New perspectives of ALT engineering

This article presents an instance of a framework on e-learning system project. We show the capabilities of the framework to support the designers team who wish to analyse the e-learning system design intentions.
The instance of the RM-ODP framework on the e-learning platform project demonstrates the four specification design steps. The effort of the OpenUSS community to communicate their e-learning platform design logics is highlighted in this example. The work of building relationships with new point of view proposed by another open source community is facilitated.
The aim is to understand and identify new perspectives on ALT engineering based on the abstraction of the design practices :

- on educational re-engineering which applies the propositions of ALT. The IMS consortium questioned its capacity to describe the *a priori* behaviour early on. One of the new perspectives is to analyse the capabilities of a generic framework like RM-ODP to instrument specification activity. For example in [8], the authors define rules to guide the observable specification based on and to extend the XML schema of IMS Learning Design language;
- on software based components engineering where each component can be reused to design another and to support the negotiation between them [1]. The integration a software tracker, itself constrained by software architecture, is a complex task. With the RM-ODP framework, we can analyse the designer practices on the OpenCPMS (open Controlling Performance Measurement System) component. It's a proposition of a tracking manager of the OpenUSS platform.
- on service engineering [11] which look to mapping the notion of business process and the business process life cycle onto learning processes and the learning process life cycle. This perspective structures and specifies the politics and the collective behaviours of a "community" defined in the business viewpoint [13]. These specifications will facilitate the exchanges between e-learning system projects;
- on model driven engineering where the difficulty is to identify the mechanisms used to model the various software artefacts [9]. The open source community OpenUSS [10] proposed one of the first contributions in the e-learning domain. One of the new perspectives is to detail this proposition by using RM-ODP framework concepts and viewpoints.

One of the stakes of the e-learning designers' open source community is to have a framework such as RM-ODP to propose a common vocabulary to share their practices and to identify new engineering and re-engineering perspectives to accommodate advances in ALT.

References

1. Szyperski. C (2003) Component Technology - What, Where, and How ? (USA). doi:10.1109/ICSE.2003.1201255
2. O'Rourke C, Fishman N; Selkow W (2003) Enterprise architecture using the Zachman framework. THOMSON LEARNING, Boston
3. ISO/IEC-10746-1 (1998) Open Distributed Processing Reference Model, Part 1: Overview. ISOIIEC JTC1 SC7
4. ISOIIEC-10746-2 (1996) Open Distributed Processing Reference Model, Part 2: Foundations. ISOIIEC JTC1 SC7
5. Koper R, Olivier B, Anderson T.(2003) IMS Learning Design Information Model, version 1.0 Final Specification.IMS Global Learning Consortium
6. Barré V, Choquet C (2005) Language Independent Rules for Suggesting and Formalizing Observed Uses In a Pedagogical Reengineering Context. doi: 10.1109/ICALT.2005.189
7. Burgos D, Koper R.(2005) Practical pedagogical uses of IMS Learning Deslgn's Level B. SIGOSSEE Conference. http://dspace.ou.nl/handle/1820/471. Accessed 01 April 2008

8. Pemin J.-P., Lejeune A. (2006) Models for the re-use of learning scenarios. http://dspace.ou.nl/handle/1820/580. Accessed 01 April 2008
9. Bézivin J.(2006) Model Driven Engineering: An Emerging Technical Space. doi:10.1007/11877028
10. Grob H. L, Bensberg F., Dewanto B. L (2005) Model Driven Architecture (MDA): Integration and Model Reuse for Open Source eLeaming Platforms. Eleed Journal. http://eleed.campussource.de/archive/1/81/. Accessed 01 April 2008
11. Helle D, Hrastnlk J, Maurer H (2005) An Analysis of Application of Business Process Management Technology in E-Learning Systems. Proceedings of E-Leam 2005 MCE Charlottesville USA 2937-2942
12. Cees V, C Jones V, van Sinderen et al (1997). Tele-education process modeling supported by the ODP viewpoint enterprise language. doi:10.1109/EDOC.1997.628341
13. ISOIIEC-15414 (2006) Open Distributed Processing Reference Model, Enterprise language. ISOIIEC JTC1 SC7

Assessing Innovation in the Software Sector: Proprietary vs. FOSS Production Mode. Preliminary Evidence from the Italian Case

Dario Lorenzi and Cristina Rossi
Department of Management, Economics, and Industrial Engineering
Politecnico di Milano

Abstract. Innovation in the software sector is a widely debated issue. Which are the most important dimensions to assess innovation in this field? Can we measure innovative processes carried out by software companies and what kind of innovation do they develop? Are FOSS solutions more innovative than proprietary ones? These are the research questions we endeavor to answer in this paper providing some empirical evidence, obtained using an original methodology of collecting experts' evaluations on the innovation level of 134 solutions provided by a group of Italian Small and Medium Enterprises.

Keywords: Innovation, Free/Open Source software, proprietary software

1 Introduction

The issue of innovation in the software industry is of great interest for both academic and practitioners (Bloch, 2007). Which is an innovative software solution? Which aspects should be considered to highlight the most important elements of innovation processes?

In this framework, the success of Free/Open Source Software (FOSS) highlights new research issues, dealing with whether and how FOSS programs turn out to be more innovative than proprietary ones (Klincewicz, 2005). The theme is intriguing as FOSS represents a disruptive process innovation affecting industrial dynamics (Dalle et al., 2007), and it can be regarded as an important instantiation of the Open Innovation model (West and Gallagher, 2006).

We focus on Italian software sector, addressing three research questions: (i) are software solutions developed by Italian SMEs' innovative? (ii) What kinds of innovations are implemented? (iii) Are FOSS programs more innovative than proprietary ones?

Please use the following format when citing this chapter:

Lorenzi, D. and Rossi, C., 2008, in IFIP International Federation for Information Processing, Volume 275; *Open Source Development, Communities and Quality*; Barbara Russo, Ernesto Damiani, Scott Hissam, Björn Lundell, Giancarlo Succi; (Boston: Springer), pp. 325–331.

2 Review of Literature

The concept of innovation is one of the mostly studied by economic scholars (Fagerberg, 2004). Particularly, it was acknowledged the complexity of the phenomenon and how to measuring it turns out to be a critical task. A short list of the most used metrics of firms' innovation effort include: (i) data on Research and Development; (ii) patents; (iii) bibliometrical data, such as publications in scientific and technical journals.

All previous indicators suffer from several shortcomings (Kleinknecht et al., 2002), in particular as far as the sectors forming the so-called *new economy* (Haskel, 2007). Indeed, the passing from a commodity-driven to a knowledge-driven economy forces to re-define innovation, considering a whole new set of variables related to how knowledge is created, managed, and passed through different actors (Bloch, 2007). Specifically, it has been noted that patents are often unable to follow the rapid evolution of the software market and to account for the complexity of complementary activities (Blind et al., 2004).

As a consequence, new indicators are needed to assess innovation in ICT fields (Maruyama et al., 2007). In the case of software, such indicators should take into account not only general aspects, but also specific elements (as the use of certain programming languages and platforms and so on).

In this framework, the rapid pace of diffusion of FOSS represents another source of complexity. Klincewicz (2005) has attempted to provide a classification of innovation in FOSS, basing on four classes: radical innovation, technological modifications, platform modifications, and new uses for existing technologies. The authors have also analysed 500 projects hosted on SourceForge[1], assessing that 436 of them are not innovative. This result can be linked to other studies showing low confidence in the innovative impact of FOSS solutions (Tuomi, 2005). In brief, the debate is far from a conclusion, even if FOSS solutions have proved to be as complex and reliable as proprietary ones.

3 Data and Methodology

The sample comes from a survey taken, in 2004, on more than 900 software firms[2] from Finland, Germany, Italy, Portugal, and Spain (Second European Libre Software Survey, ELISS II, see Bonaccorsi et al., 2006). Specifically, we focused on the 323 Italian respondents, because of database characteristics (some information are not available for all countries) and peculiarity of this software market, shaped by the presence of Small and Medium Enterprises (SMEs). More than 90% of firms have a total staff of less than 20 employees, and, in 16% of cases, they are one-man businesses. 167 of the companies provide to their customers FOSS-based software.

---

[1] http://www.sourceforge.net

[2] NACE code 72.2.

The average percentage of graduate staff is fairly high (about 36%), so as that of software developers (almost 30%). Respondents serve mainly business customers (81%), particularly SMEs (64%), while very few refer to University (3%) or end users (3%).

In order to address whether traditional innovation indicators are really not suitable for assessing innovation, data on three main metrics have been collected: (i) trademarks, using the database of the European Office for Trademarks and Design; (ii) patents, referring to the Delphion database (); (iii) scientific and technical publications hosted on Scopus[3]. Methodology is based on evaluations by software experts, basing on information recorded through the Web sites of the 323 Italian respondents. We collected comprehensive information on 134 solutions developed by a subsample of 70 companies. It is important to underline that, according to this methodology, the unit of analysis is no more the firm, but its software solutions. The 134 programs target mainly business customers: only 8% are intended for home users, and the most widespread category is managerial systems (45%), followed by Web oriented applications (9%). Moreover, most of them (107) are released under proprietary license, while the remaining ones (27) are distributed under FOSS licenses.

Three experts[4] were asked to evaluate the level of innovativeness: after an in depth colloquium, they received a table (containing the name of each product, the link to its Web page, a brief description of the product and of the producing firm) to be filled and a guide for its compilation. It is worth noting that, in order not to introduce a bias, we did not tell the experts whether a software was FOSS or not; anyway, they might find this information on the software Web site. Evaluators were asked to assign a mark between 1 (*not innovative*) to 5 (*very innovative*) to each product, referring to three main dimensions, leading to a set of five indicators. The choice of the dimensions is driven by economic literature on the topic (see, for instance, Garcia and Calantone, 2002).

The first dimension is related to the internal level of innovation, comparing each software with other programs developed by the same company (*Indicator 1: is the product new to the firm?*). The second one refers to the market in which the firm operate, comparing each product with similar available solutions. This dimension is addressed by two indicators, related to innovation in *what* a software does (*Indicator 2: is the software innovative in the sense that it better satisfies needs from users?*), and in *how* it succeeds in accomplishing a task, exploring technical aspects (*Indicator 3: is the product technologically new to the market?*).

The third dimension addresses innovation referring to the general level of tehnology and knowledge (*is the product new to the world?*). Two indicators are developed: (i) innovation in modules composing the software (*Indicator 4: is the software innovative as it contains original modules, which can be hardly found in other solutions, also in different market segments?*); (ii) innovation in what we labelled as *platform*, meaning those aspects related to the other technological characteristics, such as

[3] http://oami.eu.int, http://www.delphion.com, http://www.scopus.com/scopus/home.url

[4] Our decision to choose these experts was driven by geographic closeness and budget considerations. We are confident that they are well qualified to evaluate these products, having a long working experience in the software field.

programming languages, implemented algorithms, use of libraries, and so on (*Indicator 5: how the software platform is new with respect to those of other software solutions, also in different market segments?*).

It is useful to relate our indicators to dichotomy between *radical vs. incremental innovations*. For instance, innovations more related to technical aspects (indicator 3 and 5) can be considered as more radical innovations, with respect to a solution having original modules as the only element of novelty.

The main shortcoming of this methodology is the subjective nature of evaluations. However, all software have been evaluated by three experts: their knowledge of the market and multiple opinions mitigate the problem. Moreover, metrics of accordance of their judgement have been computed, showing that they were correlated[5]. Concluding, we chose to compute, for each indicator, the sum of the three evaluations, obtaining scores ranging between three (all experts assigned one) and fifteen (all five), and preserving variability even if mitigating the effect of outliers.

4 Empirical Results

Traditional metrics seem not to be suitable for the software sector formed. According to our investigations, only 5 companies registered, globally, 35 trademarks (26 logos and 9 names of companies). Only 3 firms hold a patent (for a total of 15 patents), and 3 were involved in scientific publications. In presenting experts' evaluations, we follow the repartition previously mentioned: innovation within the firm (dimension 1, indicator 1); innovation within the referring market (dimension 2, indicators 2 and 3); overall innovation (dimension 3, indicators 4 and 5).

Table 4.1: Descriptive statistics.

Dimension	Indicator	Min.	Max.	Std.Dev.	Median	75th	90th perc	99th
I	1	4	14	2.11	8	10	11	14
II	2	3	14	2.46	9	10.7	12.7	13.7
	3	3	14	2.78	8	10	12	13.7
III	4	5	13	2.04	8	10	11	13
	5	3	14	2.46	8	9	11	13.7

For the first dimension, 99th percentile is 14 (the highest for all dimensions). Standard deviation is low, showing concentration around mean values (more than 50% of the sample is between 6 and 8). Two indicators (innovation in *what* a software does: *indicator 2*; innovation in technical aspects: *indicator 3*) capture the second dimension. Both show equal values for minimum and mode, while differences in percentiles emerge: in 75th and 90th percentiles, indicator 2 has higher values (respec-

[5] As our study is characterised by multiple ratings per subject, we used the Spearman's rank correlation coefficient.

tively, 10.7 vs. 10, and 12.7 vs. 12). This finding is confirmed by other analysis: 69% of solutions have received a mark of 7 or more for indicator 2, while the proportion decreases to 52% for the third indicator. The innovative process seems to be more effective for aspects related to what a software does, instead of technological aspects. Third dimension was distinguished between innovation in modules (*indicator 4*) and in other technical aspects (*indicator 5*). 75th is higher for indicator 4 (10 vs. 9), but this pattern is not still true when focusing on values closer to the upper limit (99th percentile: 13 vs. 13.7). Experts claimed that sometimes Web sites provided few information about modules: this have generated a *central tendency bias,* leading evaluators to assign score 3 (confirmed by standard deviation: 2.04 for modules vs. 2.46). Indicator 4 obtains higher scores: proportion of evaluations between 5 and 7 is predominant for indicator 5 (32% vs. 38%), while indicator on modules presents more values between 7 and 9 (53% vs. 43%). This may be related to the peculiar structure of the sample: in a market dominated by SMEs, it is likely to observe more customizations and adaptations than radical innovations based on new technologies.

Summing up, data allow us to answer the first two research questions. As far as the former (*are Italian software solutions innovative?*), whilst results with traditional instruments are useless, using a methodology based on experts' evaluations, we succeed in disentangling innovation into its main dimensions. Also the latter issue (*what typologies of innovation are implemented?*) receives an answer. On one hand, when focusing on the referring market, indicator 2 shows higher values than indicator 3, supporting the idea of innovation processes more targeted to *what* a software solution does, than to *how* to do it. On the other, considering the *new to the world* dimension, innovation seems to be more focused on modules than in technical aspects. According to our findings, the Italian software sector seems to be characterized mainly by adaptations, customizations, and transfer of solutions into different platforms (an innovation that can be appointed as incremental).

In order to address our third research question (*are FOSS solutions more innovative than proprietary ones?*), we have performed comparisons between these two groups. As mentioned in the previous section, the sample of 134 software was formed by 109 proprietary and 27 FOSS solutions.

Table 4.2: Descriptive statistics. Proprietary vs. FOSS solutions

		Proprietary solutions						FOSS solutions						Mann Whitney P value	Nonparametric equality of medians P value
Dim	Ind	Min	Max	Median	Std Dev	75th per	90th per	Min	Max	Median	Std Dev	75th per	90th per		
I	1	4	14	8	2.03	10	11	6	14	10	2.15	11	12	0.007	0.027
II	2	3	14	8	2.30	10	11	5	14	11	2.66	12.5	13	0.004	0.002
	3	3	14	7	2.55	9	11	3	14	11	3.14	12	13	0.003	0.001
III	4	5	13	8	2.03	10	11	5	13	9	2.12	10	11	0.428	0.061
	5	3	14	7	2.21	9	10	4	14	10	2.58	11	12.4	0.000	0.000

FOSS solutions seem to be more innovative: in all the three dimensions, evaluations are higher for FOSS. Specifically, indicator 1 has higher median for FOSS and statistical tests show that this difference is significant. This is corroborated by data distribution: focusing on the score range 5-7, the proportion for FOSS (26%) is lower than the one for proprietary programs (44%), while the opposite emerges for values equal to 10 or more (51% vs. 27%). As far as the second dimension, FOSS solutions seem to be more innovative too. For both indicators, statistical tests confirm a higher level of innovativeness. Focusing on differences between indicators 2 and 3 within the same group, we notice that, in both cases, evaluations for indicator 3 are lower than those of indicator 2, confirming the conclusions for the entire sample. Same pattern emerges with the third dimension. However, whilst statistical tests confirm significant differences in median for indicator 5, no significant difference between the two sub-samples emerges for indicator 4, but, as mentioned above, results could be invalidated by central tendency bias. If the comparison between the two groups is interesting, it is also of interest to consider the differences between the two indicators within each group. Indeed, proprietary solutions show higher evaluations for modules, as emerged for the entire sample (e.g. values over 7 constitute the 65% for indicator 4, while only the 46% for indicator 5), while FOSS programs follow an opposite pattern. Indeed, indicator 5 shows higher values, as highlighted by median (9 for indicator 4 vs. 10 for indicator 5), 75th percentile (10 vs. 11), and 90th percentile (11 vs. 12.4). A more in depth analysis allows to notice that a large part for this difference comes from the highest values. This last consideration can be regarded as an insight that proprietary and FOSS software are also shaped by different innovative processes: radical innovation in FOSS vs. incremental innovation in proprietary field.

5 Conclusions

Innovation in software industry can be hardly defined and measured: this paper proposes an original methodology for assessing innovativeness of software solutions produced by Italian SMEs. We have provided evidence that innovative processes exist and it is possible to assess them under different perspectives and to delineate general characteristics of these processes, showing that innovations related to technical aspects are less prominent: it is possible to address these innovation processes as incremental, which is in agreement with a software sector shaped by SMEs. Moreover, our analysis has highlighted differences between innovativeness of FOSS and proprietary software. Specifically, FOSS solutions display higher level for all indicators, and almost all statistical tests indicate that the two groups are two different populations. Differences emerge in the level of innovation and in the relationships between indicators: specifically, focusing on the global level of technology, FOSS solutions show higher values for technical aspects. The characteristics of the sample made results hardly generalizable; however, they help in shed light on questions posed by the FOSS paradigm. Does the FOSS production foster innovation processes? Does the FOSS represent a valid alternative for software SMEs whishing to operate with leading-edge technologies? Hence, it would be interesting for future researches to apply a refined version of this methodology on larger database, containing data from different countries.

References

Blind K., Edler J., Friedewald M. (2004) Software Patents – An Empirical Analysis from an Economic Perspective. Stuttgart: Fraunhofer IRB Verlag

Bloch C. (2007) Assessing recent developments in innovation measurement: the third edition of the Oslo manual. Science and Public Policy, 34 (1): 23 – 34

Bonaccorsi A., Giannangeli S., Rossi C. (2006) Adaptive entry strategies under competing standards-hybrid business models in the Open Source software industry. Management Science, 52(7): 1085-1098

Dalle J.M., Rossi C., Rullani F. (2007) Toward a new industrial organization? OSS in economic and managerial perspective. In Feller J., Fitzgerald B., Scacchi W., Sillitti A. (eds.) Open Source Development, Adoption and Innovation, Springer, New York, NY

Fagerberg J. (2004) Innovation: a guide to the literature. In Fagerberg, Jan, David C. Mowery and Richard R. Nelson: The Oxford Handbook of Innovations. Oxford University Press: 1-26

Garcia R., Calantone R. (2002) A critical look at technological innovation typology and innovativeness terminology: a literature review. he journal of product innovation management, 19(2): 110-132

Haskel J. (2007) Measuring innovation and productivity in a knowledge-based service economy. Economic and Labour Market Review, 1 (7): 27-31

Kleinknecht A., van Montfort K., Brouwer E. (2002) The Non-Trivial Choice between Innovation Indicators. Economics of Innovation and New Technology, 11 (2): 109-121

Klincewicz K. (2005) Innovativeness of open source software projects, MIT online paper, Boston. Available at: http://opensource.mit.edu/papers/klincewicz.pdf

Koberg S., Detienne D., Heppard K. (2003) An empirical test of environmental, organizational, and process factors affecting incremental and radical innovation. The Journal of High Technology Management Research, 14 (1): 21-45

Maruyama, Kohda, Katsuyama (2007) Issues of Service Innovation and Its Model. The 9th IEEE International Conference on E-Commerce Technology and The 4th IEEE International Conference on Enterprise Computing, E-Commerce and E-Services: 489-490

West J., Gallagher S. (2006) Patterns of open innovation in Open Source software. In Chesbrough H., Vanhaverbeke W., West J., Eds. (2006) Open Innovation: researching a new Paradigm, Oxford University press, Cambridge

Detecting Agility of Open Source Projects Through Developer Engagement

Paul J. Adams[1], Andrea Capiluppi[2], and Adriaan de Groot[1]

[1] Sirius Corporaion Ltd., Hamm Moor Lane, Weybridge, UK, KT15 2SF
paul.adams@siriusit.co.uk, groot@kde.org
[2] Centre for Research on Open Source Software, University of Lincoln, Lincoln, UK, LN5 7TS acapiluppi@lincoln.ac.uk

Abstract. The principles behind the agile development methods and common practise within the Open Source community are vastly different. In recent years there has been a rise of interest in these, in order to detect and inform on areas of compatible shared practises. This paper argues that it is possible to quantify the level of agility displayed by Open Source projects. An indicator of agility, the Mean Developer Engagement (MDE) metric is introduced and tested through the analysis of public project data. Projects sampled from two repositories (KDE and SourceForge) are studied and a hypothesis is formulated: projects from the two samples display a similar level of MDE.

This paper provides two main contributions: first, the MDE metric is shown to vary significantly between the KDE and SourceForge projects. Second, by combining MDE with a project's lifespan, it is also shown that SourceForge projects have insufficient uptake of new developers resulting in more active, shorter, initial activity, and in a quicker "burning out" of the projects.

1 Introduction

Plan-driven approaches to software engineering emphasise large-scale planning and formal communications while agile approaches emphasise flexibility [14]. Proponents of agile processes argue that such processes respond to change and withstand the continual pressures of software evolution better than plan-driven approaches [6, 1]. Proponents of the OSS paradigm claim that it should be considered as a novel approach, and its evolution and maintenance phases should be considered different from a plan-driven approach [5].

In theory agility and Open Source are very different concepts; the latter being just a licensing paradigm with implications for code reuse and redistribution. Comparative studies have been made in the past, but the scarcity of data from Agile processes leaves most studies on the surface of theoretical discussions [19, 13].

The term "agility" has been formulated to assess how a software company locates itself in a spectrum between Agile and plan-driven. Process-related characteristics have been identified to help either in focusing on the critical factors of the development framework [4]; or in the selection itself of the most appropriate approach [7]. Agility in Open Source projects, however, is often implemented significantly differently from the canonical definition of the agile processes. Usually this occurs due to certain agile

Please use the following format when citing this chapter:

Adams, P.J., Capiluppi, A. and de Groot, A., 2008, in IFIP International Federation for Information Processing, Volume 275; *Open Source Development, Communities and Quality*; Barbara Russo, Ernesto Damiani, Scott Hissam, Björn Lundell, Giancarlo Succi; (Boston: Springer), pp. 333–341.

practises requiring team co-location [15] or smaller teams [12]. Instead agility within Open Source is often performed by much larger teams in a distributed fashion; although co-location for certain activities, like sprinting, is becoming more common [9]. The unifying aspect of all agile processes is flexibility in order to react to change (in requirements, or other conditions) [3]. We posit that this, coupled with the agile culture of producing useful, working software as quickly as possible, creates an implicit requirement for an agile project to make efficient use of its developer resource.

This paper introduces and justifies the Mean Developer Engagement (MDE) metric. Being it a process-based metric, it correlates with the effort of OSS developers along the duration of a project, and it addresses one of the relevant factors in the definition of agility [4]. The metric is not introduced per-se: it is used both to empirically evaluate the agility of OSS projects, and to compare two samples of projects extracted from two repositories (KDE and SourceForge), in order to detect differences in the agility of OSS developers. The traditional Goal-Question-Metric paradigm will be used to detect the presence of differences: a research hypothesis will be formulated and a statistical test will be evaluated to detect statistically significant differences among the samples.

This paper is structured as follows: Section 2 introduces the MDE metric and describes the factors it is built upon, showing how the data was gathered and processed. Section 3 introduces the GQM approach and tailors it into the research hypothesis which this paper explores. Section 4 evaluates the results and provides the discussion of the statistical tests used. Section 5 concludes.

2 Mean Developer Engagement

Users and developers are limited resources within the OSS environment, particularly so with regards to develoeprs [8]. However, several major OSS projects have been noted to be particularly successful at recruiting new developers [16, 17]. No empirical evidence has been given yet to a comparison of how repositories employ their resources, in terms of active developers.

In order to draw a comparison between two OSS repositories, the Mean Developer Engagement (MDE) is here proposed and analysed as a metric. MDE is a measurement of how effective (on average over time) an OSS project is at making use of its human resources and, therefore, potentially indicative of agility [7]. MDE is measured over n time periods, and each developer associated with the project is classified as active or inactive in each period. Typically, a week is used as time period; the number n ranges from 1 (a very short project) to over 600 (long-term projects). In our research we define MDE as:

$$\bar{de}_n = \frac{(n-1).\bar{de}_{n-1} + \left(\frac{\text{dev}(active)}{\text{dev}(total)}\right)_i}{n} \tag{1}$$

– dev($active$) is the number of (distinct) developers active in time period i.

- dev(*total*) is the total number of developers involved with the project in the periods $0 \ldots i$.
- n is the number of time periods over which the project has been evaluated.

An ideal project, in which every developer is active in every single time period within the range of the MDE calculation, has an MDE of 1. The primary concern with the current definition of MDE lies with the metric dev(*total*), this metric naïvely asserts that the number of accounts in the project repository is the total number of developers in the project. This is deficient as an account may remain in the repository long after a developer has left a project. To create a refined and more precise definition, $dtotal$ is augmented with the inclusion of a *grace period.*

2.1 Refined Definition – Grace Period

OSS project developers leave a trace which can be retrieved by assessing version control logs (*i.e.* their account name appears for the first time). The definition of dev(*total*), above, establishes a list of everyone who has ever been a developer in a specific project. In order to detect when a developer leaves a project, it is possible to set an arbitrary time span after which a developer who has shown no activity in that span is removed from the list of project participants.

The definition of dev(*total*), for each n, should be refined in order to detect developer inactivity. Depending on length of service, each developer shall be allowed an inactivity "grace period," as are shown in Table 1 (These figures were created as a discussion exercise between 10 Open Source developers and validated by 10 more). Only once they have been inactive for longer than this time shall they no-longer be considered as project developers. As soon as the developer commits more code, they are reconsidered as a developer and their grace period is set to one, as a new developer.

Table 1. Developer grace periods (in weeks), shorter length of service has grace period 1.

Length Of Service	Grace Period	Length Of Service	Grace Period
1024	20	208	8
520	15	104	6
416	12	52	4
260	10	24	2

By making these adjustments a more accurate measure of dev(*total*) is calculated, thus improving the overall accuracy of MDE. The downside to this adjustment, however, is an increase in overall computational complexity when automating MDE measurement. This is simply a linear increase, with n, in complexity created by the adjust being made after each time quanta.

2.2 Data Gathering and Processing

In order to calculate MDE for a project we require to know which members of the project are active and when. In this research the data has been gathered from the history of the projects' source code repositories. This data could easily be supplemented with data from mailing lists, IRC logs, etc. The history contains, for each change done to the project, at least the user name of the developer and the date/time stamp of the commit. MDE can easily be calculated using these. Most source code management tools (such as Subversion) provide a way to print out the histories in a machine-parseable form.

Figure 2.2 shows example plots of MDE (in both simple and refined forms) for the entire KDE project (`http://www.kde.org`). KDE is a very large project, with over 1600 accounts in its Subversion repository, over 760000 changes and 10 years of development history. The plot shows the change in MDE as calculated on a week-by-week basis from the beginning of the project in 1997.

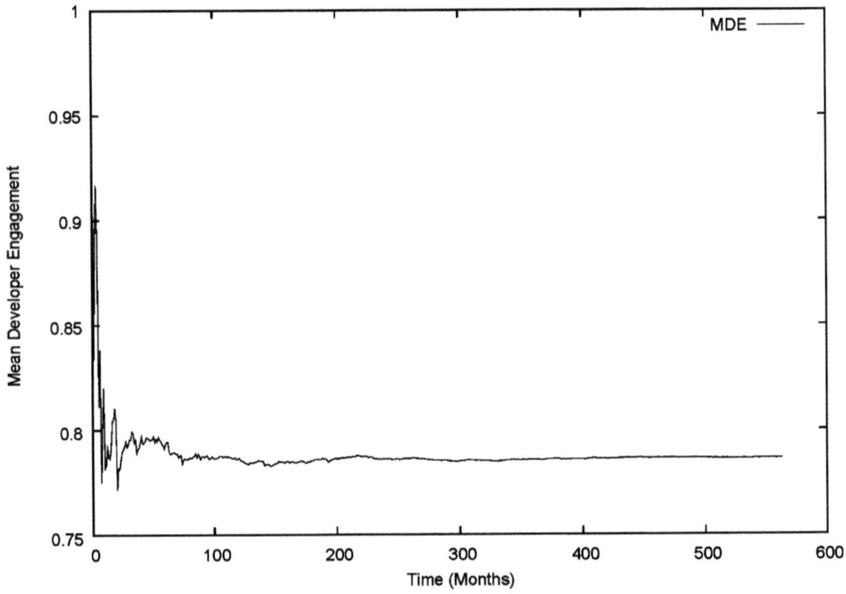

Fig. 1. MDE over the lifetime of the KDE project

The first aspect of MDE plots that should be noted is the anomalies which occurs within the data for the first year. These deviations from the trends are caused by a disproportionate shift in the number of active developers early on. Early in a project's lifetime, both n and dev(*total*) are low and any change in dev(*active*) will have a dramatic affect on MDE.

The initial period of upheaval is followed by an upturn in MDE, indicating that the project has attracted many new developers. This is shortly followed by a slightly steeper gradient in the plot, indicating increased turnover (i.e. an increased number of developers having short tenure in the project). As the project matures, this plot begins to level out as more developers maintain longer commitments to KDE. From week 300 until the end of the plot the gradient of MDE is stable. This is indicative of process (explicit or otherwise) and a stable community.

By applying the adjustments described by Table 1 the new plot is always equal to or greater than the original plot at any point in time. This is clearly shown in Figure 2.2 where the refined MDE plot is significantly higher in value. In the case of this KDE plot, the most remarkable aspect is the stability and success with which KDE has managed to engage its active developer base; this plot clearly indicating that the average regular contributor has been active nearly 80% of the time since the second year of the project.

3 MDE – Empirical Evaluation

In order to validate the MDE metric, the following Section will both apply it and study its behaviour on two samples of OSS projects: one was extracted from KDE, and the other was randomly selected from the repositories hosted at SourceForge (`http://sourceforge.net`). SourceForge (SF) hosts over 120,000 different projects; the majority of these are small projects compared with a large and long-term project like KDE (which is outside SourceForge) [10].

The MDE metric applied to the KDE project as a whole is analysed in Figure 2.2 above. The KDE project has to be considered as a collection of sub-projects, each of them much more focused on a particular goal, and with a smaller developer base. Very few of the developers in KDE are active across the entire project, as most focus on their own sub-project. This improves the accuracy of MDE for each sub-project by disregarding developers who work elsewhere in KDE.

As the data-base for the present work, 20 sub-projects from KDE and 20 SF projects were randomly sampled. Projects which had no history, (i.e. "dead on arrival" as they have not ever engaged developers) were replaced by other randomly selected projects. A research hypothesis was formulated based on the MDE behaviour on these two samples. It is tested first via a bi-directional test, to detect major differences between the two samples; then a directional test is applied to detect whether one sample statistically achieves better results in terms of the MDE metric.

3.1 Empirical Approach – Goal-Question-Metric

Metric-based evaluation of software products is well established within the software engineering research, since it allows a simple and effective means of quality evaluation [11]. The Goal-Question-Metric (GQM) approach [2, 18] is particularly popular due to its ease of automation. This research was conducted using the GQM approach, with MDE as a metric.

Goal: The goal of this research is to identify, through the application of metrics, the degree of agility displayed by an Open Source development project. Empirically comparing the Agile and OSS development approaches, finding similarities and differences, will help bridge the gap between the traditional closed-source and newer paradigms in software development.

Question: As part of a greater research programme this study is conducted to establish the statistical significance of MDE as a metric. As such, we ask: Are projects within KDE statistically different from those hosted within SourceForge with regards to MDE? Alternatively, does KDE display a different level of agility than SF projects? If a difference is found in the bi-directional comparison of the samples, a more restrictive test will be formulated, asking whether the KDE sample consistently achieves better MDE results than the SourceForge sample.

Metric: The metric applied is MDE using time quanta of one week. The metric is applied across the project lifetime and an average MDE score for each week is used.

3.2 The Samples

The complete version control log of the 20 randomly selected KDE projects and SourceForge projects were parsed to produce the MDE scores shown in Table 2. Here, the date of the first log entry, i (the duration of the log in weeks) and the MDE score are shown for each project. In addition a "effort" value is included and will be described in the following section.

4 Results and Analysis

From the SourceForge sample, one may note the relatively high incidence of projects with an MDE of 1.0, indicating "ideal" projects with total engagement of all the project developers. A closer examination of the table shows a strong correlation between an MDE of 1.0 and a lifespan of one week; a project *necessarily* has an MDE of 1.0 in its first week, as the determination of active and total developers is based on the set of developers seen in that first week. Such short-lived projects are likely "dead on arrival" as they fail to engage any long-term effort [10]. Much more interesting are the longer-lived projects with a high MDE, such as wxpropgrid (MDE=0.9968 over seven months) and shareaza (MDE=0.7830 over three years).

4.1 Testing of the Hypothesis and Discussion

The Wilcoxon two-sample test is used to assess the significance in similarity between samples from two populations. It is applied here principally in two-tail form to show that the samples are indeed significantly different and yields: $W = 97, p \leq 0.005376$. At the 95% confidence level, this is a significant result. We reject the null hypothesis that the populations display similar levels of agility. We test the hypothesis that SF

Table 2. MDE Scores Calculated for 20 Random Projects from KDE and SF.net.

KDE					*SF.net*				
Project	Start	*i*	MDE	Effort	Project	Start	*i*	MDE	Effort
dolphin	21-11-06	54	0.6799	36.7146	askcms	29-06-06	1	1.0	1.0
k3b	26-03-01	349	0.5961	208.0389	awdotnet	24-05-07	1	1.0	1.0
katomic	29-06-99	438	0.3340	146.2920	dvdshop	31-03-06	1	1.0	1.0
kcalc	13-04-97	554	0.4307	238.6078	hivex	16-07-07	1	1.0	1.0
kgeography	07-03-04	38	0.5386	20.4668	interaction	04-03-07	1	1.0	1.0
kig	15-04-02	294	0.6878	202.2132	kuragari	13-01-07	1	1.0	1.0
kivio	02-12-00	365	0.5320	194.1800	kyrios	03-07-06	74	0.5634	41.6916
kmail	18-01-03	254	0.6730	170.9420	map	06-11-05	50	0.3780	18.9000
kmoon	27-09-98	478	0.2913	139.2414	neuralbattle	14-06-06	74	0.6803	50.3422
knotes	30-06-97	544	0.4638	252.3072	opulus	25-07-07	10	0.4931	4.9310
kolourpaint	10-10-03	214	0.6269	134.1566	pwytter	09-07-07	1	1.0	1.0
konqueror	09-02-99	459	0.6610	303.3990	pyaws	11-04-06	56	0.2514	14.0784
konsole	28-10-98	474	0.6109	281.5666	rejuce	02-08-06	10	0.5554	5.5540
kontact	18-01-03	254	0.5867	149.0218	rlcyber	02-07-06	17	0.7612	12.9404
kopete	02-01-02	308	0.7142	219.9736	shareaza	02-06-04	182	0.7830	142.5060
kscd	04-07-97	542	0.4962	268.9404	stellarium	12-07-02	280	0.6183	173.1240
kspread	18-04-98	502	0.6216	312.0432	tclshp	04-10-06	1	1.0	1.0
ksudoku	03-03-07	39	0.6530	25.4670	tsg	23-03-07	19	0.6036	11.4684
kteatime	16-04-99	450	0.3299	148.4550	wxpropgrid	16-04-07	31	0.9968	30.9008
marble	29-09-06	61	0.6321	38.5581	xml-copy-editor	16-08-07	14	0.7731	10.8234

shows greater level of agility than KDE using a single-tail Wilcoxon test and find: $W = 97, p \leq 0.002688$. This is another strong result at the 95% confidence level, and we reject the null hypothesis. SF *does* show greater agility.

The Wilcoxon two-sample tests applied here strongly indicate a statistical difference between MDE in the samples from KDE and SF and potentially a difference in agility. We may say that the SF projects achieve better developer engagement in the sampled projects. It may be surprising that both null hypotheses were rejected, especially given SourceForge's notoriety for being home to low quality projects [10].

This counter-intuitive result was studied further: an analysis of the start and end dates in the projects from both samples shows that KDE projects may not be as strong at utilising developers, but typically have longer lifespans. There may be further significance to MDE in conjunction with the lifespan of a project. Using the same samples from KDE and SF, the duration of the project was multiplied by the MDE value in order to produce a new "effort" score. The weighted effort value for each project is shown within Table 2.

Even without formal statistical analysis, we see a clear separation between the new "weighted" scores for MDE. The same two-tail Wilcoxon test applied to effort returns: $W = 374, p \leq 2.455e\text{-}06$. Therefore, at the 95% confidence level we can state that a randomly selected KDE project will display better developer engagement over time than a randomly selected SourceForge project. This can be explained as follows: SF projects tend to better engage developers, but just for a limited amount of time, and its projects tend to "burn bright" but fade rather quickly. The KDE project manages instead to achieve a prolonged engagement of its developers, and this by itself represents a quality factor within different OSS repositories.

5 Conclusions and Further Work

This paper argued that it is possible to measure the agility of OSS projects by means of a metric based on developers effort. The Mean Developer Engagement (MDE) metric was introduced as a means for assessing how affectively OSS projects utilise their developer resource, if they leverage it consistently and for prolonged periods of time, and whether different OSS repositories achieve different levels of engagement of developers. Samples from two OSS repositories (KDE and SourceForge) were extracted, and the MDE's statistical significance was evaluated through a bi-directional and a single directional tests.

The empirical evaluation of the hypothesis showed at first a counter-intuitive result: if fact, it was found that SF projects are statistically better at engaging their developers than the projects from KDE. Investigating the results further, the duration of development was studied, which displayed much longer development periods in the KDE sample than in the SF one. Combining the duration with the engagement, we find that SF projects tend to better engage their developers, but only for a limited amount of time, after which it is common for the project to quit its activity. KDE projects have more overall endurance: part of the endurance beyond the lifespan of a SF project must be attributed to the more regular intake of new developers these projects have. Therefore a project is more likely to sustain MDE in a forge of related projects, such as KDE, than in a forge of unrelated projects, such as SourceForge.

Before MDE can be formally introduced as a metric further work shall be carried out to compare the results of Open Source MDE, presented here, with known agile project data from industry. This will allow us to establish upper and lower thresholds for MDE as an indicator of agility.

6 Acknowledgement

This work is partially supported by the European Community Framework Programme 6, Information Society Technologies key action, contract number IST-033331 ("SQO-OSS").

References

1. A. Capiluppi and J. Fernandez-Ramil and J. Higman and H. C. Sharp and N. Smith. An Empirical Study of the Evolution of an Agile-Developed Software System. In *International Conf. on Software Engineering*, pages 511–518, Minneapolis, Minnesota, May 2007.
2. V. Basili, G. Caldiera, and H. D. Rombach. The Goal Question Metric Approach. In *Encyclopedia of Software Engineering*, pages 528 – 532. John Wiley & Sons, Inc., 1994.

3. K. Beck and C. Andres. *Extreme Programming Explained: Embrace Change*. Addison Wesley, 2004.
4. B. Boehm and R. Turner. Using Risk to Balance Agile and Plan-Driven Methods. *IEEE Computer*, 36(6):57–66, 2003.
5. A. Capiluppi, J. Gonzales-Barahona, I. Herraiz, and G. Robles. Adapting the "Staged Model for Software Evolution" to Free/Libre/Open Source Software. In *Proc. Int'l Workshop on Principles of Software Evolution (IWPSE)*, Dubrovnik, Croatia, 3-4 Sept. 2007.
6. N. Chapin. Agile Methods' Contributions in Software Evolution. In *ICSM '04: Proceedings of the 20th IEEE International Conference on Software Maintenance*, page 522, Washington, DC, USA, 2004. IEEE Computer Society.
7. S. Datta. Agility Measurement Index: A Metric for the Crossroads of Software Development Methodologies. In *ACM-SE 44: Proceedings of the 44th annual Southeast regional conference*, pages 271–273, New York, NY, USA, 2006. ACM.
8. A. de Groot, S. Kügler, P. J. Adams, and G. Gousios. Call for Quality: Open Source Quality Observation. In E. Damiani and B. Fitzgerald and W. Scacchi and G. Scotto, editor, *IFIP International Federation for Information Processing: Open Source Systems*, pages 57 – 62, 2006.
9. B. Düring. *Extreme Programming and Agile Processes in Software Engineering*, chapter Sprint Driven Development: Agile Methodologies in a Distributed Open Source Project. Springer, 2006.
10. R. English and C. M. Schweik. Identifying Success and Tragedy of FLOSS Commons: A Preliminary Classification of Sourceforge.net Projects. In *International Workshop on Emerging Trends in FLOSS Research and Development*, 2007.
11. Norman E. Fenton. *Software Metrics: A Rigorous Approach.* Chapman & Hall, Ltd., London, UK, UK, 1991.
12. K. Schwaber and M. Beedle. *Agile Software Development with SCRUM*. Prentice Hall, 2002.
13. S. Koch. Agile Principles and Open Source Software Development: A Theoretical and Empirical Discussion. In *Extreme Programming and Agile Processes in Software Engineering: Proceedings the 5th International Conference XP 2004*, number 3092 in Lecture Notes in Computer Science (LNCS), pages 85–93. Springer Verlag, 2004.
14. M. Fowler and J. Highsmith. The Agile Manifesto. In Software Development, Issue on Agile Methodologies, `http://www.sdmagazine.com`, last accessed on March 8th,2006, August 2001.
15. M. Kircher and P. Jain and A. Corsaro and D. L. Levine. *Extreme Programming Perspectives*, chapter Distributed Extreme Programming. Pearson Education, 2002.
16. A. Mockus, R. .T. Fielding, and J. .D. Herbsleb. Two Case Studies of Open Source Software Development: Apache and Mozilla. *ACM Transactions on Software Engineering and Methodology (TOSEM)*, 11(3):309–346, 2002.
17. G. Robles and J. M. Gonzlez-Barahona. Contributor Turnover in Libre Software Projects. In Ernesto Damiani, Brian Fitzgerald, Walt Scacchi, Marco Scotto, and Giancarlo Succi, editors, *OSS*, volume 203 of *IFIP*, pages 273–286. Springer, 2006.
18. R. van Solingen. *The Goal/Question/Metric Method: A Practical Guide For Quality Improvement Of Software Development*. McGraw-Hill, 1999.
19. J. Warsta and P. Abrahamsson. Is Open Source Software Development Essentially an Agile Method? In *3rd Workshop on Open Source Software Engineering*, 2003.

Facilitating Social Network Studies of FLOSS using the OSSNetwork Environment

Marco A. Balieiro, Samuel F. de Sousa Júnior, and Cleidson R. B. de Souza
Faculdade de Computação – Universidade Federal do Pará
66075-110 – Belém – PA – Brazil,
{ma.balieiro, sfelixjr}@gmail.com, cdesouza@ufpa.br

Abstract. Open source projects are typical examples of successful distributed software development projects. Understanding how coordination in these projects takes place can provide important lessons to Software Engineering researchers and practitioners. This understanding has been achieved using different research methods, including, surveys, case studies and social network analysis. However, to conduct these studies each researcher needs to build his own infra-structure from the scratch, a time consuming and error-prone task. This paper aims to alleviate this problem by describing an environment, the OSSNetwork, which allows the automatic data collection of open source repositories. Data collected by the OSSNetwork is aimed to support the construction, visualization, and analysis of social networks. This environment is extensible, therefore facilitating empirical studies of open source projects.

1 Introduction

The Free/Libre Open Source Software (FLOSS) movement has become an economically viable and financially satisfactory alternative to proprietary software due to its reduced cost, good performance in critical operations and data manipulation, and improved security [1]. Supporters of FLOSS argue that the availability of the source code influences positively its quality, since any developer can review the code and improve it [2]. Today, the Internet infrastructure has great part of its critical elements based on FLOSS [3].

Due to these factors, researchers and practitioners of several areas (software engineering, economy, sociology, etc) are interested in understanding FLOSS projects from different viewpoints, including developers' motivation [4], the software process adopted by these communities [5], quality assurance [6], just to name a few. To address these different goals, several research methods have been used, from ethnography [7], to case studies [8], social network analysis [9], and even traditional statistical methods [10]. In particular, the use of the Social Network Analysis (SNA) allows the study of relationships among developers in these communities. For instance, Lopez-Fernandez, *et al.* [11] used social networks to understand the social relationships based on data available in CVS repositories, whereas Crowston and Howison [12] studied the networks of people who got

Please use the following format when citing this chapter:

Balieiro, M.A., Júnior, S.F. and Souza, C.R.B., 2008, in IFIP International Federation for Information Processing, Volume 275; *Open Source Development, Communities and Quality*; Barbara Russo, Ernesto Damiani, Scott Hissam, Björn Lundell, Giancarlo Succi; (Boston: Springer), pp. 343–350.

involved in bug fixing activities, and de Souza, *et al.* [13] analyzed developers' social network extracted from source-code dependency relationships.

All these approaches helped to understand important aspects of FLOSS projects. However, a limitation of these approaches is that they were conducted independently: each researcher had to build his own tools to extract, manipulate and analyze the data. To minimize this effort, Howison, *et al.* [14] developed the FLOSSmole, a tool for collect, store and distribute FLOSS data and analysis. While FLOSSMole alleviates part of this problem, researchers still face difficulties to collect data from FLOSS repositories to perform social network analysis such as: collection and storage the data which are in servers that researchers do not have direct access, differences between data models from different repositories, handling large amounts of information, treatment of specific information that can generate ambiguities (such as the problem of aliases [15]), implementation of algorithms on the data collected or even on the social networks generated, and visualization and manipulation of these networks.

The work described in this paper extends the FLOSSmole tool with an environment, called OSSNetwork, which allows the study of FLOSS communities using social network analysis. This environment is extensible so that new algorithms, visualization, and functionalities can be added. Social networks are generated with information extracted from mailing lists, forums, issue-tracking tools and chat logs. All this information is stored in a local database for future analysis. We argue that the problems faced by SNA researchers described in the previous paragraph are minimized by using the OSSNetwork environment.

The rest of this paper is organized as follows. In the next Section we will briefly present our motivation to this work. Next, a very short review of social network definition will be presented. The following section describes the OSSNetwork environment, and is followed by a case study and a discussion of the obtained results. Finally, we present our conclusions and future work.

2 Motivation

Howison, *et al.* [14] describes a research process to be used when studying FLOSS projects. This process is presented in Figure 1. According to this process, one of the most difficult tasks is the selection of projects to analyze. According to Howinson, two mechanisms can be used: *census*, where all existing projects of a particular phenomenon to be examined must be used, which is very difficult because no one knows how many projects exists; and *sampling*, where a small number of projects that represents a particular phenomenon is selected randomly. This is not an easy task, because researchers actually end up limiting their studies to a single repository. More importantly, sampling open source projects is methodologically difficult because everything FLOSS research has shown so far points to massively skewed distributions across almost all points of research interest [16][17] and even randomly selecting the projects, still, in general, does not produce a representative sample [14].

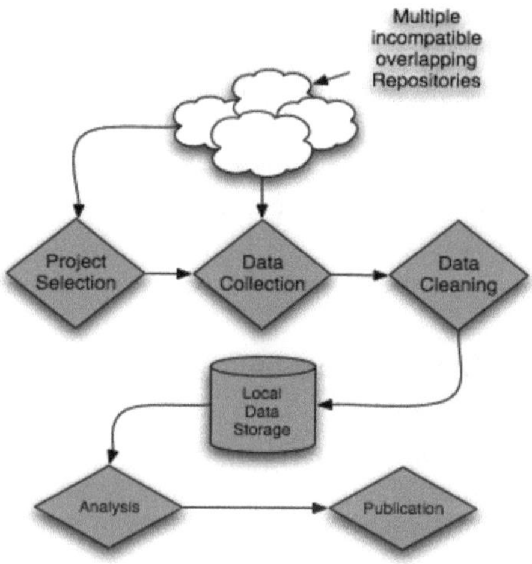

Figure 1 – Research process in FLOSS projects

Project selection becomes even more complicated because public repositories contain a large number of inactive, relocated or disabled projects. Our approach to handle this problem, detailed later, is to expand the number of supported repositories. After selecting the projects, two processes can be used for data collection: getting the databases *dumps* of the repositories or conduct a *parsing* of the repositories' web pages. Although gaining access to the databases is clearly preferable, not all repositories make their dumps available. Therefore, parsing is the data collection method that is made available by OSSNetwork, because it only requires the availability of Internet access.

3 A brief Social Network overview

A social network is broadly defined as a set of relationships [18]. A social network has a set of objects (nodes, in mathematical terms) and a description of the relationships between these objects. For example, it can be said that nodes are the people of a house and the relation that establish connection between these people is "people who use the same room".

A social network can be characterized according to structural and topological properties [19]. These properties are derived from the graph theory. The structural properties are: node degree, weighted degree of a node, distance centrality of the node, proximity degree, betweenness centrality, and others. Topological properties include: density of the network, distribution degree, network diameter, and finally, cluster degree, that it is a set of connected nodes through some way, them is considered as representative of communities.

Social networks can be classified according to two types: *1-mode networks*, which represent the relationship between social entities of the same type, for example, who is friend of who, who depends on whom; and *2-mode networks*, which represents relationships between different social entities, for example, the people who had been to a meeting, the developers that had corrected a given bug. It is important to underline here that from a 2-mode network, it is possible to easily generate a 1-mode network [20].

4 The OSSNetwork Environment

The OSSNetwork environment allows one to: (*i*) retrieve information from FLOSS repositories, (*ii*) store this information in a database, (*iii*) generate different social networks from this information, and, finally, (*iv*) analyze these networks using tools to manipulate, edit, and execute algorithms. This can be seen in the Figure 2.

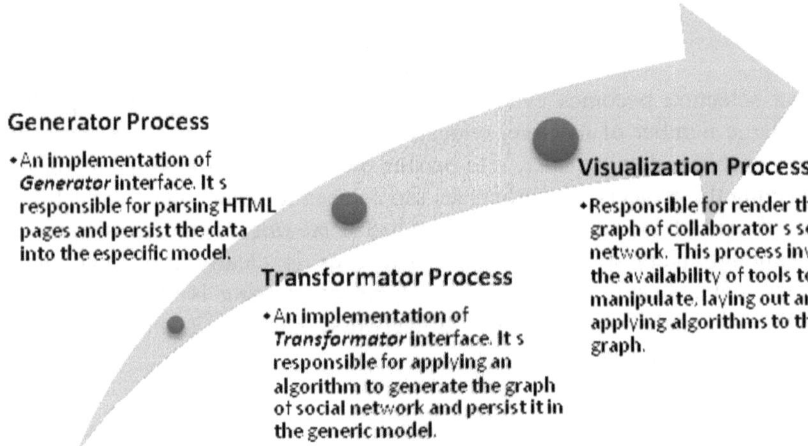

Figure 2 – The OSSNetwork approach

The OSSNetwork is implemented in Java and uses matrices to generate the social networks from the data extracted from projects repositories. Data is extracted through parsing HTML information about forums, mailing lists, bug tracking and chat.

4.1 An Example: the Apache Jackrabbit Project

Figure 3 below illustrates the social network generated with the OSSNetwork environment from the messages exchanged in the mailing list of Apache Jackrabbit project. In this figure, it is possible to observe some features already implemented, such as: handling of vertices and edges, use of geometric shapes and sizes according to some metrics, annotations, highlight of neighbor vertices, etc.

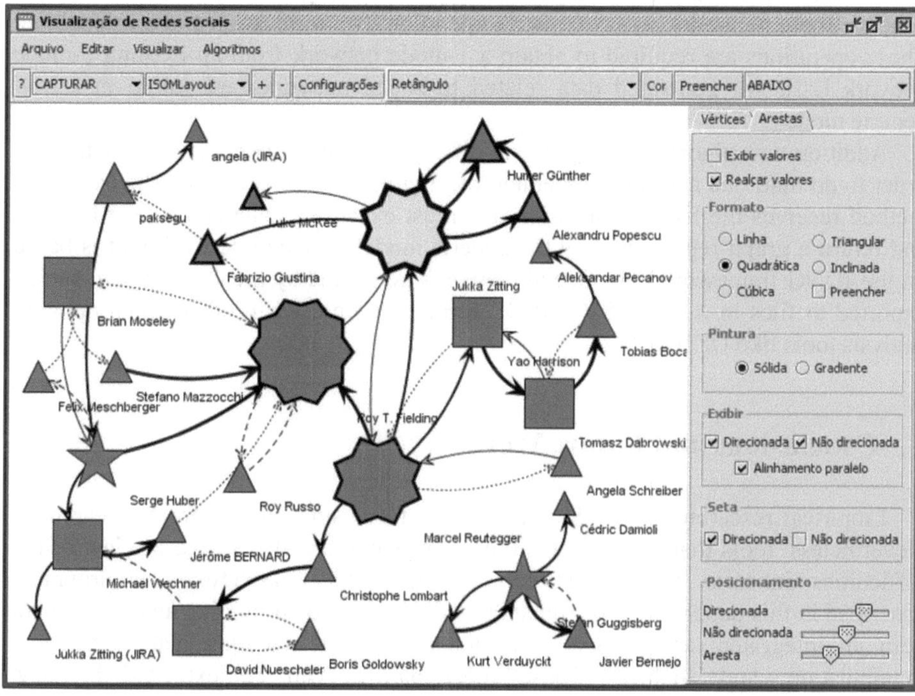

Figure 3 – The Apache Jackrabbit project in the OSSNetwork environment

4.2 Extracting Information from FLOSS Repositories

The OSSNetwork aims to minimize the effort of researchers interested in the social network analysis of FLOSS communities, which requires the extraction of information from these communities. Currently, the OSSNetwork has support for several repositories including: SourceForge, RubyForge Apache, and Microsoft Codeplex.

As mentioned earlier, the environment uses the FLOSSmole framework [14] to parse HTML web pages from the supported repositories. In addition, we implemented new parsing abilities to extract information to be used for social network analysis, for instance, information from the mailing lists which includes who sent a message, who replied to that message, etc. All these steps can be extended providing a new implementation of the *Generator* interface.

4.3 Social Network Generation

Social networks are generated from information extracted from mailing lists, forums and the discussion messages associated with bugs. The mechanism used to generate these networks uses two matrix operations: multiplication and transposition. These operations are required to obtain a 1-mode network from an existing 2-mode network [20]. All generated data related to social networks are stored in a new generic model.

Addition new algorithms to generate different social networks is an easy task. In order to do that, one needs to implement the *Transformator* interface. The *transform* method receives the list of discussion and must execute a calculation over the data and return a graph represented by the generic model of social network that is based on the JUNG framework [21]. Social networks generated by the environment can be exported to files in XML, CSV and DL formats to be used in other social network analysis tools like UCINet [22].

5 Conclusions and Future Work

Empirical research on FLOSS has aroused increasing interest from researchers. Nevertheless, tools that assist in this type of research are still scarce in view of the difficulties inherent in the research process. The OSSNetwork environment described in this paper helps to reduce these difficulties by providing an environment with an integrated set of tools and functionalities to facilitate data extraction, manipulation, and analysis. These functionalities can be extended by new implementations of some interfaces and adding new algorithms to the set of tools currently supported.

We expect that our environment will facilitate the adoption of new approaches using social network analysis. In particular, we are interested in multi-dimensional analysis of social networks extracted from FLOSS communities, that is, analysis where it is possible to take into account, at the same time, different social networks created from different data, such as a public forum, chat rooms, bug tracking systems, mailing lists, etc. We argue that a multidimensional analysis will allows us to study the relationship among different social networks. For instance, the different roles that a same developer has on different aspects (code, bug fixing, user support, etc) of a FLOSS project.

Acknowledgments

This research was supported by the Brazilian Government under grant CNPq 479206/2006-6, by the Universidade Federal do Pará, and by a Microsoft grant.

References

[1]. **Hoepman, J. and Jacobs, B.** *Increased Security Through Open Source.* Communications of the ACM, pp. 79-83, 2007.

[2]. **Raymond, E. S.** *The Cathedral and the Bazaar.* s.l. : First Monday, 1998.

[3]. **Madey, G., Freeh, V. and Tynan, R.** Modeling the F/OSS Community: A Quantitative Investigation. *Free/Open Source Software Development.* s.l. : Idea Publishing, 2004.

[4]. **Rullani, F.** *Dragging Developers Towards The Core. How The Free/Libre/Open Source Software Community Enhances Developer's Contribution.* Pisa, Italy, 2006.

[5]. **Jensen, C. and Scacchi, W.** *A Reference Model for Discovering Open Source Software Processes.* Limerick, IR. Third IFIP International Conference on Open Source Systems, 2007.

[6]. **Halloran, T. and Scherlis, W.** *High Quality and Open Source Software Practices.* Orlando, FL : s.n., Workshop on Open Source Software Engineering, 2002.

[7]. **Ducheneaut, N.** *The Reproduction of Open Source Software Programming Communities.* Berkeley, CA : UC Berkeley, School of Information Management and Systems, 2002.

[8]. **Jensen, C. and Scacchi, W.** Role Migration and Advancement Processes in OSSD Projects: A Comparative Case Study. *International Conference Software Engineering.* 2007.

[9]. **Gao, Y. and Madey, G.** *Network Analysis of the SourceForge.net Community.* Limerick, Ireland : s.n., International Conference on Open Source Systems, 2007.

[10]. **Mockus, A., Fielding, R. and Herbsleb, J.** *A Case Study of Open Source Software Development: The Apache Server.* Limerick, IR, International Conference on Software Engineering, 2000.

[11]. **Lopez-Fernandez, L., Robles, G. and Gonzalez-Barahona, J.** *Applying Social Network Analysis to the Information in CVS Repositories.* Juan Carlos, Spain : Universidad Rey Juan Carlos, 2004.

[12]. **Crowston, K. and Howison, J.** *The Social Structure of Open Source Software Development Teams.* Seattle, WA : s.n., International Conference on Information Systems, 2003.

[13]. **De Souza, C., Froehlich, J. and Dourish, P.** *Seeking the Source: Software Source Code as a Social and Technical Artifact.* Sanibel Island, FL : s.n., ACM Conference on Group Work, 2005.

[14]. **Howison, J., Conklin, M. and Crowston, K.** FLOSSmole: A Collaborative Repository for FLOSS Research Data and Analyses. *Journal of Information Technology & Web Engineering.* 2006.

[15]. **Gertz, M.** *Mining Email Social Networks in Postgres.* Shanghai, China : s.n., International Workshop on Mining Software Repositories, 2006.

[16]. **Conklin, M.** *Do the Rich Get Richer? The Impact of Power Laws on Open Source Development Projects.* Portland, Oregon : s.n., Open Source Conference (OSCON), 2004.

[17]. **Xu, J., et al.** *A Topological Analysis Of The Open Source Software Development Community.* Big Island, Hawaii : IEEE Computer Society, HICSS, 2005.

[18]. **Kadushin, C.** *Introduction to Social Network.* 2004.

[19]. **Hanneman, R. and Riddle, M.** *Introduction to Social Network Methods.* Riverside, CA : University of California, 2005.

[20]. **Wasserman, S. and Faust, K.** *Social Network Analysis: Methods and Applications.* Cambridge, UK and New York : Cambridge University Press, 1997.

[21]. **Fisher, D., et al.** Analysis and Visualization of Network Data Using JUNG. *Java Universal Nerwork/Graph Framework.* [Online] http://jung.sourceforge.net/doc/JUNG_journal.pdf.

[22]. **Borgatti, S., Everett, M. and Freeman, L.** UCINET 6 Social Network Analysis Software. *Analytic Technologies -- Social Network Analysis & Cultural Domain Analysis.* 2006.

Reflection on Knowledge Sharing in F/OSS Projects[1]

Sulayman K. Sowe and Ioannis Stamelos
Department of Informatics, Aristotle University, Greece
sksowe,stamelos{@csd.auth.gr}

Abstract. Knowledge sharing between software project participants simplifies a range of decision-making processes and helps improve the way software is being developed, distributed, and supported. However, research in this area has traditionally been very difficult because the source of knowledge, the code, has been a guarded secret and software developers and users inhabit different worlds. F/OSS projects have changed the way we perceive and understand knowledge sharing in distributed software development. This short paper presents our current understanding, and what needs to be done in terms of empirical research in knowledge sharing in F/OSS projects.

Keywords: Open Source Software Development, Open Source Software Projects, Knowledge Sharing, Knowledge Resources, Collaborative Software Development

1 Introduction

Free and Open Source Software (F/OSS) has changed the way we initiate software projects, develop, distribute, and maintain software. In a bazaar styled project roles are not clearly defined and software users are treated as co-developers. The cohabitation of both developers and users facilitates communication between all individuals involved in the software development process, thus, making it easy to study the knowledge sharing activities. Many F/OSS projects succeed because people volunteer their time and effort to share their knowledge and develop the software. Interaction between participants in the form of "talking to each other" is important for cooperation, resolution of conflicts, and the establishment of trust between project participants [1]. If F/OSS is all about coding and few project members are willing to interact and share their knowledge, questions one may ask are;

[1] This research is partly funded by the FLOSScom project (http://flosscom.net/). Grant No. 229405-CP-1-2006-1-PT-MINERVA-MPP

Please use the following format when citing this chapter:

Sowe, S.K. and Stamelos, I., 2008, in IFIP International Federation for Information Processing, Volume 275; *Open Source Development, Communities and Quality*; Barbara Russo, Ernesto Damiani, Scott Hissam, Björn Lundell, Giancarlo Succi; (Boston: Springer), pp. 351–358.

- effective communication and knowledge creation are used as measures of project success [2,3]. But is there knowledge sharing, who are the people involved, how much knowledge sharing are developers and users doing?
- how can participants at the very edge of the project's community feel that they are part of the project when they are not opportune to interact and share their knowledge with the rest?

The first step in answering these questions is to understand the nature and dynamics of knowledge sharing in F/OSS projects. The rest of the paper attempts to develop such understanding. First we argue for a paradigm shift from traditional knowledge sharing practices. Then we address knowledge sharing in F/OSS projects and use some empirical studies to reflect on our current understand and map future research directions.

2 Paradigm Shift in Knowledge Sharing in F/OSS

The importance of knowledge sharing is not unique to F/OSS projects alone. Software projects face a problem of how to leverage and transform the tacit knowledge of community members into explicit usable knowledge. Practically, a successful project needs to manage its knowledge resources (people and technologies) in order to generate an efficient and sustainable software development environment. Knowledge management (KM) practices often consider how organizational structures and processes promote collaborative learning [6] and sharing of knowledge [4]. The goal of knowledge management is to lower barriers imposed by organizational structures, format restrictions, and conceptual limitations, so that the acquisition, transfer, and sharing of knowledge can be facilitated. Thus, KM helps us understand tools, roles, and activities we need to develop in order to help individuals benefit from F/OSS. However, F/OSS projects are different entities when compared to organizational structures in which many KM studies are conduct. To address KM issues in F/OSS projects, one needs a *paradigm shift* from organizational attention and knowledge making as a manufacturing process to online interactive systems where knowledge making is characterized by the virtual presence of geographically distributed groups of volunteers. The virtual world makes hording and selling knowledge difficult, if not impossible, because someone else might be positioned to provide the same knowledge for free.

The F/OSS development process not only highlights a different way of sharing knowledge but also acquiring it is a complicated process and building on existing knowledge takes time. Software development is a human-based and knowledge-intensive activity [8,9]. In addition to sound technological infrastructure and effective tools to coordinate the collaborative software development process [1], the success of any project immensely depends on the knowledge and experience brought to it by software developers and users. F/OSS projects provide the means for members to transform their tacit knowledge into explicit [4] (**Fig. 1**). As illustrated, project participants socialize by sharing their knowledge. Individuals make their tacit knowledge explicit to the project through externalization. Combination refers to the formation and organization of abstract knowledge from explicit knowledge. Through internalization individuals will absorb explicit knowledge, combining it with their own knowledge and experiences to produce "new" tacit knowledge. Through active participation, individuals' tacit knowledge is transformed into explicit knowledge.

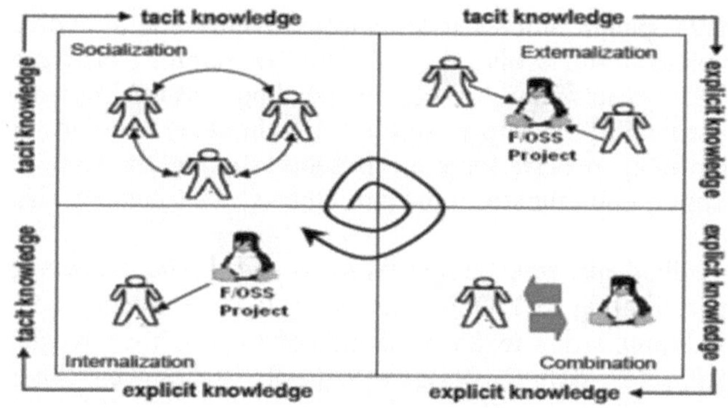

Fig. 1. Making tacit knowledge explicit in F/OSS projects

F/OSS projects are complex environments with many different actors. There is no indication that all project participants will interact and share their knowledge. When members do, *knowledge link* (***K***) is said to exist between them. The link is a reciprocal relationship of the form *A talks to B* and *B talks to A* and can be expressed as; $K_{AB} = \{^1_0$; *where* $\boldsymbol{K}_{AB}=1$ *if there is knowledge sharing between actor A and actor B, and 0 if otherwise.*

Sharing knowledge is a synergistic process. If a project participant shares his ideas or a way of configuring particular software with another person, then just the act of putting his idea into words will help him shape and improve his idea. If he enters into a dialogue with the community, then he may benefit from their knowledge, from their unique way of doing things and improve his ideas further. The benefit derived from knowledge sharing is that participants learn from each other, and the result of their interaction is archived in the project's repositories from which subsequent participants can learn.

3 Knowledge Sharing in F/OSS Projects

The F/OSS development process facilitates the creation, diffusion, and transformation of software knowledge at a rate unprecedented in the history of software development. The prospects for expert software developers and novice users to understand the software development process are now great. However, our understanding of knowledge sharing in F/OSS projects is challenged by the fact that individuals or even infrastructures are often located at large distances from each other, making traditional face-to-face knowledge sharing practices hard. Furthermore, the "babbling bazaar of differing agendas and approaches" [10] in some projects has people with varying knowledge and skills. Nevertheless, the F/OSS development process has made the empirical study of knowledge sharing possible because we can now use the freely available data in mailing lists, forums, code versioning systems, bug trackers, etc. to understand who is involved, who is talking to whom, and what is talked about. The F/OSS development process is knowledge intensive and involves real people who create, maintain and evolve the software. Therefore, focusing on knowledge sharing in F/OSS projects may shed light on pending research issues such as motivation and involvement of developers and users, community and software project formation and dynamics, reasons for projects success or failure, software engineering practicing, learning opportunities, how participants' contributions change overtime, etc.

For many individuals, developing new skills and sharing knowledge are primary motives for participating in F/OSS. Through reflective practice and collaborative learning, participants strive to improve the software in their respective projects, develop and refine their skills, challenge and question themselves. There are many opportunities for serendipity or information encountering in F/OSS projects. For example, a potential knowledge seeker [6] confronts an unfamiliar concept (or bug) in the use of an application (e.g. OpenOffice) and decides to seek help form a project's mailing list. There are two ways to look at this scenario. First, if the concept has been encountered before, it will be captured and stored in the project's knowledge base (mailing lists, forums, code repository, etc). He/she then consults and learns from the knowledge base. Second, if the concept has not been encountered, ie. the knowledge seeker's problem has not been addressed in the project before. He/she then identifies the appropriate list, posts his/her question, and exchanges ideas with list participants. Alternatively, the knowledge seeker may know a project participant with expertise in the area he is interested in and exchange direct emails with that person, with or without copies being posted to the list.

4 An Empirical Investigation of Knowledge Sharing

Methodologies suitable for investigating knowledge sharing in terms of email exchanges have been proposed [5, 6]. The intangible nature of tacit knowledge makes it very difficult, if not impossible, to measure. However, when tacit knowledge is transformed into explicit knowledge through socialization or interaction and shared by members of a project, an attempt can be made to measure how much knowledge is being shared. One approach to quantify the level of knowledge sharing in F/OSS is by analyzing substantial email exchanges between list participants. This can be achieved by

(i) Counting the total number of posts externalized to the list. That is, email messages potential knowledge seekers posted. We represented this value by the *nposts* variable.

(ii) Counting the total number of replies made by potential knowledge providers to questions posted to the lists. This value is represented by the *nreplies* variable.

The data (**Table 1**) collection, extraction, and cleaning methodology for investigating knowledge sharing in mailing lists is obtained from the Developer and User mailing lists of the Debian project [6]. The dataset was collected over 5 years (January 2000-December 2005) and consists of 3735 participants in the Developer list, who posted 29685 email messages, which generated 128933 replies. The 5970 participants in the User list posted 193276 email messages, which generated 165380 replies.

Table 1. Descriptive statistics of Developer and User mailing lists data.

		Developer	User
nposts	Mean	7.95	32.37
	Median	3.00	7.00
	Std. Dev.	21.302	121.753
	Maximum	523	4106
nreplies	Mean	34.52	27.70
	Median	6.00	5.00
	Std. Dev.	105.567	122.040
	Maximum	1517	4168

Comparatively, the mean (posts/person) and median of *nposts* are smaller for the Developer list, while the same measures have larger values for *nreplies*. Thus, the posting and replying activities of the participants are different in the two lists - further clarified in **Fig. 2**.

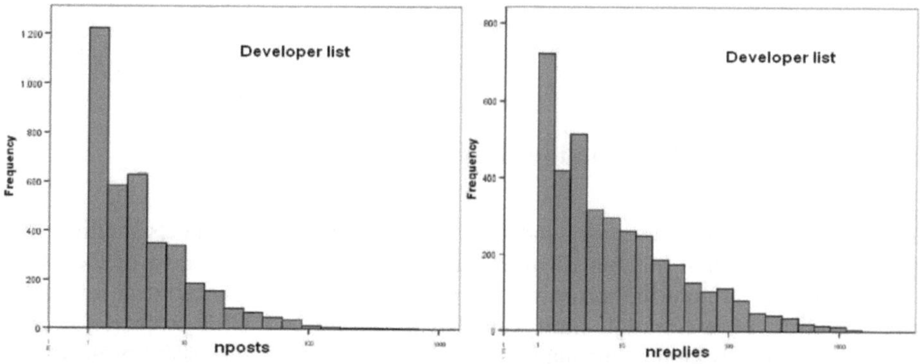

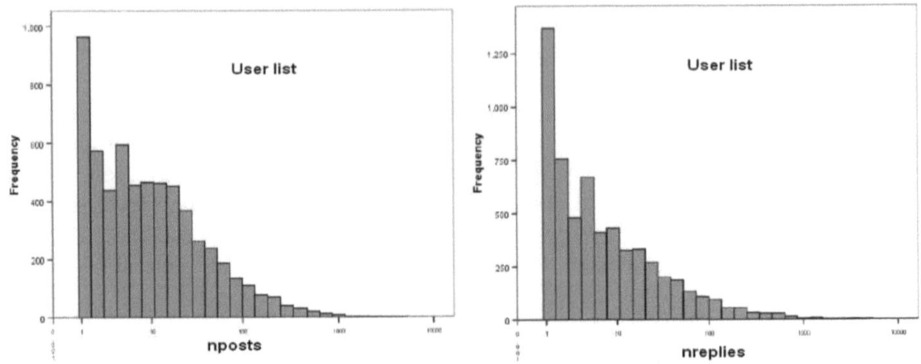

Fig. 2. Frequency distributions of posts and replies

Participants in the User list contributed small posts and small replies. For the developer list, participants' activities were characterized by a small number of posts and a large number of replies. For the relationship between posting and replying activities, Table 2 shows only the Kendall's *taub* and Spearman's *rho*, since we ranked the participants according to their positing or replying [7].

Table 2. Nonparametric correlations between posts and replies in the two lists (Sig. =0.000 for all correlations).

			Developer List		User List	
Test	Variable		nposts	nreplies	nposts	nreplies
Kandella*'s taub*	nposts	Corr. Coef.	1,000	,475*	1,000	,550*
	nreplies	Corr. Coef.	,475*	1,000	,550*	1,000
Spearmans *rho*	nposts	Corr. Coef.	1,000	,608*	1,000	,699*
	nreplies	Corr. Coef.	,608*	1,000	,699*	1,000

5 Reflection on Knowledge sharing in F/OSS Projects

Research findings on developer and user activities in F/OSS projects mailing lists point out that a small number of individuals are responsible for most of the work. This inequality in contribution raises serious concerns that concentration of development effort on a few will limit knowledge sharing in F/OSS projects [5]. The paradox is that this kind of inequality was observed in many successful projects (eg. Apache, KDE, Friefox).

- **Are Developer and User mailing lists participants doing more posting than replying to questions posited to their lists?** In the Developer list participants contributed more replies (mean=34.52) than posts (7.95). The reverse was the case in the User list. Participants posted more than they replied to questions asked in the list. One explanation for this could be that postings in the developer mailing list may contain sufficient information to allow other participants to analyze the request and are given the highest priority since the reporter is likely to be a member of the development community. Such posts receive the attention of almost all participants.

- **Is there a trend in the way individuals post and/or reply to questions in Developer and User lists?** About 32.8% (1224) of the participants in the Developer list posted one email message and 19.3% (721) contributed one reply. For the User list 16.1% (963) of the participants posted one email message and 22.9% (1369) contributed one reply. The maximum email messages posted (*nposts*) by one individual was 523 in the Developer list and 4106 in the User list. For the replies, the maximum values were 1517 in the Developer list and 4168 in the User list. In none of the lists did the individual who posted the most emails also made the most replies. For example, in the Developer list, the participant who posted the most emails (523) contributed 574 replies. While the participant with most replies (1517) contributed 79 posts.
- **How are the posts and replies of Developer and User mailing lists participants correlated?** In both lists we found that posting and replying activities of the lists participants are correlated. When posting increases, replying likewise increases. However, the correlation was stronger for the User list (ρ=0.699). This means that, for the User list more questions generate more answers.

6 Summary and Conclusion

A reflection on the empirical investigation revealed inequality in posting and replying activities in the lists studied. Investigating who was asking versus who was replying, we found out that, in the Developer list, the participant who posted the most emails (523) contributed 574 replies. While the participant with most replies (1517) contributed 79 posts. A similar trend was observed in Apache, Mozilla, KDE. What is different in this case is that we looked at knowledge sharing from the perspectives of both developers and users. Yet still, few individuals are involved in the knowledge sharing process. However, while this may be true for one kind of repository (mailing lists), the situation might be different in another kind, bug trackers or version control systems, for instance. An interesting research direction may be to simultaneously study developer and user lists in big and small, successful and unsuccessful projects to see if the pattern of knowledge sharing reported can be generalized. In addition the role of knowledge sharing for open source project success or failure should be better understood and assessed.

References

1. S. K. Sowe, I. Stamelos, I. Samoladas (Eds.) (2007). *Emerging Free and Open Source Software Practices.* Idea Global, May 2007, pp: vi-vii, 98-119.
2. Karl Fogel. (2005). *Producing Open Source Software: How to Run a Successful Free Software Project,* Creative Commons.

3. Crowston, K., Hala, A., and Howison, J. (2003). Defining Open Source Software Project Success. *Proc. of International Conference on Information Systems*, ICIS.
4. Nonaka, I. & Takeuchi, H. (1995). *The Knowledge Creating Company*. Oxford University Press.
5. Kuk, G. (2006). Strategic Interaction and Knowledge Sharing in the KDE Developer Mailing List, *MANAGEMENT SCIENCE*, Vol. 52, 1031-1042.
6. Sulayman K. Sowe, I. Stamelos, L. (2008). Angelis. Understanding Knowledge Sharing Activities in Free/Open Source Software Projects: An Empirical Study, *Journal of Systems and Software*, Vol. 81(4), 431-446.
7. Sheskin, D. J. (2000). *Handbook of parametric and nonparametric statistical procedures*, Chapman & Hall, 491-508.
8. S. K. Sowe. An Empirical Study of Knowledge Sharing in Free and Open Source Software Projects. *PhD thesis*, Department of Informatics, Aristotle University, Greece, 2007.
9. A. Aurum, R. Jeffery, C. Wohlin, and M. Handzic, editors. *Managing Software Engineering Knowledge*. Springer, 2003.
10. S. E. Raymond. The Cathedral and the Bazaar. Musings on Linux and Open Source by an Accidental Revolutionary. OReilly, Sebastopol.

Usability in Company Open Source Software Context - Initial Findings from an Empirical Case Study

Netta Iivari[1], Henrik Hedberg[1], and Tanja Kirves[1]
1 University of Oulu, Department of Information Processing Science
P.O.Box 3000, FIN-90014 University of Oulu, Finland
{netta.iivari, henrik.hedberg}@oulu.fi, tanjakir@mail.student.oulu.fi

Abstract. In the company open source software (OSS) development context, usability is becoming an important issue due to a growing user population, who is only interested in usable applications, not in their development. Companies try to gain a competitive advantage of OSS by utilizing available components, but the openness is difficult to achieve in the business world with licenses, patents and intellectual property rights. This paper analyses usability and user-interface (UI) development in the company OSS context through an interpretive case study in a software development unit of a large, global corporation. Our initial findings suggest that there is a need for human computer interaction specialists in the OSS context. It is revealed that with the software based on OSS, more time can be spent on usability and UI design. In the company's viewpoint, there are still many issues involved in deciding what parts of the product will be open source. Especially UI code may remain closed due to competitive advantage and patents.

1 Introduction

This paper analyzes how usability and user-interface (UI) development are dealt with in company open source software (OSS) development context. Company OSS development context refers to 'OSS 2.0', i.e. to the new, commercially viable OSS development, in which software (SW) development companies try to gain a competitive advantage of OSS [7]. SW development companies release the source code of their products and produce OS compliant licenses, and OSS companies develop their business around raising money through licensing [7], [15]. In OSS development, the source code needs to be 'available for anyone who wants to use or modify it', but in the company OSS context, there actually is a 'continuum of openness' [16: 151]. This paper focuses on commercial SW development utilizing OSS as part of the product, and potentially also releasing the source code for the OSS community to develop it further.

Nowadays OSS is targeted at a mass of users, not only for developers developing it for their own use. The user population of OSS is becoming larger, including a growing number of non-technical users, who are not interested in OSS development, but only in the resulting solution [4], [8], [14], [15], [18]. Therefore, usability and

---

Please use the following format when citing this chapter:

Iivari, N., Hedberg, H. and Kirves, T., 2008, in IFIP International Federation for Information Processing, Volume 275; *Open Source Development, Communities and Quality*; Barbara Russo, Ernesto Damiani, Scott Hissam, Björn Lundell, Giancarlo Succi; (Boston: Springer), pp. 359–365.

high quality UI are becoming an important issues also in OSS context [1], [14], [19], [20]. This paper reports initial findings of an interpretive case study designed to analyze usability and UI development in company OSS development context.

2 Usability and User Interface Development

The importance of usability and UI development are emphasized especially within the field of human computer interaction (HCI). Usability refers to 'the extent to which a product can be used by specified users to achieve specified goals with effectiveness, efficiency and satisfaction in a specified context of use' [10]. Another widely cited definition defines usability to consist of learnability, efficiency, memorability, errors and satisfaction; it should be easy to learn to use the system, its use should be efficient, it should be easy to remember how to use it, the users should not make errors or they should easily recover from them, and the use should be satisfactory. [16]

Different user-centered design (UCD) and usability engineering (UE) methodologies offer guidance for usability and UI development. Many differences can be identified in them, but they all emphasize the importance of gaining a detailed understanding the user, his/her tasks or work practices and the context of use as a basis. Afterwards, one should carefully redesign the tasks or work practices based on that understanding. User involvement in the design process is argued for. User feedback should be gathered early, and the design solution should be iterated based on the user feedback. [2], [12], [16], [17]

To carry out these activities, the HCI literature suggests hiring a group of specialists, variably labeled e.g. as usability, UCD or UE specialists. They are to carry out or facilitate the analysis of the users, their current tasks and work practices and the context of use, the user task redesign and the iterative usability evaluations. They are also to ensure active user involvement. [2], [9], [12], [16], [17]

Many challenges involved with usability and UI development in the OSS development context have already been revealed. In OSS development, the developers typically produce the SW for themselves. From the viewpoint of non technical users, usability of the OSS tends to be poor, and the development process anything but 'user centered' [1], [3], [4], [14], [19], [20]. Therefore, usability is becoming a relevant topic of research in the OSS context, even though, to date, it has not been examined much [1], [4], [14], [19].

Typically, the OSS developers do not have knowledge about the non technical users, their tasks and the context of use. In addition, no UCD/UE methodology is typically employed. Extensive gathering of user feedback and bug reporting have been highlighted as solutions in OSS context. However, it has also been reported that non-technical users may be intimidated or incapable to report bugs. [1], [3], [4], [13], [14], [19], [20] HCI specialists do not typically participate in the OSS development, and the OSS developers do not normally have the HCI knowledge and skills needed. The users can not replace HCI specialists either, because they are not trained for developing and ensuring usability, even thought they encounter the usability problems while using the system. [1], [4], [8], [13], [14], [19] [20].

Related to company OSS development, it has already been argued that large corporations that participate in OSS development can provide professional usability resources and HCI guidelines for OSS development [1]. However, there clearly is a lack of research on company OSS development, and particularly on usability and UI development in this context. This paper provides insights into this phenomenon.

3 Empirical Case

In this research effort an interpretive case study method is utilized. Case studies are suggested, if little is known about the phenomenon or current perspectives have little empirical evidence or conflict with each other [6]. There is a lack of research on usability in company OSS development context. Interpretive case study method was selected, since through it one can focus on the meanings attached to the phenomenon studied from 'the native's point of view', produce thick descriptions, and gain thorough understandings. The focus is on understanding and making sense, not explaining in the predictive sense. Theories are used as sensitizing devices. [5], [11]

The case involved in this study is a SW development unit of a large, global corporation that has been involved with OSS development already for few years. It has a strong background in usability and UI development. However, now the company is facing challenges in combining the worlds of commercial SW development, OSS development and usability and UI work. The case was selected, since it offers a rich setting to analyze the emerging 'company OSS' phenomenon.

Different kinds of empirical data have been gathered from the unit. This paper relies on data gathered by interviewing the personnel and by keeping field notes after joint meetings organized in the unit. Five persons were interviewed, including a project manager (denoted as [a]), two developers ([b] and [c]) and two HCI specialists ([e] and [f]). In addition, field notes from three meetings organized with the management of the unit were included in the analysis. This paper reports our initial findings related to how usability and UI development were dealt with in this particular case of company OSS.

The OSS was seen as a basis to build up something new in the company: *"From the viewpoint of the firm it is fast, time is not spent in implementation, but one gets everything ready made. One can concentrate on doing new things, not things that already exist."* [c] Typically, available solutions were evaluated and an OSS alternative chosen that was further developed to fit the company's needs. That way the development time was reduced significantly: *"Without this communication and library, [an application] would not have been possible. There was 6 months time, and it took 3 months, because there was support from the community. Otherwise it would have taken over a year."* [c] In addition to the support for the implementation of the low-level library, the OSS community gave feedback that was important for usability of the product: *"From the viewpoint of UI design there are more users, a social network of knowledge."* [e] Interestingly, OSS was seen as a source of knowledge: *"[OSS is] learning and collaboration, a place to learn from developers."* [e] *"One always learns something. One sees other people's code, their expertise."* [c]

Usability and UI design were emphasized in the case: *"[Usability is] while developing UI, one of the most essential things"* [a]. *"[The firm] makes devices for people. Why would anybody buy a product that was difficult to use, compared to competitors? So market is the reason [for usability]"* [b]. *"[Usability is] extremely important: competitive edge, brand, image."* [d] There have been recent changes to emphasize the importance of usability and UI design: *"Usability and user experience are the key, the company started to invest in them. (...) In the beginning, one person took care of everything. Now there are seven persons in the team, so the role is bigger. (...) Power has been given to designers, from developers. They have the power to figure out things, they are very concerned with usability."* [e]

The difficulties involved with usability and UI design in OSS development are acknowledged: *"Developers produced the UI. It was difficult to help them, if you were not there in the beginning. (...) [I] tried to change the code in an OSS project, but it can be bureaucratic in there, they get a lot of change requests, they do not necessarily want to implement them."* [e] *"Usability is hard in OSS projects. There are no usability professionals. (...) The main problem is the usability staff in OSS projects. Except when big companies support the OSS projects. Because the firms are interested in the end user and give help."* [c]

Therefore, the support gained from companies to OSS projects is highlighted. Especially the importance of professional HCI specialists' participation in OSS projects is emphasized: *"[Interaction designers] there should be more of them willing to help, UI designers to plan and design, and developers to sponsor them."* [e] *"Get a UI designer and a usability specialist"* [b]. There should be *"open usability work: this kind of persons could be there commenting and helping (...) Usability specialists could gain reputation, if it results in good products"* [d] *"One should attract also designers, artists, end users. All areas. Developers learn from these [other areas]"* [c].

The usage of the OSS gave more time for the usability and UI design: *"One could much earlier experiment with the finished software. One did not just use own simulation. This was a positive effect."* [d] *"Late changes are possible, because own process resembles OSS projects. OSS enables late changes. There is more design and evaluation. So, it helps usability that there is code ready-made. Time is not spent on that, you start building on top of that."* [e] *"[OSS development is] faster and closer to user"* [c]. In addition, OSS gave access to users: *"In OSS development one is always in contact with the user. One knows what they want and one knows if the wishes change."* [c] *"OSS community, users -> a rich place to gather user feedback. User-centered design in the community: wishes are ranked, [the users] are used as partners in the beginning and also during the design"* [d]. Being in contact with user is *"easier and cheaper"* [e].

UI design was a key to success: *"Designers (...) always thought of users, they thought of interaction, so that the users don't get tired. We have succeeded well. (...) Best thing of the whole project is the UI."* [c] Actually, the UI part was seen as a competitive edge for the company, and that was one factor affecting not to publish the source code: *"Usability and UI are so valuable that they are not released."* [e] The chosen model was to share improvements made into the OSS library and to keep the UI part of the application closed: *"[An application is] closed source, on top of open source."* [e] That fulfilled the license terms of the original source code also: *"Openness did not spread to the UI code."* [a] Despite the situation, the company continued to interact with the community: *"There is cooperation with the community, gathering of feedback, even if it was closed source. Bugs are fixed in the OSS."* [e]

The decision had negative impacts in the community: *"If the UI is closed that causes anger in some people"* [e], but the company had also other reasons for their decision: *"People asked for the source code, but it was not given. It was an IPR risk."* [a] Everything had to be analyzed keeping the company secrets in mind: *"In the beginning, sourceforge's cvs server was used, and everything was not thought of. It was not thought of that what is secret, proprietary (...) It was moved to the firms own server, the in-house made component was put in there also. Legal check must be made. This component is not in sourceforge."* [b] The most secure way to act is to develop the product in-house first, and then release it, if it is possible: *"Bug fixes are given back, but if there are risks, a legal check is done. Everything is not let out."* [e]

In general, the licenses were seen as an issue in company OSS development: *"License defines the openness. It is difficult"* [a] *"Sometimes there are difficulties due to the licenses. One has to know what kind of code is used, what libraries are used. Usually firms know these issues, they have to know. (...) There needs to be lawyers. One has to hire them."* [c] Sometimes the procedures needed, before the open source release can be made, were seen as too expensive and complicated, when compared to the benefits: *"[The company] has a lot of patents related to [issues related to the OSS and the application], there was no desire to carry out investigations."* [a] That encourages to keep the SW as closed as possible. The result is a hybrid SW with open and closed source parts.

4 Concluding Discussion

In the company OSS context, OSS solutions are used as part of the products, but there are many issues involved in deciding what parts of the product will be open source. Especially UI code tends to remain closed. Several reasons were identified related to that. Difficulties with licenses and patents were brought up. However, interestingly, UI was also seen as a competitive advantage, which was for that reason kept closed source. It was maintained that by putting effort into the UI design, the company can beat the competitors. However, for that reason, it is unlikely that the UI parts become open source in the company OSS context.

Regarding the field of HCI, the results of this study seem promising. If usability and UI design are becoming such central concerns in SW development as indicated by this study, the field of HCI will increase its importance. There probably will be a need for HCI methods and tools, which are particularly tailored to fit the OSS development context, as well as for HCI specialists contributing to the development. Regarding the relationship between HCI and OSS, two interesting observations are emphasized. First, the results confirm that there is a need of HCI specialists in the OSS context. The interviewees emphasized the need of professional HCI specialists (some specializing in usability, others in UI design), taking care of understanding the users, their tasks and the context use, and evaluating the solution with the users.

Another interesting issue was the benefits of OSS that can be gained by the HCI specialists in the company OSS context. It was emphasized that realistic user feedback can be gathered earlier than normally if part of the product is OSS. Therefore, OSS may reduce the development time, which enables early usability evaluation with the actual SW. In addition, it was emphasized that due to the reduced development time, more time can be spent on usability and UI design, which is also a clear benefit from the HCI viewpoint. Moreover, the possibility to concentrate on innovating new things, when utilizing OSS components as a basis, was brought up as a benefit of OSS in the company context.

This paper provided initial findings from our empirical examination. More thorough analyses will be carried out in the future. Paths for future work include also deepening the understanding of usability in the company OSS context, and devising procedures that enable HCI specialists to participate in OSS communities. In general, the effects of usability work on OSS products, communities and companies, and the means to achieve those effects are interesting, momentous research topics.

References

[1] Benson C., Müller-Prove, M., & Mzourek, J.(2004): Professional usability in open source projects: GNOME, OpenOffice.org, NetBeans. Extended Abstracts of the Conference on Human Factors in Computer Systems. New York, ACM Press. Pp. 1083-1084.

[2] Beyer, H. & Holtzblatt, K. (1998). Contextual Design: Defining Customer-Centered Systems. San Francisco: Morgan Kaufmann Publishers.

[3] Bødker, M., Nielsen, L. & Orngreen, R. (2007): Enabling User-Centered Design Processes in Open Source Communities. In N. Aykin (ed.): Proc. Human Computer Interaction International, Part I: Usability and Internationalization. LNCS 4559. Pp. 10-18.

[4] Cetin, G., Verzulli, D. & Frings, S. (2007): An Analysis of Involvement of HCI Experts in Distributed Software Development: Practical Issues. In D. Schuler (ed.): Proc. Human Computer Interaction International: Online Communities and Social Computing. LNCS 4564. Pp. 32-40.

[5] Denzin, N. & Lincoln, Y. (2000): Introduction: The Discipline and Practice of Qualitative Research. In N. Denzin, Y. Lincoln (Eds.): Handbook of Qualitative Research. 2nd edition. Thousand Oaks: Sage Publications.

[6] Eisenhardt, K. (1989): Building Theories from Case Study Research. Academy of Management Review 14(4): 532-550.

[7] Fitzgerald, B. (2006): The Transformation of Open Source Software. MIS Quarterly 30(3), 587-598.

[8] Frishberg, N., Dirks, A., Benson, C., Nickel, S. & Smith, S. (2002): Getting to know you: open source development meets usability. Extended Abstracts of the Conference on Human Factors in Computer Systems. New York: ACM Press. Pp. 932-933.

[9] Iivari, N. (2006): Discourses on 'culture' and 'usability work' in software product development. Acta Universitatis Ouluensis, Series A, Scientiae rerum naturalium nro 457.

[10] ISO 9241-11 (1998): Ergonomic requirements for office work with visual display terminals (VDT)s - Part 11 Guidance on usability. International standard.

[11] Klein, H. & Myers, M. (1999): A Set of Principles for Conducting and Evaluating Interpretive Field Studies in Information Systems. MIS Quarterly 23(1), 67-94.

[12] Mayhew, D. (1999): The Usability Engineering Lifecycle: A practitioner's handbook for user interface design, San Francisco: Morgan Kaufmann Publishers.

[13] Nichols, D., Thomson, K. & Yeates, S. (2001): Usability and Open Source Software Development. Proc. Symposium on Computer Human Interaction, Palmerston North, New Zealand, July 6. Pp. 49-54.

[14] Nichols, D. & Twidale, M. (2006): Usability Processes in Open Source Projects. Software Process Improvement and Practice 11, 149-162.

[15] Niederman, F., Davis, A. Greiner, M., Wynn, D. & York, P. (2006): A Research Agenda for Studying Open Source I: A Multilevel Framework. Communication of the Association for Information Systems 18, 129-149.

[16] Nielsen, J. (1993): Usability Engineering, Boston: Academic Press.

[17] Rosson, M. & Carroll, J. (2002): Usability Engineering: Scenario-based Development of Human-Computer Interaction, San Francisco: Morgan-Kaufman.

[18] Viorres, N., Xenofon, P., Stavrakis, M., Vlanhogiannis, E., Koutsabasis, P. & Darzentas J. (2007): Major HCI Challenges for Open Source Software Adoption and Development. In D. Schuler (Ed.): Proc. Human Computer Interaction International: Online Communities and Social Computing. LNCS 4564. Pp. 455-464.

[19] Zhao, L. & Deek, F. (2005): Improving Open Source Software Usability. Proc. 11th Americas Conference on Information Systems, Omaha, USA, August 11-14. Pp. 923-928.

[20] Zhao, L. & Deek, F. (2006): Exploratory inspection: a learning model for improving open source software usability. Extended Abstracts of the Conference on Human Factors in Computer Systems. New York: ACM Press. Pp. 1589-1594.

Willingness to Cooperate Within the Open Source Software Domain

Pascal Ravesteyn and Gilbert Silvius[1]
University of Applied Sciences Utrecht, The Netherlands
pascal.ravesteijn@hu.nl, gilbert.silvius@hu.nl

Abstract. Open Source Software (OSS) is an increasingly hot topic in the business domain. One of the key benefits mentioned is the unlimited access to the source code, which enables large communities to continuously improve a software application and prevents vendor lock-in. How attractive these benefits may be, the market for OSS however remains limited. In the Netherlands research consisting of 7 interviews and a survey among 206 Open Source Software Service providers (with a 34% response rate) was done to determine whether service providers wanted to cooperate in an Association that will set quality levels and guarantees to its members and their customers.

Keywords: Open Source Software, Communities, Quality

1 Introduction

In the last decade open source software (OSS) initiatives have been steadily growing, resulting in more and more companies that provide services, support and certification around open source applications. From a user perspective some of the most important reasons for the use of OSS are: cost effectiveness, improved flexibility, expiration of maintenance, availability of support through both software vendors and service providers, independence from software vendors, increased technical requirements, increased interoperability, security aspects and improved reliability (Ghosh et al. (2005). Probably the most important of these characteristics is the independence from software vendors which means there is no or limited vendor lock-in (Pavlicek, 2000; Raymond, 2001; Wichmann, 2002b; Goldman et al., 2005). Vendor lock-in implies that it is very hard to switch to other software and/or service providers due to high switching costs or the usage of legacy and non-standard software that is available only through the network of one vendor. Because open source software is normally based on open standards and open interfaces (Varian et al., 2003) it becomes easier to migrate to different software products. Normally communities evolve around open source software that then adapt and further develop the applica-

---

Please use the following format when citing this chapter:

Ravesteyn, P. and Silvius, G., 2008, in IFIP International Federation for Information Processing, Volume 275; *Open Source Development, Communities and Quality*; Barbara Russo, Ernesto Damiani, Scott Hissam, Björn Lundell, Giancarlo Succi; (Boston: Springer), pp. 367–373.

tions and services. Although users of open source software are not dependent on a single vendor or service provider to deliver updates with new functionality, in practice an emotional binding with one supplier still seems to exist.
Contrary to the reasons that are found for end-user adaptation, the trigger for many software providers to open sourcing their offerings are mostly internally motivated (Wijnen-Meijer and Batenburg, 2007) and based on market position, the capability for product innovation (or lack thereof) and the degree of customer independence. This seems to be supported by Cusumano (2004), who in his book The Business of Software describes several product characteristics that may be relevant for the decision of open sourcing such as (1) the fundamental difference between intended audiences: enterprises and home users (2) the difference between niche and mass audiences, and software with a horizontal or a vertical functional scope (3) the market position of a software product. This can be leading, complementary or following. Also some software providers start with using open source software internally because of its perceived cost effectiveness (Grand et al., 2004) before considering open sourcing their own offerings. Finally governments are an important trigger to vendors to provide open source software due to the value they give open source software for its conformance to open standards that help to ensure accessibility of governmental information (Varian et al., 2003).
To bridge the gap between the motivation given by end-users versus software vendors and service providers on why to adopt the open source paradigm, Rijke (2005) suggests that open source software vendors and service providers should cooperate in a more structured way to provide improved flexibility, maintenance, availability of support, increased technical requirements, increased interoperability, improved reliability and higher quality to end-users. This suggestion is based on the fact that a large majority of the open source vendors and service providers in the Netherlands are small office and home office companies. Contrary to the numerous studies on the reasons for OSS (Ghosh et al., 2005; Wichmann, 2002a), very little research is available on the cooperation between organizations and what the triggers for such cooperation are in the OSS domain. This research tries to find an answer to the question if organizations within the open source domain are willing to cooperate with their peers to improve the different aspects as mentioned with a focus on the improvement of maintenance, support, reliability and quality.
The following section elaborates further on the market for open source products and services in the Netherlands. Then the research methodology that was used is described and the results from both the interviews and the survey are given. In the final section the limitations of this research will be mentioned and some suggestions for future research are given.

2 Open Source Software Market in the Netherlands

At the start of this research only part of the Dutch market of open source software and service providers was known. This meant that the first activity was to exten-

sively map the entire market. This was done by looking at different available resources such as the governmental Program for Open Standards and Open Source Software, lists of delegates to different Open Source conferences that were available and the Internet. Besides creating an overview of the organizations that are active in the Dutch market we also determined the involvement of these organizations within the open source communities that already existed. The rate of involvement is measured on a 3 point scale (low, average and high score) and was determined based on the number of times delegates of these organizations attended conferences (e.g. Holland Open), were active speakers or were involved in professional publications.
The final result of this part of the research was an extensive overview of 222 organizations that are active in the open source domain in the Netherlands during 2006. Of each organization information was collected. Figure 1 shows a small part of the matrix that was the end result.

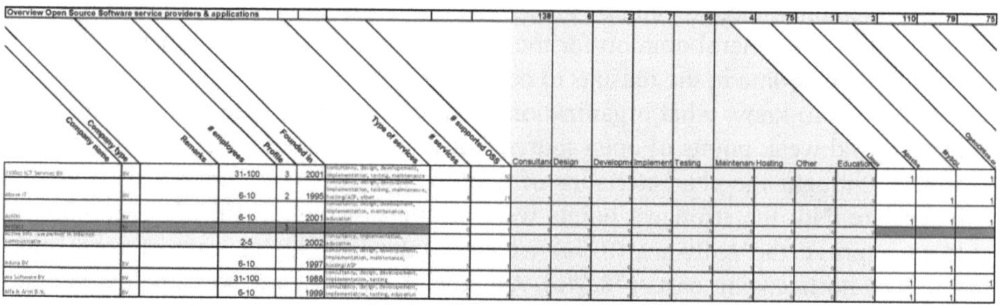

Fig. 1. Example of data collected on open source organizations in the Netherlands

3 Research Methodology

Based on the open source market overview it was determined to first do several interviews followed by a survey because by gathering data from different angles a clearer picture of the real world can be modeled and validated (Baarda et al., 2001). The interviews were semi-structured and resulted in a validated list of research questions to be used in the survey.
The interviews had two goals, first they provided us with a validation on the market overview and secondly the outcomes were used to validate and broaden the list of research topics that made up the survey. Seven organizations were sent a first draft of the survey questions to fill out and return, after which an interview was held. The interview was based on the answers the respondents provided before hand and lasted approximately for 2 hours.
The final survey consisted out of 23 questions, some of which had several sub questions. Both open and closed questions were used. Where respondents had to answer on a scale, we used a 4 point scale ranging from completely agree to completely disagree. The survey was sent to 206 mail addresses out of the 222 organizations available in the market overview (some e-mail addresses were missing), and after a re-

minder (two weeks after the first participation request a total of 70 surveys were returned. The final response rate was around 34%.

4. Results

The question that this research tries to answer is: *Are organizations within the open source domain willing to cooperate with each other to improve (amongst others) the maintenance, support, reliability and quality of open source services and software?* Based on the interviews this is not the case. According to our findings organizations are only willing to cooperate with others when this results in direct financial gains for their own company. Only two respondents also mentioned higher quality of their service or software offering important enough to consider cooperation. But the interviews were mainly used to validate the survey questions and the outcomes can not be considered as the general opinion for the entire sector. The survey however shows a more diverse outcome in the reasons to cooperate.

It is important to know what organizations within the open source domain find to be the strong and weak points of open source software. Therefore we asked what the respondents thought the characteristics of open source software versus closed source software are. Not the strongest points were: no vendor lock-in (89%), everybody is able to improve the software (82%) which results in a higher rate of innovation (84%), and no licensing costs (78.5%). Asked if there were any weak points in open source software there was a large difference in answers with 44% of the respondents stating that the quality of open source is lower than closed source software (with a small majority of 56% who think otherwise), while 40% of the respondents also thought open source software to be less safe than closed software (a small majority thinks it is better). This means that the open source community in general finds their software to be superior to closed software solutions. Of course the outcomes in this research are clearly biased because of the population that was surveyed.

To determine whether close cooperation between organizations within the open source domain is needed, several questions and propositions were part of the survey. When asked 'Which of the following 6 reasons would get your organization to cooperate with other companies in the open source domain?' more than 75% of the respondents of the survey said their primary reason to cooperate is to exchange information between peers to further improve their software (see figure 2).

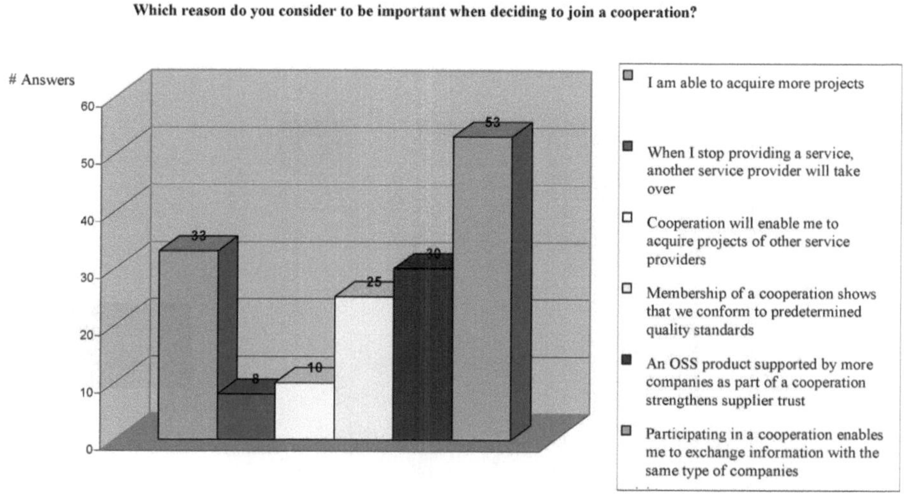

Fig. 2. Reasons to cooperate within the open source domain

The second most important reason (with 47%) is the financial gains organizations hoped to receive in the form of new projects. The continuity of services like maintenance and support that could be guaranteed by cooperating only received support of 11.4% of the respondents and although acquiring new projects is the second most important reason to cooperate not many respondents actually expect to get many new projects (only 14.5% do). The two reasons that have to do with the perceived reliability and quality of an organization by customers get respectively 43% and 35.7% of the respondents approval.

Based on this it seems that the sharing of information (with a focus on software development) is the only trigger to start cooperating. This is to be expected because it is the primary foundation of the open source community. However there is not very much support for cooperation between open source vendors and services suppliers regarding improvement of aspects like maintenance, support and quality. In these topics it seems that organizations in the open source domain stick to their existing business models in which they try to do everything themselves.

The perceived advantages of cooperation (see figure 3) show a similar result.

Although financial gains by acquiring projects via cooperation is perceived as an advantage (69%), a majority of the respondents (74%) do not expect their customers to be willing to pay a premium for such a cooperation. Still when they were asked if cooperation within the open source domain could improve the continuity and reliability of support to their customers, 78.5% agreed. When a cooperation takes the form of an organization that is responsible for maintaining quality levels (of member organizations) a large majority of the respondents (91%) stated that the trust in open source and thereby the use would be much higher. In conclusion, we can state that while organizations do think that cooperating is perceived by their customers as an added value, they are not really willing to start such cooperation because they don't perceive any benefits for themselves and can't direct any costs towards their customers.

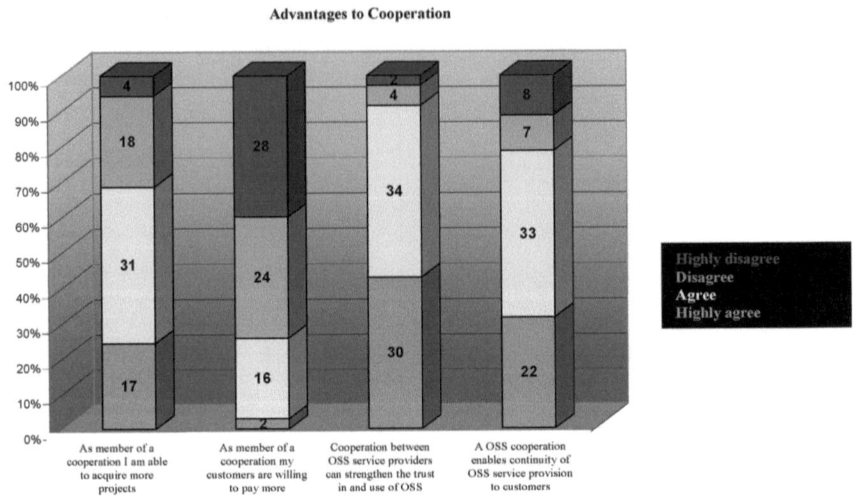

Fig. 3. Perceived advantages of cooperation within the open source domain

5. Discussion and Future Research

This paper describes the outcomes of a multi method research approach to determine if organizations within the open source domain are willing to cooperate. While such cooperation is perceived beneficial there is no positive attitude towards starting such cooperation. However the outcome of this research knows some limitations. First the respondents all are situated in the Netherlands, which makes that the findings may not be applicable to other countries or regions. Second the research is conducted solely at software developers and services providers in the open source software domain; the customers of these organizations have not participated. This means that the perceived value for customers of cooperation as seen by the respondents might be non existent. Finally this research is focused on the willingness to cooperate to improve maintenance, support, reliability and quality of the services and software, other forms of cooperation are out of scope. Therefore the results can't be interpreted as a complete unwillingness of organizations to cooperate with each other. The amount of research done on cooperation between organizations in the open source domain is limited. The findings from this research need further validation at open source users. A next step is research on cultural differences and finally in-depth studies are needed to determine whether perceived advantages and disadvantages are different depending on the type of organization or its maturity.

6. References

Baarda, DB, de Goede, MPM & Teunissen, J 2001, Basisboek: Kwalitatief Onderzoek (in Dutch), Groningen, Stenfert Kroese.

Cusumano, M.A. (2004). The Business of Software. Free Press. ISBN 0-7432-1580-X.

Ghosh, R. & Glott, R. (2005). FLOSSPOLS Deliverable D3: Results and policy paper from survey of government authorities [http://flosspols.org/deliverables/]

Goldman, R. & Gabriel R. (2005). Innovation happens elsewhere. Open source as business strategy

Grand, S., Krogh, G. v., Leonard, D. & Swap, W. (2004). Resource Allocation Beyond Firm Boundaries: A multilevel model for Open Source Innovation. Long Range Planning 37 (2004) 591–610.

Pavlicek, R.C. (2000). Embracing Insanity. Open Source Software Development. Sams. ISBN 0-672-31989-6.

Raymond, E.S. (2001). The Cathedral and the Bazaar: Musings on Linux and Open Source By an Accidental Revolutionary. O'Reilly & Associates. ISBN 0-596-00108-8.

Rijke, H. de (2005). Continuïteit in Open Source diensten. In: Holland Open.

Varian, H.R. & Shapiro, C. (2003). Linux Adoption in the Public Sector: An Economic Analysis. [http://www.sims.berkeley.edu/~hal/Papers/2004/Linuxadoptioninthepublicsector.pdf]

Wichmann T. (2002a) Use of Open Source Software in Firms and Public Institutions. Evidence from Germany, Sweden and UK. Berlecom Research GmbH [http://www.berlecon.de/studien/downloads/200207FLOSS_Use.pdf]

Wichmann T. (2002b) Firms' Open Source activities: motivations and policy implications. Berlecom Research GmbH [http://www.berlecon.de/studien/downloads/200207FLOSS_Activities.pdf]

Wijnen-Meijer, M. and R. Batenburg (2007). To open source or not to open source: that's the strategic question. Results from a Survey among eight leading software providers. In Proceedings of ECIS 2007. St. Gallen, Zwitserland.

Open Source Project Categorization Based on Growth Rate Analysis and Portfolio Planning Methods

Stefan Koch and Volker Stix
Vienna University of Economics and Business Administration
Institute for Information Business
Augasse 2-6
1090 Vienna/Austria
{stefan.koch, volker.stix}@wu-wien.ac.at

Abstract. In this paper, we propose to arrive at an assessment and evaluation of open source projects based on an analysis of their growth rates in several aspects. These include code base, developer number, bug reports and downloads. Based on this analysis and assessment, a well-known portfolio planning method, the BCG matrix, is employed for arriving at a very broad classification of open source projects. While this approach naturally results in a loss of detailed information, a top-level categorization is in some domains necessary and of interest.

1 Introduction

The adoption and evaluation of open source projects has gained increasing interest, both from an academic and business perspective. This has led to the development of assessment schemes like OpenBRR (Open Business Readiness Rating), Open Source Maturity Model, QSOS by Atos Origin, OpenBQR [8] and similar achievements. Most of these approaches are based on detailed scoring of open source products, and aggregation using some form of weightings. While some consider that features of the underlying community form an important part of an evaluation, this is not generally acknowledged. In addition, while in some approaches the use of real data, both on community and the software product itself is planned, some rely on personal rating or data entry of many features.

The approach we will present here is intended to be coupled with a repository of repositories on open source project data [7]. In this context, an enormous amount of data is collected, but this might prove to create additional problems with users of such a service, who might not be able to put it to use. Too much information could effectively hamper their use of the system for rather simple evaluation and adoption tasks or decisions. Therefore, providing a top-level, aggregate classification scheme is necessary. In this paper, we will propose to base such an effort on well-known portfolio planning techniques, especially the BCG matrix. For constructing the axis of such a matrix, several possibilities exist, but in our case we will argue for applying the results of growth rate analysis.

Please use the following format when citing this chapter:

Koch, S. and Stix, V., 2008, in IFIP International Federation for Information Processing, Volume 275; *Open Source Development, Communities and Quality*; Barbara Russo, Ernesto Damiani, Scott Hissam, Björn Lundell, Giancarlo Succi; (Boston: Springer), pp. 375–380.

2 Growth Rate Analysis

For performing the proposed analysis of open source software projects, the information contained in software development repositories will be used. These repositories contain a plethora of information on the underlying software and the associated development processes [2]. Studying software systems and development processes using these sources of data is very cost-effective and does not influence the software process under consideration. In addition, longitudinal data is available, allowing for analyses considering the project history. Depending on the tools used in a project, possible repositories available for analysis include source code versioning systems, bug reporting systems, or mailing lists.

In open source software development projects, repositories in several forms are also in use, in fact form the most important communication and coordination channels. Therefore only a small amount of information can not be captured by repository analyses because it is transmitted inter-personally. As a side effect, the repositories in use must be available openly and publicly. Therefore open source software development repositories form an optimal data source for studying the associated type of software development. Currently, efforts are underway to consolidate information from diverse sources, in building RoRs (repositories of repositories) [7]. In this pa-per, we propose to build on this infrastructure using appropriate techniques.

For characterising the past development, and also gain an understanding of possible future developments, growth rates can be computed for several aspects like source code, contributors, bug reports, mailing list postings or downloads. All of these might give some insight, while of course the growth in size (of source code) is most often cited (software evolution). For computing and characterising the growth rates, the following methodology will be adopted. This is taken from a prior study of one of the project participants [4] on growth in size.

The first step is to analyse whether a linear or other growth pattern is present in the data. To this end, both a linear and a quadratic model are computed for each project, taking the size in lines-of-code S as a function of the time in days since the first commit t, which is used as project start date, and using one month as time window. Therefore model A is formulated simply as SA(t) = a * t + b and model B as SB(t) = a * t2 + t *b + c. The necessary parameters are to be estimated using regression techniques. As a next step, it is necessary to explore whether the growth rate is decreasing over time. This can be done by analysing the second derivative of the quadratic model *SB(t)'*, or directly the coefficient of the quadratic term a.

The sharp distinction between two groups of projects might prove too inflexible. A new group is therefore introduced representing linear growth in contrast to sub- and super-linear rates. This group is defined as those projects having either a better fit for the linear than the quadratic model, or a coefficient of the quadratic term between -0.1 and 0.1, thus being very near to zero. This allows for arriving, for each project and each aspect of interest, at a classification for the evolutionary behavior as being either sub-linear, linear, or super-linear.

3 Portfolio Planning and the BCG Matrix

Portfolio planning methods have been applied in strategic decision making for over 20 years [1,9] although they have little theoretical support. They are presented in the literature as diagnostic aids and as prescriptive guides for selecting strategic options [5]. The general idea is to classify positions of products along two dimensions to form a matrix: attractiveness of the market and ability of the product to compete within that market, and to derive insights into strategic actions in this way. Managers often neglect to use a rational economic approach, instead applying un-structured judgmental processes. They may base their decisions on power or emotional factors, which might lead to many of their decisions as being irrational. Thus, portfolio planning methods, such as the BCG matrix, may lead managers to make decisions that are less irrational.

Maybe the most well-known portfolio planning method is the Boston Consulting Group (BCG) method [3], the most widely used portfolio method in US firms [1]. It is based on measuring market attractiveness by market growth rate, and it assesses the firm's ability to compete by its relative market share. The BCG matrix assumes a causal relationship between market share and profitability. It is based on product life cycle theory that can be used to determine what priorities should be given to different products. To ensure long-term value creation, a company should construct a portfolio using products that contains both high-growth products in need of cash inputs and low-growth products that generate cash. Each of the two axes is normally divided into a high and a low portion, resulting in four different quadrants. Each quadrant is assigned both a catching name and a general strategy (see also Figure 1):

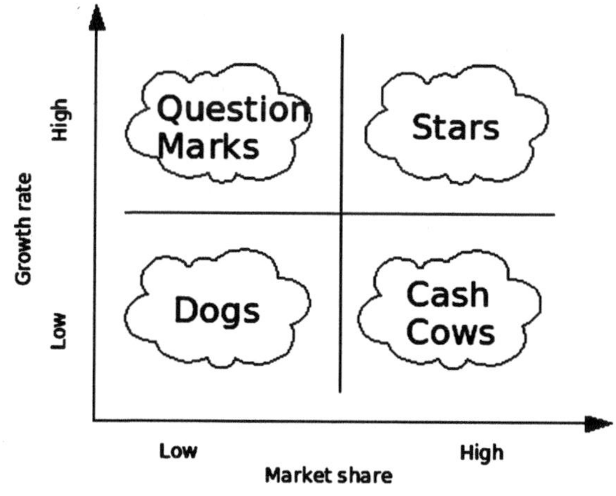

Fig. 1. BCG matrix

Stars are located in the high growth and high market share area. Normally, the cash flow is rather balanced or even, but a position in stars should be maintained. Cash Cows are placed in low growth area coupled with high market share. Profits and cash generation will generally be high, with relatively small investment due to low growth, translating into a very desirable type. Dogs are placed in low growth and low market share quadrant, which are normally associated with a de-invest strategy. Question Marks are enjoying high growth but low market share, resulting in demand for cash but low profits. This kind of product over time might turn into either star or dog, so careful considerations is advised to invest or liquidate.

A review of previously published evaluations of the BCG matrix can be found in [6]. Actual practical use of the BCG matrix is often found to be inhibited by difficulties in measurement of market growth rates and relative market shares. The results are highly sensitive on these measurements. As a result, different matrix methods are likely to yield different recommendations for the same situation.

4 Open Source Matrix and Classification

In this paper, we propose to adopt the BCG matrix approach for classifying open source projects. There are two main aspects to discuss and decide: The construction of the axes, and results of the classification. For constructing and measuring the axes, we propose to use the results of a growth rate analysis. The growth rate of an open source project is constructed using the growth rate in source code (which equals the software evolution viewpoint of software engineering research) and the growth rate of developers. For market share, we propose to use growth rates of bug reports and downloads. Bug reports normally are associated with usage of a product, especially by interested individuals, but might also signal a product with problems.

As each growth rate of the four types used here is classified in one of three steps, conversion into a single measure needed. We propose to use the mean of both rates, with source code respectively downloads taking priority in ties. Using this approach, an open source project matrix can be constructed, with the standard names having been replaced by possible release numbers (see Figure 2).

As can be seen, the classification results in four possible types of projects. This has to be translated into strategies. We need to differentiate between two possible uses, the first one being simple adoption, in which a company or individual wants to decide on which project within a given domain to adopt for a certain task. In the second case, a company wants to build a portfolio of projects. Possible reasons for this include a business model based on a range of software, cooperation with the open source world within a given area, or an application in marketing. Also a company that might pursue a development based on open source, but wants to keep open to several projects might pursue this idea. This leads to the following strategies as-signed to the different types of projects.

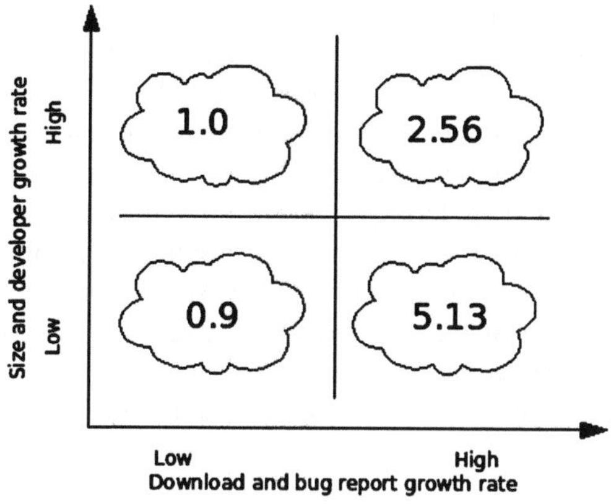

Fig. 2. Open source project matrix

1.0 (Question Marks) currently enjoy huge growth in size and participants, but have not achieved widespread adoption yet. Therefore they might become quite successful, but might fail. For a separate adoption decision, these projects pose considerable risk, while adding 1.0 projects to a portfolio might be interesting.

2.56 (Stars) enjoy both considerable growth and adoption. This makes them interesting candidates for any portfolio selection decision, and candidates for a singular adoption consideration.

5.13 (Cash Cows) have somewhat stabilized in their code and developer growth, but have achieved widespread adoption. This means that normally a mature solution has been found, with less emphasis on introducing new functionalities. This makes these projects prime candidates for consideration for a single adoption decision, and an interesting candidate for portfolio selection. On the other hand, there might be the need for maintenance at a later stage, maybe due to technological changes, but the community is not that active any more.

0.9 (Dogs) have neither huge growth nor adoption, meaning that they prove to be of interest to neither adoption or portfolio considerations. These projects could be termed as failed.

5 Conclusion and Future Research

In this paper we have argued for constructing a top-level open source project classification based on growth rate analyses of several project aspects, and using portfolio planning techniques, especially the BCG matrix. Given current efforts of constructing the databases necessary to support the kind of analyses that form the basis of this approach, pursuing this road seems worthwhile. Portfolio planning approaches have been in business use since several decades, and despite some shortcomings, have provided value and are in wide-spread use. Given that software adoption decisions on organisational levels are often decisions made on a management level, adopting these common approaches might prove beneficial for communication between technical evaluation level and decision authorities.

In future research, an empirical evaluation of the proposed approach would be very important. This would include performing the necessary analyses based on a database, and presenting the results of categorization to decision-makers. There are several possible ways of refinement of the approach that could be pursued: On the one hand, the construction of the axes could be discussed by adding or substituting aspects of projects or communities. On the other hand, there are other portfolio planning approaches besides the BCG matrix that could be explored.

Acknowledgments

This work is partially supported by the Free / libre / open source software metrics and benchmarking study (FLOSSMETRICS), funded by the European Commission under con-tract number FP6-033982 (www.flossmetrics.org).

References

1. Armstrong, J.S., & Brodie, R.J. (1994) Effects of portfolio planning meth-ods on decision making: experimental results. International Journal of Re-search in Marketing, 11(1):73-84.
2. Cook, J.E., Votta, L.G., & Wolf, A.L. (1998) Cost-effective analysis of in-place software processes. IEEE Transactions on Software Engineering, 24 (8):650-663.
3. Day, G. (1986) Analysis for strategic market decisions. St. Paul: West.
4. Koch, S. (2007) Software Evolution in Open Source Projects - A Large-Scale Investigation. Journal of Software Maintenance and Evolution, 19(6):361-382.
5. Kotler, P. (1984) Marketing Management. 5th ed. Englewood Cliffs, NJ: Prentice-Hall.
6. Morrison, A. & Wensley, R. (1991) Boxing up or boxed in? A short history of the Boston Consulting Group share/growth matrix. Journal of Marketing Management, 7:105-129.
7. Sowe, S.K., Angelis, L., Stamelos, I., & Manolopoulos, Y. (2007) Using Repository of Repositories (RoRs) to Study the Growth of F/OSS Projects: A Meta-Analysis Research Approach. In Open Source Development, Adoption and Innovation, pp. 147-160, Boston: Springer.
8. Taibi, D., Lavazza, L., & Morasca, S. (2007) OpenBQR: a framework for the assessment of OSS. In Open Source Development, Adoption and Innovation, pp. 173-186, Boston: Springer.
9. Wind, Y., & Mahajan, V. (1981) Designing product and business portfolios.

Applying Open Source Development Practices Inside a Company

Juho Lindman[1], Matti Rossi[1], and Pentti Marttiin[2]
[1] Helsinki School of Economics, Information Systems Science, PO Box 1210, 00101 Helsinki, Finland. {}@hse.fi, http://www.hse.fi
[2] Nokia Siemens Networks, PO Box 31, 02022 Nokia Siemens Networks, Finland. {}@nsn.com, http://www.nsn.com

Abstract. Open Source Software development is seen as a panacea by many companies. The promise of community-style development, innovation and cost savings drive the wider adoption of OSS in companies. However, it is still difficult to institutionalize the open and agile culture of sharing innovation especially into larger departmentalized organizations. The aim of this research paper is to investigate the characteristics of one successful OSS development implementation approach limited inside a company (Inner source). Based on our data, we argue that there are possibilities for employing OSS as a new kind of development process within a company and leveraging thus the innovation potential inside the company.

1 Introduction

It is currently virtually impossible to conduct any business without encountering software created using OSS development methods. Companies are becoming more interested in understanding how to use OSS development inside their organizations or in inter-company development activities [2] [5] [6]. Research indicates that it is possible to build solid business cases around OSS [4].

However, researchers and practitioners are still struggling with the challenge of deploying OSS development practises inside companies. This study aims to provide some initial answers by describing the adoption of inner source portal in a case company. Our viewpoint is that of a support service organization launching new tools for business unit use. The specific case is Nokia, a leading telecommunications company using adopted OSS development process called iSource. We aim to provide an account of the intra-company portal usage and what kind of projects seem to benefit. Findings indicate that 1) there is a growing interest towards iSource, 2) projects that use the portal are heterogeneous, and 3) projects seem to benefit from openness enabled by OSS tooling.

Please use the following format when citing this chapter:

Lindman, J., Rossi, M. and Marttiin, P., 2008, in IFIP International Federation for Information Processing, Volume 275; *Open Source Development, Communities and Quality*; Barbara Russo, Ernesto Damiani, Scott Hissam, Björn Lundell, Giancarlo Succi; (Boston: Springer), pp. 381–387.

2 Research methodology

Our goal is to provide an account of a successful implementation of OSS practices inside a company. This is necessary because it is widely believed that OSS development will gain more footing in different kinds of organizations [5]. Taking account our goal, we select to conduct an interpretative case study on Nokia iSource service organization [16]. Interpretative approach helped us to take into account the interplay of the service organization and its environment [14]. We also used other methods and sources of evidence to develop our understanding of the events and to ensure the validity of our findings [3].

We started out with managerial interviews and direct key user contacts. Our informants included people from the service organization and business units to build solid case description. The respondents were selected to represent the different levels of inner customers and service organizations. We conducted four interviews and reviewed usage data provided by the technology platform to corroborate the interview findings. Usage data consists of user information, number of projects created and their activity. One of the researchers was working for the company and thus has a very good view of the situation and context of the case from the inside. This might cause bias, but that is offset by the depth gained by being an insider.

As the results from the different data sources seem to be aligned, we assume that the findings support each other. We aimed to make analytical, not statistical generalizations. Statistics offered by the platform did not yet enable developing understanding of models and causal relationships between different data. Thus these two were used in conjunction with interviews and participant observation to validate the case findings.

3 Review of literature

Theories describing OSS phenomenon sometimes suffer from a promoted assumption that OSS communities and processes would be a priori similar [10] [12] [13]. In contrast, it has been shown that OSS communities, software companies and the relations between them are not homogeneous [1]. Thus it seems plausible to presume that also inner source communities are heterogeneous.

The companies that wish to launch communities are in different position than those that wish to benefit from existing OSS software [4]. Also the challenges related to the processes are different depending on whether company has outbound or inbound OSS approach [4]. Commercial context enables different roles for companies using OSS [7] and companies have a variety of choice regarding integrating their operations with the selected business model [9] [11].

Hierarchical organizations benefit from open development communities that promote flow of information and ideas between professionals [15]. In traditional proprietary software development software is developed and maintained centrally in a selected business unit or program. Development community is a way to respond to the misalignment of experience, skills and interests [8]. This is especially beneficial to large organizations prone to re-organization. Company's priorities might change due to market conditions, often leading to the reallocation of developers into different projects.

Inner Source aims to leverage the power of open source practices, methods and tools in company context [7] [5]. This means in practice: 1) software produced is open to everyone working for a company to use and develop. More accurately, all activities relating to the software development are open and visible to everyone, and 2) interest to develop software initiates a community to take care of the development.

4 Nokia iSource

We selected for analysis a successful OSS inspired implementation, Nokia iSource. Nokia is the world leader in mobile communications. It is a publicly held company with listings in five major exchanges. Today the iSource portal has two instances one for Nokia and another for Nokia Siemens Networks (NSN). NSN is a company created in a merger between Nokia Networks and a part of Siemens in 2007. Our data focuses mainly on events that happened before the merger.

iSource is a company wide portal created in 2001 for managing and working with software assets. Its introduction was originally encouraged by HP's good experiences [2]. Technically, at the time of the study, iSource was a fork of OSS version of Sourceforge portal dated back to 2001 and maintained separately from the mainline. The idea behind iSource was to provide a portal enabling visibility of software and the source code. The goals were to increase individual engineers' awareness of software developed inside the company, and to boost innovation by avoiding the problem of re-implementing the wheel. Currently, projects are counted in hundreds and users in thousands, but activity status varies depending on the project life-cycle and funding. iSource has a support service, that promote iSource service and champions its adoption among business.

5 Observations from cases

5.1 Increase in adoption

According to the user and project statistics iSource has enjoyed stable increase in use. This trend can be observed from Figure 1 below, which shows the number of new projects created per year (the exact numbers were omitted to protect company confidential information, but the trend is visible).

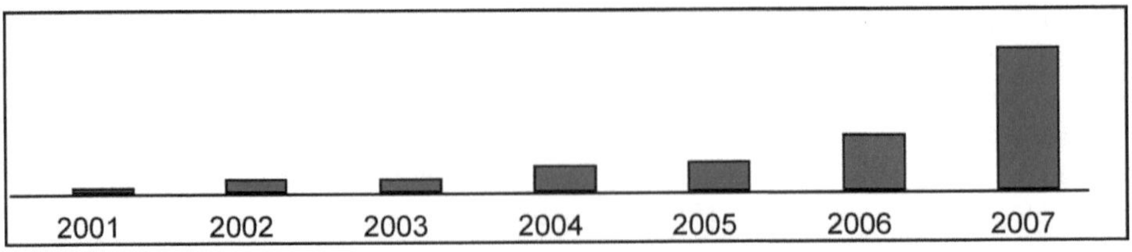

Fig. 1. New iSource projects with their creation year

5.2 Project heterogeneity and openness

iSource has been used for different kinds of projects. This variety can be observed for example when comparing the number of developers and the administrators or the ratio of the two. Figure 2 shows the numbers of developer per project and Figure 3 the number of administrators.

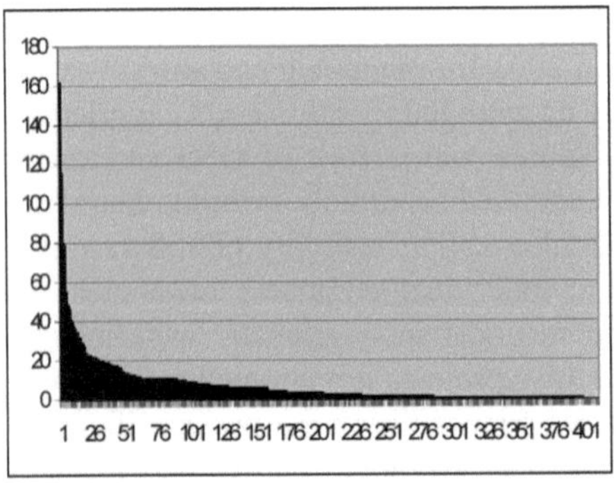

Fig. 2. The number of developers/project

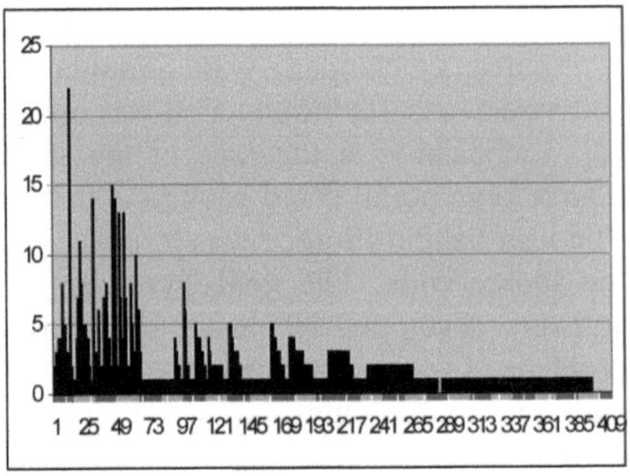

Fig. 3. The number of admins/project number

Most projects using iSource are having one or more of the following characteristics:

1. Projects have selected Subversion or CVS (Concurrent Version System) as their SCM tool (iSource service is the official one for hosting these SCM repositories).
2. Projects are distributed to multiple sites and continents (open source tools require less bandwidth)
3. Projects are using agile development methods (OSS tooling attracts agile projects) or take advance of continuous integration tools (e.g. CruiseControl or Bamboo)
4. Software is developed in inter-company collaboration (iSource is opened to collaborators)

5. Projects are advancing Inner Source (openness when sharing e.g. scripts and libraries; OSS development model in platform development)

The following table shows three top-10 lists of iSource projects. It was what kinds of projects have most developers, are benefitting of file downloading, and are using CVS. The project identification (or categorization) and is done by selecting a key word form the project's public summary.

Table 1. Breakdown of top-10 lists: # of developers, file downloads and CVS usage (commits).

Categorization (Most developers)	#	**Categorization (File Downloads)**	#	**Categorization (CVS commits)**	#
Platform	6	Framework	3	Platform	4
Simulator	2	Scripts and libraries	2	Framework	2
Reference Implementation	1	SDK	1	Emulator	1
Testing environment	1	Software suite	1	Simulator	1
		Platform	1	Language	1
		Emulator	1	Protocol architecture	1
		Language	1		

First, 10 projects with the biggest developer number were overviewed. It seemed that among the biggest projects there were several platform projects as indicated in Table 1. Not all the projects are ranked in downloads list. This probably means that no files are stored. The projects on this list are different from those that have the most developers. Smaller projects are able to generate interest and share for example emulators, scripts and libraries. Downloads also correlate with project age. Projects may use the portal with or without SCM. Based on our statistics less than 50% of projects have used or at least tried CVS (Subversion was just introduced by the service). Some projects in our table 1 have also been transferred to Sourceforge at some point of their life-cycle. Two open sourced projects (Sofia SIP http://sourceforge.net/projects/sofia-sip/ and Python for S60 http://sourceforge.net/projects/pys60/) are the top of the iSource lists.

6 Findings and discussion

The aim of our research was to describe usage and show what kind of projects benefit from intra-company portal. There is a clear growing trend in iSource usage. As projects adopted it voluntarily, there is clearly an expectation of benefit. The portal launch needs to be planned, projects need support and there needs to be a robust technical support and evangelists to keep the platform alive.

Projects inside iSource are heterogeneous: most of the biggest projects are platform projects, but on the other hand frameworks and libraries are more downloaded. So, we cannot claim homogeneity between projects. One way to characterize the different project types would be to divide them into: 1) SCM projects, 2) distributed projects, 3) agile projects, 4) intra-company collaboration projects, and 5) Inner Source projects utilizing the full potential of OSS approach.

Openness seems to support adoption of the project results. Not only have projects been able to gain visibility inside the company, but some iSource projects have been moved into open domain once tested inside the global company.

When describing one case study, there is always a question of how to transfer the findings into other companies. This is especially true when dealing with global company tool adoption. However, from our industrial experience and discussions with several other companies in scope of a European research project, it seems that similar challenges need to be solved when moving towards developer communities. The experience of the companies already implementing inner source are very valuable to other industry actors considering moving towards similar development practices.

Acknowledgements

The authors would like to thank the ITEA-COSI project.

References

1. L. Dahlander, M. Magnusson. Relationships Between Open Source Companies and Communities: Observations from Nordic Firms. *Research Policy*, 34(4): 481-493, 2005.
2. J. Dinkelacker, P. Garg, R. Miller, D. Nelson. Progressive Open Source. *Proceedings of the 24th International Conference on Software Engineering, Buenos Aires, Argentina,* May 2002.
3. K. M. Eisenhardt. Building Theories from Case Study Research. *Academy of Management Review* 14 (4): 532-550, 1989.
4. M. Fink. *The Business and Economics of Linux and Open Source*. Prentice Hall, New Jersey, 2002.
5. B. Fitzgerald. The Transformation of Open Source Software. MIS Quarterly, 30(2):587-598, 2006.
6. V. Gurbani, A. Garvert, and J. Herbsleb. A Case Study of Open Source Tools and Practices in a Commercial Setting. In *Open Source Application Spaces: Proceeding of the Fifth Workshop on Open Source Software Engineering. St Louis, USA, 17-21 May 2005.*
7. Ø. Hauge, C. Sørensen, and A. Røsdal. Surveying Industrial Roles in Open Source Software Development. *OSS 2007. June 11-14 2007*, Limerick, Ireland.
8. C. Melian, CB. Ammirati, P. Garg, and G. Sevon. Building Networks of Software Communities in a Large Corporation. Hewlet Packard POS, 2001.

9. A. Osterwalder, Y. Pigneur. Clarifying Business Models: Origins, Present and Future of the Concept. Communications of the AIS, v. 15, May 2005.
10. B. Perens. The open source definition. In C. DiBona, S. Ockman, and M. Stone, eds, Open Sources: Voices from the Open Source Revolution. O'Reilly & Associates, Sebastapol, CA, 1999.
11. R. Rajala, M. Westerlund, and J. Nissilä, Software for Free? Revenue Models In The Open Source Software Business. Proceedings of the 5th Global Conference on Business&Economics, Cambridge University, Cambridge, UK, 2006.
12. E.S. Raymond. The Cathedral and The Bazaar – Musings on Linux and Open Source by Accidential Revolutionary, O'Reilly&Associates, Sebastopol, CA., 1999.
13. A.M. Szczepanska, M. Bergquist and , J. Ljunberg. High Noon at OS Corral: Duels and Shoot-Outs in Open Source Discours. In: J. Feller, B. Fitzgerald., S. A. Hissam, and K. R. Lakhani, eds. *Perspectives on Free and Open Source Software,* MIT Press, Cambridge, Mass., 2005.
14. G. Walsham. *Interpreting Information Systems in Organizations*. Cichester, Wiley&Sons. 1993.
15. G. von Krogh, E. von Hippel. The Promise of Research on Open Source Software. *Management Science*, 52(7): 975-983, July 2006.
16. R. K. Yin, Case Study Research, Design and Methods, 2nd ed., Sage Publications, Newbury Park, 1994.

Towards The Evaluation of OSS Trustworthiness: Lessons Learned From The Observation of Relevant OSS Projects

Davide Taibi[1], Vieri del Bianco[1], Davide Dalle Carbonare[2], Luigi Lavazza[1], and Sandro Morasca[1]
[1] University of Insubria
davide.taibi | vieri.delbianco | luigi.lavazza | sandro.morasca@uninsubria.it
WWW home page: http://www.uninsubria.it
[2] Engineering Ingegneria Informatica S.p.A.
davide.dallecarbonare@eng.it
WWW home page: http://www.eng.it

Abstract. To facilitate the adoption of open-source software (OSS) in industry, it is important to provide potential users (i.e., those who could decide to adopt OSS) with the means for evaluating the trustworthiness of OS products. This paper presents part of the work done in the QualiPSo project for this purpose. A set of factors that are believed to affect the perception of trustworthiness are introduced. In order to test the feasibility of deriving a correct, complete and reliable evaluation of trustworthiness on the basis of these factors, a set of well-known OSS projects have been chosen. Then, the possibility to assess the proposed factors on each project was verified: not all the factors appear to be observable or measurable. The paper reports what information is available to support the evaluation and what is not. This knowledge is considered to be useful to users, who are warned that there are still dark areas in the characterization of OSS products, and to developers, who should provide more data and characteristics on their products in order to support their adoption.

Keywords: OSS trustworthiness, OSS quality, OSS adoption

1 Introduction

The success of OSS is due to multiple reasons, ranging from technical qualities to financial, ethical and political motivations. Nonetheless, the adoption of OSS is still limited. The reason is that, in several cases, OSS fails to convince potential users that its adoption is safe and poses no more risks than purchasing commercial software. In this paper, we report on the initial work, carried out in the QualiPSo project, that focuses specifically on the characteristics of OSS products and artefacts, in order to identify the ones most closely related to trustworthiness. The QualiPSo (Quality Platform for Open Source Software) project 0 is an ongoing initiative that proposes a

Please use the following format when citing this chapter:

Taibi, D., del Bianco, V., Carbonare, D.D., Lavazza, L. and Morasca, S., 2008, in IFIP International Federation for Information Processing, Volume 275; *Open Source Development, Communities and Quality*; Barbara Russo, Ernesto Damiani, Scott Hissam, Björn Lundell, Giancarlo Succi; (Boston: Springer), pp. 389–395.

coherent and systematic evaluation of the trustworthiness of OSS projects, and aims at promoting the diffusion of OSS by focusing on OSS trustworthiness.

We name "trustworthiness" the set of qualities that are of interest for the users, especially in the process of deciding whether a given OS program (or library, or other piece of software) is "good enough" to be used in an industrial or professional context.

Firstly, we defined the set of factors that were believed to be the most closely related to the perceived trustworthiness 0; then we identified a set of OSS projects, widely adopted and generally considered trustable, to be used as references. Afterwards, a first quick analysis was carried out, checking which factors were readily available on each project's web site. The idea was to emulate the search for information carried out by a potential user, who browses the project's web sites, but is not willing to spend too much effort and time in carrying out a complete analysis. Since the view of trustworthiness factors emerging from the analysis seemed too subjective, it was decided to precisely define measures specifying how to evaluate the OSS characteristics, and how to collect data that could be effectively used in the analysis phase, to be performed according to some statistical methods.

2 Project Selection and Analysis

The selection of projects addressed different types of software applications, generally considered stable and mature. The complete set of projects comprises 32 products, different with respect to age, implementation language, size of developers and users communities, etc.

Here the criteria used to select a representative set of OSS projects are reported. Projects have a set of characterising attributes. The selection criteria aimed at:

- Including a reasonably small set of projects.
- Including at least a couple of projects for every possible value of any attribute.

For instance, an attribute is the size of the development team. Four possible values were defined: 0 (inactive project), no more than ten people, up to 50 people, more than 50 people. Therefore, we took care to include at least two projects for each of the four mentioned classes. The complete set of attributes is reported in Table 1.

Table 1. The projects' attributes.

Attribute	Possible values
Repository	SourceForge, Apache, Java.net, FreshMeat, Rubyforge, ObjectWeb, Free Software Foundation, SourceKibitzer, other
Standalone	Yes/No (Part of a Project family)
Type	Web Server, Operating System, ERP, CSM, …
Developer organization type	Sponsored/foundation, spontaneous, other
Cost	Free; pay for services and features; pay for everything
Size of the development team	0 (abandoned/closed project), 1–10, 11–50, >50

User community size	Small (<51), Medium (51–250), Large (>250)
Programming language	Java, C#, C/C++, scripting languages, Visual Basic, other
Tool support(*)	little use of tools (0-4 tools used); extensive use of tools (5-7)
Innovation	Traditional application (existing before 2003); Emerging application (only proprietary solutions before 2003)
Age	Project started before 1998; between 1998 and 2003; after 2003

(*) the potentially supported activities are: continuous integration (supported by Cruise Control, Damage Control, Continuum, …), building (Ant, make, …), code documentation (Doxygen, Javadoc, …), testing (JUnit/NUnit/PhpUnit, …), version control (CVS, Subversion, …), bug tracking (Jira, Bugzilla, …), static code analysis (Spoon, Checkstyle,…).

We analyzed the 32 selected projects, considering the information concerning the trustworthiness factors. The analysis was carried out by looking for information that was readily available in the project web sites.

Table 2 lists the factors that are believed to determine trustworthiness, and reports, for each factor, how many projects provided (in the official web site) enough information to evaluate the factor.

Table 2. Number of projects that provide data about the considered factors

Factor	N° of projects supporting the evaluation of the factor
Type of licenses used	32
Facilities for developing modifying...	10
Technical manual	2
Mid/long term existence of a user community	Not Found
Existence of a sufficiently large community	Not Found
Short term support	Not Found
Mid/long term existence of a maintainer organization	Not Found
Use of standard architecture	11
Usage of patterns	6
Programming language uniformity	25*
Complexity	Not Found
Size	Not Found
Reliability	8
Maintainability	7
Modularity	18
Usability	9
Portability	15
Performances	8
Functional requirements satisfaction	11
Customer satisfaction	Not Found
Interoperability with external systems/integration ease	10

Availability of user manual	30
Standard compliance	10
Availability of best practices	17
Human interface language/localization	15
Self containedness	15
Existence of benchmarks or test suites that witness quality	5
Availability of training, guidelines, use cases, tutorial	20
Distribution channel	31
Number of downloads	32

* Only a few of these projects explicitly declare to use one language for the whole project.

3 Factor Refinement

The experience of the quick project analysis showed that for several factors it was necessary to define more precise and specific measures. The need to base evaluations on more objective data also emerged. Accordingly, whenever a factor proved not to be directly measurable, a set of 'proxies' was defined. Some proxies can be assessed in a simple and direct manner, while others need specific tools. Table 3 reports both the new measures and the unchanged ones defined for OSS product trustworthiness. The idea is that for each OSS project the factors are evaluated according to these measurement definitions.

Table 3. New criteria for the evaluation of trustworthiness factors

Factor	Basic indicators
Functional requirements satisfaction degree	Availability of: feature list, free text description, release notes, product example/demo
Customer Satisfaction	List of organizations, testimonials and other projects using this software, case studies, usage histories User community satisfaction (according to forums, blogs, mailing lists, newsgroups, magazine/scientific articles)
Interoperability	Communication with other systems supported by suitable mechanisms (SOAP, Web services, protocols, public interfaces, ...); Ease of integration with other products and possibility to migrate to other product with little effort
Reliability	Development status, frequency of patches, average bug time solving
Maintainability	Existence of a guide to extend/adapt the OSS product, maintenance releases and architectural documentation. Coherent usage of coding guidelines/standard, source code quality and programming language uniformity
Modularity	The product provides plug-in interface(s)
Standard Architecture	Availability of architectural documentation and usage of architectural standard/pattern

Mid Long Term Existence of a User Community	Project Age; Trend of the number of users; Number of patches/releases in the last 6 month; Number of developers involved; Average bug solving time
Availability of technical and user documentation	Availability of: up to date technical/user manual, getting started guide, installation guide, Technical/User related F.A.Q., Technical/user forum and mailing list
Standard Compliance	Any information about standard implemented (like HTTP 1.0, SQL 97...) and coding standards
Existence of a sufficiently large community of users	Number of posts available on forums/blogs/newsgroups and related activity
Performance	Existence of performance tests and/or scenarios, specific performance-related documentation Implementation -Any best practices, concerning design and product construction, aimed at boosting performance.
Type of License	Main and sub license used
Short Term Support	Bug number, bug removal rate, availability of professional services
Availability of facilities for developing, modifying, and customizing the product	General purpose build tools applicable to the product, build script, built-in customization facility (configuration API, …)
Usability	Detailed feature description and user manual Ease of installation/configuration, ease of use.
Portability	Supported environments, usage of a portable language (like Java), environment-dependent implementation (e.g., usage of hardware/software dependent libraries)
OSS Provider Reputation	Opinion and feedback from other users
Best Practices	Availability of best practices, code examples/tutorials
Programming language uniformity	Number of languages used in the project
Complexity	McCabe complexity number or any related information available on the web site
Human Interface Language Localization	Localization support availability (e.g., are language files provided?)
Self Containedness	Can the product be installed and executed "out of the box" or does it require other software? Are dependencies documented?
Existence of benchmarks/test suites that witness for the quality	Availability of test suites/benchmarks, Usage of a test framework (JUnit, DejaGNU,…), results of tests published (on the project site), existence of initiatives to encourage the community to contribute to quality efforts
Mid/long term existence of a maintainer / sponsor	Active maintainer organization / sponsor
Availability of training, guidelines, use cases, tutorial etc.	Up to date training materials, manuals and guidelines available free of charge Availability of official training courses
The distribution media	Source code download; Binaries download Access to the project repository; CD/DVD distribution
Size	Number of Lines of code, source files and functions (or classes and methods, for object oriented code)
Popularity of the product	Number of downloads

The main areas that could not be covered in the previous analysis were those related to the quality of the product and the user community. In no project website we found any indication about the user community size, the internal software quality and complexity, or the vitality of the project.

Proxy definitions were conceived to make the assessment as easy and objective as possible. The possibility of employing tools –possibly specifically developed for this purpose– was also taken into account. Considering for instance the evaluation of *the mid/long term existence of a user community*, we suggest checking the following indicators: the growth rate of the community, the number of patches/releases during the last 6 months, the number of developers involved, the average bug solving time and the project age. In order to assess the growth trend of the user community we shall develop a specific tool, which –by digging into the web portals, official forums and blogs– computes the number of unique users in the last months.

Unfortunately, some information considered important is never exposed on the project websites; therefore we wish to throw a suggestion to the Open Source community, recommending the leaders of OSS projects who would like to publicize the trustworthiness of their products to publish all the useful data. In any case, there are some factors that are inherently difficult to evaluate: for instance, it is quite hard to evaluate the quality of the supplied user manual. This task could be made much easier if it were possible to collect feedback from users: it is thus important to make the users aware that the usage of some feedback collector would be beneficial to the whole user community.

4 Conclusions

In order to favour the adoption of OSS, it is necessary to assure the potential users that the OSS products do meet their expectations under several respects. In the QualiPSo project, the notion of "trustworthiness" is meant to include several qualities of the OSS, ranging from training support to the possibility of modifying/adapting the programs, to the availability of support from the producer, etc. Since the notion of trustworthiness is quite broad, it is necessary to fully understand what factors contribute to making a product trustworthy. For this purpose, in the QualiPSo project several OSS products have been examined: a set of factors that are believed to affect the perceived trustworthiness were identified, a set of outstanding OSS project were selected and are being analysed with respect to the mentioned factors.

Here we reported the preliminary results of the analysis of OSS products and artifacts. Next steps will include a second analysis round, based on the usage of the newly defined measures, possibly along with a campaign, addressed to OSS developers, to provide more information on the characteristics that affect the trustworthiness of their products. A number of OSS code repositories will also be analyzed, with the aid of automated tools.

The collected data will be analyzed, with the objective of identifying commonalities and differences in the characteristics and usage of OSS products, to prepare the ground for the creation of a trustworthiness model encompassing the characteristics and factors that have been observed to actually affect the perception of trustworthiness in OSS products and artifacts.

Although the analysis is not yet complete, we were able to make some preliminary observations. A first result is that by browsing the information provided by the projects' web sites, only a relatively small set of the interesting factors could be evaluated: several factors appear not to be observable or measurable. The paper reports what information is not available: developers should provide the missing information in order to support the adoption of their products. Since some of the trustworthiness factors could not be evaluated because of their subjectivity, we began a more precise definition of the measures – illustrated in Table 3 – that should be used to capture these factors.

References

1. V. del Bianco, M. Chinosi, L. Lavazza, S. Morasca, D. Taibi, "How European software industry perceives OSS trustworthiness and what are the specific criteria to establish trust in OSS", October 2007, available on-line at http://qualipso.semanticdesktop.org/xwiki/bin/view/Wiki/WP51.
2. QualiPSo project web site: http://www.qualipso.eu

Open Source Reference Systems for Biometric Verification of Identity

Aurélien Mayoue and Dijana Petrovska-Delacrétaz
TELECOM & Management SudParis,
9 rue Charles Fourier,
91011 Evry Cedex, France

Abstract. This paper focuses on the common evaluation framework which was developed by the BioSecure Network of Excellence during the European FP6 project BioSecure (Biometrics for Secure authentication). This framework, which is composed of open-source reference systems, publicly available databases, assessment protocols and benchmarking results, introduces a new experimental methodology for conducting, reporting and comparing experiments for biometric systems, participating to standardisation efforts. Its use will permit to make a link between different published works. It provides also the necessary tools to assure the reproducibility of the benchmarking biometric experiments. This framework can be considered as a re-liable and innovative process to evaluate the progress of research in the field of bio-metrics.

1 Introduction

With the widespread use of biometric systems in our society, a lot of articles about this topic have been published in the last years. Among all the algorithms presented in the literature, it seems essential to know which one performs better, hence the need for a common evaluation framework which would enable a fair comparison between biometric algorithms. Indeed, the performance of two biometric verification systems can only be fairly compared in the case where these both systems have been evaluated in the same experimental conditions, i.e. applied on the same database according to the same protocol. That's why several biometric evaluation campaigns have been launched during the last years. But in the existing ongoing evaluation programs, such as NIST-SRE [1] for speaker recognition, BANCA [2], M2VTS [3] and FRVT [4] for face, FVC [5] for fingerprint, SVC [6] for signature and ICE [7] for iris, the databases used are often not publicly available and there is no systematic usage of a state-of-the-art algorithm to calibrate both the performance of the evaluated systems and the 'difficulty' of the evaluation database and protocol. Therefore, it is impossible to reproduce the experiments and to measure the progress (in comparison with the current state of the art) done by the newly developed research prototypes which are tested during these evaluation campaigns. In this way, such evaluations can not be considered as an universal evaluation tool.

Please use the following format when citing this chapter:

Mayoue, A. and Petrovska-Delacrétaz, D., 2008, in IFIP International Federation for Information Processing, Volume 275; *Open Source Development, Communities and Quality*; Barbara Russo, Ernesto Damiani, Scott Hissam, Björn Lundell, Giancarlo Succi; (Boston: Springer), pp. 397–404.

From these observations, the partners of the BioSecure Network of Excellence (NoE) [8] have brought together the expertise in a wide range of biometric modalities in order to make available to the biometric community a new open-source evaluation tool, which enables a fair comparison of the biometric algorithms being tested. In this way, the NoE has taken in charge the development or improvement of existing open-source identity verification systems (softwares) for the most widely used biometric modalities (2D and 3D faces, fingerprint, hand, iris, signature, speech and talking-face). These open-source systems are based on principles that have proven their efficiency and their purpose is to serve as comparison point to measure the real progress achieved with new research methods. Consequently, these open-source systems are known as reference systems. These systems accompanied with benchmarking (calibration) publicly available databases and benchmarking (calibration) assessment protocols define the building blocks of the evaluation framework, which also reports benchmarking results (i.e. results obtained by applying the reference system on the benchmarking database according to the benchmarking protocol).

From now on, any research laboratory can evaluate their own biometric algorithms using the benchmarking database in accordance with the benchmarking protocol and then compare their results to the performance of the reference system. This is a new way to calibrate the performance of an algorithm.

The outline of this paper is as follows. In Sect. 2, the objectives of the proposed evaluation framework are developed. Then, the open-source reference systems, which compose this framework, are briefly presented in Sect. 3 whereas in Sect. 4 we explain how to use the evaluation tool in practice. Section 5 ends up with conclusions and perspectives.

2 Objectives

2.1 Properties of the evaluation framework

In the framework of identity verification, it is very difficult to compare two different methods from two different articles in the literature, even though they deal with the very same task. It raises a real problem when one wants to know if a new original method performs better than the current state of the art for example. This can be explained by the fact that a lot of researchers have recorded their own test data-base and are the only one performing experiments on it, which are subsequently impossible to reproduce.

Our evaluation framework brings an easy yet efficient answer to this problem. As it is composed (for each modality) of a reference system, a publicly available database and an evaluation protocol accompanied with a documentation which reports performance of the reference system, our evaluation framework can be used in two ways:

- in the case where someone publishes results on a specific database according to a specific protocol, experiments using the reference system have to be added as a way of calibrating the difficulty of this particular task.
- in the case where someone publishes results using the benchmarking data-base and protocol, the benchmarking results of the reference system can be used as a way of calibrating the performance.

In both cases, the results of the reference systems permit to measure the progress achieved with the newly developed algorithm being tested. Now, it is hoped that the published results of a new biometric algorithm will be systematically accompanied with the results obtained by the reference system in the same experimental conditions. Such a methodology for reporting experimental results will facilitate deeply advances of the state of the art.

Through our framework, an absolute reproducibility of the benchmarking results is also assured. Indeed, an explanatory documentation is available for each modality to avoid any possible misinterpretation of the proposed evaluation framework. In this way, the properties of our framework are the following:

- its universal use: for each modality, it is comprised of an open-source reference system, a publicly available database and a well defined evaluation protocol.
- it enables a fair comparison of the biometric algorithms being tested.
- it evaluates the real progress achieved with new research prototypes.
- its easy use: for each modality, a document explains in details the evaluation protocol and how to install and use the reference system.
- the full reproducibility of the benchmarking results.

2.2 Relevance of using open-source reference systems

The fact that the proposed reference systems are open-source and made of replaceable C/C++ software modules with well defined inputs/outputs is of great interest. Indeed, researchers often work on a specific part of the system and do not have the time nor the interest in building a complete system. In this way, a researcher could show the improvement of his new features extraction algorithm (for example) simply by replacing the corresponding module in the reference system and without having to bother about the pattern recognition algorithm. This new methodology for conducting research and experiments will enable to assess the contribution of each module to the final performance of a biometric system.

Using an open-source reference system as a basis for researching a specific area is also a good way to save time, human resources and money. For example, young researchers who are just starting in the field of biometrics, could immediately be faced with the reference system and they could put all their efforts to improve our efficient system rather than developing a state-of-the-art algorithm from A to Z again. In this way, the main advantages of our reference systems are the following:

- development as open-source software.

- easy implementation: in general, a reference system is composed of four replaceable modules (pre-processing, features extraction, model building and matching).
- time saving: a reference system can be considered as a starting point for the development of a more efficient system.

3 The Open-source Reference Systems

At time of writing, the evaluation framework concerns eight biometric modalities. It is comprised of five publicly available databases and ten benchmarking open-source reference systems. Among these systems, eight were developed within the framework of the BioSecure NoE and only three were existing ones (the fingerprint and speech reference systems) but all systems are accompanied with a benchmarking database, assessment protocol and benchmarking results to compose our evaluation framework:

1. For the 2D face modality, the BioSecure reference system is based on the Eigenface approach [9] and the BANCA database [10] is chosen for the benchmarking experiments.
2. For the 3D face modality, the BioSecure reference system [11] uses both Iterative Closest Points [12] and Thin Plate Spline warping [14] algorithms. The associated database is the 3D RMA database [13].
3. For the fingerprint modality, the NIST reference system (NFIS2 [15]) uses a standard minutiae based approach. MCYT-100 [16] is selected as the benchmarking database.
4. For the hand modality, the BioSecure reference system [17] uses geometry of fingers for recognition purposes. The selected database is the Biosecure database [17].
5. For the iris modality, the BioSecure reference system (OSIRIS [18]) is deeply inspired by Daugman's works [19] and the database used for the benchmarking experiments is CBS [20].
6. For the signature modality, two reference systems developed by BioSecure members are available. The first one [21] is based on the Hidden Markov Model [22] whereas the second one [23] uses the Levenshtein distance [24]. The MCYT-100 [16] database is chosen for the benchmarking experiments.
7. For the speech modality, the evaluation framework is composed of two open-source softwares: ALIZE [25] and BECARS [27]. Both systems are based on the Gaussian Mixture Models approach [26]. The reference data-base is the speech part of the BANCA database [10].
8. For the talking-face modality, the BioSecure reference system [28] is based on the fusion of face and speech scores. The BANCA database [10] is used for the benchmarking experiments.

Some of the open-source reference systems available in the benchmarking framework have been already used in major existing evaluation campaigns. For example, the ALIZE software [25] is consistently used during the NIST-SRE [1] and it exhibits state-of-the-art performance. The iris reference system [18] has been tested with the ICE'2005 database and it has a quite good ranking compared to the results re-ported in [7]. Endless, the signature reference system based on HMM [21] has obtained good performance at the SVC'2004 competition [6]. More details about performance of all reference systems can be found in [29].

4 Use of the Evaluation Tool

The source code of the ten reference systems described in Sect. 3 are available at [30]. Scripts (required to run a full experiment with the reference system), lists of tests (impostor and genuine trials) to be done and all the necessary information needed to fully reproduce the benchmarking results are also available at this adress. Endless, for each modality, a document explains how to install and use the reference system. In practice, the user of our evaluation framework can be confronted with three different scenarios:

1. He wants to evaluate his new biometric algorithm using our reference data-base and protocol to calibrate the performance of his algorithm. In this case, he has to process as follows:
   - run the evaluated system on the reference database using the list of trials provided within the evaluation framework.
   - compare the obtained results to the benchmarking results provided within the evaluation framework to measure the progress achieved with the new algorithm.
2. He wants to test the reference system on his own database according to his own protocol in order to calibrate this particular task. In this case, he has to process as follows:
   - run the reference system using his own database and protocol.
   - compare the obtained results to those provided within the evaluation framework to evaluate the 'difficulty' of these particular database and protocol.
   - use the obtained results as comparison point for the other experiments carried out in the same conditions.
3. He wants simply to reproduce the benchmarking results to be convinced of the good installation and use of the reference system:
   - run the reference system on the reference database using the scripts and lists of trials provided within the evaluation framework.
   - verify that the obtained results are the same as the benchmarking results.

Since the reference systems are open-source, other scenarios are of course conceivable. Some parameters or even some modules of the reference systems can be changed in order to improve their basic performances.

5. Conclusions and Perspectives

In the field of biometry, the BioSecure NoE has developed an universal evaluation framework based on open-source reference systems, publicly available data-bases, evaluation protocols and benchmarking results. This framework enables a fair comparison of the performance of biometric systems and its widespread use would facilitate the advances of the biometric state of the art.

This framework has been used for the first time during the BioSecure Multimodal Evaluation Campaign (BMEC) 2007. The organizers of this competition have systematically used the reference systems to calibrate the 'difficulty' of the newly constituted BioSecure database and protocol. Then, the results of the reference systems have been used for measuring the improvements acquired with each submitted re-search system. All results of this evaluation are available on the BMEC's web site [31].

As the research advances, the reference systems should be updated in order to remain competitive. The development of reference systems for the newly appeared modalities (such as palm vein) is also part of our future plans.

Acknowledgments

Biosecure is a project of the 6th Framework Programme of the European Un-ion. We thank in particular all the universities which participated in the development of the BioSe-cure reference systems.

References

1. NIST Speaker Recognition Evaluations. http://www.nist.gov/speech/tests/spk.
2. BANCA: Biometric Access control for Networked and e-Comerce Applications. http://www.ee.surrey.ac.uk/CVSSP/banca/.
3. M2VTS: Multi Modal Verification for Teleservices and Security applications. http://www.ee.surrey.ac.uk/CVSSP/xm2vtsdb/.
4. FRVT: Face Recognition Vendor Test. http://www.frvt.org/.
5. FVC: Fingerprint Verification Competition. http://bias.csr.unibo.it/fvc2006/.
6. SVC: Signature Verification Competition. http://www.cse.ust.hk/svc2004/.
7. ICE: Iris Challenge Evaluation. http://iris.nist.gov/ice/.
8. BioSecure Network of Excellence. http://biosecure.info/.

9. M. Turk and A. Pentland. Eigenfaces for recognition. Journal of Cognitive Neuroscience, 3(1):71-86, 1991.
10. E. Bailly-Baillière, S. Bengio, F. Bimbot, M. Hamouz, J. Kittler, J. Mariéthoz, J. Matas, K. Messer, V. Popovici, F. Porée, B. Ruiz, and J.-P. Thiran. The BANCA Database and Evaluation Protocol. In 4th International Conference on Audio-and Video-Based Biometric Person Authen-tication (AVBPA'03), volume 2688 of Lecture Notes in Computer Science, pages 625-638, Guild-ford, UK, January 2003. Springer.
11. M.O Irfanoglu, B. Gokberk, and L. Akarun. 3d Shape-based Face Recognition Using Automatically Registered Facial Surfaces. In Proc. 17th International Conference on Pattern Recognition, Cambridge, UK, 2004.
12. P. Besl and N. McKay. A Method for Registration of 3-D Shapes. IEEE Transactions on Pat-tern Analysis and Machine Intelligence, 14(2):239-256, 1992.
13. 3D RMA database. http://www.sic.rma.ac.be/~beumier/DB/3d_rma.html.
14. F.L. Bookstein. Principal Warps: Thin-Plate Splines and the Decomposition of Deformations. IEEE Transactions on Pattern Analysis and Machine Intelligence, 11:567-585, 1989.
15. C. Watson, M. Garris, E. Tabassi, C. Wilson, R. McCabe, and S. Janet. Guide to NIST Finger-print Image Software 2 (NFIS2) - http://fingerprint.nist.gov/NFIS.
16. J. Ortega-Garcia, J. Fierrez-Aguilar, D. Simon, M.F.J. Gonzalez, V. Espinosa, A. Satue, I. Hernaez, J. J. Igarza, C. Vivaracho, D. Escudero, and Q. I. Moro. MCYT baseline corpus: A bi-modal biometric database. IEE Proceedings Vision, Image and Signal Processing, Special Issue on Biometrics on the Internet, 150(6):395-401, December 2003.
17. G. Fouquier, L. Likforman, J. Darbon, and B. Sankur. The Biosecure Geometry-based System for Hand Modality. In the Proceedings of 32nd International Conference on Acoustics, Speech and Signal Processing (ICASSP), Honolulu, Hawai, USA, april 2007.
18. E. Krichen. Reconnaissance des personnes par l'iris en mode dégradé. Thèse de doctorat, Institut National des Télécommunications, 2007.
19. J.G. Daugman. High confidence visual recognition of persons by a test of statistical independ-ence. IEEE Trans. Patt. Ana. Mach. Intell., 15(11):1148-1161, 1993.
20. CASIA iris image database. http://www.cbsr.ia.ac.cn/IrisDatabase.htm.
21. B. Ly Van, S. Garcia-Salicetti, and B. Dorizzi. On using the Viterbi Path along with HMM Likelihood Information for On-line Signature Verification. In Proceedings of the IEEE Transactions on Systems, Man and Cybernetics, Part B, to appear.
22. L. Rabiner and B.H. Juang. Fundamentals of Speech Recognition. Prentice Hall Signal Processing Series. 1993.
23. S. Schimke, C. Vielhauer, and J. Dittmann. Using Adapted Levenshtein Distance for On-Line Signature Authentication. In Proceedings of the ICPR 2004, IEEE 17th International Confer-ence on Pattern Recognition, ISBN 0-7695-2128-2, 2004.
24. V.I. Levenshtein. Binary Codes Capable of Correcting Deletions, Insertions and Reversals. Soviet Physics, 10:707-710, 1966.
25. ALIZE software. http://www.lia.univ-avignon.fr/heberges/ALIZE/.
26. D.A. Reynolds. A Gaussian Mixture Modeling Approach to Text-Independent Speaker Identification. Ph.D. Thesis, Georgia Institute of Technology, 1992.
27. BECARS software. http://www.tsi.enst.fr/becars/index.php.
28. Hervé Bredin, Guido Aversano, Chafic Mokbel, and Gérard Chollet. The Biosecure Talking-Face Reference System. In 2nd Workshop on Multimodal User Authentication (MMUA'06), Toulouse, France, May 2006.
29. D. Petrovska-Delacrétaz, G. Chollet, and B. Dorizzi, editors. Guide to Biometric Reference Systems and Performance Evaluation. Springer-Verlag, London, to be published.

30. BioSecure Reference Systems. http://share.int-evry.fr/svnview-eph/.
31. BioSecure Mutimodal Evaluation Campaign 2007 (BMEC'2007). http://biometrics.it-sudparis.eu/BMEC2007/.

eResearch Workflows for Studying Free and Open Source Software Development

James Howison, Andrea Wiggins, and Kevin Crowston

School of Information Studies
Syracuse University
{jhowison|awiggins|crowston}@syr.edu

Abstract. This paper introduces eResearch workflow tools as a model for the research community studying free and open source software and its development. The paper first introduces eResearch as increasingly practiced in fields such as astrophysics and biology, then contrasts the practice of research on free and open source software. After outlining suitable research data sets the paper introduces a class of tools known as scientific workflow frameworks, focusing on one—Taverna—and introducing its features. To further explain the tool a complete workflow used for original research on FLOSS is described. Finally the paper considers the trade-offs inherent in these tools.[1]

eResearch refers to a set of scientific practices and technologies, sometimes called eScience or Cyberinfrastructure, which allow distributed groups of scientists to bring to bear large shared data sets, computational resources and shared workflows for scientific inquiry. A prototypical example of such research is the Upper Atmospheric Research Collaboratory (UARC) and the NSF has produced a series of reports on the topic (eg [4]). The hallmarks of eResearch are: a) broad community-level collaborations between distributed scientists, b) large-scale broadly available data sets c) shared computational analysis tools and workflows, and d) replicable research with clear provenance metadata.

While the FLOSS research community has taken some steps towards this goal we have not yet fully embraced this model of inquiry. Given that we study highly effective distributed collaborators and collaborative technologies in the FLOSS community, we have good understanding of solutions to the challenges faced by such distributed collaborations. Figure 1 shows an envisioned workflow repository which allows the discovery, replication, extension and publication of research workflows, drawing on shared components. It is time to build further towards eResearch.

1 Current FLOSS research practices

A series of papers has examined the current research practices in the investigation of FLOSS and its development [1, 2][2]. In general this research has been, and continues

[1] This work is supported by NSF grant #0708437. A longer version of this paper is available at http://floss.syr.edu/publications/HowisonTavernaDemoIFIP.pdf

[2] See also the report of the FOSSRRI workshop at http://fossrri.rotterdam.ics.uci.edu/ and the Research Room @ FOSSDEM: http://libresoft.es/Activities/Research_activities/fosdem2008

Please use the following format when citing this chapter:

Howison, J., Wiggins, A. and Crowston, K., 2008, in IFIP International Federation for Information Processing, Volume 275; *Open Source Development, Communities and Quality*; Barbara Russo, Ernesto Damiani, Scott Hissam, Björn Lundell, Giancarlo Succi; (Boston: Springer), pp. 405–411.

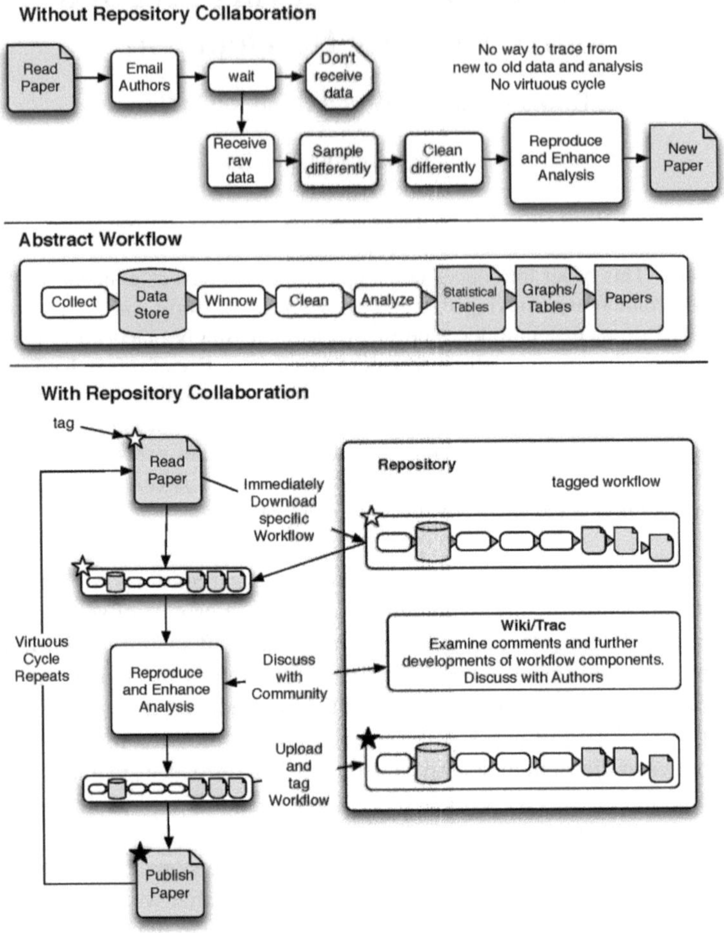

Fig. 1. Envisioned improvements in FLOSS research practices

to be, undertaken by separate groups and has involved substantial re-collection of very similar data, usually through spidering Sourceforge or similar sites.

In the past three years significant progress has been made towards shared datasets held in what have been called Repositories of Repositories [1]. At the IFIP 2.13 conference in 2007 a workshop was held for research based on public databases, including FLOSSMole and CVSanalY. In addition, the Notre Dame Sourceforge database dumps are available under an academic sub-license. These data sources provide an excellent foundation for moving research in this field towards eResearch. Figure 2 summarizes the impressive and substantial amount of data available in these RoRs, and points out gaps in data availability. Of course not all researchers use these databases, with many continuing to spider their own data sets, especially outside of such communities as IFIP 2.13 and the Mining Software Repositories workshops.

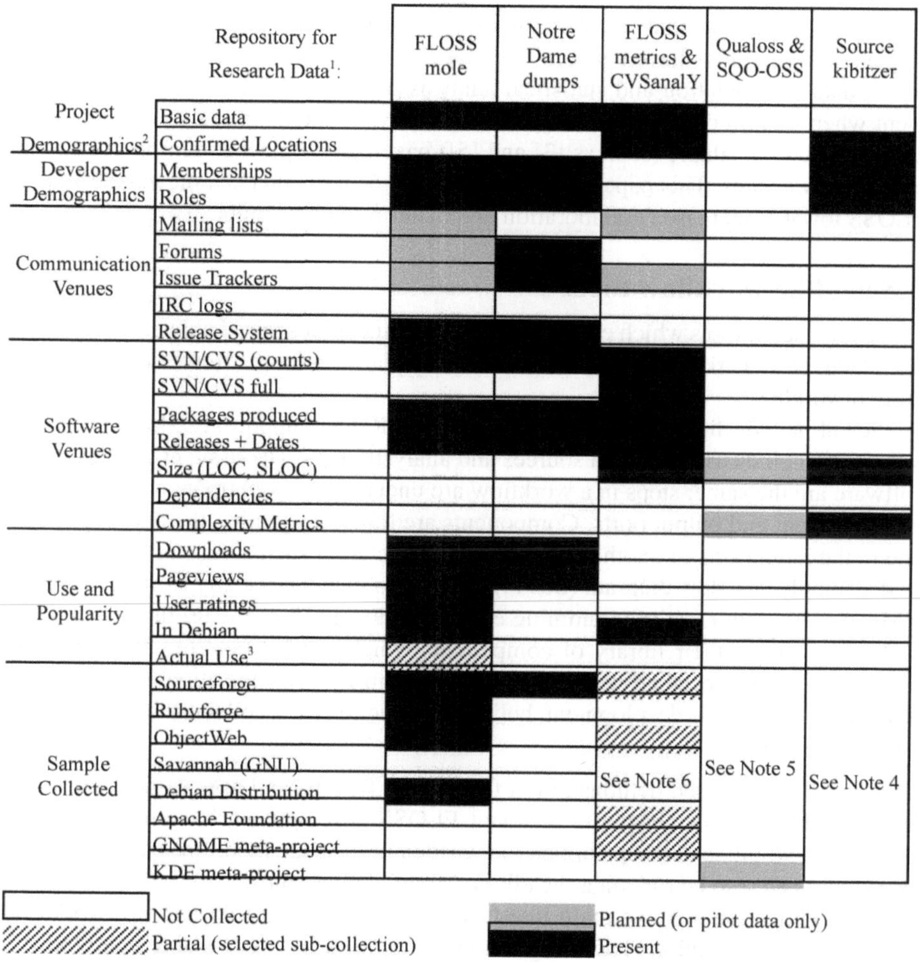

1. This table excludes services with data not easily available to researchers. Ohloh, for example, was excluded for this reason. The Notre Dame dumps require signing a research usage agreement. Sourcekitbizer was included insofar as it provides public access to data via the FLOSSmole project. FLOSSmetrics includes the earlier sets released by the Libre Software engineering group (CVSanalY and Debian Counts). Qualoss and SQO-OSS are included together for reasons of space, they are separate projects, but they are collaborating.

2. Project Demographics include Names, Descriptions, Founding date, Intended Audience, Operating System/environment, License, Programming language, Maturity/Status and Donors. Projects are often hosted on more than one service, or provide their own services (such as Trac, SVN etc) Confirmed Locations refers to a human effort to identify the locations actually used by each project.

3. Actual use as measured, for example, by the Debian Popularity contest which has a voluntary agent installed by some Debian users that reports frequency of package use.

4. Sourcekibitzer samples only Java projects and accepts user contributions (specify project, SCM location, homepage)

5. Qualoss intends to implement their measures on 50 projects, currently there are 5 available as pilot data. SQO-OSS works closely with the KDE meta-project.

6. FLOSSmetrics aims to have validated data for 3,000 and currently has partial data available (primarily CVSanalY) for 100 projects.

URLS: FLOSSmole: ossmole.sf.net, Notre Dame: nd.edu/~oss/, FLOSSmetrics: data.flossmetrics.com, CVSanalY: libresoft.es/Results/CVSAnalY_SF, Qualoss: qualoss.org, SQO-OSS: www.sqo-oss.eu, Sourcekibitzer: sourcekibitzer.org. Thanks to Jesus González-Barahona, Gregorio Robles and Megan Conklin for assistance in preparing this table.

Fig. 2. Table showing repositories available for FLOSS research

While progress has been made in data availability there is little sharing of analyses, including components that calculate important measures such as project effectiveness. In general researchers have stuck to their (or perhaps to their graduate students) preferred data manipulation and statistical analysis tools, conducting in-house development where required. Those researchers which have made their analysis components and workflows available (such as [3] and [5]) have merely placed such bespoke tools on project websites. This paper now turns to describe tools that can move research on FLOSS towards increased collaboration and better research results.

2 Scientific workflow tools

There are a set of tools which contribute to solving the issues raised above. This section introduces two: workflow tools and a community platform for distributed collaboration around workflows.

Scientific workflow tools such as Taverna and Kepler support high-level programming which binds together data sources and analysis steps. The basic principles of the software are the same: steps in a workflow are undertaken by components which have multiple input and output ports. Components are linked by joining the output ports of one to the input ports of another. A workflow made up in such a manner can be represented simply as a flow diagram (See Figure 3, below) and is usually stored in a single XML file. As with most programming environments, much of the usefulness of these tools comes from their library of components which can be local (eg Java or *R*) or remote (eg SOAP accessed web-services). The high-level composition also promotes modularity in analysis development, believed to lead to easier collaboration and higher quality products.

Taverna The proposed demonstration focuses on Taverna and uses workflows developed to address research questions about FLOSS development. Taverna is instantiated as a stand-alone desktop application, written in Java and therefore cross-platform. Workflows can also be run via a 'headless' server application.

The application has two main interface modes: one for the design of a workflow and one for its execution. The design mode provides a list of available components, the workflow definition, and an automatically rendered diagram of the workflow. Input and output ports are typed through the familiar MIME typing system. For simplicity and sharing, components can be grouped into sub-workflows, with a single set of input and output ports.

Taverna supports workflows with both remote and local components. Remote services can be gathered ('scavenged' in Taverna parlance) by entering URLs including Web Services Description Language (WSDL), or from other workflows. It is anticipated that the development of remote services in the FLOSS domain will utilize the WSDL/SOAP combination, standard in many server technologies. Taverna parses the WSDL description file to make multiple components available, each with named input and output ports.

Local services include a library of components dealing with standard operations such as file IO, string and list manipulation. Customized local components can be written in Java, via a scripting syntax called Beanshell, and in the statistical package *R*. Data fed into a component's input ports are available as local variables of the same name and, similarly, output is automatically taken from variables with the same name as the output port at the end of a script. Workflows are able to incorporate typical flow of control methods, such as iteration and conditional branching. There are no global variables and components do not communicate except via their ports.

A designed workflow is executed by first providing any initial workflow inputs (such as a set of FLOSS project names or sampling criteria). An animated step-by-step process monitor summarizes analysis progress until the final outputs of the workflow are displayed. One excellent feature of the software is that during and after the execution, the full set of intermediate input and output variables can be viewed for each component, significantly improving workflow debugging and verification. An XML status report is available for each component, and the full set of status, intermediate and final results can be saved as an XML file for archiving or sharing.

Taverna provides significant metadata facilities. Firstly, a workflow or component designer can provide metadata about the workflow or individual ports, both in unstructured text descriptions and using scientific ontologies based on RDF/OWL. Secondly, the system provides a unique identifier for the workflow and a unique identifier for each and every workflow execution. These identifiers are standardized by the Object Management Group and can be used in papers to point to a specific workflow as well as the specific execution used to produce the results in the paper.

The group that developed Taverna has also developed a social networking site called MyExperiment to encourage sharing of workflows. The site allows the creation of profiles for individual researchers, groups (such as our FLOSS group), and the upload of Taverna workflows. Users can tag their contributed workflows with metadata for discovery and can download, rate, and comment on workflows. If the workflow is later used as a sub-workflow, a citation is displayed on the site.

Example workflow The authors are working to replicate a small number of FLOSS studies with Taverna workflows. These studies draw on large federated data sets (FLOSSMole, CVSanalY and the Notre Dame dumps) and will assist in the prototyping of SOAP access and a library of reusable local components. The discussion below presents a workflow prepared for a companion scientific paper [6], also published in these proceedings.

The workflow draws on FLOSSmole data to produce a time-series graph of social network centralization through a project's lifetime, based on evidence from project communications. Figure 3 shows the workflow graphic saved directly from Taverna. Workflow inputs are boxed at the top, and the final graphical output boxed at the bottom. There are three types of components used: 1) WebServices accessed via SOAP (eg GetPeriods) 2) Rshell components (eg CalculateWeight) and 3) Local components used for splitting XML results and managing iteration.

The basic flow is as follows. The user specifies a project and a start and end date, for which GeneratePeriods provides a set of overlapping periods. Then for each period, the events (dated from-to relations in project communications) are accessed from FLOSSmole by EventsForProjectInPeriod, which returns an XML document of the events. The XML is split into individual events, used by CalulateWeight to calculate a recency based edge weight, such that less recent events are lower weighted.

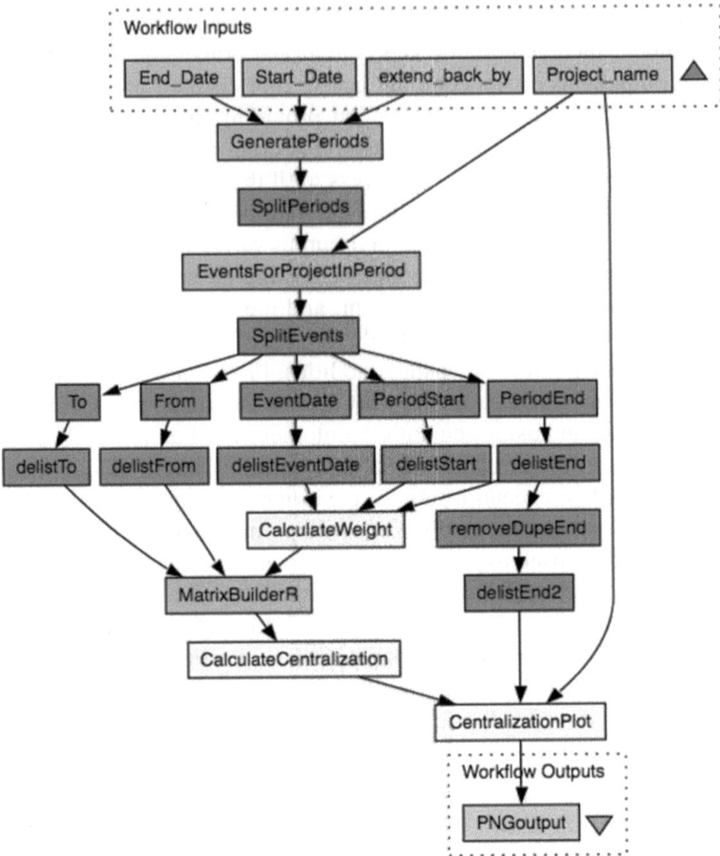

Fig. 3. An example Taverna workflow for analysis of FLOSS communications social networks over time, saved directly from the Taverna interface

The MatrixBuilderR component uses the dates and weights to generate an aggregated socio-matrix. A local *Rserve* instance uses the matrix to calculate network centralization, which is passed with an associated date to the CentralizationPlot component to produce a time-series graph and summary measures. The workflow and the workflow execution XML files that produced this diagram are available in the FLOSSmole SVN (see [6]).

3 Conclusion

The combination of growing large-scale public data sets and workflow tools such as Taverna and MyExperiment.org present a great opportunity for eResearch on FLOSS and its development. There are, of course, issues to be worked through, including a) building common interfaces to public datasets, b) creating ontologies for naming parts of datasets, such as project and developer identifiers, c) incorporating metadata gathered about projects, such as their patch submission procedures and the location of their repositories at different times and d) incorporating social science data, such as content analytic schemas. While data sets and demonstrations are vital to encouraging researcher involvement, editors and reviewers should feel empowered to request complete workflows and insist that papers draw on available datasets, where available.

There are clearly trade-offs in standardizing on analysis technologies. For example, there is a substantial store of experience and skills with individual researcher's tools of choice. Standardization promotes collaboration but also asks research groups to move towards the standard tools, in order to benefit from the work of the collaborators. While standardization has some costs, the benefits of the collaboration it supports aren't limited to working with other research groups. Many groups have also had the experience of losing their main programmer, subsequently facing a lack of knowledge about their own systems. Indeed while it is commonly acknowledged that any form of collaboration can benefit from standardization, it is also true that programmers returning to their own work months later can also benefit from standardized approaches, enabling one to quickly build on one's own earlier work.

eResearch presents a significant opportunity for research on FLOSS development. This paper outlines what is meant by a call for a move towards eResearch techniques and describes tools and ongoing work to kickstart that process. Finally it proposes a demonstration session for the IFIP 2.13 conference in 2008 to make these ideas and tools concrete to the FLOSS research community.

References

[1] Antoniades I, Samoladas I, Sowe SK, Robles G, Koch S, Fraczek K, Hadzisalihovic A (2007) D1.1 study of available tools. EU Framework deliverable, FLOSSmetrics, URL http://flossmetrics.org/sections/deliverables/docs/deliverables/WP1/D1.1-Study_of_Available_Tools.pdf

[2] Howison J, Conklin M, Crowston K (2006) FLOSSmole: A collaborative repository for FLOSS research data and analysis. International Journal of Information Technology and Web Engineering 1(3):17–26

[3] Howison J, Inoue K, Crowston K (2006) Social dynamics of free and open source team communications. In: Damiani E, Fitzgerald B, Scacchi W, Scotto M (eds) Proceedings of the IFIP 2nd International Conference on Open Source Software (Lake Como, Italy), IFIP International Federation for Information Processing, vol 203/2006, Springer, Boston, USA, pp 319–330, URL http://floss.syr.edu/publications/howison_dynamic_sna_intoss_ifip_short.pdf

[4] NSF Cyberinfrastructure Council (2007) Cyberinfrastructure vision for 21st century discovery. URL http://netstats.ucar.edu/cyrdas/report/cyrdas_report_final.pdf, NSF Report 0728

[5] Robles G, Amor JJ, González-Barahona JM, Herraiz I (2005) Evolution and growth in large libre software projects. In: The 8th International Workshop on Principles of Software Evolution, Lisbon, Portugal

[6] Wiggins A, Howison J, Crowston K (2008) Social dynamics of FLOSS team communication across channels. In: Proceedings of the Fourth International Conference on Open Source Software (IFIP 2.13), Milan, Italy

Panel: Opportunities and Risks for Open Source Software in Industry

Joseph Feller[1], Björn Lundell[2], Pentti Marttiin[3], Walt Scacchi[4], and Nico Schellingerhout[5]
[1] University College Cork, Ireland, JFeller@afis.ucc.ie,
[2] University of Skövde, Sweden, bjorn.lundell@his.se,
[3] Nokia Siemens Networks, Finland, pentti.marttiin@nsn.com,
[4] University of California Irvine, USA, wscacchi@uci.edu,
[5] Philips Medical Systems, The Netherlands, nico.schellingerhout@philips.com

1 Introduction

Open Source Software (OSS) is a multi-faceted phenomenon which has become an issue of strategic importance for many commercial organisations. Stemming from an ideological issue, with emphasis on freedom and community values, we have recently seen a broader interest in the Open Source phenomenon amongst practitioners in many companies. A number of SMEs and large companies are currently exploring the potential of Open Source, and for some it has become core to their business and development activities.

Open Source is currently evolving and we have yet to see its full potential. In this panel, the goal is to stimulate discussion on the opportunities and risks to be considered with the wider adoption of Open Source systems and methods in the development of software systems in commercial organisations. In particular, the discussion will address the following issues:

- There are many different ways in which Open Source ideas can be adopted by companies, and influence the way in which companies do business and develop software systems. How can firms utilize OSS practices and tools?
- Open Source licensing has created a large commons of public software goods. How can firms create sustainable business models predicated on productizing these "commodities"?
- Open Source utilizes a legal, social and technological architecture to enable a community-based peer-production process. How can firms create sustainable business models predicated on effectively leveraging this process (either through participation or emulation)?

The panel will include short position statements by the panellists and a dialogue between them, followed by a discussion with the audience. Significant time will be allocated to an open discussion on the issues with the audience, and those attending are invited to raise their own concerns and share their own experiences.

Please use the following format when citing this chapter:

Feller, J., Lundell, B., Marttiin, P., Scacchi, W. and Schellingerhout, N., 2008, in IFIP International Federation for Information Processing, Volume 275; *Open Source Development, Communities and Quality*; Barbara Russo, Ernesto Damiani, Scott Hissam, Björn Lundell, Giancarlo Succi; (Boston: Springer), pp. 413–414.

2 About the Panellists

On this international panel, the five panellists are: Joseph Feller (University College Cork), Björn Lundell (University of Skövde), Pentti Marttiin (Nokia Siemens Networks), Walt Scacchi (University of California Irvine), and Nico Schellingerhout (Philips Medical Systems). The panel will be chaired by Walt Scacchi.

Joseph Feller is a Senior Lecturer in Business Information Systems, University College Cork, Ireland. He has co-authored/edited three books on open source. He chaired the IEE/ACM workshop series on Open Source Software Engineering (2001-2005), served as Program Co-Chair for the Third International Conference on Open Source Systems, and is the co-chair for the Open Source and Innovation track at ECIS 2008. Dr. Feller was a principle investigator in the EU FP6 CALIBRE project, and is currently a principle investigator in Open Code, Content and Commerce (O3C) Business Models, a three year project funded by the Irish Research Council for the Humanities and Social Sciences.

Björn Lundell has been involved in a number of collaborations on open source, including the EU FP6 CALIBRE project (2004-2006) and the industrial (ITEA) research project COSI (2005-2008). He is a founding member of the IFIP Working Group 2.13 on Open Source Software, and the founding chair of Open Source Sweden, an industry association established by Swedish Open Source companies.

Pentti Marttiin is a Manager in Nokia Siemens Networks. He has been responsible for deploying OSS based Inner Source and SCM services in Nokia and Nokia Siemens Networks. He received his PhD in information systems (1998), and holds Docent position at Helsinki School of Economics, Finland. He has actively participated in EU projects (IST-MOTION, IST-Tellmaris, ITEA-MOOSE, ITEA-COSI).

Walt Scacchi is senior research scientist and research faculty member in the Institute for Software Research, and also research director of the Computer Game Culture and Technology Laboratory, both at UC Irvine. He received a Ph.D. in Information and Computer Science at University of California, Irvine in 1981. His research interests include open source software development, computer game culture and technology, knowledge-based systems for modeling and simulating complex engineering and business processes, and software acquisition and electronic commerce/business. Last, he was Program Co-Chair of the 2006 Intern. Conf. on Open Source Systems, Como, Italy June 2006, and is General Chair of the 2007 Intern. Conf. on Open Source Systems, Limerick, IR, June 2007.

Nico Schellingerhout is a software team leader and responsible for the InnerSource initiative in Philips Healthcare. He is a task leader in ITEA COSI and has been involved in System Simulation and Software architectures research for over 10 years. He received his training in Computational Physics at the University of Groningen (M.Sc. 1988, Ph.D. 1995). His recent research interest is collaboration of distributed teams and the application of OSS practices in a corporate setting.

Open Source Environments for Collaborative Experiments in e-Science

Andrea Bosin[1], Nicoletta Dessì[1], Maria Grazia Fugini[2], Diego Liberati[3], and Barbara Pes[1]
[1] Università degli Studi di Cagliari, Dipartimento di Matematica e Informatica,
Via Ospedale 72, 09124 Cagliari
andrea.bosin@dsf.unica.it,
{dessi,pes}@unica.it
[2] Politecnico di Milano, Dipartimento di Elettronica e Informazione,
Piazza da Vinci 32, I-20133 MILANO
fugini@elet.polimi.it
[3] IEIIT CNR c/o Politecnico di Milano, Piazza da Vinci 32, I-20133 MILANO
liberati@elet.polimi.it

Open Source Software (OSS) for e-Science should make reference to the paradigm of a distributed surrounding over a multi system mix of Web Services and Grid technologies, allowing data exchanging through services, according to standards in the area of the Grid and of Service Oriented Computing (SOC). In fact, biologists, medical doctors, and scientists are often involved in time consuming experiments and are aware of the degree of difficulty in validating or rejecting a given hypothesis by lab experiments. The benefits of OSS for e-Science consider that as many operating nodes as possible can work cooperatively sharing data, resources, and software, thus avoiding the bottleneck of licenses for distributed use of tools needed to perform *cooperative scientific experiments*. In particular, this chapter presents an architecture based on nodes equipped with a Grid and with Web Services in order to access OSS, showing how scientific experiments can be enacted through the use of a cooperation among OSS sites. Such a choice, besides reducing the cost of the experiments, would support distributed introduction of OSS among other actors of the dynamical networks, thus supporting the awareness about OSS and their diffusion. An OSS environment for cooperative scientific experiments (*e-experiments)* can effectively support the distributed execution of different classes of experiments, from visualization to model identification through clustering and rules generation, in various application fields, such as bioinformatics, neuro-informatics, tele-monitoring, or drug discovery. By applying Web Services and Grid computing, an experiment or a simulation can be executed in a cooperative way on various computation nodes of a network equipped with OSS, allowing data exchange among researchers. Our environment formalizes experiments as *cooperative services* on various computational nodes of a grid network. Basic elements are models, languages, and support tools creating a virtual network of organizational responsibility of the global experiments, according to rules under which each node can execute local services to be accessed by other nodes in order to achieve the whole experiment's results.

The OSS environment supports the simulation/execution of different classes of experiments in bioinformatics (drug discovering, micro-array data analysis,

---

Please use the following format when citing this chapter:

Bosin, A., Dessì, N., Fugini, M.G., Liberati, D. and Pes, B., 2008, in IFIP International Federation for Information Processing, Volume 275; *Open Source Development, Communities and Quality*; Barbara Russo, Ernesto Damiani, Scott Hissam, Björn Lundell, Giancarlo Succi; (Boston: Springer), pp. 415–416.

molecular docking). Each experiment ranges from visualization (browsing and search interfaces), to model identification through clustering and rules generation, and requires tools for correct design and set up of the experiment workflow and for information retrieval (e.g., for searching similar protocols, or descriptive datasheets for chemical reactors). Cooperating scientists who perform joint experiments may require specialized tools (e.g., data mining, or database tools) or computational power (e.g., long calculi for protein analysis based on their forms, or for discarding the irrelevant experiments in drug study) available only at specific nodes. The visualization part is given special attention, considering friendly interfaces and graphical simulations enabling an improved comprehension of currently textual explanations. Also privacy and data security are a major concern in our environment, considering both methods to select trusted nodes within the cooperation network, and/or to obscure or encrypt the transmitted and stored data, to preserve their sensitivity, according to user-formulated security requirements.

The environment supports experiments defined as numerical evaluations carried out on selected data sets according to available methodological approaches. The experiment execution platform is composed of: 1) a distributed workflow; 2) the involved nodes and their relative roles in the experiment; 3) the set of involved resources (data areas, data repositories and e-services). Experiments have some portions, both of processes and of data or knowledge, that can be shared in a collaborative environment. One of the reasons for executing an experiment in a distributed way might be that one organization would need to process data under a specific costly product available on a node because of its lack of skill for developing or using open source equivalent; rather than acquiring the product (e.g. SAS, ORACLE, or MATLAB), the organization might invoke a remote service as OSS available on the remote node. Another reason is that some cooperating organizations might want to inspect data dispersed on their databases, with no changes to their local computational environment. Although heterogeneous services can provide similar capabilities, the researcher is in charge of choosing the most suitable methods to accomplish each task, that is, he is in charge of designing the workflow of the scientific experiment. The run time OSS platform performs service discovery, meeting functional and non functional (e.g., price, security, quality) parameters. If the researcher wants to rerun an experiment, the workflow must take into account the changes in the choice of methods as well as in the availability of services and tools. The researcher interacts and chooses services, workflows, and data in an experimental scenario whose cooperative framework has been defined to extend the integration of scientific experiments to a level of scenario-based interaction. This scenario is profitable for many reasons, like exchanging scientific data and processing tools which results in a reduced number of software acquisitions, load balancing work between specialized researchers, and so on.

List of Demonstrations at The Fourth International Conference on Open Source Software

eResearch Workflows for Studying Free and Open Source Software Development

- James Howison, Syracuse University, US, jhowison@syr.edu
- Andrea Wiggins, Syracuse University, US, awiggins@syr.edu
- Kevin Crowston, Syracuse University, US, crowston@syr.edu

Facilitating Social Network Studies of FLOSS using the OSSNetwork Environment

- Marco A. Balieiro, Faculdade de Computação – Universidade Federal do Pará, BR, ma.balieiro@gmail.com
- Samuel F. de Sousa Júnior, Faculdade de Computação – Universidade Federal do Pará, BR, sfelixjr@gmail.com
- Cleidson R. B. de Souza, Faculdade de Computação – Universidade Federal do Pará, BR, cdesouza@ufpa.br

MIX
Papier aus verantwortungsvollen Quellen
Paper from responsible sources
FSC® C105338

If you have any concerns about our products,
you can contact us on
ProductSafety@springernature.com

In case Publisher is established outside the EU,
the EU authorized representative is:
Springer Nature Customer Service Center GmbH
Europaplatz 3, 69115 Heidelberg, Germany

Printed by Libri Plureos GmbH
in Hamburg, Germany

Paediatric Nephrology

Winnie Kwai Yu Chan
Manson Chon In Kuok

Paediatric Nephrology

Case Studies

Springer

Winnie Kwai Yu Chan, MBBS, FRCP, FRCPCH
Department of Paediatrics
Queen Elizabeth Hospital
Hong Kong, China

Manson Chon In Kuok, MBBS, MPH, MRCPCH
Department of Paediatrics
Queen Elizabeth Hospital
Hong Kong, China

ISBN 978-981-95-5059-3 ISBN 978-981-95-5060-9 (eBook)
https://doi.org/10.1007/978-981-95-5060-9

This Springer imprint is published by the registered company Springer Nature Singapore Pte Ltd.
The registered company address is: 152 Beach Road, #21-01/04 Gateway East, Singapore 189721, Singapore

Foreword

This book focuses on common as well as rare paediatric kidney disorders. The patients are neonates, infants and children cared for by Doctor Winnie K. Y. Chan and her team at Queen Elizabeth Hospital (QEH), Kowloon, Hong Kong.

I met Winnie Chan, MB,BS, FRCPCH, through the Hong Kong Pediatric Nephrology Society (HKPNS). I was born and raised in Hong Kong and am grateful to have received my early medical education at the University of Hong Kong (HKU). Since moving to North America, every time I return to Hong Kong, I would visit my nephrology colleagues at QEH, Princess Margaret Hospital, Prince of Wales Hospital and HKU. More often than not, I would attend HKPNS meetings, where I got to interact with Dr. Chan.

Dr. Winnie Chan is Honorary Assistant Professor at HKU and The Chinese University of Hong Kong. In the early 2000s, she was elected Honorary Secretary and Council Member of HKPNS.

She received the MB, BS medical degree from HKU. Later, she earned a Master of Health Administration degree from the University of New South Wales, Sydney, Australia. She was awarded the MRCP (UK); FRCP (Edin); FHKAM; FHKCP; MRCP Child Heath; and FRCP Child Heath. Moreover, she obtained advanced training in nephrology in 1996 at Mayo Clinic, Rochester, MN, USA; in rheumatology in 2016 at Ann & Robert Lurie Children's Hospital, Chicago, IL, USA; and in 2017 at Hamburg Center for Pediatric & Adolescent Rheumatology, Hamburg, Germany.

With this expertise, it naturally follows that she would be giving courses in nephrology and rheumatology at QEH and be invited to review for local and international medical journals. In the meantime, she found time to complete more than 70 publications in medical journals and book chapters, representing her clinical and research interests.

In summary, this book explores the diverse presentations of kidney disorders in neonates, infants and children. The clarity of the tables and updates on diagnostic work up, treatment and prognosis are superb. Chronic kidney diseases are often silent. Early recognition is crucial in preventing and slowing the rate of progression to end-stage kidney failure. This book paves the way for a more thorough understanding of acute and chronic kidney disorders. It will be immensely useful for nephrologists, paediatricians, general practitioners, medical and nursing clinicians in training.

James C. Chan, M.D., D.Sc.

Professor of Pediatrics,
Tufts University, Courtesy Staff,
Barbara Bush Children's Hospital,
Maine Medical Center
Portland, Maine, USA

Preface

With the advancement in internet technology and easy access to information, we are now overwhelmed with a vast amount of information. Anyone can access medical information without needing to read chapters of medical books. Even without a clear understanding of this information, one can write paragraphs and chapters on any topic in the literature. Information may provide you with data and facts, but it is not knowledge. Medical knowledge requires a deeper understanding, which involves clinical skills, problem-solving techniques, effective interpersonal communication and clinical experience. These clinical skills are not just important; they are integral to the medical field. No patient is the same. With a particular diagnosis, we can obtain millions of pieces of information from the internet, which provides hundreds of articles in a short time. However, in real life, our patients present to us with a complaint, a physical sign and a problem, not a diagnosis. Physicians are like medical detectives. We gather symptoms from the history and identify physical signs to arrive at a differential diagnosis. These skills need training, clinical exposure and experience to develop. Through investigations, we confirm the diagnosis and treat the patient accordingly. Our daily medical decisions are the result of a continuous risk-benefit balance based on various information we gathered and experienced in the past.

Case Studies in Paediatric Nephrology is a series designed for you, the reader. It provides a range of clinical scenarios in general nephrology, from everyday encounters to rare cases, and from a single patient's history to a constellation of patients' clinical courses. Through these case-based discussions, we invite you to engage actively and discover the art in medicine. Our patients, who are our unique and invaluable teachers, have made this series possible. We express our heartfelt gratitude to them once again. By sharing their stories, we learn and develop into better medical doctors, and we hope you will enjoy reading it.

Hong Kong, China Winnie Kwai Yu Chan, MBBS, FRCP, FRCPCH

Contents

Part I

Urinary Tract Infection and CAKUT

Fever Without Localizing Signs

1

1.1 Case Description

Kaiden is a 3-month-old boy born at full term with a birth weight of 3.2 kg. He is breastfeeding and thrives satisfactorily. He was admitted for sudden onset of high fever up to 39 °C for 1 day. Her mother had mild upper respiratory symptoms, which has been resolved a few days ago. Kaiden did not have any respiratory symptoms. Apart from the fever, he appeared well. His feeding was normal, and there was no vomiting or diarrhoea. He passed urine normally. He was given some antipyretic, but the fever persisted; today, the temperature has risen to 40 °C. He was found to be more irritable and behaved unusually; hence, he was brought to the emergency department. Physical examination was uneventful, and he was admitted despite the absence of focalising signs for the infection. His nasopharyngeal swab for microarray of respiratory virus panel was negative. His urine test for nitrite was positive, and the leucocyte was 1+.

1.2 Interactive Case Discussion

How likely is Kaiden to suffer from a urinary tract infection (UTI)?
The diagnosis of urinary tract infection required the isolation of pure growth of bacteria in an uncontaminated sample of urine using a semiquantitative culture method. As the urine culture takes at least 24–48 h before a result is available, the probability of UTI can be supported by clinical diagnosis and laboratory findings (Table 1.1). UTI Calculator (https://uticalc.pitt.edu/) is a web-based calculator developed to help doctors estimate the risk of urinary tract infection in children 2–23 months of age. However, estimation is only a probability that can be used as

W. K. Y. Chan, M. C. I. Kuok, *Paediatric Nephrology*,
https://doi.org/10.1007/978-981-95-5060-9_1

Table 1.1 Features that increase the probability of UTI

Clinical features that increase the likelihood of UTI in children	Laboratory features that increase the possibility of UTI in children
Symptoms present at <12 months old	Urine nitrite positive
Maximum temperature ≥39 °C	Leucocyte esterase positive
History of previous UTI	Presence of white blood cells in urine
Female or uncircumcised male	Positive Gram stain for bacteria
Absence of other foci of infection Acute illnesses like acute otitis media, upper respiratory tract infection, gastroenteritis, pneumonia, meningitis, bronchiolitis and viral syndrome are excluded	
Duration of fever ≥48 hours	

an aid, and the tool is not intended to be (nor should it be used as) a substitute for the exercise of professional judgment. From the clinical presentation, Kaiden is highly likely to get a urinary tract infection.

How do the bedside urine leukocyte esterase and nitrite tests assist in the diagnosis of UTI in children?
Both tests are urine dipstick screening tests for the detection of bacteria in the urine. The urine nitrate reductase test detects the reduction of nitrate to nitrite by the nitrate reductase enzyme present in bacteria. The test has a sensitivity of around 53% and a specificity of 98% in detecting UTI. A urine leukocyte test is used to detect leukocytes in the urine. It has a sensitivity of around 83% and a specificity of 78%. The combination of both tests has a sensitivity of 72% and a specificity of 96% for diagnosing UTI (Table 1.2).

What are the risk factors for urinary tract infections in children?
Risk factors for UTI can be divided into host factors and bacterial factors.

1. Host factors that predispose an infant, a child or an adolescent to UTI include the following:
   (a) Uncircumcised male neonates (foreskin as the site for bacteria colonisation).
   (b) Female after 1 year old (shorter urethra).
   Females <1 year old and uncircumcised males <3 months old have a higher prevalence of urinary tract infection.
   (c) The presence of congenital abnormalities of the kidney and urinary tract (CAKUT) like obstructive uropathy or vesicoureteric reflux.
   (d) Spinal dysraphism and other neurological causes leading to neurogenic bladder and resulting in dysfunctional voiding.
   (e) Immunodeficiency.
   (f) Diabetes mellitus.

Table 1.2 Estimated sensitivity and specificity of the combined urine dipstick tests

Urine leukocyte esterase	Urine nitrate	Likelihood ratio for UTI	Sensitivity of the combined urine tests (%)	Specificity of the combined urine tests (%)
Positive	Positive	28.2	72	96
Positive	Negative	5.5	83	78
Negative	Positive	15.9	53	98

   (g) Sick cell disease.
   (h) Renal or bladder stones.
   (i) Sexual activity.
   (j) Recent urinary tract instrumentation, hospitalisation, or use of antibiotics.
2. Factors that affect the virulent of the bacteria.
   (a) Uropathogenic *Escherichia coli* (UPEC) with the P fimbriae.
   (b) Bacteria lipopolysaccharide.
   (c) Role of Toll-like receptor 4 in the immune defence system.

What are the common organisms for UTI in children?
Gram-negative bacteria are common organisms for UTI in children. These include *Escherichia coli*, *Klebsiella pneumoniae*, *Enterococcus faecalis* and *Proteus mirabilis*. Bacteria like coagulase-negative Staphylococi, *Lactobacillus* and *Corynebacterium* are likely contaminants.

Kaiden had a bag urine culture saved, and it showed >10 epithelial cells/HPF, the presence of a mixed growth of *Corynebacterium* and *Escherichia coli* with a bacterial colony count of 10^5. You are not sure whether this could be a contaminated urine, so a catheterised urine sample was saved to repeat the urine culture, and an empirical antibiotic was given.

How would the method of urine collection affect the diagnosis of UTI?
The method of urine collection is important in making the diagnosis, as a contaminated urine sample will give a false positive result. Table 1.3 summarises the pros and cons of the method of urine collection.

How would you decide the reliability of the urine culture?
The method and technique of urine collection will affect the reliability of urine culture.

Scenarios that may suggest a high probability of contamination instead of a genuine urinary tract infection are as follows;

- Gram-positive bacteria growth from the urine culture
- The presence of epithelial cells in the urine sample instead of white blood cells
- Presence of > one organism isolated in the urine culture
- Low bacterial colony count* (refer to Table 1.4)
- Unusual microorganisms which are not uropathogenic

Table 1.3 Advantages and disadvantages of the different methods of urine collection

Suprapubic tap urine for culture	– Least contaminated urine sample – Invasive procedure – It may not be practical as there is a need to wait for a full bladder after a feed and perform the tap before the urine is voided when a needle is inserted into the bladder
Transurethral catheterisation urine for culture	– The next best test for saving a urine sample. It has a lower chance of contamination, provided the catheterisation is performed under a good aseptic technique – Sometimes technically challenging, especially in male infants with phimosis
Voided sample (clean catch)	– Clean catch urine required a cooperative patient and parents – Only children >2 years old can cooperate to save a midstream urine – Requires the technique of parents and is time-consuming – May not have time to wait for sick children who need immediate treatment – Combine with the voiding stimulating method may improve the speed and success in obtaining a proper urine sample
Voided sample (bag urine)	– The highest rate of contamination – Non-invasive – Least cost-effective – Useful for dipstick urine screening but not for culture

Table 1.4 Bacterial colony forming units suggesting UTI in various methods of urine collection

Method of urine collection	Number of bacterial colony forming units (CFU)/ml of urine suggesting UTI
Sterile supra-pubic tap urine	Any growth
Midstream urine	$>10^5$ CFU/ml of urine
Catheterised urine	$>10^5$ CFU/ml of urine
Bag urine	High contamination rate and is not suitable for diagnosis of UTI

What bacterial colony counts on urine culture represent a urinary tract infection?

Urine is sterile; hence, the presence of bacteria in urine suggests a UTI. However, the method of urine collection and periurethral colonisation may affect the bacterial colony count by contamination. In general, a positive urine culture with ≥100,000 colony-forming units (CFU)/ml of a single pathogen on properly collected urine is considered significant (Table 1.4). The bacterial colony counts need to be interpreted with other clinical features to confirm a diagnosis of UTI. In appropriate clinical context, the diagnosis of UTI can be made even with a lower bacterial colony counts of 10^3–10^4 CFU/mL.

What features suggest acute pyelonephritis instead of cystitis in Kaiden?

In nonverbal patients and small infants, it is difficult to differentiate an infection in the upper urinary tract (acute pyelonephritis) from a lower urinary tract infection (cystitis, urethritis). A patient with a lower urinary tract infection typically is not septic and complains of dysuria, suprapubic pain, urinary frequency and haematuria. Systemic features, including fever, poor oral feeding, vomiting and lethargy, are features of acute pyelonephritis. In adolescent, loin pain may present. In acute pyelonephritis, inflammatory markers like c-reactive protein and procalcitonin may increase, and in severe cases, serum creatinine may be elevated. Hence, in Kaiden's scenarios, apart from a proper urine culture, blood culture, blood test for electrolytes, serum urea, creatinine and blood counts would be helpful in his management.

What empirical antibiotics would you choose to treat Kaiden?

In view of their young age, persistent high fever and decreased activity of Kaiden, intravenous antibiotics would be commenced after sepsis work, including saving a catheterised urine for culture. The choice of antibiotics depends on the antibiotic resistance pattern in each region. Since *E. coli* is likely to be the pathogen, the recommended starting antibiotics are listed in Table 1.5. Kaiden was treated with intravenous cefuroxime and his fever subsided within 24 hours. His catheterized urine grew *Escherichia coli* which is sensitive to most commonly used antibiotics.

Will you arrange any further investigation on Kaiden?

The investigations after a urinary tract infection include performing an ultrasound of the urinary tract, micturating cystourethrogram (MCUG), voiding urosonography (VUS) and DMSA renal scan. This imaging helps to assess the risk of recurrent urinary tract infection and the extent of renal damage after a urinary tract infection, especially post-acute pyelonephritis.

The extent and recommendation of investigation vary, and there are different recommendations from different guidelines, depending on the risk factors for recurrent UTI. The indications, advantages and disadvantages of each imaging modality are summarised in Table 1.6.

Table 1.5 Common antibiotics and doses for treatment of UTI in children. Dose adjustment is required for impaired renal function

Antibiotics	Dose (mg/kg/dose)	Dose frequency
Co-amoxiclav (amoxicillin +clavulanate)	25 mg	Every 8 hours
Cefuroxime	30–50 mg	Every 8 hours
Cefotaxime	30–50 mg	Every 8 hours
Ceftriaxone	50 mg	Every 12 or 24 hours
Amikacin	15 mg	Every 24 hours

Table 1.6 The roles of different radiological investigations in assessing a child with urinary tract infection

Imaging modalities	Indications	Advantages and disadvantages
Ultrasound (USG)	– Detect genitourinary anomalies, including duplex kidneys, hydronephrosis and hydroureters – Assess bladder wall thickness – Measure post-void residual urine	– Non-invasive, easy-to-repeat examination – Can be performed by bedside as the point of care
Micturating cystourethrogram (MCUG)	– Better visualisation of the bladder structure, capacity, trabeculations or sacculations of the bladder wall – Detection of vesicoureteric reflux and grade of the severity—the gold standard – Better detection of post-urethral valve	– A fluoroscopic study exposes the patient to irradiation, especially over the genetalia, which is exposed during the MCUG study – Invasive examination as it involves bladder catheterisation
Voiding ultrasonography (VUS)	– Detect vesicoureteric reflux	– Radiation-free examination as it uses intravesical ultrasound contrast – Still needs bladder catheterisation – Can be performed in the same setting as USG kidney and bladder examination
Dimercaptosuccinate scan (DMSA)	– Detect acute pyelonephritis at the acute phase and any renal scarring 3–6 months after an episode of acute pyelonephritis – Give information on the differential function of individual kidneys – Detect renal agenesis, ectopic kidney or horseshoe kidney	– Involve the setup of intravenous access for DMSA injection

1.3 Case Illustrations

The case illustrates the common difficulties encountered in diagnosing urinary tract infection in daily practice. It also exemplifies how vigilant clinical observation and appropriate laboratory testing can help diagnose and address potentially serious conditions such as urinary tract infections in infants.

Suggested Further Readings

1. Kaufman J, Temple-Smith M, Sanci L. Urinary tract infections in children: an overview of diagnosis and management. BMJ Paediatr Open. 2019;3(1):e000487.
2. A't Hoen L, Bogaert G, Radmayr C, Dogan HS, Nijman RJ, Quaedackers J, et al. Update of the EAU/ESPU guidelines on urinary tract infections in children. J Pediatr Urol. 2021;17(2):200–7.
3. Mattoo TK, Shaikh N, Nelson CP. Contemporary management of urinary tract infection in children. Pediatrics. 2021;147(2):e2020012138.
4. Yang SS, Tsai JD, Kanematsu A, Han CH. Asian guidelines for urinary tract infection in children. J Infect Chemother. 2021;27(11):1543–54.
5. Oliveira EA, Mak RH. Urinary tract infection in pediatrics: an overview. J Pediatr. 2020;96:65–79.

2 An Unusual Neonatal Fever

2.1 Case Description

Baby Jordan was born at full term with a birth weight of 3.2 kg. The antenatal history was uneventful, and antenatal ultrasound scans were normal. He was well after birth and was discharged home on day 3 with his mother uneventfully. He was well until 25 days old when he was noticed to kick up a temperature of 38.9 °C. He was brought to see a private doctor, and a bag of urine was saved. The urine microscopy showed numerous white blood cells. He was then referred to the emergency department and was admitted. Upon examination, Joran had a fever of up to 40 °C, his heart rate increased to 200 beats per minute with sinus rhythm, respiratory rate increased to 50 breaths per minute, and oxygen saturation was 94% in room air. He was tired-looking with skill mottling, and the blood pressure was 65/45 mmHg. He was resuscitated with nasal oxygen and intravenous normal saline bolus at 20 ml/kg infusion. His heart rate improved to 180 beats per minute. Initial blood test showed haemoglobin 10 g/dL, white blood cell of 2.3×10^9/L, platelet 65×10^9/L, aPTT 74.7 s, PT of 18 s, INR 1.7, D-dimer 4686 ng/ml and serum lactate 3.6 mmol/L. His chest X-ray was normal.

2.2 Interactive Case Discussion

What did the clinical picture suggest?
Baby Jordan was having severe septicaemia with septic shock and disseminated intravascular coagulopathy. He has to be resuscitated with the following:

- Fluid boluses to correct the hypotension and a vasopressor like noradrenaline infusion may be needed if his blood pressure was persistently low after adequate fluid resuscitation.

W. K. Y. Chan, M. C. I. Kuok, *Paediatric Nephrology*,
https://doi.org/10.1007/978-981-95-5060-9_2

- Fresh frozen plasma infusion to correct the deranged clotting profile.
- Sepsis workup including catheterised urine culture and blood culture.
- Started intravenous board spectrum antibiotics immediately after sepsis workup.

After initial stabilisation, intravenous ampicillin and meropenem were commenced. His blood test showed raised urea to 8 mmol/L, creatinine to 60 umol/L and C-reactive protein to 226 mg/L (normal < 5mg/L). Bedside USG kidneys were normal. Subsequent blood and urine cultures grew *Escherichia coli* sensitive to cefuroxime, amoxicillin-clavulanic acid and amikacin. The antibiotics were adjusted accordingly. Jordan was diagnosed with an *E. coli* UTI with septicaemia. After 14 days of antibiotics, a USG kidney was repeated in Fig. 2.1.

Will you perform a further investigation on baby Jordan after the USG examination?

The clinical picture of baby Jordan suggested acute pyelonephritis with septicaemia. A normal USG kidney does not exclude vesicoureteric reflux. A full workup for urogenital abnormalities should proceed, especially. Hence, a MCUG and a Tc-99m DMSA were arranged (Figs. 2.2 and 2.3).

What is vesicoureteric reflux (VUR), and what are its causes?

Vesicoureteric reflux is the retrograde urine flow from the urinary bladder to the upper urinary tract.

Anatomically, the ureter is a tubular structure connecting the renal pelvis proximally to the bladder distally. It serves as the pipe that drains urine from the kidneys and into the urinary bladder. The ureteric openings are located just lateral to the bladder trigone. The distal-most part of the ureter is continuous as an oblique tunnel within the urinary bladder. It is known as the intramural or the intravesical part. This oblique insertion is of utmost importance as the orifice typically is functionally closed when the bladder contracts to empty the urine. Hence, the retrograde flow of

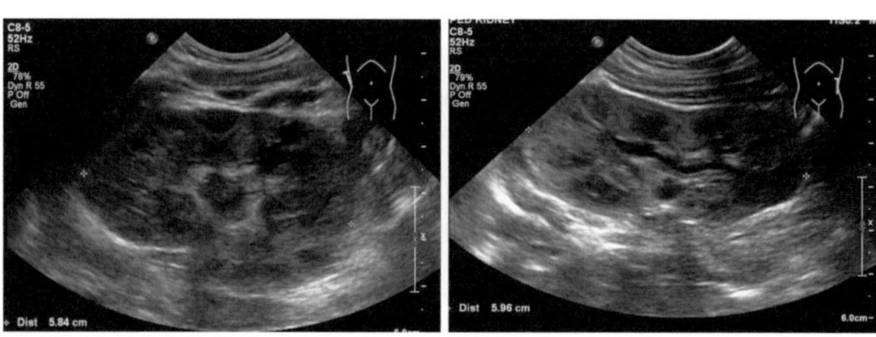

Fig. 2.1 The ultrasound of both kidneys showed normal size (left kidney 5.96 cm, right kidney 5.84 cm). The echogenicity of both kidneys was normal, with normal cortico-medullary differentiation. The central sinus of the left kidney was prominent; otherwise, there was no hydronephrosis or renal stone

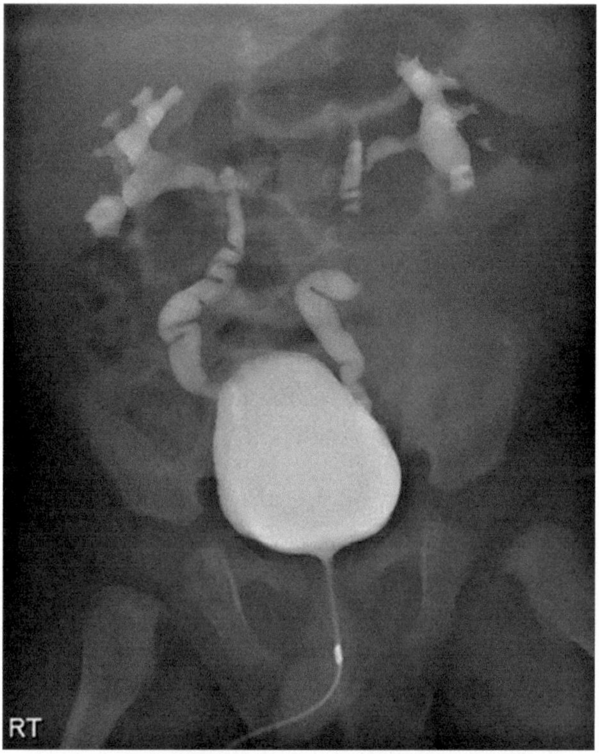

Fig. 2.2 The micturating cystourethrogram (MCUG) showed bilateral grade 4 VUR with tortuous ureters and blunting of fornices. The bladder contour appeared normal, and the posterior urethra was of normal size

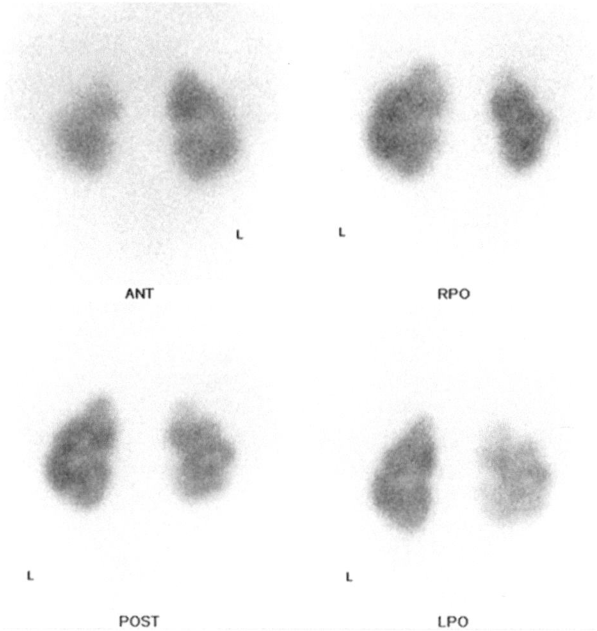

Fig. 2.3 The Tc-99m DMSA scan, which was performed 3 months after the episode of acute pyelonephritis, showed a multifocal decrease in cortical uptakes in both kidneys. Scarring was more severe over the right kidney than the left kidney. The differential renal cortical mass ratio, left-to-right, was 58%:42%

urine is prevented. During the ureteric peristalsis, ureteric pressure increases and opens the orifice momentarily to propel urine into the bladder. After urine propulsion, the ureter loses its pressure. The intravesical pressure will then close the intramural ureteral part. The approximate ratio of intramural tunnel length to the ureteral diameter is approximately 5 to 1. A decrease in this ratio is believed to be one of the reasons for this urinary reflux.

Other causes of vesicoureteric reflux include the following:

- Ectopic ureteric opening, e.g. duplex kidney and drainage system resulting in ectopic ureter
- Immature bladder discoordination
- Bladder dysfunction or neurogenic bladder due to underlying neurological disease (e.g. myelomeningocele)
- Bladder outlet obstruction, like posterior urethral valve

How would you classify VUR, and why is it important to classify different grades of VUR?

MCUG, with fluoroscopy, is the gold standard for diagnosing and grading VUR. The international grading system grades VUR into five grades with progression in the severity of the retrograde of urine flow and associated ureter and renal pyelocalyceal system. The descriptions of the grades are listed in Table 2.1.

How would you manage baby Jordan?

There has yet to be a universal consensus on managing primary VUR. The approach can be observational with or without antibiotic prophylaxis or surgical intervention.

Antibiotic prophylaxis aims to prevent recurrent pyelonephritis that causes renal scarring. The surgical approach corrects the VUR. Several surgical techniques are available, including endoscopic Deflux™ injection at the vesicoureteric junction or laparoscopic reimplantation of the ureters. Rarely open laparotomy is required nowadays. The choice of surgical intervention depends on the severity of VUR, surgical fitness of the patient, the surgeon's experience and expertise.

Table 2.1 The international grading system of VUR

Gradings	Description of the gradings
Grade 1	Reflux only into the non-dilated ureter
Grade 2	Reflux into the ureter and the renal pelvis without dilatation
Grade 3	Reflux with mildly dilated ureter and pelvicalyceal system
Grade 4	Reflux with the tortuous and moderately dilated ureter with blunting of renal fornices. The papillary impression is preserved
Grade 5	Reflux with the tortuous and severely dilated ureter, dilatation of pelvicalyces with loss of fornices and papillary impression

Will baby Jordan develop into renal failure?

Both VUR and UTI are common in children. The prevalence of VUR in the general paediatric population has been estimated to be around 17–20%. Some patients with VUR develop into reflux nephropathy (RN), some patients with RN develop chronic kidney disease and rarely, some patients (<1%) will develop end-stage renal disease.

What is reflux nephropathy?

When a patient with VUR has repeated urinary tract infections, he may develop progressive renal scars, which is acquired reflux nephropathy. In this group of patients, we may try to correct the VUR and start antibiotic prophylaxis to avoid repeated urinary tract infections, hoping it works.

However, there is another group of patients born with "congenital scarring" or renal dysplasia associated with prenatal VUR. It is postulated that the mechanical high pressure of the sterile fetal urine and the abnormal bladder hypertonicity with uncoordinated voiding during the fetal period may interfere with the development of the renal parenchyma and its interaction with the ureteric bud, causing abnormal differentiation of renal parenchyma. This type of congenital reflux nephropathy is more commonly seen in males.

Baby Jordan developed another episode of UTI shortly after the first UTI, which was managed with systemic antibiotics again. Hence, he was put on long-term prophylactic antibiotics, i.e. oral trimethoprim at 1–2 mg/kg nocte. He developed the third episode of UTI 2 months after the second episode. Hence, transurethral Deflux™ injections were performed. A DMSA scan performed 6 months after the first UTI showed diffuse renal scarring. A repeated MCUG showed persistently bilateral VUR post-Deflux™ injection. Hence, a laparoscopic reimplantation of both ureters was performed. He was thriving, and there was no recurrence of urinary tract infection after the surgical intervention.

Who is at higher risk of progressing to chronic kidney disease or even end-stage renal disease in patients with VUR?

Several groups of patients are more prone to develop renal impairment as they grow up. They are as follows:

- Children with high grade VUR, i.e. grade IV–V
- VUR secondary to other organic causes like urinary outflow tract obstruction (e.g. posterior urethral valve), neurogenic bladder with detrusor instability
- Presence of bilateral renal scarring
- Presence of renal hypoplasia
- Reduced GFR at early presentation
- Persistent proteinuria, which signifies ongoing renal damage

How would you manage children with reflux nephropathy?
As there is a risk of progressive deterioration in renal function in this group of patients. One has to do the following:

- Evaluate and treat any voiding dysfunction.
- Treat every acute pyelonephritis promptly, and a delay in treatment increases the risk of scar formation.
- Consider surgical intervention to correct VUR.
- Consider the use of prophylactic antibiotics to prevent recurrent UTI, especially in high-grade VUR.
- Correct underlying secondary causes for the VUR if there are any, like ablation of the posterior urethral value, treatment of neurogenic bladder.
- Control blood pressure.
- Monitor the degree of proteinuria and control proteinuria with an angiotensin-converting enzyme inhibitor.

What is the prognosis for Jordan?
With the correction of VUR, further urinary tract infection is unlikely, and most children remain stable after surgical correction. However, Jordan's DMSA scans showed multifocal scarring after repeated urinary tract infections. Hence, he needs regular follow-up to assess his subsequent renal function. Besides blood tests for eGFR, regular ultrasound scans are advised to monitor kidney growth, and DMSA scans to assess subsequent differentiated renal function. Children with bilateral scarred kidneys, due to reflux nephropathy, will have a higher risk for hypertension and proteinuria, which have to be monitored and treated accordingly in the long run.

2.3 Case Illustrations

This case illustrates an infant with vesicoureteric reflux presented as severe urinary tract infection complicated by septic shock and disseminated intravascular coagulopathy in the neonatal period. A normal renal ultrasound does not exclude VUR; given the severity of the urinary tract infection and the age of baby Jordan, a more extensive workup is warranted.

Suggested Further Readings

1. Hari P, Meena J, Kumar M, Sinha A, Thergaonkar RW, Iyengar A, et al. Evidence-based clinical practice guideline for management of urinary tract infection and primary vesicoureteric reflux. Pediatr Nephrol. 2024;39(5):1639–68.
2. Läckgren G, Cooper CS, Neveus T, Kirsch AJ. Management of vesicoureteral reflux: what have we learned over the last 20 years? Front Pediatr. 2021;9:650326.

Near Miss

3

3.1 Case Description

A previously well 16-year-old girl was admitted for fever for 2 days with progressive 'weakness'. She had coryzal symptoms for 2–3 weeks before admission and started to have a high fever 2 days ago. She felt nauseous and vomited undigested food several times, but there was no diarrhoea. She had poor appetite and felt weak. There was no urinary frequency or dysuria. Her menstrual period was normal, and she denied any sexual activity.

Upon admission, she was conscious, with a GCS of 15/15 and a high fever of up to 40.5 °C. Her blood pressure was low at 85/40 mmHg with tachycardia up to 140 beats per minute. She was resuscitated with a fluid bolus of normal saline, and her blood pressure increased back to 90/45 mmHg, but she remained in tachycardia with a heart rate of 140 bpm. Physical examination did not detect any focus of infection. There was no loin pain. On physical examination, her abdomen was soft, and signs of peritonitis were absent. Her lower limbs showed a muscle power 4/5, and peripheral jerks were depressed. Her urine pregnancy test was negative, and her urine routine was negative.

Her initial blood test showed a white cell count (WCC) of 13.3×10^9/L, with neutrophils of 11.7×10^9/L and lymphocytes of 0.6×10^9/L. Her haemoglobin and platelet counts were normal. The C-reactive protein (CRP) was 244 mg/L (normal: <5 mg/L), and procalcitonin was 80.2 ng/mL (normal <2 ng/mL). Her renal function test showed normal electrolytes, but her urea was 8.5 mmol/L (3.0–7.4 mmol/L), and creatinine was 92 µmol/L (48–75 µmol/L). Her liver function test, serum albumin and amylase were normal. Her chest X-ray and KUB were normal. Sepsis workup, including blood culture and urine culture, were obtained. Her vitals were stabilised with noradrenaline infusion, intravenous board spectrum antibiotic, hydrocortisone and gamma-globulin infusion was empirically commenced for a suspicion of neurological disease.

W. K. Y. Chan, M. C. I. Kuok, *Paediatric Nephrology*,
https://doi.org/10.1007/978-981-95-5060-9_3

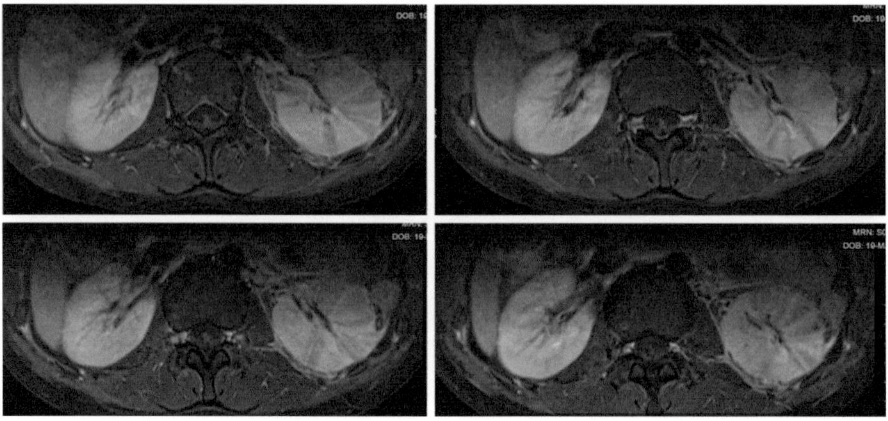

Fig. 3.1 These are the T1 with contrast MRI films of the lumbar spine. It incidentally picked up the images of the kidneys. The left kidney showed multifocal hypo-enhancing areas, which were compatible with acute pyelonephritis of the left kidney

While awaiting the results of the sepsis workup, an urgent MRI of the spine was taken to exclude the possibility of Guillain-Barre syndrome causing the lower limb areflexia and weakness. The brain and spinal cord MRI were normal, but the left kidney was incidentally found to have abnormal signals (Fig. 3.1).

3.2 Interactive Case Discussion

An urgent CT abdomen was performed to identify the pathology better and detect any other intra-abdominal pathology. What did the film show?
The CT abdomen showed evidence of acute pyelonephritis of the left kidney, with the whole left kidney swollen, and this was the cause of septic shock in this patient. The patient has undergone several neurological investigations, including lumbar puncture, nerve conduction velocity and autoimmune encephalitis panels. All these investigations were negative. Hence, the lower limbs weakness was just one of the manifestations of septic shock in this patient (Fig. 3.2a, b).

What is acute pyelonephritis? How does it occur?
It is a severe bacterial infection causing acute inflammation of the kidneys. It usually occurs as a complication of lower urinary tract infection such that the infection ascends to cause acute pyelonephritis. The spread of disease and seed of the kidney hematogenous is another possibility, though less common.

What are the possible organisms causing acute pyelonephritis?
Escherichia coli is by far the most common cause of acute pyelonephritis and urinary tract infections in children. *Klebsiella pneumoniae* is the second most common

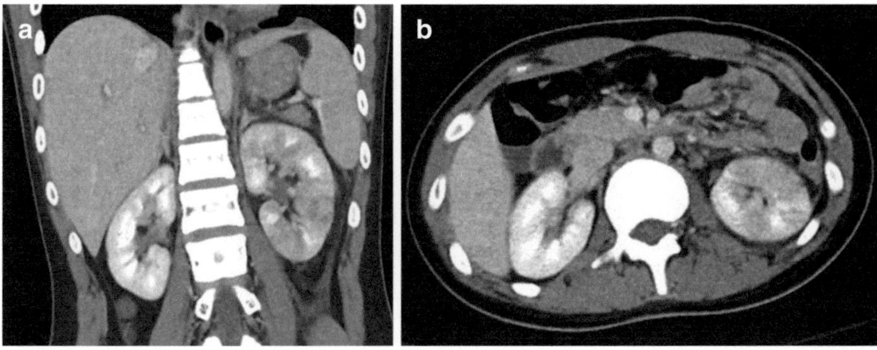

Fig. 3.2 (**a**) In contrast, the CT abdomen's coronal plane showed the left kidney was swollen with areas of hypo-enhancement over the upper, middle and lower poles of the kidney. There was no hydronephrosis, and no renal stone was identified. (**b**) In contrast, the axial plane of the CT abdomen showed the left kidney with areas of hypo-enhancement and perinephric strandings. The right kidney was normal

Table 3.1 Common organisms that cause acute pyelonephritis

	Organisms
Gram-negative bacteria	Uropathogenic *Escherichia coli* (UPEC), *Klebsiella pneumoniae*, *Proteus mirabilis*, *Pseudomonas aeruginosa*
Gram-positive bacteria	*Staphylococcus saprophyticus*, *Enterococcus* spp., Group B streptococcus, *Staphylococcus aureus*
Fungi	*Candida* spp.

causative organism, followed by *Proteus*, *Pseudomonas*, *Enterococci*, *Staphylococci* and other enterobacteria. In recent years, extended-spectrum beta-lactamase (ESBL)-producing bacteria has become an increasing concern, especially in the choice of initial antibiotics treatment. It was reported that around 14% of paediatric UTIs are caused by ESBL-producing Enterobacteriaceae [2]. They are associated with prolonged hospital stays. The presence of vesicoureteral reflux, previous UTI and recent antibiotic use are risk factors for ESBL urinary tract infection (Table 3.1).

Why is Escherichia coli so virulent and causes acute pyelonephritis?

Uropathogenic *Escherichia coli* (UPEC) is the leading causative agent of UTI. It initially colonises the human host by adhering to the bladder epithelium. The bacterial invasion of the urothelial epithelial cells then follows adhesion. Uropathogenic *Escherichia coli* possesses several characteristics that account for its virulence, including the following:

- Adhesive structure: flagella, outer membrane vesicles, pili and non-pili adhesin and lipopolysaccharides [3]
- Toxin: α-haemolysin, cytotoxic necrotizing factor 1 (CNF1) and vacuolating autotransporter cytotoxin [3]

- Iron-acquisition system: To ensure adequate levels of intracellular iron by upregulating the expression of genes involved in iron acquisition in response to iron limitation encountered within the human urinary tract [3]
- Biofilms formation: to allow bacteria to survive antimicrobial treatments and resist the host immune response

What are the risk factors for acute pyelonephritis?
The cystitis risk factors apply to acute pyelonephritis and are summarised in Table 3.2.

Was the patient's clinical picture classical for acute pyelonephritis?
Pyelonephritis typically manifests acutely with signs and symptoms of both systemic inflammation and bladder infection. Hence, affected patients will have systemic signs of fever, chills, rigour and symptoms of bladder inflammation like urinary frequency, urgency and dysuria. In young infants, the symptoms and signs of acute pyelonephritis and cystitis may NOT be easily differentiated; hence, most febrile urinary tract infections are treated as acute pyelonephritis. Theoretically, as the patient grows older, it is easier to distinguish the two.

However, the clinical presentation and disease severity vary widely, from mild flank pain with low-grade fever or no fever to septic shock. Up to 20% of adult patients with acute pyelonephritis do not have bladder symptoms, making the diagnosis difficult at the initial presentation. Our adolescent patient presented with septic shock without initial symptoms and signs to suggest pyelonephritis; though rare, it is not uncommonly encountered. Her initial symptoms of lower limb weakness misled the management team.

How do the different imaging modalities help you in the management of a child suspected to have acute pyelonephritis?
The diagnosis of acute pyelonephritis is clinical and based on the microbiological result. Radiological investigations help in the management of complicated scenarios and guide treatment options. The information obtained from various radiological imaging is summarised in Table 3.3.
A Technetium-99m dimercaptosuccinic acid (DMSA) renal scan was performed for the patient 1 week after admission (Fig. 3.3).

Table 3.2 Risk factors for acute pyelonephritis

Female Sexual activity
CAKUT, especially lesions with urinary outflow tract obstruction or obstructive uropathy
Neurogenic bladder
Foreign body like Foley's catheter in situ, double J catheters in the urinary system
Vesico-ureteric reflux
Renal stone
Post renal transplant
Immunocompromised patients
Diabetes mellitus (emphysematous pyelonephritis is a rare, necrotizing, gas-forming infection associated with diabetes reported in adults)

Table 3.3 Roles of different radiological modalities in the management of acute pyelonephritis

Radiological modalities	Indication and information obtained
Plain X-ray	May detect urinary tract calculi and occasionally may demonstrate gas within the collecting system (emphysematous pyelonephritis), which is a rare complication of diabetes mellitus
Ultrasound of the kidneys and urinary tract system	Ultrasound is insensitive to the changes of acute pyelonephritis, with most patients having 'normal' scans. Abnormalities are identified in only ~25% of cases. Possible features include the following: – Particulate matter or debris detected in an obstructed collecting system may indicate a pyonephrosis – Reduced areas of cortical vascularity detected by power Doppler – Gas bubbles (emphysematous pyelonephritis) may be detected – Abnormal echogenicity of the renal parenchyma, for example, focal hypoechoic regions, may indicate focal oedema or hyperechoic regions may indicate local bleeding. Ultrasound is, however, useful in assessing local complications such as the following: – Hydronephrosis – Renal abscess formation – Renal infarction – Perinephric collections
CT scan with contrast	Post-contrast CT: – In acute pyelonephritis, one or more focal wedge-like regions may appear swollen and demonstrate reduced enhancement compared with the normal portions of the kidney – If imaged during the excretory phase, a striated nephrogram may also be visible
MRI	In acute pyelonephritis, the kidney demonstrates wedge-shaped regions of altered signal: – T1: affected region(s) appear hypointense compared with the normal kidney parenchyma – T2: hyperintense compared to normal kidney parenchyma – T1 C+: reduced enhancement – DWI: round or wedge-shaped parenchymal areas, hyperintense on DWI with corresponding low ADC due to oedema
DMSA	Technetium-99m dimercaptosuccinic acid (DMSA) demonstrates a similar reduction in renal perfusion and function, which appears as one or more patchy scintigraphy defects in the outline of the kidneys

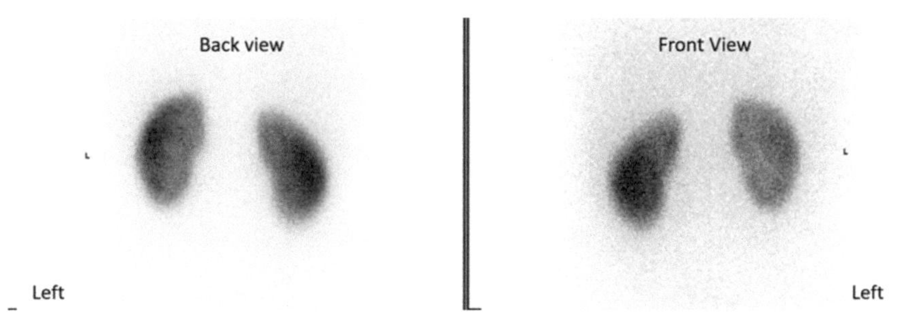

Fig. 3.3 Mild to moderate decreased DMSA uptakes in the left kidney, more severe over the lower 1/3 and lower pole compatible with acute pyelonephritis. The differential cortical mass ratio was 43% (left):57% (right)

The urine culture of the patient came back to have ESBL-producing *Escherichia coli*. She received vancomycin and meropenem at admission for coverage of her septic shock. The antibiotics was narrowed down to meropenem according to antibiotic sensitivity. She recovered uneventfully and was discharged with a follow up DMSA scan, which performed 6 months later and was normal.

What is the prognosis of the patient?
Mild acute kidney injury from inflammation-related hemodynamic shifts is common, and the damage resolves quickly with treatment. Long-term renal scarring is not common in the absence of coexisting urinary tract obstruction. Recurrent pyelonephritis is also uncommon, and the reported recurrence rate is <10% in general. If there was recurrent acute pyelonephritis, a detailed assessment is needed as there is likely a predisposing cause. Our patient had a normal DMSA scan 6 months later; hence, her prognosis is good.

3.3 Case Illustrations

Acute pyelonephritis has the potential to cause septicemia, septic shock and even death if the patient was not managed promptly. Patients with acute pyelonephritis may have ambiguous symptoms and are at major risk of serious complications if left undiagnosed. This case illustrates an uncommon and extreme presentation of acute pyelonephritis. The rising prevalence of *Escherichia coli* resistant to fluoroquinolones and trimethoprim-sulfamethoxazole complicates empirical oral therapy. A board spectrum antibiotic which covers ESBL-*E Coli* is necessary in critically ill patient with the suspicion of acute pyelonephritis.

Suggested Further Readings

1. Morello W, La Scola C, Alberici I, Montini G. Acute pyelonephritis in children. Pediatr Nephrol. 2016;31:1253–65.
2. Flokas ME, Detsis M, Alevizakos M, Mylonakis E. Prevalence of ESBL-producing Enterobacteriaceae in paediatric urinary tract infections: a systematic review and meta-analysis. J Infect. 2016;73(6):547–57.
3. Zagaglia C, Ammendolia MG, Maurizi L, Nicoletti M, Longhi C. Urinary tract infections caused by uropathogenic Escherichia coli strains—new strategies for an old pathogen. Microorganisms. 2022;10(7):1425.

4 Double the Drain, Double the Drama

4.1 Case Description

Dorothy was delivered at term via vaginal birth, weighing 3.5 kg. Antenatal imaging raised suspicion of a left duplex kidney; otherwise, the antenatal course was unremarkable. A postnatal ultrasound at 2 weeks of age confirmed the presence of a left duplex kidney, showing a dilated renal pelvis measuring 1.6 cm in the upper moiety with hydroureter. The central calyces over the left lower moiety also appeared prominent (Fig. 4.1).

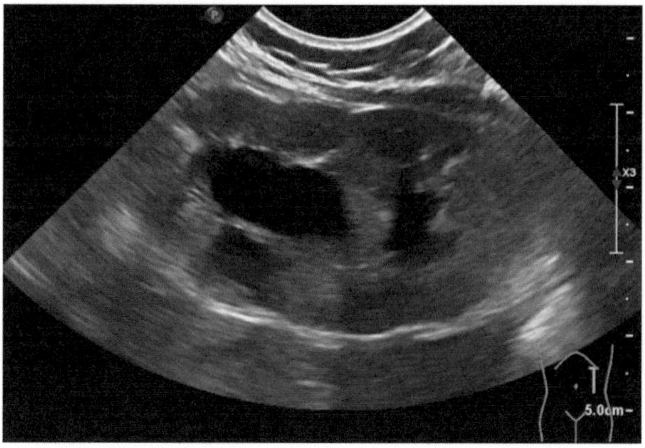

Fig. 4.1 Ultrasound showed a duplex kidney with hydronephrosis over the left upper moiety

W. K. Y. Chan, M. C. I. Kuok, *Paediatric Nephrology*,
https://doi.org/10.1007/978-981-95-5060-9_4

4.2 Interactive Case Discussion

What is a duplex kidney, and how common is it?
A duplex kidney is a type of congenital anomaly of the kidney and urinary tract (CAKUT) characterised by the presence of two pelvicalyceal systems in a single kidney, typically referred to as the upper and lower moieties. The condition can be classified into (i) a complete duplex kidney, where two ureters drain separately into the bladder, and (ii) an incomplete duplex kidney, where two ureters join before entering the bladder as a single ureter.

The reported prevalence of duplex kidney is around 1–2% in the general population. However, the actual prevalence may be even higher as some patients remain asymptomatic and undiagnosed without imaging. The condition seems to be more commonly detected in females, possibly due to a higher incidence of urinary tract infections in adult women, prompting further investigations. The left kidney is more commonly affected than the right kidney, although the underlying cause for this laterality remains unclear. Bilateral duplex systems are observed in about 10–20% of cases.

What are the common clinical presentations in these patients?
Urinary tract infections (UTI) have traditionally been the classical clinical presentation of a duplex kidney. However, with advancements in antenatal imaging and increased awareness, prenatal detection has become the most frequent mode of detection before the patients have any symptoms. Abdominal mass from an obstructed moiety and continuous urinary dribbling due to an ectopic ureter are other recognised but less common presentations. In our experience, around one-third of duplex kidneys were discovered incidentally during imaging for unrelated issues, highlighting the benign and asymptomatic nature of this condition in some patients.

Dorothy underwent further investigations to evaluate the presence of associated anomalies in the setting of a duplex kidney with hydronephrosis. A micturating cystourethrogram (MCUG) revealed left grade 2 vesicoureteral reflux (VUR). A MAG-3 (mercaptoacetyltriglycine) radioisotope renogram scan showed impaired perfusion in the left upper moiety, while the lower moiety had preserved perfusion and function, with no evidence of outflow obstruction. A DMSA (dimercaptosuccinic acid) scan performed at 6 months of age showed a cortical mass ratio of 45% (left) to 55% (right), with the left upper moiety to lower moiety ratio of 15% to 85% (Fig. 4.2).

What other conditions are commonly associated with a duplex kidney?
Ureterocele and ectopic ureter are two conditions commonly associated with duplex kidneys, occurring in approximately one-fifth of patients with duplex kidneys. A ureterocele is a cystic dilatation of the intravesical portion of the distal ureter, forming a sac-like pouch within the bladder. It may cause partial or complete urinary obstruction, leading to hydroureteronephrosis, and can be associated with

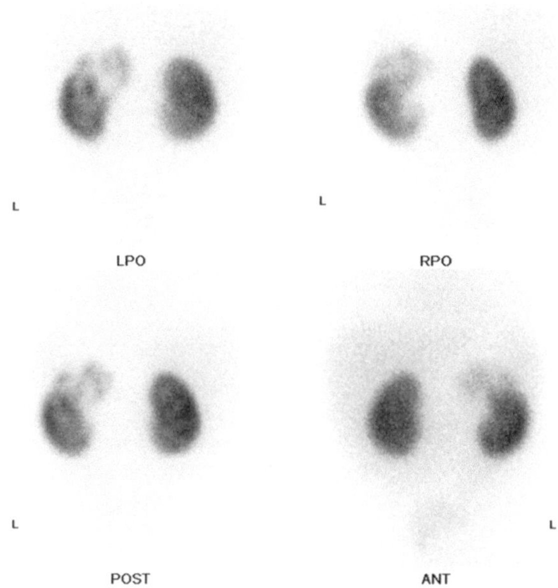

Fig. 4.2 A DMSA scan showed markedly decreased uptake at the upper moiety of the left duplex kidney. The cortical mass ratio of upper-to-lower moiety was 15%:85%

vesicoureteral reflux (VUR). In rare cases, a large ureterocele may prolapse into the bladder neck or urethra, resulting in urinary retention.

An ectopic ureter refers to an abnormal distal ureteral insertion, most often involving the ureter from the upper moiety of a duplex kidney. It typically inserts medially and inferior to the orthotopic ureter from the lower moiety. This observation is also known as the Weigert-Meyer rule, though exceptions have been reported as well. Ectopic ureters may coexist with a ureterocele and are associated with urinary tract obstruction. Urinary incontinence or continuous dribbling may occur if the ureteral insertion is distal to the external sphincter in female patients. Besides, a megaureter, with dilated (>7 mm), elongated and tortuous course, is also seen in some of these ectopic ureters.

Vesicoureteral reflux is another frequent finding in duplex systems. It typically affects the lower moiety of the ureter, which inserts laterally with a shorter intramural course, compromising the anti-reflux mechanism. It is also noteworthy that up to 25% of patients may also have contralateral VUR, highlighting the need for thorough evaluation, particularly in those presenting with urinary tract infections.

Both urinary obstruction and VUR increase the risk of progressive hydronephrosis, hydroureter and recurrent UTIs. High-grade VUR is particularly concerning due to its association with renal scarring, hypertension and potential progression to chronic kidney disease.

What investigations are considered in the assessment of a duplex kidney?
Various imaging and diagnostic studies are utilised to define the anatomical configuration of the duplex system and to evaluate functional abnormalities (Table 4.1).

Table 4.1 The role of different modalities in the investigation of children with duplex kidneys

Modality	Roles
Ultrasound	– Measure kidney size (duplex kidneys are often larger) – Identify two collecting systems – Detect and assess the severity of hydronephrosis or dilated ureter – May detect a ureterocele as a cystic structure projecting into the bladder
Micturating cystourethrogram (MCUG)	– Detect vesicoureteral reflux (in both duplex kidney and contralateral kidney) – Help identify the refluxing moiety in the duplex system – Visualise ureterocele as a filling defect within the bladder
MAG3 scan	– A dynamic scan to detect urinary tract obstruction – Provides an estimate of differential kidney functions
DMSA scan	– Quantify the cortical mass ratio between the left and right kidney and between the upper and lower moieties of the duplex kidney – Identify any renal scarring
MR urography	– Outline the details of anatomical features in duplex kidneys, in particular for the ectopic insertion of ureters and ureteroceles – Can estimate differential renal function by assessing differences in uptake or clearance of contrast between two kidneys and between moieties
Cystoscopy	– Direct visualisation of bladder anatomy and ureteric orifices – Can identify ureterocele and ectopic ureter opening – A retrograde pyelogram can be performed

Dorothy had an episode of *Klebsiella* UTI at 9 months of age. A repeat MCUG at 1 year of age demonstrated a grade 4 left-sided vesicoureteral reflux. She was commenced on prophylactic nitrofurantoin. A follow-up DMSA scan showed an upper-to-lower moiety cortical mass ratio of 8%:92% on the left side. To better delineate the anatomy, a magnetic resonance urography (MRU) was arranged. The MRU showed that the left kidney measured 7.1 cm, and the right kidney 5.6 cm. The left upper moiety was hydronephrotic (AP diameter 1 cm) with central calyceal dilatation, a dilated and tortuous ureter and ureteric insertion into the bladder, which was medial and inferior compared to the lower moiety (Fig. 4.3). The right kidney appeared normal. Dorothy underwent robotic-assisted laparoscopic nephroureterectomy of the left upper moiety at 2 years of age.

What are the management options for duplex kidneys?

The primary goals of treatment are to prevent recurrent infections, manage functional abnormalities such as reflux and obstruction and preserve renal function. For asymptomatic patients with normal renal function and no evidence of functional abnormalities, a watchful waiting approach may be appropriate. Parents should be educated about the warning signs of urinary tract infections to ensure prompt medical attention. Prophylactic antibiotics may be considered in patients with refluxing ureterocele. Surgical interventions are indicated in patients with symptoms (such as UTI and urinary incontinence) and the presence of obstruction or VUR.

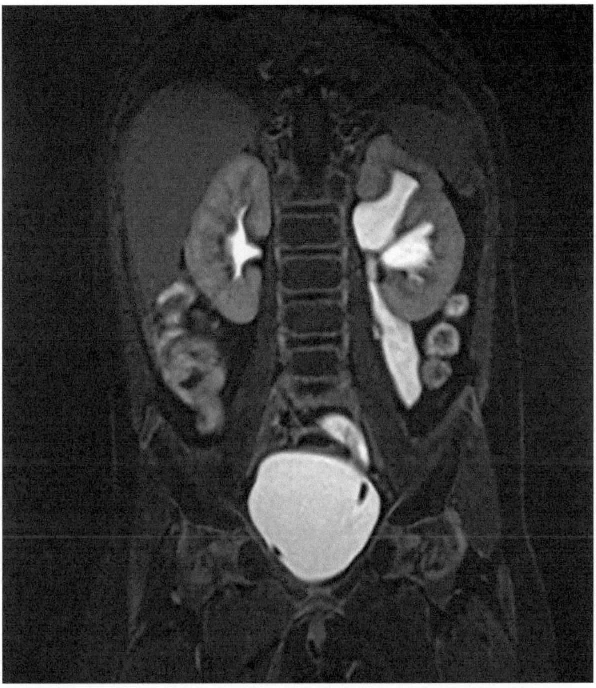

Fig. 4.3 MR urography showed a left duplex kidney with hydronephrosis at the upper moiety. The ureter from the upper moiety was dilated and tortuous

In cases of duplex kidney with ureterocele, a transurethral incision is commonly recommended for symptomatic patients or in the presence of progressive hydronephrosis which suggests urinary tract obstruction. This minimally invasive procedure is typically the initial intervention, especially in infants, due to its lower morbidity and faster recovery. The goal is to relieve obstruction while minimising the risk of postoperative reflux caused by the incision. If an ectopic ureter is also present, other procedures such as ureteral reimplantation, ureteroureterostomy (connecting the upper moiety's ectopic ureter to the lower moiety ureter) or upper pole heminephrectomy (in cases of poor upper moiety function) may be indicated. Treatment strategies are guided by factors including the patient's symptoms, age, severity of reflux or obstruction and the relative function of the renal moieties, and therefore need to be individualised.

What are the outcomes of patients with a duplex kidney?

Around 60% of patients with duplex kidney remain asymptomatic, have no associated renal anomalies and thus require no interventions. These duplex kidneys are sometimes regarded as a normal variant. However, it is important to look for associated functional anomalies (including VUR and urinary tract obstruction) and structural anomalies (including ureterocele, ectopic ureter and megaureter), as these conditions may increase the risk of recurrent urinary tract infections and renal scarring with subsequent functional loss and hypertension. Timely surgical intervention in such cases is essential to prevent long-term renal damage.

Studies from different paediatric centres report that around 20–40% of patients with duplex kidneys require surgical management, with the variation possibly due to the differences in the indications for initial imaging (e.g. antenatal scans versus evaluation for urinary tract infections). Among those requiring surgery, outcomes are generally favourable, including those receiving ureteral reimplantation or upper pole heminephrectomy. While long-term outcome data remain limited, patients with high-grade VUR or renal scarring should undergo continued follow-up to monitor for potential renal complications later in life.

4.3 Case Illustrations

While many patients with a duplex kidney remain asymptomatic, the condition can be associated with anomalies such as ureterocele, ectopic ureter and vesicoureteral reflux. Different imaging modalities are important for evaluating these anomalies. Timely surgical intervention in symptomatic or complicated cases is crucial to preserve renal function and prevent long-term damage.

Suggested Further Readings

1. Doery AJ, Ang E, Ditchfield MR. Duplex kidney: not just a drooping lily. J Med Imaging Radiat Oncol. 2015;59(2):149–53.
2. Siomou E, Papadopoulou F, Kollios KD, Photopoulos A, Evagelidou E, Androulakakis P, Siamopoulou A. Duplex collecting system diagnosed during the first 6 years of life after a first urinary tract infection: a study of 63 children. J Urol. 2006;175(2):678–82.
3. Kolvenbach CM, Shril S, Hildebrandt F. The genetics and pathogenesis of CAKUT. Nat Rev Nephrol. 2023;19(11):709–20.

Is the Kidney Absent?

5

5.1 Case Description

Ken is a baby boy born at full term by normal spontaneous delivery with a birth weight of 2.8 kg. His antenatal ultrasound suspected left kidney agenesis, and after delivery, physical examination showed right preaxial polydactyly and right undescended testes. Hence, you were consulted to assess Ken.

5.2 Interactive Case Discussion

How common is a solitary kidney in a newborn?
Congenital anomalies of the kidney and urinary tract (CAKUT) are among newborns' most common congenital malformations. The incidence of congenital solitary kidney has been reported as 1 in 1500 newborns annually. However, before we conclude that one kidney is absent, we have to make sure that we did not miss an undiagnosed ectopic kidney.

What is an ectopic kidney?
An ectopic kidney, also known as renal ectopia, is a kidney that fails to migrate to its normal position and may sometimes be mistaken as 'missing' when it cannot be identified in its usual position during an ultrasound examination. During normal embryogenesis, the kidney migrates cephalically to its normal retroperitoneal position. However, this migration may be in the wrong direction or arrested during the process of migration, resulting in resting in the pelvic (ectopic pelvic kidney), in the iliac region (ectopic iliac kidney), inside the thorax (ectopic thoracic kidney) or even cross the midline (crossed renal ectopia) and fused with the contralateral kidney to form a horseshoe kidney.

W. K. Y. Chan, M. C. I. Kuok, *Paediatric Nephrology*,
https://doi.org/10.1007/978-981-95-5060-9_5

How would you manage Ken?

To confirm whether Ken has a solitary kidney or an ectopic kidney, an ultrasound and DMSA scan were arranged to evaluate his kidney condition.

An ultrasound of the baby boy was performed. The left kidney was not found in the left renal fossa and a normal right kidney was detected (Fig. 5.1).

A renal cortical scintiscan with Tc99m-DMSA was performed to identify any functioning ectopic kidney, and cortical uptake was noted in the infra-medial aspect of the left kidney (Fig. 5.2).

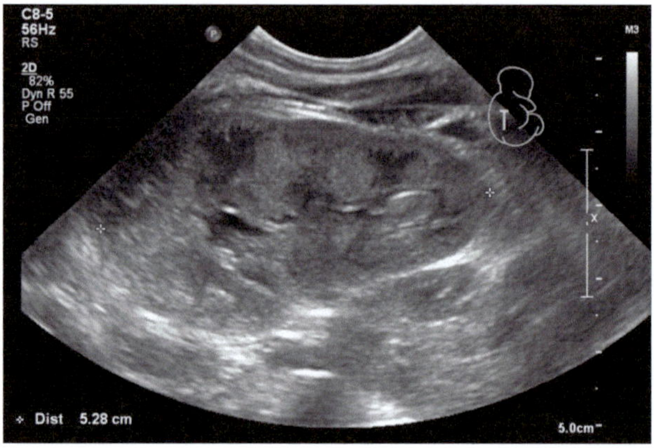

Fig. 5.1 An ultrasound of the baby performed at 1 month old showed a normal right kidney, measured at 5.28 cm, with normal corticomedullary differentiation. There was no hydronephrosis. The left kidney cannot be located at the left renal fossa

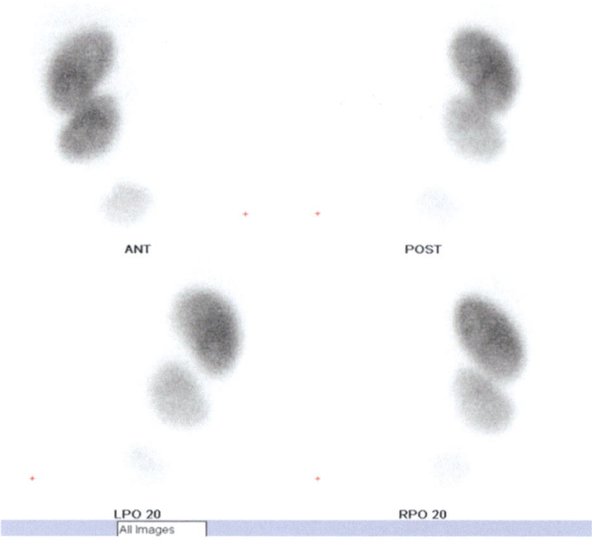

Fig. 5.2 The left kidney is inferior to the right kidney and not fused with the right kidney. It is smallish in size and smooth in outline. Cortical uptake of function is mildly impaired compared to the normal right kidney. Differentiate renal cortical mass ratio (left-to-tight) = 35%:65%. Hence, the left kidney is not absent. It is a crossed ectopic of the left kidney

What are the clinical significances of ectopic kidney?
Most ectopic kidneys are asymptomatic and can function normally even if not in their normal position. However, it may cause the following:

- Persistent or recurrent abdominal pain
- Urinary tract infection
- Renal stone and
- Prone to trauma

An ectopic kidney is more likely to be associated with the following

- Other urogenital abnormalities, like UPJO, VUJO, ectopic ureters, and VUR
- Impaired renal function
- Associates with other congenital malformations

An ectopic kidney is more likely to have an abnormal vascular supply, such as having more than one accessory, and polar arteries may arise.

- During embryogenesis, while the kidneys ascend through the pelvis, they receive new branches from the nearby iliac arteries and aorta. When they reach the highest point, they receive new branches from the aorta, and the former branches degenerate. In the case of failure of normal kidney migration, the vascular supplies will be abnormal. These are of clinical importance during any surgical intervention on the ectopic kidney. These abnormal vessels may also predispose to early-onset hypertension.

What kind of abnormalities may be associated with an ectopic kidney?
Ectopic kidney may be part of the features in multisystem congenital syndromes such as the following:

- CHARGE (coloboma, heart disease, atresia choanae, retarded growth, genital hypoplasia, and ear abnormalities)
- VACTERL malformations (vertebral, anal, cardiac, tracheal, oesophageal, renal, and limb anomalies)
- Mayer-Rokitansky-Küster-Hauser (MRKH) syndrome in a girl, i.e. absence or underdevelopment of the vagina and uterus

Hence, it is important to look out for other congenital defects in patients with ectopic kidneys.

Ken's MCUG and MAG3 scans were normal, and his renal function was normal. As Ken has polydactyly, further investigation of related congenital abnormalities was performed. The X-ray of his spine was normal, with vertebral height preserved. His chest X-ray showed 12 pairs of ribs. The right hand has five metacarpal bones, but there were an osseous oval structure and a tiny triangular bony structure at the right thumb, between the proximal and distal phalanx (Fig. 5.3).

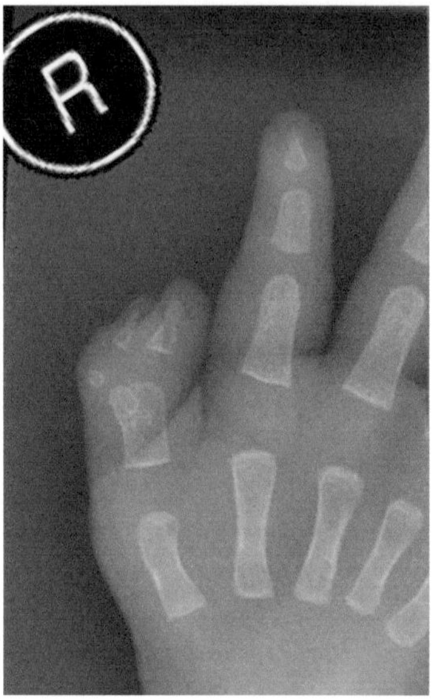

Fig. 5.3 The X-ray of the right hand showed five metacarpal bones. An osseous oval structure and a tiny triangular bony structure were noted at the right thumb, between the proximal and distal phalanx

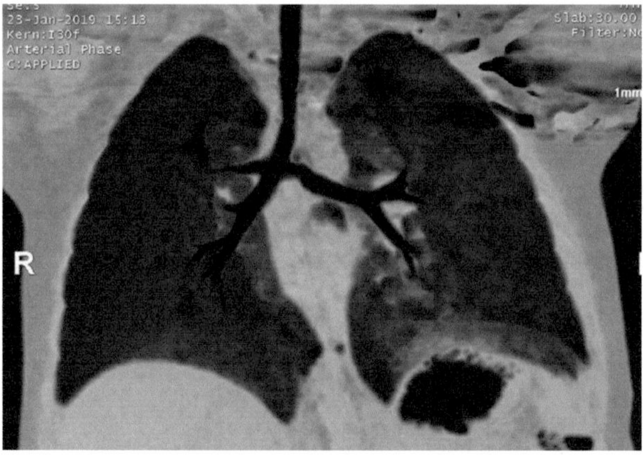

Fig. 5.4 The CT aortic angiogram and bronchogram showed mild narrowing of the trachea at the level of the aortic arch. Bronchus suis arose from the level of the carina, giving rise to the trifurcating appearance of the trachea. A mild narrowing of the left proximal bronchus is also noted. The trachea and other major airways were remarkable. The right lung was trilobed, and the left lung was bilobed typically

His echocardiogram showed a right-sided aortic arch with situs solitus, and a vascular ring was suspected. A subsequent CT aortic and pulmonary angiogram showed a mild narrowing at the left proximal bronchus, and no vascular ring was present. Serial bronchoscopy did not show any progression of the narrowing (Fig. 5.4).

What treatment options are available for managing an ectopic kidney?
Since there is no obstruction to the urinary flow in the ectopic kidney, no surgical intervention is needed. Ken has to be monitored for any urinary tract infection and possible renal stone formation in the abnormal urinary tract. He is also prone to develop early hypertension and proteinuria. These comorbidities need to be monitored, and early intervention may improve overall health outcomes.

Are there any long-term implications or risks associated with Ken's condition?
Since Ken does not have any significant associated congenital abnormalities, this combination of congenital anomalies will not have a severe impact on his future health. Apart from monitoring the possible complications of the ectopic kidney, Ken has to be aware that the abnormal position of the kidney is prone to external injuries. Fitness in contact sports and possible sequelae of kidney injury have to be thoughtfully discussed. The abnormal kidney position and different vascular supply also warrant surgical attention in the case there is a need for any abdominal surgery.

5.3 Case Illustrations

Ectopic kidneys may be mistaken for absent kidneys. A static functional renal scan, such as Tc-99m DMSA scintigraphy, is useful for identifying functioning renal tissue in an abnormal position. Many congenital abnormalities are associated with CAKUT, ranging from simple polydactyly to severe malformations like a vascular ring. Furthermore work up for associated abnormalities may be needed.

Suggested Further Readings

1. Rodriguez MM. Congenital anomalies of the kidney and the urinary tract (CAKUT). Fetal Pediatr Pathol. 2014;33(5–6):293–320.
2. Kagan M, Pleniceanu O, Vivante A. The genetic basis of congenital anomalies of the kidney and urinary tract. Pediatr Nephrol. 2022;37(10):2231–43.

Palpable K&B at Birth

6

6.1 Case Description

Tim was born at full term with a birth weight of 3.6 kg. His antenatal ultrasound scan performed at 21 weeks of gestation was normal with adequate liquor volume. At birth, the paediatrician was consulted to stand by the delivery of meconium-stained liquor. Tim developed respiratory distress after birth with an Apgar score of six at 1 minute, seven at 5 minutes and eight at 10 minutes. He was intubated and required invasive ventilatory support. Chest X-ray showed a right pneumothorax, which was managed with a chest drain insertion. After stabilisation, a physical examination revealed a markedly distended abdomen with palpable masses. His blood test showed serum sodium of 134 mmol/L, potassium of 5.4 mmol/L, urea of 5.1 mmol/L and serum creatinine of 120 umol/L. His mother's blood test for renal function was normal, with urea at 6 mmol/L and creatinine at 70 umol/L.

6.2 Interactive Case Discussion

What is the correlation of maternal-fetal serum creatinine? Did Tim's blood result suggest renal impairment?

Newborns can have high serum creatinine levels during the first week of life due to residual levels transferred from mothers through the placenta. Studies have shown that newborn and maternal serum creatinine correlate tightly for more than 72 hours after delivery, rendering this biomarker unsuitable for assessing neonatal renal function. Cystatin C does not cross the placenta and may be the preferred biomarker in the neonate. Postnatally, glomerular function rate (GFR) increases daily, doubles by 2 weeks and slowly reaches full maturity at 18 months. Yet, Tim's serum creatinine was higher than his mother's serum creatinine, making one caution about his renal function.

An urgent abdominal ultrasound was performed, and it showed bilaterally enlarged kidneys and a distended bladder. There were bilateral hydronephrosis with

W. K. Y. Chan, M. C. I. Kuok, *Paediatric Nephrology*, https://doi.org/10.1007/978-981-95-5060-9_6

cortical thinning, bilateral tortuous ureters and a distended bladder (Figs. 6.1a, b, 6.2a, b, and 6.3a, b).

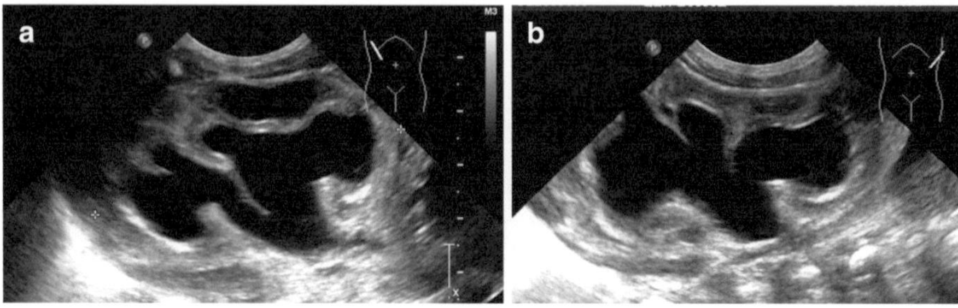

Fig. 6.1 (**a**) Marked right hydronephrosis, calyceal dilatation and cortical thinning. (**b**) Marked left hydronephrosis, calyceal dilation and cortical thinning with debris inside the renal pelvis

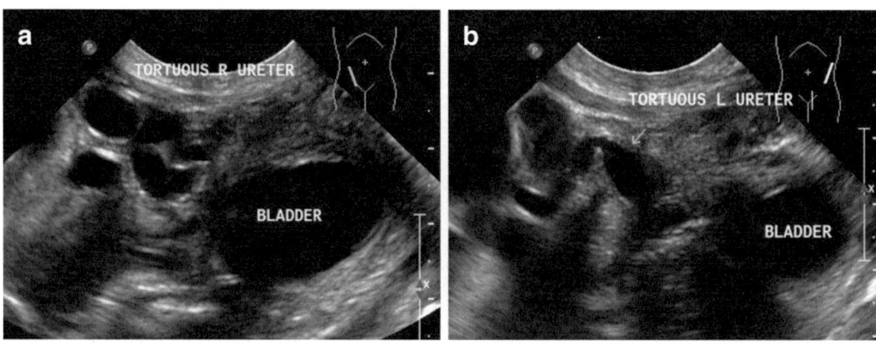

Fig. 6.2 (**a**) Dilated and tortuous right ureter entering the bladder. (**b**) Dilated and tortuous left ureter entered the bladder

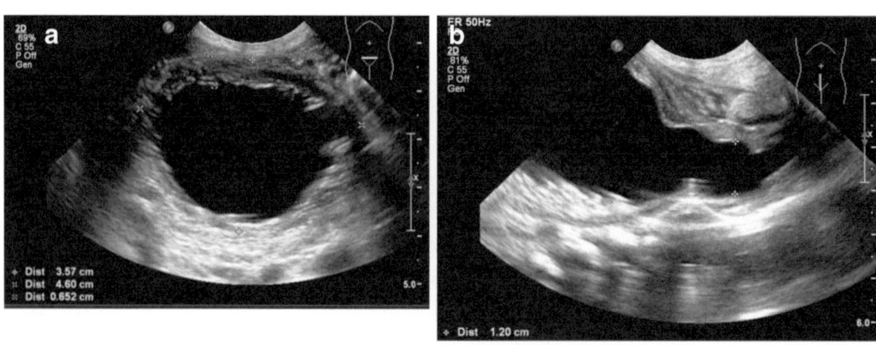

Fig. 6.3 (**a**) Distended bladder with thickened bladder wall and trabeculated appearance. The bladder measured 3.57 cm x 4.60 cm in two dimensions. The bladder wall thickness measured 0.652 cm. Normal bladder wall should measured less than 0.3 cm. (**b**) Distended bladder neck with dilated poster urethra, i.e. the keyhole sign was shown and the posterior urethra measured 1.2 cm. Normal diameter of the posterior urethra should measure less than 0.6 cm

In view of the USG finding suspecting a posterior urethral valve, a micturating cystourethrogram (Fig. 6.4) was performed. The bladder wall was irregular, and the bladder volume was small. There was a high resistance to contrast infusing, and vesicoureteric refluxes were not noted. The bladder neck and posterior urethra were dilated, which was compatible with the presence of a posterior urethral valve.

What is the posterior urethral valve (PUV)?

The posterior urethral valve occurs exclusively in males. It is an obstructing membranous fold in the lumen of the posterior part of the urethra. It is a congenital malformation, but there is no consensus regarding the origin of PUV. The early theory proposed that PUV either represents the persistent attachment of the verumontanum to the roof of the urethra or a persistent urogenital membrane. Later theory also suggests that it can result from the Wolffian ducts' failure to integrate into the urethra properly, resulting in a membrane obstructing the lower urinary tract.

Posterior urethral valves are classically split into three subtypes by Young's criteria according to the orientation of the valves within the urethra (Table 6.1).

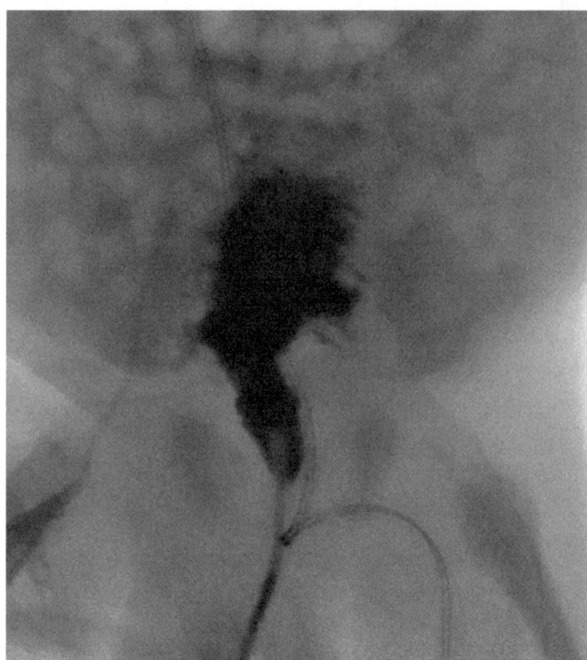

Fig. 6.4 The micturating cystourethrogram showed a small elongated bladder with trabeculations and sacculations. The posterior urethra was distended, suggesting a urethral outflow tract obstruction. Because of the high bladder pressure, there is a high resistance to instilling X-ray contrast and the classical bilateral high-grade vesicoureteric reflux was not demonstrated in this MCUG. This micturating cystourethrogram findings were compatible the diagnosis of posterior urethral valve

Table 6.1 Young's classification of PUV

Type 1	The most common type of PUV, accounting for almost 95% of patients The folds arise from the caudal verumontanum along the lateral margins of the urethra and fuse anteriorly, causing the obstruction
Type 2	It is rare and is now considered as a normal variant as it does not cause obstruction
Type 3	It accounts for around 5% of cases. It is a round membrane at the caudal verumontanum with a hole in the middle that is either above or below it. It is sometimes referred to as Cobb's collar

How common is PUV, and can it be detected antenatally?
The incidence of PUV reported is around 1 in 7000–8000 live births. The presence of PUV causes variable degrees of bladder outlet obstruction (BOO). The most severe case presents in early pregnancy, causing oligohydramnios, pulmonary hypoplasia and even Potter sequence.

On antenatal ultrasound, there may be the presence of marked distention and hypertrophy of the bladder. There may be hydronephrosis and hydroureter. In severe cases, there is oligohydramnios and renal dysplasia. The typical keyhole sign may be seen on ultrasound due to the distention of both the bladder and the urethra immediately proximal to the valve. Unfortunately, such findings are generally not seen before 26 weeks of gestation and, as such, are not frequently identified on routine morphology screening, usually carried out around 18 weeks gestation.

Is it possible to offer treatment before the birth of the fetus if PUV is detected early?
In selected patients, after parental counselling, one may propose a fetal vesico-amniotic shunting procedure in those experience centres. The method is to decompress the bladder to avoid further damage to the renal growth and to divert the fetal urine to the amniotic cavity to allow the normal growth of the fetal lung. Two other in utero procedures, i.e. valve ablation via fetal cystoscopy and fetal vesicotomy, have been proposed to be feasible options in dedicated fetal surgery centres, but both procedures carry significant maternal and fetal morbidity.

Tim has poor urine output before the surgical intervention. Only a Fr 6 urinary catheter could be inserted, and gross haematuria was noted after the bladder catheterisation. The initial urine output was only 0.5 mL/kg/hr, and hence frusemide infusion was started at 0.5 mg/kg/hr. Tim underwent an urgent cystoscopy, and it showed a type 1 posterior urethral valve extending from the verumontanum to the 4 and 8 o'clock, obstructing the dilated and trabeculated posterior urethra. The bladder mucosa was severely trabeculated with multiple diverticulitis. The ureteral openings were not identified because of the thickened bladder mucosa. Valve ablation was performed with a gush of strong urine stream, and a larger Fr 8 bladder catheter was inserted.

What are the precautions for starting frusemide in Tim?
After the release of the bladder outlet obstruction, there may be severe post-obstructive diuresis and severe electrolyte disturbances due to impaired tubular function. Hence, adequate volume replacement is essential to avoid renal damage.

The urine output dramatically improved, and progressive diuresis was noted even after stopping the frusemide infusion. Tim developed severe post-obstructive diuresis with urine output up to 16 mL/kg/hr. His serum creatinine increased to 187 umol/L transiently but it slowly normalised over 2 weeks' time.

What is Tim's long-term prognosis?
Despite the timely and complete removal of the bladder outlet obstruction, it is well-known that long-term sequelae occur in patients with PUV. Tom is prone to develop

the following problems, which require continuous monitoring, support and intervention from a multidisciplinary team.

1. *Deterioration in renal function*
    - In general, up to 50% of these patients progress to chronic kidney disease and up to 10–15% of them require kidney replacement therapy in subsequent life.
    - The renal impairment is secondary to the impaired pre-renal nephrogenesis, cystic dysplasia and persistent bladder dysfunction.
    - Hence, regular monitoring of renal function, blood pressure and proteinuria are required. Early intervention, according to the chronic kidney disease guideline, is advised.
2. *Lower urinary tract dysfunction—the valve bladder syndrome*
    - The valve bladder syndrome describes the thick-walled, poorly complained bladder with high resting pressure, resulting in hydroureteronephrosis and renal failure.
    - Three typical urodynamic patterns are observed in valve bladder syndrome. These patterns change with the patient's age and may overlap.
        - Pattern 1: Detrusor overactivity and hypercontractility
        - Pattern 2: Normal. Low compliant bladder
        - Pattern 3: Detrusor hypocontractivity leads to myogenic failure due to bladder overdistension.
    - Other problems include urinary incontinence, enuresis and frequent urinary tract infection.
    - Hence, frequent urodynamic assessment will be needed. The management of valve bladder syndrome is similar to the management of neurogenic bladder.
        - Need for behavioural modification: timed voiding, clean intermittent bladder catheterisation and overnight catheter drainage.
        - Medical treatment: the use of medication like anticholinergics or α-blockers.
        - Surgical interventions: botulinum toxin injection, bladder augmentation and creation of catheterised conduit and bladder neck incision.

The urodynamic study of Tim was performed at 2 months old with a suprapubic bladder catheter. In the fill phase, the bladder end-fill Pdet was 14 cmH_2O at 26 mL; the voided urine volume was 16 mL with a residue of 7 mL. The bladder emptying efficiency was only 69%. With this poor bladder compliance, a suprapubic cystostomy (vesicostomy) was performed. His DMSA performed at 2 months old (Fig. 6.5) showed multiple cortical defects in both kidneys, yet his serum creatinine and blood pressure were normal. He was then regularly followed up in a combined nephron-urology clinic for monitoring of his kidney and bladder problems.

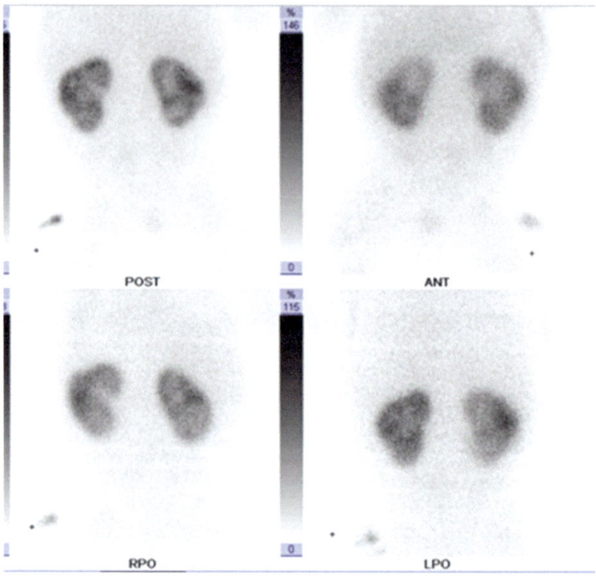

Fig. 6.5 Technetium-99m DMSA renal scan performed at 2 months old showed multiple cortical uptake defects in both kidneys. The differential renal cortical mass ratio, left-to-right, was 55%:45%. The findings suggested a generalized renal scarring affecting both kidneys

6.3 Case Illustrations

Patients suffering from serious obstructive uropathy may present at birth as an abdominal mass and impaired renal function. Tim's case highlights a severe form of posterior urethral valve presents at birth, which requires immediate medical attention and surgical intervention. Even after ablation of the posterior urethral valves, this group of patients suffers from variable severity of bladder dysfunction, and 50% of them may progress into chronic kidney disease, which needs to be managed accordingly.

Suggested Further Readings

1. Pereira PL, Urrutia MM, Espinosa L, Jaureguizar E. Long-term consequences of posterior urethral valves. J Pediatr Urol. 2013;9(5):590–6.
2. Chan EP, Wang PZT, Dave S. Valve bladder syndrome associated with posterior urethral valves: natural history, work-up, and management. Curr Bladder Dysfunction Rep. 2020;15:76–82.

7 From Distension to Obstruction

7.1 Case Description

Karl was a baby boy, born at full term with a birth weight of 3.2 kg via caesarean section for fetal distress. The delivery was uneventful, and he started breastfeeding as usual. His antenatal ultrasound showed hydronephrosis in the third trimester. A paediatrician was consulted to assess the baby after delivery.

7.2 Interactive Case Discussion

How common is antenatal hydronephrosis?
With the universal antenatal ultrasound examination, antenatal hydronephrosis is the most common type of kidney abnormality detected. The incidence depends on the accessibility and timing of fetal ultrasound. Some quoted a high incidence of up to 1 in 100 pregnancies.

Is antenatal hydronephrosis a serious condition?
Hydronephrosis refers to the dilation of the renal pelvis and calyces. It represents a broad spectrum of urological conditions and is a surrogate marker for congenital abnormalities. Most antenatal hydronephrosis is mild, transient and eventually resolves; however, some may persist and even progress, especially in those with underlying obstructive uropathies. Careful evaluation of the severity, improvement of the hydronephrosis and association of other congenital abnormalities is recommended.

W. K. Y. Chan, M. C. I. Kuok, *Paediatric Nephrology*,
https://doi.org/10.1007/978-981-95-5060-9_7

The causes of antenatal hydronephrosis and related CAKUT or abnormalities are as follows:

- Transient antenatal hydronephrosis
  - It resolves prenatal.
- Isolated antenatal hydronephrosis
  - Hydronephrosis persists in the postnatal period, but most resolve in the first few years of life.
- Ureteropelvic junction obstruction (UPJO)
- Ureterovesical junction obstruction (UVJO)
- Megaureter (obstructed or non-obstructed, refluxing or non-refluxing)
- Urinary outflow tract obstruction—posterior urethral valve and urogenital sinus
- Vesicoureteral reflux (VUR)
- Multicystic dysplastic kidney
- Associated with syndromal diagnoses such as Prune-Belly syndrome
- Associated genital abnormalities

What will you look for in the clinical history?
The history will help explore the possibilities of associated abnormalities and any damage caused by the hydronephrosis, especially any impact on fetal kidney function.

- When was the hydronephrosis picked up? (the trimester)
- What is the severity of the degree of the hydronephrosis?
  - Any progression or resolution of the hydronephrosis during antenatal ultrasound follow-up
- Bilateral or unilateral renal involvement
- Any associated kidney abnormalities, like duplex kidneys, ectopic kidneys and renal hypoplasia
- Any oligohydramnios
- Any other structural abnormalities detected
- Any family history of CAKUT
- Any antenatal fetal intervention, such as the insertion of vesico-amniotic shunts

How do we assess the severity of hydronephrosis antenatally?
The Society of Fetal Urology (SFU) first set up the diagnostic criteria for hydronephrosis in 1993. They used the degree of anteroposterior diameter (APD) of the renal pelvis in different trimesters to classify the severity of hydronephrosis into mild, moderate and severe (Table 7.1).

In the literature, there are other classifications, such as the ONEN classification (2007 and updated in 2016), RAD (Radiology Hydronephrosis Classification) in 2008 and UTD (Urinary Tract Dilatation) classification in 2014.

These classifications may be confusing without understanding their descriptions and clinical significance.

Table 7.1 The Society of Fetal Urology used the anteroposterior diameter (APD) to classify the severity of antenatal hydronephrosis in 1993

	Second trimester	Third trimester
Mild	4–7 mm	7–9 mm
Moderate	7–10 mm	9–15 mm
Severe	>10 mm	>15 mm

Implications and the Interpretation of the Ultrasound Findings

- Pelvic dilatation and the appearance of the pelvic
  - The compliance of the renal pelvis is high and distensible if it is extrarenal. The high expandability of the pelvis will protect the renal parenchyma from pressure damage.
- Calyceal dilatation
  - The expandability of the calyces is lower than that of the renal pelvis. Hence, the dilatation of the calyces will exert a higher pressure on the renal parenchyma, causing more damage.
- The thickness of the renal parenchyma
  - The medulla region is more expandable than the renal cortex, but if under high pressure for a prolonged time, the medulla will shorten and lose its pyramidal form.
  - The renal cortex is the most crucial part of the kidney where most glomeruli are situated. It represents the functional part of the kidney, and its thinning suggests significant damage to the kidney function. It is an objective parameter to measure as it is not affected by hydration status, bladder filling, position and respiratory stage of the patients.
- The ureter and the bladder
  - Dilated and tortuous ureters may represent megaureters ± UVJO or high-grade VUR.
  - A dilated proximal ureter may present an obstruction or stenosis at the ureteropelvic junction (UPJ).
  - A ureterocele suggests abnormal insertion of the ureter into the bladder.
  - An increase in bladder wall thickness and abnormal shape suggests urinary outflow tract obstruction.

The APD was once the primary parameter in assessing the severity of hydronephrosis; however, in Onen's most recent classification, APD was no longer considered as important as before because of the following:

- The rate of inter-operator variation is high.
- There is an absence of consensus on the measurement of APD.
- The configuration of the pelvis is equally important as an isolated APD measurement.
  - In extrarenal pelvic, even with a high APD, may not cause parenchymal injury.
  - In intrarenal pelvic, a low APD with parenchyma injury may indicate the loss of kidney function.

- The pelvis is highly distensible, and its measurement can be affected significantly by external parameters.
  - The APD may be lower when the patient is dehydrated, in an empty bladder or breathing at the expiratory phase.

The Red Flags

The various classifications help in professional communication and research studies. In clinical practice, it is essential to look at the ultrasound findings of the urinary tract, rather than relying solely on the grading (Table 7.2). The red flag signs in ultrasound include the following:

- The presence of oligohydramnios.
- An APD >15 mm, especially in the intrarenal pelvis. The larger the APD, the more likely it is to be caused by obstruction and the lower the chance of spontaneous resolution.
- Thinning of the renal medulla.
- Loss of corticomedullary differentiation.
- Thinning of the renal cortex.

Table 7.2 Comparing the different classifications of the severity of hydronephrosis

SFU classification 1993		UTD classification 2014		Onen classification 2016 (APD is not important)	
Grade 1	Visualised only the renal pelvis	UTD-P1 (low risk)	APD 10 to <15 mm or pelviectasis, pelvicaliectasis	Grade 1	Pelvis dilated
Grade 2	+ A few calyceal dilatations	UTD-P2 Intermittent risk	APD 10 to $\geq$15 mm or peripheral dilation of calyces or ureter $\geq$4 mm	Grade 2	Additional calyceal dilation
Grade 3	All calyceal dilatation	UTD-P3 (high risk)	APD $\geq$15mm or any calyceal dilation and parenchymal abnormality, bladder abnormality or prenatal oligohydramnios	Grade 3	*Medulla is thin* Cortex is normal Corticomedullary differentiation is normal
Grade 4	+ Parenchymal thinning			Grade 4	*Cortex is thin* There is no corticomedullary differentiation Prenatal 2nd trimester <2 mm Prenatal 3rd trimester <2.5 mm Postnatal period <3 mm

SFU The Society for Fetal Urology, *UTD* Urinary Tract Dilatation, UTD-P1, UTD-P2 and UTD-P3 represent the three postnatal categories described by the UTD classification

What will you look for in the physical examination?
In most newborns with simple hydronephrosis, physical examination was unremarkable, and we can then focus on identifying clinical features that may suggest a severe renal disease or associated congenital abnormalities:

- General appearance of the baby, to look for any Potter's facies.
- Any single umbilical artery.
- Abnormal ears.
- Abdomen: any lax abdominal wall, abdominal distension and palpable kidneys or bladder.
- Examine the urethral opening and look for any hypospadias or urogenital sinus.
- Check for any abnormal site of the anal opening.

What is the prognosis of antenatal hydronephrosis?
In most fetuses with antenatal hydronephrosis, the renal pelvic dilatation is transient. Some resolve after birth, and persistence of hydronephrosis is not unusual. In the majority of babies, even if the hydronephrosis persists, it does not cause significant clinical problems and usually resolves spontaneously over the first few years of life. However, if there is urinary tract obstruction or urinary reflux, they may cause repeated urinary tract infection or even progress to deterioration in renal function. To correctly predict the clinical course of hydronephrosis, we need serial USG to monitor for any progression, a MAG3 renal scan to assess the drainage half-time, and split renal function. Sometimes, a MCUG is needed to detect any vesicoureteric reflux that may cause the hydronephrosis.

Both the history and physical examination of Karl were unremarkable. The hydronephrosis was detected at the third trimester, and both APD measured 7 mm. A postnatal ultrasound performed on day 7 of life showed a similar degree of hydronephrosis. Karl was then discharged with outpatient follow-up. However, he defaulted after 1 year old as the ultrasound findings appeared static.

At the age of 7 years old, Karl had an episode of gross haematuria triggered by a minor body contact while he was playing football with his schoolmates. He was then referred back for assessment. Upon physical examination, the right kidney was palpable, and Karl's blood pressure was high at 130/85 mmHg. His blood test for serum urea, creatinine and electrolytes was normal. An ultrasound of the kidneys was repeated (Fig. 7.1a, b).

It showed a gross hydronephrotic right kidney, and the left kidney had an extrarenal pelvis. Subsequently, both DTPA and DMSA scans showed minimal function of the right kidney (Figs. 7.2 and 7.3).

Karl was diagnosed with a right UPJO, causing gross hydronephrosis and poor urinary drainage. The right kidney function was impaired. After discussion with the family, Karl underwent a laparoscopic right pyeloplasty. However, the drainage did not improve. Repeated ultrasound examination (Fig. 7.4) showed progression of the right hydronephrosis.

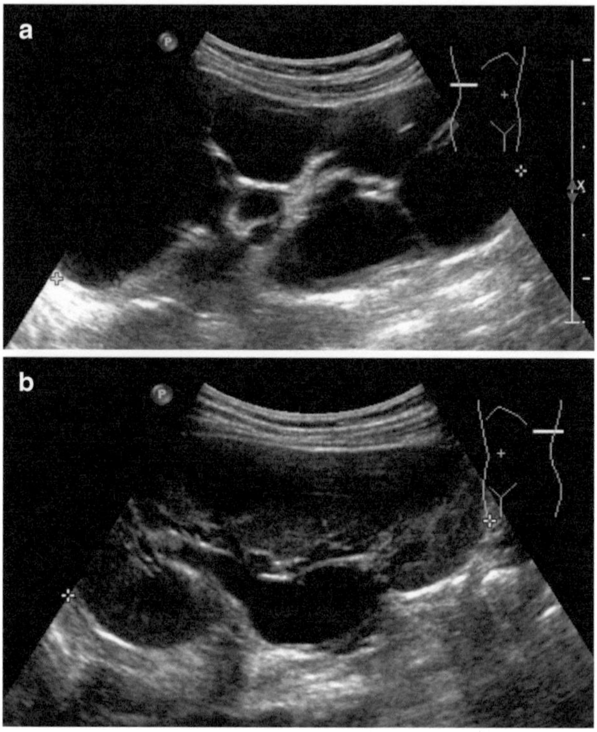

Fig. 7.1 (**a**) Ultrasound showed an enlarged right kidney, measuring up to 11 cm in length. It was grossly hydronephrotic. Most of the renal parenchyma was replaced by the distended collecting system, and only a very thin cortex remained. (**b**) Ultrasound of the left kidney, which measured 8.7 cm in length. The renal pelvis was extra-renal, and the anteroposterior diameter was 0.7 cm. The left kidney showed normal echogenicity and normal corticomedullary differentiation. The renal cortex was normal

Given the risk of trauma, gross haematuria, early hypertension and the UPJO was unlikely to be amendable by repeating the pyeloplasty, a right nephrectomy was decided.

Why is the ureteropelvic junction obstructed?
UPJO is a congenital abnormality, and it has been reported to account for up to two-thirds of patients with antenatal hydronephrosis and is recognised as a common cause of CAKUT.

The exact mechanism of UPJO is unclear, but the causes of obstruction can be categorised into intramural, mural and extramural.

- Intramural obstruction is extremely rare in children.
- Mural obstruction is postulated to be caused by several mechanisms, such as the following:
  - Intramural obliteration at the ureteropelvic junction related to failure of recanalisation in the fetal development.

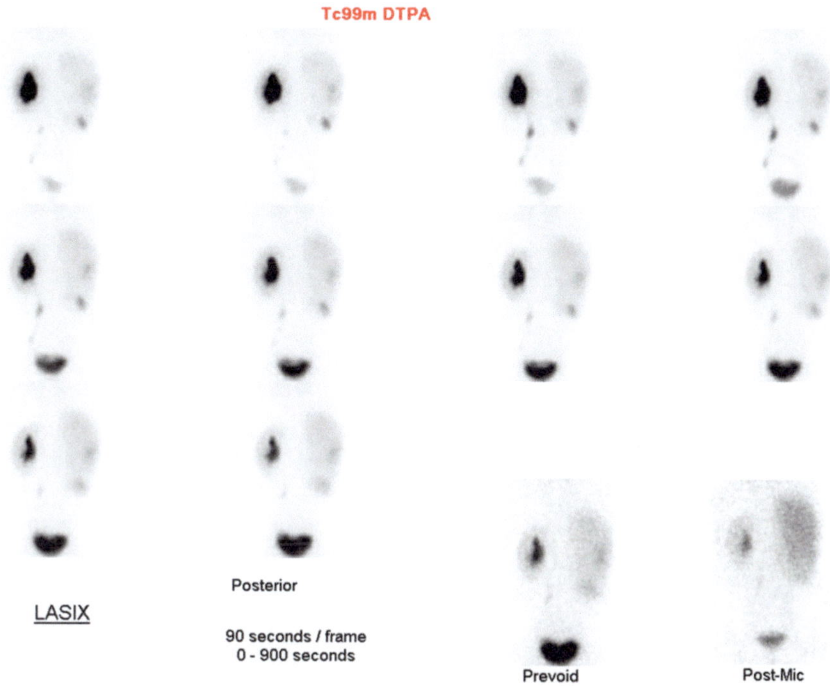

Fig. 7.2 The figure showed the Tc99m-DTPA renal scan with intravenous furosemide for the diuretic renogram study. The left kidney showed normal dynamic perfusion and glomerular function. The left ureter was not dilated. Renogram phase 2 was upward, phase 3 was flat, and diuretic renogram T1/2 was 4.8 min. The right kidney showed markedly decreased dynamic perfusion, with markedly decreased glomerular function. The right ureter was not seen. Renogram phase 2 and phase 3 were slowly upward. There was marked right hydronephrosis with post-micturition urine hold up in the right kidney. The differentiate GFR left:right was 87.3%:12.7%

  - The presence of abnormal musculature in the ureteric wall. It forms an aperistaltic ureteric segment which affects the efficiency of peristaltic waves. Hence, the lumen is not obliterated but is narrowed, creating a functional obstruction which can progress over time. In the abnormal segment, the normal spiral musculature of the ureter is replaced by longitudinal muscle or fibrous tissue.
- Extramural obstruction by aberrant vessels or adhesive bands.
  - The involvement of crossing vessels is not conclusive. Whether a crossing vessel can pose a purely mechanical obstruction is uncertain, but it may trigger surrounding inflammation, fibrosis and smooth muscle hypertrophy at the UPJ, leading to obstruction.

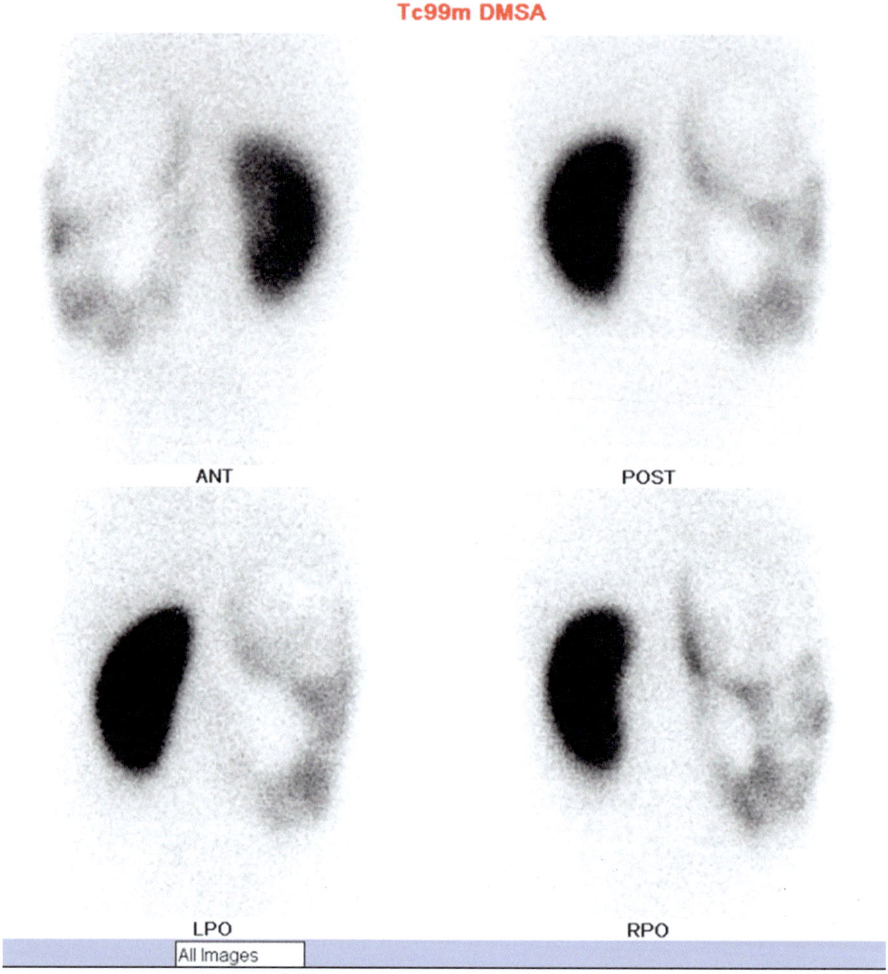

Fig. 7.3 The Tc99m DMSA of the patient. The left kidney showed normal uptake, with a functional height of 10.7 cm. The right kidney had markedly decreased in DMSA uptake, with a "functional height" of 17.8 cm. The cortical mass ratio left:right was 81.7%:18.3%

What are the indications for pyeloplasty for ureteropelvic obstruction?
Most patients with UPJO are managed conservatively. Indications for surgical repair include the following:

- Complications of the severe hydronephrosis, such as recurrent pain crises, recurrent gross haematuria, nephrolithiasis and recurrent urinary tract infection
- Differential renal function decreases to less than 40%
- Decline in renal function over time
- Worsening hydronephrosis

The decision for surgical repair has to be carefully balanced between risk and benefit in individual patients.

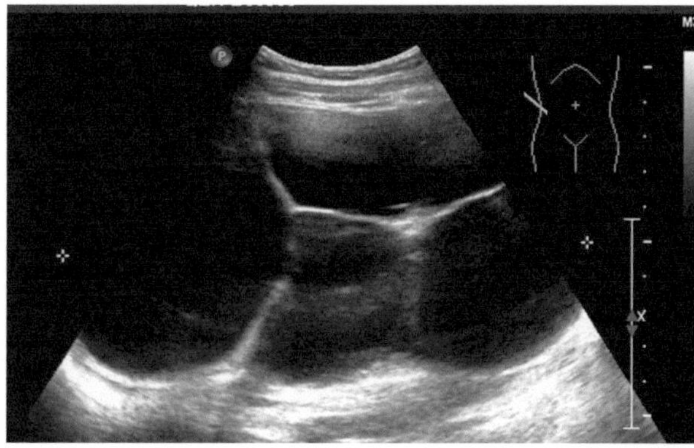

Fig. 7.4 USG of the right kidney showed further increase in renal size to 15 cm with gross hydronephrosis, and the renal cortex was paper thin

7.3 Case Illustrations

Despite antenatal hydronephrosis being a common diagnosis, there are many differential diagnoses for causing it. UPJO is one of the common causes of congenital hydronephrosis. Although most children with congenital hydronephrosis will do well, there are individual patients with UPJO who only progress after birth and may have a serious outcome later in life if undetected. This case demonstrates the unforeseen worsening of hydronephrosis attributable to UPJO. Hence, regular monitoring for the severity of hydronephrosis with further imaging is necessary. Parents should be educated about the natural history and possible course to avoid handling the problem lightly.

Suggested Further Readings

1. Costigan CS, Rosenblum ND. Understanding ureteropelvic junction obstruction: how far have we come? Front Urol. 2023;3:1154740.
2. Cai PY, Lee RS. Ureteropelvic junction obstruction/hydronephrosis. Urol Clin. 2023;50(3):361–9.
3. Drake K. Updates in the management of antenatal hydronephrosis—from current practices to on-going challenges. Curr Treat Options Pediatr. 2022;8(1):1–16.

Part II

Glomerulonephritis and Related Problems

8 When Frothy Urine Is Not Frothy

8.1 Case Description

Alex was a 9-year-old boy who was referred for management of frothy urine. Alex was well all along. His neonatal history was uneventful, except there was transient dilatation of the right renal pelvis detected by the antenatal ultrasound. His postnatal ultrasound kidney was normal, and he did not have any regular follow-up by the paediatrician thereafter. He thrives and enters into regular primary school. He did not have any significant illness except occasional upper respiratory tract symptoms that required medical consultations. Otherwise, he has been doing well all along.

One year ago, his father was diagnosed to have diabetes and was told to have excessive protein in the urine. Thereafter, Alex's mother became very anxious and obsessed with 'protein in the urine'. She watched videos about diabetes-related renal problems and got worried about possible kidney problems. She checked Alex's urine every night after he returned home from school. She became increasingly nervous when she observed Alex's on-and-off 'frothy urine' over the past few months. She brought over-the-counter urine test strips and was upset about the colour change detected in the urinary dipsticks.

8.2 Interactive Case Discussion

Is it reasonable for Alex's mother to worry about the presence of protein in Alex's urine?
If there is genuine proteinuria, Alex may need to refer to a medical doctor for advice and further workup for any underlying renal causes.

Proteinuria is an important biomarker for detecting renal disease in children. In normal circumstances, very little protein is lost in the urine despite many grams of plasma protein delivered daily to the nephrons. There is only a minimal amount of protein found in normal human beings such as the following:

W. K. Y. Chan, M. C. I. Kuok, *Paediatric Nephrology*, https://doi.org/10.1007/978-981-95-5060-9_8

1. The glomerulus restricts the filtration of protein (the filtration barrier).
2. The renal tubules will reabsorb most of the filtrated protein in the urine.

Hence, Alex's mother's concern is reasonable and should be addressed appropriately.

What could be the causes of frothy or foamy urine?

Although protein in the urine is a concern, other trivial causes can cause foamy urine and do not indicate any underlying health issues.

The following are causes of foamy urine:

1. Speedy urination as the force of urine entering the water in the toilet can cause a bubble of urine.
2. Dehydration can cause more concentrated urine and bubbles in the urine.
3. The presence of toilet cleaning chemicals or soap in the toilet may create bubbles in the voided urine.
4. Semen in the urine may cause bubbles in the urine.
5. Medical causes include proteinuria and urinary tract infection.

What is the urinary protein dipstick test?

Urine protein dipstick is the most common screening test for proteinuria. Despite these over-the-counter dipstick tests are commercially available and have different brands, they share similar principles.

The dipstick is impregnated with tetrabromophenol blue (TBPB) as a pH indicator. It is most sensitive in detecting albumin in the urine. Urine albumin binds to the reagent (TBPB) and changes its pH. It then causes a colour change in the strips. The colour changes are proportional to the amount of protein in the urine. The urine dipsticks come equipped with a colour chart that helps to make a semi-quantitative estimate of the amount of albumin in the urine (Fig. 8.1).

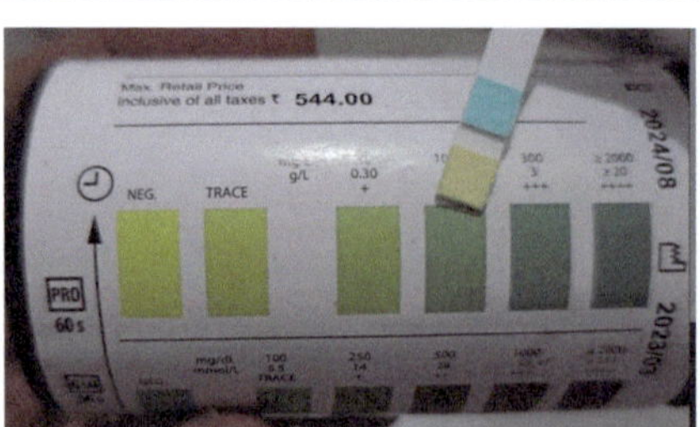

Scale	The concentration of protein assumed
Trace	10 mg/dL
+	30 mg/dL
++	100 mg/dL
+++	300 mg/dL
++++	>1g/dL

Fig. 8.1 An example of a commercially available dipstick test for testing protein in urine. The dipstick measures albumin concentration as a protein surrogate, turning different shades of green according to the urine albumin concentration that reacts with tetrabromophenol

How accurate are these dipsticks in detecting protein in the urine?
The dipsticks are sensitive to albumin at a concentration of approximately 10–15 mg/dL or a total albumin excretion of roughly 300–500 mg per day. This method measures protein concentration in the urine and is only a screening test. There exist false positives and false negatives.

False positive tests occur due to the following:

- The dipstick is left in the urine for too long.
- In the presence of gross haematuria, pyuria or bacteriuria.
- The urine specimen is contaminated with antiseptics.
- History of recent ingestion of drugs like penicillin, cephalosporin or sulphonamides.
- The urine is too concentrated with a specific gravity >1.025.
- The urine is too alkaline with pH >8.0.
- Post-administration of radiographic contrast.

False negative tests occur due to the following:

- The urine is too diluted with specific gravity <1.002.
- The urine is too acidic with pH <4.5.
- The presence of non-albumin proteinuria, such as globulin, mucoprotein and Bence-Jones protein, is not detectable by this dipstick test and may give a false negative impression.

How to perform a urine dipstick test?
To perform a proper urine dipstick test

1. Save the test urine in a proper container.
2. Urine dipstick should be performed on a freshly voided urine sample within 2 hours of collection.
3. Check the expiry date of the test strip before use.
4. Remove one test strip from the bottle. Put the bottle cap back on right away so that it fits tightly.
5. Hold the strip by the end opposite the colour blocks.
6. Briefly dip the strip in the urine to moisten the colour blocks.
7. All pads of the dipsticks are fully immersed in the urine and then immediately removed from the specimen container.
8. Lightly tap the strip against the inside of the cup to remove excess urine.
9. Then, hold the strip sideways for only a few seconds to prevent mixing the chemicals from each of the colour blocks.
10. If you have only a tiny amount of urine, tilt the cup on its side and dip the strip into the pool of urine. Do not void directly to the test stick.
11. Make sure to wet all of the blocks in the test strip, especially if the test strip has multiple purposes.

12. Use a clock or watch with a second hand to help count the seconds for each test you are doing.
13. Match the bottom block on the test strip to the bottom block of the colour chart. It will be easier to time each test correctly this way.
14. Starting from the bottom block, compare the test strip to the correct colour chart on the bottle when the time is up for each test.
15. The scale of the colour refers to a corresponding concentration of protein measured.

What is the other semi-quantitative method for measuring urinary protein?
The sulfosalicylic acid (SSA) test is another semi-quantitative measurement of urinary protein. SSA detects all types of protein and is also helpful in diseases that cause significant non-albumin proteinuria, like in myeloma kidney.

The SSA test is performed by mixing the urine supernatant with 3% sulfosalicylic acid in a ratio of 1:3 or around three drops of 20% SSA into 5 mL of the test urine to measure the turbidity of the suspension. The grading of turbidity can be assessed by visual observation (Table 8.1). For an accurate result, the turbidity of the urine can be measured by a turbidimeter. Turbidity level increases in proportion to the protein concentration in the urine.

What are the quantitative measurements of urine protein?
There are several methods for quantitative measurements of urine protein, and each method has pros and cons. The quantitative measurements of urine protein include the following:

1. *24-hour urine protein*

   A 24-hour urine collection for proteinuria is the traditional reference standard. However, carrying out a 24-hour urine collection may be challenging, especially in young children without bladder catheterization (Table 8.2).
2. *Spot urine measurements*
   - Spot urine samples are easier to collect than a 24-hour urine sample.
   - To avoid diurnal variation, the first void morning sample is advised.
   - To account for day-to-day variation in a person, multiple sampling may give a better idea of the clinical picture.

Table 8.1 Sulfosalicylic acid (SSA) test and its interpretation

Grade	Appearance of urine suspension by visual observation	Urine protein concentration (g/L)
0	No turbidity	0
Trace	Slight turbidity	0.01–0.1
+	Turbidity through which print can be read	0.15–0.3
++	White cloud without precipitate through which black lines on a background can be read	0.4–1
+++	White cloud with precipitate through which black lines on a background cannot be read	1.5–3.5
++++	Flocculent precipitates	>5

Table 8.2 Reference range of proteinuria in a 24-hour urine collection

24-hour urine protein should be <4 mg/m^2 per hour or <100 mg/m^2 per day or a total of <150 mg per day	Normal
24-hour urine protein excretion from 4 to 40 mg/m^2 per hour or 100–999 mg $/m^2/day$	Significant proteinuria
24-hour urine protein excretion >40 mg/m^2 per hour or ≥1000 mg/m^2 per day	Nephrotic range proteinuria

Table 8.3 Commonly used reference for Urine-protein-creatinine ratio (UPCR)in children and adolescent

	Normal reference	
	6–24 months	Older than 24 months
UPCR (mg/mg)	<0.5	<0.2
UPCR (mg/mmol)	50	20
UPCR (mg/g)	500	200

3. *Spot urine protein to creatinine ratio (UPCR) and spot urine albumin to creatinine ratio (UACR)*

   Both UPCR and UACR are commonly used parameters to measure urine protein/albumin. Using the ratio to urine creatinine, one can adjust spot urine concentration for the urinary flow rate as the concurrent increase in the urine creatinine concentration balances out the hydration-induced variation in the urine protein concentration.

   Measuring urine total protein includes measuring both urine albumin and other proteins in the urine, but for measuring albuminuria, only albumin in the urine is measured. Among adults, albuminuria correlates more closely with end-stage renal disease, and the measurement of this low level of albuminuria (microalbuminuria) has replaced the measurement of total protein, especially in diabetic patients.

   As normal individuals have minimal protein excreted in the urine, the urine protein excretion in the population will have a skewed distribution. Racial differences, variations in dietary intake, muscular mass and physical activity may all affect the degree of urine protein detected in normal populations. The reference of 'normal' for 'cut-off' for 'significant proteinuria' will usually take the upper percentile limit.

   The National Kidney Foundation practice guidelines recommend that UPCR be measured instead of 24-hour UP in most cases of children and adults with CKD, and the recommended normal reference value is lower than 200 mg/g (0.2 mg/mg). However, another widely used normal reference value is lower than 150 mg/g (Tables 8.3 and 8.4).

Table 8.4 Comparing the reference for various measurements of protein in urine

Degree of proteinuria	Normal to mild	Moderately increase	Severely increase
Spot albumin to creatinine UACR	<30 mg/g	30–299 mg/g	≥300 mg/g
Spot urine protein to creatinine UPCR	<150 mg/g	150–499 mg/g	>500 mg/g
Urine dipstick	Negative to trace	Trace to +	>++

8.3 Case Illustrations

Frothy urine is a common complaint for referral to paediatricians. Understanding the different methods of detecting proteinuria is crucial in counselling the family to avoid over-investigations, yet proteinuria is an important presentation for underlying renal disease and some children may need careful evaluation.

Suggested Further Readings

1. Leung AK, Wong AH, Barg SS. Proteinuria in children: evaluation and differential diagnosis. Am Fam Physician. 2017;95(4):248–54.
2. Bökenkamp A. Proteinuria—take a closer look! Pediatr Nephrol. 2020;35(4):533–41.

When Frothy Urine Means Proteinuria

9

9.1 Case Description

Alex, a 9-year-old boy who was suspected to have frothy urine, was brought to you for assessment. His mother has appropriately performed the urine dipstick test, showing two plus (++) to three plus (+++) on various occasions. Alex was then referred to you for further assessment.

9.2 Interactive Case Discussion

What could be the possible reasons for Alex's positive urine albustix?
When proteinuria is detected, we need to determine whether it is transient, orthostatic or persistent. It is also important to determine whether the patient has a nephrotic or acute nephritic syndrome that requires immediate medical attention, and the approach in management will be different. If the child is stable, we then need to quantitatively assess the degree of proteinuria and monitor whether the proteinuria is persistent (Fig. 9.1 and Table 9.1).

When a child's UPCR is more than 0.2 mg/mg (more than 0.5 for children from 6 to 24 months of age) or the urinalysis results are abnormal, further evaluation with history, physical examination and additional blood work is recommended to rule out significant renal disease. Once persistent proteinuria is confirmed, an important initial step is to quantify the degree of proteinuria. Proteinuria >3.5 g/24 hour/1.73 m^2 and the presence of red cell cast are nearly always due to an underlying glomerular disease. The causes of persistent proteinuria are summarized in Table 9.2.

How to differentiate glomerular proteinuria from non-glomerular proteinuria?
Glomerular proteinuria is due to damage or change in the charge or size of the filtration barrier, leading to loss of serum protein in the urine. In most situations, the

W. K. Y. Chan, M. C. I. Kuok, *Paediatric Nephrology*,
https://doi.org/10.1007/978-981-95-5060-9_9

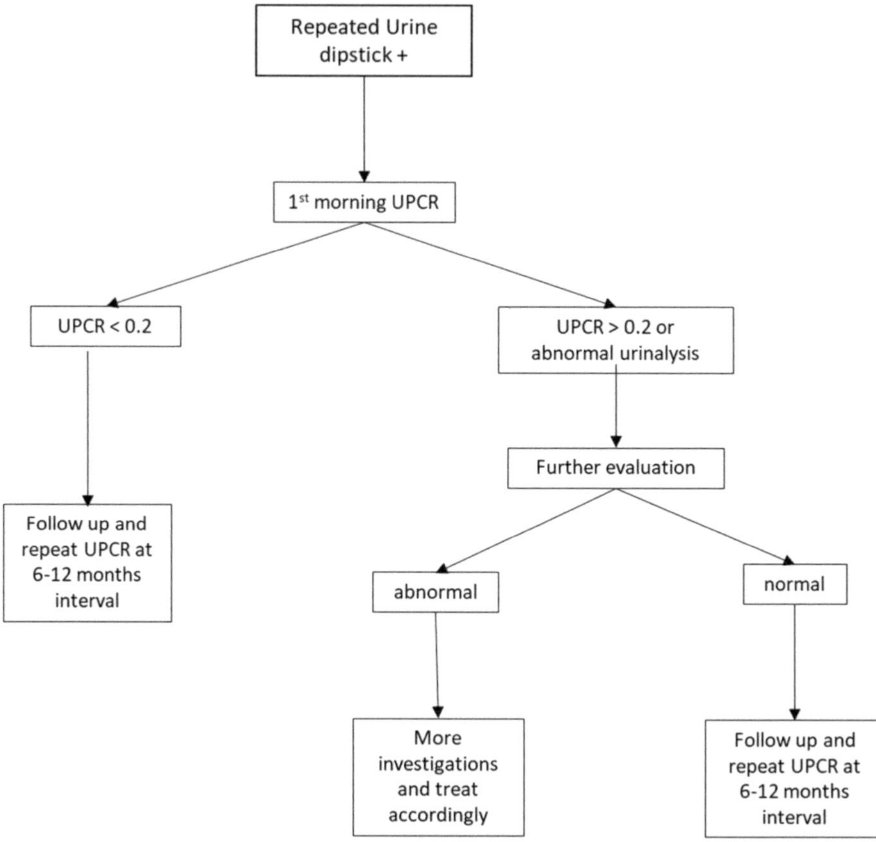

Fig. 9.1 Algorithm shows the approach to children with positive urine dipstick for protein. It begins with a first morning urine protein-to-creatinine ratio (UPCR). If UPCR is less then 0.2, follow-up and repeat UPCR at 6-12 months intervals. If UPCR is greater than 0.2 or urinalysis is abnormal, further evaluation is needed

protein loss is a small molecular protein like albumin called selective proteinuria. Patients with minimal change disease generally have highly selective proteinuria and are usually responsive to steroid treatment. In some glomerular diseases, there is leakage of both small and large molecular weight proteins known as non-selective proteinuria. Patients with non-selective proteinuria are generally less responsive to steroid therapy. The selectivity of proteinuria index (SPI) can be measured by determining the clearance of a small molecular weight protein like transferrin and a large molecular weight protein like IgG. A selective protein index of <0.1 denotes highly selective proteinuria, and a ratio of >0.3 indicates non-selective proteinuria.

Tubular proteinuria is the loss of the small molecular weight protein in the urine. Small molecular weight proteins like light chains of immunoglobulins, β2microglobulin and lysozyme are usually filtered at the glomeruli and reabsorbed at the proximal renal tubules. The presence of these proteins in urine is an indicator

Table 9.1 Characteristics and underlying causes of different types of proteinuria

	Characteristics features	Causes
Transient proteinuria	Temporary and resolves when the triggering factor remits or is removed	Fever, exercise, stress, dehydration, cold exposure or after a seizure. Sometimes idiopathic
Orthostatic proteinuria	Most common in children, especially in adolescent males The first morning urine sample after the patient has been supine for the whole night is normal, but there is an increase in urinary protein at least 4–6 hours after the patient has been in an upright posture	Idiopathic and usually benign without clinical significance
Persistent proteinuria	UPCR is persistently more than 0.2 (mg/mg) on different occasions	Glomerular proteinuria Non-glomerular proteinuria • Tubular proteinuria • Overflow proteinuria (very rare in children)

Table 9.2 Examples of the causes of persistent glomerular and tubular proteinuria

Glomerular proteinuria

1. Congenital or genetic: congenital nephrotic syndrome. Alport syndrome
2. Acquired
   (a) Primary or idiopathic
   Minimal change disease, focal segmental glomerulosclerosis, membranoproliferative glomerulonephritis, membranous nephropathy, mesangial proliferative glomerulonephritis and IgA nephropathy
   (b) Secondary
   (i) Infection: post-streptococcal glomerulonephritis, shunt nephritis, hepatitis-related, subacute bacterial endocarditis, malaria, dengue fever, AIDs, etc.
   (ii) Multisystem disease: systemic lupus erythematosus, Henoch-Scholein purpura, vasculitis disease like polyarteritis nodosa, ANCA-associated vasculitis, haemolytic-uremic syndrome
   (iii) Drugs: non-steroidal anti-inflammatory drugs, penicillamine, gold, lithium and street drugs
   (iv) Malignancy related like leukaemia, lymphoma and carcinoma
   (v) Others: chronic renal failure, reflux nephropathy

Tubular proteinuria

1. Congenial or genetic: Fanconi syndrome, Lowe syndrome, Lawrence-Moon-Biedl syndrome, renal tubular acidosis, cystinosis, Wilson's disease, tyrosinemia, glycogen storage disease and Dent's disease
2. Acquired: interstitial nephritis, pyelonephritis, acute tubular necrosis, nephrocalcinosis, drugs like NSAIDs, lithium, gentamycin, vancomycin, ifosfamide, cisplatin and tenofovir

of proximal renal tubular diseases. The causes of tubular disease causing proteinuria are listed in Table 9.2.

Overload proteinuria occurs when the normally filtered protein (low-molecular-weight protein) exceeds and overwhelms the reabsorption capacity of the proximal renal tubules; proteinuria will occur. This is rare in the paediatric population but may appear in scenarios such as the following:

- Excessive light chains (Bence-Jones protein) in multiple myeloma
- Excessive lysozymes in myelocytic leukaemia
- Excessive macroglobulin in rhabdomyolysis or
- Excess hemoglobulin in haemolysis

How would you assess the significance of Alex's proteinuria?
To evaluate a child with persistent proteinuria, we need to take a detailed history and physical examination as the initial evaluation, followed by laboratory investigation and radiological examination as required.

The history and physical examination should address the following issues:

1. The nature and severity of the symptoms
2. Temporal sequence and chronicity of the problem
3. Features of underlying causes

History and Physical Examination

Most children with isolated proteinuria are asymptomatic and only detected during check-ups for other reasons. The history and physical examination have to focus on the possible aetiology that causes persistent proteinuria, as listed in Table 9.3. Special attention should be given to the following:

- Any features suggestive of autoimmune disease (fever, skin rash, arthritis)
- Features of systemic diseases like diabetes or hypertension
- The presence of any red flags for specific organ involvement
- A complete history of drugs
- Any significant past medical history that may cause kidney injury
- Family history like hereditary nephritis, nail-patella syndrome and polycystic kidney disease (ADPKD, ARPKD and syndrome-related cystic kidney disease)

Urinalysis

Urinalysis is a simple yet highly informative diagnostic test, and the following general principles may aid in interpreting the results with respect to their clinical relevance.

Table 9.3 Summary of the evaluation of children with persistent proteinuria

History and physical examination
Urinalysis
Quantitative measurement of proteinuria
Blood test: complete blood counts and serum chemistries including sodium, potassium, chloride, calcium, phosphate and bicarbonate, urea or BUN, creatinine, uric acid, total protein, serum albumin, globulin and serum cholesterol
Immune workup includes a blood test for antinuclear antibody, anti-streptococcal antibodies (ASOT), total haemolytic complement, C3 and C4
Hepatitis serology screening
Test for urine selectivity by urine electrophoresis
Renal ultrasound
Renal biopsy in a specific group of patients

- Urine albustix of 4+ is more likely seen in glomerular rather than tubular disease.
- If oedema is present with isolated proteinuria, the patient probably suffers from nephrotic syndrome and should be managed accordingly.
- The presence of RBCs and RBC casts indicate glomerular disease or glomerulonephritis.
- Proteinuria with haematuria, particularly 3+ to 4+ in urine albustix, almost always suggests an underlying glomerular disease.
- The presence of WBC or WBC casts suggests tubulointerstitial disease or pyelonephritis.
- Muddy brown granular casts are seen in acute tubular necrosis.
- The presence of glucose in urine suggests either diabetes mellitus or renal glycosuria related to proximal tubular disease.

Alex's first-morning UPCR was 0.49 mg/mg. The history was unremarkable, except his father has diabetes. Physical examination of Alex was normal. He is not obese, with his growth centiles at the 50th. His blood pressure was 90/45 mmHg, which is normal for his age and body height. He has his blood test for blood chemistry, BUN and creatinine which were normal. His fasting blood sugar and lipid profile were normal. His ultrasound kidneys were normal, and there was no hydronephrosis. His urine microscopy and urine culture were negative. Autoimmune worker up was all normal. Hepatitis B, hepatitis C and HIV serology were negative. He was then reviewed in 3 months time. His UPCR increased to 0.88 mg/mg. A 24-hour urine showed proteinuria of 0.94 g/day (30 mg/m^2/hr) and his serum albumin was 32 g/dL.

Did Alex need a renal biopsy?
In general, proteinuria is considered damaging to renal function and a strong predictor of progressive renal damage. Renal biopsy is usually indicated in situations like the following:

- Children with severe disease, for example nephrotic syndrome, acute nephritic syndrome, nephrotic-nephritis syndrome and acute renal failure, such that a renal biopsy for the underlying renal pathology guide the treatment options
- Children with chronic kidney disease with an unknown aetiology
- Children suspected to have renal involvement as part of an autoimmune disease

The indication in children with isolated and asymptomatic proteinuria is more controversial than those symptomatic scenarios. There is no consensus on the optimal cutoff maximum urinary protein/creatinine ratio (UP/Cr) to separate minor glomerular abnormalities (MGA) and other significant glomerular changes. A 'too early renal biopsy' may not reveal substantial pathologies, and a 'too late renal biopsy' may miss the golden time for treatment. The decision dilemma is also complicated as renal biopsy is an invasive procedure, not without risk. Recently with the advance of genetic study, some children may benefit from a genetic test before an invasive kidney biopsy.

Alex has persistent and significant proteinuria, which appears to be progressive. Although he did not have nephrotic syndrome and his proteinuria did not reach nephrotic range proteinuria, a discussion on the possible renal biopsy was initiated with the parents.

What are the common renal pathologies seen in patients with asymptomatic isolated proteinuria like Alex?
The possible and more common kidney histology are as follows:

- Minor glomerular abnormalities (MGA)
- Focal segmental glomerulosclerosis (FSGS)
- IgA glomerulonephritis
- Membranous nephropathy
- Diffuse mesangial proliferative glomerulonephritis without IgA

Alex's parents agreed to a renal biopsy which showed minor glomerular abnormalities (MGA). The light microscopic examination of the kidney biopsy showed focal segmental mild mesangial hypercellularity and matrix expansion. The immunofluorescent studies showed diffuse global mesangial granular 1+ staining for IgA. The ultrastructural examination revealed focal effacement of podocytes' foot processes. In view of the renal histology, Alex was treated with an angiotensin-converting enzyme inhibitor (ACE), ramipril at 5 mg daily. His 24-hour urine proteinuria dropped to 0.25 g/day and remained stable. Alex needs continuous monitoring, and in the case his proteinuria progresses or renal function deteriorates, he may need another kidney biopsy to guide subsequent treatment. Minor glomerular abnormalities may represent an early phase of primary glomerulonephritis like IgA nephropathy or FSGS.

9.3 Case Illustrations

Isolated asymptomatic proteinuria is not an uncommon complaint in children. Careful evaluation and monitoring of the severity of proteinuria is needed as some patients may continue to deteriorate and subsequently warrant a renal biopsy. The early use of ACEI helps to control the progression of proteinuria.

Suggested Further Readings

1. Hogg RJ, Portman RJ, Milliner D, Lemley KV, Eddy A, Ingelfinger J. Evaluation and management of proteinuria and nephrotic syndrome in children: recommendations from a pediatric nephrology panel established at the National Kidney Foundation conference on proteinuria, albuminuria, risk, assessment, detection, and elimination (PARADE). Pediatrics. 2000;105(6):1242–9.
2. Larkins NG, Teixeira-Pinto A, Craig JC. A narrative review of proteinuria and albuminuria as clinical biomarkers in children. J Paediatr Child Health. 2019;55(2):136–42.

Fluid in the Third Space—From Theories to Treatment

10

10.1 Case Description

Isabella is an 11-year-old girl who has been healthy all along. She had a history of a febrile upper respiratory infection 2 weeks before admission, and she recovered with a residual cough. She complained of puffy eyelids and abdominal fullness for 2 days. Hence, she was admitted to the emergency department. She had a chest X-ray taken in the emergency room. The duty house officer assessed her and informed the paediatric resident as she was not sure about the chest X-ray findings (Fig. 10.1a). Isabella looked puffy and gained 2 kg in the past 1 week. Her blood

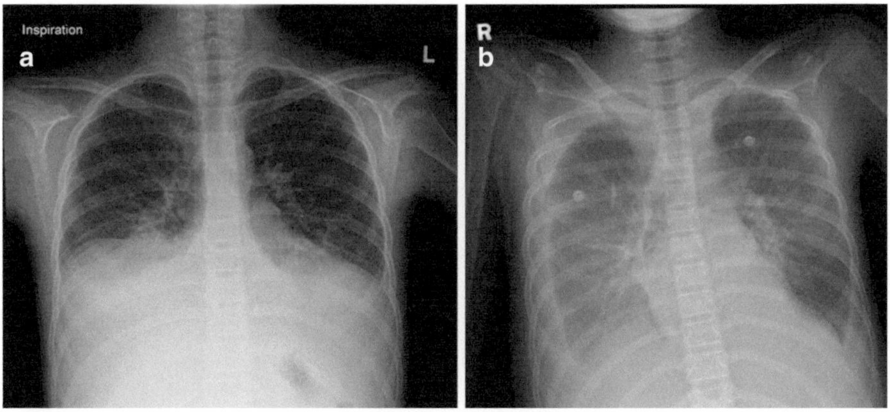

Fig. 10.1 (**a**) Showed a postero–anterior (PA) view of the chest X-ray, a standard frontal view where the X-ray beam passes through the patient from back to front. It showed bilateral pleural effusion, and the subpleural fluid caused apparent elevation and flattening of the diaphragm. (**b**) showed a CXR taken with the patient supine. There were bilateral pleural effusion, more severe on the right side with a fluid level and blunted the left costophrenic angle. The lung field was congested

W. K. Y. Chan, M. C. I. Kuok, *Paediatric Nephrology*,
https://doi.org/10.1007/978-981-95-5060-9_10

pressure was 90/60 mmHg with a heart rate of 110 bpm. Her oxygen saturation was 92% in room air.

The paediatric resident ordered another CXR, and a portable chest X-ray was performed 2 hours later (Fig. 10.1b). Isabella's emergency blood test showed serum sodium 140 mmol/L, potassium 4.2 mmol/L, creatinine 45 μmol/L, urea 4.3 mmol/L, albumin 7 g/L, globulin 42 g/L, cholesterol 12.7 mmol/L and urine protein-creatinine ratio 15.2 g/g. With these laboratory results, the resident diagnosed Isabella to have nephrotic syndrome.

10.2 Interactive Case Discussion

What is the definition of nephrotic syndrome?
The combination of four classical features defines nephrotic syndrome. They are the following:

1. Oedema
2. Nephrotic range proteinuria (urine protein >40 mg/m^2/hr or spot urine protein-to-creatinine ratio ≥2 mg/mg)
3. Hypoalbuminemia of <25 g/L
4. Hyperlipidaemia with total cholesterol ≥5.2 mmol/L or ≥200 mg/dL

What did the chest X-ray show, and what were the differences?

How would you assess Isabella with the diagnosis of nephrotic syndrome at admission?
Oedema, proteinuria, hypoalbuminaemia and hypercholesterolaemia are the four defining features of nephrotic syndrome. The initial assessment of the disease severity would focus on the patient's clinical symptoms and vital signs. The initial assessment would evaluate the following:

1. Features of intravascular volume depletion
   - Dizziness and abdominal cramps.
   - Cold hands, mottling skin and capillary refill more than 2 seconds suggest hypoperfusion.
   - Tachycardia, decreased urine output and hypotension suggest low intravascular volume.
2. Symptoms related to the oedema
   - Discomfort related to abdominal distension, genital oedema and limbs oedema. Severe oedema results in functional restraint and restricted leg movements and may even impair the mobility of the patient.
   - Interstitial oedema will increase tension in the skin, especially over the lower limbs, leading to blistering, skin breakage and exudate extrusion. This may further be complicated by secondary bacterial infection and cellulitis.
3. Potential problems related to nephrotic syndrome
   - Watch out for infection risk and thrombotic risk.

4. Features suggest secondary causes for the nephrotic syndrome include skin rash, arthritis, livedo reticularis, oral ulcers and alopecia.

What are the causes of oedema in nephrotic syndrome?
The two major contributors to oedema in nephrotic syndrome are the loss of serum albumin and the retention of sodium. There are two major theories explaining the pathophysiology.

The Underfilling Theory
When there is low serum albumin, the capillary oncotic pressure will decrease, and fluid leakage to the interstitial space causing a drop in the circulatory volume (Starling's law). Because of renal hypoperfusion, the renin-angiotensin-aldosterone system (RAAS) becomes active, causing secondary sodium and water retention. In this theory, there is increased synthesis/activity of the RASS, anti-diuretic hormone (ADH) and catecholamines but a decrease in atrial natriuretic peptide (ANP) synthesis.

The Overfilling Theory
In the overfilling theory, there is a primary defect in sodium and water retention leads to hypervolaemia. There is no increased synthesis in RASS, ADH and catecholamines; instead, ANP resistance is observed which leads to fluid retention and oedema.

These two mechanisms are not mutually exclusive. They may co-exist in the same patient at different stages of the disease (Fig. 10.2).

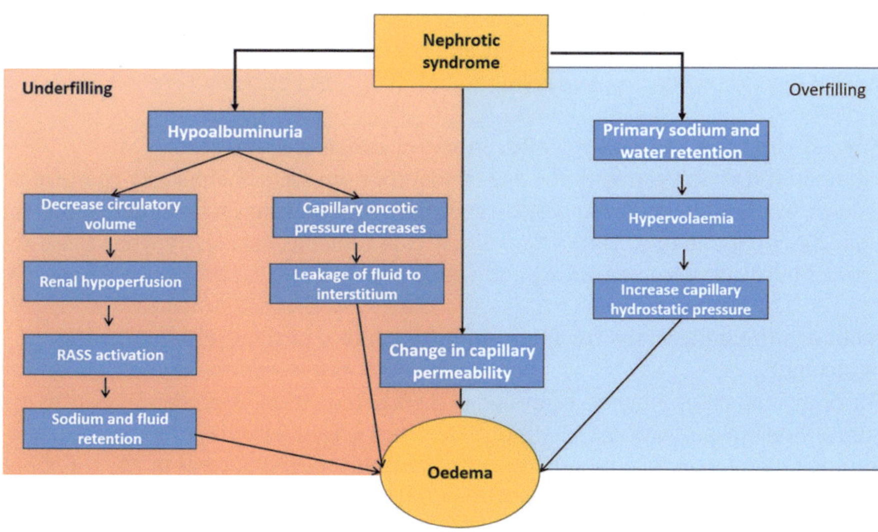

Fig. 10.2 The diagram shows the overfilling and underfilling theories in causing oedema in nephrotic syndrome

What were the possible causes of pleural effusion in Isabella? How would you manage her pleural effusion?

Bilateral pleural effusion can be part of the feature of nephrotic syndrome. Although the causes for oedema in nephrotic syndrome are complicated, the ultimate pathway is leakage of body fluid into the following:

- The subcutaneous tissue, causing a puffy face and eyelids
- Body-dependent areas causing ankle oedema, sacral oedema, bilateral hydrocele and scrotal oedema in males and vulva oedema in females
- Body cavities cause pericardial effusion, pleural effusion and ascites

Other causes of pleural effusion, like pneumonic pleural effusion, are possible differential diagnoses, especially in children with nephrotic syndrome, who are prone to pneumococcus infection. Clinical features help to differentiate the two clinical situations.

- Parapneumonic pleural effusion tends to occur unilaterally, though bilateral involvement is possible.
- The presence of fever, increased white cell counts, high C-reactive protein, ESR and procalcitonin would support an underlying infective complication.

However, the definitive diagnosis could only be made by obtaining the pleural fluid for biochemistry, cell counts and culture. Because of the low serum albumin in nephrotic syndrome, the biochemistry of the pleural effusion was expected to have low albumin; hence, in the case of suspicion of an infection, a cell count study, bacterial PCR and culture would be helpful. However, an invasive procedure of pleural tapping had to be performed to obtain the pleural fluid.

Since Isabella had no fever and the white cell counts were normal, she was given 20% albumin infusion at 1 g/kg over 6 hours with intravenous frusemide at 1 mg/kg per dose during and after the albumin infusion. A chest X-ray repeated on the subsequent days showed complete resolution of the pleural effusion (Fig. 10.3).

How do you treat oedema in children with nephrotic syndrome?

Salt and fluid restriction with the use of diuretics are the principal management of oedema in children with nephrotic syndrome. The addition of albumin infusion, typically in combination with a loop diuretic, is valuable, especially when there are signs of intravascular underfilling and severe oedema.

What are the indications for albumin infusion in a patient with nephrotic syndrome?

The body content of albumin is around 4–5 g/kg. It distributes predominantly in the extracellular space. Around 30–40% of albumin is found in the intravascular compartment, corresponds to around 40–50 g/L of plasma and is responsible for about 80% of the osmotic pressure of the plasma. This oncotic activity remains physiologically adequate if serum albumin is kept ≥20 g/L and the total proteins ≥35 g/L. As serum albumin drops, the oncotic pressure of the intravascular compartment will decrease significantly.

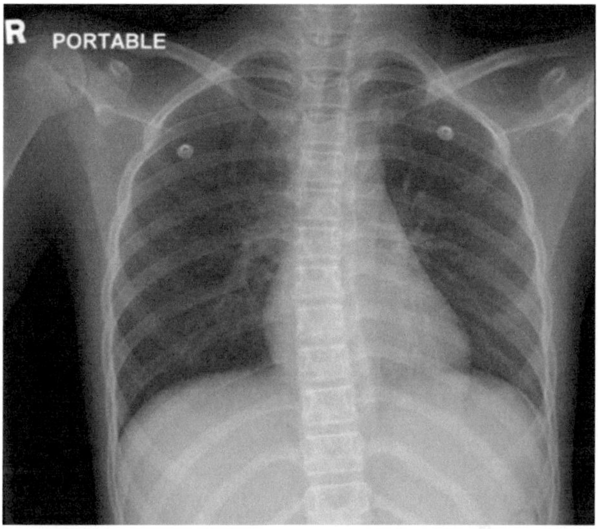

Fig. 10.3 A chest X-ray of Isabella showed resolution to the pleural effusion. The lung field was less congested

The concept of albumin infusion is to replenish the serum albumin lost in the urine and restore the body's oncotic pressure when the underlying cause of albumin loss is corrected simultaneously. The infusion of human albumin will cause the shifting of fluids from the interstitial space into the circulation within a few minutes after the onset of infusion. However, this fluid passage is limited or absent in dehydrated patients unless the dehydration is corrected. The half-life of endogenous albumin is about 3 weeks. In contrast, blood-derived albumin's half-life is only 12–16 hours and is reduced notably in conditions of increased capillary permeability or persistent albumin loss from the body. Repeated albumin infusion may be needed in individual patients. Short-term infusion of albumin 20–25%, together with diuretics, is usually reserved for patients with serum albumin <20 g/L, with marked hypovolaemia and significant symptoms.

Hypoalbuminemia also decreases the amount of loop diuretics delivered to their action site in the tubular lumen. The albumin infusion helps to enhance the delivery of diuretics to their site of action and maximise the diuretic effect.

Indications for albumin infusion with diuretics include the following:

- Decrease in effective intravascular volume (present as symptoms of abdominal pain, vomiting, lethargy, tachycardia, prolonged capillary refill and low blood pressure)
- Debilitating oedema like pleural effusion, ascites, genital oedema or anasarca
- Hypovolemic hyponatremia
- Diuretic-refractory oedema
- Hepatorenal syndrome
- Hypoperfusion renal failure
- Spontaneous bacterial peritonitis

Albumin preparations are available in 5%, 20% and 25% concentrations. The sodium concentration in these preparations is between 130 and 160 mEq/L. The dosage for albumin infusion is 0.5–1 g/kg per dose infused over a few hours. We should avoid rapid infusion of hyper-oncotic albumin as it may cause acute fluid overload, especially in patients with 'overfilling' pathophysiology, causing acute pulmonary oedema and heart failure. Albumin infusion may also cause a rapid rise in serum sodium, and some patients may develop hypersensitivity reactions. An infusion rate not to exceed 2–3 mL/min is advisable. Hyper-oncotic albumin preparations are contraindicated in premature neonates, as they may cause intraventricular haemorrhage in the premature brains.

Would you perform a renal biopsy for Isabella?

Most children of steroid-sensitive nephrotic syndrome (SSNS) did not require a renal biopsy, as most renal pathology is minimal change disease. Renal biopsy is usually reserved for those patients whose clinical presentations suggest renal pathology other than minimal change disease. In general, a renal biopsy will be considered in the following situations.

- Age <1 or >12 years
- Persistent or sustained elevation in serum creatinine
- Significant haematuria or gross haematuria
- Hypocomplementaemia or the presence of any features that suggest an autoimmune disease
- Infection with hepatitis B or C, HIV or tuberculosis that may account for the nephrotic syndrome
- Steroid resistance, which is defined as the absence of clinical remission after an 8-week steroid treatment
- Acute kidney injury that is not related to hypovolemia

What are the possible renal histopathologies in idiopathic primary nephrotic syndrome?

There are four typical types of non-inflammatory glomerulonephritis manifest as primary nephrotic syndrome in children. They are the following:

1. Minimal change disease (MCD)
   - This is the most common renal histology, and it accounts for around 90% of children <10 years old as the cause of nephrotic syndrome.
   - Greater than 90% of children with MCD are steroid-sensitive.
2. Focal segmental glomerulonephritis (FSGS)
   - Because of its focal nature, an adequate renal biopsy that requires at least 20 glomeruli and preferably includes the cortico-medullary junction, the common site for FSGS, is required to exclude the diagnosis.
   - Around 30% of children with FSGS are steroid-sensitive.
3. Membranoproliferative glomerulonephritis (MPGN/ C3 glomerulonephritis)
   - Around 50% of children with MPGN are steroid-sensitive.
   - There are three subtypes of MPGN:

- Immune complex-mediated MPGN
- Complement -mediated MPGN
- Dense deposit disease (MPGN II)
- Both complement-mediated MPGN and dense deposit disease are characterised by dysregulation in the complement system, especially C3. They showed characteristic features in the renal histology, which helped to differentiate them.

4. Membranous glomerulonephritis
   - Primary membranous glomerulonephritis is rare in children and needs to exclude hepatitis B-related membranous glomerulonephritis, especially in endemic areas.

For secondary causes, isolated nephrotic syndrome may be the first presentation in adolescents with systemic lupus erythematosus and IgA nephropathy (Table 10.1).

Further history revealed that Isabella has a half-brother who is now 24 years old and has a history of nephrotic syndrome diagnosed at 3 years old. He had frequent relapses and had two renal biopsies performed, which showed minimal change disease. He is currently on steroids and immunosuppressive agents for his frequent relapses.

When would you consider genetic tests for Isabella?
Most children with idiopathic nephrotic syndrome present in early childhood and are frequently precipitated by an upper respiratory tract infection. Before a genetic test is offered to Isabella, a detailed history, clinical assessment and renal histology of Isabella's brother should be reviewed. In general, genetic tests would be considered in a child with the following:

- A positive family history of nephrotic syndrome
- Congenital nephrotic syndrome (the patient may present in utero or shortly after birth)
- Infantile onset (<1 year) nephrotic syndrome
- Steroid resistant nephrotic syndrome
- Persistent abnormal renal function
- Other features suggestive of a known syndrome

What are the common genetic panels for nephrotic syndrome?
The genetic cause of nephrotic syndrome is mainly related to monogenic congenital nephrotic syndrome, FSGS-related or syndrome-related kidney disease, which may present as nephrotic syndrome. The list has expanded over the years with advances in molecular genetics and a better understanding of molecular biology. An example of the genetic mutation associated with childhood-onset nephrotic syndrome is listed below (Table 10.2). The repertoire of genetic mutation is anticipated to grow over time.

Given the history, FSGS could not be excluded in Isabella's brother. Isabella underwent a genetic panel test for nephrotic syndrome, but it did not detect any mutation.

Table 10.1 The four common kidney pathologies in children with idiopathic nephrotic syndrome

Diagnosis	Light microscopy	Immunofluorescence	Electron microscopy
Minimal change disease (MCD)	Normal	Negative	Podocyte with diffuse foot process effacement No electron-dense deposits
Focal segmental glomerulosclerosis (FSGS)	Segmental, focal or global glomerulosclerosis	Typically shows limited or no immune complex deposition, with nonspecific IgM and C3 staining in sclerotic areas	Extensive effacement of the podocyte foot processes
Membranoproliferative (MPGN)	Hypercellularity with mesangial cell proliferation, and the glomerular basement membrane (GBM) is thickened Appearance of 'tram-tracking' or splitting of the GBM due to subendothelial deposits and mesangial cell interposition	Positive staining for immunoglobulins (IgG, IgA, IgM) and C3 or predominant C3 staining with minimal or no immunoglobulin staining	Electron-dense deposits primarily in the subendothelial and mesangial regions of the glomeruli Double contours, or 'tram-tracking,' are observed on EM due to subendothelial deposits and new GBM formation underneath
Membranous (MG)	Diffuse thickening of the GBM Small deposits may be visualised as pinpoint 'holes' and GBM reaction to the deposits as 'spikes' appearance on the silver stain	Granular capillary wall deposits of IgG and sometimes C3 along the GBM	Extensive foot process effacement and subepithelial electron-dense deposits as a 'spike and dome' appearance

GBM glomerular basement membrane

Table 10.2 Genetic mutation associated with nephrotic syndrome in children

	Genetic mutation associated
Congenital nephrotic syndrome-related gene mutation	NPHS1, NPHS2, PDCN, SRN1, ITGA3, WT1, LAMB2, PLCE1
FSGS-related gene mutations	APOL1, MYH9, NPHS2, CD151, PTPRO, MYO1E, CD2AP, INF2, TRPC6, FSGS2, ACTN4, NUP93, NUP205, NUP107, COQ8B

How would you treat Isabella's nephrotic syndrome?

The original work of the International Study of Kidney Diseases in Children (ISKDC), followed by a series of studies by the Arbeitsgemeinschaft für Padiatrische Nephrologie (APN), formed the foundation for the management of children with nephrotic syndrome. They set up protocols on the steroid regimen in managing the first presentation and subsequent relapses of nephrotic syndrome in children and remain the cornerstone for following guidelines.

- Oral prednisolone at 60 mg/m^2 or 2 mg/kg (maximum dose of 60 mg/day) per day for 4–6 weeks, followed by alternate-day prednisolone at 40 mg/m^2 or 1.5 mg/kg (a maximum dose of 40 mg on alternate days) per day for 4–6 weeks.

There was a period of enthusiasm in maintaining a prolonged steroid tapering course after the 4–6 weeks of alternate-day steroids, and this was supported by meta-analysis and some studies in the past years. However, with the emergence of recent evidence, prolonged steroid tapering did not show any beneficial effect, and recent guidelines have dropped this recommendation (Table 10.3).

After the exclusion of secondary causes of nephrotic syndrome, Isabella was treated with the standard prednisolone regimen (an 8-week regimen). She responded well to the steroid and remitted within the second week of daily prednisolone.

What is the prognosis for idiopathic nephrotic syndrome, and how would you counsel the family?

Remission of proteinuria to steroid therapy is the most significant predictor of long-term prognosis. The majority of children (80–90%) with idiopathic nephrotic syndrome are steroid responsive (SSNS) and remit within 4 weeks of steroid therapy. However, most children relapse, and around 50% will become steroid-dependent, and 50% will have frequent relapses. A small percentage of children (around 3–10%) will become late steroid-resistant.

In correlation with the renal pathology, ≥90% of MCD respond to steroid treatment. Around 50% of children with MPGN respond to steroids, and only 30% of FSGS respond to steroids.

Most children with SSNS improve with age. Less than 10% of children continue to relapse in adulthood, and less than 5% will end up in renal impairment in adulthood.

In contrast, children with steroid-resistant nephrotic syndrome (SRNS) are more likely to progress, and some may go into renal failure.

Although Isabella responded well to prednisolone, she had a relapse of proteinuria 4 months after stopping steroid therapy. How do you define relapse of nephrotic syndrome, and how would you treat her?

In a child who has previously achieved complete remission, relapse of nephrotic syndrome is defined as urine dipstick ≥3+ or urine protein-creatinine ratio ≥2 mg/mg on a spot urine sample on 3 consecutive days, with or without the reappearance of oedema.

Table 10.3 Steroid regimes in the treatment of childhood idiopathic nephrotic syndrome

Steroid regime	Steroid regimen in the initial episode
ISKDC (1981)	*An 8-week regimen* 60 mg/m^2/day for 4 weeks, followed by intermittent prednisone 40 mg/m^2/day on 3 consecutive days out of 7 days for 4 weeks
APN (1988) A shorter steroid regimen	Prednisone 60 mg/m^2/day until proteinuria had disappeared for 3 days, followed by 40 mg/m^2/day every 48 hours until complete remission had occurred
APN (1993)	*A 12-week regime* 60 mg/m^2/day for 6 weeks, followed by 40 mg/m^2/day on alternative days for 6 weeks
Cochrane data-based meta-analysis 2007	Prolonged alternate-day steroid therapy for 6 months
KDIGO 2012	Oral prednisone be administered as a single daily dose starting at 60 mg/m^2/day or 2 mg/kg/day to a maximum of 60 mg/day for 4–6 weeks, followed by alternate-day medication as a single daily dose starting at 40 mg/m^2 or 1.5 mg/kg (maximum 40 mg on alternate days) and continued for 2–5 months with tapering of the dose
KDIGO 2021	Oral prednisolone daily dose ([a]BSA or weight-based dosing) for 4–6 weeks, followed by alternate day doses ([b]BSA or weight-based dosing) for 4–6 weeks. Prolonged therapy for 16–24 weeks if <4–6 years old or if delayed remission
IPNA 2022	Oral prednisolone daily dose ([a]BSA or weight-based dosing) for 4–6 weeks, followed by alternate day doses ([b]BSA or weight-based dosing) for 4–6 weeks, then off No prolonged tapering regime
KDIGO 2025	Oral prednisolone daily dose ([a]BSA or weight-based dosing) for 4–6 weeks, followed by alternate day doses ([b]BSA or weight-based dosing) for 4–6 weeks No prolonged tapering regime

ISKDC International Study of Kidney Diseases in Children, *APN* Arbeitsgemeinschaft für Pädiatrische Nephrologie, *KDIGO* Kidney disease improving global outcomes, *IPNA* International Paediatric Nephrology Association, *BSA* body surface area

[a]Daily dose (BSA or weight-based) dosing: 60 mg/m^2/day or 2 mg/kg/day to a maximum of 60 mg/day

[b]Alternate-day dose (BSA or weight-based) dosing 40 mg/m^2 or 1.5 mg/kg to a maximum of 40 mg on alternate days

In the treatment of relapse, most protocols are similar.

Oral prednisolone at 60 mg/m^2/day until urine protein-free for 3–5 days, followed by 40 mg/m^2/day on alternative days for 4 weeks

How would you define frequent relapse?

Frequent relapse is defined as ≥2 relapses in the first 6 months following remission of the initial episode or ≥3 relapses in any 12 months.

Upon subsequent follow-up, Isabella had three relapses in 12 months. A renal biopsy was performed, and it was confirmed that the kidney histology was MCD. What are the possible second-line treatment options for her?

Children with SSNS who have relapsing courses require repeated steroid cycles, and this may cause significant steroid toxicity. To minimise steroid complications, immunosuppressive agents, like levamisole, mycophenolate mofetil, calcineurin inhibitors, cyclophosphamide and anti-CD20 monoclonal antibodies have been used as steroid-sparing agents to reduce morbidity (Table 10.4).

Table 10.4 Immunosuppressive agents for SSNS with frequent relapses

Drugs	Mechanism of action	Dose	Indications	Side effects
Levamisole	Antihelminthic drug with immunomodulatory properties	2–2.5 mg/kg alternate day (maximum 150 mg per dose)	Mild disease of SSNS-frequent relapses	Neutropenia
Mycophenolate mofetil	Inhibits the de novo synthesis of guanine nucleotides	600–1200 mg/m^2/day in 2 divided doses	Mild disease of SSNS-frequent relapses	Abdominal pain, diarrhoea, bone marrow suppression Toxic hepatitis
Cyclosporin A	Calcineurin inhibitor inhibits the synthesis of interleukins like IL-2, inhibits TH1, TH2, APC and B lymphocyte	3–5 mg/kg/day in two divided doses and monitor drug level, C_0 at 60–100 ng/ml and maintain the lowest possible drug level	The first line in SRNS, SSNS-frequent relapses	Nephrotoxicity, gingival hypertrophy, hypertrichosis, hypertension, PRES
Tacrolimus	Calcineurin inhibitor	0.1–0.2 mg/kg/day in 2 divided doses and monitor drug level with C_0 at 3–7 ng/ml and lowest possible drug level	The first line in SRNS, SSNS-frequent relapses	Nephrotoxicity, hypertension, PRES
Cyclophosphamide	Alkylating agent	2 mg/kg for 12 weeks in SSNS and 3 mg/kg for 8 weeks in SRNS (cumulative dose not to exceed 168 mg/kg)	SSNS-frequent relapse; SRNS	Neutropenia and bone marrow suppression, gonadal toxicity, particularly in pubertal boys

(continued)

Table 10.4 (continued)

Drugs	Mechanism of action	Dose	Indications	Side effects
Rituximab	The chimeric mouse-human monoclonal antibody targets CD20, which induces B-cell apoptosis	375 mg/m^2 for 1–4 doses per course at weekly intervals, aiming for depletion of CD20-positive B cells	SSNS-frequent relapse	Need premedication for infusion reaction Persistent IgG deficiency, activation of tuberculosis, hepatitis and opportunistic infections
Ofatumumab	Human anti-CD20 monoclonal antibody	300 mg/1.73m^2	Refractory NS	Hypersensitivity, bronchospasm, dyspnoea

SSNS Steroid-sensitive nephrotic syndrome, *SRNS* Steroid-resistant nephrotic syndrome, *PRES* posterior reversible encephalopathy syndrome, *NS* nephrotic syndrome, C_0 drug trough level

How would you advise on Isabella's vaccination?

In general, live attenuated vaccinations should be avoided. As Isabella has reached 12 years old, she must have received most of her childhood vaccinations. At the same time, the 'acquired-immunity deficiency' state of nephrotic syndrome, due to the loss of immunoglobin in urine and the use of immunosuppressive agents, makes her vulnerable to opportunistic infections and encapsulated bacteria. Hence, she will be advised to receive the following:

- Vaccination against *Streptococcus pneumoniae*, *Haemophilus influenzae* and *Neisseria meningitidis*
- Yearly seasonal inactivated influenzae vaccine (not the inhalation preparation, which is live attenuated)
- COVID-19 vaccination
- The hepatitis B vaccination
- Avoid live vaccines or boosters (measles, rubeola, mumps, varicella, rotavirus and oral polio)

10.3 Case Illustrations

Idiopathic nephrotic syndrome is a common renal problem in childhood. This case guides the reader through the journey of a patient with nephrotic syndrome, encompassing the clinical presentation, theoretical background and therapeutic options. While most paediatricians are familiar with the features of anasarca, sometimes pleural effusion is overlooked, especially when a supine film is taken.

Suggested Further Readings

1. Floege J, Gibson KL, Vivarelli M, Liew A, Radhakrishnan J, Balk EM, Gordon CE, et al. Executive summary of the KDIGO 2025 clinical practice guideline for the management of nephrotic syndrome in children. Kidney Int. 2025;107(5):806–8.
2. Trautmann A, Boyer O, Hodson E, Bagga A, Gipson DS, Samuel S, Wetzels J, et al. IPNA clinical practice recommendations for the diagnosis and management of children with steroid-sensitive nephrotic syndrome. Pediatr Nephrol. 2023;38(3):877–919.
3. Vivarelli M, Gibson K, Sinha A, Boyer O. Childhood nephrotic syndrome. Lancet. 2023;402(10404):809–24.
4. Hahn D, Samuel SM, Willis NS, Craig JC, Hodson EM. Corticosteroid therapy for nephrotic syndrome in children. Cochrane Database Syst Rev. 2024;8:CD001533.
5. Kallash M, Mahan JD. Mechanisms and management of edema in pediatric nephrotic syndrome. Pediatr Nephrol. 2021;36(7):1719–30.

It May Not Be a Simple Seizure

11

11.1 Case Description

Beatrice is a 27-month-old girl admitted in the morning for an episode of generalized-tonic clonic (GTC) seizure with uprolling eyes and loss of consciousness for 3–4 min. The seizure stopped spontaneously but recurred an hour later and was aborted by rectal diazepam at the A&E department. She developed the third episode of GTC, and a dose of intravenous phenytoin aborted it. The history revealed low-grade fever, cough, running nose and gastroenteritis symptoms lasting 3 days before admission. Her blood test showed a serum albumin of 14 g/dL and urine albustix of 4+. Upon further questioning, the parents noticed Beatrice had puffy eyelids for almost 2 weeks.

11.2 Interactive Case Discussion

What is nephrotic syndrome of childhood?
Nephrotic syndrome describes a clinical syndrome characterized by massive protein loss in the urine, leading to generalized oedema, hypoalbuminemia and hyperlipidaemia. It results from abnormally increased permeability in the glomerular filtration barrier, which causes loss of albumin and other negatively charged proteins in urine.

Nephrotic syndrome is characterized by the following:

1. Clinical oedema includes puffy faces, swollen eyelids, pitting oedema over lower limbs, sacral oedema (dependent oedema), ascites, vulval oedema in females, penile and scrotal oedema in males. Sometimes, there may be pleural effusion.
2. Nephrotic range proteinuria is defined as 24-hour urine protein $\geq$40 mg/m^2/hr or a spot urine protein/creatinine ratio of $\geq$2 mg/mg.
3. Hypoalbuminemia with serum albumin <25 g/L.
4. Hyperlipidaemia—raised serum cholesterol ± triglyceride.

W. K. Y. Chan, M. C. I. Kuok, *Paediatric Nephrology*,
https://doi.org/10.1007/978-981-95-5060-9_11

What are the causes of nephrotic syndrome, and how would you classify nephrotic syndrome in children?

According to its underlying aetiology, nephrotic syndrome can be classified as primary or secondary to a systemic disease (Table 11.1). It can also be classified according to its age of onset (Table 11.2) or by its clinical responsiveness to steroid therapy (Table 11.3). These classifications are not mutually exclusive; for example, a patient with a renal history of FSGS may have an underlying genetic (idiopathic) or a secondary cause, and he can be steroid-responsive or steroid-resistant.

Table 11.1 Classification of nephrotic syndrome by aetiology

Primary (no secondary cause was identified, and the classification is based on renal histology)	Minimal change nephrotic syndrome (MCNS) Other primary glomerulonephritis – Focal segmental glomerulosclerosis (FSGS) – Membranous glomerulonephritis – Membranoproliferative glomerulonephritis – Mesangial proliferative glomerulonephritis (with IgM or IgA-IgG deposit)
Secondary to renal involvement in systemic diseases	Henoch-SchÖnlein purpura Systemic lupus erythematosus and other systemic vasculitis Diabetic mellitus Chronic infections like hepatitis B, malaria, HIV, syphilis Drugs like penicillamine, gold, mercury, heroin Malignancy like lymphoma, myeloma Chronic inflammation with amyloidosis

Table 11.2 Classification of nephrotic syndrome by age of onset of disease

Age of onset	Nephrotic syndrome type	Underlying causes
<3 months	Congenital nephrotic syndrome	Genetic cause (Finnish type) Congenital infection
4 months–1 year	Infantile nephrotic syndrome	Likely has a genetic cause
Greater than 1 year	Childhood nephrotic syndrome	Idiopathic nephrotic syndrome most commonly has a childhood onset time between 2 and 7 years old

Table 11.3 Classification of nephrotic syndrome according to its responsiveness to high-dose steroid therapy

Steroid responsiveness	Nephrotic syndrome type	Clinical importance
Remission is achieved within 4 weeks of daily high-dose steroid therapy	Steroid sensitive (SSNS)	As most patients have minimal change in glomerulonephritis, a steroid trial without a renal biopsy is the option.
Remission not achieved after 4 weeks of daily high-dose steroid	Steroid resistant (SRNS)	A renal biopsy is indicated, and the prognosis is less favourable. Workup for genetic causes may be needed

What are the genetic causes of nephrotic syndrome in childhood?
With the advances in podocytology study and genetic techniques, our understanding of the pathogenesis of hereditary nephrotic syndrome has increased. Most of these children are steroid-resistant with renal histology of FSGS. When a genetic mutation causes a structural and functional change in the podocyte molecules, it will cause podocyte injury, leading to sclerosis and progress to FSGS. Some well-known genetic mutations include NPHS1 in Finnish-type congenital nephrotic syndrome, NPHS2 in early onset SRNS and WT1 gene mutation in Denys-Drash and Frasier syndrome.

Beatrice was in a post-ictal state, and her vital signs were stable. There was no focal neurological sign. Her BP was 100/60, and her heart rate was 110 bpm. There were puffy eyelids with ankle oedema. Her abdomen was distended with ascites. Blood test showed white blood cell 10.6×10^9/L, platelet 1064×10^9/L, haemoglobin 9.6 g/dL, MCV 62.3 fL, sodium 133 mmol/L, potassium 4.1 mmol/L, urea 3.3 mmol/L, creatinine 15 umol/L. serum albumin 14 g/L, globulin 37 g/L, calcium 2.18 mmol/L, phosphate 1.13 mmol/L, Ig A 0.77 g/L (Ref: 0.2–1.0 g/L), Ig G 3.02 g/L (Ref: 3.17–9.94 g/L), Ig M 1.08 g/L (Ref: 0.19–1.46 g/L) and a random serum cholesterol was 6 mmol/L. Her spot urine protein/creatinine ratio was 19.1 g/g Cr (Ref: <0.4 g/g Cr), and 24-hour urine was 3.25 g/day (270 mg/m^2/hr). Hence, Beatrice suffered from nephrotic syndrome in childhood.

If Beatrice has nephrotic syndrome, what could be the causes of her seizure?
In general, seizures may be caused by the following:

- Electrolytes disturbances, like hyponatremia, hypocalcaemia and hypomagnesium
- Infection like meningitis and encephalitis
- Cerebral vascular events
- Space-occupying lesions in the CNS
- Metabolic encephalopathy
- Epileptic syndrome

Concerning the setting of a child with nephrotic syndrome, the following have to be considered.

- Electrolyte disturbance: Hyponatraemia is common in children with nephrotic syndrome. The severity of hyponatremia correlates with the degree of fluid retention and hyperlipidaemia, which may cause pseudo-hyponatremia.
- Nephrotic syndrome shifts the body's haemostasis towards a hypercoagulable state. Children with NS have an imbalance between prothrombogenic and antithrombotic factors. They also have thrombocytosis and increased platelet activation, making them prone to venous thromboembolism.
- With the loss of immunoglobin IgG in the urine, the affected child may have defective opsonization of bacteria, rendering the child prone to infection by organisms like *streptococcus pneumoniae* and *E. coli*. Hence, infective meningitis is a possible differential diagnosis.

- If the patient is on steroid or calcineurin inhibition, posterior reversible encephalopathy syndrome (PRES) is another possible cause of seizure.

Review Beatrice's investigation on admission. She had a high platelet count at admission, but her white cell counts were normal. Her IgG was low, her fibrinogen was 4.5 g/L (Ref: 1.5–3.6 g/L); PT, aPTT and INR were normal. Her urgent CT brain was normal. A lumbar puncture showed low CSF protein and normal glucose; no white blood cell was in the CSF, and subsequent CSF culture and blood culture were negative. Her nasopharyngeal swab, however, was positive for enterovirus. Her EEG showed a post-ictal state and no features of status epilepticus. The cause of her seizure could be enterovirus-related encephalopathy or atypical febrile convulsion.

Why the risk of thromboembolism is increased in patients with nephrotic syndrome?

The pathogenesis of thromboembolism risk needs to be better understood. When the permeability in the glomerular filtration membrane increases and other negatively charged proteins are lost together with albumin, like prothrombin III and other antithrombotic factors, the liver will increase the synthesis of the proteins, leading to the imbalance between the thrombotic and antithrombotic factors. Mechanisms for procoagulopathy could be as follows:

- Liver synthesis of pro-coagulants increases (increase fibrinogen, factor II, V, VII and VIII)
- Decrease anti-coagulant synthesis (loss of antithrombin III in urine)
- Defective fibrinogenesis (decrease plasminogen and hyperfibrinogenaemia)

Other contributing factors to thrombosis are intravascular dehydration, thrombocytosis, use of steroids and central venous catheters, if any.

Where are the possible sites for thromboembolism in a nephrotic child?

Theoretically, all vessels can be affected, including both arteries and veins.

- Renal vein thrombosis (causes sudden gross haematuria with a congested kidney)
- Deep vein thrombosis (especially if a central venous catheter was placed)
- Pulmonary embolism (this could be fatal if left untreated)
- Central sinovenous thrombosis (rare but could be fatal; the most common site is the superior sagittal sinus)
- Central retinal vein thrombosis (rare but has serious consequences)

Beatrice was started on intravenous methylprednisolone with a dose equivalent to prednisolone at 60 $mg/m^2/day$ initially and put back to oral prednisolone when she can tolerate oral feeding. A blood test for iron profile was taken as her MCV was low at 62.3 fl. Her serum iron was 2 μmol/L (Ref: 7–26 μmol/L), TIBC was 32 umol/L (Ref: 41–77), iron saturation was 6% (Ref: 10–50%), and ferritin was low at 10 pmol/L (Ref:14–151 pmol/L).

What was the cause of Beatrice's iron deficiency anaemia?

In nephrotic syndrome, there is a loss of transferrin and iron in the urine, giving rise to iron deficiency anaemia. This usually is not problematic in steroid-responsive nephrotic syndrome, as the permeability of glomerular filtration members will normalize over time. However, this will be an important issue to address in children with congenital nephrotic syndrome or steroid-resistant nephrotic syndrome.

What kind of protein is lost in nephrotic syndrome?

Because of the altered filtration barrier, many other proteins are lost in urine besides albumin. Therefore, nephrotic patients could have low levels of binding proteins for ions (iron, copper, zinc), vitamins (vitamin D) and hormones (steroid or thyroid hormones). As most childhood-onset nephrotic syndrome is resolved with steroid therapy, the loss of these proteins is transient and may not cause a long-term impact. However, the significance of these protein losses is important in managing congenital nephrotic syndrome (Table 11.4).

Beatrice's nephrotic syndrome remitted on day 10 after steroid treatment. She returned for a follow-up after a 3-week course of prednisolone at 60 mg/m^2/day. Her serum albumin was normalized to 34 g/dL with a urine protein/creatinine ratio of 0.13 g/g (normal). Her total cholesterol remained high at 9.3 mmol/L with LDL-cholesterol 5.8 mmol/L. She had a palpable liver, and she had a private ultrasound that showed a fatty liver. Her parents were worried.

How would you advise the parent about the hepatomegaly and fatty liver in a child with nephrotic syndrome?

Hepatomegaly is common in children with nephrotic syndrome, especially when there is increased protein synthesis in response to various protein loss and disturbed lipid metabolism. Minimal change disease in childhood nephrotic syndrome was once called lipoid nephrosis in the old days, meaning fatty infiltration to the kidney in untreated patients with prolonged disease course .

As Beatrice's nephrotic syndrome responded to steroid therapy, her abnormal lipid metabolism and hepatomegaly should be transient and would resolve after remission of her nephrotic syndrome.

Table 11.4 Protein loss in nephrotic syndrome

Protein	Clinical significance
Albumin	Hypoalbuminemia and oedema
Lecithin cholesterol acyltransferase and high-density lipoprotein	Hyperlipidaemia
Ig G and factor B	Hypoglobulinaemia and altered opsonization lead to an increased risk of infection like pneumococcal infection
Transferrin, iron	Iron-resistant anaemia
Thyroxin-binding globulin	Altered thyroid function
Vitamin D binding protein	Risk of metabolic bone disease

Given the persistently high total cholesterol, cholestyramine was started. Repeated total cholesterol dropped to 6.5 mmol/L before starting HMGC$_O$A reductase, so she was kept on cholestyramine only. Follow-up USG showed resolution of the fatty infiltration.

What is your plan of steroid therapy in Beatrice?

Since Beatrice's nephrotic syndrome is steroid responsive, we would complete a 4–6-week daily prednisolone at 60 mg/m^2/day, followed by prednisolone 40 mg/m^2 on alternate day for another 4–6 weeks and then stop as recommended in the standard treatment. Steroid tapering regime over a period of 2–3 months may be adopted by some centres.

What is the long-term prognosis of Beatrice?

Patients with steroid sensitive nephrotic syndrome has a better overall prognosis than steroid resistant children. In general, 85% of children with idiopathic nephrotic syndrome are steroid sensitive. For those steroid sensitive patients, around 75% may have a relapse during the follow up period and 50% of them may be frequent relapsers.

For those steroid-dependent patients or frequent relapsers, alternative immunosuppressive agents may be needed as steroid sparing agents. The long-term kidney outcome is overall excellent for steroid responsive patients.

11.3 Case Illustrations

This case highlights some of the common yet often overlooked features associated with nephrotic syndrome. Seizure in children with nephrotic syndrome need careful evaluation because of the potential serious complications seen in this group of children. Apart from albumin, the loss of other proteins in urine may cause clinical concerns, and the managing doctors should be aware of these complications to avoid unnecessary investigations.

Suggested Further Readings

1. Noone DG, Iijima K, Parekh R. Idiopathic nephrotic syndrome in children. Lancet. 2018;392(10141):61–74.
2. Trautmann A, Boyer O, Hodson E, Bagga A, Gipson DS, Samuel S, et al. IPNA clinical practice recommendations for the diagnosis and management of children with steroid-sensitive nephrotic syndrome. Pediatr Nephrol. 2023;38(3):877–919.
3. Rodriguez-Ballestas E, Reid-Adam J. Nephrotic syndrome. Pediatr Rev. 2022;43(2):87–99.

Blood Leaks in the Urine 12

12.1 Case Description

Elizabeth is a 14-year-old girl referred to our clinic as her urine dipstick test was positive for red blood cells during the routine check-up in her family doctor's clinic. Elizabeth was initially reassured as the family doctor suspected the urine test may be contaminated with menstrual blood. The test was repeated several weeks later. However, it was still positive, so Elizabeth was referred for further assessment.

12.2 Interactive Case Discussion

What is the dipstick test for detecting blood in urine?

A urine dipstick is a convenient way to screen urine for red blood cells. Detection of red blood cells in the urine is based on the peroxidase activity of *Heme*, which is the core component of haemoglobin, to catalyse a reaction between hydrogen peroxide and a chromogen, such as tetramethylbenzidine, causing a green colour change in the test strips. The degree of colour change correlates with the amount of *Heme* in the urine. A spotted pattern indicates intact RBCs and a uniform pattern indicates free haemoglobin.

As the test detects the presence of Heme, a positive test may indicate the presence of RBC, haemoglobin or myoglobin.

Does a positive urine dipstick test indicate haematuria?

Urinary dipstick tests for haematuria have a high false positive rate; patients with positive dipstick results require microscopic urinalysis before diagnosing haematuria (Fig. 12.1).

W. K. Y. Chan, M. C. I. Kuok, *Paediatric Nephrology*,
https://doi.org/10.1007/978-981-95-5060-9_12

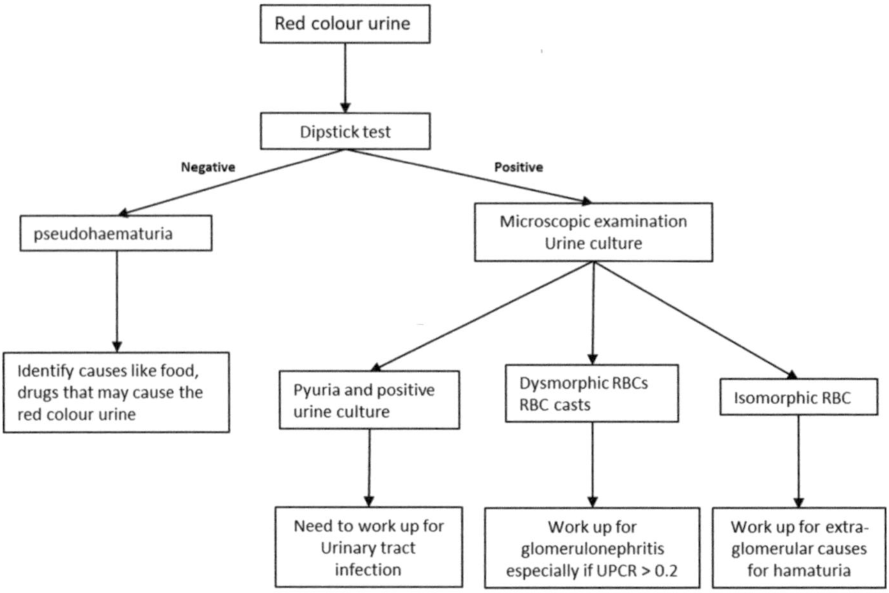

Fig. 12.1 A diagrammatic approach to red-coloured urine

False Positive Test

- Due to the presence of myoglobin, haemoglobin and contaminants such as hypochlorite in the containers, menstrual blood, trauma and bacterial peroxidase
- Dehydration with a highly concentrated urine

False Negative Test

- Ingestion of ascorbic acid or other reducing agents
- Low urine pH

What is pseudo-hematuria?

There are two clinical scenarios in which the patient is misinterpreted as having blood in urine, but she is not.

- Scenario 1
  The urine looks bloody, but the urine dipstick is negative. Many different drugs, foods and additives may cause a colour change in the urine. This is benign and does not indicate any pathology.
- Scenario 2
  The urine dipstick was positive, but urine microscopy for RBC was negative. 'Dipstick haematuria' or pseudo-haematuria describes patients with no symptoms but a positive dipstick test and negative microscopic urinalysis. This kind of dipstick pseudo-haematuria (false positive dipstick test) is a clinically insignificant finding.

What kind of food can cause red-coloured urine?
Food like beets, fava beans, blackberries and rhubarb may cause red-coloured urine, not haematuria.

What kind of drugs can cause red-coloured urine?
There are numerous medications that can cause red urine discolouration, and they are harmless. The most common drugs are rifampin and pyridium (phenazopyridine). Others include chlorpromazine, thioridazine, senna and laxatives with a phenolphthalein component, which turns pink in alkaline urine.

What are the differences between gross hematuria and microscopic hematuria?
The difference between the two is based on the visibility to the naked eye during urine inspection. There are different aetiology and underlying causes between the two. Significant and persistent haematuria may be a marker for underlying renal pathologies, no matter its gross or microscopic haematuria (Tables 12.1 and 12.2).

On repeated urinary examination, Elizabeth's urine showed persistent microscopic haematuria. How would you evaluate her problem?
Evaluation of Elizabeth's problem starts with a comprehensive history taking and physical examination, which includes the following.

1. Any change in the colour of urine?
   - The urine colour may remain yellow in microhaematuria. As the red blood cells increase in urine, the urine colour may change to a pinkish, bloody or even coke-like colour, which may indicate an underlying glomerulonephritis.

Table 12.1 The difference between gross and microscopic haematuria

	Appearance and significance	Remarks
Gross haematuria	Urine looks bloody upon visual inspection. The bloody urine may appear pink or red but may also appear tea-coloured or dark-cola-coloured, indicating underlying glomerular pathologies	One ml of blood per litre of urine can induce a visible colour change
Microscopic haematuria	The amount of RBC in the urine does not cause a colour change in the urine, so it cannot be visualised with the naked eye. The presence of RBC in urine can only be detected by a microscope. Microscopic examination of RBC in the urine: – The morphologic features of RBCs are best seen through phase-contrast microscopy – The presence of dysmorphic RBC (RBC with irregular cell membranes) and RBC casts are highly suggestive of the glomerular origin of the RBC	The presence of 2–3 RBC per high power field (HPF) under microscopy can make the urine dipstick positive. The definition of microscopic haematuria varies depending on the amount of RBC that can be detected by microscopic examination. A common definition is 5 RBC/mm^3 in uncentrifuged urine or 5 RBC/HPF in centrifuged urine on at least 2–3 different occasions.

Table 12.2 The different causes of persistent haematuria

Site of bleeding	Aetiology

Urinary tract -Kidney causes	Glomerular Diseases
	– Hereditary: Alport syndrome, familial benign haematuria syndrome, nail-patella syndrome
	– Primary glomerulonephritis:
	– Membranoproliferative glomerulonephritis, mesangial proliferative glomerulonephritis, IgA nephropathy, crescentic glomerulonephritis, focal glomerulosclerosis, minimal change disease
	– Secondary glomerulonephritis
	  – Infection-related: post-streptococcal glomerulonephritis, shunt nephritis, hepatitis-related, subacute bacterial endocarditis, malaria, dengue fever, hepatitis B-associated glomerulonephritis, AIDs, etc.
	  – Multisystem diseases: systemic lupus erythematosus, Henoch-Schonlein purpura, vasculitis disease like polyarteritis nodosa, ANCA-associated vasculitis, haemolytic-uremic syndrome
	  – Drugs-related: non-steroidal anti-inflammatory drugs, cyclosporin A, aminoglycosides

	Non-glomerular Disease – Hypercalciuria – Nephrocalcinosis – Vascular causes: nutcracker syndrome, renal vein thrombosis, sickle cell disease – Cystic kidney disease: polycystic kidney disease, medullary cystic disease – Tubulointerstitial nephritis – Renal tumours like Wilms tumour – Papillary necrosis
Urinary tract -Non-kidney causes	Ureter: ureteric stone, UPJO, UVJO, ureterocele
	Bladder: bladder stone, cystitis
	Urethra: urethral strictures, trauma
Non-urinary tract causes	Bleeding and coagulation defect – Congenital diseases : haemophilia A, haemophilia B, platelet function disorders – Acquired diseases: idiopathic thrombocytopenic purpura, disseminated intravascular coagulopathy

2. Timing of urine colour change related to the urinary streams
   - Haematuria noted at the onset of micturition indicates a urethral problem.
   - Terminal haematuria with super-pubic pain indicates cystitis.
   - Haematuria throughout the micturition (whole stream haematuria) indicates bleeding from any site along the urinary tract.
   - The presence of blood clots in urine usually indicates bleeding in the bladder.
3. The temporal relationship of urine colour change to an infection like a sore throat
   - The temporal relation to sore throat of a viral infection may indicate the underlying glomerulonephritis. Post-infectious glomerulonephritis typically occurs 10–14 days after an infection, while haematuria occurs at the time of infection (synpharyngitic)may indicate an underlying IgA glomerulonephritis.

4. Association of pain
   - Loin pain may indicate acute pyelonephritis, renal stone or papillary necrosis.
   - The radiation of pain from the loin downwards to the suprapubic region may indicate the passage of a renal stone down to the ureter (renal colic).
   - Suprapubic pain may indicate cystitis.
5. Association with exercise may indicate exercise-induced haematuria
6. A family history of renal disease, renal stones, cystic kidney disease or hearing impairment may indicate genetic causes of renal disease, like hereditary nephritis or polycystic kidney diseases.

   A focused physical examination to detect any of the following:

- Signs of chronic kidney disease—like growth failure, pallor and even rickets
- Hypertension
- Palpable kidneys or bladders
- Systemic features that may relate to systemic renal disease, like systemic lupus erythematosus, Henoch-Schonlein purpura, etc.

What initial investigations would you perform?
Apart from urinary examination, the following radiological imaging may be helpful.

- A plain X-ray (KUB) to detect any renal calculi
- Ultrasound of the urinary system to assess any CAKUT, kidney stones, renal mass and measure the kidney size
- Appropriate laboratory tests, which may include BUN; creatinine; electrolytes; serum calcium; phosphate; autoimmune markers (ANA, ANCA and anti-dsDNA); immunoglobin pattern including IgA, anti-streptolysin O titer (ASOT), complements (C3, C4, CH50), hepatitis B and hepatitis C serology, urine protein-to-creatinine ratio and urine calcium-to-creatinine ratio; urine culture and throat swab for culture.

How would you manage Elizabeth if all the history, physical examination and investigations were negative?
Few differential diagnoses for isolated microhaematuria begin in childhood and are of glomerular origin. They are hereditary nephritis (Alport syndrome), IgA glomerulonephritis and benign familial haematuria (thin membrane disease). As Elizabeth just has isolated persistent microhaematuria with normal renal function, no secondary causes are identified, and there was no significant family history; she was regularly followed up to assess any progression of the disease. In some patients, a renal biopsy may be indicated.

Elizabeth's condition remained stable over the years of follow-up. She had persistent isolated microhaematuria. There was no proteinuria, and her renal function remained stable. Does she suffer from thin membrane disease?

What is thin membrane disease?

Thin membrane disease was described more than 80 years ago, with different names, such as congenital hereditary haematuria, familial benign haematuria, thin membrane nephropathy, etc.

The hallmark of thin membrane nephropathy is a generalised thinning of the glomerular basement membrane (GBM) without any other glomerular abnormalities detected in the kidney biopsy. The clinical features are characterised by

- Persistent microhaematuria
- Episodic gross haematuria is rare
- Proteinuria is absent
- Non-progressive renal failure
- Absent of extra-renal disease
- Positive familial history and disease run a 'benign' course

Thin basement membrane disease is often diagnosed on clinical grounds when there is persistent dysmorphic or glomerular haematuria, minimal or no proteinuria, normal kidney function and no other apparent cause. Over the past decades, it once was believed to run a benign clinical course. However, recent advances in genetic and molecular studies have revealed the spectrum of renal disease related to the mutation of collagen IV. Thin membrane disease may not be as benign as we previously thought.

12.3 Case Illustrations

Microscopic haematuria is a common finding in children. This case demonstrates the evaluation steps in children with microhaematuria and raises the question on whether microscopic haematuria is a benign entity as it has long been assumed. Most of the patients with microhaematuria do not have a serious disease; however, it could be an early presentation of a progressive glomerulopathy.

Suggested Further Readings

1. Viteri B, Reid-Adam J. Hematuria and proteinuria in children. Pediatr Rev. 2018;39(12):573–87.
2. Horváth O, Szabó AJ, Reusz GS. How to define and assess the clinically significant causes of hematuria in childhood. Pediatr Nephrol. 2023;38(8):2549–62.
3. Uzzo M, Moroni G, Ponticelli C. Thin basement membrane: an underrated cause of end-stage renal disease. Nephron. 2023;147(7):383–91.

Benign or Not Benign

13

13.1 Case Description

Elizabeth was the 14-year-old girl who was previously referred for evaluation of microhaematuria. She was followed up regularly in the outpatient clinic and remained well all along. Her renal function test was normal, and her urine protein creatinine ratio was <0.2 (mg/mg). Her microhaematuria persisted with 5–15 RBC per high-power field. Does Elizabeth suffer from thin membrane nephropathy?

13.2 Interactive Case Discussion

What is thin membrane nephropathy?

Thin basement membrane disease was first described in the 1960s when several families with isolated haematuria were classified as benign familial haematuria. These patients had persistent microscopic haematuria for years without disease progression. Since then, different names like congenital hereditary haematuria, familial benign haematuria, thin membrane disease, thin basement membrane disease and thin membrane nephropathy have been used to describe this 'benign' condition interchangeably.

Before we can define the thinning of the glomerular basement membrane (GBM), we have to know the normal range of the thickness of GBM. The thickness of GBM depends on the age and sex of the person. It is also affected by the method by which the renal tissue is fixed. The World Health Organisation (WHO) defines a thin basement membrane with a threshold of 250 nm for adults and 180 nm for children between 2 and 11 years of age (Table 13.1).

The pathognomonic feature of thin membrane nephropathy is the uniform thinning of the glomerular basement membrane (GBM) without any other glomerular

W. K. Y. Chan, M. C. I. Kuok, *Paediatric Nephrology*,
https://doi.org/10.1007/978-981-95-5060-9_13

Table 13.1 Normal thickness of the glomerular basement membrane for different age groups and sex

Subject groups	Thickness of glomerular basement membrane (GBM)
Children at birth	150 nm
Children at 1 year	200 nm
Children from 2 to 11 years	GBM grows into adult GBM thickness
Female adult	320 ± 50 nm
Male adult	370 ± 50 nm

Table 13.2 Pathology of thin basement membrane disease

Light microscopy	The glomeruli appear normal or with mild mesangial cell proliferation or matrix expansion
Immunofluorescence study	Negative
Electronic microscopy	Uniform thinning of GBM appears as a trilaminar structure made up of the following: – An outer lamina rara externa – A central lamina densa – An inner lamina rara interna The appearance of these changes cannot be differentiated from the early stage of classical Alport syndrome

abnormalities detected in the kidney biopsy (Table 13.2). The clinical features described in the classical thin membrane disease are characterised by the following:

- Persistent microhaematuria and episodic gross haematuria are rare.
- Proteinuria is usually absent.
- The disease is non-progressive and will not go into renal failure.
- Extra-renal manifestations are absent.
- The presence of a positive familial history such that the disease runs a 'benign' course.

When will a renal biopsy be indicated in Elizabeth?

The traditional approach is that if Elizabeth runs a benign clinical course compatible with typical thin basement membrane disease, a renal biopsy may not be necessary. If there are atypical clinical features like progression in proteinuria, deterioration in renal function or the inability to exclude IgA glomerulonephritis or Alport syndrome clinically, then a renal biopsy is needed to make the diagnosis. With the advancement in genetic study, sometimes a renal biopsy may be replaced by it.

How can the family history help in making the diagnosis?

Over 50% of patients with thin basement membrane disease are inherited in an autosomal dominant pattern. However, a negative family history does not exclude the diagnosis. Patients without an identifiable family history may have a de novo mutation. The disease can also exhibit incomplete penetrance, which might explain a negative family history in some patients. The affected relative's phenotype may help predict Elizabeth's prognosis.

How can genetic tests help to manage the disease? Is thin basement membrane disease (TBMD) benign?

Genetic mutations in COL4A3 and COL4A4 have been found in patients with TBMD. These genes are located on chromosome 2 at 2q35–37 and encode for two different chains of type IV collagen. The mutations are heterozygous, involving a single allele, and can include various types of mutation, such as splice variants, missense mutations or frameshift mutations.

Thin basement membrane disease may not be as benign as we initially thought as follows:

1. Thin basement membrane disease shares and overlaps with Alport syndrome in the mutation of the collagen IV molecule.
2. There were reports of patients diagnosed with TBMD but who continued to progress to proteinuria and renal failure in later life. Some authors described this phenotype as late Alport syndrome.
3. There were also reports of TBMD associated with focal segmental glomerulonephritis and other glomerulonephritis resulting in impaired renal function and chronic kidney disease.
4. Genetic studies of patients with TBMD have shown heterozygous variants in the COL4A3 and COL4A4. These mutations were found to be associated with a spectrum of nephropathy, which may be clinically indistinguishable from Alport syndrome.

What is the relationship between Collagen IV and the basement membrane?

Collagen IV is the principal collagenous constituent of the glomerular basement membrane. Each COL4 molecule is a heterotrimer made up of three α chains (α-3, α-4 and α-5), which form triple helices and interact with the laminin to form the basement membrane. A distinct gene encodes each α chain. For α-3 and α-4 chains, the genes are located on chromosome 2, whereas the α-5 gene is located on the X chromosome.

What is the Collagen IV nephropathy?

As collagen type IV is the major constituent of the glomerular basement membrane, any abnormalities of it will affect the function of the GBM. The collagen type IV is made up of a repetitive triplet sequence glycine-Xaa-Yaa in which Xaa and Yaa represent a variety of other amino acids; a C-terminal non-collagenous (NC1) domain of about 230 residues and a non-collagenous N-terminal sequence of 15–20 residues. The NC1 terminal end of the molecule plays a key role in the assembly of the collagen network, and the N-terminal end is involved in the interactions that help stabilise the network (Fig. 13.1).

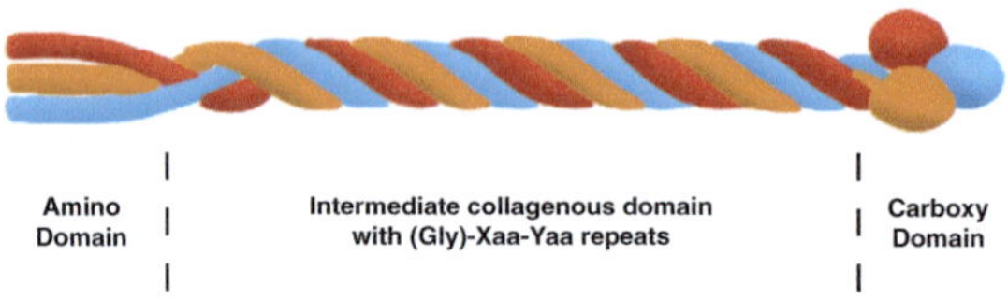

Fig. 13.1 Schematic diagram of collage IV protomer (Reproduced with permission from Dr. James Simon, MD of Cleveland Clinic, Ohio, USA and the Alport Syndrome Foundation)

Table 13.3 Genotype-phenotype correlation in collagen IV nephropathy

Gene	Mutations	Phenotype
COL4A3 and COL4A4	Heterozygous mutations	Thin basement membrane disease
	Homozygous or heterozygous mutations	AR or AD-Alport syndrome
COL4A5	α-5 mutation	X-linked Alport syndrome

With increasing knowledge in the molecular biology and genetics of collagen IV, it was found that mutations in the collagen type IV α-3, α-4 and α-5 genes account for a broad spectrum of nephropathy, ranging from microhaematuria to end-stage renal disease. The diversity of this genetic-phenotypic relationship is currently grouped under the name of collagen IV nephropathy or Collagen IV (α-3, α-4, α-5) nephropathy (Table 13.3). Hence, TBMD, previously known as Benign Familial Haematuria, may not be as benign as we initially thought.

How would you follow up with Elizabeth, and how would you counsel the long-term outcome of Elizabeth?
Exploring the family history of Elizabeth, no relatives are having any microhaematuria, nephritis or renal failure. There is no specific treatment for isolated asymptomatic microhaematuria or TBMD. However, because of the uncertainty of clinical progress, the management should involve regular monitoring for the development of hypertension, proteinuria and renal impairment as in Alport syndrome. If the diagnosis is uncertain, a renal biopsy or even genetic testing may be helpful.

13.3 Case Illustrations

Elizabeth's case highlights the need for proactive and vigilant patient management. The importance of regular monitoring in patients with isolated microhaematuria should not be overlooked, as, despite the apparent normal renal function, her persistent microhaematuria still raises the concern of thin membrane nephropathy.

Suggested Further Readings

1. Gregory MC. The clinical features of thin basement membrane nephropathy. Semin Nephrol. 2005;25(3):140–5. WB Saunders.
2. Qazi RA, Bastani B. Co-existence of thin basement membrane nephropathy with other glomerular pathologies: a single centre experience. J Nephropathol. 2015;4(2):43.
3. Savige J, Rana K, Tonna S, Buzza M, Dagher H, Wang YY. Thin basement membrane nephropathy. Kidney Int. 2003;64(4):1169–78.
4. Uzzo M, Moroni G, Ponticelli C. Thin basement membrane: an underrated cause of end-stage renal disease. Nephron. 2023;147(7):383–91.
5. Lusco MA, Fogo AB. Hereditary nephritis and thin glomerular basement membrane lesion. Glomerular Dis. 2021;1(3):135–44.

The Cyst Is Not the Culprit 14

14.1 Case Description

Tina was a 12-year-old girl referred for assessment of persistent microhaematuria. Tina was well all along without significant illness. She went for an insurance check-up, and a urinalysis by haemastix showed 2+. Urine microscopy showed RBC 11 cells/μL, and 80% were dysmorphic RBCs. Tina had no gross haematuria, loin pain or renal stones. There were no symptoms to suggest a urinary tract infection. Physical examination showed a normal-sized girl with body height and weight at the 50th percentile. Her blood pressure was 110/66 mmHg. There were no dysmorphic facial features, and systems reviews were normal. Urine examination showed persistent microhaematuria; the urine protein-creatinine ratio was <0.2 mg/mg.

From the family history, however, Tina's father had a history of chronic kidney disease and recently had to be put on haemodialysis. The ultrasound of her father showed some renal cysts, but the definitive cause of his renal failure was uncertain. Tina's mother had performed a health check-up recently; a urinalysis and a blood test were normal.

14.2 Interactive Case Discussion

Could Tina suffer from cystic kidney disease?

With such a significant family history, Tina's microscopic haematuria needs careful evaluation. It may signify an underlying genetic renal disease. With the possible cystic kidney disease in her father, autosomal dominant polycystic kidney disease (ADPKD) could be a differential diagnosis.

Tina's ultrasound kidneys was, however, normal. There was no renal cyst. A genetic test for ADPKD was negative. Renal cysts may be found in any kidneys in end-stage renal disease and may be associated with other genetic diseases that may run in the family. A detailed family history of Tina showed that her father had ESRD

W. K. Y. Chan, M. C. I. Kuok, *Paediatric Nephrology*,
https://doi.org/10.1007/978-981-95-5060-9_14

at the age of 40 years old without a definitive diagnosis. Her uncle had undergone renal transplantation at the age of 48 years old, but the exact underlying aetiology of ESRD was not known. Tina has a cousin who also has abnormal renal function. The grandmother of the family passed away many years ago, and the cause of her death was uncertain.

The family pedigree shown in Fig. 14.1 suggested an X-linked or autosomal dominant (AD) inherited medical condition; hence, a genetic study using the next-generation sequencing was explicitly ordered to look for X-linked Alport syndrome.

The genetic test subsequently revealed a heterozygous NM_000495.5 (COL4A5):c 358G >A p. (Gly 120 Ser) mutation. Tina was diagnosed with X-linked Alport syndrome.

What is Alport syndrome?

Alport syndrome is a basement membrane disease caused by an inherited defect in the collagen IV, leading to a syndrome characterised by renal, cochlear and ocular involvement. The genetic defect is due to the variations in genes encoding the COL4 α3, α4 and α5 chains, resulting in X-linked, autosomal recessive (AR) or autosomal dominant (AD) forms of Alport syndrome.

How does collagen IV contribute to the structure of the glomerular basement membrane (GBM)?

Type IV collagen is the major structural protein of the GBM. There are six types of collagen IV isoform, α1 (IV) to α6 (IV) chains. Each monomer will twist with the other two monomers to form a trimer (a rope of three proteins). Trimers assemble

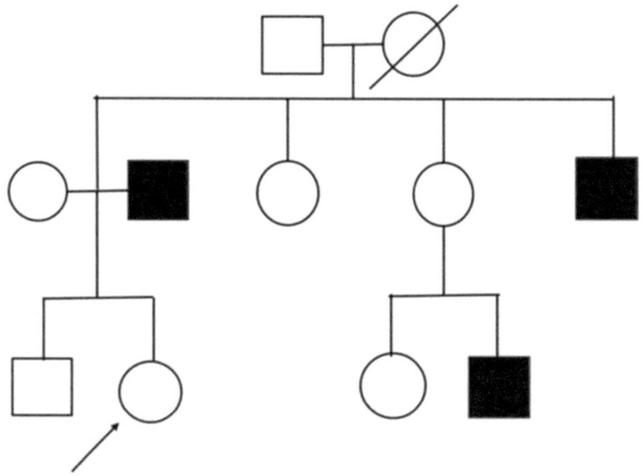

Fig. 14.1 Family pedigree of Tina, showing the family relationships and genetic traits. Squares represent males, and circles represent females. Filled shapes indicate individuals expressing the trait (renal disease), while unfilled shapes indicate those who do not have or not yet confirmed to have the disease. A diagonal line through a shape signifies a deceased individual. The arrow points to the proband, Tina

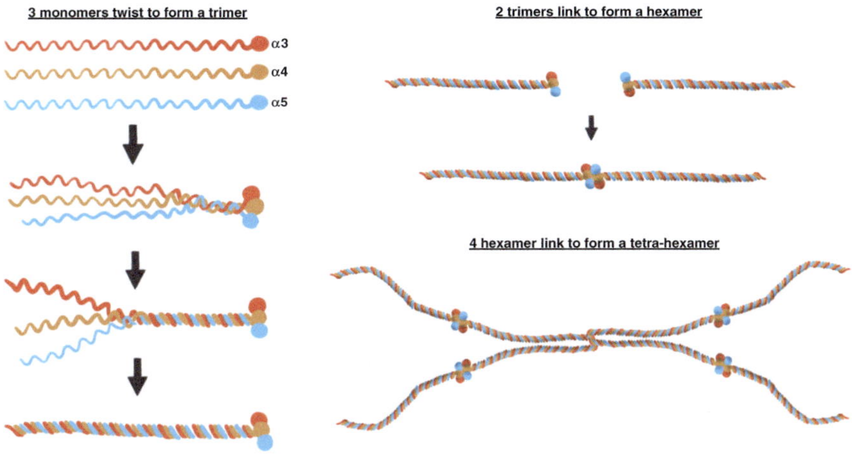

Fig. 14.2 Formation of the tetra-hexamer network from the collagen IV isomers. Three monomers α3, α4 and α5 twist to form a trimer. Two trimers link to form a hexamer, and four hexamers link to form a tetra-hexamer which is then released from the podocytes to the GBM. (Reproduced with permission from Dr. James Simon, MD of Cleveland Clinic, Ohio, USA and the Alport Syndrome Foundation

into hexamers, which further combine into tetra-hexamers that constitute the glomerular basement membrane (GBM) (Fig. 14.2)

Each collagen IV monomer shares a similar structure composed of the following:

- A C-terminal non-collagenous (NC1) domain
- A collagenous Gly-X-Y repeats that form a triple helix with the two other monomers
- An N-terminal '7S' domain

The α1-α1-α2 heterotrimers make up the GBM in utero, but after birth, the gene switches to produce α3-α4-α5 heterotrimers, making the GBM thicker and more complex to handle the increasing filtration pressure over the GBM as the child grows into adulthood.

The glycine residue in the monomer chain is a common site for mutation in Alport syndrome. If a mutation (usually a nonsense or deletion mutation) leads to failure of synthesis of any one of the isomers α3, α4 and α5, the trimer cannot be formed. In that situation, the podocytes will shift back to produce the α1-α1-α2 heterotrimers; hence, the GBM will be 'weaker' as compared with the α3-α4-α5 heterotrimers network.

Alport syndrome follows three types of inheritance patterns, i.e. the X-linked, autosomal recessive (AR) and autosomal dominant (AD)

Table 14.1 The genetics of different types of Alport syndrome

Gene	COL4A1, COL4A2	COL4A3, COL4A4	COL4A5, COL4A6
Chromosome	13	2q36	Xq22
Protein	COL4A1, COL4A2	COL4A3, COL4A4	COL4A5, COL4A6
Trimers form to hexamers and tetra-hexamers	α1-α1-α2(IV) heterotrimers	α3-α4-α5 (IV) heterotrimers	α5 α5-α6 (IV) heterotrimers
Site of the basement membrane	Immature glomerular basement membrane	Mature glomerular basement membrane	The basement membrane of Bowman's capsule
Disease caused by pathogenic variants		ARAS, ADAS Digenic AS	X-linked AS or digenic AS or diffuse leiomyomatosis associated with AS

ARAS autosomal recessive Alport syndrome, *ADAS* autosomal dominant Alport syndrome, *AS* Alport syndrome

- X-linked Alport syndrome is caused by a pathogenic variant in COL4A5 and was considered the most typical type of Alport syndrome. Some authors have reported that up to 80% of Alport syndrome patients are actually inherited in an X-linked pattern.
- AR Alport syndrome is caused by homozygous or compound heterozygous rare variants in COL4A3 or COL4A4 genes.
- AD Alport syndrome results from heterozygous rare variants in COL4A3 or COL4A4 genes.

Alport syndrome can also follow digenic inheritance, that is, the presence of 2 pathogenic variants in different type IV collagen genes (Table 14.1).

Being a "carrier" of X-linked Alport syndrome, will Tina have a milder disease or remain oligo-symptomatic?

With previous clinical observations and a recent understanding of the genetics of Alport syndrome, the phenotypes of patients with Alport syndrome do not follow the classical Mendelian pattern and are more consistent with additive inheritance. Some authors opined that there is no actual 'carrier' of the disease. The 'carriers' have the disease and they can progress to renal impairment. Hence, long-term follow-up with regular monitoring and early intervention for any proteinuria is recommended.

What are the extra-renal manifestations of Alport syndrome?

As collagen IV is also a major component in the basement membrane of the cochlea and the base of the ocular lens, sensory hearing loss and ocular lesions are part of the clinical triad of Alport syndrome (Table 14.2).

Table 14.2 Extra-renal involvement of Alport syndrome

Organ	Site of collagen IV	Disease
Ocular	Lens' capsule Descemet's membrane Bowman's membrane Retinal pigment epithelium	Corneal opacity Anterior lenticonus Cataract Retinal abnormalities
Cochlear	The basilar membrane in the cochlea	Sensorineural hearing loss

Table 14.3 Drug trials that showed protective effects on patients with Alport syndrome

Drugs	Trials	Results
Ramipril	EARLY PRO-TECT Alport [2] (Early Prospective Therapy European Community Trial on Alport Syndrome) – Study ramipril in Alport patients aged 2–18 years old and with eGFR >90 ml/min/1.73 m^2	↓ albuminuria ↓ decline in eGFR Emphasis on the value of pre-emptive treatment
Empagliflozin	EMPA-KIDNEY [3]	↓ albuminuria

How would you manage Tina?

To date, there is no specific treatment for Alport syndrome. Once diagnosed, management involves regular clinical monitoring for the development of hypertension, proteinuria and renal impairment. Regular laboratory studies should include serum creatinine and blood urea nitrogen tests, as well as urinalyses with urine protein-to-creatinine ratio assessments. With the increasing accessibility of genetic testing, early diagnosis of Alport syndrome is advocated, as early initiation of angiotensin-converting enzyme inhibitors significantly delays the onset of renal failure. Treatment includes the following:

- Tight blood pressure management, with a goal of less than 130/80 mmHg in children >13 years old and for younger children, BP should be kept at around the 50th percentile of the nomogram.
- Pharmacological therapy would involve the use of renin-angiotensin system inhibitors, such as angiotensin-converting enzyme (ACE) inhibitors or angiotensin receptor blockers (ARBs).
- New agents under investigation include: SGLT2 inhibitor (empagliflozin), endothelin A receptor antagonist (atrasentan), dual endothelin angiotensin receptor antagonist (sparsentan), hydroxychloroquine, lipid modifying agents and even gene therapy (Table 14.3).

14.3 Case Illustrations

This case guides the reader through the journey of a patient with Alport syndrome who presented with microhaematuria. It illustrates the importance of having a good family history. The history of a renal cyst in the father has misled the doctor on the diagnosis of ADPKD and overlooked the possibility of Alport syndrome in the family. Early recognition of Alport syndrome helps to retard disease progression in the patient.

Suggested Further Readings

1. De Gregorio V, Caparali EB, Shojaei A, Ricardo S, Barua M. Alport syndrome: clinical spectrum and therapeutic advances. Kidney Med. 2023;5(5):100631.
2. Gross O, Friede T, Hilgers R, Görlitz A, Gavénis K, Ahmed R, Dürr U. Safety and efficacy of the ACE-inhibitor Ramipril in Alport Syndrome: the double-blind, randomised, placebo-controlled, multicenter phase III EARLY PRO-TECT Alport trial in pediatric patients. Int Sch Res Notices. 2012;2012(1):436046.
3. Fernández-Fernandez B, Sarafidis P, Soler MJ, Ortiz A. EMPA-KIDNEY: expanding the range of kidney protection by SGLT2 inhibitors. Clin Kidney J. 2023;16(8):1187–98.
4. ESCAPE Trial Group. Strict blood-pressure control and progression of renal failure in children. N Engl J Med. 2009;361(17):1639–50.

When the Glomeruli Inflamed 15

15.1 Case Description

Olivia was previously well. At 10 years old, she was admitted for peri-orbital swelling and facial puffiness for 1 week. There was a history of transient erythematous rash over the elbows, but it subsided uneventfully, and there was no preceding sore throat or respiratory tract infection. There was no facial rash, oral ulcers or unexplained fever. Her urine was blood-stained, and it terrified the family; hence, she was brought to medical attention. Physical examination showed a normal body build for a 10-year-old girl. She had gained 2 kg in the past 2 weeks. Her blood pressure was at 140/90 mmHg. She had a puffy face, and her eyelids were swollen. There was bilateral pitting ankle oedema but no detectable ascites. Her urine examination showed a red cell granular cast and 3+ albustix. She was diagnosed with acute glomerulonephritis.

15.2 Interactive Case Discussion

How do you navigate the intricate classification of glomerulonephritis (GN)?
The aetiology of glomerulonephritis is broad. One can classify it according to the clinical presentation, renal history and underlying causes (Table 15.1).

How would you differentiate the different clinical presentations of glomerulonephritis?
The clinical presentation of GN could be described as acute nephritic syndrome, nephrotic syndrome or nephritic-nephrotic syndrome, depending on the severity of proteinuria and the aetiology of the fluid retention (Table 15.2).

- Nephritic syndrome is a clinical syndrome that describes a triad of haematuria, elevated blood pressure, and oedema. Other features include decreased urine out-

W. K. Y. Chan, M. C. I. Kuok, *Paediatric Nephrology*,
https://doi.org/10.1007/978-981-95-5060-9_15

Table 15.1 Approach to classifying glomerulonephritis by clinical presentation, aetiology and renal histology

Clinical presentation	Nephritic syndrome Nephrotic syndrome Nephritic-nephrotic syndrome Rapidly progressive GN Chronic GN
Aetiology	Primary: the disease is restricted to the kidney Secondary: the renal disease is part of the systemic presentations or secondary drug toxicity
Renal histology	Proliferative GN: endocapillary proliferative, mesangial proliferation Crescentic GN Minimal change disease Glomerulosclerosis: focal segmental Membranous GN Membranoproliferative GN Other specific histology like C1q GN, C3 GN, IgA glomerulonephritis

put and a variable degree of azotaemia. The major underlying pathology is glomeruli inflammation, resulting in glomerular haematuria, i.e. the appearance of red blood cell (RBC) casts, and red blood cells in urine is the hallmark with variable degrees of proteinuria in the urine. Oedema is due to fluid retention.

- Nephrotic syndrome is characterised by the kidneys leaking a large amount of protein in the urine, leading to a loss of serum albumin, raised serum cholesterol and generalised oedema. The oedema is due to the drop of oncotic pressure in the blood vessels, and fluid leaks into the third space.
- Nephrotic-nephritic is a combination of clinical features seen in both syndromes.

What are the mechanisms and pathogenesis of glomerulonephritis?

In glomerulonephritis, the glomerular basement membranes are disrupted, leading to the loss of red blood cells, albumin and large molecules in the urine. The glomerular basement membrane is a ribbon-like extracellular matrix between the endothelium and the foot process of the podocytes. The mechanisms of injuries can be the following:

- Direct damage to the endothelial cell layer of the glomerular capillaries
- Deposition of immune complex in the subendothelial, subepithelial and mesangial space or
- Disruption of the glomerular basement membrane by primary or secondary causes

Table 15.2 Differentiate nephritic and nephrotic syndrome

	Clinical features and definitions	Underlying pathology and causes
Nephritic syndrome	– Fluid retention with clinical oedema – Significant haematuria, usually gross haematuria with red cell casts and granular casts, may be present. The gross haematuria is usually described as cola-coloured urine – Variable degree of proteinuria, but does not reach the degree of nephrotic range proteinuria (4–40 $mg/m^2/hr$) – Hypertension – Variable degree of impaired renal function – Oliguria related to decreased glomerular filtration	Inflammation of the glomeruli is usually a proliferative type of glomerulonephritis (GN), with structural disruption of the glomerular basement membrane *Underlying causes*: – Acute post-infectious GN – Immune-medicated GN – Crescentic GN
Nephrotic syndrome	– A combination of clinical features of the following: – Fluid retention with variable degrees of clinical oedema, – Frothy urine with significant proteinuria up to >40 $mg/m^2/hr$ – Low serum albumin of <25 g/dL – Elevated serum cholesterol – Haematuria is less prominent and usually absent – Oliguria is common due to decreased capillary oncotic pressure and decreased glomerular filtration – Blood pressure could be low, normal or even high depending on the circulatory intravascular volume state	Damage to the glomerular filtration membrane, i.e. usually at the slit membrane, is related to pathology at the podocytes, also called podocytopathies *Underlying causes*: – Minimal change glomerulonephritis in children – Focal segmental glomerulonephritis-primary or secondary – Membranous glomerulonephritis
Nephritic-nephrotic syndrome	Mix features of nephritic and nephrotic syndrome with proteinuria >40 $mg/m^2/hr$	Mostly glomerulonephritis with structural damage to the glomerular basement membrane

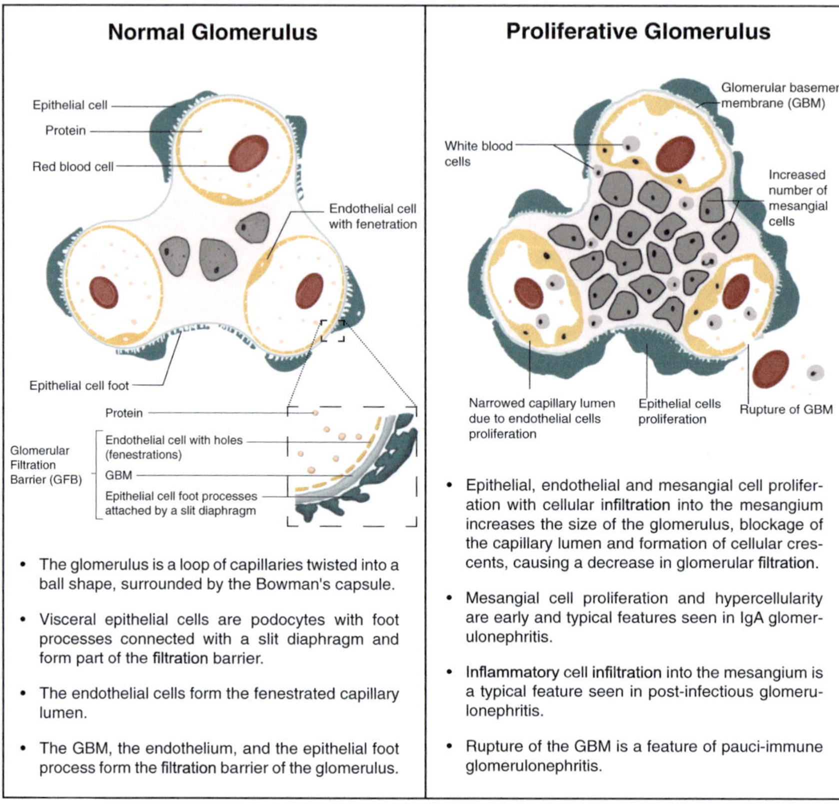

Fig. 15.1 Diagram illustrating the differences between a normal and a proliferative glomerulus

In proliferative glomerulonephritis, the possible pathological features are as follows (Fig 15.1):

- Cellular proliferation of endothelial cells and mesangial cells
- Cellular infiltration by plasma cells, neutrophils and lymphocytes, depending on the types of glomerulonephritis
- The capillary lumens are obliterated by the cellular infiltrate and proliferation, leading to a decrease in glomerular filtration
- Glomerular membranes may rupture, or their structures may be distorted by immune-complex depositions at the subepithelial or subendothelial sides of the GBM
- When the inflammatory process continues, it eventually results in glomerular sclerosis and loss of glomerular function

Olivia suffers from acute nephritic syndrome. What could be the causes for it?

The most common cause of acute nephritic syndrome is acute glomerulonephritis, and the clinical features and laboratory investigation will help to arrive at the diagnosis.

Glomerulonephritis presents as acute nephritic syndrome	Clinical features	Laboratory investigations
Primary glomerulonephritis		
Membranoproliferative GN (Type I, II, III)	Absence of systemic symptoms	– Complements can be normal or decreased – Other autoimmune markers are negative – The diagnosis is made by renal histology
Secondary glomerulonephritis		
Post-infectious GN	– History of recent infections, such as sore throat in post-streptococcal GN, skin infection in post-staphylococcal GN – Absence of other systemic features	– Low C3 but normal C4 – Evidence of recent infection, such as raised ASOT – Other autoimmune markers are negative
Ig A GN	– Syn-pharyngitis gross haematuria	– Normal complements – Negative autoimmune markers – IgA may be elevated
Henoch-SchÖnlein GN	– Presence of purpuric rash typical of HSP	– Normal complements – Negative autoimmune markers – IgA may be elevated
Systemic lupus erythematosus	– Presence of systemic features of SLE	– Low C3 and C4 – Positive serology for SLE – Negative serology of ANCA
Pauci-immune GN	– Presence of systemic features related to underlying vasculitis	– Normal complements – Negative serology for SLE – Positive ANCA serology

Olivia's first blood test showed serum urea of 10 mmol/L, creatinine of 90 μmol/L and electrolytes were normal. The serum albumin was 26 g/dL (decreased), and globulin was 50 g/L (elevated). She showed progressive deterioration in renal function, with urea increased to 21.8 mmol/L and creatinine to 150 μmol/L in a week. The 24-hour urine was 1.43 g/day (>60 mg/m^2/hr). Her haemoglobin was slightly low at 10.6 g/dL, reticulocyte 1.7%, direct comb test positive (score 5), anti-IgG (score 5) and anti-C3d (score 3). The anti-nuclear antibody was 1:1280, anti-dsDNA was >300 IU/mL (normal <50 IU/mL) and anti-Ro antibody was positive. Lupus anticoagulant was not detected. Anticardiolipin IgG and IgM were within normal limits. Her complements showed extremely low C3 of 0.12 g/L (RI: 0.9–1.6 g/L) and C4 of 0.02 g/L (RI: 0.13–0.38 g/L). Her IgG was 22.4 g/L (elevated), and her IgM was 2.33 g/L (elevated). The p-ANCA-positive but anti-myeloperoxidase and anti-PR3 antibodies were all within normal limits.

What is Olivia's diagnosis, and how can it be confirmed?
Olivia has hypocomplementemic glomerulonephritis with raised anti-dsDNA and positive anti-Ro antibody. She suffered from lupus nephritis, even though other clinical features of systemic lupus erythematosus were lacking. A renal biopsy would help confirm the diagnosis, classify the type of lupus nephritis and guide the subsequent treatment.

How would you manage Olivia at this juncture while awaiting renal histology results?
Olivia is most likely experiencing proliferative lupus nephritis, consistent with either Class III or Class IV disease. Initiation of Prednisolone at 2 mg/kg/day, or an equivalent corticosteroid regimen, can be considered while concurrently addressing her other clinical issues. This approach should be maintained as we await confirmation from the definitive renal biopsy results.

1. Control of her hypertension by antihypertensive agents.
2. Improve urine output with diuretics.
3. Control azotaemia by protein restriction.
4. Minimise fluid retention by a low salt diet and limiting fluid intake.
5. Control hyperlipidaemia with statins if there is no contraindication.
6. Pre-steroid workup, including tuberculosis screening by IGRA and hepatitis B and C screening.
7. Genetic screening for TPMT or NUDT15 genotype for possible use of azathioprine.
8. Consult an ophthalmologist for screening of lupus involvement and as a baseline before commencing hydroxychloroquine.
9. A systems review will be performed to assess the extent of organ involvement in patients with systemic lupus erythematosus, including an echocardiogram and chest X-ray.
10. Kidney supportive therapy if the disease progresses.
11. Start hydroxychloroquine (HCQ) at 5 mg/kg/day and adjust the dose according to eGFR.
12. Be cautious when receiving blood transfusions and avoid them as much as possible.

What are the indications of renal supportive therapy in Olivia?

Before definitive treatment has an effect in controlling the activity of lupus nephritis, Olivia may need temporary renal supportive therapy, especially in situations like the following:

- Significant fluid overload that causes pulmonary oedema, heart failure and uncontrolled hypertension
- Electrolyte disturbances, especially hyperkalaemia, hyponatremia and hyperphosphatemia
- Uremic symptoms

What is the prognosis of Olivia?

The prognosis of Olivia depends on the severity of renal histology. Her clinical picture is compatible with proliferative lupus nephritis, which requires intensive treatment with immunosuppressive agents, including pulse or high-dose steroids, cyclophosphamide, mycophenolate mofetil and azathioprine and rituximab. The choice of drug therapy depends on the disease's progression and the patient's response to the initial treatment.

15.3 Case Illustrations

This case demonstrates how readers can integrate glomerular pathology with clinical presentations to reach a diagnosis. Olivia's case also illustrates lupus nephritis can mimic other types of acute nephritis and present without any other clinical features of systemic lupus erythematosus. Early disease identification is essential, as intensive immunosuppressive agents will alter the disease outcome.

Suggested Further Readings

1. Sethi S, De Vriese AS, Fervenza FC. Acute glomerulonephritis. The Lancet. 2022;399(10335):1646–63.
2. Pesce F, Stea ED, Rossini M, Fiorentino M, Piancone F, Infante B, et al. Glomerulonephritis in AKI: from pathogenesis to therapeutic intervention. Fron Med. 2021;7:582272.

When the Glomeruli Were Inflamed and Damaged

16

16.1 Case Description

Olivia was diagnosed with lupus nephritis. The histology of the renal biopsy showed class IV lupus nephritis with an activity score of 6/24 and a chronicity score of 0/52.

Olivia's renal histology was shown below (Figs. 16.1a, b and 16.2a–d).

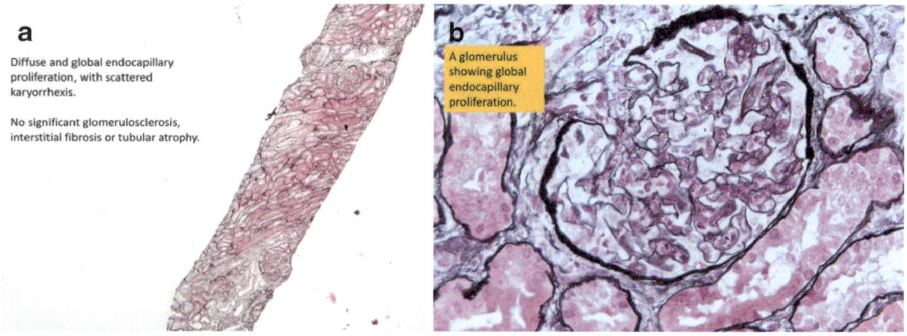

Fig. 16.1 (**a**) Renal histology under low power view, with H&E staining. (**b**) Haematoxylin and eosin staining at ×400 showed a glomerulus; cut at the glomerular stalk region. It showed global endocapillary proliferation with scattered karyorrhexis. There was no signficant glomerulosclerosis, interstitial fibrosis or tubular atrophy. (Pathology slides courtesy of Dr. Lau Wing Hung, Department of Pathology, Queen Elizabeth Hospital, Hong Kong)

W. K. Y. Chan, M. C. I. Kuok, *Paediatric Nephrology*, https://doi.org/10.1007/978-981-95-5060-9_16

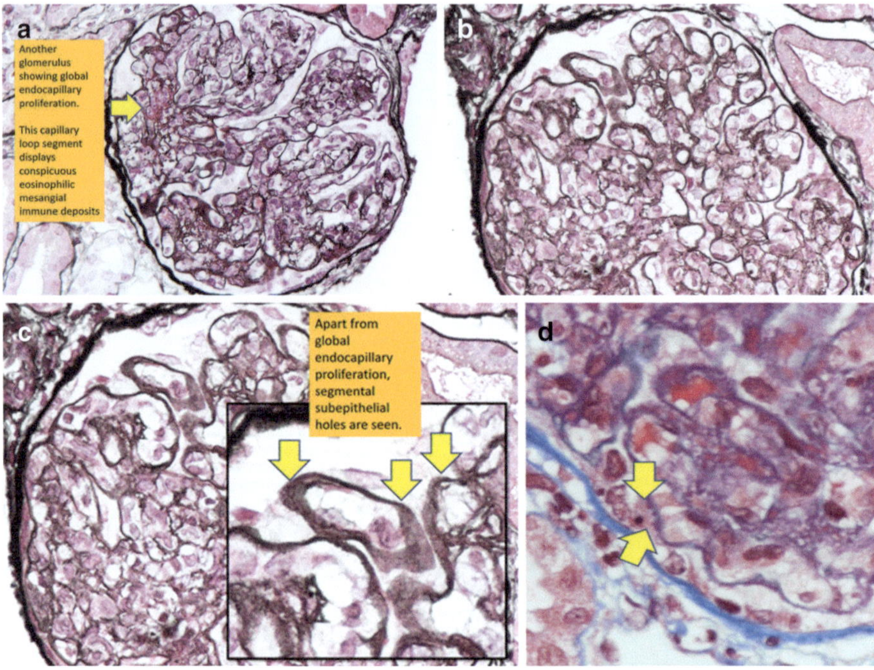

Fig. 16.2 (**a**) Haematoxylin and eosin staining at ×400, staining in light microscopy showed diffuse endocapillary proliferation. The yellow arrow pointed to the eosinophilic mesangial immune deposits. (**b**) Haematoxylin and eosin staining at ×400, staining in light microscopy with another glomerulus showing diffuse endocapillary proliferation. (**c**) Further magnification showed the thickening of basement membranous. The yellow arrows pointed to the subepithelial holes. (**d**) CAB stain showed the subepithelial deposits in the capillary lumen (yellow arrows). (Pathology slides courtesy of Dr. Lau Wing Hung, Department of Pathology, Queen Elizabeth Hospital, Hong Kong)

16.2 Interactive Case Discussion

What are the diagnostic features of lupus nephritis in renal pathology?

Lupus nephritis (LN) may affect different compartments of the kidney, including the glomeruli, interstitium, tubules and capillary loops. Aside from anti-dsDNA immune complex deposits, immunoglobulin G (IgG), immunoglobulin A (IgA), immunoglobulin M (IgM) and complement (C1, C3, and properdin) are commonly found as mesangial, subendothelial and subepithelial deposits. Full-house immunofluorescence staining, significant C1q positivity, extraglomerular immunostaining and the finding of tubuloreticular inclusions by electron microscopy establish the lupus aetiology of the nephritis.

What are the classifications of lupus nephritis, and what are the activity and chronicity scores?

The WHO morphological classification of lupus nephritis is one of the most widely used classifications in the past century. It divided LN into six different classes. The classification was further modified in 2003 by the International Society of Nephrology/Renal Pathology Society (ISN/RPS), which has better descriptions of the acute and chronic elements seen in lupus nephritis. The classification system is based on the glomerular morphologic changes seen on light microscopy, immune deposits seen on immunofluorescence and electron microscopy findings (Table 16.1).

Active lesions in lupus nephritis are described below, and each active lesion is further graded from 0 to 3. Hence, the highest possible active score will be 24. There are five descriptions in the chronicity score. Each score is a maximum of 2 points, making a total of 10 points (Table 16.2).

Table 16.1 WHO and ISN/RPS classification of lupus nephritis

WHO morphological classification of lupus nephritis (modified in 1982)		International Society of Nephrology/ Renal Pathology Society (ISN//RPS) Classification of Lupus Nephritis (2003)	
Class I	Normal (by Light microscopy)	Class I	Minimal mesangial
Class II	Pure mesangial	Class II	Mesangial proliferative
Class III	Focal segmental glomerulonephritis with mild to moderate mesangial alterations	Class III	Focal lupus nephritis Active (A) lesions Chronic (C) lesions
Class IV	Diffuse glomerulonephritis with severe mesangial, endocapillary or mesangiocapillary proliferation and/or extensive subendothelial deposit	Class IV	Diffuse segmental (IV-S) or diffuse global (IV-G) lupus nephritis Active (A) lesions Chronic (C) lesions
Class V	Diffuse membranous glomerulonephritis	Class V	Membranous lupus nephritis
Class VI	Advanced sclerosing glomerulonephritis	Class VI	Advanced sclerosing lupus nephritis

Table 16.2 Active and chronic lesions described by ISN/RPS 2003

Active lesions in lupus nephritis	Chronic lesions in lupus nephritis
1. Endocapillary hypercellularity with or without leucocyte infiltration and with a reduction in the capillary lumen 2. Karyorrhexis 3. Fibrinoid necrosis 4. Rupture of the glomerular basement membrane 5. Crescents formation—cellular or fibrocellular 6. Subendothelial deposits identifiable by light microscopy (wire loop lesions) 7. Intraluminal immune aggregates (hyaline thrombi)	1. Glomerular sclerosis 2. Fibrous adhesions 3. Fibrous crescents 4. Interstitial fibrosis 5. Tubular atrophy
Active lesion is further graded from 0 to 3; cellular crescents and necrosis are graded from 0 to 6; the maximum activity score is 24	Chronic lesions, maximum score 10

What are the other non-classifiable forms of lupus nephritis?
Several lupus renal involvements are not classifiable by the WHO or the ISN/RPS. These lesions include the following:

1. Lupus vasculitis
   - It is not immune-mediated; the renal histology belongs to the pauci-immune type and necrotising glomerulonephritis.
2. Lupus thrombotic microangiopathy
   - Intra-glomerular fibrin will be associated with microangiopathic haemolytic anaemia and thrombocytopenia.
   - It is often associated with antiphospholipid syndrome with anticardiolipin antibody, anti-β2 glycoprotein antibody or lupus anticoagulant.
3. Lupus podocytopathy
   - In renal histology, podocyte foot process effacement with minimal change and mesangial or focal segmental glomerulosclerosis. Clinically, proteinuria is the predominant clinical feature.

How would you treat Olivia with proliferative lupus nephritis and what are your treatment goals ?
Children and adolescent patients are given the same immunosuppressive agents as adult SLE patients and generally require more aggressive treatment to achieve disease control than adult SLE populations. Unlike adult lupus nephritis, most treatments in paediatric patients are off-label drugs with recommendations based on inadequately powered studies, therapeutic consensus guidelines or case series. Nevertheless, the treatment goals are the same:

- To alleviate the signs and symptoms
- Rapidly control the disease activity
- Minimise drug-induced complications
- Prevent long-term damage
- Minimise disease relapses and
- Improve the quality of life of the patient

The Principle of Treatment What are the principles in treating Lupus Nephritis?

- Lupus proliferative glomerulonephritis (Class III/IV) with high disease activity scores requires more aggressive treatment as the renal disease is more likely to progress rapidly, resulting in higher morbidity or mortality.
- Steroids are the mainstay of treatment, and additional immunosuppressive agents are used to control lupus activity.
- Hydroxychloroquine at 5 mg/kg/day (maximum 400 mg/day) is indicated for all lupus patients without contraindication.

- The treatment plan includes an initial 'induction phase' followed by a 'maintenance phase'.
- The treatment plan should be individualised as the severity of renal disease and extra-renal disease varies among different patients.

Treatment for proliferative lupus nephritis will be aggressive, as halting the disease progression could be life-saving. The treatment options are listed in Table 16.3.

Concerning the treatment for non-proliferative lupus nephritis Class I and II, it will depend on the severity of other systemic manifestations, and usually, steroids alone are adequate for this mild type of nephritis.

For the non-proliferative Class V lupus nephritis, if it has a mixed feature of Class III or IV, the treatment plan will be the same as proliferative lupus nephritis. It is less common to have pure Class V lupus nephritis in childhood-onset systemic lupus erythematosus; the treatment plan will be similar to proliferative lupus nephritis, except intravenous pulse methylprednisolone is usually not required, as membranous LN is less aggressive than proliferative LN.

If a child has a sclerosing type of lupus nephritis, the renal function is unlikely to be salvageable, and the indication of immunosuppression will depend on the extra-renal lupus disease.

In some patients, combination or sequential therapy may be needed to put the disease under control especially in resistant cases. The degree of immunosuppression needs to be balanced with the risk of opportunistic infections. Recent FDA-approved immunosuppressive agents, including Obinutuzumab (anti-CD20), Anifrolumab (Type 1 interferon receptor antagonist), and Voclosporin, have expanded treatment options for adult lupus nephritis. Their use in pediatric patients—especially those with resistant disease—is anticipated to increase in the coming years. Additionally, CAR-T cell therapy, once considered experimental, is likely to be incorporated into treatment algorithms in the near future.

What are the adjuvant therapies for lupus nephritis?

Apart from immunosuppressive agents, the following therapies need to be considered.

- Tight control of blood pressure, especially the use of renin-angiotensin blockade (ACEI/ARB) to reduce proteinuria.
- Use of an anticoagulant if antiphospholipid antibodies are positive.
- Calcium and vitamin D supplements to avoid osteoporosis and improve bone health.
- Antibiotic prophylaxis if the child is severely immunocompromised.
- Monitor serum immunoglobulin pattern after rituximab infusion and give Immunoglobulin replacement at 400 mg/kg if deficiency is observed.
- Immunisation against common pathogens. Hence, routine non-live vaccinations, such as influenza, tetanus, hepatitis A and B, meningococcal, pneumococcal, quadrivalent human papillomavirus and COVID-19 vaccination, should be recommended.

Table 16.3 Treatment for proliferative lupus nephritis (Class III/ IV or mixed III/V, IV/V)

	Steroid	In addition to steroid therapy
Initial induction therapy – Aims to prompt dampening of the inflammation in the kidney to minimise renal damage	– High-dose IV methylprednisolone (solumedrol) 10–30 mg/kg per dose (maximum 1 g per dose) for 3–5 days, followed by high-dose oral prednisolone 1–2 mg/kg/day (maximum 60 mg daily) for 4 weeks is the standard regime. In some centers, regular weekly pulse methylprednisolone (10-30mg/kg/dose) may be incorporated in the early weeks of treatment in order to control the disease rapidly. – A lower dose of pulse methylprednisolone has been advocated to avoid steroid toxicity, especially in late adolescents reaching adulthood	– NIH's regime of monthly IV cyclophosphamide (CYC) at 0.5–1 g/m^2, adjusted according to the white cell counts, for six doses Or – The Euro-Lupus protocol of low-dose IV cyclophosphamide at 500 mg every 2 weeks (for six doses, total 3 g) Or – Mycophenolate mofetil at 1200–1800 $mg/m^2/day$ (max 2 g daily in Asian and 3 g in Caucasians) Or – Multi-targeted therapy with low-dose mycophenolate mofetil with tacrolimus (TAC)
Maintenance therapy – To consolidate remission and to reduce the risk of renal flares	– Tapering the dose of steroids depends on the severity of the disease – Usually, reduce prednisolone 10 mg every 2 weeks and reach a dose of 10 mg at 3–6 months	– NIH regimen with IVI cyclophosphamide every 3 months Or – Mycophenolate mofetil Or – Multi-targeted therapy: mycophenolate mofetil with tacrolimus (TAC) Or – Azathioprine 2–2.5 mg/kg day, maximum 100 mg daily (check TPMT and NUDT15 genotype) And/or – Belimumab IVI at 10 mg/kg every 4 weeks
Resistant lupus nephritis		– Oral cyclophosphamide at 2 mg/kg daily for 12 weeks (168 mg/kg) in resistant lupus nephritis Or – IVI rituximab at 750 mg/m^2 (max 1 g) every 2 weeks for two doses or 375 mg/m^2 every week for four doses Or – Therapeutic plasmapheresis (TPE) may be considered, especially in patients with features of thrombotic microangiopathy

How would you monitor Olivia during follow-up and assess the impact of disease activity?

The patient would be evaluated clinically for any systemic features of active lupus in every clinic visit.

We would do the following:

- Monitor any symptoms and signs of lupus relapse
  - Systemic features of lupus erythematosus, like fever, facial rash, joint pain and involvement of other organs.
  - Blood pressure measurement.
  - Any clinical features of oedema or fluid retention.
  - Urine microscopy for any haematuria and red cell casts.
  - Regular serum albumin and urine protein excretion by spot urine protein creatinine ratio or 24-h urine protein excretion.
  - Regular C3 complement and anti-dsDNA. These markers are usually abnormal in proliferative GN but normalised when the disease is under control, burnt-out disease or membranous glomerulonephritis.
  - Regular blood chemistry, serum urea and creatinine and estimated glomerular filtration rate.
  - Regular screening for infections involves blood tests, such as C-reactive protein, and cultures as indicated.
  - High index of suspicion for opportunistic infections.

The Systemic Lupus International Collaborating Clinics/American College of Rheumatology (SLICC/ACR) Damage Index (SDI) was developed in 1996 to assess the ongoing disease activity in SLE patients and to measure irreversible damage resulting from SLE disease activity and its treatment. The SDI contains items that represent permanent, irreversible damage in a lupus patient. Items should be present for at least 6 months, with the exception that manifestations such as myocardial infarction and stroke are recorded once they occur. Damage score is defined for 12 organ systems:

1. Ocular (range 0–2 points)
2. Neuropsychiatric (0–6 points)
3. Renal (0–3 points)
4. Pulmonary (0–5 points)
5. Cardiovascular (0–6 points)
6. Peripheral vascular (0–5 points)
7. Gastrointestinal (0–6 points)
8. Musculoskeletal (0–7 points)
9. Skin (0–3 points)
10. Endocrine (diabetes) (0–1 points)
11. Gonadal (0–1 points)
12. Malignancies (0–2 points)

Damage over time can only be stable or increase, theoretically to a maximum of 47 points.

What is the prognosis of Olivia?

Irreversible organ damage, reduced health-related quality of life and diminished life expectancy, mainly due to infections and recurrence of disease activity, are not uncommon in patients with systemic lupus erythematosus. Children with both CNS lupus and lupus nephritis carry a less favourable prognosis. With the treat-to-target approach, rapid control of the lupus activity, relapse prevention, minimising drug toxicity (especially steroids) and prevention of infection are of utmost importance in Olivia's long-term management. Over time, strict drug compliance should be reinforced to minimize the risk of disease relapse.

Olivia was treated with pulse methylprednisolone at 500 mg intravenous for three doses followed by oral prednisolone at 2 mg/kg/day for 4 weeks and then tapered down to low dose over 3–6 months. Intravenous cyclophosphamide using the EULAR regimen was given for six doses. She achieved clinical and serological remission and was maintained in remission with a low-dose oral prednisolone, mycophenolate mofetil and hydroxychloroquine.

16.3 Case Illustrations

By using Olivia's case, we review the the key aspects in managing lupus nephritis with the readers and illustrates that lupus nephritis can present without other features of systemic lupus erythematosus. The renal histology not only helps to confirm the diagnosis but also guides the plan of management.

Suggested Further Readings

1. Markowitz GS, D'agati VD. The ISN/RPS 2003 classification of lupus nephritis: an assessment at 3 years. Kidney Int. 2007;71(6):491–5.
2. Groot N, De Graeff N, Marks SD, Brogan P, Avcin T, Bader-Meunier B, et al. European evidence-based recommendations for the diagnosis and treatment of childhood-onset lupus nephritis: the SHARE initiative. Ann Rheum Dis. 2017;76:1965–73.
3. Bomback AS. An update on therapies for proliferative lupus nephritis: how certain can we be about the evidence? Am J Kidney Dis. 2018;72(5):758–60.
4. Trindade VC, Carneiro-Sampaio M, Bonfa E, Silva CA. An update on the management of childhood-onset systemic lupus erythematosus. Pediatr Drugs. 2021;23(4):331–47.

Polar Views in Treatment 17

17.1 Case Description

Derick is a 15-year-old boy who was previously healthy. Three months ago, he noticed a foaming appearance to his urine, and the condition was worsening. He sought advice from a private doctor. Upon examination, his urine albustix was 4+, with a trace of red blood cells, and he was referred. There was no history of gross haematuria, no skin rash, nor any arthritis. There was no preceding history of respiratory tract infection. There were no urinary symptoms. He has no hearing problem, and a family history of renal disease was absent. Upon physical examination, his vitals were stable. His body weight was 42.4 kg (10th centile), body height 160 cm (10th centile), and office blood pressure was 121/77 mmHg. There was no ankle oedema, no puffy face, and abdominal examination was uneventful. Laboratory tests showed the following:

- Serum albumin 24 g/L (reference range: 33–48 g/L).
- Urea 6.0 mmol/L, creatinine 90 μmol/L.
- eGFR by modified Schwartz formula = 65 mL/min/1.73 m^2 (stage2 CKD).
- Twenty-four-hour urine 3.6 g/day (107 mg/m^2/hr) and UPCR 560 mg/mmol Cr.
- Cholesterol increased to 9 mmol/L.
- Electrolytes were normal.
- Antinuclear factor, anti-dsDNA, ANCA, ASOT, complement C3 and C4, hepatitis B, hepatitis C and HIV serology were all negative. Serum IgA increased to 2.65 g/L (reference range: 0.47–2.49 g/L).
- The Mantoux test was negative, and the CXR was normal.

The laboratory features were compatible with nephrotic syndrome, although there was no detectable oedema. A renal biopsy was performed.

W. K. Y. Chan, M. C. I. Kuok, *Paediatric Nephrology*,
https://doi.org/10.1007/978-981-95-5060-9_17

The histology showed 23 glomeruli, with 15% of which 15% are grossly sclerosed. The viable glomeruli showed diffuse global mesangial proliferation, mesangial matrix expansion and remodelling, mesangial deposits and silver-negative paramesangial nodules. Around 40% of viable glomeruli showed endocapillary proliferation, predominantly segmental. Fibrocellular crescent is noted in 15% of the viable glomeruli. Segmental sclerosis was seen in 55% of the viable glomeruli. Around 10% of the cortex is affected by tubular atrophy. In the immunofluorescence staining, there was diffuse global IgA (3+ granular) mesangial and capillary loop staining, IgM (1+ granular), IgG with slight linear accentuation along the glomerular basement membrane and C3 (trace granular) focal segmental mesangial and capillary loop staining. C1q is nonspecific. The diagnosis was primary IgA nephropathy with the Oxford MEST-C scores of M1, E1, S1, T0 and C1 (Figs. 17.1, 17.2, 17.3, and 17.4).

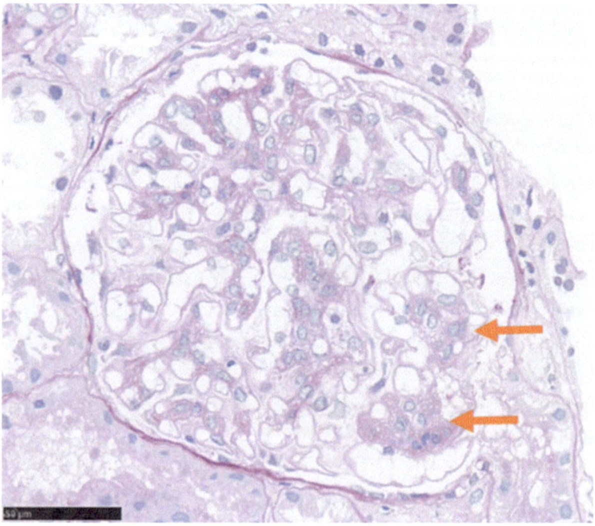

Fig. 17.1 Microscopic examination of a viable glomerulus, showing patent capillary lumens with focal mesangial hypercellularity. Solid orange arrow: mesangial hypercellularity. (H&E, X400). (Pathology slides courtesy of Dr Ho Tin Wai, Elson and Dr Cheuk Wah, Department of Pathology, Queen Elizabeth Hospital, Hong Kong)

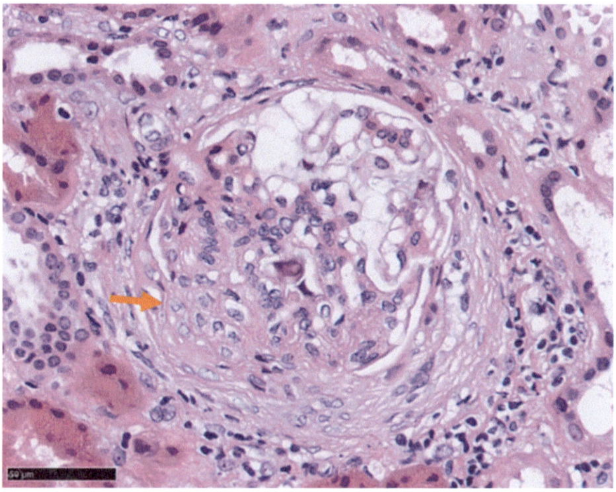

Fig. 17.2 Microscopic examination of a viable glomerulus, with significant cellular crescent obliterating >50% of the capillary lumens. The solid orange arrow: fibrocellular crescents. (H&E, X400). (Pathology slides courtesy of Dr Ho Tin Wai, Elson and Dr Cheuk Wah, Department of Pathology, Queen Elizabeth Hospital, Hong Kong)

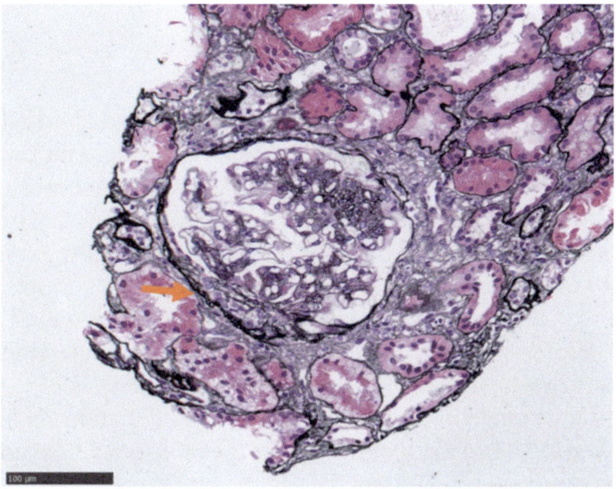

Fig. 17.3 Microscopic examination of a viable glomerulus with mild surrounding tubular atrophy. A small fibrocellular crescent was seen at the left lower quadrant. The solid orange arrow: segmental sclerosis associated with capsular adhesion and fibrocellular crescent (silver stain x400). (Pathology slides courtesy of Dr Ho Tin Wai, Elson and Dr Cheuk Wah, Department of Pathology, Queen Elizabeth Hospital, Hong Kong)

Fig. 17.4 Microscopic examination of two viable glomeruli with focal mesangial proliferation and cellular crescents. The orange arrows: segmental sclerosis associated with capsular adhesion and fibrocellular crescent (trichrome, X400). (Pathology slides courtesy of Dr Ho Tin Wai, Elson and Dr Cheuk Wah, Department of Pathology, Queen Elizabeth Hospital, Hong Kong)

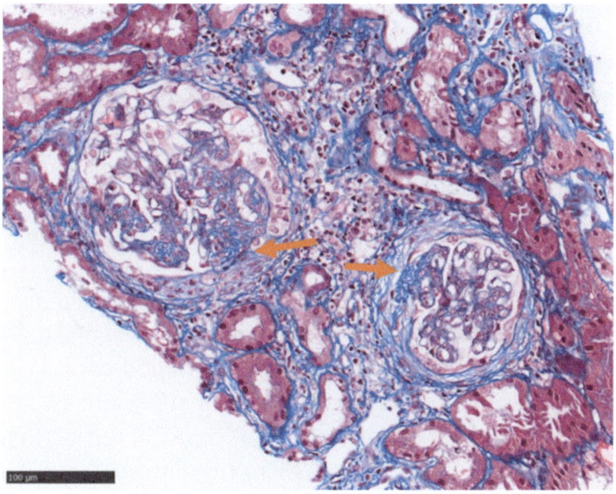

With these clinical and pathological parameters, there is a risk of a 30% decline in estimated glomerular filtration rate or 6.11% of progression to end-stage renal disease after renal biopsy in 1 year and 24.59% in 5 years (online calculation by International IgAN Prediction Tool. https://qxmd.com/calculate/calculator_713/international-igan-prediction-tool-at-biopsy-pediatrics).

17.2 Interactive Case Discussion

What is immunoglobulin A nephropathy (IgAN)?

IgA nephropathy is an autoimmune glomerulonephritis characterised by mesangial cell proliferation with predominant IgA deposition. It was first described by the French renal pathologist Jean Berger (1930–2011) in 1968 and was once known as Berger's disease. Nowadays, IgA nephropathy is known as the most common primary glomerulonephritis worldwide and a leading cause of chronic kidney disease. It is estimated that around 20–40% of patients with IgAN progress to end-stage renal disease in 20–30 years after diagnosis. Despite tremendous effort, the pathogenesis is still mysterious. The presence of IgA deposits in the glomeruli remains the only means to diagnose IgA nephropathy. The pathogenesis of IgA nephropathy is complex and still unclear; however, immune dysregulation mediated by aberrantly glycosylated IgA1 in the hinge region is a characteristic feature.

IgAN most commonly presents in the second and third decades of life. In children, the median age is around 10–11 years old. The incidence of IgAN varies among different ethnic groups and is affected by the following:

- Whether mass urine screening is routinely performed in the country
- The practice of kidney biopsy in suspected cases

These practices affect the incidence of IgAN in different populations.

What is the pathophysiology of IgA nephropathy?

The pathophysiological mechanisms of IgAN are complex and incompletely understood. A common observation is an elevated level of galactose-deficiency (Gd-IgA1). The multi-hit hypothesis suggests the following:

1. Synthesis of aberrantly glycosylated IgA1, leading to Galactose-deficient IgA1 (Gd-IgA1).
   - Gd-IgA1 lacks galactose in the hinge region of IgA1
   - The aberrant hinge region enables diversification of the structure and acts as an epitope for anti-IgA-IgG formation
   - Gd-IgA1 also escapes the normal hepatic clearance of IgA1, resulting in an overwhelming amount of Gd-IgA1 in the circulation
2. Development of antibodies against Gd-IgA1.
3. Formation of Gd-IgA1 immune complexes.
4. These immune complexes deposit at the vessel wall and the mesangium of the glomeruli, triggering the inflammation cascades.

What are the clinical presentations of IgA nephropathy?

There is a significant variability in the clinical presentation of patients with IgA nephropathy, from asymptomatic, mild disease to a severe form of rapid progression to renal failure. The spectrum of presentation covers all possible clinical presentations of glomerulonephritis, including the following:

- Microscopic haematuria
- Recurrent gross haematuria
- Proteinuria (non-nephrotic range or nephrotic range proteinuria)
- Nephrotic syndrome
- Nephritic syndrome
- Nephritic-nephrotic syndrome
- Acute kidney injury
- Rapidly progressive glomerulonephritis (RPGN)
- Chronic kidney disease, and
- End-stage renal failure

What is secondary IgA nephropathy?

IgAN has been described in patients with other comorbidities. It is sometimes referred to as secondary IgA nephropathy, but there are no specific features differentiating primary or secondary causes of mesangial IgA deposition in proliferative glomerulonephritis. Hence, it is not clear whether the association of systemic disease relates to an exacerbation or a recognition of coincidental primary IgAN. Examples of common 'secondary IgAN' are as follows:

- Liver disease: inflammatory bowel disease and celiac disease
- Viral infections: hepatitis B, hepatitis C, HIV, chronic staphylococcus infection
- Autoimmune disease: systemic lupus erythematosus, ankylosing spondylitis, rheumatoid arthritis, psoriasis
- Chronic respiratory disease: chronic obstructive bronchiolitis, cystic fibrosis
- Neoplasia: IgA myeloma, Hodgkin's and Non-Hodgkin's lymphoma

Is there any difference between childhood-onset and adult-onset IgAN?

Recurrent gross haematuria is more common in children than in adults, leading to early diagnosis by renal biopsy. The gross haematuria in IgAN is usually triggered by a concurrent upper respiratory tract infection (synpharyngitic macrohaematuria). This characteristic helps to distinguish IgAN from post-infectious glomerulonephritis, in which gross haematuria usually occurs 10–14 days after an upper respiratory tract infection.

Mesangial, endocapillary and extra-capillary hypercellularity are more common in the paediatric population than in adults. In contrast, chronic features like tubular atrophy and interstitial fibrosis are more frequently described in adults. Hence, the renal biopsy in children with IgA nephropathy is usually more intensely inflamed and has less chronic changes as compared with adults at the time of diagnosis, implying children with IgAN may justify a more aggressive anti-inflammatory approach than the adult counterpart.

What are the risk factors for progression in IgAN?

Risk factors for disease progression include the following:

- Ongoing high level of proteinuria (sustained proteinuria >1 g/day is strongly associated with progression of chronic kidney disease).
- Ongoing haematuria.
- Hypertension, especially >140/90 mmHg,
- Decreased renal function at the time of renal biopsy (high serum creatinine/reduced eGFR).
- Severe histological lesions.

What is the Oxford classification MEST-C scoring system in IgA nephropathy?

The Oxford MEST-C classification was first published in 2009. It initially described four morphologic features in the renal histology of patients with IgAN. These four features are the following:

- Mesangial cellularity (M).
- Endocapillary hypercellularity (E).
- Segmental sclerosis (S).
- The interstitial fibrosis/tubular atrophy (T) form the MEST score.

A revised version in 2016 added the fifth parameter, cellular/fibrocellular Crescents (C), to form the current MEST-C score, and the S score was revised to consider the absence or presence of podocytopathic features (podocyte hypertrophy/tip lesions). The MEST-C scoring has been validated by many adult studies and a few paediatric studies in predicting the prognosis of IgAN; hence it is widely used both in clinical and research settings (Table 17.1).

Table 17.1 The Oxford MEST-C classification

M	*Mesangial hypercellularity* (≥4 mesangial cells in any mesangial area of a glomerulus)	M0: ≤50% glomeruli M1: >50% glomeruli
E	*Endocapillary hypercellularity* (increase the number of cells within the glomerular capillary lumen)	E0: absent E1: any present
S	*Segmental glomerulosclerosis* (adhesion or sclerosis in a segment of the glomerular tuft)	S0: absent S1: any present Presence or absence of podocyte hypertrophy/tip lesion in biopsies with S1
T	*Interstitial fibrosis/tubular atrophy* (% of cortical area with tubular atrophy or interstitial fibrosis, whichever is greater)	T0: absent or <25% of the cortex T1: 26–50% of the cortex T2: >50% of the cortex
C	*Crescents* (% of glomeruli with cellular or fibrocellular crescents)	C0: absent C1: 1–24% glomeruli with cellular/fibrocellular crescents C2: >25% glomeruli with cellular/fibrocellular crescents

A higher MEST-C score generally indicates a poorer prognosis.
Active glomerular lesion: M1, E1, C1/C2
IgAN S1 and podocytopathy have higher levels of proteinuria and worse outcomes.

What is the treatment option for IgA nephropathy?

Corticosteroids have been the standard treatment for IgAN over the decades, especially in paediatrics. However, in recent years, there has been a polarised view on whether steroid and immunosuppressive agents should be used in the treatment of IgA nephropathy. Some studies have shown that despite the use of corticosteroids, which can decrease the severity of proteinuria in the short term, proteinuria may recur after stopping treatment, and corticosteroid use did not translate to a long-term benefit in delaying the loss in glomerular filtration rate. With the side effects of steroids, especially infection, there was a strong view of optimising supportive therapy and stopping immunosuppression in adult IgAN patients.

However, there are still high-proteinuric patients despite supportive care having been optimised, and the value of immunosuppression in patients with rapidly progressive disease remains uncertain. The complete exclusion of immunosuppressive agents in treating IgAN in paediatric patients remains sceptical, as follows:

- There is a lack of high-quality evidence in paediatric patients.
- The fear of losing the window of opportunity for treatment in children.
- Compared to adults, children with IgAN usually have a more acute presentation and histologically, glomeruli are more intensely inflamed, and there is less chronic damage.
- Many paediatric data reported improvement in renal function and a decrease in proteinuria with the use of corticosteroids.
- The heterogeneity in clinical pictures and the remitting-relapsing pattern in proteinuria may warrant individualised therapy and repeated renal biopsy to guide further treatment.

Hence, paediatric nephrologists are more likely to start corticosteroids in children with IgA nephropathy. IPNA recommended the use of corticosteroid and immunosuppressive drugs in selected paediatric patients with a risk-benefit balance of immunosuppression and disease progression. Treatment decision depends on the amount of proteinuria, blood pressure, renal function/glomerular filtration rate and risk factors in the kidney biopsy.

A brief summary of recent guidelines is shown in Table 17.2. These guidelines recommend observation over a few months after RASB treatment before starting steroids. Waiting for the action of RASB for a few months without steroids may result in losing the golden period to treat acute inflammation; hence some paediatric nephrologists would suggest early use of steroid therapy after renal biopsy.

How would you treat Derick?

Derick has stage 2 CKD, proteinuria >1 g/day and a high Oxford MEST-C score at biopsy. Hence, he was treated with oral Ramipril, an ACEI and oral Prednisolone 60 mg/day at the same time. Prednisolone was tapered over 6 months.

Table 17.2 Highlights of International guidelines in the recommendation of treatment

International guidelines	Extract of recommendations	
KDIGO 2021 guideline	*ACEIs or ARBs as the first-line treatment for* – All patients with proteinuria of *>0.5 g/day*, regardless of whether there is hypertension (recommendation level 1B) – Up-titrating ACEIs or ARBs to a maximum recommended dose of the maximum tolerated dose to reduce proteinuria to <0.75–1 g/day (recommendation 1B) *Systemic corticosteroid* – Can be considered for 6 months if proteinuria is >0.75–1 g/day despite optimised RASB for 3 months	
IPNA recommendation (2025)	**Scenarios**	**Treatment recommended**
	UPCR 20–50 mg/mmol (0.2–0.5 mg/mg) for 2–3 weeks on ≥2 occasions	Start ACIEs/ARBs and monitor or perform a kidney biopsy
	Renal biopsy with ≥1 of M1, E1, S1 and C1 ± UPCR consistently >100 mg/mmol, *without RPGN*, start RASB if not yet commenced +	
	Persistent UPCR 50–100 mg/mmol (0.5–1 mg/mg) despite 3–6 months of RASB or Persistent UPCR >100 mg/mmol (1 mg/mg) despite 4 weeks of RASB	IV methylprednisolone pulse ± prednisolone for 4–6 months + RASB ± combination treatment in case of nephrotic syndrome In the case of no remission – Consider a repeat kidney biopsy – Additional IS drugs – Enrolled in clinical trials – Supportive care only if T2 on biopsy and continuously decline in GFR <30 mL/min/1.73 m^2
	Renal biopsy with ≥1 of M1, E1, S1 and C1 ± UPCR consistently >100 mg/mmol *with RPGN or C2 irrespective proteinuria*	Start RASB if stable GFR + IV methylprednisolone pulse + prednisolone for 3–6 months ± cyclophosphamide pulse ± MMF/MPS
	M0, E0, S0, T0, C0 and UPCR ≥200 mg/mmol or 2 g/g	Treated as minimal change disease with steroids
	M0, E0, C0 and T2 only with no active lesion	Continue RASB and supportive care
KDIGO 2024 under public review	Recommendation on the use of new therapeutic agents in progress	

KDIGO kidney disease: improving global outcomes, *IPNA* International Pediatric Nephrology Association, *UPCR* urine protein creatinine ratio, *RASB* renin-angiotensin system blockage, *ACEIs* angiotensin-converting enzyme inhibitors, *ARBs* angiotensin receptor blockers, *RASB* renin-angiotensin system blockage, MMF mycophenolate mofetil, MPS mycophenolate sodium.

The principle of treatment in children with IgAN is summarised below:

1. Lifestyle modification
   - Sodium restriction
     - Dietary counselling to keep a moderate salt intake below 3–5 g/day
   - Weight control
     - Target to maintain ideal body weight, as being overweight and obese increases the risk of progression of renal disease
   - Regular exercise
     - Regular aerobic exercise
   - Advice against smoking and no vaping
2. Tight blood pressure control
   - In children with CKD stage 2 or higher, the target is to keep arterial BP ≤50th percentile for age, sex and height by ambulatory BP monitoring in patients with proteinuria and keep BP ≤75th percentile in patients without proteinuria.
3. Use of antiproteinuric agents
   - Treatment with renin-angiotensin system blockers (RASB), either as an ACE inhibitor (ACEIs) or angiotensin receptor blockers (ARBs), at maximally tolerated dose, aims to keep UPCR <0.2 mg/mg (20 mg/mmol) even without hypertension.
4. The use of corticosteroids, especially in nephrotic range proteinuria and actively inflamed glomeruli. However, there is no consensus or data to support which regime is superior to the other. Examples of pulse and oral steroid regimes are listed below.
   - An example of steroid regime: Prednisolone at 0.8–1 mg/kg/day (max 60 mg/day) for 4–6 weeks, then tapered by 5 mg every 2 weeks until reaching 0.5 mg/kg/day, followed by a reduction of 2.5–5 mg every 2–4 weeks until discontinuation, with a total treatment duration of 6 months.
   - Oral Prednisolone at 2 mg/kg/day max 60 mg/day for 4 weeks, followed by alternate day dosing and tapered over 5–6 months.
   - Oral Prednisolone at 0.4 mg/kg/day for 2 months, tapering over 6 months (TESTING Trial).
   - Intravenous methylprednisolone 1000 mg for 3 consecutive days on months 1, 3 and 5 with oral Prednisolone at 0.5 mg/kg on alternate days, for a total of 6 months (Pozzi Protocol).
5. Use of second-line immunosuppressive agents
   - Second-line therapy, especially cyclophosphamide, has been used in rapidly progressive IgA nephritis. Other immunosuppressive treatments, such as mycophenolate mofetil, azathioprine and calcineurin inhibitors, have been reported.

6. Future therapeutic options
    - Now steroid therapy: targeted-release formulation of budesonide (Nefecon®)
    - Anti-proteinuria drugs: SGLT2 inhibitors (Empagliflozin, Dapagliflozin), dual endothelin and angiotensin blocker: Sparsentan
    - Complement inhibitors: factor D and B inhibitors, C3 and C5 inhibitors, C5 receptor inhibitor
    - Targeting B-cell lineage: anti-CD 20, anti-APRIL, BAFF/APRIL: inhibitor

Dereck's renal function and proteinuria improved with oral steroids. As the steroid tapered, he was given mycophenolate mofetil for steroid sparing. He remained stable for around 1 year, but then developed repeated relapses once steroid was tapered off. Each relapse was accompanied by worsening in eGFR and increasing proteinuria. He responded to repeated steroid therapy with the addition of immunosuppressive agents, including a calcineurin inhibitor. A second renal biopsy was performed 2 years after the first biopsy. The Oxford MEST-C score was M1, E0, S1, T0 and C0. Despite the improvement in renal histology, there was persistent proteinuria at 3–4 g/day, and he was dependent on immunosuppressive therapy. Empagliflozin 10 mg daily per oral was then started, and the aim was to taper down the immunosuppressive agents.

What is empagliflozin and dapagliflozin?
Empagliflozin and dapagliflozin are SGLT2 inhibitors initially developed for the treatment of diabetes mellitus. In clinical trials, like EMPA-KIDNEY, empagliflozin has been shown to reduce the progression of proteinuria and lower the risk of progression of kidney disease or death from cardiovascular causes compared to placebo.

What are the limitations of the new anti-proteinuria agent and dual endothelin/angiotensin blockers?
These drugs theoretically do not control active glomerular lesions, but proteinuria will improve. Hence, one has to wait for data on the long-term outcome of eGFR. Other limitations include the following:

- They are not available in many countries.
- They are expensive and may not be covered by insurance.
- They are not approved for use in children.

What is the role of budesonide in treating IgAN?
Budesonide is a steroid which have been sold under the brand name Pulmocort® for years in treating childhood asthma. Targeted-release formulation of budesonide (Nefecon®) is a new preparation, which delivers the drug to the Peyer's patches at the distal ileum and proximal colon. This is the first treatment approved by the US Food and Drug Administration and European Medicines Agency for patients with primary IgAN at risk of rapid disease progression. As the steroid formulation targets

the Peyer's patches, it may minimise systemic side effects of corticosteroids. Although a beneficial role in adults has been demonstrated, data in children are still lacking.

What is the outcome of patients with IgAN?

Large-scale epidemiology studies have shown an increasing percentage of children with IgAN developing chronic disease during follow-up for 5, 10 and 15 years. Time average proteinuria (TAP) is the mean of every 6 months of proteinuria. Renal survival is inversely proportional to the values of TAP during follow-up, and a value of <1 g/day is associated with better renal survival. Urinary abnormalities may reappear, and progression in renal damage was observed in children who showed complete remission. Hence, long-term follow-up for children with IgAN is necessary even in those with minimal kidney dysfunction or mild proteinuria.

17.3 Case Illustrations

This case provides an overview on the clinical presentation, renal histology and treatment options for paediatric IgA glomerulonephritis. Because of the broad spectrum in clinical severity and remitting-relapsing nature of IgA nephropathy, existing guidelines may not cover all the clinical scenarios, making the need for individualisation of treatment therapy. Some patients may have repeated relapses with worsening in proteinuria and renal function. Some patients have active proliferative lesions in renal histology, and with the fear of missing a treatment opportunity, use of corticosteroids and second-line immunosuppressive agents may be unavoidable. For patients with mild disease or advanced disease, conventional therapy with RASB and optimal blood pressure control may be the treatment of choice. New therapeutic agents will become available in the market and will modify the current treatment options.

Suggested Further Readings

1. Rauen T, Eitner F, Fitzner C, Sommerer C, Zeier M, Otte B, et al. Intensive supportive care plus immunosuppression in IgA nephropathy. N Engl J Med. 2015;373(23):2225–36.
2. Pozzi C. Pro: STOP immunosuppression in IgA nephropathy? Nephrol Dial Transplant. 2016;31(11):1766–70.
3. Rauen T, Eitner F, Fitzner C, Floege J. Con: STOP immunosuppression in IgA nephropathy. Nephrol Dial Transplant. 2016;31(11):1771–4.
4. Vivarelli M, Samuel S, Coppo R, Barratt J, Bonilla-Felix M, Haffner D, et al. IPNA clinical practice recommendations for the diagnosis and management of children with IgA nephropathy and IgA vasculitis nephritis. Pediatr Nephrol. 2025;40(2):533–69.
5. EMPA-KIDNEY Collaborative Group. Long-term effects of empagliflozin in patients with chronic kidney disease. N Engl J Med. 2025;392(8):777–87.

18 Same Diseases with Different Treatments?

18.1 Case Description

Joan is a 15-year-old girl who complained of a purpuric rash over both lower limbs with bilateral ankle pain and abdominal pain for 4 days. She was diagnosed with Henoch-Schönlein purpura. Her initial blood test, including a routine urine test, was normal. Her arthritis progressed to affect both knees, and the purpuric rash became more extensive. Her abdominal pain was getting worse. Her abdominal ultrasound was normal. Because of the progression of vasculitis, she was treated with a short course of oral Prednisolone and tapered off in 2 weeks. However, a few days after taking off the steroid, she got another relapse of purpuric rash and abdominal pain. She was treated with another short course of oral Prednisolone and tapered again, yet she had a third relapse, but the symptoms were less severe. She was managed conservatively. However, her urine started to show microscopic haematuria and proteinuria. The proteinuria increased to >0.5 g/day. Her blood test for immunological markers, including antinuclear factor, anti-dsDNA, ANCA, anti-ENA, complements, ASOT, immunoglobulin pattern, hepatitis B and hepatitis C, were all negative. Her skin biopsy confirmed leukocytoclastic vasculitis with predominantly IgA deposition, compatible with Henoch-Schönlein purpura.

18.2 Interactive Case Discussion

What is Henoch-Schönlein purpura (HSP) and related nephritis?

In 1837, a German physician, Johann Lukas Schönlein (1793–1864), first described the clinical association of purpura, arthralgia and arthritis. A few years later, in 1874, Eduard Henoch (1820–1910), a student of Schönlein, reported cases of children with purpura, abdominal pain, bloody diarrhoea and joint pain. The constellation of clinical features was then named Henoch-Schönlein purpura, and this name has been used for decades. With the better understanding on the pathogenesis,

W. K. Y. Chan, M. C. I. Kuok, *Paediatric Nephrology*,
https://doi.org/10.1007/978-981-95-5060-9_18

developments in immunology and immune markers on tissue biopsies, the American College of Rheumatology (ACR) proposed HSP to be classified as IgA vasculitis in 1990, then the European League Against Rheumatism (EULAR) and the Pediatric Rheumatology Society (PRES) in 2006, followed by 2012 revised Chapel Hill Consensus Conference defined IgA Vasculitis as a vasculitis with IgA-dominant immune deposits affecting small vessels (capillaries, venules and arterioles) involving the skin, gut and glomeruli, associated with arthritis or arthralgia. Since then, IgA vasculitis (IgAV) and IgA vasculitis-related nephritis (IgAVN) have replaced the terminology of HSP and HSP-related nephritis.

IgA vasculitis is the most common systemic vasculitis in children. It typically occurs in children between 2 and 18 years, with the peak age at 6 years. The clinical features of IgA vasculitis consist of a tetrad of the following:

1. Cutaneous palpable purpura
   - Most commonly affect the buttocks and lower extremities—particularly the extensor surfaces.
   - The platelet count and clotting factors are normal.
2. Gastrointestinal manifestations such as abdominal pain and bleeding
   - Potential life-threatening complications include intussusception, bowel perforation, bowel gangrene and massive haemorrhage
3. Arthritis or arthralgia
   - Painful and swollen joints, most commonly affect the knees, ankles, hands and feet.
   - Typically, the arthritis is transient, responds to NSAID treatment and is non-destructive.
4. Glomerulonephritis
   - Renal symptoms typically occur 1–3 months after the development of purpuric rash.
   - Renal manifestations include haematuria, proteinuria, nephrotic syndrome, nephritic syndrome and renal failure.
   - The most common renal presentation is microhaematuria.
   - Spontaneous remission is not uncommon.

IgA vasculitis is typically self-limiting. The prognosis largely depends on renal involvement and the involvement of the major organs, such as the pulmonary and central nervous systems, but these complications are extremely rare.

What is the clinical presentation of IgAV-nephritis?

The renal manifestations of IgAV-nephritis were classified into five grades according to the initial presentation by the modified Meadow Classification.

Grade 1: microscopic haematuria
Grade 2: persistent mild proteinuria (<20 mg/m^2/hr) $\pm$ haematuria
Grade 3: nephritic syndrome
Grade 4: nephrotic syndrome
Grade 5: mixed nephritic-nephrotic syndrome

What are the indications for renal biopsy in IgA vasculitis-nephritis?
The indication for renal biopsy in IgA vasculitis-nephritis varies among different centres, especially for patients whose presentation is classified as Grade 1 in the modified Meadow classification. Other common indications are the following:

- Rapidly progressive glomerulonephritis (RPGN)
- Nephritic-nephrotic syndrome
- Nephrotic syndrome
- Progressive/persistent proteinuria
- Nonresponsive to steroid therapy
- Uncertainty of diagnosis

However, IgAV is a self-limiting disease, and there is no consensus on how long one can observe before performing a renal biopsy until the recent IPNA recommendations. IPNA in 2025 recommended performing a renal biopsy in children with IgAV-nephritis when:

- eGFR <90 mL/min/1.73 m^2 irrespective the degree of proteinuria
- Presence of nephrotic range proteinuria (UPCR >2 mg/mg or 200 mg/mmol)
- Moderate proteinuria (UPCR 1–2 mg/mg or 100–200 mg/mmol) lasts for 2–4 weeks
- Mild proteinuria (UPCR 0.2–0.5 mg/mg or 20–50 mg/mmol) lasts for >4 weeks

What is the histological classification for IgA vasculitis-nephritis?
Confirmation of IgAV-nephritis requires a kidney biopsy. There are several histological classifications for HSP-nephritis. The International Study of Kidney Disease in Children (ISKDC) remains the best studied classification. It classified Henoch-Schönlein purpura nephritis/IgAV nephritis into six grades based on renal biopsy findings. Unlike the Oxford MEST-C classification for IgA nephropathy, the ISKDC classification in IgAV nephritis focuses on the degree of active inflammatory process in the glomeruli, especially on the degree of crescent formation. The degree of tubular atrophy or interstitial fibrosis, which has implications for chronicity and long-term prognosis, is not addressed (Table 18.1).

The working group of Oxford MEST-C in IgA nephropathy did not recommend extending its use to children with HSP-nephritis, as they did not include children in their validation cohort. However, due to the shared histological findings, the Oxford classification has increasingly been used in IgAV-Nephritis in clinical practice.

Table 18.1 The ISKDC classification of IgAV-nephritis

Grades of ISKDC classification	Description in renal histology
Grade I	Minimal glomerular abnormalities
Grade II	Focal or diffuse mesangial proliferation
Grade III	Focal or diffuse mesangial proliferation with <50% crescents
Grade IV	Focal or diffuse mesangial proliferation with <50–75% crescents
Grade V	Focal or diffuse mesangial proliferation with >75% crescents
Grade VI	Membranoproliferative-like glomerulonephritis

Is IgA vasculitis-nephritis and IgA nephropathy the same disease?

Both diseases showed IgA deposits in the glomeruli, but whether the two diseases are distinct entities or represent a spectrum of the same condition is debatable. Many studies have looked into the similarities and differences between the two diseases, yet no universal consensus has been reached. IgA vasculitis is more commonly seen in children and presents acutely. The extra-renal manifestations often bring early attention to the kidney involvement. The renal histology in IgAV-nephritis may show more inflammatory pictures, making the use of corticosteroids more common. At the same time, corticosteroid and immunosuppressive agents may be used for extra-renal disease and their complications. The prior use of corticosteroids may affect the renal histology before biopsy (Table 18.2).

What is the pathophysiology of IgAV-nephritis?

The pathophysiology of IgAV-nephritis is similar to that of IgA nephropathy. It is multifactorial, involves immune complex formation and deposition, in patients with genetic predisposition and environmental triggers. The hallmark of IgAV-nephritis is the deposition of IgA1-dominant immune complexes in small vessels, causing inflammation. Many future drugs are being developed to target various sites in the pathogenetic pathway.

- Mucosa-associated lymphatic tissue (MALT) and gut-associated lymphatic tissue (GALT) are closely related to the environmental triggers in the production of galatose-deficient-IgA1.

Table 18.2 Differences and similarities between IgAV-nephritis and IgA nephropathy

	HSP-nephritis/IgAV-nephritis	IgA nephropathy
Age of onset	Have two peaks, one in childhood (1–18 years), with a typical age between 4 and 7 years, and another age peak is at older adults from 60 to 69 years	15–35 years
Renal presentation	Mainly present acutely as a nephrotic/nephritic picture	Mostly present as a chronic progressive disease
Extra-renal presentation	Skin, gastrointestinal, musculoskeletal, neurological and pulmonary	No extra-renal involvement
Pathophysiology	Multi-hit model involving overproduction of galactose-deficient IgA1 (Gd-IgA1)	
Renal histology	Necrotising changes, fibrin deposits in glomeruli ± endocapillary proliferation ± crescents are more common	More likely glomerulosclerosis and tubular atrophy at the time of renal biopsy
Mechanism of damage	Glomerular endothelial lesions may heal or progress to fibrosis	Damage predominantly in the mesangium and gradually progresses to glomerulosclerosis and interstitial fibrosis
Prognosis	Higher incidence of remission	Higher incidence of Progression to CKD

- Gd-IgA1 interacts with autoantibodies (either IgA1 or IgG antibodies), forming circulating immune complexes.
- Deposition of circulating immune complexes in tissue triggers an inflammatory process, which involves the following:
  - Stimulation of Toll-like receptors
  - Proliferation of B cells
  - Complement activation
  - Cytokines such as IL-6, IL-10, B-cell activation factor (BAFF) and a proliferation-inducing ligand (APRIL)

What is the treatment of IgAV-nephritis?
As in patients with IgA nephropathy, tight blood pressure control, lifestyle modification and anti-proteinuric agents are the mainstay of treatment. There are three main categories of anti-proteinuric medications.

1. Renin-angiotensin system blockers (RASB)
   - RASB includes angiotensin converting enzyme inhibitors (ACEIs) and angiotensin receptor blockers (ARBs).
   - RASB is the only treatment that has been well studied and widely used in children with both IgA nephropathy and IgAV nephritis.
   - The combination of ACEIs and ARBs is not well studied, and because of the risk of renal damage, it is not routinely recommended in children.
2. Sodium-glucose cotransporter 2 (SGLT2) inhibitors
   - Like dapagliflozin and empagliflozin, which showed beneficial effects in adult studies.
   - They are less well studied in children.
3. Endothelin receptor antagonists
   - Like Sparsentan (a dual endothelin receptor and angiotensin receptor blocker)
   - Less studied in children

Conventional immunosuppressive therapy, including corticosteroid (GS) and immunosuppressive (IS) agents such as cyclophosphamide, mycophenolate mofetil, azathioprine and calcineurin inhibitors, has been used in children with severe disease and in those children who have an unfavourable prognosis in renal function. The choice of GS and IS is usually based on histology and clinical severity after consideration of the risk-and-benefit profile for the individual patient (Table 18.3).

Joan was started on losartan when she had proteinuria >0.5 g/day. However, despite treatment with ARB, her urine proteinuria continued to increase to 1.2 g/day. A renal biopsy was suggested, but Joan refused as she is asymptomatic. However, her rash reappeared, and she agreed on empirical treatment with oral Prednisolone at 1 mg/kg/day for 4 weeks and tapered. Tacrolimus was added for steroid sparing. She then became disease-free. Finally, she agreed on a kidney biopsy, and it showed ISKDC grade 1 and Oxford MEST-C classification with M0, E0, S0, T0 and C0. Immunosuppressive agents and steroid was tapered off. Joan was treated with losartan and her proteinuria remained <0.5 g/day.

Table 18.3 Highlights of the ISKDC 2025 recommendations on the treatment of IgA vasculitis-related nephritis

Renal biopsy gradings	Treatment recommendations
ISKDC Grade I histology	Use of RASB
ISKDC Grade II–III and UPCR <200 mg/mmol (2 mg/mg)	RASB + consideration use of Prednisolone (3–6 months) ± steroid-sparing agents, like MMF, mizoribine, CNI
ISKDC Grade III, ± UPCR ≥200 mg/mmol (2 mg/mg)	RASB + Prednisolone (3–6 months) and consider pulse methylprednisolone ± steroid-sparing agents, like MMF, mizoribine and CNI
ISKDC Grade IV and V ± RPGN	RASB if stable eGFR + pulse methylprednisolone then prednisolone for 3–6 months + pulse cyclophosphamide ± MMF
Only have sclerotic lesions	RASB if GFR >30 mL/min/1.73 m^2 Supportive treatment

ISKDC international study of kidney disease in children, *RPGN* rapidly progressive glomerulonephritis, *RASB* renin-angiotensin system blockers, *MMF* mycophenolate mofetil, *CNI* calcineurin inhibitor

Table 18.4 Brief outline of the novel treatment for IgAV-nephritis in recent years

The pathophysiological mechanisms	Targeted novel therapies
Microorganisms binding to toll-like receptors (TLR) might be a trigger for the production of Gd-IgA1	Silencing APRIL by siRNA and neutralisation of IL-6 signalling, as it may reduce TLR-9-stimulated Gd-IgA1 production
Mucosa-associated lymphatic tissue (MALT) stimulation increases Gd-IgA1 production	Tonsillectomy
Gut-associated lymphatic tissue (GALT) is associated with increased memory B cells	Target-release formulation-budesonide
BAFF and APRIL's role in T-cell-independent IgA switch of B cells	Anti-CD antibodies (e.g. rituximab and ofatumumab) Anti-APRIL antibodies (e.g. sibeprenimab) BAFF/APRIL inhibition (e.g. telitaciept and atacicept) BLyS-neutralising monoclonal antibody (e.g. belimumab)
Activation of the alternate and lectin pathways	Complement inhibitors

TLR Toll-like receptor, *siRNA* small interfering RNA, *MALT* mucosa-associated lymphatic tissue, *GALT* gut-associated lymphatic tissue, *APRIL* a proliferation-inducing ligand, *BAFF* B-cell activating factor

What are the novel agents for the treatment of IgAV-nephritis?

In recent years, many agents have been developed to target different sites of the pathogenic pathway of IgAV-nephritis/IgA nephropathy. The FDA has approved some drugs, and some are in various stages of clinical trials with promising results. More clinical evidence is likely to come out in the coming years and will give more insight to modify the treatment recommendations. Table 18.4 is a summary of the novel drug development, and the list is not exclusive, as more information on the treatment is likely to be revealed in the future.

18.3 Case Illustrations

Although it is still debatable whether IgAV-nephritis and IgA nephropathy represent the spectrum of the same disease, clinically, these patients may follow distinct courses, implying different treatment strategies. Early use of RASB, tight BP control and lifestyle modification are the cornerstones in the management of both IgAV-nephritis and IgA Nephropathy. However, in selected patients, corticosteroid remains the mainstay of treatment, and immunosuppressive agents may be needed in patients with severe disease and have a poorer prognosis. With the exciting development in novel drugs that target multiple levels of the pathogenesis, future recommendations would be very different when more data and evidence are published.

Suggested Further Readings

1. Vivarelli M, Samuel S, Coppo R, Barratt J, Bonilla-Felix M, Haffner D, et al. IPNA clinical practice recommendations for the diagnosis and management of children with IgA nephropathy and IgA vasculitis nephritis. Pediatr Nephrol. 2025;40(2):533–69.
2. Peruzzi L, Coppo R. IgA vasculitis nephritis in children and adults: one or different entities? Pediatr Nephrol. 2021;36(9):2615–25.
3. Nüsken E, Weber LT. IgA vasculitis nephritis. Curr Opin Pediatr. 2022;34(2):209–16.
4. Ozen S, Marks SD, Brogan P, Groot N, de Graeff N, Avcin T, et al. European consensus-based recommendations for diagnosis and treatment of immunoglobulin A vasculitis—the SHARE initiative. Rheumatology. 2019;58(9):1607–16.

Part III

Cystic Kidneys and Genetic Diseases

When It Is Solitary

19

19.1 Case Description

Danny is a 14-year-old boy, previously healthy but obese since childhood. He was detected to have hypertension with a blood pressure of 140/85 mmHg by routine health check, and he was referred for assessment. The clinical history was insignificant, and physical examination only showed a body mass index of 30.2 kg/m^2. The blood test showed normal renal function, and urine protein/creatinine was normal. A USG kidney was ordered to work up his hypertension. It showed a normal-sized kidney, but a renal cyst was detected in the left kidney (Fig. 19.1).

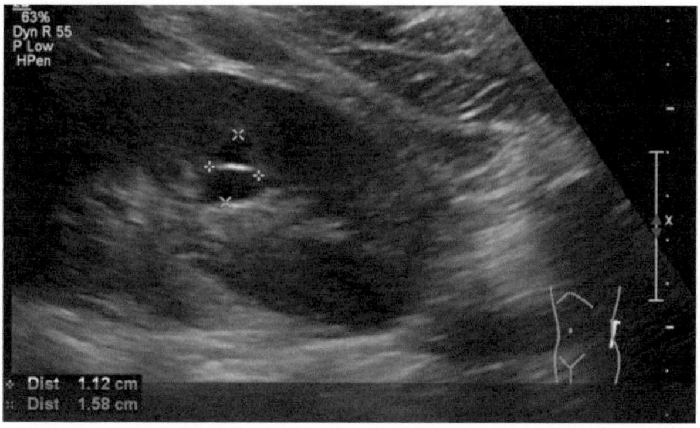

Fig. 19.1 A solitary renal cyst measured 1.12 cm × 1.58 cm with a thin calcified septum. According to the Bosniak classification system, it is a type II single renal cyst

W. K. Y. Chan, M. C. I. Kuok, *Paediatric Nephrology*,
https://doi.org/10.1007/978-981-95-5060-9_19

19.2 Interactive Case Discussion

How common is a simple renal cyst found in the Paediatric population?
Renal cysts are more common in adults, and the incidence increases with age. It has been reported as 20% at 40 years old and up to 50% in the 50-year-old population. However, renal cysts are less common in children. The true incidence of simple renal cysts in paediatrics is not known, as most of the time the solitary renal cyst is asymptomatic, and only detected incidentally by renal ultrasound. The indication for renal ultrasound becomes the determinant for picking up a simple renal cyst. Furthermore, the variation in ultrasound technique also affects the detection of a small single renal cyst. Yet, in general, the incidence of solitary renal cysts ranged from 0.2% to 5% of the paediatric population.

What is the classification of a solitary renal cyst?
The Bosniak classification system of renal cystic mass has been used for more than 30 years, especially by radiologists and urologists, to describe the appearance of a renal cystic mass and stratify the risk of malignancy. It divides renal cystic masses into five categories based on contrast-enhanced computed tomography (CT) imaging characteristics. In the latest version (The Bosniak v2019), the characteristics of MRI were incorporated into the classification to improve its precision and accuracy for the likelihood of cancer in each class. The use of ultrasound in the classification has been controversial, but ultrasound has a higher sensitivity for intralesional septa than CT or MRI; hence, its use is also common. As the majority of simple renal cysts in children do not progress, using ultrasound-based classification allows regular surveillance without unnecessary exposure of the child to irradiation. The contrast-enhanced CT, however, remains the gold standard of the classification. For classes III and IV, surgical intervention is indicated as they have a higher risk of malignancy (Table 19.1, Fig. 19.2).

Table 19.1 The Bosniak v2019 and its correlation to malignancy potential

Bosniak classification	Description in CT	Doppler US	Malignancy potential
I	Benign simple cyst – Well-defined thin wall, hairline thin wall of <2 mm – Water content, homogeneous simple fluid – No septa, no calcification or solid mass – The wall may be enhanced after contrast	No flow	No
II	Benign cyst: minimally complex – Well-defined with thin (≤2 mm) smooth walls – May have thin (<1 mm) septations or fine calcifications	No flow	No
IIF	Minimally complex cyst (increased number of septae and thickened with nodular or thick calcifications) – Cystic masses with a smooth, minimally thickened (3 mm) enhancing wall, or smooth minimal thickening (3 mm) of one or more enhancing septa. – Cystic masses with many (≥4) smooth thin (≤2 mm) enhancing septa	No flow	~5%
III	Indeterminate – One or more enhancing thick (≥4 mm width) or enhancing irregular (displaying ≤3 mm obtusely margined convex protrusion(s)) walls or septa	Flow detected	~50%
IV	Clearly malignant – One or more enhancing nodules (≥4-mm convex protrusion with obtuse margins, or a convex protrusion of any size that has acute margins)	Flow detected	~100%

The Bosniak classification should not be applied to lesions with an infectious, inflammatory or vascular aetiology

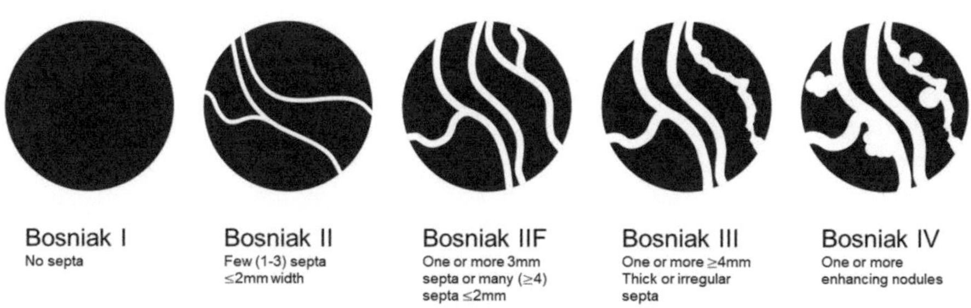

Fig. 19.2 The diagrammatic explanation of the Bosniak classification of renal cysts

What are the possible causes of a single kidney cyst in children?
The differential diagnoses of renal cysts in children are summarised below.

Simple renal cysts (commonest)
Polycystic kidney disease – ADPKD at an early stage – ARPKD is rare and unlikely to present as a single renal cyst – Other ciliopathies: rare and have other clinical features
Syndrome-related cystic kidney disease – Tuberous sclerosis – Von Hippel-Lindau
Cystic dysplasia with or without other CAKUT
Calyceal diverticulum
Acquired renal cyst related to trauma, infection or end-stage renal disease
Cystic renal tumour (rare) – Cystic nephroblastoma – Cystic adenoma – Metanephric adenoma – Multicystic nephrogenic rest – Juxtaglomerular tumour – Mature teratoma

What are the risks of malignancy?
There are several clinical features that suggest a higher risk of malignancy, and these patients either require early surgical intervention/biopsy or need more frequent imaging follow-up and surveillance. These clinical features include the following:

- The presence of a syndrome diagnosis, such as Von Hippel-Lindau and tuberous sclerosis
- Bosniak classification of III and IV, with larger cyst/cystic mass, more septae, more solid component of the cyst and the presence of blood flow inside the cyst/mass

How would you manage Danny?
Danny was asymptomatic, and his renal cyst was detected incidentally by ultrasound, which was initially performed for his hypertension workup. There was no family history of cystic kidney disease, and physical examination did not reveal any syndromal diagnoses.

Since he currently does not have other at-risk clinical features, a regular ultrasound to monitor the size and number of the cyst would be suggested. If the number of renal cysts increases, the workup for ADPKD should be considered, especially since Danny is only 14 years old, and his obesity may not solely explain his hypertension. This single renal cyst could be the early presentation of ADPKD. Screening of the parents by ultrasonography to detect any renal cysts will be helpful. A negative ultrasound scan with parental age >40 years old, then ADPKD is unlikely.

Although rare, complications of renal cysts like infection, bleeding and rupture should be kept in mind as these complications, if they occurred, would change the conservative plan of management. Early involvement of interventional radiologists and urologists may be needed.

19.3 Case Illustrations

Ultrasound usually picks up a single renal cyst during workup for other problems like urinary tract infection or hypertension. Understanding the importance and clinical implications of a renal cyst helps in deciding the follow-up plan for each patient.

Suggested Further Readings

1. Bosniak MA. The use of the Bosniak classification system for renal cysts and cystic tumors. J Urol. 1997;157(5):1852–3.
2. McHugh K, Stringer DA, Hebert D, Babiak CA. Simple renal cysts in children: diagnosis and follow-up with US. Radiology. 1991;178(2):383–5.
3. Wallis MC, Lorenzo AJ, Farhat WA, Bägli DJ, Khoury AE, Pippi Salle JL. Risk assessment of incidentally detected complex renal cysts in children: potential role for a modification of the Bosniak classification. J Urol. 2008;180(1):317–21.
4. Peard L, Gargollo P, Grant C, Strine A, De Loof M, Sinatti C, et al. Validation of the modified Bosniak classification system to risk stratify pediatric cystic renal masses: an international, multi-site study from the Pediatric Urologic Oncology Working Group of the societies for pediatric urology. J Pediatr Urol. 2022;18(2):180.e1–7.

The MCDK 20

20.1 Case Description

Helena, the first child in the family, was born at full term by normal spontaneous vaginal delivery. She was found to have cysts in the kidneys and was promptly referred to the paediatrician for further management. Helena's birth weight was 3.2 kg with an Apgar score of 9 at the first minute. Her perinatal and neonatal period was uneventful. Physical examination was unremarkable. Her blood pressure was normal at 65/35 mmHg at birth. Her renal function test and urinalysis were normal. There was no family history of polycystic kidney disease or chronic kidney disease.

20.2 Interactive Case Discussion

How would you investigate Helena's renal problem?
Helena had an ultrasound examination in the first week. This is the most essential and informative investigation that not only provides early diagnosis and enables us to give proper counselling to the family. The images of USG were shown in Fig. 20.1. A Tc-99m DMSA scan was also performed (Fig. 20.2).

What is multicystic dysplastic kidney disease (MCDK)?
MCDK is a type of non-hereditary cystic renal disease seen in paediatric patients. It results from multiple cysts being formed in the affected kidney. With the increasing use of antenatal ultrasonography, the incidence of MCDK reported is around 1:4000. It is the most severe form of cystic renal dysplasia, and unilateral MCDK is the most common cystic renal disease seen in children. Bilateral MCDK is lethal and will result in Potter syndrome as both kidneys are not functioning.

W. K. Y. Chan, M. C. I. Kuok, *Paediatric Nephrology*,
https://doi.org/10.1007/978-981-95-5060-9_20

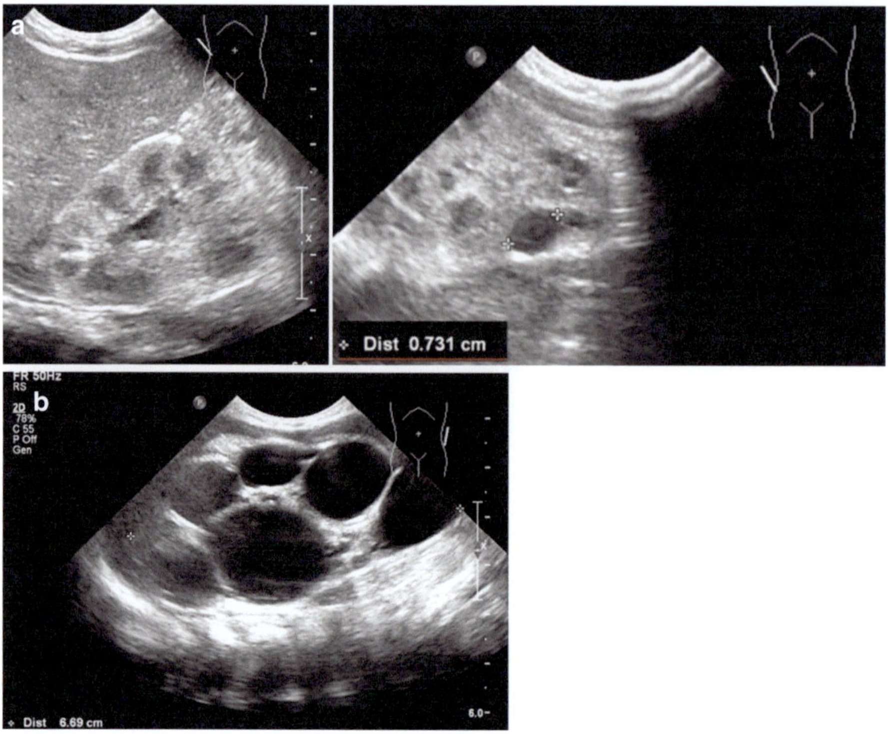

Fig. 20.1 An ultrasound of the kidneys was performed 1 week after birth. (**a**) The right kidney was normal in size and echo pattern, and there was no hydronephrosis. However, a cluster of small cysts with the largest size measured up to 0.73 cm in the interpolar region was noted. (**b**) An aggregate of non-communicating cysts of varying sizes occupied the left renal bed. The entire aggregate measured approximately 6.69 cm, with the largest cyst reaching 2 cm in size

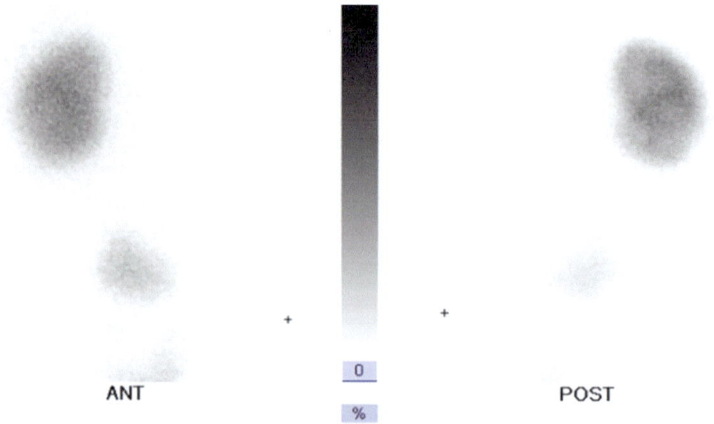

Fig. 20.2 A Tc-99m DMSA kidney scan was performed when Helena was 1 month old, revealed a non-functioning left kidney with a differential renal cortical mass ratio (left-to-right) of 0–100%

What is the natural history of MCDK?
The cysts of the MCDK will involute over the years. With monitoring by serial ultrasonography, 10% of MCDK involuted in the first year, 35% in the second year, up to 50% in the third year and 60% when followed up to 10–15 years old. In general, the rate of involution is highest in the first 30 months. The rate of involution decreases with age.

What is the pathogenesis of MCDK?
The exact mechanism causing MCDK is unknown, but several theories are attempting to explain its pathogenesis.

1. Ureteric bud theory
   The ureteric bud is atretic or connects abnormally with the metanephric mesenchyme.
2. Obstruction
   Ureteric or bladder obstruction in early nephrogenesis leads to cystic renal dysplasia.
3. Genetic
   Pathogenic variation in the developmental genes like TCF2, PAX2 and uroplakins. The TCF2 gene encodes the transcription factor hepatocyte nuclear factor-1β (HNF1β), which regulates the development and function of epithelia in the kidney, liver, pancreas and genitourinary tract.
4. Exposure teratogens
   Congenital viral infection and maternal use of anti-epileptic drugs have been reported to cause MCDK.

How would you diagnose MCDK?
Usually, ultrasound alone is sufficient to make the diagnosis. The typical features of MCDK are as follows:

- Lobulate renal contour
- Multiple internal cysts of variable sizes and shapes
- Cysts are typically non-communicating and do not communicate with the ureter
- The renal parenchyma is usually fibrous and echogenic without blood flow

The primary differential diagnosis is a hydronephrotic obstructive kidney. In a doubtful situation, a functional scan like MAG3 or DMSA renal scan will detect the presence of renal function in the obstructed kidney and aid in diagnosis. MAG3 is particularly useful for detecting drainage obstructions.

What is the objective of serial ultrasonography monitoring in Helena?
Apart from monitoring the involution of the CDK, the aim of serial USG is to monitor the compensatory hypertrophy in the normal kidney and detect any renal abnormalities in the contralateral kidney. Although the mechanism of compensatory hypertrophy is uncertain, there is a linear relationship between the rate of involution of the MCDK and the compensatory hypertrophy in the normal kidney.

Most children with unilateral MCDK and a contralateral normal kidney can maintain a near-normal eGFR. However, in patients with significant renal abnormalities in the contralateral kidney, they may progress into chronic kidney disease. For patients without compensatory hypertrophy of the contralateral kidney, renal hypoplasia may be a possibility, and these patients are at a higher risk of hypertension and renal insufficiency in future life.

What are the common associated abnormalities in the contralateral kidney?
Common associated abnormalities include the following:

- Vesicoureteric reflux
- Pelviureteric junction objection
- Ureteral ectopia or ureterocele
- Renal hypoplasia

What are the diseases that may be associated with MCDK?
Even though the majority of MCDK occurs sporadically and non-familially, some MCDK occurs in association with syndromes like the following:

- Meckel-Gruber syndrome
- Joubert syndrome
- Zellweger syndrome
- Branchiootorenal syndrome (BOR)
- VACTERL

Bilateral MCDK is more likely associated with syndromal disease, whereas unilateral MCDK is more likely sporadic.

What is the malignant risk in the MCDK?
Cases of Wilms' tumour, renal cell carcinoma and renal transitional cell carcinoma have been reported in the literature. However, long-term follow-up of patients with MCDK has a malignancy risk comparable to that of the general population.

What was the diagnosis of Helena?
Helena had a multicystic dysplastic left kidney which was non-functioning. The few small cysts in the right kidney remain static and are likely a focal cystic dysplasia of the right kidney.

Helena underwent serial follow-up USG examinations. Her USG at 3 years old showed progressive shrinkage in the MCDK. The right kidney showed compensatory hypertrophy, and the few cystic structures in the interpolar region remained static (Fig. 20.3).

How would you manage Helena?
Historically, nephrectomy is advocated for children whose MCDK does not involute due to the concern of infection, hypertension and malignant changes. However, data

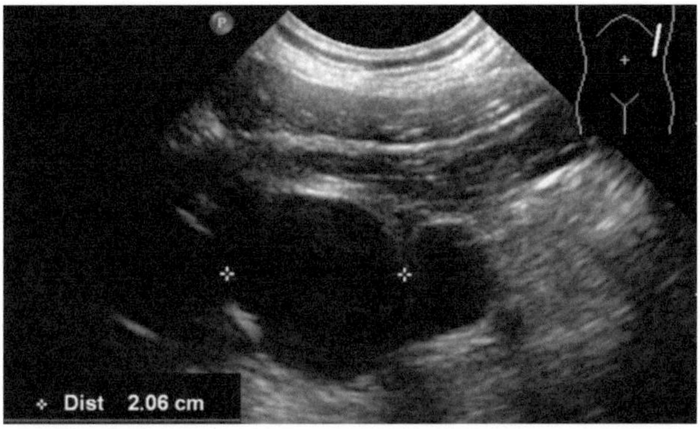

Fig. 20.3 There was progressive shrinkage in the number and size of the cystic aggregates in the left renal bed, and the largest cyst remained at around 2 cm in diameter

from the long-term follow-up of these patients suggest that the risk of hypertension and malignant change in these patients is not higher than that of the normal population. Nowadays, a conservative approach is a common management alternative. Helena underwent a laparoscopic removal of the left MCDK at the age of 10 years after detailed discussion with the family and the urologist. Despite the MCDK being removed, she needs to continue monitoring her blood pressure, renal function, urine protein and serial ultrasonography for the growth of the contralateral kidney and the few cysts in the right kidney.

20.3 Case Illustrations

This case walks the readers through the presentation and management of a common renal consultation: multicystic dysplastic kidney (MCDK). Most patients with a unilateral MCDK and a normal contralateral kidney remain healthy. However, some patients, like Helena, may have renal abnormalities in the contralateral kidney, and they need regular follow-up. This regular follow-up is crucial to ensure the remaining renal function is not jeopardised, and it should provide reassurance and confidence in the chosen approach.

Suggested Further Readings

1. Chang A, Sivananthan D, Nataraja RM, Johnstone L, Webb N, Lopez PJ. Evidence-based treatment of multicystic dysplastic kidney: a systematic review. J Pediatr Urol. 2018;14(6):510–9.
2. Winyard P, Chitty LS. Dysplastic kidneys. Semin Fetal Neonatal Med. 2008;13(3):142–51. WB Saunders.
3. Satariano M, Ghose S, Raina R. The pathophysiology of inherited renal cystic diseases. Genes. 2024;15(1):91.

The Potter

21

21.1 Case Description

A 32-year-old primigravida woman was admitted for rupture of the membrane. She did not have regular antenatal follow-up. Because of fetal distress, the obstetrician decided on an emergency caesarean section. A baby with an estimated maturity of 36 weeks was delivered. The birth weight of the baby was 2.85 kg. He was flaccid and cyanotic at birth and required immediate resuscitation. The baby was intubated at 1 min of life and was transferred to the neonatal intensive care unit. His Apgar score was four at 1 min, seven at 5, and eight at 10 min.

Despite being intubated, he remained in marked respiratory distress with severe chest retraction. He was noticed to have a depressed nose, a small rib cage and poor lung expansion. His abdomen was markedly distended with two huge palpable masses, which were likely kidneys.

Initial laboratory results showed a white cell count of 31.8×10^9/L, haemoglobin14 g/dL and platelet count of 230×10^9/L. His serum urea was 6 mmol/L, and serum creatinine was 98 μmol/L at 7 hours of life. Urea increased to 8 mmol/L, and creatinine increased to 116 μmol/L at 11 hours of life. Liver function test showed ALT at 83 iu/L. There was persistent mixed respiratory and metabolic acidosis with a base excess of −8 and $PaCO_2$ of 11 Kpa and PaO_2 of 6 KPa. His serum sodium was 129 mmol/L, and potassium was 7.1 mmol/L.

Despite putting on 100% oxygen with a high ventilatory setting, the baby's oxygen saturation remained at around 60%. The bedside echocardiogram showed a normal structural heart. Serial urgent CXRs were taken during resuscitation. What did they show (Figs. 21.1 and 21.2)?

W. K. Y. Chan, M. C. I. Kuok, *Paediatric Nephrology*,
https://doi.org/10.1007/978-981-95-5060-9_21

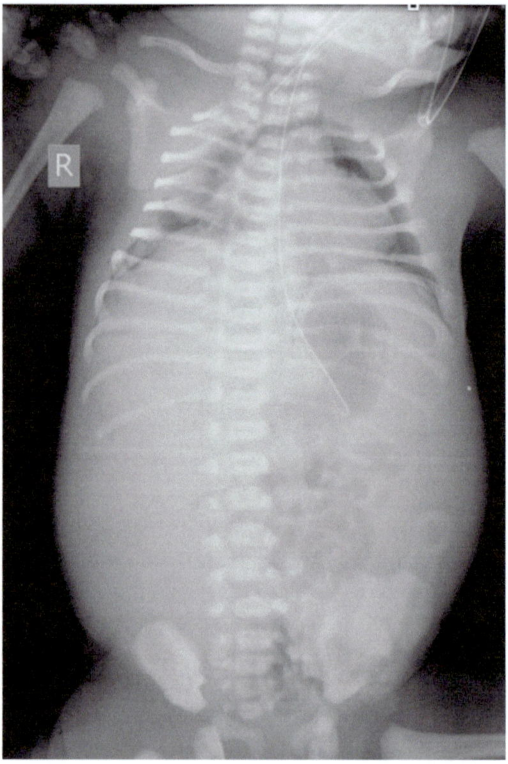

Fig. 21.1 The baby's chest X-ray (AP view) showed a rotated film. An endotracheal tube and a nasogastric tube were in situ. The lung volumes were small, and there was bilateral pneumothorax and pneumomediastinum. The abdominal X-ray showed central bowel gas likely displaced by large abdominal masses

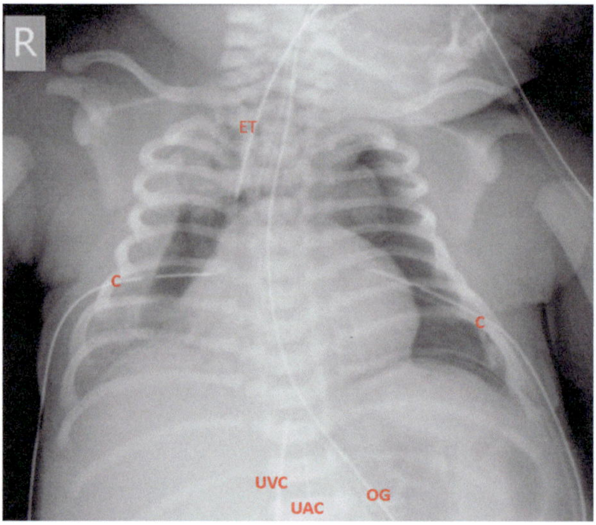

Fig. 21.2 The chest X-ray of the patient with an endotracheal tube (ET) appeared too advanced in the right lung. There was pneumothorax in both lungs with two chest drains (C) inserted. Two umbilical catheters (UVC and UAC) were inserted. OG: orogastric tube

21.2 Interactive Case Discussion

What is the Potter sequence and Potter facies?

Potter's sequence was first described by Edith Potter (1901–1993) in 1946, in newborns with bilateral renal agenesis or other kidney abnormalities [1]. Babies born with this condition are either stillborn or die very early within the neonatal period. The terms Potter sequence and Potter syndrome are interchangeable as they describe the same clinical features and results of chronic and severe oligohydramnios in the growing fetus. The reported incidence of Potter syndrome varies from 1 in 2000 to 1 in 5000 deliveries. With the routine use of antenatal ultrasound, affected pregnancies are terminated earlier. In the autopsies of stillbirth, the reported incidence was around 0.2–0.4%.

The Potter's sequence describes a constellation of features born to a baby with severe oligohydramnios in utero as the fetal kidneys produce most amniotic fluid. The causes of Potter's sequence are usually the consequence of fetal renal failure caused by conditions like bilateral renal agenesis, polycystic kidneys and severe obstructive renal diseases. Hence, Potter syndrome's classification was based on the causes of renal anomalies (Table 21.1).

With the marked reduction in the production of amniotic fluid, the baby's lungs were unable to develop. Severe respiratory insufficiency due to pulmonary hypoplasia leads to a fatal outcome in most infants. The stage of lung development, degree and duration of oligohydramnios are determining factors for the extent of pulmonary hypoplasia.

The oligohydramnios causes fetal compression in the uterus by limiting the movement of the fetus. These babies were born prematurely and have special facial features and limb malformations. Potter facies are characterised by prominent epicanthic folds, low-set ears, a flattened nose due to uterine pressure and a recessed

Table 21.1 Classification of the Potter syndrome (Potter sequence)

	Causes for renal failure and oligohydramnios
Classical Potter syndrome	Bilateral renal agenesis (failure of the metanephros to develop into kidneys)
Potter syndrome subtype 1	Autosomal recessive polycystic kidney (ARPKD)
Potter syndrome subtype II	Renal dysplasia
Potter syndrome subtype III	Autosomal dominant polycystic kidney (ADPKD) Although the typical age of presentation of ADPKD is between the third and fifth decades of life, ADPKD can present in utero or in the neonatal period, with ultrasound changes similar to ARPKD
Potter syndrome subtype IV	Related to obstruction of the ureter or pelvis, causing hydronephrosis

chin. Limb anomalies, hip dislocation, short lower limbs and clubbed feet are related to the abnormal positioning of the fetus. Other associated common abnormalities include absent anal opening, hemivertebrae and sacral agenesis.

What is the prognosis of the Potter sequence?

The outcome of Potter syndrome is poor. All the babies born are either stillborn or die very early after birth. Neonates associated with hypoplastic lungs are at very high risk, and the primary cause of death is due to respiratory distress syndrome within hours or days after birth. Even if the newborn survives, there is still a high mortality in infancy related to respiratory failure and renal failure.

Despite the full ventilatory support with high-frequency ventilation and inhalational nitric oxygen, the baby's oxygenation decreased progressively, and he remained anuric. He finally succumbed at 18 hours post-delivery. The genetic test confirmed a truncated mutation of the PKHD1. Post-mortem examination of the newborn showed (Fig. 21.3a, b).

- The left and right lungs weighed 9.1 g and 13.1 g, respectively. The lung/body weight ratio is 0.0078 (the normal lung/body weight ratio in a term infant is 0.222 ± 0.002), confirming lung hypoplasia. Histological examination showed a diffuse coating of eosinophilic to hyaline material on the wall of the alveoli, and the changes were consistent with respiratory distress syndrome.
- The liver weighed 116.6 g. The extra-hepatic biliary systems were unremarkable. The liver tissue showed an increase in intrahepatic bile ducts and occasional angulated branching and cystic dilatation. The findings are consistent with congenital hepatic fibrosis.
- Gross features of the kidneys were typical of autosomal recessive polycystic kidney disease (ARPKD). The microscopic examination showed non-obstructive dilatation or ectasia of the collecting tubules located in the renal medulla, resulting in microcysts up to 2–3 mm in diameter. These cysts expand into the cortex.

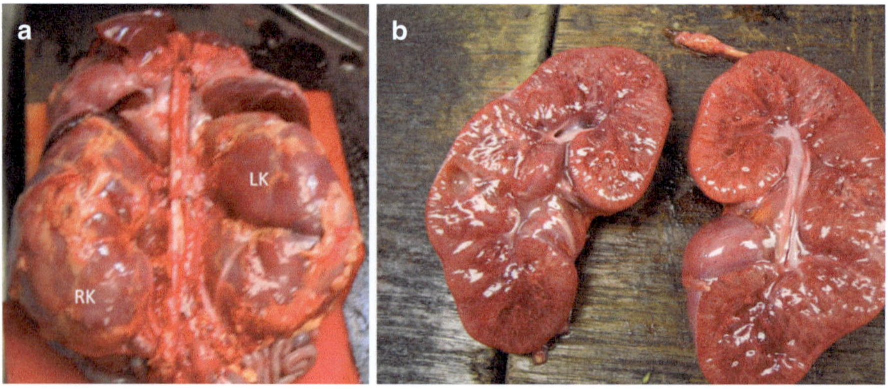

Fig. 21.3 (**a**) The kidneys were markedly enlarged and occupied the whole abdomen; the reniform shape with fetal lobulation remained. RK: right kidney; LK: left kidney (**b**) The cut section of the kidneys showed that the renal cysts were pretty small and uniformly distributed throughout the renal parenchyma

Table 21.2 Classification of autosomal recessive polycystic kidney disease

Perinatal type	Most common Present as oligohydramnios and pulmonary hypoplasia Minimal hepatic fibrosis 75% of affected foetuses die within 24 hours after birth
Neonatal type	Minimal hepatic fibrosis with renal disease predominant
Infantile type	Moderate periportal fibrosis, progressive renal failure and eventually reach end-stage renal disease at an early age
Juvenile type	Gross hepatic fibrosis Portal hypertension with splenomegaly and portosystemic varices Progressive renal failure and eventually reach end-stage renal disease

What is autosomal recessive polycystic kidney disease (ARPKD)?

ARPKD is one of the most common inheritable infantile cystic renal diseases, but it is far less common than autosomal dominant polycystic kidney disease (ADPKD), which mainly affects adults. The incidence is estimated at ~1:20,000–50,000 [2]. Despite it being a rare disease, it is one of the common diseases of ciliopathies affecting both the kidneys and the liver.

ARPKD is caused by mutations in the PKHD1 (polycystic kidney and hepatic disease) gene, located on chromosome 6p12.3-p12.2, and this encodes the protein fibrocystin, which is typically expressed in the primary cilia and the basal body of the renal and bile duct epithelial cells.

The genetic mutation in the PKHD1 gene results in the development of symmetric microcystic disease affecting the distal convoluted tubules and collecting ducts of the kidneys. The phenotype of ARPKD is variable, and based on the age of presentation, ARPKD can be classified into perinatal, neonatal, infantile and juvenile forms. In the perinatal and neonatal forms, renal disease dominates, while in the infantile and juvenile forms, liver disease dominates the clinical picture (Table 21.2).

Can Potter syndrome be diagnosed antenatally?

Oligohydramnios, which can be picked up by antenatal ultrasound, is the cardinal sign in a fetus with Potter syndrome. The structural abnormalities of the face, lungs and limbs are secondary to oligohydramnios.

Antenatal ultrasound features in kidney agenesis

- The absent kidneys may be challenging to pick up, especially if there is compensatory adrenal hyperplasia. The adrenal gland takes an ovoid, elongated or discoid shape and may be mistaken as a reniform structure on parasagittal and transverse scans in the renal fossae, i.e. the 'lying down adrenal sign'.

Antenatal ultrasound features of ARPKD include the following:

- Increase in fetal abdominal circumference.
- Oligohydramnios.
- Bilateral enlarged echogenic kidneys with loss of corticomedullary differentiation and multiple small cysts replacing the normal renal parenchyma. Using a

high-resolution ultrasound (linear-array transducer, 7.5 MHz or greater) may allow visualisation of numerous cylindrical cysts in the medulla and cortex, representing ectatic collecting ducts.
- Hyperechogenicity of the kidneys can be demonstrated as early as 12–16 weeks, but renal enlargement with increased echogenicity is usually evidenced by 24 weeks of gestation.
- The renal cysts are rarely greater than 1–2 cm, and the kidneys retain the reniform shape.
- There may be an empty bladder.
- Both lung volumes are small, with possible pleural effusion.
- Hepatic hyper-echogenicity indicating hepatic fibrosis.

For other subtypes of Porter syndrome, features may include the following:
- Obstructive hydronephrosis, hydroureters, thickened bladder wall
- Large non-communicating cystic structures, distorting the kidney shapes
- Extra-renal abnormalities

How would one manage if the diagnosis of perinatal ARPKD is made antenatally?
Once the diagnosis is made or suspected, the patient and the family should be managed and supported by a multidisciplinary team consisting of fetal medicine subspecialists, obstetricians, midwives, paediatric renal specialists, neonatologists and geneticists.

1. *Antenatal fetal monitoring*
    - Ultrasound should be performed every 2–3 weeks for serial assessment of the renal size and amniotic fluid volume. In severe oligohydramnios, fetal MRI may be a better alternative to delineating the renal structure. Systematic evaluation should be undertaken for extra-renal anomalies because other fetal conditions have been associated with renal hyperechogenicity.
    - A genetic study should be performed urgently to provide better counselling on the prognosis of the baby. Termination of pregnancy is an option when there are poor prognostic factors, such as progressive oligo or anhydramnios with massive nephromegaly and severe pulmonary hypoplasia.
2. Perinatal plan and post-delivery support involve a multidisciplinary team
    Obstetrics
    - The baby should be delivered in a unit with high-level neonatal intensive care unit support.
    - A caesarean section may be needed for fetal abdominal dystocia with enlarged kidneys.

    Neonatology
    - After delivery, neonatal pulmonary status will usually dictate early management.
    - A milder form of pulmonary hypoplasia may respond to high-frequency ventilation and inhalational nitric oxide.

- Extracorporeal membrane oxygenation may be appropriate if respiratory failure and/or pulmonary HTN are not thought to be attributable to lethal lung hypoplasia.

Nephrology

- The need for dialysis depends on the remaining renal function.
- The decision to offer (or withhold) dialysis should be made jointly by the treating physicians and the infant's parents.
- If dialysis is needed, peritoneal dialysis is the preferred modality.
- Unilateral or bilateral nephrectomy has been suggested to improve respiratory function and feeding problems, but the decision has to be carefully discussed with the parents and management team.

21.3 Case Illustrations

This case highlights how in-utero renal disease can impair pulmonary development and shape the clinical outcome of a newborn. Potter syndrome is a fatal congenital disorder characterised by changes in the physical appearance of neonates due to oligohydramnios caused by renal agenesis or severe renal impairment. The severity of pulmonary hypoplasia and renal impairment determines the prognosis of the patient.

Suggested Further Readings

1. Bhandari J, Thada PK, Sergent SR. Potter Syndrome. 2023 Aug 8. In: StatPearls [Internet]. Treasure Island (FL): StatPearls Publishing; 2025. PMID: 32809693.
2. Wicher D, Obrycki Ł, Jankowska I. Autosomal recessive polycystic kidney disease—the clinical aspects and diagnostic challenges. J Pediatr Genet. 2021;10(01):001–8.
3. Yulia A, Winyard P. Management of antenatally detected kidney malformations. Early Hum Dev. 2018;126:38–46.

Cysts and the Cilia

22

22.1 Case Description

Lucas was born at 37 weeks of gestation, with a birth weight of 2.8 kg, by Caesarean section for maternal fever and rupture of the membrane. He cried immediately after birth and was noted to have respiratory distress. Initial workup showed a raised white cell count of 20×10^9/L, and maternal high vaginal swab grew *Group B streptococcus* colonisation. Lucas was managed as suffering from a perinatal infection with intravenous antibiotics, and a chest X-ray was taken (Fig. 22.1).

Lucas did well after the intravenous antibiotics. The blood culture was negative. However, physical examination showed a progressive increase in his blood pressure, with mean arterial pressure increasing to 70 mmHg. Physical examination of the cardiovascular system and the echocardiogram were normal. However, the abdominal examination revealed bilaterally enlarged kidneys and liver. His renal function test was normal, with serum urea at 2.2 mmol/L and creatinine at 40 μmol/L. Serum sodium once dropped to 132 mmol/L and potassium 4.2 mmol/L, and other electrolytes were normal. An ultrasound of the urinary system was performed on day 3, and a CT of the abdomen was performed at 1 month. What did they show (Figs. 22.2 and 22.3)?

W. K. Y. Chan, M. C. I. Kuok, *Paediatric Nephrology*,
https://doi.org/10.1007/978-981-95-5060-9_22

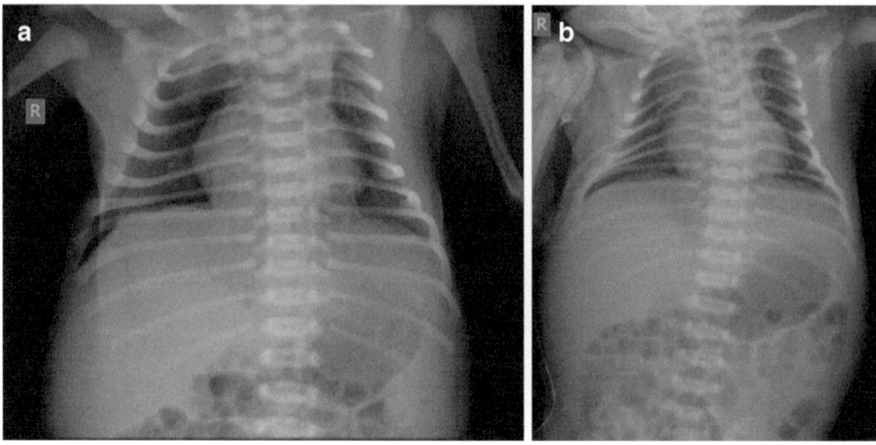

Fig. 22.1 (**a**) Chest X-ray showed right pneumothorax with pneumomediastinum. The liver shadow was prominent. (**b**) A right chest drain was inserted, and the pneumothorax resolved. The liver shadow was prominent

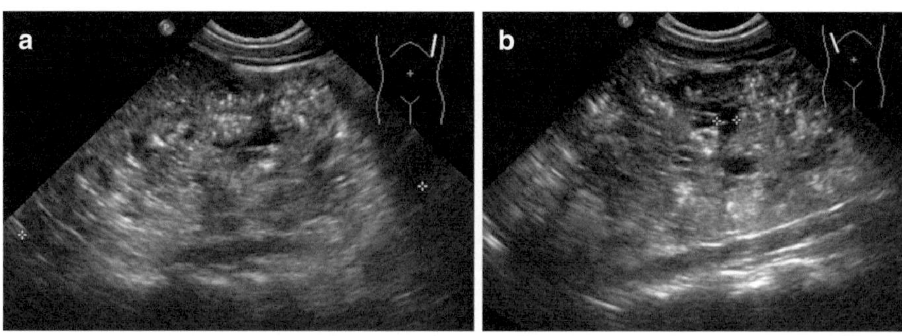

Fig. 22.2 (**a**, **b**) Ultrasound of the left kidney and right kidney. Both kidneys are grossly and symmetrically enlarged. They measured 6.6 cm and 6.2 cm in length, respectively. The kidneys retained the reniform shape. The corticomedullary differentiation was lost, and there is a generalised increase in echo pattern with multiple small cystic lesions in the renal parenchyma (salt-and-pepper appearance). The largest cyst measured 0.4 cm over the right kidney. These features are indicative of autosomal recessive polycystic kidney disease (ARPKD)

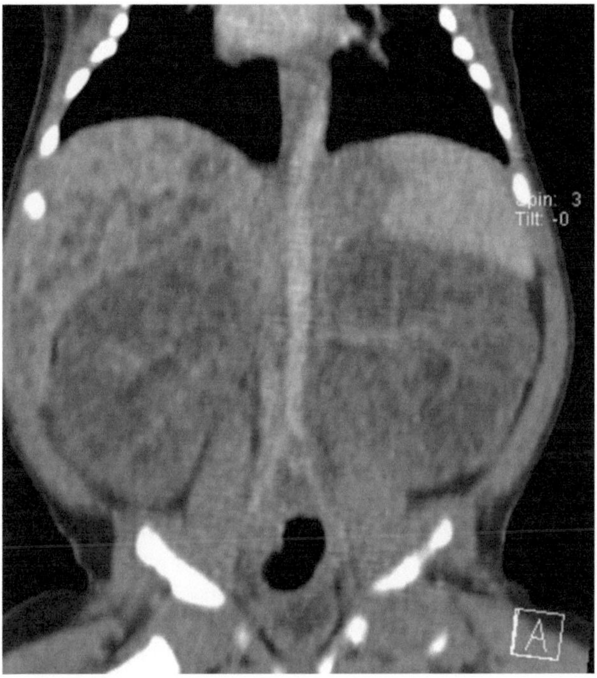

Fig. 22.3 Plan CT abdomen of Lucas performed at 1 month old showed symmetrically enlarged kidneys, with reniform shapes maintained and loss of corticomedullary differentiation. The features were compatible with ARPKD, and there were ill-defined areas of hypodense areas over both lobes of the liver, which are compatible with ductal ectasia seen in ARPKD

22.2 Interactive Case Discussion

Why were the abnormalities of the kidneys not detected by antenatal ultrasound?

Diagnosing the abnormalities of the kidneys in ARPKD is not straightforward. Antenatal ultrasound scans in the first trimester could appear normal in patients with ARPKD. The abnormality may only become visible and more apparent at around 20 weeks of gestation, or even in the late second trimester and beyond, making termination of pregnancy not possible. Hence, a normal antenatal ultrasound does not rule out the diagnosis of ARPKD, emphasising the need for a comprehensive and ongoing patient evaluation.

Why did Lucas have respiratory distress shortly after birth?

The causes of Lucas' respiratory distress can be related to the following:

- Perinatal infection and pneumonia
- Pneumothorax and pneumomediastinum
- Pulmonary hypoplasia
- Enlarged kidneys may compress the diaphragm and restrict the thorax expansion

What is autosomal recessive polycystic kidney disease (ARPKD)?
ARPKD is a rare inherited disease compared to autosomal dominant polycystic kidney disease (ADPKD). Its incidence ranges from 1 in 10,000 to 40,000 live births. In most patients, the disease is caused by the mutation of the PKHD-1 gene on chromosome 6; recently, the DZIP1L mutation accounts for some of the ARPKD patients. Despite the rarity of ARPKD, it is the most common ciliopathy reported.

What are the renal cysts and hepatic cysts seen in ARPKD?
The renal cysts in ARPKD represent the cystic dilatation of the distal tubules and the collecting ducts. These fusiform dilations or cysts are arranged radially through the renal parenchyma, from the medulla to the renal cortex, giving it a bilateral 'striated nephrogram' in a contrast-enhanced CT scan. The cysts in the liver are the ductal ectasia and the bile duct cysts (Fig. 22.4).

What is the clinical presentation of ARPKD?
The clinical spectrum seen in ARPKD is very variable. Severely affected individuals will present in late pregnancy or at birth, the Potter syndrome/Potter sequence with pulmonary hypoplasia, massively enlarged kidneys and characteristic facial and musculoskeletal deformities related to the pressure effect of oligohydramnios. Up to 30–50% of affected neonates die shortly after birth due to respiratory failure. Some patients survive the neonatal period but suffer from progressive kidney failure and liver fibrosis. In some patients, the diagnosis of ARPKD is only made during childhood or even the adolescent period.

Apart from progressive renal failure, ARPKD patients tend to have early-onset arterial hypertension, which is difficult to control, especially in the first month of age. Although the exact aetiology of the hypertension is not fully understood, the underlying cause of this hypertension is not solely related to the deteriorating renal function. The causes of this arterial hypertension may be attributed to the following:

- An increase in intrarenal angiotensin activities
- Impaired urinary dilution with associated fluid retention and dysregulation of the collecting duct epithelial sodium channel

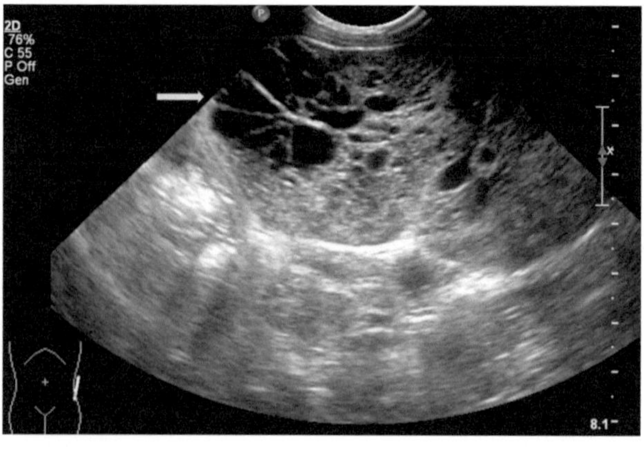

Fig. 22.4 USG of the left kidney of a patient with genetically confirmed ARPKD. It showed numerous cylindrical cysts in the medulla and cortex, representing the characteristic ectatic collecting ducts (yellow arrow)

Survived patients with ARPKD face a variety of hepatobiliary problems, including progressive hepatic fibrosis, portal hypertension, hypersplenism, oesophageal varices, recurrent cholangitis and liver failure. Managing these conditions can be challenging, especially in children. The diagnosis of cholangitis, for instance, can be difficult to establish. The classical triad of fever, increasing jaundice and right upper quadrant abdominal pain may be absent.

Feeding problems are inevitable in patients with ARPKD. Commonly, these children require a long course of nasogastric tube feeding because of the following:

- Prematurity
- On prolonged ventilatory support
- Early uremia
- Massive kidneys occupy the abdomen

There are specific concerns about performing gastrostomy in this group of children, such as the possible increase in infection risk for gastrostomy in patients on peritoneal dialysis. The gastrostomy should preferably be performed before a peritoneal dialysis catheter is placed. In patients with portal hypertension, the decision on gastrostomy has to balance between the possible increased risk of variceal bleeding, damage to the enlarged spleen and development of stomal varices (Table 22.1).

What is the genotype-phenotype relationship in ARPKD?

ARPKD is caused by the mutation in the PKHD1 gene that leads to the malfunction of the protein polyductin or fibrocystin. The PKHD1 gene is one of the largest human genes. There are different types of variants, including missense and truncating (nonsense, frameshift, splice site) mutations, distributed along the whole gene of PKHD1. Around 40% of PKHD1 mutations are truncating, and 60% are missense mutations. Two truncating mutations are the most severe phenotype, usually resulting in neonatal death.

What is the prognosis of Lucas?

The cause of immediate mortality in ARPKD after birth is usually related to pulmonary hypoplasia, which could be so severe that the infant dies shortly after birth. Those with less severe lung involvement may be born with impaired renal function or with normal renal function.

For ARPKD patients who survive the perinatal period with abnormal renal function, some may require early renal replacement therapy in infancy, and some children's renal function may improve in the first year of life as the glomerular filtration improves with kidney maturation. However, their renal function will continue to deteriorate over the years. Around 50% of these patients require renal replacement therapy in the first decade of life.

Lucas, with ARPKD, survived the perinatal period as his pulmonary function was minimally affected. Despite his renal function being normal at birth, it deteriorated over the years, and most children reached end-stage renal disease within the first decade. The hepatic disease will become a prominent feature, such as portal

Table 22.1 Clinical problems and management of patients with ARPKD

Clinical problems	Management
Respiratory failure Pulmonary hypertension	– For pulmonary hypertension (PHT), high-frequency ventilation (HFV), inhaled nitric oxide and even ECMO may be considered in individual cases, especially if the PHT is unrelated to pulmonary hypoplasia – Tracheostomy may be needed for prolonged ventilation – Unilateral nephrectomy to facilitate ventilation may be considered in selected cases
Arterial hypertension	– ACEI or ARB, Ca-channel blockers and beta-blockers add on to anti-hypertension medications as indicated – Arterial hypertension may become less resistant to treatment after infancy
Hyponatremia (especially in infancy)	– Supplement with sodium may worsen hypertension unless in the state of hypovolemia, as hyponatremia may be related to impaired urinary dilution, leading to water overload – Fluid restriction with adequate nutritional intake
Progressive chronic kidney disease	– Usual management for children with chronic kidney disease – If early renal dialysis therapy is needed, peritoneal dialysis is the treatment choice. Because of the enlarged kidneys, sequential nephrectomy or bilateral nephrectomy may need to be considered
Feeding problem	– May need prolonged nasogastric tube feeding – Assess the benefits of gastrostomy insertion with potential complications and risks; an individual assessment is needed
Hepatic disease and its complications	
Congenital hepatic fibrosis (CHF) with progressive portal hypertension and its complications, like hypersplenism, oesophageal varices and hepatopulmonary syndrome	– Routine screening for liver disease and complications of congenital hepatic fibrosis – Liver biochemistries are typically not informative – Regular monitoring of complete blood cell and platelet count – Regularly screening for splenomegaly and portal hypertension – Screening for gastric and oesophageal varices once portal hypertension is confirmed. Pre-emptive ligation of varices to avoid life-threatening bleeding – In severe hypersplenism and/or splenomegaly, splenectomy or splenic embolisation may be beneficial in some patients. – The use of a non-selective β-blocker (propranolol) for portal hypertension

(continued)

Table 22.1 (continued)

Clinical problems	Management
Acute or recurrent cholangitis (Caroli disease)	– Acute cholangitis necessitates a prolonged course of intravenous antibiotics, and potentially worsens the prognosis of the CHF – Routine antibiotic prophylaxis for cholangitis is not indicated, except for recurrent disease in some patients – Antibiotic prophylaxis for 6–12 weeks after a cholangitis episode, immediately after transplantation, or in the context of enhanced immunosuppression may be considered
Growth failure (multifactorial)	– Early use of growth hormone – Adequate nutritional support
Vaccination for splenic dysfunction	– Immunisation against encapsulated bacteria like pneumococcus, meningococcus and Haemophilus influenzae type B is indicated

hypertension and recurrent cholangitis. In the long run, the child may need a sequential renal-liver transplant or a combined renal-liver transplant.

Concerning the lung problem, most survivors will not have a significant impairment in lung function and have a long-term prognosis comparable to the general population.

The genetic study of Lucas showed heterozygous PKHD1: c.1123C>T (p. Arg375Trp) and PKHD1: c10058T>G (p.leu33353Arg). Both mutations are pathogenic. Lucas had normal renal function after birth, but he developed significant hypertension and transient hyponatremia. His initial hypertension was so severe that it caused significant left ventricular hypertrophy, which subsequently resolved after controlling his blood pressure with captopril, amlodipine and hydralazine. At 6 years old, he had an episode of massive variceal bleeding that required resuscitation. He then underwent regular endoscopy with prophylactic variceal sclerotherapy. He underwent a splenectomy for hypersplenism at the age of 9 for severe thrombocytopenia. At the age of 10, he reached end-stage renal disease and received regular haemodialysis.

What are the ciliopathies?

Ciliopathies refer to cilia-related disorders, most of which have cystic kidneys as part of the clinical features, making kidney cysts a hallmark of ciliopathies.

Epithelial cells lining the ducts and tubules of the kidney nephrons and collecting ducts have a single non-motile cilium projecting from their surfaces into the lumen of the tubule. These cilia were long considered vestigial remnants left due to evolution from a ciliated ancestor, but we now recognise them as critical sensory antennae. These non-motile cilia are small antennae that detect various extracellular stimuli and orchestrate multiple signalling pathways with the nuclear trafficking of some molecules. Cilia regulate the planar cell polarity and control the orientation of cell division, which is crucial for establishing renal tubule development in the shape of a tubule and not a cyst.

The axoneme defines the inner ciliary structure, composed of nine microtubule doublets (9 + 0) structures derived from the basal body and mother centriole of the centrosome. Along this microtubule core, the transport of proteins in the anterograde direction towards the tip of the cilium and in the retrograde direction towards the cell body is organised by an elaborate process called intraflagellar transport. Mutations in these complex ciliary proteins result in phenotypes affecting the kidney and other organs.

Ciliopathy involves a core set of tissues, including the kidneys, central nervous system, liver and other systems (Table 22.2), and this also sheds light on a better understanding of syndrome-related cystic kidney diseases like Bardet-Biedl syndrome, Joubert syndrome, Meckel-Gruber syndrome and nephronophthisis (Tables 22.3 and 22.4).

Table 22.2 The spectrum of disease manifestations in ciliopathies

System anomalies	Clinical features
Kidney	Renal cysts, interstitial fibrosis
Central nervous system	Encephalocele, cerebellar anomalies, intellectual disability
Liver	Hepatic fibrosis, liver cysts
Ocular	Retinal degeneration, retinitis pigmentosa
Ear	Hearing loss
Cardiovascular	Congenital heart disease
Skeletal	Polydactyly
Reproductive	Hypogonadism
Others	Situs inversus

Table 22.3 The genotype and phenotypes of some common ciliopathies

Phenotype	Inherited pattern	Gene	Protein	Site of cysts
ADPKD	Autosomal dominant	PKD1. PKD2 (~91%) NMD (~9%)	Polycystin 1, polycystin 2	Anywhere along the nephrons
ARPKD	Autosomal recessive	PKHD1	Polyductin or Fibrocystin	Cystic dilatation of the collecting tubules
Nephronophthisis	Autosomal recessive	NPHP1 to NPHP16	Nephrocystin, inversin	Cysts at the corticomedullary juncture

NMD no mutation detected

Table 22.4 The differential diagnosis of ARPKD and other ciliopathies

Disease	Clinical similarity and difference
Early onset ADPKD	Most patients present in adulthood, but around 5% of patients may present in childhood or even at birth. ADPKD patients rarely develop hepatobiliary complications. They are more likely to have intracranial aneurysms
PKD due to TSC2-PKD1 deletion	PKD1 and TSC2 genes are adjacent to each other. Deletion affecting these genes causes an early onset of PKD. Clinical symptoms will be between PKD and TSC. Hence, they will have seizures, brain and renal tumours
Hepatocyte nuclear factor 1 β (HNF1β) related disease	This genetic mutation can have a very similar phenotype to ARPKD with prenatal hyperechogenic kidneys and Potter sequence, which can confuse the diagnosis of ARPKD, as HNF1β is a transcription factor that regulates PKHD1 expression. It can have a wide range of manifestations
Nephronophthisis (NPHP)	An autosomal recessive cystic kidney disease. Unlike ARPKD, the affected kidneys in NPHP are usually small because of progressive renal fibrosis, cysts (medullary) and hypertension manifested in late disease. However, some patients may present early with features similar to ARPKD with Potter syndrome
Bardet-Biedl (BBS)	Mental retardation, obesity, polydactyly, situs inversus, retinal degeneration, gonadal abnormalities and renal failure. Recessively inherited
Joubert syndrome (JBTS)	Characterised by cerebellar vermis hypoplasia with developmental delay, hypotonia, ataxia and cysts in the kidneys. Recessively inherited
Meckel-Gruber syndrome (MKS)	A lethal autosomal recessive disease with posterior fossa abnormalities (usually occipital encephalocele), bilaterally enlarged polycystic kidneys, hepatic ductal plate malformation with hepatic fibrosis and hepatic cysts, polydactyly and shortening of long bones
Senior-Loken syndrome (SLS)	Nephronophthisis with retinitis pigmentosa

ADPKD autosomal dominant polycystic kidney disease, *ARPKD* autosomal recessive polycystic kidney disease, *BBS* Bardet-Biedl syndrome, *CNS* central nervous system, *JBTS* Joubert syndrome, *MKS* Meckel-Gruber syndrome, *NPHP* nephronophthisis, *SLS* Senior-Loken syndrome

22.3 Case Illustrations

This case begins with a common perinatal presentation, where careful physical examination reveals bilaterally enlarged kidneys, leading to the diagnosis of ARPKD. The discussion enhances the reader's understanding of the long-term management of ARPKD and places the condition within the broader framework of ciliopathies. ARPKD is a rare polycystic kidney disease which has a broad spectrum of both kidney and liver presentations. The management required a team of multidisciplinary experts. Ciliopathies describe a group of diseases that share various genetic mutations in the ciliary proteins. Understanding the function of the primary cilia brought insight into the molecular pathology of many inherited cystic kidney diseases, including ARPKD.

Suggested Further Readings

1. Guay-Woodford LM, Bissler JJ, Braun MC, Bockenhauer D, Cadnapaphornchai MA, Dell KM, et al. Consensus expert recommendations for the diagnosis and management of autosomal recessive polycystic kidney disease: report of an international conference. J Pediatr. 2014;165(3):611–7.
2. Raina R, Chakraborty R, Sethi SK, Kumar D, Gibson K, Bergmann C. Diagnosis and management of renal cystic disease of the newborn: core curriculum 2021. Am J Kidney Dis. 2021;78(1):125–41.
3. Cordido A, Vizoso-Gonzalez M, Garcia-Gonzalez MA. Molecular pathophysiology of autosomal recessive polycystic kidney disease. Int J Mol Sci. 2021;22(12):6523.
4. Büscher R, Büscher AK, Weber S, Mohr J, Hegen B, Vester U, Hoyer PF. Clinical manifestations of autosomal recessive polycystic kidney disease (ARPKD): kidney-related and non-kidney-related phenotypes. Pediatr Nephrol. 2014;29:1915–25.
5. McConnachie DJ, Stow JL, Mallett AJ. Ciliopathies and the kidney: a review. Am J Kidney Dis. 2021;77(3):410–9.

The Dominant Cyst 23

23.1 Case Description

Wyatt, now 16, was first referred to nephrology at 2 years old due to a family history of ADPKD. His father and paternal aunt were diagnosed with ADPKD and chronic kidney disease at 35 and 30, respectively. His paternal grandma died at 70 due to renal failure. Despite this, Wyatt was healthy, with no history of haematuria or urinary tract infection, and his growth was normal.

23.2 Interactive Case Discussion

With the strong family history of ADPKD, will you perform a USG examination for Wyatt at this early age?

Wyatt was asymptomatic. Because of the strong family history, he has a 50% chance of inheriting the disease from his father. USG examination of the kidneys would help in making the diagnosis; however, the absence of cysts at this early age does not rule out the diagnosis of ADPKD. The practice of regular surveillance in an asymptomatic child and early genetic diagnosis at this early age needs careful discussion with the parents and the family. The psychological impact and anxiety imposed on the child and the family have to be considered, especially when limited treatment is available to stop the progression of the disease.

Counselling with the parents and family should be a non-directional discussion, fostering shared decision-making and respecting the autonomy of the child. The best interests of the child should guide the decisions. The outlines of the discussion should include the followings and a symptomatology approach is suggested as below (Table 23.1).

- The possibilities, limitations and consequences of genetic and clinical testing.
- The screening methods do not always yield definite results.

W. K. Y. Chan, M. C. I. Kuok, *Paediatric Nephrology*,
https://doi.org/10.1007/978-981-95-5060-9_23

Table 23.1 Approach based on family history and symptomatology

	Suggested approach
Asymptomatic child with a positive family history	Ongoing surveillance ± immediate diagnostic screening are acceptable approaches and need careful counselling with the family and patient
Symptomatic or very-early-onset disease, or rapidly progressive with negative family history	Genetic diagnosis is recommended, as the very-early-onset or rapidly progressive disease may be due to the following: – Unusual biallelic mutation – Contiguous gene deletion syndrome (PKD1-TSC2) – HNF1β mutation, which mimics ADPKD but is associated with other comorbidities

- A normal kidney ultrasound has a low negative predictive value in children.
- Failure to detect a genetic mutation did not rule out the disease.
- Possible impact on securing insurance coverage, especially having a genetic diagnosis.
- Despite the lack of definitive treatment, early integration of low salt and adequate fluid intake as a protective eating habit can delay disease progression and improve the patient's quality of life.
- Early identification of hypertension and proteinuria is amenable to medical treatment with the potential benefit of a decrease in disease progression.
- Tolvaptan is used in adults, but it currently lacks data support in children.

Wyatt did not receive the ultrasound examination when he was first seen at 2 years old. However, as the child grew older to 5 years old, the parents decided to perform an ultrasound examination of the kidneys. The images showed the USG findings when Wyatt was 5 years old (Fig. 23.1).

Did Wyatt suffer from ADPKD?

With the strong family history and three sizable cysts detected at this young age, Wyatt likely suffered from ADPKD.

Wyatt subsequently underwent a genetic study, and it showed a mutation with heterozygous PKD1 NM_001009944.2: c.8362_8371delTCGGACCCGC p.(Ser2788Glyfs*84) in exon 23. The diagnosis of ADPKD was confirmed.

What are the differences between ADPKD and ARPKD?

Both ADPKD and ARPKD are polycystic kidney diseases related to ciliopathies. Before the availability of genetic diagnosis, we could differentiate these two polycystic kidney diseases on clinical grounds (Table 23.2).

What are the differences in the clinical presentations between 'adult onset' and 'childhood onset' ADPKD?

Historically, ADPKD is considered a disease of adults. Most children are 'asymptomatic', and even if they have symptoms, the symptoms may be misinterpreted or overlooked as other common complaints in normal children (Table 23.3).

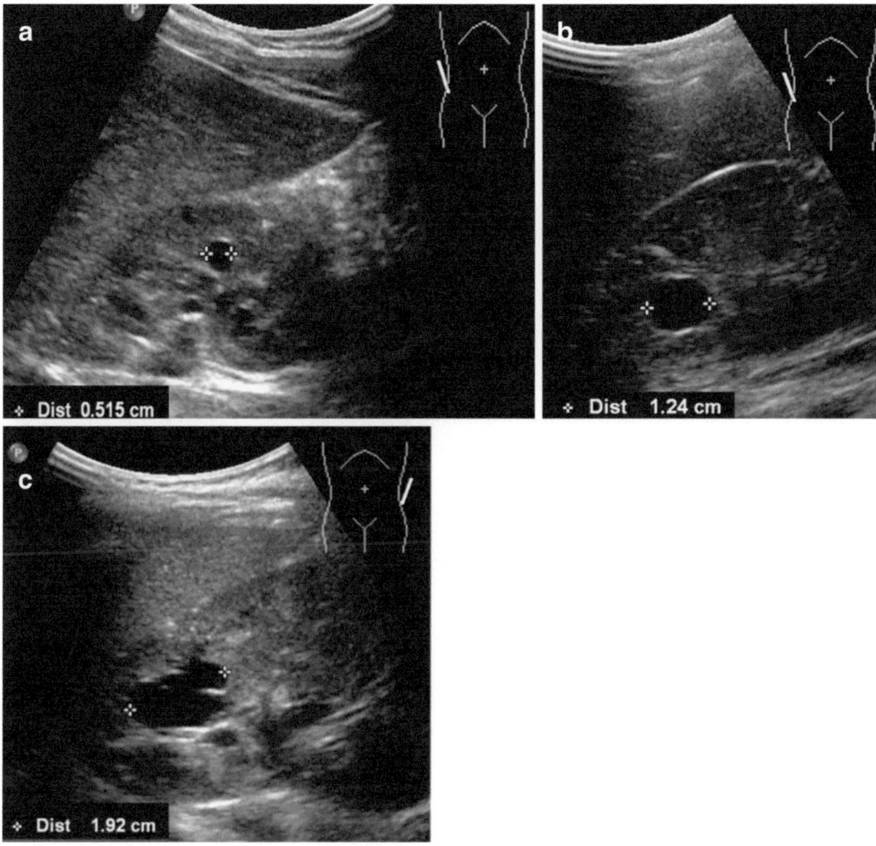

Fig. 23.1 (**a**, **b**) The USG of the right kidney. The right kidney was of normal size and echopattern, but there were several cystic structures, with two large cysts measuring 0.515 cm and 1.24 cm in diameter, respectively. (**c**) USG of the left kidney showed a large cyst measuring 1.92 cm in diameter with a thin septum inside

Table 23.2 Differentiate ADPKD and ARPDK based on phenotypes

	ADPKD	ARPKD
Inheritance	Autosomal dominant (50% chance of offspring affected)	Autosomal recessive (25% chance of offspring affected)
Incidence	1:1000 to 1:2500 (the most common inherited kidney disease, which accounts for ~10% of ESRD in adults)	1: 10,000 to 40,000 (a rarer disease)
Main responsible gene	PKD1 (~85%) and PKD2 (~15%)	PKHD1
Age of onset	Usually, in adults, early neonatal presentation is rare	Perinatal, neonatal, infantile and juvenile types

(continued)

Table 23.2 (continued)

	ADPKD	ARPKD
The affected kidneys	Both kidneys are affected by multiple cysts of variable numbers and sizes. The kidney shapes are distorted. When more cysts develop, the total kidney volume increases and the renal function deteriorates	Both kidneys are enlarged with tiny cysts and remain in a reniform shape
Sites of the cysts	Cysts come from all parts of the nephrons	Cysts are the dilated distal tubules and the collecting ducts
The liver manifestation	Cysts in the liver	Congenital hepatic fibrosis, portal hypertension Recurrent cholangitis
Extra-renal manifestation	Heart: mitral valve prolapse and mitral valve regurgitation CNS: intracranial aneurysm	Not present

Table 23.3 Symptoms of ADPKD in children and adults

	Similarities and differences
Symptomatology Symptoms of ADPKD are nonspecific in children	(i) Abdominal pain: it is difficult to differentiate whether this is a symptom of the ADPKD, as abdominal pain is so common in children. Use of NSAIDs needs careful consideration. Prolonged use or high doses of NSAIDs are not recommended (ii) Enuresis and urinary frequency, which are common childhood complaints, may indicate poor urinary concentration ability in ADPKD (iii) Urinary tract infection can be the cause of performing the USG instead of a complication. Cyst infection is rare in children (iv) Microhaematuria does not necessarily indicate cyst haemorrhage. In adults, gross haematuria with enlarged kidney volume indicates cyst haemorrhage, which is extremely rare in children (v) Nephrolithiasis is rare in children
Hypertension	(i) Same as the adult population, hypertension and hypertensive vascular damage often precede kidney damage (ii) The incidence of hypertension increases with age, and the possible causes of early hypertension are due to the following: (a) The activation of the intrarenal renin-angiotensin system is related to the compression of renal tissue by the enlarging renal cysts (b) The loss of PKD1/2-dependent nitric oxide production by the vascular smooth muscle cells (iii) The first presentation of hypertension is an isolated nocturnal hypertension, which can only be detected by a 24-hour BP study, and a normal office BP may overlook the diagnosis (iv) As with adults, BP control is recommended. A BP >95th percentile for age, sex and height needs early treatment and with a tight control of BP to ≤75th percentile is recommended

(continued)

Table 23.3 (continued)

	Similarities and differences
Reduce renal function	Usually not a feature in childhood, except in very-early-onset ADPKD
Glomerular hyperfiltration	In the early stage of ADPKD, glomerular hyperfiltration may overestimate and mask the loss of GFR. Hence, eGFR may not be a reliable parameter to monitor disease progression
Hepatic cyst	Uncommon in childhood
Intracranial aneurysms	Negligible incidence in children

What is 'very-early-onset' ADPKD? What is its clinical significance?
Unlike the previous understanding of ADPKD, there is increasing evidence that ADPKD is not an 'adult' disease; some children can progress to early onset of renal failure. The term very-early-onset ADPKD (ADPKDveo) is used to describe this spectrum of the disease.

ADPKDveo is defined as follows:

- Diagnosis and onset of disease before 18 months of age.
- Children with this type of disease onset have a more severe ADPKD disease than the classical one.
- They suffer from an early onset of kidney failure.
- Some patients may present like the ARPKD with in utero oligohydramnios, pulmonary hypoplasia and severe respiratory disease or even the Potter syndrome at birth.

What are the possible complications of ADPKD, and how would you manage these complications?
Most children remain asymptomatic until they reach adulthood and enter their 30s. With advances in age, the cysts grow in size and number, replacing the normal renal tissues. The complications are related to the large kidney size, the cysts and associated extra-renal involvement (Table 23.4).
Follow-up USG of Wyatt at 16 years old showed an increasing number of renal cysts (Figs. 23.2 and 23.3).

How does the measurement of total kidney volume (TKV) help in the management of ADPKD?
A normal total kidney volume is 250–350 mL in a normal adult. Increasing size and number of cysts cause progressive renal failure. Total kidney volume is a validated prognostic biomarker for autosomal dominant polycystic kidney disease in adults. The Mayo Imaging Classification (MIC) is a model that predicts the rate of progression among ADPKD patients. This model helps identify rapid progressors and has been used as a valuable clinical indicator for the use of tolvaptan. With this prediction model, patients with typical ADPKD can be subclassified into classes 1A through 1E according to height-adjusted total kidney volume (htTKV) for age, measured by either CT/MRI. The MIC model assumes that htTKV increases

Table 23.4 Complications of ADPKD and its management

Complications		Management
Complications of the cysts	Cyst infection	– Use of broad-spectrum antibiotics that cover Gram-negative bacteria. – Difficult to identify the 'infected cysts' among all the cysts. – Long-term antibiotic prophylaxis is not recommended. – Drainage of an infected cyst may be needed in selected cases.
	Cyst bleeding	– The use of oral or intravenous tranexamic acid can usually achieve haemostasis. Rarely is surgical intervention needed.
	Urolithiasis	– Prevention is always better. Hence, there is a need for advice on adequate fluid intake.
Complications of a large kidney		– There is a progressive increase in kidney volume due to the increasing number and size of the cysts. – The large kidneys are prone to trauma and bleeding – Hence, there is a need to advise against contact sports.
Renal complication	Blood pressure	– A 24-hour BP study helps to detect nocturnal hypertension. – Regularly monitor blood pressure and keep BP<110/70 at adolescent age or ≤75th percentile. – Early use of ACEI/ ARB for BP control.
	Proteinuria and progressive deterioation of renal function to reach ESRD	Regular monitoring of total kidney volume (in adults). Regular monitoring and use of ACE/ ARB when there is proteinuria. Consider the use of tolvaptan in selected adult patients.
Extra-renal complications	Mitral valve prolapse (MVP) and regurgitation (MR)	In the absence of a heart murmur, MVP or MR are not likely. Regular echocardiogram according to clinical condition.
	Intracranial aneurysm	Routine screening is not necessary; however, with a positive family history of subarachnoid or intracranial aneurysm, MRA screening may be required.
	Hepatic cysts	Avoidance of high oestrogen-containing contraceptive methods in adolescent/adult females because of the potential exacerbation of liver disease.

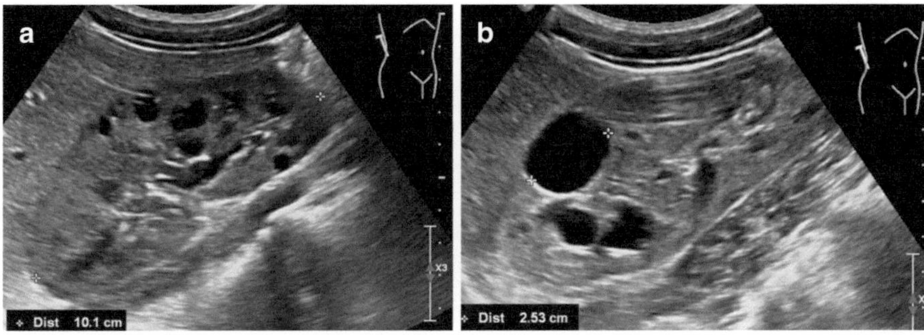

Fig. 23.2 (**a**) (left) and (**b**) (right). The USG images showed the right kidney, which measured 10.1 cm in length, with increasing number of cysts in it. The cysts are of variable sizes, with a large cyst measuring 2.53 cm in the right kidney. The reniform shape was not distorted, but there was a generalised increase in the echogenicity of the renal parenchyma, and the cysts disrupted the corticomedullary architecture

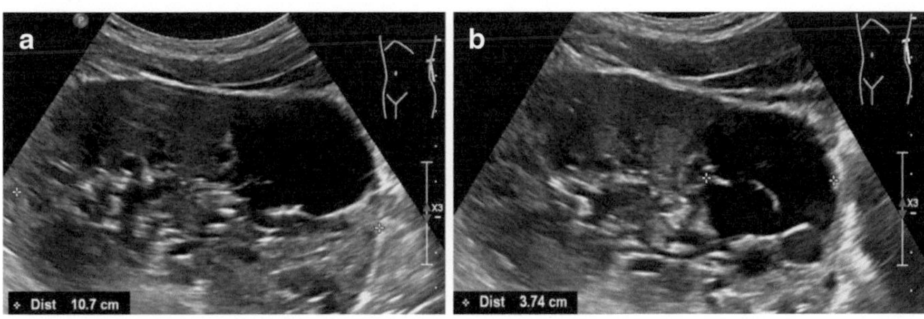

Fig. 23.3 (**a**) (left) and (**b**) (right). The USG images showed the left kidney, which measured 10.7 cm in length. The reniform shape was still maintained, but there were numerous cysts in the left kidney, with a large cyst measuring up to 3.74 cm and a thin septum inside the cyst

continuously and exponentially at an annual kidney growth rate of α (%/year) from htTKV of 150 mL/m at age 0. A total kidney volume of ≥750 mL and a TKV increase of 5% per year indicate intractable disease.

Mayo Clinic Classification for the Growth in htTKV Per Year

Class 1A: Slowest progression (<1.5% growth per year)
Class 1B: Slow progression (1.5–3% growth per year)
Class 1C: Intermediate progression (3–4.5% growth per year)
Class 1D: Rapid progression (4.5–6% growth/year)
Class 1E: Fastest progression (>6% growth/year)

Although the TKV measured by magnetic resonance imaging (MRI)/computed tomography (CT) and manual segmentation is considered the 'reference standard', this method is time-consuming and may not be readily accessible. The use of this

Table 23.5 The PRO-PKD score

Variable		Points
Male		1
Hypertension before the age of 35 years		2
First urologic events before 35 years of age		2
Mutation study	PKD 2 mutation	0
	Non-truncating PKD1 mutation	2
	Truncating PKD 1 mutation	4

The PRO-PKD score from 0 to 3 is low risk, 4 to 6 is intermediate risk, and 7 to 9 is high risk

method in young children may require sedation, and there is a concern of frequent exposure to irradiation. To simplify the study method, the ellipsoid formula (i.e. length × width × depth × $\pi/6$), which only involves the measurement of the three dimensions of a kidney, has been developed to determine the TKV. This method can also be performed by using an ultrasound machine, which facilitates monitoring TKV. Although measuring htTKV has become a regular monitoring in adult patients, there is no validated data on its use in children.

What is the PRO-PKD score?
The PROPKD score is another scoring system developed in adults to predict the likelihood of renal failure before age 60. With multivariate survival analysis, four variables significantly associated with the age of onset for end-stage renal failure were identified in this group of patients. A scoring system from 0 to 9 was developed (Table 23.5).

What is tolvaptan?
Tolvaptan is a vasopressin-2 receptor antagonist. It has been used to prevent deterioration of kidney function in adult ARPKD patients who have a poor prognosis or rapidly progressive disease. The significant adverse effect is hepatotoxicity, which is dose-unrelated and will resolve when tolvaptan is discontinued. Symptoms of polyuria, polydipsia and nocturia may be substantial and result in treatment discontinuation in some adult patients.

23.3 Case Illustrations

In this case study, we invite readers to follow the journey of a child with ADPKD, illustrating how cystic changes progress in kidneys that initially appear normal. The art of treating children with suspected ADPKD is the balance between 'not medicalising currently healthy individuals and not treating disease manifestation in those affected at an early age'.

Despite the majority of ADPKD patients having symptoms in adulthood, a substantial number of adolescents may have hypertension and proteinuria, which are treatable by medication. There is also a small proportion of children with very-early-onset disease who require early treatment and even dialysis therapy.

Suggested Further Readings

1. Nishio S, Tsuchiya K, Nakatani S, Muto S, Mochizuki T, Kawano H, et al. A digest from the evidence-based clinical practice guideline for polycystic kidney disease 2020. Clin Exp Nephrol. 2021;25:1292–302.
2. Gimpel C, Bergmann C, Bockenhauer D, Breysem L, Cadnapaphornchai MA, Cetiner M, et al. International consensus statement on the diagnosis and management of autosomal dominant polycystic kidney disease in children and young people. Nat Rev Nephrol. 2019;15(11):713–26.
3. Torres VE, Ahn C, Barten TR, Brosnahan G, Cadnapaphornchai MA, Chapman AB, et al. KDIGO 2025 clinical practice guideline for the evaluation, management, and treatment of autosomal dominant polycystic kidney disease (ADPKD): executive summary. Kidney Int. 2025;107(2):234–54.
4. De Rechter S, Bockenhauer D, Guay-Woodford LM, Liu I, Mallett AJ, Soliman NA, et al. ADPedKD: a global online platform on the management of children with ADPKD. Kidney Int Rep. 2019;4(9):1271–84.
5. Cornec-Le Gall E, Audrézet MP, Rousseau A, Hourmant M, Renaudineau E, Charasse C, et al. The PROPKD score: a new algorithm to predict renal survival in autosomal dominant polycystic kidney disease. J Am Soc Nephrol. 2016;27(3):942–51.

Vessel-Muscle and Lipid

24

24.1 Case Description

A 15-year-old young lady, Camila, was admitted through the accident and emergency department for gross haematuria for 2 days. She was a new immigrant to the city 1 month ago. She was diagnosed with tuberous sclerosis at 2 years old in her home town when she first presented as developmental delay and repeated twitching of the limbs. She was on regular anti-epileptic medications to control her seizures. She can walk independently but needs supervision in all daily activities and cannot communicate verbally. Two days ago, she was noticed to have unusual behaviour, which suggested she was not feeling well. Her pants were blood-stained, and the parents were not sure whether she had dysmenorrhea, causing her discomfort. Hence, a few tablets of painkillers were given to her for pain control. However, the bleeding increased in amount, and she looked increasingly unwell; thus, she was brought to the hospital.

Upon arrival, she looked extremely pale. Her extremities were cold, and she had a poor capillary refill. Her blood pressure was 80/40 mmHg with a heart rate of 140 bpm. Her oxygen saturation was 89% on 2 L/min nasal oxygen. She was afebrile and had tenderness over her right flank on physical examination. She had multiple angiofibromas over her face and a periungual fibroma over her fingers. She was immediately resuscitated with intravenous normal saline 500 mL given at full rate for two times. Her blood pressure improved to 90/45 mmHg, and her heart rate dropped back to 120 bpm. Her haemoglobin was 6 g/dL and she was urgently transfused with two units of packed cells. After initial stabilisation, an urgent CT abdomen was performed. (Fig. 24.1).

W. K. Y. Chan, M. C. I. Kuok, *Paediatric Nephrology*,
https://doi.org/10.1007/978-981-95-5060-9_24

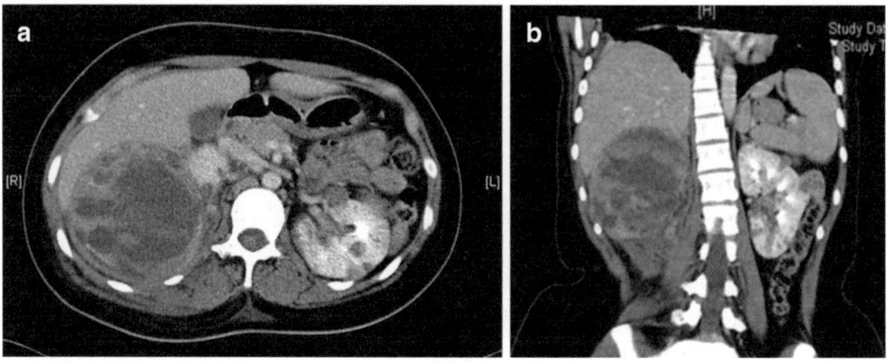

Fig. 24.1 (**a**) Axial contrast-enhanced CT of the abdomen showed the right kidney was enlarged and replaced with a large heterogeneous mass likely to be a haemorrhagic tumour. The left kidney showed multiple small hypodense nodular lesions. (**b**) Coronal contrast-enhanced abdomen CT showed the same huge mass replacing the upper pole of the right kidney, with mixed heterogeneity. The left kidney had multiple small hypodense nodular lesions and one relatively larger lesion with mixed densities was found at the mid-outer cortical region

24.2 Interactive Case Discussion

What is tuberous sclerosis complex?
Tuberous sclerosis complex (TSC) is a multisystem hereditary disease, presented as growth of benign tumours in multiple organs, including the central nervous system, the kidneys, the skin, the heart and the lungs (Table 24.1). With the advancement in understanding the pathophysiology and use of mTOR inhibitors, there is a paradigm shift in early screening and treatment of the disease.

How do you diagnose tuberous sclerosis complex (TSC)?
The International Tuberous Sclerosis Complex consensus group set up diagnostic criteria for TSC in 1998. Genetic criteria were added as a distinct diagnostic criterion in the 2012 consensus, and recently, in 2018–2021, the diagnostic criteria were reconfirmed with additional clarification and emphasis.

For genetic criteria, the identification of either a TSC1 or TSC2 pathogenic mutation is sufficient to make a definitive diagnosis of tuberous sclerosis (Table 24.2).

Without genetic criteria, major and minor criteria support definite and possible diagnoses.

Definite TSC is made with the following:

- A combination of the TWO major clinical features (except AML + LAM)
- One major feature with more or equal to two minor features

Table 24.1 Summary of the genetic and clinical features of TSC

Genetics of TSC	
Incidence	1: 6000 to 1:10,000 live births (a rare disease)
Inheritance	Autosomal dominant with complete penetrance but variable expressivity, leading to variable severity in clinical manifestations even within the same family
Genetics	TSC1 is located at 9q24, and TSC2 is located at 16p13 TSC2 gene mutation is more common, accounts for around 70% of mutations, and the disease is more severe than with the TSC1 gene mutation Proteins produced by these genes are hamartin and tuberin. They are tumour suppressors in the mTOR pathway
Pathogenesis	Loss of function of the tumour suppressor genes (TSC1/TSC2) causes upregulation of the mTOR signalling pathway, which accelerates cell growth, proliferation and subsequent formation of hamartomatous tumours in the brain, skin, kidney, eyes, heart and the lung
Clinical features of TSC	
Skin	– Hypomelanotic macules and patches (ash leaf spots) are usually present at birth and become evident during infancy – Ash leaf spots are best visualised and detected by a Wood's lamp, which uses ultraviolet light to detect skin pigment disorders – Facial angiofibroma ('adenoma sebaceum') – Fibrous cephalic plaques – Shagreen patches over the lower back or flank – Ungual fibroma
CNS	– Infantile spasm or early onset epilepsy syndrome, focal seizure, drug-resistant epilepsy – Focal cortical dysplasia – Cortical tubers – Subependymal giant cell astrocytoma (SEGA) – Intellectual disability – Neuropsychiatric disorder, autism
CVS	– Cardiac rhabdomyoma (prenatally/neonatally) is more often present in the ventricles and may cause ventricular outflow tract obstruction – Has a propensity to involute with age
Kidney	– Angiomyolipoma – Renal cysts
Eyes	– Retinal hamartoma, which is unlikely to affect vision
Lung	– Pulmonary lymphangioleiomyomatosis, which may cause haemoptysis, pneumothorax and progressive dyspnoea

mTOR mechanistic target of rapamycin or mammalian target of rapamycin, *CNS* central nervous system, *CVS* cardiovascular system

Table 24.2 Diagnostic criteria for tuberous sclerosis complex by the International Tuberous Sclerosis Complex Consensus group in 2012, and with updates in 2021

A. Genetic diagnostic criteria	– Identifying either a TSC1 or TSC2 pathogenic mutation is a definitive diagnosis – A pathogenic mutation is defined as a mutation that inactivates the function of the TSC1 or TSC2 protein – Failure to identify a pathogenic variant in TSC1 or TSC2 does not exclude a diagnosis of TSC, as 10–25% of TSC patients have no mutation identified by a conventional genetic test	
B. Clinical diagnostic criteria	**Major criteria**	**Minor criteria**
	1. Hypomelanotic macules (≥3, at least 5-mm diameter) 2. Angiofibromas (≥3) or fibrous cephalic plaque 3. Ungual fibromas (≥2) 4. Shagreen patch 5. Multiple retinal hamartomas 6. Multiple cortical tubers and/or radial migration lines[a] 7. Subependymal nodules 8. Subependymal giant cell astrocytoma (SEGA) 9. Cardiac rhabdomyoma 10. Lymphangioleiomyomatosis (LAM)[b] 11. Angiomyolipomas (AML) (≥2)	1. 'Confetti' skin lesions[c] 2. Dental enamel pits (≥3) 3. Intraoral fibromas (≥2) 4. Retinal achromic patch 5. Multiple renal cysts 6. Nonrenal hamartomas 7. Sclerotic bone lesions[d]

[a]Cortical dysplasia is used in the 2012 diagnostic criteria, but was found to be too nonspecific; hence, it was replaced by 'multiple cortical tubers and/or radial migration lines', which are more specific for TSC.
[b]A combination of the two major clinical features (LAM and AML) without other features does not meet criteria for a definitive diagnosis.
[c]'Confetti' skin lesions refer to 1- to 3-mm hypopigmented macules scattered over regions of the body such as the arms and legs.
[d]Sclerotic bone lesions are relatively common and specific for TBS. It was added back to the diagnostic minor criteria to alert clinicians that these lesions are not surprising in TSC and rarely require intervention, and they should not raise undue alarm of possible cancer.

Possible TSC is made by the following:

- One major feature or
- More or equal to two minor features

What are the renal manifestations of tuberous sclerosis complex?

Renal disease is a significant cause of morbidity and mortality in tuberous sclerosis. In the adult population, renal complication is the major cause of death in TSC patients. Renal manifestations in TSC include the following:

- Angiomyolipomas
  - It is the most common renal presentation. AMLs are benign tumours with three components (abnormal blood vessels, immature smooth muscle cells and lipid cells). They are typically bilateral and multiple. They grow continu-

ously, increase in size and are prone to developing intra-tumour aneurysms with the tendency to bleed.

- Renal cysts
  - These are also common and have an onset in childhood. Most of the time, these cysts are small, have no clinical consequences and will not affect renal function. However, if these cysts continue to enlarge and grow, they may cause renal impairment. This is typically observed in patients with a contiguous deletion of TSC2 and the adjacent PKD1 gene; these patients may have a clinical presentation as early-onset polycystic kidney disease.
- TSC-associated renal cell carcinoma (RCC)
  - This is rare in children and has a reported incidence of 1–3%.
  - CT/MRI scans may sometimes be challenging to differentiate a benign AML from an RCC, especially in fat-poor AML.
  - The high vascularity may increase the risk of bleeding for a tumour biopsy.

What was the diagnosis of Camila?

Since Camila has tuberous sclerosis, the renal pathology was likely a bleeding angiomyolipoma of the right kidney. If a fat attenuation MRI/CT examination were available, the fat component of the angiomyolipoma would be better demonstrated. A genetic test can be performed to confirm the diagnosis further, and the information would be helpful in family genetic counselling. However, a negative genetic test did not rule out the diagnosis. Even without a genetic diagnosis, Camila has fulfilled the clinical criteria for tuberous sclerosis complex.

What is the risk of bleeding in AML?

Renal angiolipoma is a benign renal tumour of vascular tissue, smooth muscle cells and fat tissue. Most (~80%) of AMLs are sporadic, while around 20% of AMLs are associated with tuberous sclerosis complex.

Renal AML is prone to bleeding because of the hypervascularity inside the tumour. The vascular structures are tortuous and lack an elastic membrane, making them prone to developing aneurysms. The neovascularisation can lead to spontaneous haemorrhage, causing haematuria and retroperitoneal hematoma.

The risk of bleeding increases with the following:

- The size of the tumour
  - Tumour size >4 cm has a 50% higher risk, whereas tumours <4 cm only have around a 13% risk of bleeding.
- The grade of the angiogenic component of the tumour
- The presence of TSC
  - AML in association with TSC grows faster and is usually bilateral as compared with sporadic isolated AML.
- The presence and size of vascular aneurysms within the AML

Wunderlich's syndrome, which describes an acute onset of spontaneous, non-traumatic renal haemorrhage, is a rare but potentially life-threatening complication of renal angiomyolipoma in the setting of tumours >4 cm. Clinical manifestations usually include flank pain, a palpable mass, gross haematuria and hypovolemic shock as in our patient.

How would you manage the bleeding renal angiomyolipoma in Camila?
Camila had to be urgently resuscitated to stabilise her vital signs. The subsequent plan will consider the following.

- Stop the bleeding urgently.
- Reserve the kidney as much as possible.
- Possible nature of the tumour—managing bleeding from a benign tumour would differ from managing bleeding from a renal cell carcinoma (RCC).

An urgent diagnostic renal arteriogram with embolisation of the bleeding vessels would be one of the treatment options, and it helps to preserve renal function.

The cornerstone of diagnosis of AML in all radiological modalities is the demonstration of macroscopic fat in the tumour; however, in the setting of haemorrhage, or when lesions contain little fat (fat-poor AML), it may be difficult to distinguish an angiomyolipoma from a renal cell carcinoma.

Despite Camila's condition was stabilised after blood transfusion; her bleeding did not stop. Given the emergency, an urgent laparotomy for surgical removal of the right renal mass was decided. Unfortunately, the tumour was massive and adhered to the surrounding tissue. It ended up with a total nephrectomy of the right kidney. The renal histology confirmed massive bleeding from a benign renal angiomyolipoma. Camila recovered well from the surgery. She was regularly monitored for her blood pressure, renal function, size of the AMLs and cysts in the left kidney. Seven years later, the CT abdomen showed progression of the AML in her remaining left kidney. Camila was then treated with an mTOR inhibitor (everolimus) at 10 mg daily. She tolerated the treatment without significant side effects (Fig. 24.2).

What is the conventional method for treating AML in tuberous sclerosis?
Before mTOR inhibitors is available, TSC patients with AML were monitored regularly. AML lesions >3 cm are typically managed by arterial embolisation or surgical resection, such as partial nephrectomy. However, these lesions are usually bilateral and multiple. They will regrow even after embolisation. Recurrent interventions will cause progressive loss of renal function.

With the discovery of the pathophysiological role of the mTOR pathway in TSC, new treatment with mTOR inhibitors has changed the management of AML. Embolisation is only reserved in emergency situations for acute bleeding, and partial nephrectomy is no longer desirable for kidney preservation.

What is the role of the mTOR inhibitor in managing AMLs in tuberous sclerosis?
The hyperactivation of the mammalian target of rapamycin (mTOR) signalling pathway is a key factor in the development of various clinical manifestations.

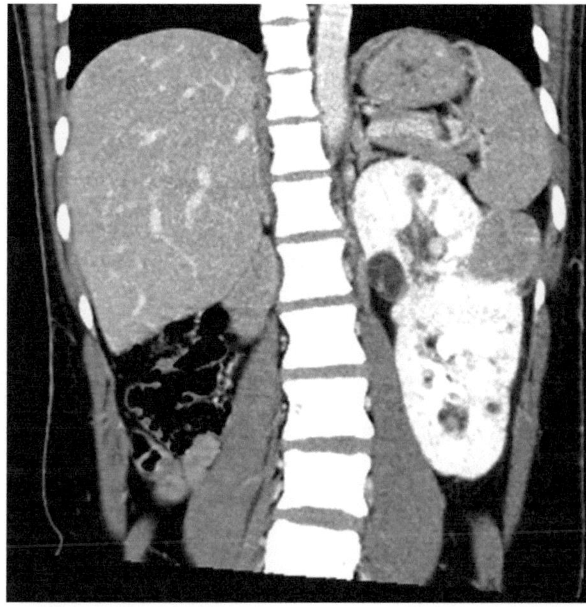

Fig. 24.2 Seven years later, a repeated CT scan showed status post right nephrectomy. There was progressive enlargement of the AML especially the one near the outer cortical region of the left kidney and there were multiple renal cysts

Everolimus (EVE), an mTOR inhibitor, has been extensively studied and has shown efficacy in TSC-associated disorders, including renal angiomyolipoma.

The EXIST-1 and EXIST-2 studies were the two randomised, placebo-controlled, international trials investigating the efficacy and safety of everolimus for treating tuberous sclerosis complex (TSC). The EXIST-1 study focused on subependymal giant cell astrocytomas (SEGAs), while the EXIST-2 study focused on renal angiomyolipomas. Everolimus was used at a dose of 10 mg per day or 4.5 mg/m^2, and the target trough level was between 5 and 15 ng/mL. The international consensus suggested starting everolimus at 2.5 mg/m^2 or 5 mg daily to minimise side effects. The dose is then titrated according to efficacy and side effects. Sirolimus, also a mTOR inhibitor, is a reasonable alternative to everolimus.

What are the side effects of everolimus?

Most side effects of everolimus are dose-dependent; hence, significant side effects can be managed by lowering the dosage or even temporary cessation of the medication. The reported side effects of everolimus include the following:

- Stomatitis (most common)
- Infection risk
- Menstrual irregularity
- Maculopapular or acneiform rashes
- Hyperlipidaemia
- Hyperglycaemia
- Proteinuria

What are the principles in treating AML in TSC?
The management plan is as follows.

1. For asymptomatic, growing angiomyolipoma measuring larger than 3 cm in diameter, treatment with an mTORi is recommended as the first-line therapy. Clinicians can consider starting everolimus at a low dose of 2.5 mg/m^2 and then titrating accordingly.
2. Continue regular surveillance with abdominal MRI or CT scan. The frequency of surveillance depends on the size of AML.
3. Control of blood pressure with renin-aldosterone-angiotensin inhibitors as the first-line therapy.
4. Second-line treatment includes selective embolisation followed by a short course of corticosteroid, kidney-sparing resection and ablative therapy for exophytic lesions. The second line of treatment is usually reserved for patients for whom an mTOR inhibitor is contraindicated.
5. Acute haemorrhage can be managed by arterial embolisation with a short course of steroids.

24.3 Case Illustrations

By sharing Camila's story, we emphasis the need for ongoing surveillance to improve outcome of patients with this complicated disease. Undiagnosed angiomyolipoma in tuberous sclerosis complex can present as a life-threatening event. The advances in understanding the dysregulation of the mTOR pathway in TSC have led to enormous progress in the management. Kidney surveillance of children with TSC now provides the opportunity for timely interventions with evolimus to preserve kidney function and reduce the impact of renal failure in adulthood.

Suggested Further Readings

1. Northrup H, Aronow ME, Bebin EM, Bissler J, Darling TN, de Vries PJ, et al. Updated international tuberous sclerosis complex diagnostic criteria and surveillance and management recommendations. Pediatr Neurol. 2021;123:50–66.
2. Trnka P, Kennedy SE. Renal tumors in tuberous sclerosis complex. Pediatr Nephrol. 2021;36(6):1427–38.
3. Luo C, Ye WR, Shi W, Yin P, Chen C, He YB, et al. Perfect match: mTOR inhibitors and tuberous sclerosis complex. Orphanet J Rare Dis. 2022;17(1):106.
4. Mekahli D, Müller RU, Marlais M, Wlodkowski T, Haeberle S, de Argumedo ML, et al. Clinical practice recommendations for kidney involvement in tuberous sclerosis complex: a consensus statement by the ERKNet Working Group for Autosomal Dominant Structural Kidney Disorders and the ERA Genes & Kidney Working Group. Nat Rev. Nephrol. 2024;20(6):402–20.

Do Not Miss the KUB

25

25.1 Case Description

Ramesh was a 17-month-old boy who was first brought to our attention at 6 months old for an episode of *Escherichia coli* urinary tract infection. He was treated with antibiotics and recovered uneventfully. His ultrasound of the kidneys was normal at that time. He presented to us again for two more episodes of urinary tract infection at 12 months and 14 months old, respectively, and recovered uneventfully. This time, he was admitted again for a febrile urinary tract infection, and his urine culture grew Proteus mirabilis.

He underwent a USG kidney, KUB and MCUG examination to evaluate his recurrent urinary tract infection. What did they show (Figs. 25.1, 25.2, 25.3, and 25.4)?

W. K. Y. Chan, M. C. I. Kuok, *Paediatric Nephrology*,
https://doi.org/10.1007/978-981-95-5060-9_25

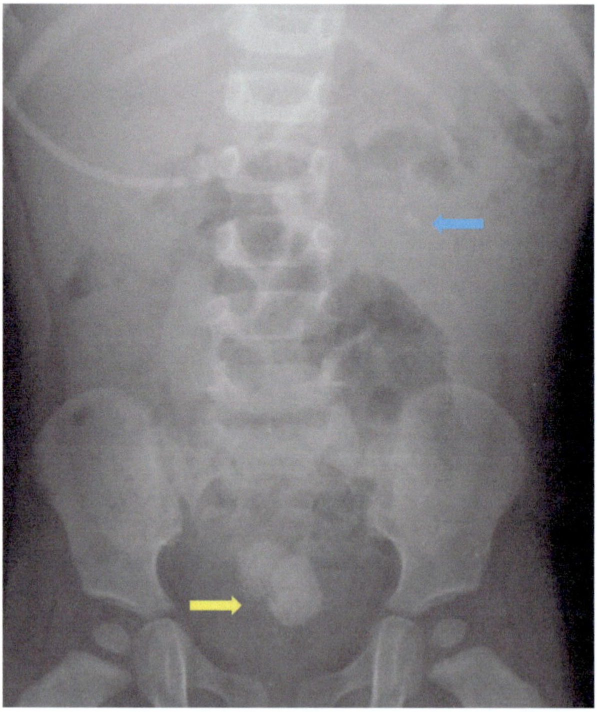

Fig. 25.1 KUB showed two radio-opaque shadows ~1.6 cm each, located in the central pelvic (yellow arrow), likely representing two bladder stones. Another faint opacity measured around 0.5 cm at the left L2/3 level could be a renal stone (blue arrow)

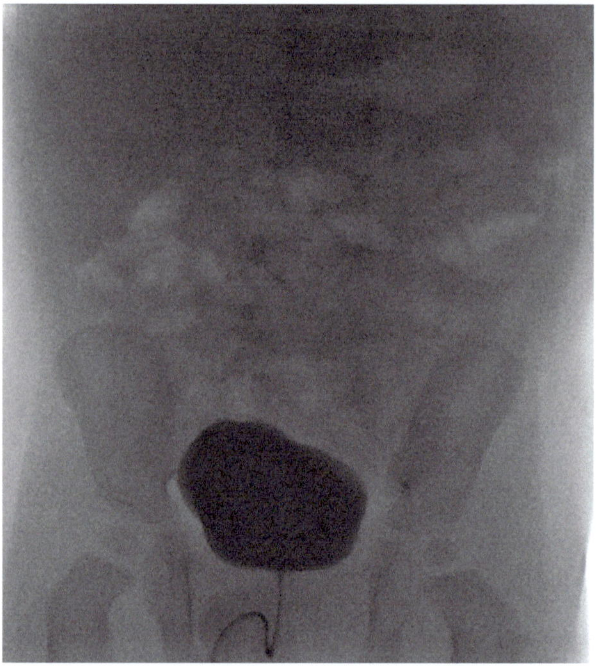

Fig. 25.2 MCUG of the patient did not show any vesicoureteric reflux, and the bladder outline appeared smooth and regular. No contrast-filling defect in the bladder was detected

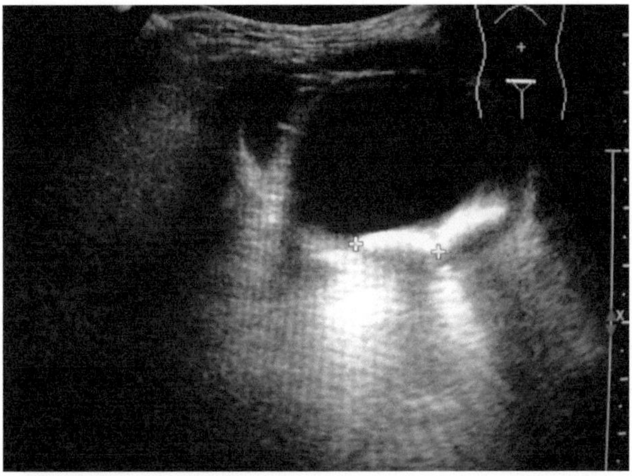

Fig. 25.3 Ultrasound of the urinary bladder showed two echogenic foci with posterior shadowing inside, suggestive of bladder stones and measured 1.4 and 1.5 cm respectively

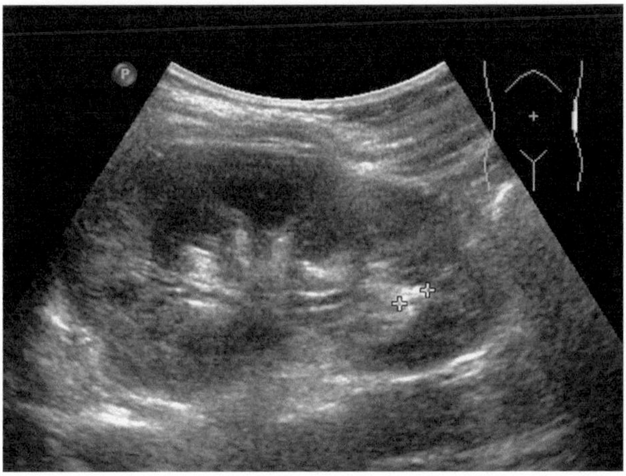

Fig. 25.4 A kidney ultrasound showed an echogenic focus in the left kidney, consistent with a renal stone, which corresponded to the renal stone identified in the KUB. It measured 0.5cm in diameter by the markers

25.2 Interactive Case Discussion

What are infection stones?

Urinary stones that develop due to a urinary tract infection are called infection stones. Infection stones are complex aggregates of crystals amalgamated in an organic matrix that is strictly associated with urinary tract infections. These stones are primarily made up of struvite or magnesium ammonium phosphate ($NH_4MgPO_4 \cdot 6H_2O$), but calcium-containing apatite or hydroxyapatite may also be present. These stones are typically large and irregular (staghorn stones) and occasionally occupy the entire renal pelvis.

The mechanism of infection stone formation is complicated and multifactorial. Factors include the following:

- Change in urine chemistry and pH
- Change in urine microenvironment
- Decrease in stone-forming inhibitors
- The presence of stone-forming modulators
- Biofilm of bacteria

Managing patients who form infection stones is challenging owing to the complexity of the calculi and high recurrence rates.

What are the risk factors for nephrolithiasis/renal stones in children?
Contrary to the adult population, renal stones in children are not common. Risk factors associated with stone formation include the following:

- Children with an abnormal and obstructed urinary tract, causing stasis of urine in the urinary tract
- Children with cystic kidney disease, medullary sponge kidneys
- Children required chronic urinary catheter insertion or a nephrostomy tube (i.e. the presence of a foreign body)
- Metabolic disorders like hyperoxaluria, cystinuria, hypercalcemia and hypercalciuria (primary or secondary)
- Genetic tubular disorders like distal renal tubular acidosis, and Bartter syndrome

Which organisms can form infection stones (struvite stone) and why?
Organisms that produce the enzyme ‘urease’ can form struvite urinary stones. The most common urease-producing bacteria are Proteus species like *Proteus mirabilis*. Other organisms that may also be associated with infection stones are *Staphylococcus aureus*, *Klebsiella pneumoniae*, *Serratia marcescens*, *Pseudomonas aeruginosa*, *Ureaplasma urealyticum* and some strains of *Candida*. As *Escherichia coli* does not produce urease, it will not cause infection stones.

Urease catalyses the hydrolysis of urea to ammonia and carbamate, generating the preferred nitrogen source of many organisms. It also acts as a virulence factor for these organisms (Fig. 25.5).

Why did the MCUG not detect the bladder stones?
In the presence of a bladder stone, a well-performed MCUG should be able to show the contrast-filling defect. However, if too much contrast is injected into the bladder, the filling defects may be obscured.

$$\mathrm{CO\,(NH_2)_2} + H_2O \overset{\text{Urease}}{\rightleftharpoons} CO_2 + 2\,NH_3$$

Fig. 25.5 The action of urease and stone formation. Urease splits urea into ammonia and carbon dioxide, which reacts with water to generate bicarbonate, resulting in a rise in the urinary pH. In alkaline pH, the supersaturated urine precipitates magnesium, ammonium, calcium and phosphate, leading to struvite stone formation

Table 25.1 The urine amino acid profile showed raised levels of cysteine, ornithine, lysine and arginine

Urine amino acid	Value (μM/mmol Cr)	Normal reference range (μM/mmol Cr)
Cystine	681	1–20
Ornithine	599	1–8
Lysine	1934	3–22
Arginine	1318	<11

To screen for other metabolic causes of renal stone, urine for amino acids was tested, and the results are shown in Table 25.1.

The bladder stones of Ramesh were removed surgically, and the stone analysis showed two pieces of bladder stone. They were whitish in colour and oval in shape. The stone texture was brittle. Chemical analysis showed 10% calcium, 40% oxalate, 3% ammonium, 20% phosphate, 5% magnesium and 60% cysteine. Stone-type analysis showed 25% calcium oxalate, 30% struvite (magnesium, ammonium phosphate) and 45% cysteine. Further genetic tests showed a compound heterozygous for two missense mutations in the SLC3A1 gene (genotype AA). The diagnosis was cystinuria. So, in Ramesh's case, the presence of cystine stones predisposes him to repeated UTIs because the stones both harbor bacteria and interfere with normal urine flow.

What is cystinuria?

Cystinuria is an autosomal recessive disease caused by a defective common transport mechanism of the dibasic amino acids (including cystine, lysine, arginine and ornithine) in the proximal renal tubules and small intestine. Only cystine causes medical problems among these amino acids because of its relative insolubility at the usual urine pH. Cystinuria has been described as one of the most common genetic disorders in amino acid transport. Overall prevalence has been reported to be 1 in 7000 in the general population of Europe and America. The figures for the Chinese population are lacking. It generally accounts for 6–8% of urinary stones in paediatric patients and 1–2% in adults. Although the incidence of cystinuria is the same in males and females, males are more severely affected than females. It is not certain whether men's narrower urethra causes this difference in outcome. Men are more prone to having cystine stones than women.

How would you diagnose cystinuria?

Cystinuria can be diagnosed by the following:

1. The presence of typical hexagonal crystals in the urine. It appears in almost 25% of patients with cystinuria in early urine samples.
2. Stone analysis by Infrared spectroscopy and X-ray diffraction offers the highest degree of certainty for determining cystine stone composition. However, in children, it is often difficult to obtain a stone for analysis without surgical intervention.

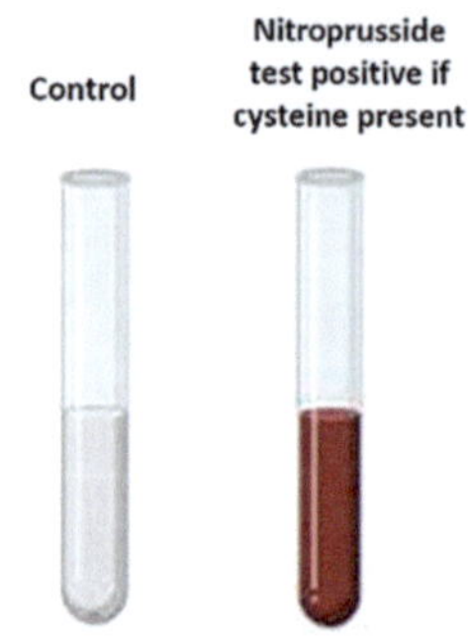

Fig. 25.6 Cyanide converts cystine to cysteine, binding to the nitroprusside, creating an intense purple colour in just a few minutes

3. Measurement of the increased levels of cystine and dibasic amino acids (ornithine, lysine and arginine) in a 24-hour urine specimen or a spot urine sample as the amino acid-creatinine ratio.
4. Sodium cyanide-nitroprusside test (Fig. 25.6).
   - The test typically turns urine deep purple-red if cystine levels exceed 75 mg/gm creatinine. It is a rapid test.
   - False positives are possible in Fanconi syndrome or when the patient is taking sulfur-based medication like ampicillin and N-acetylcysteine.
   - Because of its low reproducibility and the use of a potentially hazardous agent, it became an obsolete method of detecting cystinuria.
5. Genetic study.

   Genetic mutations at the SLC3A1 gene on chromosome 2 and the SLC7A9 gene on chromosome 19 are classically reported as responsible genes.

What is the best imaging to detect cystine stones?

Cystine stones tend to be larger relative to the other aetiologies for stone disease and frequently coalesce to form large, branching staghorn calculi. Pure cystine stones are only faintly radio-opaque because of their disulfur content. A plain X-ray of the abdomen will not show a cystine stone well. USG can identify them if they are large enough or cause hydronephrosis. CT scan without contrast remains the gold standard and will show cystine stones clearly.

How would you manage acute renal colic?

The treatment of acute renal colic includes the following:

1. Use of analgesics, especially a non-steroidal anti-inflammatory drug, for pain relief.
2. Treat any possible urinary tract infection.
3. Assess the need for urgent decompression, like putting in a ureteric stent or a nephrostomy tube.

4. Assess the need for surgical stone removal, ureteroscopically or by extracorporeal shock wave lithotripsy (ESWL). Because cystine stones are highly recurrent, complete stone clearance should be achieved whenever possible.

How would you manage a patient with cystinuria in the long run?

1. Enhance hydration
   - Fluid intake should guarantee a urine output large enough to maintain a cystine concentration of <250 mg/L (1 mmol/L) in the 24-h urine.
     - In adults, 3 L of urine is required to excrete 1–1.5 g (2–3 mmol) cysteine daily.
     - In children, urine volume should be higher than 2 L/1.73 m^2.
2. Decrease the amount of cystine in urine by reducing both cystine and sodium intake.
   - Decrease sodium intake to 1–1.5 mEq/kg.
   - Decrease methionine intake to lower cystine production, or decrease protein intake to <20 g/day
3. Increase the solubility of cystine by increasing the urine pH—the cornerstone for treatment (Table 25.2).
   - Use potassium citrate, 60–80 mEq/day or 60–80 mEq/m^2/day, diluted in a large volume of water, given in 3–4 doses per day, as the alkalinising agent and adjusted until therapeutic urine pH values (7.5–8.0) are reached.
   - Acetazolamide may be considered as an additional means to alkalinise the urine.
   - Urinary pH should be measured in freshly voided urine.
4. Cystine-binding thiol drugs (CBTD) to enhance cystine solubility

   Tiopronin and D-penicillamine are the sulfhydryl drugs that cleave cystine into two cysteines, and by forming compounds with these drugs, higher solubility compounds are formed, and free cystine in urine is decreased.
   - Tiopronin (α-mercaptopropionyl glycine): 15–40 mg/kg per day in three divided doses
   - D-penicillamine: 20–30 mg/kg per day in four divided doses

Table 25.2 The solubility of cystine increases as urine pH increases. However, as the urine becomes more alkaline, the possibility of calcium stone precipitation also increases

Urine pH	Solubility of cystine
7	1 L of urine can dissolve 250 mg of cystine
7.5	1 L of urine can dissolve 500 mg of cystine
8	1 L of urine can dissolve 750 mg of cystine

How would you monitor the patient?

Conservative treatment is based on a stepwise strategy, using hydration, diet and alkalinisation as basic measures, adding thiol derivatives in refractory cases. The patient has to be regularly reviewed on the following:

1. Compliance with conservative treatment by regular urine pH measurement and assessment of urine output.
2. Formation of any new stones or complications like urinary tract infection.
3. The side effects of CBTD are monitored by checking the complete blood cell count and urinary protein excretion.
4. Periodic ultrasound and non-contrast CT for stone evaluation.
5. The risk of CKD is higher in this group of patients and is related to the severity of renal parenchymal damage, including previous nephrectomies and underlying congenital abnormalities or renal hypoplasia.
6. Blood pressure measurement as hypertension is not uncommonly observed in this group of patients.

25.3 Case Illustrations

This case illustrates the importance of identifying secondary causes that can predispose a child to repeated urinary tract infections. With the recurrence of infection by the urea-splitting organisms, underlying infection stones have to be excluded. The KUB film is sometimes informative in identifying kidney or bladder stones and should not be missed. A metabolic workup is crucial in evaluating these stones, as prompt management helps prevent further renal damage. Through Ramesh's story, we review the principles of managing cystinuria, hoping it will be of value to the readers.

Suggested Further Readings

1. Servais A, Thomas K, Strologo LD, Sayer JA, Bekri S, Bertholet-Thomas A, et al. Cystinuria: clinical practice recommendation. Kidney Int. 2021;99(1):48–58.
2. Moussa M, Papatsoris AG, Abou Chakra M, Moussa Y. Update on cystine stones: current and future concepts in treatment. Intractable Rare Dis Res. 2020;9(2):71–8.
3. Bhatt NP, Deshpande AV, Starkey MR. Pharmacological interventions for the management of cystinuria: a systematic review. J Nephrol. 2024;37:208–293.

Even 3.1 Matters 26

26.1 Case Description

Arlo is the family's first child, born in a non-consanguineous marriage. His perinatal history was uneventful, and he was born at full term with a birth weight of 3.2 kg. Arlo first attended the Paediatric clinic for poor weight gain at 17 months old. Physical examination showed his body height and weight were at the third centile. Initial screening tests, including complete blood counts, liver enzymes, urea, creatinine, electrolytes and thyroid function tests, were normal. Arlo's mother described him as a picky eater. He has his weight gain along the third centile, but her body height dropped off during the follow-up.

At 25 months old, Arlo's bone age showed a delay of 1 year. His blood test showed serum potassium at 3.0 mmol/L, but it spontaneously normalised to 3.5 mmol/L upon repeated testing. Other blood tests were normal. A glucagon stimulation test showed a growth hormone (GH) peak at 7.1 μg/L (borderline response). An additional arginine infusion test showed a peak GH response at 10.1 μg/L. Neither test supports the diagnosis of GH deficiency. Arlo was then referred to a dietitian for advice and monitoring of the growth parameters. At the age of 8, there was a marked deviation of his body height to 8 cm below the third centile (Fig. 26.1). His blood test was repeated, and the only abnormality detected was a serum potassium of 3.1 mmol/L.

W. K. Y. Chan, M. C. I. Kuok, *Paediatric Nephrology*,
https://doi.org/10.1007/978-981-95-5060-9_26

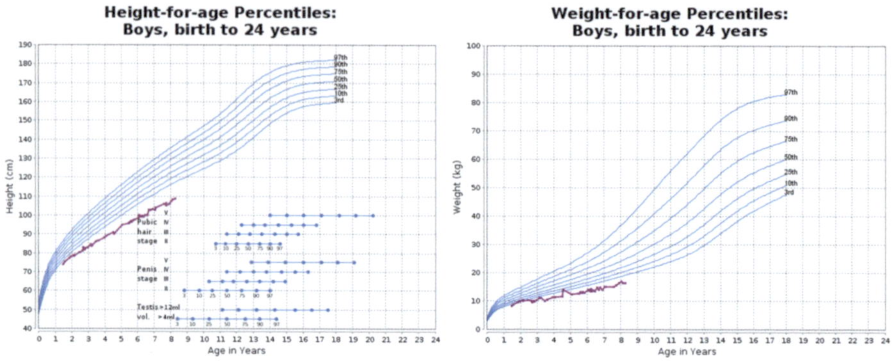

Fig. 26.1 Growth parameters of Arlo. He has been dropping off his height and weight centiles since 2 years old

26.2 Interactive Case Discussion

Is this degree of hypokalaemia significant, and what are the causes of hypokalaemia?

Mild hypokalaemia is often asymptomatic. A serum potassium of <3.5 mmol/L is considered hypokalaemia and is substantial. Patients with this degree of hypokalaemia may present with generalised weakness, fatigue and constipation. In this patient, the growth delay may be attributed to the hypokalaemia. The more acute the hypokalaemia, the more likely it will be symptomatic.

How would you work up for his hypokalaemia?

It is essential, firstly, to exclude spurious and transcellular potassium shifts. Spurious hypokalaemia occurs when there are abnormally high white blood cells, like leukaemia, which may take up extracellular potassium after blood is taken and kept at room temperature. Some medications may cause a transcellular shift of potassium, like salbutamol and insulin, causing hypokalaemia, but these causes will be obvious. In this patient, the hypokalaemia may be related to his growth failure.

What is the most helpful test to identify the cause of hypokalaemia?

Apart from the transcellular shift, potassium can be lost in the urine or gastrointestinal tract. Assessing renal potassium excretion is the most crucial step in evaluating hypokalaemia. If there is excess renal excretion in low serum potassium, renal loss would be the underlying cause.

Urine potassium excretion can be assessed with a 24-hour urine potassium excretion or by a spot urine potassium test. There are four spot urine indices to assess urine potassium excretion.

1. Spot urine potassium excretion

   Renal K >15 mmol/L suggests renal potassium loss.

   Renal K <15 mmol/L suggests appropriate renal conservation of potassium.

2. Spot urine potassium/creatinine (K/Cr) ratio

   Urine K/Cr <1.5 suggests renal conservation, but this value may vary with age, renal failure and muscle mass.
3. Fractional excretion of potassium (FeK)—usually should be <3%:

$$\text{FeK} = \frac{\text{Urinary potassium} \times \text{serum creatinine}}{\text{Serum potassium} \times \text{urine creatinine}}$$

4. Transtubular potassium gradient (TTKG): a value >2.5 would suggest renal wasting.

   TTKG is used to assess renal potassium excretion by the cortical collecting duct. It indirectly estimates the aldosterone activity.

$$\text{TTKG} = \frac{\text{Urine potassium} \times \text{serum osmolality}}{\text{Serum potassium} \times \text{urine osmolality}}$$

There are two prerequisites for TTKG measurement:

- Urine osmolality > serum osmolality.
- Urine sodium >25 mmol/L to ensure sufficient sodium is delivered to the distal tubules.

Arlo's blood test showed serum sodium of 142 mmol/L (normal), chloride 94 mmol/L (RI: 98–107), bicarbonate was normal at 24 mmol/L, urea was slightly high at 6.9 mmol/L (RI: 1.8–6.4), creatinine was 44 umol/L (RI: 28–52), calcium was 2.4 mmol/L (normal), phosphate was 1.4 mmol/L (normal), serum osmolality was 282 mOsmol/kg (normal), and serum magnesium was 0.63 mmol/L (RI: 0.7–0.95). His spot urine test showed potassium 45.2 mmol/L, with an osmolality of 674 mOsm/kg. His urine calcium/creatinine ratio is 0.2 mg/mg (normal).

How would you interpret these laboratory tests?

Arlo's urine potassium excretion was unusually high at 45.2 mmol/L, given his low serum potassium. His calculated TTKG was 6. Hence, he was having renal potassium wasting. The serum chloride was also low. Therefore, one needs to consider salt-losing tubulopathy with hypokalaemia. The slightly raised serum urea may also indicate mild intravascular dehydration despite our inability to elicit a history of polyuria and salt craving in Arlo.

Arlo's blood pressure measurements were normal, but sometimes they were on the low side. There was no history of ever using diuretics. Further blood tests showed plasma renin was 19.9 ng/mL/hr (RI: 0.5–5.9) and aldosterone was 613 pmol/L (RI: <250). Hence, a genetic test for Bartter and Gitelman syndrome was performed. Arlo's genetic test revealed one pathogenic variant SLC12A3 c.179C>T p.(Thr60Met) and one likely pathogenic variant SLC12A3 c.602-16G>A in the SLC12A3 gene. The result confirmed a diagnosis of SLC12A3-related Gitelman syndrome.

What is Gitelman syndrome?

Gitelman syndrome (GS) is a rare autosomal recessive, salt-losing tubulopathy characterised by renal potassium wasting, leading to hypokalaemia and metabolic alkalosis. Other features include hypocalciuria, hypomagnesemia and hyperaldosteronism. Phenotypically, it mimics thiazide toxicity. The degree of hypomagnesium and hypocalciuria may vary, making it sometimes difficult to differentiate from other types of salt-losing tubulopathy.

Gitelman syndrome results from mutations of the genes that encode Na^+, Cl^- and Mg^{++} transporters in the apical membrane of the distal convoluted tubules (DCT).

The mutations include the following:

- SLC12A3, which encodes the thiazide-sensitive NaCl co-transporter (NCC)
- The TRPM6 gene, which results in distal tubular magnesium loss

The movement of ions across the renal tubular system primarily occurs through cotransporters and ion channels, driven mainly by the electrochemical gradient established by the basolateral sodium-potassium ATPase (Na+/K+-ATPase). The flow of ions across the tubular and capillary members is shown in the diagram (Fig. 26.2). SLC12A3 encodes the NCC channel in the apical membrane of the DCT. Mutations in the SLC12A3 gene result in a loss of function of the NCC, such that sodium and chloride are not absorbed in the DCT, causing volume contraction and increasing delivery of sodium and chloride to the collecting tubule. This leads to an increase in aldosterone secretion, causing hypokalaemia and metabolic alkalosis.

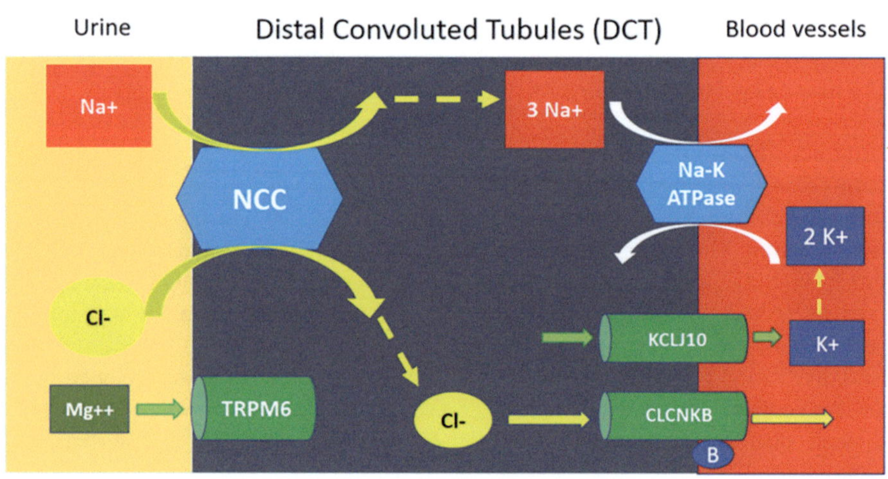

Fig. 26.2 The diagram shows the different electrolyte transporters and movement of ions at the DCT. NCC: sodium chloride cotransporter; TRPM6: transient receptor potential cation channel subfamily M member 6; CLCNKB: chloride channel; B: Barttin. The arrows indicate the direction of ion movement between urine, DCT and blood vessels. The basolateral sodium-potassium ATPase (Na+/K+-ATPase) provides the driving force

TRPM6 magnesium-permeable channels are located at the DCT. In Gitelman syndrome, there is a reduced expression of TRPM6 channels. Downregulation of these channels in the distal tubule results in wasting urinary and intestinal magnesium, leading to hypomagnesemia in Gitelman syndrome. The hypomagnesium will suppress PTH action, decreasing calcium mobilisation from bone and hypocalciuria. However, there is variation in clinical expression of the degree of hypomagnesemia and hypocalciuria.

Is Arlo's clinical presentation classical?

Most patients with Gitelman syndrome present at an adolescent or adult age, with hypokalaemia detected incidentally. Arlo has an early presentation (before 6 years old) associated with growth failure. In addition to this, his serum potassium was normal initially, and it took years for the hypokalaemia to become apparent. Arlo also did not have any symptoms related to his hypokalaemia.

What are the symptoms of Gitelman syndrome?

Because of the salt-losing property, affected individuals will have polyuria, nocturia and salt cravings. Muscle cramps, tetany, paresthesia, seizure and carpopedal spasms may occur. If there is severe hypomagnesium, positive Chvostek's and Trousseau's signs may be demonstrated. Because of the hypokalaemia, muscle weakness, cardiac arrhythmia and prolonged QTc may also occur.

How do you differentiate Gitelman syndrome from Bartter syndrome?

Bartter and Gitelman syndromes (BS and GS) are inherited disorders affecting the renal tubular handling of sodium, potassium and chloride. They share the same characteristic metabolic abnormalities, such as hypokalaemia, metabolic alkalosis and hyperplasia of the juxtaglomerular apparatus with hyperreninemia and hyperaldosteronism. The clinical and laboratory manifestations may only sometimes allow distinction between them. Despite the similarities in their phenotypes, they have different genetic defects (Table 26.1).

What are the treatments for Gitelman syndrome?

The goal of treatment is to maintain normal electrolytes as much as possible to allow normal growth and be free of symptoms. The treatment methods include the following:

1. Potassium and magnesium supplements
    - According to the patient's preference, KCl supplements can be administered as syrup, in water or a slow-release formulation. The dose will be titrated individually. The maintenance dose may be high. Hence, a reasonable target for potassium is 3.0 mmol/L.
    - A target magnesium level of 0.6 mmol/L (1.46 mg/dL) is recommended. Oral administration of magnesium supplements is preferred. All magnesium salts are effective; however, their bioavailability is highly variable, causing osmotic diarrhoea at higher doses.

Table 26.1 Differentiation between Bartter syndrome and Gitelman syndrome

Characteristics	Bartter syndrome	Gitelman syndrome
Usual age at presentation	From birth to early childhood	From late childhood to adulthood
Neuromuscular symptoms (muscle spasm, weakness)	Infrequent or less serious	More common
Serum magnesium	Normal or diminished	Diminished due to an increase in urine magnesium
Urine calcium excretion	Normal or increased. Nephrocalcinosis in some types of BS	Diminished Nephrocalcinosis is not a feature
Renal production of prostaglandin E2	Increased	Normal
The site of the tubules affected	Thick ascending limb of the Loop of Henle	Distal convoluted tubules
Transporter affected	Na-K-2Cl cotransporter	Na-Cl cotransporter
Diuretics mimics	Loop diuretics	Thiazide diuretics
Subtypes	Bartter syndrome has five subtypes reported	No other subtypes were reported
Genetic defect	Type 1: SLC12A1 Type 2: KCNJ1 Type 3: CLCNKB Type 4: BSND Type 5: CASR	SLC12A3

2. Use of NSAIDs like indomethacin (to increase serum potassium) is an alternative.
3. Potassium-sparing diuretics like aldactone or eplerenone are usually needed.
4. Epithelial sodium channel blocker—amiloride (to decrease potassium excretion), but use with caution as it has a sodium-wasting property.
5. Avoid medication that may prolong QTc, like macrolides and antihistamines.
6. Encourage NaCl intake and keep the salt-craving behaviour, as salt loss is the underlying pathology.

What are the possible long-term complications and prognosis of Gitelman syndrome?
Possible long-term complications of GS are the following:

- Growth retardation and delayed puberty.
- Rhabdomyolysis.
- Weakness and fatigue may affect daily activities.
- Chondrocalcinosis.
- Medical compliance and psychosocial issues.

Arlo was treated with potassium and magnesium supplements, aldactone and amiloride. He gained weight and height satisfactorily and was free of symptoms.

What is the prognosis of Arlo?

In general, patients with GS have a favourable prognosis after treatment. Renal failure is rare despite proteinuria, which may present because of long-term tubulopathy. Cardiac death, which may be related to cardiac arrhythmia, has been reported. Compliance is often an issue because of the lifelong medication.

26.3 Case Illustrations

Ultimately, Arlo's growth failure was attributed to an underlying diagnosis of Gitelman syndrome. Despite hypokalaemia being the most prominent electrolyte abnormality leading to the diagnosis of Gitelman syndrome, it may not be apparent initially, and the serum potassium may fluctuate at the beginning of the disease.

Suggested Further Readings

1. Fulchiero R, Seo-Mayer P. Bartter syndrome and Gitelman syndrome. Pediatr Clin. 2019;66(1):121–34.
2. Besouw MT, Kleta R, Bockenhauer D. Bartter and Gitelman syndromes: Questions of class. Pediatr Nephrol. 2020;35:1815–24.

The Bowlegs 27

27.1 Case Description

Dickson is a 3-year-old boy, referred by the orthopaedic surgeon to the paediatric clinic for short stature and suspected bowlegs. He was delivered at full term by Caesarean section for maternal short stature. His birth weight was 2.8 kg, and the neonatal history was uneventful. He was thriving well, with satisfactory weight gain; however, his knees appeared to be bent outward and were worsening. Hence, the parents sought medical advice from a paediatric orthopaedic surgeon, who referred him for the management of bowlegs. Upon physical examination, the child weighed 12.7 kg (25th centile), his body height was 93.5 cm (3rd centile), and his head circumference was 53 cm (97th centile). His mother's height was 144 cm, and his father's height was 168 cm. He had bilateral genu varum (bowlegs), a bulged forehead, pectus carinatum (pigeon chest), rachitic rosary, exaggerated lumbar lordosis and his wrists appeared swollen. In what ways might Dickson's skeletal problem be associated with underlying kidney disorders?

27.2 Interactive Case Discussion

What are the causes of bowlegs in children?

Bowlegs, also known as genu varum, is a description of the outward curvature of the legs with the knees appearing to be farther apart than the ankles when the child stands with feet together. It can be normal in infancy and early childhood, but it usually resolves as the child grows older. If the bowing persisted after the age of 2, it could be abnormal and medical attention is advised. The possible causes of bowlegs are the following:

- Physiological bowing
- Rickets related to various underlying aetiologies
- Metaphyseal dysplasia

W. K. Y. Chan, M. C. I. Kuok, *Paediatric Nephrology*,
https://doi.org/10.1007/978-981-95-5060-9_27

What is rickets?

Rickets is a bone disease that affects bone mineralisation, resulting in soft and weakened bones in children. Osteomalacia is the adult form of rickets. The structure of bone is a mixture of the following:

- Organic matrix (osteoid), which is composed of type 1 collagen and other non-collagenous proteins.
- Inorganic mineral component (hydroxyapatite) with the chemical formula of $Ca_{10}(PO_4)_6(OH)_2$.
- Cellular components include osteoblasts (cells that produce osteoid), osteocytes (mature bone cells) and osteoclasts (bone-resorbing cells).
- Water.

Osteoblasts are bone-forming cells that secrete the extracellular matrix, and the osteoid is mineralised by calcium salt, making it harder and stronger to support the body. In rickets, the process of mineralisation is impaired, leading to a mess of osteoid beneath the growth plate. Hence, abnormalities in calcium and phosphate metabolism can cause rickets. Rickets is traditionally divided into calcipenic rickets and phosphopenic rickets, depending on whether the cause of impaired mineralisation is related to calcium (calcipenic) or phosphate metabolism (phosphopenic).

How do you diagnose rickets?

The diagnosis of rickets is based on medical history, physical examination, biochemical tests and radiology. Genetic tests will help in identifying the genetic form of rickets.

The clinical features of rickets are the following:

- Growth failure, especially short stature.
- Waddling gait.
- Bowlegged (genu varum) or knock-knees (genu valgum).
- Thickened metaphyseal of wrists and ankles.
- Rachitic rosary (enlarged, bead-like appearance of the costochondral junctions in children).
- Bone pain.
- Muscle weakness.
- Delayed closure of fontanelles in infancy.
- Soft skull bone in infancy (craniotabes).
- Poor dentition.
- Craniosynostosis, sensorineural hearing loss and dental abscess are specific features in patients with X-linked hypophosphatemia (XLH) and should be assessed.

Typical radiological features of poor mineralisation of the growth plate are as follows:

- Metaphyseal cupping, fraying and splaying of the long bones (especially over the wrists and knees)
- Widening and irregularity of the growth plates
- Enlargement of the costochondral juncture (rachitic rosary)
- Decreased bone density

Biochemically, serum alkaline phosphatase (ALP) level is elevated, indicating an increased activity of osteoblasts. Depending on the underlying causes, abnormalities in serum calcium, phosphate, vitamin D metabolites, parathyroid hormones, FGF23 levels, urinary calcium and urinary phosphate excretion help making the diagnosis. A genetic test may help to identify genetic causes of rickets.

Calculation of tubular reabsorption of phosphate (TRP) and the maximum rate of tubular reabsorption of phosphate per glomerular filtration rate (TmP/GFR) are useful formulae to diagnose abnormally increased phosphate wasting. There are online calculators and reference ranges available on the web, such as https://gpn.de/service/tmp-gfr-calculator, to ease the calculation.

The formulae are as follows

$$\text{TRP} = 1 - \left[\left(\text{Up}/\text{Pp}\right) \times \left(\text{Pcr}/\text{Ucr}\right)\right], \text{and normal TRP}: 85-95\%$$

$$\text{TmP}/\text{GFR} = \text{Pp} - \left(\text{Up}/\text{Ucr}\right) \times \text{Pcr}$$

- TmP/GFR varies with age in children; therefore, it is important to use appropriate normative data for interpretation.
- A high TmP/GFR indicates appropriate renal phosphate conservation, whereas a low TmP/GFR below 0.8 mmol/L often indicates inappropriate renal phosphate wasting.

TRP: tubular reabsorption of phosphate
Up: urine phosphate
Pp: plasma phosphate
Pcr: plasma creatinine
Ucr: urine creatinine
TmP/GFR: the maximum rate of tubular reabsorption of phosphate per glomerular filtration rate

What is calcipenic rickets?

- Calcipenic rickets is related to calcium insufficiency, most commonly due to low availability or defective functioning of vitamin D.
- In calcipenic rickets, the serum calcium is low and parathyroid hormone (PTH) is always increased.

- There is a variation in the level of vitamin D, 25-hydroxy-vitamin D and 1,25-dihydroxy-vitamin D, depending on the underlying causes.
- In addition to the clinical features of rickets, this group of patients may develop symptoms related to hypocalcaemia like tetany, seizure and even heart failure.
- The causes of calcipenic rickets are related to vitamin D metabolism. They are as follows:
  - Vitamin D deficiency or dependent
    - Dietary deficiency (nutritional rickets)
    - Malabsorption
    - Vitamin D-dependent rickets 1 (VDDR 1) and vitamin D-dependent rickets II (VDDR II)
  - Calcium deficiency
  - Renal rickets secondary to chronic kidney disease (deficiency in1-α hydroxylase leads to failure to produce active 1,25-dihydroxy-vitamin D)
  - Rickets secondary to chronic liver disease (defective 25-hydroxylation of vitamin D)
- The most common cause of calcipenic rickets worldwide is nutritional rickets.
- Treatment of calcipenic rickets involves supplementing native or active vitamin D, depending on the underlying pathophysiology, in combination with an adequate calcium supplement.

What is phosphopenic rickets (hypophosphatemic rickets)?

- Phosphopenic rickets is related to low serum phosphate. Serum calcium is usually normal or slightly elevated, and PTH is typically normal or may be slightly suppressed if serum calcium levels are elevated.
- Urine phosphate excretion is usually increased.
- Causes of hypophosphatemic rickets are:
  - Dietary phosphate deficiency
    - This is uncommon as there is an abundant source of phosphate in usual diet. However, preterm infants using amino-acid elemental milk formula like Neocate® may be prone to developing hypophosphatemia.
    - Malabsorption, e.g. secondary to short gut syndrome
  - FGF23 mediated renal phosphate wasting.
    - The most common cause is X-linked hypophosphatemia (XLH).
  - Primary or secondary tubular phosphate wasting related to proximal tubular disorders. These disorders are non-FGF23 mediated, and hypercalciuria may be a feature before any treatment.
  - Treatment of phosphopenic rickets includes oral phosphate ± active vitamin D or burosumab, depending on the underlying pathophysiology.

Dickson's blood test showed an alkaline phosphatase level of 638 IU/L (RI: 104–345 IU/L), and his X-rays showed a generalised decrease in bone density. The metaphyses of humeri, proximal femurs, radii and tibias showed typical features of splaying and fraying. He was diagnosed with rickets.

His serum calcium was 2.6 mmol/L (RI: 2.19–2.64 mmol/L); phosphate was 0.5 mmol/L (RI: 1.0–1.85 mmol/L); serum creatinine was 28 μmol/L (RI: 21–36 μmol/L); other electrolytes, liver function and renal function test were normal. His PTH was suppressed at 0.5 pmol/L (RI: 1.6–6.9 pmol/L). There was no metabolic acidosis. Urine phosphate excretion was 19.2 mmol/day with tubular reabsorption of phosphate 52.2%. Urine calcium excretion decreased to 0.2 mmol/day (RI: 2.5–7.5 mmol/day). There was no glucosuria, proteinuria or amniaciduria to suggest a proximal renal tubular defect. The first ultrasound of the kidney, performed prior to treatment, was normal, with no evidence of nephrocalcinosis. Dickson was diagnosed with hypophosphatemic rickets. The genetic study showed a nonsense mutation in the PHEX gene; his mother is the carrier of the mutation.

What are the genetic causes of rickets?
The genetic and inherited causes of rickets usually involve vitamin D metabolism, renal phosphate reabsorption or degradation of FGF23, a phosphaturic hormone. A summary of these inherited genetic causes is laid out in Table 27.1. However, with advancements in genetic study, more genetic abnormalities may be revealed in the future, and the list is never complete.

What is X-linked hypophosphatemia (XLH)?
X-linked hypophosphatemia is a prototypical disorder of renal phosphate wasting that affects the growth of the skeleton and teeth in children. It was also known as vitamin D-resistant rickets, as the rickets did not respond to vitamin D treatment. It is the most common type of hereditary rickets, caused by mutations in the PHEX (phosphate-regulating endopeptidase homolog, X-linked) gene. The normal process of FGF23 inactivation is impaired. Elevated FGF23 causes renal phosphate wasting and hypophosphatemia.

What is the treatment for XLH?
The conventional treatment for XLH is the use of phosphate supplements with active vitamin D, especially before the discovery of the genetic abnormalities related to FGF23 and the availability of burosumab in recent years.

The conventional treatment involves administering frequent doses of oral phosphate salts with active vitamin D supplements. Side effects of this combination treatment include the following:

- Diarrhoea and gastrointestinal discomfort related to frequent phosphate doses
- Secondary hyperparathyroidism, hypercalciuria and then the development of nephrocalcinosis or nephrolithiasis

In general, normalisation of serum alkaline phosphatase, calcium, phosphate and PTH indicates healing of the rickets. However, in XLH, normalisation of serum phosphate is almost an impractical goal, as serum phosphate level drops again shortly after each phosphate dose. The dosage of phosphate salt and active vitamin D is titrated with laboratory monitoring. Conventional therapy does not correct the phosphaturia. It targets the healing of the rickets (Table 27.2).

Table 27.1 Genetic causes for different types of rickets

	Gene affected	Pathology
(I) Vitamin D-dependent rickets (VDDR)	**Genetic mutations that affect vitamin D metabolism**	
VDDR1A	CYP27B1	Impaired synthesis of 1,25-$(OH)_2$D
VDDR1B	CYP2R1	Impaired synthesis of 25-(OH) D
VDDR2A	VDR	Affect vitamin D receptors, leading to resistance to the active form of vitamin D
VDDR2B	HNRNPC	Impaired signalling of the vitamin D receptor
VDDR3	CYP3A4	Increased inactivation of 1,25-$(OH)_2$D
(II) Hypophosphatemic rickets due to mutations causing elevated or abnormal signalling of FGF23		
X-linked hypophosphatemic rickets (XLH)	PHEX	Increase FGF23 and excessive phosphate loss
Autosomal recessive hypophosphatemic rickets 1 (ARHR1)	DMP1	Increased FGF23 expression in bone
Autosomal recessive hypophosphatemic rickets 2 (ARHR2)	ENPP1	Increased FGF23 expression in bone
Autosomal dominant hypophosphatemic rickets (ADHR)	FGF23	Due to activating mutations in FGF23 leading to FGF23 protein resistant to degradation
(III) Hypophosphatemic rickets related to mutations causing primary renal tubular phosphate wasting (non-FGF23 mediated)		
Hereditary hypophosphatemic rickets and hypercalciuria	SLC34A3	Loss of function of NaPi2c in the proximal renal tubules
X-linked recessive hypophosphatemic rickets (Dent disease 1)	CLCN5	Loss of function of the CLCN5 in the proximal tubules
Hypophosphatemia and nephrocalcinosis	SLC34A1	Loss of function of NaPi2c in the proximal renal tubules
(IV) Various genetic causes of Fanconi syndrome include cystinosis, Lowe's syndrome, galactosemia and Wilson's disease. There are other features of Fanconi syndrome		

CYP27B1 Cytochrome P450 family 27 subfamily B member 1, *CYP2R1* Cytochrome P450 family 2 subfamily R member 1, *PHEX* Phosphate-regulating neutral endopeptidase homolog, *DMP1* Dentin matrix acidic phosphoprotein 1, *ENPP1* Ectonucleotide pyrophosphatase/phosphodiesterase 1, *FGF23* Fibroblast growth factor 23, *VDR* Vitamin D receptor, *SLC34A3* Solute carrier family 34 member 3, *SLC34A1* Solute Carrier family 34 member 1, *CLCN5* Chloride voltage-gated channel 5

Table 27.2 Conventional treatment for XLH with the standard dosage of oral phosphate and active vitamin D supplements

Medication	Dose	Complications
Phosphate	20–60 (max: 80 mg/kg/day) in 4–6 doses per day	Diarrhoea, gastrointestinal upset, secondary hyperparathyroidism
1,25-dihyroxy-vitamin D (calcitriol)	20–30 ng/kg/day in 2–3 doses, or 0.5–1.5 µg per day in twice divided doses	The dosage needs to be adjusted to maintain a normal PTH level and prevent hypercalciuria – In the case of hypercalciuria, the vitamin D dosage needs to be decreased – When the PTH level is elevated, either increase the active vitamin D dosage or decrease the phosphate dosage
1 (OH) vitamin D (alfacalcidol)	40–60 ng/kg/day, or 1–3 µg daily	

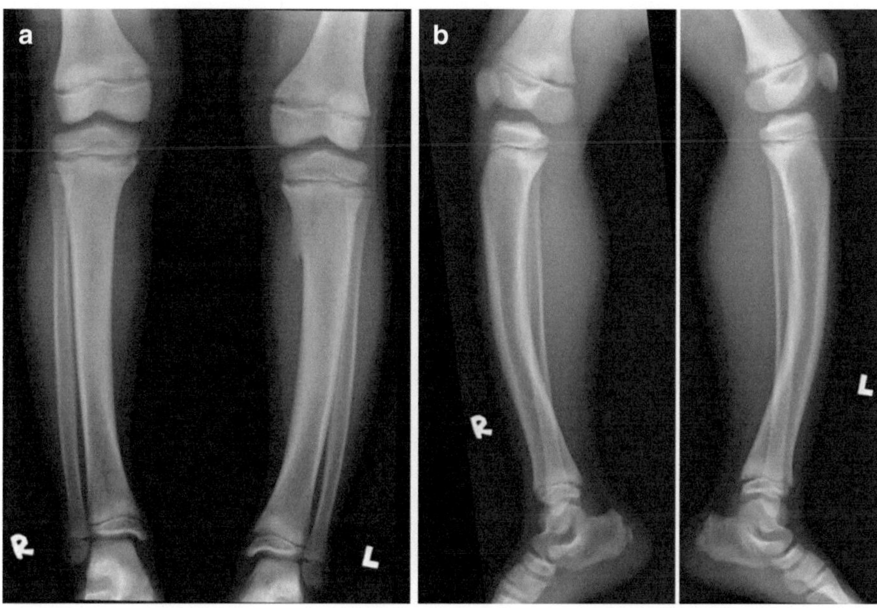

Fig. 27.1 (**a**) AP view of the X-rays of both distal femurs, tibias and fibulas, taken 1 year after conventional treatment. The bone density normalised. There was no metaphyseal fraying or spraying. The bowing of the tibias was still there. A small cortical outgrowth at the medial metaphysis of the left tibia could be an exostosis. (**b**) Lateral view of the right leg and left leg, respectively. They showed persistent anterior bowing of both tibias. Other radiological signs of rickets resolved

Dickson was treated with the conventional treatment since he was 3 years old. His serum alkaline phosphate level normalised, but serum phosphate was challenging to keep within the normal range. Skeletal X-rays taken 1 year later showed complete healing of the rickets, despite the mild bowing of the legs remained (Fig. 27.1). He has regular urine calcium and ultrasound kidney monitoring for any hypercalciuria and nephrocalcinosis yet, three years after conventional treatment, he started to have nephrocalcinosis and it progressed over the years.

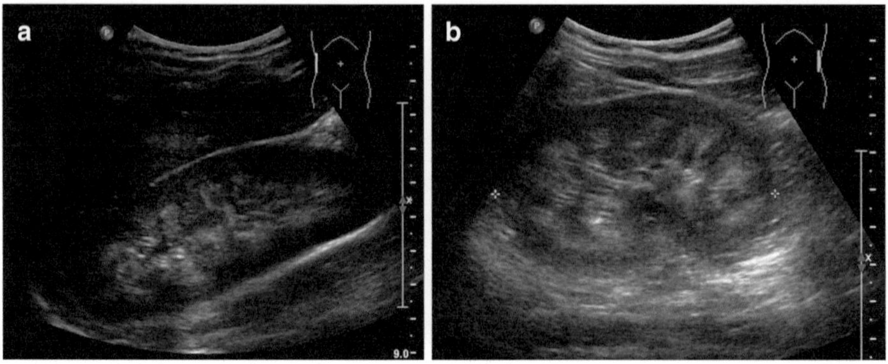

Fig. 27.2 Two USG images with (**a**) indicates the right kidney and (**b**) indicates the left kidney. In both images, the pyramids of the kidneys are diffusely echogenic suggesting bilateral medullary nephrocalcinosis

Figure 27.2 showed the bilateral medullary nephrocalcinosis in both kidneys of Dickson, after 8 years of conventional treatment, which caused significant hypercalciuria and secondary hyperparathyroidism.

What is Burosumab?
Burosumab is a fully humanised FGF23 antibody that antagonises the action of FGF23. With the availability of Burosumab, the management of children with XLH has changed in recent years. However, the high cost of Burosumab makes it unaffordable without insurance coverage or government funding.

List the precautions that need to be considered when prescribing burosumab

- If the patient is on calcitriol and phosphate treatment, these drugs should be stopped 1 week before starting burosumab.
- In children, the starting dose of burosumab is usually 0.8 mg/kg subcutaneously every 2 weeks and then titrated up to 2 mg/kg every 2 weeks, targeting to maintain a low to mid-normal serum phosphate concentration while avoiding hyperphosphatemia.
- The standard adult dose is 1 mg/kg every 4 weeks, with a maximum weight-based dose of 90 mg.
- Serial monitoring for serum phosphate, vitamin D metabolites, PTH, hypercalcemia and hypercalciuria is needed.
- The dose of burosumab has to be lowered when there is nephrocalcinosis or hypercalcemia.

Does burosumab replace the conventional treatment?
With a better understanding of FGF23' role in the pathogenesis of XLH and the development of burosumab as the targeted therapy, the most recent international guideline recommends burosumab over conventional treatment in XLH

children aged >1 year and even down to XLH children aged 6–12 months old. If burosumab is not available or accessible, conventional therapy is better than no treatment.

The clinical severity of XLH varies, and so does the response to conventional treatment. Both burosumab and conventional treatments show healing of rickets and normalisation of alkaline phosphatase, but with greater effect from burosumab. Most patients tolerate burosumab well, and the side effects include fever, myalgia, headache, cough and transient site reaction. Hypersensitivity reaction is rare. However, nephrocalcinosis is still a potential risk as hyperphosphatemia may occur, and 1,25-dihydroxyvitamin D level may increase.

In clinical practice, the effectiveness and complications of both treatment options, as well as the cost of burosumab, which is very expensive, need to be carefully discussed with the family. Different countries or health authorities may set different criteria for the use of burosumab.

Some recommended criteria for the use of burosumab in XLH children who are >1 year old includes

- There is radiographic evidence of overt bone disease or those with severe rickets.
- Disease that is refractory to conventional therapy.
- There are complications related to conventional therapy.
- Patient's inability to adhere to conventional therapy.

In general, it is reasonable to start conventional therapy in all children diagnosed with XLH to avoid delay in treatment while waiting for the financial support for Burosumab.

What is the prognosis and long-term management plan for Dickson?

Children with XLH often remain short with persistence of childhood skeletal abnormalities even when they reach adulthood. Chronic hypophosphatemia causes osteomalacia, and they may have related symptoms in adulthood. Some of the symptoms of XLH are typically present in adulthood. Hence, monitoring of these features and complications of medications is also necessary.

Long-term complications that need regular monitoring include the following:

- Musculoskeletal pain, bone pain associated with fracture or pseudo-fracture.
- Osteoarthritis.
- Enthesopathy.
- Dental diseases like dental abscesses and periodontal disease, which remain common in adult XLH.
- Nephrocalcinosis and possible impaired renal function (regular monitoring of serum calcium, urine calcium-creatinine ratio, renal function test, glomerular filtration rate and ultrasound kidney).
- Hypertension.
- Skeletal deformities that may require corrective osteotomies.
- Spinal stenosis.

- Hearing loss and tinnitus.
- Secondary hyperparathyroidism, and if tertiary hyperparathyroidism developed, a calcimimetic drug like cinacalcet may be considered, as once autonomy of parathyroid hormone is established, Burosumab will not normalise the PTH level.
- Specific features in XLH, like hearing impairment, craniosynostosis, Chiari malformation type 1 and intracranial hypertension, may be present and need medical attention.

27.3 Case Illustrations

By examining Dickson's case, we aim to shed light on the diverse causes of rickets and highlight the kidney's dual role: both as a contributor to the disease and as an organ susceptible to the side effects of standard treatments. X-linked hypophosphatemic rickets is the most common genetic cause of hypophosphatemic rickets in children. Although the previous treatment with phosphate and active vitamin D supplements is not ideal, they used to be the standard therapy, and they healed the rickets and improved bone growth. However, long-term complications, including nephrocalcinosis, are a concern, especially in adult patients. With the availability of burosumab, the targeted therapy, the management algorithm and outcome of this group of patients may change considerably.

Suggested Further Readings

1. Chanchlani R, Nemer P, Sinha R, Nemer L, Krishnappa V, Sochett E, et al. An overview of rickets in children. Kidney Int Rep. 2020;5(7):980–90.
2. Carpenter TO, Whyte MP, Imel EA, Boot AM, Högler W, Linglart A, et al. Burosumab therapy in children with X-linked hypophosphatemia. N Engl J Med. 2018;378(21):1987–98.
3. Ackah SA, Imel EA. Approach to hypophosphatemic rickets. J Clin Endocrinol Metabol. 2023;108(1):209–20.
4. Ali DS, Carpenter TO, Imel EA, Ward LM, Appelman-Dijkstra NM, Chaussain C, et al. X-linked hypophosphatemia management in children: an International Working Group Clinical Practice Guideline. J Clin Endocrinol Metabol. 2025;110(7):2055–70.

Part IV

Kidneys and the ICU

It Is Not Just RAS

28

28.1 Case Description

Emma is a 15-year-old young lady who presented to the accident and emergency department (AED) for the sudden onset of limb twitching with loss of consciousness, which lasted for 2–3 minutes. Emma has had a history of headaches for 6 months. The headache was dull in nature and bilateral over both occipital regions. There was no association with vomiting or vision disturbances. She had a decrease in appetite and a weight loss of 3–4 kg with night sweats in the past 3 months. The system review had no other significant history. When Emma was assessed at AED, her Glasgow coma scale (GCS) was 15, but she was tired-looking. She was afebrile, and her blood pressure (BP) by oscillometric method was 211/131 mmHg with a pulse rate of 120 bpm. Emma was then admitted to the intensive care unit for the management of hypertensive crisis. What might be causing her hypertension, and how can it be treated?

28.2 Interactive Case Discussion

What was your differential diagnosis?

Emma had a seizure with high blood pressure. We have to decide whether the high blood pressure causes the seizure or if there is an intracranial lesion that causes the high blood pressure and seizure. In a focused assessment, we would try to identify the following:

- Any features suggestive of chronic hypertension or pointing to an underlying cause of the hypertension.
- Any features of hypertensive-related end-organ damage that signify a hypertensive emergency and require immediate treatment.

W. K. Y. Chan, M. C. I. Kuok, *Paediatric Nephrology*,
https://doi.org/10.1007/978-981-95-5060-9_28

After resting for 15 minutes, Emma's blood pressure remained high. Her peripheral pulses were equally strong without radio-femoral delay. The cardiovascular examination was normal. Her kidneys were not palpable, but a bruit was apparent over the left paraumbilical region. Fundoscopic examination showed bilateral papilledema, but without retinal haemorrhage.

What are these physical signs suggestive of?
The papilledema in fundoscopic examination suggests a hypertensive emergency, and the bruit may indicate renal artery stenosis (RAS). If the blood test shows low serum potassium, then the likelihood of RAS will increase.

What could be the causes of the convulsion?
Given the hypertension and seizure, hypertensive encephalopathy and posterior reversible encephalopathy syndrome (PRES) are the possible diagnoses. PRES most commonly presents with visual disturbance, seizures and altered consciousness with typical radiological changes, especially over the occipital regions. The typical radiological findings of PRES inlcude symmetrical cortical and subcortical hyperintense signals on T2 and FLAIR-weighted MR images in the parieto-occipital lobes of both hemispheres.

Other possible causes for hypertension and seizure include cerebral vascular events, like intracranial haemorrhage, infarction and brain tumours, which a brain CT scan can quickly rule out. As Emma, has a GCS of 15/15, cerebral vascular events are unlikely.

What are the differences between hypertensive encephalopathy and PRES?
Hypertensive encephalopathy and PRES were first described at different historical times. They have several similarities in clinical presentations and overlap with cerebral hyperperfusion syndrome. Despite being described in various clinical scenarios, they share similar pathophysiological mechanisms with endothelial damage, cerebral vasoconstriction, blood-brain barrier disturbances and cerebral oedema.

The first blood test of Emma showed a serum sodium of 134 mmol/L, potassium 3.0 mmol/L, urea 7.6 mmol/L, creatinine 65 umol/L, ESR 40 mm/hr, C-reactive protein of 20 mg/L (normal <5 mg/L) and 24-hour urine protein was 0.12 g/day. Spot cortisol was 665 nmol/L (normal), and thyroid-stimulating hormone was 1.2 miu/L (normal). His chest X-ray showed a normal cardiothoracic ratio of 0.43. Her CT brain and MRI brain were also normal. Hence, hypertensive encephalopathy is likely the cause of her seizure.

How would you treat this patient?
As the patient has end-organ damage with markedly elevated blood pressure, she was managed as a hypertensive crisis with encephalopathy. The management principles would be the following:

1. Stepwise, lower the high blood pressure over 24–48 hours to the target blood pressure
2. Prevent further convulsions by starting anticonvulsant

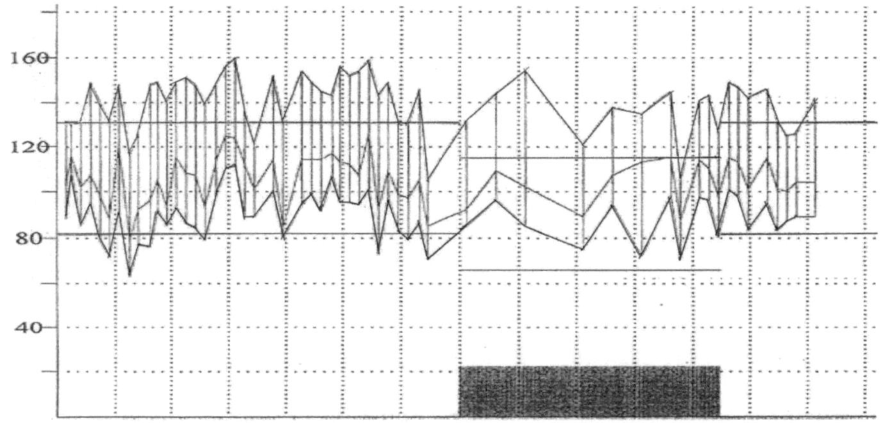

Fig. 28.1 The 24-hour blood pressure readings showed poor control of BP while Emma was taking amlodipine 10 mg daily, labetalol 200 mg q12h and aldactone 25 mg bd. The average 24-hour blood pressure was 139/88 mmHg, the MAP was 105 mmHg, the systolic BP load was 82.1% (majority of the SBP readings were above 130mmHg), and the DBP load was 82% (majority of DBP readings were above 80mmHg). The MAP showed a nocturnal dip of 2.9% only (non-dipping). SBP systolic blood pressure; DBP diastolic blood pressure; MAP mean arterial pressure

3. Work up the underlying causes of the hypertension
4. Assess the degree of end-organ damage and the possible reversibility of the damage

Labetalol infusion was started at 0.25 mg/kg/hr, and intravenous levetiracetam was started to prevent further convulsions. Her blood pressure dropped in a controlled manner, and she was then put on oral amlodipine 10 mg daily, labetalol 200 mg q12h and aldactone 25 mg twice daily. A 24-hour ambulatory blood pressure monitoring was performed (Fig. 28.1).

Her first ultrasound of the kidneys with a Doppler scan showed normal-sized kidneys. The proximal left main renal artery was not well visualised, but hemodynamically significant stenosis was not detected in those visualised segments of the main renal arteries. A captopril challenge DTPA scan was arranged. She omitted her morning dose of antihypertensive agents before her baseline Tc99m DTPA scintiscan, which was followed by an oral dose of captopril 25 mg. Blood pressure was measured every 15 minutes for one hour. While Emma was waiting for a rescan, she felt severe dizziness and fainted after taking the captopril. Her blood pressure dropped to 85/40 mmHg, which normalised after fluid resuscitation.

What is the Captopril Challenge test? What lessons can we learn from Emma?

The captopril challenge test is a non-invasive medical test that measures the changes in the blood flow between the kidneys (measured by the DTPA scan in this patient) after giving a standard dose of captopril. It is usually performed to diagnose renal artery stenosis.

When hemodynamically significant RAS is present, renal perfusion is reduced. The affected kidneys attempt to maintain adequate intrarenal perfusion by constricting the efferent arterioles. This autoregulation mechanism maintains the GFR, and routine isotope scans to detect renal perfusion may be normal. Captopril is a short-acting renin-angiotensin blocker which causes dilatation of the efferent arterioles, causing a decrease in the transcapillary pressure gradient, leading to a decrease but reversible deterioration in renal perfusion, which becomes easily detectable in the isotope scan.

Although Doppler ultrasonography can directly evaluate the renal arteries and kidney perfusion, it remains an operator-dependent procedure, and sometimes significant stenosis may not be detected even by skilful hands. Emma has a substantial drop in blood pressure to captopril; hence, the presence of RAS is highly suspected.

What are the contraindications and precautions for captopril DTPA scan in patients suspicious of RAS?

Before a Captopril DTPA scan, the patient has to be well hydrated and should stop antihypertensive drugs, especially ACEI, if possible. As the captopril challenge test reduces renal perfusion, it should be avoided in patients suspected of having bilateral RAS, as it may cause significant hypotension and even impair renal function. Luckily, our patient's renal function was not affected.

Emma's DTPA scan revealed a marked decrease in glomerular function of the left kidney before and after the captopril challenge. The right kidney also showed an abnormal renogram after captopril. These suggested bilateral renovascular stenosis. Plasma renin came back to be high at >10.5 ng/ml/hr (supine normal range: 0.51–2.64 ng/ml/hr) and plasma aldosterone 1689 pmol/L (supine normal range: <444 pmo/L). MR angiogram showed bilateral renal artery stenosis with smooth narrowing of the abdominal aorta (Fig. 28.2).

How did the MR abdominal aorta help you manage the patient?

The MR angiogram showed a narrowing of the abdominal aorta extending from the celiac to the infrarenal level, leading to bilateral RAS. Further assessment of the big branches from the aorta was needed. Different diagnoses include fibromuscular dysplasia (FMD) and other causes of aortitis. Given the raised inflammatory markers and significant weight loss in this patient, one has to be careful with underlying vasculitis.

The CT aortogram of Emma also detected stenosis over the lower cervical part of the left common carotid artery. Takayasu arteritis was then a more likely diagnosis than fibromuscular hyperplasia. Emma's autoimmune markers were negative, but her ESR and CRP remained high. A fluorodeoxyglucose PET (18FDG-PET) confirmed the inflammation in the vascular wall of the affected aorta and carotid artery. Her MT2 showed 10-mm induration with a positive interferon-gamma releasing assay, but her sputum AFB cultures were negative. Prophylactic isoniazid was started before commencement of steroid therapy.

Emma was treated with oral prednisolone at 0.8 mg/kg/day (40 mg daily) for 4 weeks and tapered off over 6 months before consideration of radiological intervention. Her repeated 18FDG-PET scan became normal. A renal arteriogram with percutaneous angioplasty was then performed. Her blood pressure was much better controlled after balloon angioplasty (Fig. 28.3). Her plasma renin dropped to 1.88 ng/ml/hr (erect normal range: 0.98–4.18) and aldosterone normalised at 334 pmol/L (erect normal range: 111–860 pmol/L).

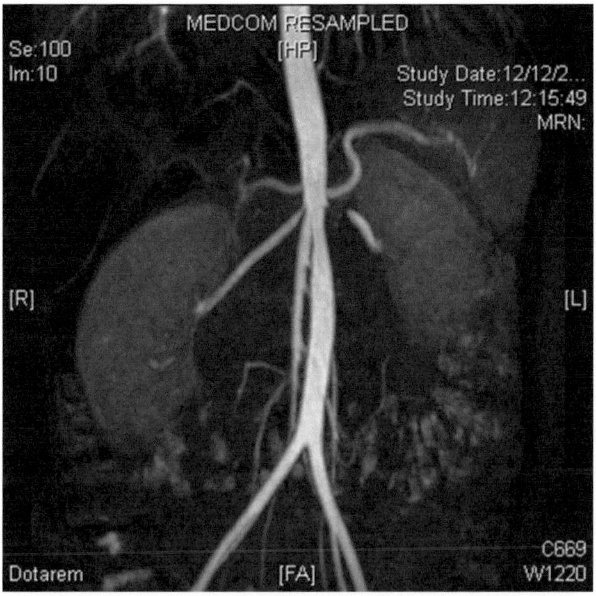

Fig. 28.2 MR arteriography with contrast: a short segment of moderate (~50%) stenosis at the proximal right main renal artery at the origin. This segment measured about 5 mm in length. There was a segment of severe stenosis (>70%) at the proximal left main renal artery at the origin. The narrowed segment measured about 9–10 mm in length. No beading appearance in both renal arteries was noted. There was a smooth narrowing of the abdominal aorta extending from the celiac to the infrarenal level (about 4.5 cm in length). The narrowest segment was at the infrarenal level (8 mm in calibre, 1.5 cm in length) and the proximal abdominal aorta measured 14 mm in calibre

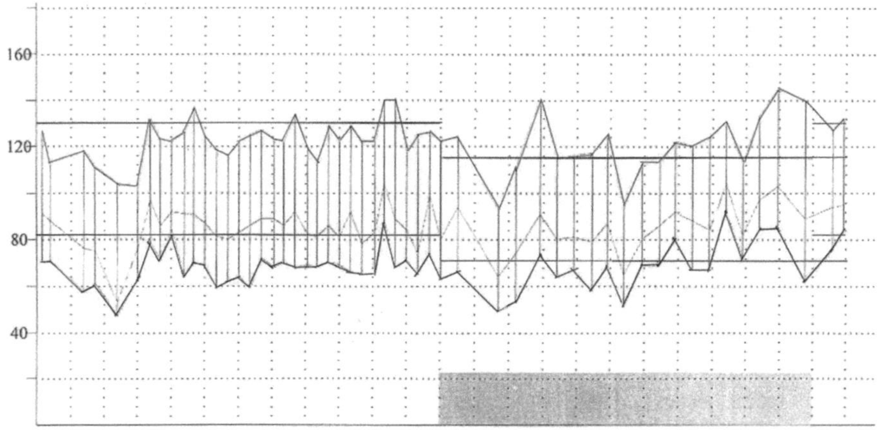

Fig. 28.3 After balloon angioplasty, the 24-hour BP graph showed significant improvement in BP control. The average BP dropped to 121/67 mmHg, MAP 84 mmHg, SBP load was 35.2%, and DBP load was 16.7%. There was no significant nocturnal dip in MAP. The patient was taking amlodipine 5 mg daily and labetalol 200 mg bid during the examination

What is the long-term care plan for Emma?

We have to monitor the long-term control and complications of hypertension and, simultaneously, the disease activity and control of the Takayasu arteritis.

For monitoring of blood pressure control and end-organ damage, she needs the following:

- Regular blood tests to assess the renal function, including eGFR
- Urine test for microalbuminuria
- Regular renal ultrasound and Doppler study to assess renal growth and the severity of RAS
- Regular renal perfusion scan to evaluate renal perfusion
- An echocardiogram to assess left ventricular hypertrophy
- Eye assessment for any retinopathy
- Regular 24-hour ambulatory blood pressure monitoring to determine control of her blood pressure

For monitoring the disease activity of Takayasu arteritis, she needs the following:

- Regular blood tests for inflammatory markers
- If there is suspicion of a relapse of disease with progressive aortitis or arteritis, a fluorodeoxyglucose PET (18FDG-PET)scan may be needed. MR angiogram has to be considered to assess the big vessels arising from the aortic arch, especially if clinically indicated.
- Second-line immunosuppressive therapy is likely needed for steroid-sparing and control of the disease.

28.3 Case Illustrations

Determining Emma's ultimate diagnosis was challenging. She presented with hypertensive crisis and end-organ damage, requiring urgent control of blood pressure in the intensive care unit. The hypertension was caused by bilateral renal artery stenosis, which was secondary to Takayasu arteritis. The initial low serum potassium and a positive abdominal bruit helped to make the diagnosis of RAS, and the elevated inflammatory markers suggested an underlying vasculitis.

Suggested Further Readings

1. Safian RD, Textor SC. Renal-artery stenosis. N Engl J Med. 2001;344(6):431–42.
2. Colbert GB, Abra G, Lerma EV. Update and review of renal artery stenosis. Dis Mon. 2021;67(6):101118.
3. Chen TH. Childhood posterior reversible encephalopathy syndrome: clinicoradiological characteristics, management, and outcome. Front Pediatr. 2020;8:585.

29 Hypertension and Low Salt

29.1 Case Description

Quinlee was a baby born prematurely at 30 weeks of gestation because of maternal pre-eclampsia. Her birth weight was 1.5 kg. She suffered from several complications of prematurity, including respiratory distress syndrome, which required surfactant therapy and ventilatory support. She also has a patent ductus arteriosus, which closed spontaneously without any medication. She has an episode of suspected necrotising enterocolitis and has been put on parental nutrition for several weeks. Because of the prematurity, an umbilical artery catheter (UAC) and an umbilical venous catheter (UVC) were inserted for close monitoring and intravenous nutrition. She was stable initially until she was 3 weeks old; her blood pressure was noticed to be on the high side and progressively increased to a mean blood pressure of 60–85 mmHg, systolic blood pressure up to 90–120 mmHg. Because of the hypertension, her UAC was removed and replaced by a peripheral arterial line.

29.2 Interactive Case Discussion

What are the normal processes of adaptation to the environment upon delivery, and how do they affect the blood pressure of preterm infants?
Blood pressure (BP) is determined by the systemic vascular resistance (SVR) and cardiac output (CO), i.e.

$$BP = SVR \times CO$$

As cardiac output depends on heart rate (HR) and stroke volume (SV)

$$BP = SVR \times HR \times SV$$

W. K. Y. Chan, M. C. I. Kuok, *Paediatric Nephrology*,
https://doi.org/10.1007/978-981-95-5060-9_29

At birth, with the first breath, there is a complex process for the cardiovascular system to adapt to the extrauterine environment, and a smooth transition is required for normal functioning of the newborn. These processes include the following:

- A decrease in the vascular resistance in the lung and peripheral tissue/organs.
- An increase in the systemic vascular resistance and the umbilical vessels. The heart has to pump against a higher pressure.
- Blood flow redirects from the placenta to the lung for oxygenation (increase pulmonary blood flow).
- The ductus arteriosus will close spontaneously.
- Because of the increased pressure in the right atrium, the foramen ovale will close functionally and then permanently.
- Initially, the blood flow to the kidney is low, but it increases over the first week of life as the vascular resistance in the kidneys drops, and urine output will increase accordingly when the glomerular filtration increases.

These processes require the interactions between various vasoconstricting and vasodilating substances, like the following:

- Prostaglandins
- Endothelin
- Nitric oxide
- Catecholamines
- Renin
- Vasopressin

In a preterm baby, other factors that occur during the perinatal period will also affect the blood pressure of the infant.

- The myocardium may have impaired contractility and function.
- The peripheral vascular beds may fail to decrease the vascular resistance.
- The fetal shunting pathways (ductus arteriosus and foramen ovale) may fail to close.
- The metabolic and endocrine response to the environment may not respond appropriately.

Hence, the blood pressure of infants changes significantly shortly after birth and in the initial few days and weeks after birth. The variation in blood pressure is more significant in preterm infants than in term infants.

What is the normal BP pattern observed after birth?
Blood pressure in a neonate depends on the gestation age, postnatal age, weight and medications used. There is a variation in defining hypotension and hypertension in neonates. For hypotension, a commonly used guide based on consensus suggested the minimum mean arterial pressure (MAP) equals the postmenstrual age in weeks.

Another proposed threshold for intervention is a MAP of less than 30 mmHg. However, in defining high blood pressure, there is a much broader variation in the range for 'normal blood pressure' as blood pressure changes over the initial 24 hours and the first few days after birth.

When a term infant is born, his blood pressure will increase over the first 24 hours and the first few days. After that, the normal BP will continue to rise slowly and steadily in the first 2 months post-delivery. Thereafter, the blood pressure will be more constant.

Premature infants and low birth weight infants are observed to have a period of rapid increase in BP during the early postnatal days and the first 1–2 weeks. The rise is more rapid in the more premature and lower birth weight infants. This apparent BP 'catch-up' period may represent a normal adaptation to the environmental changes, and when the BP catches up to that of a term infant, it will follow a similar pattern to that of the term infants.

How to measure blood pressure in a neonate?

As expected, an accurate blood pressure measurement is difficult in neonates and infants. The gold standard in measuring blood pressure is by direct intra-arterial BP measurement, and both the umbilical artery and the peripheral artery reflect similar blood pressure. However, intra-arterial BP is an invasive procedure that carries certain risks to the infant. Most BP measurements in neonates still rely on oscillometric machines, which are noninvasive and easy to use. Oscillometric machines measure the MAP and use the device-specific algorithms to calculate the systolic and diastolic blood pressure, respectively. The MAP of neonates is usually in the range of 30–50 mmHg. A deviation from this range requires further evaluation.

Infants' blood pressure is affected by the measurement techniques and their daily activities.

- Blood pressure will be higher when an infant is awake, during feeding, sucking and crying.
- Blood pressure will be higher when the infants are receiving painful or uncomfortable procedures like suctioning and heel prick procedures.
- BP taken from the arm is best correlated with the arterial pressure.
- Calf BP is similar and correlates well with the arm BP, especially in the first few days of life, but thereafter, the discrepancy will be higher.
- Choose an appropriate size and length of BP cuff to minimise erroneously high or low BP.

To obtain a reliable BP, it is advised to connect the BP cuff to the baby's right arm and allow her to settle before taking any measurement. After she is asleep or quietly awake, three consecutive measurements should be taken, and an average for the readings is suggested. If the first BP reading is unusually high, it can be discarded, and the average of the last two readings would be obtained.

Is hypertension a common problem in neonates?

Neonatal hypertension is uncommon and is mostly described in the neonatal intensive care units (NICUs). The incidence has been reported to be around 1–2% of the population. Data from the Assessment of Worldwide Acute Kidney Injury Epidemiology in Neonates (AWAKEN) cohort study reported an incidence of 1.8%. However, with the increase in survivors of premature babies and more awareness of the underdiagnosed infants, the incidence of neonatal hypertension would be expected to be higher than reported.

How to define hypertension in neonates?

Although there is a lack of robust normative data on blood pressure for both term and preterm infants, various reference BP tables are still available in the literature and can be used as a reference. The definition of hypertension in neonates is similar to that in older children. Hypertension in neonates is defined as persistent high BP >95th percentile for postmenstrual age.

- Infants with BP values >95th percentile need close monitoring.
- Infants with BP values >99th percentile require further investigations.
- Hypertensive infants with evidence of end-organ dysfunction require intravenous antihypertensive therapy.

What are the risk factors for neonatal hypertension?

There were many factors affecting the blood pressure in the neonate.

1. Genetic

   CYP2D6 CC genotype has been reported to be closely associated with higher BP in preterm infants.
2. Possible antenatal/maternal factors:
   - Maternal body mass index >30 kg/m^2
   - Maternal hypertension
   - Maternal drug use, such as steroids and substance abuse
   - Maternal chorioamnionitis, HELLP syndrome
   - Maternal smoking
3. Neonatal risk factors include the following:
   - Umbilical artery catheter insertion
   - Acute kidney injury due to various reasons
   - Chronic lung disease
   - Congenital renal disease, CAKUT
   - ECMO patients
   - Congenital heart disease, especially coarctation of the aorta

What are the causes of hypertension in neonates?

Renal artery thrombosis/stenosis, chronic lung disease and acute kidney injury are the three most common causes of hypertension in NICU. Renovascular hypertension in neonates is typically related to renal artery 'thrombus' formation after insertion of the umbilical artery, though fibromuscular dysplasia is still a possible differential diagnosis. In reality, identification of actual thrombus in the renal artery is only present in around 25% of cases. Although in the conventional practice, the tip of UAC is recommended to be placed in the thoracic aorta between the sixth and tenth ribs in the chest X-ray, there appears to be no relationship to the position of the UAC. Both 'high approach' and 'low approach' on the position of UAC carry similar risk in developing UAC thrombi. The reason for causing hypertension is believed to be related to endothelial damage during umbilical artery catheter insertion. The risk is higher in preterm babies and in those with a long duration of UAC placement.

There are other possible causes of hypertension in neonates and are listed in Table 29.1.

With the persistently high BP above the 99th percentile, Quinlee was diagnosed with hypertension. Her physical examination did not reveal any underlying cause. In reviewing the drug history, she was taking a low dose of caffeine and a standard dose of vitamin D supplement. A dose of dexamethasone was given to her mother shortly before delivery; otherwise, Quinlee did not receive any steroid therapy.

Alarmingly, Quinlee's blood test showed a sudden drop in serum sodium from 137 mmol/L to 126 mmol/L in 2 days. Serum chloride dropped from 99 mmol/L to 90 mmol/L (RI: 98–107 mmol/L), potassium remained stable at 3.6 mmol/L, serum

Table 29.1 Various causes of hypertension in neonates

	Causes of neonatal hypertension
Renovascular	Thromboembolism, related to UAC insertion Fibromuscular dysplasia Renal vein thrombosis Renal artery compression by an external mass
Renal	CAKUT, unilateral MCDK Renal hypoplasia Polycystic kidney disease (ARPKD, ADPKD) Acute kidney injury due to various causes Cortical necrosis Obstructive uropathy: posterior urethral valve, ureteropelvic junction obstruction
Pulmonary	Bronchopulmonary dysplasia
Cardiac	Coarctation of the aorta, ECMO-related hypertension
Endocrine	Congenital adrenal hyperplasia—11 β hydroxylase deficiency Hyperaldosteronism, pseudohypoaldosteronism type II Hyperthyroidism
Malignancy	Wilms tumour, neuroblastoma, mesoblastic nephroma, pheochromocytoma
Drugs	Dexamethasone, caffeine, vitamin D intoxication, theophylline, phenylephrine eye drops, pancuronium and neonatal abstinence syndrome Salt and fluid overload from parenteral nutrition
Neurological	Seizure, intracranial hypertension, subdural hematoma
Idiopathic	No pathological cause identified

CAKUT congenital anomalies of the kidney and urinary tract, *ARPKD* Autosomal recessive polycystic kidney disease, *ADPKD* Autosomal dominant polycystic kidney disease, *ECMO* Extracorporeal membrane oxygenation, *MCDK* Multicystic dysplastic kidney

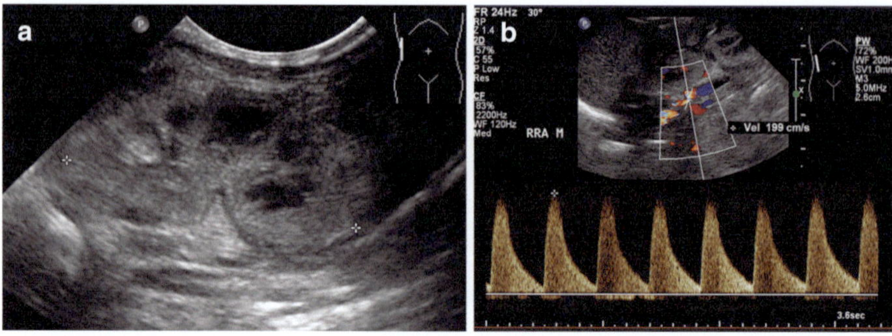

Fig. 29.1 Ultrasound images of the right kidney. (**a**) The greyscale image showed the right kidney was smaller in size (4.2 cm in length) with increased cortical echogenicity. (**b**) The colour Doppler ultrasound showed a focal aliasing (a region with high velocity) detected at the middle segment of the right main renal artery. The peak systolic velocity (PSV) was markedly elevated at 199 cm/s

calcium was stable at 2.4 mmol/L, phosphate 1.4 mmol/L, spot cortisol was 373 nmo/L (normal), renin rose to >35 ng/ml/hr (RI: 2.4–35 ng/ml/hr), aldosterone elevated to 3113 pmol/L (RI: 56–1943 pmol/L), and urine sodium excretion was 85 mmol/L with FeNa 7.5%. Her echocardiogram was normal with no coarctation of the aorta. An ultrasound of the kidney with Doppler examination was performed.

The left kidney was 4.7 cm long with normal echogenicity. The right kidney was 4.2 cm long with an increase in echogenicity. The Doppler ultrasound of the kidneys showed increased flow velocity over the right renal artery, whereas the left side was normal. A diagnosis of right renal artery stenosis was made (Fig. 29.1).

What are the causes of hypertension with hyponatremia?

Concurrent hypertension and hyponatremia can occur in certain clinical conditions like the following:

- Acute kidney injury or chronic kidney disease of various causes
- Malignant hypertension
- Renin-secreting tumour
- Hyponatremia secondary to the usage of antihypertensive medication like diuretics
- Renal ischemia causes hyperreninemia and activation of the renin-angiotensin-aldosterone system (RAAS). Renal artery stenosis is usually the underlying cause and has been described as the cause of hyponatremic hypertensive syndrome
- Intracranial lesions causing hypertension and inappropriate antidiuretic hormone secretion

Hyponatremic hypertensive syndrome (HHS) is a disorder of severe hypertension with hyponatremia. It is usually a result of any cause that triggers a high renin secretion. Renal artery stenosis and renin-secreting tumour are the two most common aetiologies. Hyponatremic hypertension syndrome has been well described in adult patients with unilateral renal artery stenosis, but reports in children and neonates are scanty and probably underreported.

The typical features of hyponatremic hypertension syndrome are hyperreninemic hypertension and natriuretic hyponatremia. The associated clinical features include hypokalaemia, polyuria and proteinuria. The intravascular volume of the patient is depleted. In hypertension caused by intracranial haemorrhage or intracranial lesion, the hyponatremia is secondary to fluid retention by the secretion of antidiuretic hormone. Instead of polyuria and volume depletion, the patient will have low urine output and high intravascular volume.

Although the exact pathophysiology of HHS is not well understood, sequences of events have been proposed in the literature.

- When a kidney with renal artery stenosis suffers from critical renal ischemia, it stimulates renin secretion and causes a sudden rise in arterial blood pressure.
- The high blood pressure will induce a pressure natriuretic effect in the normal kidney, causing polyuria and sodium loss.
- The decrease in intravascular volume further triggers renin secretion, then angiotensin II and aldosterone, intensifying the vicious cycle.
- Hypokalaemia will occur when there is hyperaldosteronism.
- Hyponatremia continue to get worse as volume depletion will trigger the secretion of antidiuretic hormone and intensify the direct effect of angiotensin II on the kidney to retain free water.

Proof of the sequence of these events will be difficult, yet it provides a plausible explanation.

Back to Quinlee's medical problem, she was managed with the following:

- Blood pressure control: Initially with intravenous hydralazine (vasodilator) and amlodipine (calcium channel blocker).
- Because of the polyuria, her volume state was resuscitated with volume and sodium replacement.

Her electrolytes and urine output normalised as her blood pressure was better controlled. At last, she was discharged from the NICU uneventfully with oral antihypertensive agents.

On subsequent ultrasound follow-up, her right kidney remained small. The left kidney thrived normally (Fig. 29.2).

What is the prognosis for Quinlee's renal problem?

Quinlee is at risk of developing early-onset hypertension, despite being able to take off antihypertensive medications at around 1 year old. Her risk factors for early hypertension include the following:

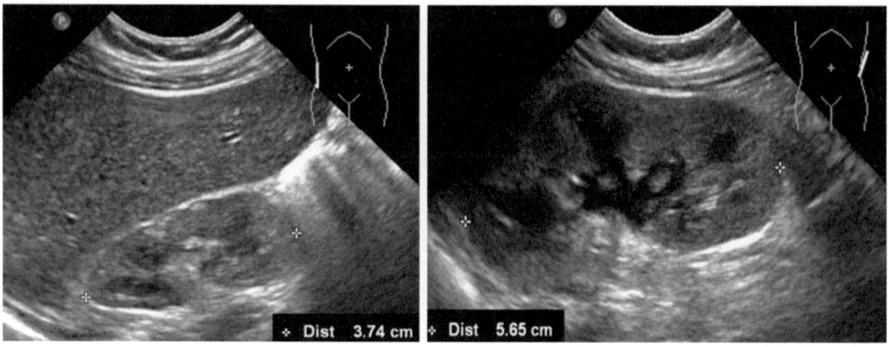

Fig. 29.2 Follow-up ultrasound 6 months later showed shrinkage in size of the right kidney, which measured 3.74 cm in length. The left kidney measured 5.65 cm in length and showed normal growth with compensatory hypertrophy

- Prematurity
- History of right renal artery stenosis with renal ischemia
- An ischemic right kidney which does not grow normally

Long-term follow-up for her blood pressure, proteinuria, renal function and renal growth is needed.

29.3 Case Illustrations

By reviewing Quinlee's case history, we explore the challenges of defining hypertension in premature infants and outline a stepwise approach to identifying its causes. Hypertension associated with profound hyponatremia is an uncommon disorder. When it occurs, we have to raise the suspicion of unilateral renovascular hypertension. Renal artery stenosis can be a complication of umbilical artery catheterisation in newborns. Apart from causing hypertension and electrolyte changes, the obstructed renal perfusion may affect the growth of the affected kidney. Long-term follow-up for their renal function, subsequent hypertension and proteinuria is needed.

Suggested Further Readings

1. Batton B. Neonatal blood pressure standards: what is "normal"? Clin Perinatol. 2020;47(3):469–85.
2. Sharma D, Farahbakhsh N, Shastri S, Sharma P. Neonatal hypertension. J Matern Fetal Neonatal Med. 2017;30(5):540–50.
3. Flynn J. Neonatal hypertension: diagnosis and management. In: Nephrology and fluid/electrolyte physiology. Elsevier; 2019. p. 255–70.
4. Starr MC, Flynn JT. Neonatal hypertension: cases, causes, and clinical approach. Pediatr Nephrol. 2019;34(5):787–99.

She Has Difficulty in Breathing

30

30.1 Case Description

Sumaira was born at 32 weeks by emergency caesarean section for fetal stress. The family was a new immigrant, and from the medical history, antenatal ultrasound showed polyhydramnios with an amniotic fluid index up to 50, which is twice the upper limit of normal. Intervention by amnioreduction therapy has been performed twice before the delivery. A fetal detail scan performed at 21 weeks of gestation did not detect any underlying cause for the polyhydramnios. Sumaira's birth weight was 2 kg, and the Apgar score was 6 at 1 min and 9 at 5 min. Sumaira developed repeated desaturation despite being put on nasal oxygen; hence, she was admitted to the intensive care unit and managed with continuous positive airway pressure support (CPAP). A CXR and an AXR were taken. The reported history of polyhydramnios raises concerns. What underlying conditions could explain Sumaira's respiratory distress?

30.2 Interactive Case Discussion

What did the CXR and AXR show?
The CXR and AXR films below were shown from a posterior-anterior view (Fig. 30.1a) and a cross-table lateral view (Fig. 30.1b). A right upper quadrant abdominal mass was suspected in both films.

Sumaira developed grunting at 6 hours of life, which required invasive ventilatory support and a dose of surfactant was given. Her abdomen was severely distended, which made ventilation challenging despite her RDS being only mild. An urgent USG examination was performed on days 1 and then 2 weeks after birth to monitor her condition.

W. K. Y. Chan, M. C. I. Kuok, *Paediatric Nephrology*,
https://doi.org/10.1007/978-981-95-5060-9_30

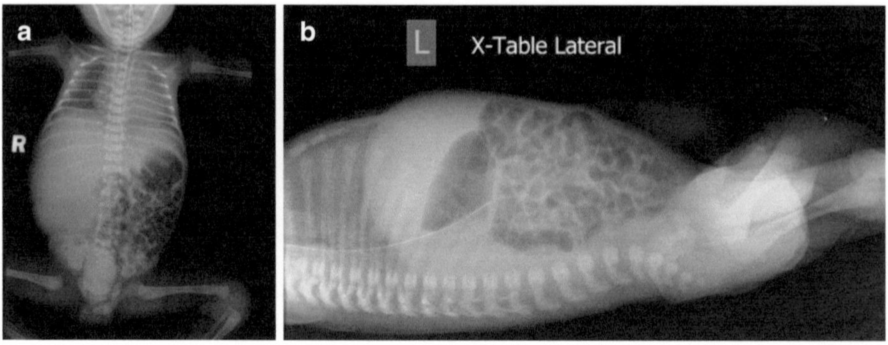

Fig. 30.1 (**a**) AXR and CXR taken after birth showed Grade 1 respiratory distress syndrome (RDS)and an opacity, suggesting a mass over the right side of the abdomen, displacing the bowel loop to the left side. There was no calcification over the mass (**b**) Cross-table lateral view showed similar opacity over the upper part of the abdomen. No calcification was noted in this view either

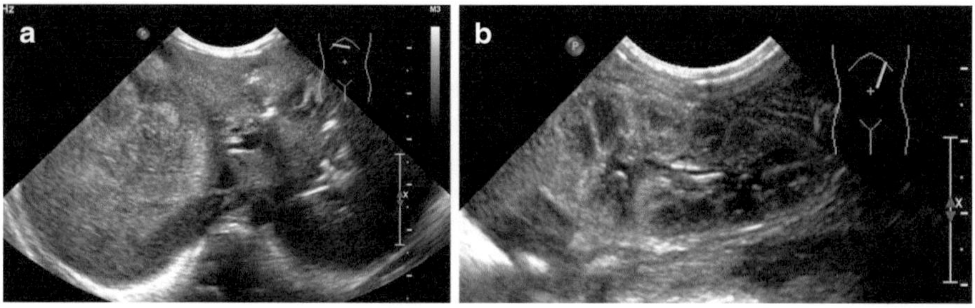

Fig. 30.2 (**a**) The USG kidney showed a 5.4-cm × 4.9-cm solid mass in the right upper quadrant of the abdomen displacing the right kidney. There was no crossing of midline, and inferiorly, the mass extended to the level of the iliac bone. There were no hyperechoic foci with shadows to suggest calcification. There were no ascites and no enlarged lymph nodes. There was no liver mass (**b**) The USG left kidney was normal in size with normal corticomedullary differentiation

What did the ultrasound show?

The USG showed a mass rising from the right kidney replacing most of the normal renal tissue, and the left kidney was normal (Fig. 30.2).

What was the most likely diagnosis?

The diagnosis is most likely a renal tumour, despite a considerable adrenal mass, such as neuroblastoma, that may displace the kidney like that.

What are the differential diagnoses for neonatal renal tumours?

Neonatal renal tumours are extremely rare, especially renal tumours that likely presented in utero, leading to polyhydramnios. Despite the widespread use of antenatal ultrasound to evaluate fetal growth and detect fetal abnormalities, only around 15% of renal masses were identified antenatally, with the remaining cases discovered postnatally as renal masses or associated abnormalities.

What are the clinical presentations of neonatal renal tumours?
As antenatal ultrasound only detected around 15% of renal tumours, the majority of patients present in the postnatal period as follows:

1. Nonspecific symptoms like pallor, vomiting, lethargy, abdominal distension and failure to thrive. Extreme cases may present after delivery, such as hydrops fetalis, respiratory distress and circulatory decompensation due to a huge abdominal mass.
2. Specific symptoms like abdominal mass, haematuria and hypertension.
3. Coexisting syndrome or abnormalities like Aniridia, Beckwith-Wiedemann syndrome, Denys-Drash syndrome and Simpson-Golabi-Behmel syndrome.

What are the types of fetal and neonatal renal tumours, and what is the most likely diagnosis for the renal tumour in Sumaira?
In the first year of life, the principal kidney neoplasms include Wilms tumour (WT), congenital mesoblastic nephroma (CMN) and rhabdoid tumour of the kidney (RTK). Although Wilms tumour is the most common renal malignancy of childhood, accounting for almost 90% of paediatric renal tumours, congenital mesoblastic nephroma is the most common renal neoplasm in neonates and the perinatal period (Table 30.1).

Sumaira had her USG repeated at 2 weeks old and confirmed a large infiltrative renal mass, measuring 70 mm × 57 mm × 67 mm, occupying the central sinus of the right kidney, causing dilatation and displacement of the renal calyces. The mass showed a heterogeneous echo pattern with internal vascularity, and it crossed the midline. The aorta and the IVC, which lie posteriorly, were patent. The right renal vein could not be visualised, but both renal arteries were patent. There was no aliasing or dampened waveform to suggest renal artery stenosis. The adrenal glands were normal. The diagnosis was a primary renal tumour, likely a congenital mesoblastic nephroma.

Sumaira's initial blood test showed a sky-high α-fetoprotein level of 327,711 iu/ml and β-HCG of 92 iu/L. Her serum urea and creatinine were normal, sodium and potassium were normal, but serum calcium was persistently high at 3.0–3.2 mmol/L, and the parathyroid hormone was suppressed to <0.5 pmol/L. Her blood pressure was high at 110/70 mmHg, with plasma renin elevated to 147 ng/ml/hr (RI: 2–35 ng/ml/hr) and aldosterone 23,846 pmol/L (RI: 190–5100 pmol/L). Urine catecholamines, adrenaline, noradrenaline, dopamine and metabolites were within normal range.

How would you explain the hypertension and hypercalcemia in Sumaira?
The elevated serum renin and aldosterone can explain Sumaira's hypertension. Hypertension is also observed in other renal tumours and is not specific to CMN; however, hypertension in patients with CMN is secondary to renin secretion from the entrapped juxtaglomerular cells. Sumaira's blood pressure was subsequently in reasonable control with oral captopril.

Hypercalcaemia has been described as a paraneoplastic phenomenon due to the secretion of parathyroid hormone-related protein (PTHrP) or prostaglandins. In

Table 30.1 The different types of perinatal and neonatal renal tumours

Tumour type	Classification	Clinical features
Congenital mesoblastic nephroma (CMN)	– Classic mesoblastic nephroma (one-third of cases) – Cellular mesoblastic nephroma (increased incidence of recurrence and metastasis) – Mixed classic and cellular	– It is the most common renal tumour in the neonatal period and the first 3 months of age. – None reported after 2 years of age. – All variants are generally benign in nature. – Primary surgical resection by radical nephroureterectomy is the mainstay of treatment. – The outcome is generally excellent, with event-free survival of 95% quoted.
Wilms tumour (WT)	– Triphasic – Blastemal – Epithelial (monomorphous) – Fetal rhabdomyomatous	– The most common renal tumour in childhood. – The second most common renal tumour presenting in the neonatal population. – Half of the patients present with an abdominal mass, which may be indistinguishable from CMN. – Findings of tumour thrombus in the inferior vena cava or renal vein will be more suggestive of WT than CMN. – May be associated with the congenital syndrome include WAGR, Denys-Drash and Beckwith-Wiedemann. – Hypertension is due to excess renin production directly by the tumour cells. – Treatment is mainly surgical removal and postoperative chemotherapy. – The prognosis depends on the staging of the disease and any related syndromal diagnosis. – In general, neonatal WT has a good prognosis with event-free survival of around 85%.
Nephroblastomatosis complex		– The persistence of metanephric blastema beyond 36 weeks of gestation. – It is also seen in a variety of syndromes associated with renal tumour development. – A pre-malignant tumour may not need prophylactic treatment.

(continued)

Table 30.1 (continued)

Tumour type	Classification	Clinical features
Cystic renal tumour	– Cystic nephroma (multilocular cyst) – Cystic partially differentiated nephroblastoma – Cystic Wilm's tumour	– It may be challenging to differentiate the different types of cystic renal tumours without a histological examination after the excision of the cystic lesions. – Surgical removal is the treatment option.
Rhabdoid tumour of the kidney		– Malignant rhabdoid tumour of the kidney is very rare. Histologically resembles rhabdomyosarcoma. – It may be associated with chromosomal deletion. – Poor outcome, especially in the presence of metastases, as it is relatively chemoresistant.

some cases, hypercalcemia may be symptomatic and require urgent treatment, but it typically resolves when the tumor is removed. Elevated serum calcium does not have any prognostic significance; however, it can be followed up as a tumour marker for individual patient.

What were the treatment options for Sumaira?

The mainstay of treatment for congenital mesoblastic nephroma was surgical resection of the tumour with radical nephrectomy, followed by monitoring with serial imaging. Most typical CMN are low-grade tumours, and metastases are uncommon. Adjuvant chemotherapy is generally reserved for children with high-stage disease or cellular subtype of CMN or patients with evidence of recurrence. Chemotherapeutic agents include cyclophosphamide, vincristine, dactinomycin and doxorubicin. The role of radiotherapy has yet to be clearly established.

What was the prognosis of Sumaira?

The outcome of a child with a renal tumour depends on the type of tumour, maturity and condition of the patient. In general, neonates with renal tumours have an excellent prognosis due to their low stage at presentation and more favourable biological features. Most neonates are cured by surgery alone and may be able to avoid cytotoxic chemotherapy, except when there is bilateral renal involvement.

Sumaira was successfully extubated 1 week after birth. She finally underwent a radical right nephrectomy. She was doing well afterwards and thrived satisfactorily with normal renal function. She was regularly followed up for any disease recurrence, and her renal function and blood pressure were closely monitored.

30.3 Case Illustrations

This case illustrates an uncommon cause of an enlarged kidney in the newborn. Despite being rare, renal tumours like congenital mesoblastic nephroma can present during the prenatal and postnatal periods. Careful physical examination helps detect the abnormally enlarged kidney promptly and allows for the early resection of the tumour. Using this case history, we guide readers through the approach to neonatal renal tumors. We also explain the causes of hypertension and the paraneoplastic phenomenon of hypercalcemia in Sumaira.

Suggested Further Readings

1. Sze SGK. Neonatal renal tumors. Clin Perinatol. 2021;48(1):71–81.
2. Isaacs H Jr. Fetal and neonatal renal tumors. J Pediatr Surg. 2008;43(9):1587–95.

Pneumonia Beyond the Lungs

31

31.1 Case Description

Henry, a 2.5-year-old boy, presented with a 4-day history of fever and cough. He had been seen by a general practitioner and was prescribed oral antibiotics and antipyretics. On the morning of admission, he developed shortness of breath and was brought to the hospital. On examination, he was febrile with a temperature of 39.7 °C, appeared pale and exhibited marked subcostal insucking with a respiratory rate of 72 breaths per minute. Chest auscultation revealed reduced air entry over the right lung field, accompanied by stony dullness on percussion. An urgent chest X-ray confirmed right-sided pneumonia with significant pleural effusion (Fig. 31.1). Laboratory investigations showed a haemoglobin level of 6.9 g/dL, a platelet count of 18×10^9/L and an elevated white cell count of 20.1×10^9/L, which was neutrophil predominant. Renal function tests revealed an elevated urea level of 10.7 mmol/L and a creatinine level of 143 μmol/L.

31.2 Interactive Case Discussion

What are the likely underlying causes of the biochemical and haematological derangements?

Henry had significantly impaired kidney function with an estimated glomerular filtration rate (GFR) of 23 ml/min/1.73 m^2. Development of acute kidney injury (AKI) in these contexts is usually multifactorial, with contributing factors such as sepsis, shock with hypoperfusion, dehydration due to poor oral intake and possible drug-induced nephrotoxicity. The combination of pneumonia, AKI, anaemia and thrombocytopenia in Henry's laboratory findings raises clinical suspicion for haemolytic uraemic syndrome (HUS), potentially secondary to *Streptococcus pneumoniae* infection. An alternative differential diagnosis is disseminated intravascular coagulation (DIC) with organ dysfunction.

W. K. Y. Chan, M. C. I. Kuok, *Paediatric Nephrology*,
https://doi.org/10.1007/978-981-95-5060-9_31

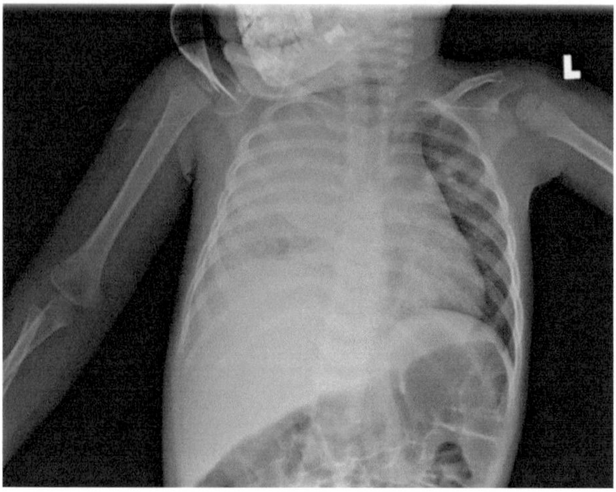

Fig. 31.1 Chest X-ray showing right-sided pneumonia with pleural effusion

What is haemolytic uraemic syndrome?

HUS is a form of thrombotic microangiopathy (TMA) characterised by a classical triad of (i) the presence of microangiopathic haemolytic anaemia (MAHA), (ii) thrombocytopenia and (iii) acute kidney injury. Schistocytes (fragmented red blood cells) seen on a peripheral blood smear are a key indicator of microangiopathic haemolysis. Additional laboratory evidence of haemolysis includes elevated serum indirect bilirubin and lactate dehydrogenase (LDH) levels, with a decreased serum haptoglobin concentration.

What are the different causes of HUS?

'Typical' HUS, also known as diarrhoea-associated or diarrhoea-positive HUS, is classically linked to infections with Shiga toxin-producing *Escherichia coli* (STEC) and *Shigella dysenteriae*. This form of HUS mainly affects children under 5 years old and typically presents 5–10 days after the onset of gastrointestinal symptoms, including bloody diarrhoea. It remains the most common cause of paediatric HUS in many European countries. In contrast, *Streptococcus pneumoniae*-associated HUS (SpHUS) is the more frequently encountered in our locality and many Asian cities.

Other acquired causes of HUS include the following:

- Drug-induced HUS, associated with medications such as cyclosporin, tacrolimus, quinine and some cytotoxic drugs
- Infectious causes such as HIV
- Autoimmune disease-related, such as systemic lupus erythematosus and antiphospholipid syndrome

Hereditary forms of HUS are linked to the following:

- Mutations in complement regulatory genes
- Inborn errors of cobalamin C metabolism
- Mutations in the DGKE (diacylglycerol kinase epsilon) gene

What is the epidemiology and clinical pattern of SpHUS?
The reported annual incidence of SpHUS is estimated at 0.4–0.6% following invasive pneumococcal infections. However, it is likely underestimated due to limited clinical and diagnostic awareness. Although the introduction of pneumococcal conjugate vaccines has reduced the incidence of invasive pneumococcal diseases, the burden of SpHUS remains high. Some epidemiological studies have reported a rising trend in SpHUS in certain countries, highlighting the need for continued surveillance and clinical vigilance.

SpHUS affects boys and girls equally and is more commonly encountered in children under 2 years old. Clinically, SpHUS often occurs in the setting of complicated pneumonia with parapneumonic empyema. It may also occur in patients with pneumococcal meningitis, but is rarely seen in cases of isolated *Streptococcus pneumoniae* bacteraemia. Symptoms of SpHUS typically develop between 3 and 13 days (most frequently 7–9 days) after the onset of infection symptoms. Serotypes 3 and 19A are the most common serotypes associated with SpHUS.

What is the pathogenesis of SpHUS?
The pathogenesis of SpHUS has classically been explained by the action of pneumococcal neuraminidase. Thomsen-Friedenreich antigen (T-antigen), normally present on the surfaces of erythrocytes, platelets and glomerular endothelial cells, is typically hidden by a coating of neuraminic acid. *Streptococcus pneumoniae* bacteria can express neuraminidases, encoded by three genes (nanA, nanB and nanC), which cleave neuraminic acid from glycoproteins and glycolipids, exposing the previously hidden T-antigen. Naturally occurring anti-T IgM antibodies in the host then bind to these exposed antigens, which initiate a cascade of haemolysis, platelet consumption, as well as endothelial injury in the glomeruli, leading to acute kidney injury.

Although this pneumococcal neuraminidase activity mechanism is well supported, recent studies also suggest that it may not fully account for the pathophysiology of SpHUS. Additional contributing factors, such as complement pathway dysregulation, have been increasingly recognised in SpHUS as a host factor. There is evidence of reduced complement levels in some patients, reflecting complement activation and consumption during the active phase, which tend to normalise during the recovery. Specifically, the loss of endothelial surface sialic acid due to neuraminidase activity impairs the binding of Factor H, a key regulator of the alternative complement pathway. This diminished regulation promotes uncontrolled complement activation and subsequent tissue injuries. Furthermore, genetic predispositions affecting complement regulation have also been proposed, with some patients demonstrating inherited variants in complement-related genes, potentially increasing susceptibility to HUS in pneumococcal infections.

Other mechanisms, such as pneumococcal surface protein C (PspC), have been implicated in the pathogenesis, although its exact role remains under investigation. Overall, the development of SpHUS is likely multifactorial, involving a complex interplay of bacterial virulence factors and host immune responses. Further studies are ongoing to elucidate these mechanisms at the cellular and molecular levels.

How can HUS be differentiated from disseminated intravascular coagulation (DIC) in cases of Streptococcus pneumoniae sepsis?

Disseminated intravascular coagulation is characterised by systemic activation of the coagulation cascade, leading to microvascular thrombus formation, consumption of coagulation factors and potentially multi-organ dysfunction. Both HUS and DIC can present with overlapping features, including microangiopathic haemolytic anaemia, thrombocytopenia and AKI, making the differentiation challenging. Importantly, the two conditions may also occur concurrently in some patients; thus, a high index of suspicion is needed for a diagnosis of SpHUS.

There are some distinguishing features which can help guide the diagnosis. DIC typically presents with prolonged prothrombin time (PT) and activated partial thromboplastin time (APTT), with low fibrinogen levels due to consumptive coagulopathy. In contrast, coagulation parameters in SpHUS are generally normal or only mildly deranged.

Additional diagnostic clues for SpHUS include direct Coomb's test and T-antigen activation tests. A positive direct Coomb's test reflects the binding of anti-T IgM antibodies to erythrocytes, consistent with T-antigen exposure following neuraminidase activity. The T-antigen activation test provides more specific evidence of this mechanism. Positive results for both tests are highly suggestive of SpHUS in the setting of invasive pneumococcal diseases. These tests are positive only in SpHUS, and not in other forms of HUS.

Henry was intubated and started on mechanical ventilation for respiratory support. A chest drain was inserted to manage his significant pleural effusion. He received antibiotic therapy, including penicillin G infusion and meropenem. Clinically, he remained oliguric and showed signs of progressive fluid overload. His serum creatinine increased further to 240 μmol/L, and his haemoglobin level dropped significantly to 3 g/dL. A peripheral blood smear revealed the presence of schistocytes, indicating microangiopathic haemolysis. Both the direct Coombs test and the T-antigen activation test returned positive, supporting a diagnosis of SpHUS.

What are the possible risks for blood transfusion in these patients?

In patients with SpHUS, there is a theoretical risk associated with blood transfusion due to the presence of naturally occurring anti-T IgM antibodies in usual blood products. These antibodies may bind to exposed T-antigens on erythrocytes and endothelial cells, potentially exacerbating haemolysis and tissue damage. Therefore, washed blood products with removal of plasma from packed cell and platelet concentrate are preferable when transfusion is indicated. However, preparation of washed components can be time-consuming and may not be immediately available in some clinical settings. In urgent or life-threatening situations, such as active bleeding, haemodynamic instability or need for emergency procedures, the benefits of transfusing unwashed blood products may outweigh the theoretical risks, and transfusion should not be delayed. Clinical decisions should be made on a case-by-case basis, and post-transfusion cell counts should be monitored.

What are the treatment options for his condition?

Initial management focuses on supportive care for septic shock and respiratory failure. These include fluid resuscitation and inotropic support for haemodynamic instability, mechanical ventilation and chest drain insertion for respiratory failure and significant pleural effusions, and appropriate antimicrobial therapy according to the clinical suspicion and local bacterial resistance patterns.

In managing AKI, close monitoring of fluid balance and electrolytes is crucial to prevent volume overload and further renal insults. Nephrotoxic medications should be avoided, and drug dosing should be adjusted based on the patient's renal function. Early anticipation for kidney replacement therapy (KRT) is essential, as fluid overload is significantly associated with increased mortality. Emerging evidence suggests that haemoadsorption therapies may provide adjunctive benefits in paediatric septic shock by removing circulating inflammatory cytokines, thereby stabilising haemodynamics and reducing the risk of organ damage.

Regarding SpHUS specifically, plasmapheresis can theoretically remove anti-T antibodies and neuraminidase. However, its benefit has not been substantially proven in clinical studies, and the current evidence offers only a weak recommendation (Grade 2C) according to the American Society for Apheresis. It should be noted that when plasmapheresis is considered in children with SpHUS, the use of plasma-free replacement fluids is recommended to avoid inadvertent transfer of anti-T antibodies from the donor plasma.

Given the increasing recognition of complement dysregulation in SpHUS, eculizumab has been reported as a potential therapeutic option. Eculizumab is a humanised monoclonal antibody which inhibits the cleavage of C5, thereby blocking the formation of proinflammatory C5a and the terminal complement complex C5b-9. Case reports have demonstrated rapid improvements in haematological parameters and renal function following eculizumab administration, which facilitate the weaning of kidney replacement therapy. Currently, there is a lack of well-designed clinical trials evaluating the efficacy of eculizumab in these patients. Therefore, the clinical decision should be individualised with a careful balance of benefits and potential risks.

Henry's pleural fluid PCR testing showed *Streptococcus pneumoniae* serotype 19A. He received continuous kidney replacement therapy for 7 days, during which there was a gradual improvement in renal function, and his urine output returned to normal. He was followed up in our outpatient clinic after discharge. At his 2-year follow-up, his urine test showed mild proteinuria, with a protein to creatinine ratio of 0.75 g/g Cr (reference <0.40 g/g Cr).

What is the outcome and prognosis of SpHUS?

Early studies from the 1980s reported a mortality rate up to 50% in patients with SpHUS. With advances in intensive care, antimicrobial therapy and supportive renal management, more recent data suggest a reduction in mortality to around 5–15%. The risk of death remains highest during the acute phase of illness, particularly in patients with pneumococcal meningitis.

Despite improved survival, long-term renal morbidity remains a significant concern. Around 30–45% of survivors develop long-term renal sequelae, including proteinuria, persistent hypertension and chronic kidney disease. Around 10% of SpHUS had end-stage renal failure requiring dialysis or kidney transplantation. As these kidney insufficiencies may not be clinically apparent during the first few years after the initial insult, long-term follow-up with monitoring of urinalysis and blood pressure is warranted in high-risk patients.

31.3 Case Illustrations

SpHUS is an uncommon but serious complication of invasive pneumococcal disease, presenting with a triad of microangiopathic haemolytic anaemia, thrombocytopenia and acute kidney injury. A positive direct Coombs test and T-antigen activation tests support the diagnosis. Despite improved survival rates, long-term renal complications remain common, highlighting the need for follow-up and monitoring.

Suggested Further Readings

1. Scobell RR, Kaplan BS, Copelovitch L. New insights into the pathogenesis of Streptococcus pneumoniae–associated hemolytic uremic syndrome. Pediatr Nephrol. 2020;35:1585–91.
2. Palma LMP, Vaisbich-Guimarães MH, Sridharan M, Tran CL, Sethi S. Thrombotic microangiopathy in children. Pediatr Nephrol. 2022;37(9):1967–80.
3. Agarwal HS, Latifi SQ. Streptococcus pneumoniae-associated hemolytic uremic syndrome in the era of pneumococcal vaccine. Pathogens. 2021;10(6):727.

The Hike to the Peak and the ICU

32

32.1 Case Description

Ronnie is a 15-year-old boy with no significant past medical history. He was admitted to the hospital following a collapse during a hiking trip from 10:00 am to 3:00 pm, on a day with a temperature of 33 °C and relative humidity of 90%. He experienced profuse sweating but consumed only 500 mL of fluid throughout the hike. Upon arrival at the emergency department, he had regained consciousness, with a body temperature of 40.1 °C. He was transferred to the PICU, where physical cooling measures were initiated for suspected heat stroke. Tea-coloured urine was observed (Fig. 32.1), and urine dipstick testing was positive for 'red blood cells'. Rhabdomyolysis was suspected.

W. K. Y. Chan, M. C. I. Kuok, *Paediatric Nephrology*, https://doi.org/10.1007/978-981-95-5060-9_32

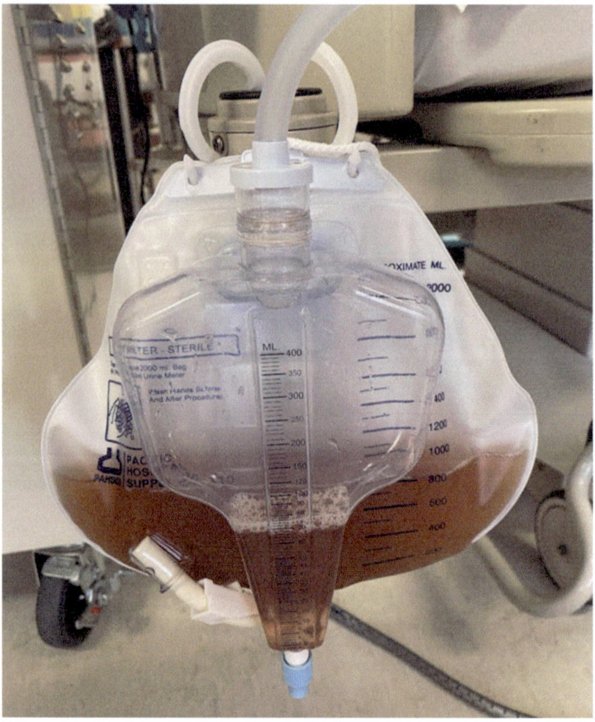

Fig. 32.1 Tea-coloured urine was noted on admission

32.2 Interactive Case Discussion

What is rhabdomyolysis?

Rhabdomyolysis refers to skeletal muscle injury resulting in the release of intracellular contents into the blood circulation. It is commonly defined by a creatine kinase (CK) level greater than 1000 IU/L, or more than five times the upper limit of normal based on local laboratory reference values, in the context of muscle injury or muscle-related symptoms. Release of myoglobin is pathognomonic of rhabdomyolysis; however, its usage for diagnosing rhabdomyolysis is limited by its relatively short half-life (1 to 3 hours), and the quantitative measurements of myoglobin may not be available in many healthcare settings.

What is the likely cause of his urine colour change?

Given the history of intense exercise and heat stroke, the change in urine colour is likely due to exertional rhabdomyolysis leading to myoglobinuria. Muscle damage releases myoglobin into the bloodstream, which is filtered by the kidneys and appears in the urine when serum levels exceed the renal threshold of 0.5–1.5 mg/dL. Visible urine discolouration typically occurs when serum myoglobin exceeds 100 mg/dL. Myoglobin, which is haem-containing, can cause a positive result for 'blood' on urine dipstick testing. However, this is not true haematuria and can be distinguished by the absence of red blood cells on urine microscopy.

Ronnie's blood tests showed deranged kidney function with urea 8.5 mmol/L and creatinine 260 μmol/L. The serum sodium and potassium were mildly elevated at 148 mmol/L and 5.2 mmol/L, respectively. His CK level was markedly elevated to around 100,000 IU/L, consistent with severe rhabdomyolysis. His white cell count was elevated to 28.7×10^9/L with neutrophil predominance (22.1×10^9/L). His haemoglobin level, platelet count and coagulation profiles were unremarkable.

How does rhabdomyolysis cause acute kidney injury (AKI)?
The development of acute kidney injury secondary to rhabdomyolysis is likely multi-factorial, and three major mechanisms have been proposed in its pathogenesis.

1. *Renal vasoconstriction:* Activation of the renin-angiotensin-aldosterone system due to fluid sequestration in damaged muscle tissues, resulting in renal vasoconstriction and reduced blood flow.
2. *Tubular obstruction:* Precipitation of urine, myoglobin and Tamm-Horsfall protein in the distal tubules, particularly in an acidic environment, leading to intratubular obstruction.
3. *Tubular toxicity:* Direct toxic effects on renal tubules by free radicals and reactive oxygen species from damaged muscle cells.

How common is AKI in paediatric rhabdomyolysis? What are the risk factors?
Recent studies have reported that the prevalence of AKI in paediatric rhabdomyolysis ranges from 7% to 45%. This wide variation is likely due to differences in study populations, clinical settings and the diagnostic criteria used for AKI. Among those who develop AKI, 20% to 67% required kidney replacement therapy in paediatric reviews.

Children who develop rhabdomyolysis secondary to high-impact trauma or seizures are at a higher risk of developing AKI. Additionally, higher peak CK levels, higher blood or urine myoglobin levels, metabolic acidosis and hypocalcaemia have all been associated with an increased risk of AKI. These factors reflect the severity of rhabdomyolysis. Other factors such as dehydration, sepsis, exposure to nephrotoxic drugs and intravenous contrast can further increase the risk of AKI in these patients.

In addition to AKI, what other complications should be monitored in patients with rhabdomyolysis?
Rhabdomyolysis can lead to other complications, including the following:

- Hyperkalaemia.
- Hyperphosphataemia.
- Early hypocalcaemia followed by hypercalcaemia.
- Compartment syndrome.
- Disseminated intravascular coagulopathy (DIC).

During muscle injury, intracellular contents such as potassium and phosphate are released into the blood, causing hyperkalaemia and hyperphosphataemia. Life-threatening hyperkalaemia with ventricular arrhythmia has been reported. Hypocalcaemia is frequently observed in the early stages of rhabdomyolysis. It is primarily due to the influx of calcium into damaged muscle cells and the precipitation of calcium phosphate in muscle tissue. Hypocalcaemia can further exacerbate the cardiac toxicity of concurrent hyperkalaemia. During the recovery phase, serum calcium levels may rebound due to the remobilisation of previously deposited calcium. Metabolic acidosis is another common complication, arising from muscle ischaemia and organic acids released by damaged muscle. It can also exacerbate hyperkalaemia in rhabdomyolysis.

Compartment syndrome and DIC are considered late complications of rhabdomyolysis. Compartment syndrome typically affects the extremities and occurs due to fluid sequestration and swelling within muscle compartments. This can impair the perfusion and result in a vicious cycle of further muscle injury. DIC has been reported in approximately 5% to 15% of paediatric rhabdomyolysis cases and is often associated with the development of AKI.

Ronnie received intravenous isotonic solution at a rate of 200 ml/hour, and urine output was closely monitored. His CK level further increased to 150,000 IU/L, and his renal function deteriorated with urea 15.5 mmol/L and creatinine 303 μmol/L. He developed oliguria despite administration of intravenous furosemide.

What is the treatment approach for rhabdomyolysis?

General Management

- Identify and treat the underlying cause of rhabdomyolysis, which may include physical cooling for heat stroke, antibiotics for sepsis, medical treatment for acute dystonia, etc.
- Monitor and correct electrolyte disturbances, particularly hyperkalaemia, which can be life-threatening.
- Avoid nephrotoxic agents.

Fluid Replacement

- Give fluid resuscitation with crystalloid in patients with hypovolaemic shock.
- Use potassium-free isotonic solutions for intravenous fluid replacement.
- Administer intravenous fluid at 1.5 to 2 times the usual maintenance rate.
- Monitor urine output closely, targeting 2 to 4 ml/kg/hour in children, or up to 200–300 ml/hour in older children/adults.
- Consider the use of intravenous diuretics if there is concern for fluid overload.
- Regularly monitor fluid status, renal function and electrolytes. Early anticipation of kidney replacement therapy.
- Evidence of intravenous mannitol remains inconclusive, particularly in the paediatric population.

Metabolic Acidosis and Urinary Alkalinisation

The administration of sodium bicarbonate for urine alkalinisation(aiming for a urine pH > 7) has been proposed to mitigate the risk of rhabdomyolysis-related AKI. It is proposed that urine alkalinisation can reduce the precipitation of myoglobin and Tamm-Horsfall protein, which is favoured in an acidic environment, and limit redox cycling of myoglobin, lipid peroxidation and subsequent oxidative stress to the renal tubules. However, clinical trials have not consistently shown the superiority of sodium bicarbonate over aggressive hydration alone.

- Despite that, it is reasonable to give sodium bicarbonate, particularly in patients with significant metabolic acidosis and severe hyperkalaemia.
- Monitor potential side effects of sodium bicarbonate, including hypernatraemia and hypocalcaemia (especially where there is a risk of hypocalcaemia in early rhabdomyolysis).

Kidney Replacement Therapy (KRT)

- The decision to initiate KRT should be guided by usual clinical indications rather than the CK level alone. These indications include oliguria, AKI, fluid overload, significant hyperkalaemia or metabolic acidosis.

What is the role of haemoadsorption in rhabdomyolysis?

Conventional KRT is generally suboptimal for clearing myoglobin due to its relatively large molecular weight of approximately 17,000 Daltons (for comparison: ammonia 17 Daltons, urea 60 Daltons, creatinine 113 Daltons). There have been recent advances in haemoperfusion filters, which are capable of adsorbing molecules up to 55,000 Daltons, making them much more effective in myoglobin removal, the primary nephrotoxin in rhabdomyolysis-associated AKI. Besides, the larger surface area of these adsorption columns further enhances their ability to eliminate circulating myoglobin. In addition to myoglobin, these blood purification systems can also eliminate pro-inflammatory cytokines, which are believed to play a key role in the pathogenesis of AKI in critically ill patients.

There have been several case reports demonstrating the successful use of haemoadsorption in paediatric patients with rhabdomyolysis. However, the optimal timing for initiation and discontinuation, as well as the overall efficacy in preventing or treating AKI, remains uncertain and requires validation through prospective studies.

Ronnie eventually required continuous venovenous haemofiltration (CVVH) for 48 hours. His urine output improved subsequently, with normalisation of renal function parameters. His CK levels gradually declined, and he was discharged from the hospital after 1 week.

What is the prognosis of rhabdomyolysis-associated AKI?

Mortality is relatively rare, with most cases attributed to underlying conditions such as sepsis or trauma, rather than rhabdomyolysis itself. While most patients recover fully upon discharge, long-term renal sequelae have been documented. Literature has reported a decline in estimated GFR of more than 20 mL/min/1.73 m^2 following rhabdomyolysis-associated AKI in adults. Persistent renal complications such as proteinuria, hypertension and chronic kidney disease have been reported in children. For patients complicated with AKI, particularly those requiring KRT, they are at a higher risk of progressing to CKD; hence, follow-up is recommended to monitor kidney function and blood pressure.

Besides heat stroke, what are the other common causes of rhabdomyolysis in children?

The causes of rhabdomyolysis can largely be divided into three categories

Direct muscle injury	Physical trauma (e.g. falls, road traffic accidents and natural disasters) Burns Electrical shock
Exertional injury	Strenuous and repetitive exercises Hyperkinetic states (e.g. status epilepticus and status dystonicus)
Non-traumatic and non-exertional	Infections (most commonly viral myositis) Inborn error of metabolism Toxins (e.g. snake or insect bites) Medications (e.g. statins, anti-psychotics and macrolides) Drug-related syndromes (e.g. malignant hyperthermia, neuroleptic malignant syndrome and serotonin syndrome) Status asthmaticus

In adults, the most common causes of rhabdomyolysis are sepsis and drug-related effects. In contrast, viral infections and trauma are the leading causes in the paediatric population. Among children, viral infections are more frequent in those under 12 years, while trauma becomes a more common trigger in older children and adolescents.

Although metabolic disorders account for only 3–5% of paediatric rhabdomyolysis cases, they are clinically significant due to the risk of recurrent episodes. Early recognition is crucial, as preventive strategies can be implemented. Common metabolic causes include the following:

- Glycogen metabolism disorders (e.g. McArdle's disease and Tarui's disease).
- Fatty acid oxidation disorders (e.g. carnitine palmitoyltransferase II deficiency).
- Mitochondrial disorders.

These conditions impair muscle energy metabolism, leading to energy depletion and subsequent muscle breakdown. Rhabdomyolysis can be triggered by fasting, febrile illness or even brief isometric exercises. A high index of suspicion is warranted, especially in individuals with recurrent rhabdomyolysis, a family history of rhabdomyolysis and episodes precipitated by fasting. Further workup and discussion with metabolic specialists are warranted.

32.3 Case Illustrations

Rhabdomyolysis is a serious condition caused by muscle injury, leading to the release of intracellular contents such as potassium, phosphate and myoglobin. It can result in acute kidney injury, and severe cases may require kidney replacement therapy. Early recognition, aggressive fluid resuscitation and close monitoring of urine output, electrolytes and renal function are critical for management. Patients with recurrent episodes should be evaluated for underlying metabolic disorders.

Suggested Further Readings

1. Szugye HS. Pediatric rhabdomyolysis. Pediatrics Rev. 2020;41(6):265–75.
2. Elsayed EF, Reilly RF. Rhabdomyolysis: a review, with emphasis on the pediatric population. Pediatric Nephrol. 2010;25(1):7–18.
3. Kuok MCI, Chan WKY. Rhabdomyolysis in children: a state-of-the-art review. Children. 2025;12(4):492.

33 Beyond the Sore Throat

33.1 Case Description

Ruby was a 5-year-old girl with good past health. She had insect bites on her feet 2 weeks ago, and her feet became swollen. Her family doctor treated her with oral antihistamines and antibiotics. Her symptoms improved, but 2 days ago, she started vomiting repeatedly, up to 10–20 times per day. On admission, her body weight was 20 kg, and her height was 110 cm. Her blood pressure was 120/80 mmHg, and her pulse rate was 100 bpm. Her initial blood test showed a normal cell count. However, her serum urea was 24 mmol/L (RI: 1.6–6.4 mmol/L), serum creatinine 184 umol/L (RI: 28–52 umol/L), sodium 130 mmol/L (RI:136–145 mmol/L), potassium 4.2 mmol/L (RI: 3.5–5 mmol/L), venous pH 7.3, bicarbonate 19 mmol/L (RI: 22–25 mmol/L) and serum albumin 29 g/L (RI: 38–54 g/L).

33.2 Interactive Case Discussion

What is Acute Kidney Injury (AKI)?
AKI, previously called acute renal failure, is a sudden reduction in renal function, causing a decrease in urine output and sometimes an increase in blood urea nitrogen and creatinine. There are several criteria to define and stage AKI in children: the pRIFLE (paediatric Risk, Injury, Failure, Loss, End-stage renal failure), AKIN (Acute Kidney Injury Network) and KDIGO (Kidney Disease: Improving Global Outcome). KDIGO is the most commonly used formula in children (Table 33.1).

What were the causes of Ruby's acute kidney injury?
Although it was difficult to obtain an accurate history of urine output, Ruby's serum creatinine was more than three times normal, suggesting renal failure. Using the modified Schwartz formula, her estimated GFR was only 30 ml/min/1.73 m^2.

W. K. Y. Chan, M. C. I. Kuok, *Paediatric Nephrology*,
https://doi.org/10.1007/978-981-95-5060-9_33

Table 33.1 Standardised staged definition of acute kidney injury

Classification	Staging	Creatinine criteria	Urine output criteria
pRIFLE	Risk	eGFR decreased by ≥25%	0.5 ml/kg/hr × 8 hours
	Injury	eGFR decreased by ≥50%	0.5 ml/kg/hr × 16 hours
	Failure	eGFR decreased by ≥75% or (<35 ml/min/1.73 m^2)	0.3 ml/kg/hr × 24 hours or anuria for 12 hours
	Loss	Persistent failure >4 weeks	
	ESRD	Persistent failure >3 months	
AKIN	1	Increase in creatinine of ≥50% or an absolute increase in creatinine of 0.3 mg/dL over 48 hours	
	2	Increase in creatinine of ≥100%	
	3	Increase in creatinine of ≥200%	
KDIGO	1	Increase in serum creatinine by 0.3 mg/dL or more, 26.5 umol/L within 48 hours Increase in serum creatinine to ≥1.5 times baseline within the prior seven days	0.5 ml/kg/hr for 6 hours
	2	Increase in creatinine ≥100%	>0.3 ml and ≤0.5 ml/kg/hr
	3	Increase in creatinine ≥200% or SCr ≥4 mg/dL or receipt of dialysis with eGFR <35 ml/min/1.73 m^2	≤0.3 ml/kg/hr

pRIFLE pediatric risk, injury, failure, loss, end-stage, *AKIN* acute kidney injury network, *KDIGO* kidney disease improving global outcomes

Table 33.2 The implications of various clinical features in helping to differentiate acute versus acute on chronic renal disease. BOR: Branchio-Oto-Renal; LVH: left Ventricular Hypertrophy; FSGS: Focal Segmental Glomerulosclerosis

Clinical features	Implications
Short stature or failure to thrive	Suggesting a chronic disease
Hearing loss	Hereditary nephritis, BOR syndrome
Syndromic features	Renal dysplasia, hypoplasia, FSGS or other genetic renal diseases
Pallor	Anaemia of chronic renal disease
Pallor and petechiae	Haemolytic-uremic syndrome, hence likely an acute insult
Features of chronic hypertension-like papilloedema, LVH	Likely an underlying long-standing renal disease with chronic hypertension
Generalised oedema	Fluid retention in acute glomerulonephritis/renal failure or hypoalbuminemia in nephrotic syndrome
Gross haematuria	Acute nephritic syndrome or acute tubular necrosis
Vasculitic rash	Vasculitis, pauci- or immune-mediated glomerulonephritis
Palpable kidneys	Cystic kidney disease or obstructive uropathy

The possible aetiology of her renal failure can be classified into pre-renal, renal and post-renal causes. With the absence of a history of renal disease and lack of information on her previous renal function test, we have to differentiate whether Ruby was having acute renal failure or acute on chronic renal failure. Despite the symptoms of uraemia being nonspecific, there are clinical features that help reveal the disease's underlying causes and duration, as listed in Table 33.2.

How would you manage Ruby initially?

Apart from treating life-threatening electrolyte disturbances, the goal of initial management would be to correct any treatable causes for renal injury, to avoid further renal damage and to assess the need for renal supportive therapies. Hence, the following had to be considered.

- Assess any element of hypovolaemia or dehydration and correct it as needed.
  - Given the history of poor oral intake and vomiting, a bolus of fluid challenge with crystalloid at 20 ml/kg would help correct hypovolaemia and test for reversible renal injury.
  - A bedside ultrasound can assess the volume state of the patient.
  - Observe the response of urine output after a fluid challenge.
- Insert a Foley catheter to monitor urine output and to bypass any urinary outflow tract obstruction if present.
- Nephrotoxic medication should be stopped and avoided.
  - The dose of medication should be adjusted for eGFR, except for the initial loading doses for antibiotics.
- Her blood pressure should be controlled with antihypertensive agents to avoid hypertensive encephalopathy or pulmonary oedema.
- Electrolytes should be carefully monitored to prevent life-threatening cardiac arrhythmia.
- A bedside USG of the kidneys would be helpful to assess the size of the kidneys. A small kidney size would suggest chronic kidney disease. The presence of cysts or other abnormalities may help diagnose underlying renal disease.
- Further, workup for the underlying causes of renal failure, including blood tests for autoimmune markers and serum complements. Ruby underwent an USG examination (Fig. 33.1). Her left kidney showed similar findings.

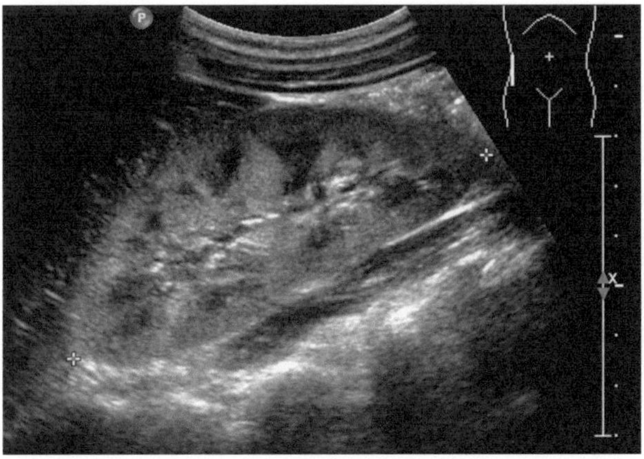

Fig. 33.1 Greyscale USG showed the right kidney of the patient. The right kidney was enlarged, measuring 9.2 cm in length with generalized increase in echogenicity suggesting renal parenchymal disease

How could this USG kidney help you in the management?

The USG kidney did not show any hydronephrosis or post-renal cause to account for the renal failure. The kidneys did not have any mass or cysts. The kidneys were not small; hence, chronic renal disease was unlikely. The nephromegaly was likely related to oedema in the kidneys or increased cellular elements due to proliferation or infiltration. Ruby likely suffered from acute kidney failure with these enlarged kidneys instead of acute-on-chronic renal failure.

Ruby's condition and renal function did not improve with initial fluid challenges. She had generalised anasarca. Her urine output dropped to 0.2 ml/kg per hour. Her BP was elevated to 160/90 mmHg. Her urine routine showed ++ albustix and +++ haemastix, and urine microscopy showed red cell casts. The autoimmune marker workup was negative, including ANA, anti-dsDNA, anti-ENA, p-ANCA and c-ANCA. The anti-GBM was normal at 1.1 u/ml (RI: <7 u/ml). The immunoglobulin pattern was within the normal range. Her ASOT, however, was 800 IU/ml (elevated), complement C3 dropped to 0.2 g/L (RI: 0.9–1.5 g/L), and C4 was 0.09 g/L (RI: 0.1–0.4 g/L). Her throat swab showed *Streptococcus pyogenes.*

What is your diagnosis at this juncture, and how would you manage?

Ruby likely suffered from post-streptococcus glomerulonephritis, resulting in this acute kidney failure. Hence, we have to do the following:

- Put her on fluid restriction, low salt and low protein diet.
- Control her blood pressure with antihypertensive agents like amlodipine or hydralazine and diuretics. The use of ACEI may not be appropriate given the risk of hyperkalaemia and low GFR in this situation.
- A course of antibiotics like penicillin or amoxicillin-clavulanic acid to clear up the *streptococcus pyogenes.*

Ruby's serum sodium progressively dropped to 125 mmol/L, potassium increased to 5.0 mmol/L, urea increased to 30 mmol/L, creatinine increased to 350 umol/L, ionised calcium dropped to 0.9 mmol/L, and phosphate increased to 3 mmol/L (RI: 1.05–1.8 mmol/L). She was put on intermittent renal supportive therapy (IRST) for better fluid and electrolyte control. Given the rapid deterioration in renal function, a renal biopsy was performed to confirm the diagnosis and assess the severity of renal damage. In the case of progression to crescentic glomerulonephritis, immunosuppressive treatment may be needed.

The light microscopic examination of the renal tissues is shown in Figs. 33.2 and 33.3. The electron microscopic examination is shown in Fig. 33.4. The kidney tissue's immunofluorescence (IF) staining showed prominent IgG and C3 staining with diffuse global 3+ granular mesangial deposits on the capillary loops. IgM and Ig A staining was weak at 1+. The pattern confirmed post-infectious glomerulonephritis. With the microbiology and serology results, the diagnosis is acute post-streptococcus glomerulonephritis (APSGN).

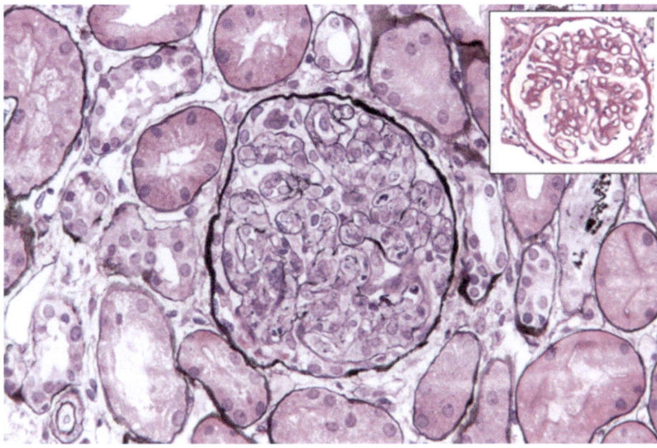

Fig. 33.2 Light microscopy showed the glomerulus was enlarged with accentuation of lobularity. Global endocapillary hypercellularity was caused by endothelial cell swelling and the infiltration of neutrophils and macrophages. The picture in the upper right corner is a normal glomerulus for comparison. A normal glomerulus has only 1–2 cells per capillary tuft. The capillary lumens are patent. The mesangial cells and matrix are located in the capillary tuft's central or stalk region, and the glomerular wall's thickness is similar to that of the tubular basement membrane. (Pathology slides courtesy of Dr Lau Wing Hung, Department of Pathology, Queen Elizabeth Hospital, Hong Kong)

Fig. 33.3 A high-power view to show the subepithelial immune complex deposit (yellow arrow). (Pathology slides courtesy of Dr Lau Wing Hung, Department of Pathology, Queen Elizabeth Hospital, Hong Kong)

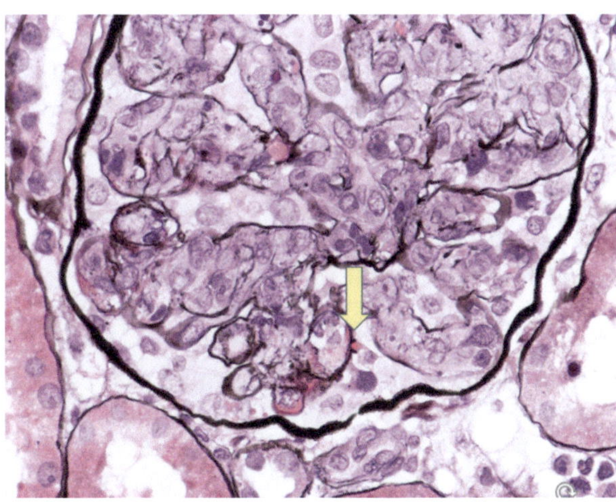

What is the cause of APSGN?

APSGN is identified as a prototype of immune-complex-mediated glomerulonephritis. It is typically triggered after a streptococcus infection. It usually occurs 10–14 days after streptococcal pharyngitis, but can occur 2–3 weeks after pyoderma caused by streptococcus. Two nephritogenic streptococcal antigens have been studied extensively as putative nephrotoxins. They are the pyogenic exotoxin B (SPeB) and the glyceraldehyde-3-phosphate dehydrogenase (GAPDH).

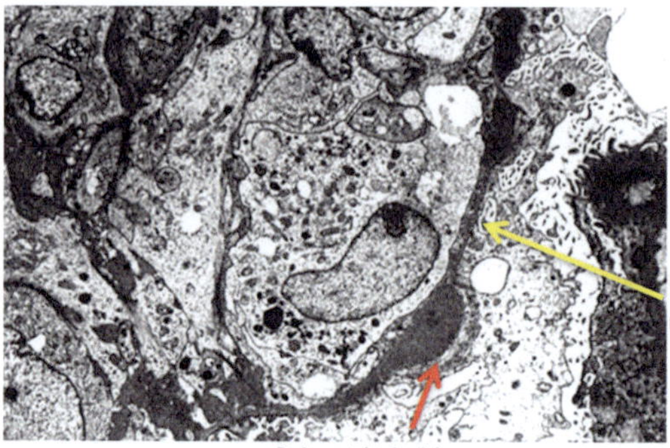

Fig. 33.4 Electronic microscopy showed the electron-dense subepithelial hump (red arrow) and the basement membrane (yellow arrow). (Pathology slides courtesy of Dr Lau Wing Hung, Department of Pathology, Queen Elizabeth Hospital, Hong Kong)

Glomerulonephritis can result from the glomerular deposition of the immune complexes or the in situ formation of immune complexes. The cationic antigens, facilitated by their charges, can penetrate the poly-anionic glomerular basement membrane. The immune complexes then trigger a variable inflammatory response with leucocyte infiltration, endocapillary cell proliferation and complement-IgG, -IgM or -IgA depositions.

What are the differential diagnoses for APSGN?
Many bacterial and viral infections can cause acute glomerulonephritis, with the clinical picture identical to APSGN. The temporal relationship of a preceding infection may be challenging to identify. Post-infectious glomerulonephritis is a general term. Shunt nephritis and bacterial endocarditis-related GN are two well-known infection-related GN with low serum C3 seen in children. Other differential diagnoses include primary C3-glomerulonephritis, which had a dominant C3 in the IF-staining of the renal histology. Membranoproliferative glomerulonephritis also has a low C3 ± low C4. A lupus nephritis patient also has low serum C3 and C4. The immunofluorescence staining of the glomeruli typically shows a full house of IgG, IgA, IgM, C3, C4 and C1q in lupus nephritis. (Table 33.3).

What are the common organisms that cause post-infectious glomerulonephritis?
Both bacterial, viral and parasitic infections can cause post-infectious glomerulonephritis, but post-streptococcal infection is the most common cause in the paediatric group. Various infections associated with post-infectious GN are listed in Table 33.4.

What are the complications of acute post-streptococcal glomerulonephritis?
Although most patients with post-streptococcal glomerulonephritis run a benign course, some children run into life-threatening complications that could be fatal in rare cases. Prompt identification of the complications and treatment accordingly is of crucial importance (Table 33.5).

Table 33.3 Relationship of serum complements with different types of glomerulonephritis (GN)

Complement level	Normal C3 and C4	Low C3 and normal C4	Low C3 and Low C4
Type of glomerulonephritis	– Ig A GN – Henoch-Schonlein nephritis – ANCA-associated GN	– Post-infectious GN – MPGN types 2 and 3 – C3 nephritis	– SLE – Shunt nephritis – Infective endocarditis-related GN – MPGN type 1

GN glomerulonephritis, *C3* complement C3, *C4* complement C4, *MPGN* membranoproliferative glomerulonephritis, *SLE* systemic lupus erythematosus

Table 33.4 Examples of infectious organisms that are associated with post-infectious glomerulonephritis

Bacterial causes	
Pharyngitis-related	*Group A streptococcus, streptococcus pyogenes*
Endocarditis-related	Group C and D streptococcus, *Streptococcus viridans*
Shunt infection-related	*Staphylococcus aureus, staphylococcus epidermis*
Abscess related	Gramme-negative bacillus
Pneumonia-related	*Streptococcus pneumoniae, mycoplasma pneumoniae*
Viral causes	Hepatitis B Hepatitis C Human immunodeficiency virus Human parvovirus B19 Cytomegalovirus
Parasites	Malaria Toxoplasmosis

Table 33.5 Complications of post-infectious glomerulonephritis

Pathophysiology	Problems	Interventions
Severe fluid retention	Pulmonary oedema	Ventilator support Removal of fluid by renal supportive therapies
Hypertension	Hypertensive heart failure Posterior reversible encephalopathy, hypertensive encephalopathy	Antihypertensive treatment to control blood pressure
Renal failure	Uremia, electrolyte disturbance, especially hyperkalaemia and hyponatremia	Medical treatment and renal supportive therapies

What is the difference between IgA-dominant post-infectious glomerulonephritis (APIGN) and APSGN?

With a shift in epidemiology and bacteriology of infection-related glomerulonephritis, IgA-dominant APIGN is increasingly described in adults. Unlike in children, the triggering infection is not *streptococcus* but is usually caused by *staphylococcus*. In kidney histology, the IF-staining has an IgA-dominant picture. It can be differentiated from IgA nephropathy by its low serum C3, which is usually not seen in IgA nephropathy (Table 33.6).

Table 33.6 Difference between APIGN and APSGN

	Acute post-streptococcus GN	IgA-dominant post-infectious GN
Epidemiology	Children	Adult
Bacteriology	*Streptococcus*	*Staphylococcus* and gramme-negative bacteria
Temporal relationship to the infection	Post-infection	Infection ongoing at the time of diagnosis
Site of infections	Pharyngitis or pyoderma	The site of infection is more heterogeneous; skin infection is most common
Associated morbidity	Usually healthy before the presentation	Diabetes mellitus, immunocompromised, elderly, HIV-related, malignancy
Immunofluorescein staining in renal histology	Predominant IgG and C3	Predominant Ig A
Outcome	The favourable outcome is that most people recover	Less favourable, some patients may go into chronic kidney disease

What is the prognosis for Ruby?
The overall prognosis of post-infectious glomerulonephritis is good. Typically, the renal function will spontaneously improve over 3–4 weeks. The volume overload will resolve as the serum urea and creatinine normalise and urine output increases. Sometimes, associated proteinuria may linger for a few weeks after normalisation of serum creatinine. Microscopic haematuria may persist for months to years. Fatality in post-infectious glomerulonephritis is rare and usually occurs in the acute stage. Most children recover without subsequent renal impairment. Ruby's renal function improved and started to recover after 2 weeks of dialysis support. She recovered uneventfully and her renal function remained normal during follow up.

33.3 Case Illustrations

Using Ruby's history and management as a guide, we present a practical approach to evaluating and managing a child with acute kidney injury secondary to post-infectious glomerulonephritis. APSGN, although decreasing in developed countries, still occurs and can present as life-threatening complications. It is important to differentiate various causes of acute glomerulonephritis as the treatment will be very different.

Suggested Further Readings

1. Rodriguez Iturbe B, Najafian B, Silva A, Alpers CE. Acute post-infectious glomerulonephritis in children. Pediatr Nephrol. 2016;7:959–81.
2. Nasr SH, D'Agati VD. IgA-dominant post-infectious glomerulonephritis: a new twist on an old disease. Nephron Clin Pract. 2011;119(1):c18–26.
3. VanDeVoorde RG III. Acute poststreptococcal glomerulonephritis: the most common acute glomerulonephritis. Pediatr Rev. 2015;36(1):3–13.

Rescuing Kidneys in Sepsis

34

34.1 Case Description

Emma was a 5-year-old girl who previously enjoyed good health. She had been having fever for 4 days without localising symptoms. She had received oral paracetamol and ibuprofen from a pharmacy, but her fever persisted. She was increasingly lethargic with poor appetite and was admitted via the emergency department. On arrival, Emma appeared tired with poor perfusion and a capillary refill time of 3 seconds. Her blood pressure was 74/34 mmHg, and she was tachycardic at 150 beats per minute. Systemic examination was otherwise unremarkable. Initial blood tests showed sodium 145 mmol/L, potassium 4.9 mmol/L, urea 12 mmol/L (RI: 1.8–6.4 mmol/L), creatinine 120 μmol/L (RI: 33–59 μmol/L) and lactate 3.0 mmol/L (RI: 0.5–2.2 mmol/L). Her venous blood gas showed metabolic acidosis with pH 7.24, pCO_2 3.1 kPa (RI: 4.7–6.0 kPa), bicarbonate 9.5 mmol/L (RI: 22–26 mmol/L) and base excess −15.9 mmol/L (RI: -2–2.0 mmol/L). Her urine dipstick was positive for leukocytes and nitrite.

34.2 Interactive Case Discussion

What's your clinical impression, and what would you do next?

Emma was in septic shock complicated by lactic acidosis and acute kidney injury (AKI). The most likely source of sepsis was a urinary tract infection, as suggested by her positive dipstick results. Her AKI was likely multi-factorial, which could possibly be related to her sepsis, hypotension with hypoperfusion, exposure to nephrotoxic medication use (ibuprofen) and urinary tract infection with possible upper tract involvement.

Management should include immediate resuscitation, including fluid resuscitation at 10 to 20 ml/kg as an initial bolus with close monitoring of vital signs and clinical condition. Repeated boluses, up to a total of 40 to 60 ml/kg, may be required

W. K. Y. Chan, M. C. I. Kuok, *Paediatric Nephrology*,
https://doi.org/10.1007/978-981-95-5060-9_34

in severe septic shock, and inotropic support should be considered early if there is a suboptimal response to fluid resuscitation. Urine output and fluid balance should be strictly monitored to prevent fluid overload. Intravenous antibiotics should be commenced as soon as possible, preferably after sepsis workup, but the initiation must not be delayed. Nephrotoxic medication should be avoided, and the dosage of medications should be reviewed for the need of renal adjustment.

Is AKI common in paediatric patients?
The reported incidence of AKI varies across studies, possibly explained by differences in clinical settings, patient population, disease severity and definition of AKI used. Meta-analyses suggested that approximately one-quarter to one-third of hospitalised paediatric patients developed AKI, with incidence reaching 70% in paediatric sepsis in some studies. Despite these variations, the evidence consistently demonstrated that paediatric AKI patients had increased mortality, worse short-term outcomes such as hospital stays and mechanical ventilation and a higher risk of long-term complications.

How does sepsis lead to AKI?
Previously, sepsis-related AKI was believed to result from reduced effective renal blood flow (RBF) secondary to vasodilatation and hypotension, leading to acute tubular necrosis. While this mechanism remains valid in some patients, studies have shown that sepsis-related AKI can still occur despite preserved or even increased RBF. Other pathogenic mechanisms have been proposed, and current understanding suggests that sepsis-related AKI arises from a complex interplay of mechanisms at cellular and molecular levels (Table 34.1).

Table 34.1 Proposed mechanisms for sepsis-induced acute kidney injury

Dysregulated inflammatory and immune response	– Sepsis can trigger an overwhelming release of pro-inflammatory cytokines, including IL-6, IL-8, IL-18 and TNF-α – Exposure to these mediators results in increased oxidative stress, reactive oxygen species production and mitochondrial injury, all of which can potentiate renal tubular epithelial cell damage
Haemodynamic alterations	– Some patients have decreased effective circulating volume due to systemic vasodilatation and reduced peripheral vascular resistance, leading to macrovascular haemodynamic instability and renal hypoperfusion – As kidneys are encapsulated organs, fluid retention and tissue oedema can significantly alter transmural pressure and worsen venous congestion, further impairing perfusion – Sepsis can also lead to microcirculatory dysfunction, compromising peritubular capillary flow and oxygen saturation, resulting in tissue hypoxia
Endothelial dysfunction	– Increased vascular permeability in sepsis can lead to interstitial oedema, which impairs oxygen delivery to target cells – Endothelial damage promotes platelet activation and adhesion, which can cause microthrombi formation and capillary occlusion

In addition, other mechanisms have been implicated in sepsis-related AKI, including metabolic reprogramming from oxidative phosphorylation to glycolysis in sepsis, and dysregulation in autophagy in the regulation of cell death. A detailed discussion of these processes is beyond the scope of this chapter.

What are the complications of AKI?
AKI can lead to serious, potentially life-threatening acute complications and can involve multiple organ systems.

- Electrolyte disturbances: Hyperkalaemia is a critical complication, as it can precipitate life-threatening arrhythmia requiring prompt recognition and treatment. Metabolic acidosis in AKI can further potentiate hyperkalaemia and cardiac instability.
- Uraemia: Though less common in children, severe AKI can lead to uraemic complications such as pericarditis, encephalopathy and platelet dysfunction.
- Fluid overload: Oliguria and anuria can result in significant fluid overload, especially with excessive fluid administration. Pulmonary oedema can cause hypoxaemia and respiratory failure.
- Hypertension: This is commonly encountered in patients with AKI and may persist even after recovery of renal function.

Emma received 40 ml/kg of PlasmaLyte-A, followed by noradrenaline infusion for her hypotension. She received renal-adjusted dose of intravenous meropenem after sepsis workup. Her blood pressure subsequently improved to 90/50 mmHg, with improvement in capillary refill time and clinical status. A urinary catheter was inserted to monitor her urine output. Despite the improvement of blood pressure, her renal function deteriorated, with urea rising to 20 mmol/L and creatinine to 250 μmol/L. Her urine output remained low at 0.3 ml/kg/hour over the past 12 hours.

What are the indications for acute kidney replacement therapy (KRT)?
Indications of acute KRT are commonly categorised into renal and non-renal causes.

Renal causes
- Severe or refractory hyperkalaemia (usually >6.5 mmol/L or with ECG changes).
- Severe metabolic acidosis not responding to medical treatment.
- Oliguria/anuria; fluid overload.
- Significant symptomatic uraemia.

Non-renal causes
- Inborn error of metabolism, e.g. severe hyperammonaemia and/or lactic acidosis.
- Removal of drugs and toxins, e.g. lithium, salicylate.
- Endotoxin and cytokines clearance in sepsis.
- Myoglobin removal in rhabdomyolysis.
- Temperature control for hyperthermia via extracorporeal cooling.

Table 34.2 Comparing different modalities of acute kidney replacement therapy

	Mechanism	Pros	Cons
PD	Gradual fluid removal and solute clearance through diffusion and ultrafiltration across the peritoneal membrane	Relatively simple setup; does not require vascular access (advantageous in small patients with difficult access and preserves vasculature for patients for potential future chronic dialysis); has less haemodynamic effects	Slow solute clearance; risk of peritonitis, possible catheter malfunction affecting filling or drainage
IHD	Solute clearance in short sessions (2 to 4 hours) via diffusion	Rapid correction of electrolytes and removal of small solutes	Higher risk of haemodynamic instability or dialysis disequilibrium syndrome due to rapid shifts; need vascular access with risk of line-related complications; anticoagulation often required
CKRT	Continuous solute and fluid removal, the solute clearance mechanism (diffusion and/or convection) depends on the modality of CKRT	More gentle and steady fluid and solute shift with less risk of haemodynamic instability; achieve more precise fluid balance control	Need vascular access with risk of line-related complications; anticoagulation often required

What are the different modalities for acute KRT?
Peritoneal dialysis (PD), intermittent haemodialysis (IHD) and continuous kidney replacement therapy (CKRT) are the three primary modalities of acute KRT. Their characteristics are summarised below (Table 34.2).

What are the basic principles of CKRT?
The solute clearance in CKRT is achieved through two main mechanisms: diffusion and convection.

Diffusion	– Solute movement from high concentration to low concentration across the semipermeable membrane, which separates the blood and dialysate compartments – Most effective for solutes with low molecular weight (e.g. urea, creatinine and potassium) – Used in continuous veno-venous haemodialysis (CVVHD)
Convection	– Solutes are transported with plasma water across the membrane driven by hydrostatic pressure gradient – Replacement fluid (pre-filter or post-filter, or both) is infused into the circulatory system to maintain the intravascular volume and regulate solute concentration – Most effective for solutes with a middle molecular weight (e.g. certain cytokines and β_2-microglobulin) – Used in continuous veno-venous haemofiltration (CVVH)

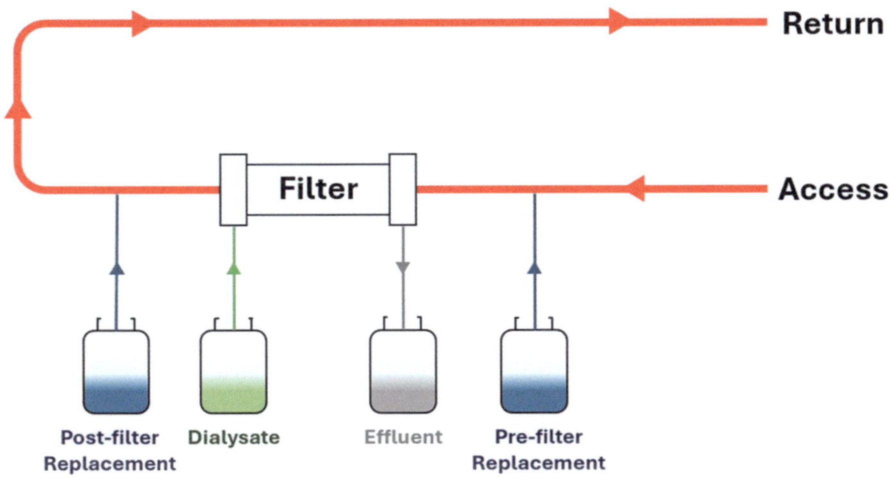

Fig. 34.1 Simplified illustration showing continuous veno-venous haemodiafiltration (CVVHDF) circuit

Continuous veno-venous haemodiafiltration (CVVHDF) combines the advantages of diffusion and convection to enhance solute clearance with a broader range of molecular sizes. Figure 34.1 illustrates a simplified CVVHDF circuit. The fluid removal rate can be adjusted to control fluid balance, particularly in patients with anuria and fluid overload.

Emma received CVVHDF with a targeted fluid removal rate set to remove fluid in a controlled manner gradually. The laboratory called and reported positive *Escherichia coli* growth in her blood culture. While her urea and creatinine dropped with CKRT as expected, her fever persisted and urine output remained low. You are considering whether haemoadsorption may be beneficial.

What is haemoadsorption?
Haemoadsorption is an extracorporeal blood purification technique that removes substances from the circulation by binding them to adsorptive materials in the cartridge. It is effective in eliminating substances of medium to high molecular weight, including myoglobin, cytokines and bilirubin, which are not efficiently removed by conventional diffusion and convection mechanisms. In sepsis, where pro-inflammatory cytokines play a significant role in sepsis-associated AKI, haemoadsorption provides an additional means to control inflammatory response and associated tissue damage. Paediatric studies have shown promising results in cytokine removal and improvement in clinical outcome in sepsis. However, large-scale trials are still lacking, and the optimal timing for initiation and discontinuation, as well as the safety profiles, particularly in smaller children, warrant further evaluation.

Emma received 1 week of CKRT, and her urine output gradually improved. Her kidney ultrasound showed normal size of both kidneys with no hydronephrosis, but increased parenchymal echogenicity consistent with AKI. Her blood pressure remained stable after weaning off inotropic support, and she did not develop hypertension. Her serum urea and creatinine levels remained normal after discontinuation of CKRT.

What are the long-term outcomes of AKI?
Growing research shows that paediatric AKI is associated with long-term adverse health outcomes, with the prognosis affected by the aetiologies, severity and duration of AKI. Different longitudinal studies have demonstrated increased risk of proteinuria, hypertension and chronic kidney disease (CKD) among AKI survivors. In one study with a mean follow-up of 6.5 years, 13.2% of patients developed proteinuria and 6.6% developed hypertension. CKD was observed in 28.0% with eGFR < 90 ml/min/1.73 m^2 and 3.6% with eGFR < 60 ml/min/1.73 m^2. As hypertension and proteinuria can be associated with further decline in renal function, ongoing follow-up with urine tests and blood pressure monitoring is advocated in patients who have developed significant AKI.

What are some advances in paediatric AKI?
As AKI can lead to significant adverse outcomes, there has been a paradigm shift toward early detection of subclinical AKI. While serum creatinine is widely used and remains the gold standard in the KDIGO criteria, it is a relatively insensitive marker of kidney injury, sometimes taking 2–3 days to rise after insult, by which time the GFR has declined by 50%. Newer biomarkers, including neutrophil gelatinase-associated lipocalin (NGAL), tissue inhibitor of metalloproteinases-2 (TIMP-2) and insulin-like growth factor-binding protein (IGFBP-7) have been studied and introduced as early indicators for tubular injuries. These markers typically rise within hours of renal insult, offering greater sensitivity for AKI detection before overt or irreversible damage occurs. Besides, there is growing evidence supporting the integration of artificial intelligence and machine learning, which analyse clinical and laboratory data to predict AKI development. This can potentially enable earlier interventions to prevent AKI or reduce its severity and damage.

34.3 Case Illustrations

Sepsis is a common cause of paediatric AKI, with pathogenesis involving a complex interplay of inflammatory, haemodynamic and endothelial mechanisms. Early recognition and prompt management, including fluid resuscitation, sepsis control and avoidance of nephrotoxic agents, are crucial to prevent progression of AKI. Some patients may need kidney replacement therapy, and the risk of long-term sequelae in severe AKI patients highlights the need for further follow-up.

Suggested Further Readings

1. Kuwabara S, Goggins E, Okusa MD. The pathophysiology of sepsis-associated AKI. Clin J Am Soc Nephrol. 2022;17(7):1050–69.
2. Schuermans A, Van den Eynde J, Mekahli D, Vlasselaers D. Long-term outcomes of acute kidney injury in children. Curr Opin Pediatr. 2023;35(2):259–67.Table 34.1 (continued)

Part V

Bladder and Urinary Continence

35 Dreams and Dribbles

35.1 Case Description

Ryan, a 10-year-old boy, was brought to your clinic by his parents due to concerns about bedwetting. He was toilet-trained in daytime by 3 years old, but has never been dry at night for more than 2 consecutive weeks. Currently, he wets the bed almost every night.

35.2 Interactive Case Discussion

How do we classify enuresis?
Enuresis is classified according to the following:

(i) Time of appearance.
  - Primary enuresis: The child has never been consistently dry at night for more than 6 months.
  - Secondary enuresis: Occurs in a child who previously achieved nighttime dryness for ≥6 months but has relapsed.

(ii) Symptoms.
  - Monosymptomatic: Nocturnal enuresis is the only symptom.
  - Non-monosymptomatic: Nocturnal enuresis is accompanied by other daytime lower urinary tract symptoms.

Definition of primary monosymptomatic nocturnal enuresis (PMNE).

- Intermittent involuntary urination during sleep in children aged ≥5 years old
- In a child who has never achieved a consistent dry period of ≥6 months at night
- Without any other lower urinary tract symptoms (LUTS)

W. K. Y. Chan, M. C. I. Kuok, *Paediatric Nephrology*,
https://doi.org/10.1007/978-981-95-5060-9_35

Before diagnosing PMNE, it is essential to exclude underlying organic causes, including urinary tract infections, bladder dysfunction (such as detrusor overactivity or bladder-bowel dysfunction) and different causes of polyuria, such as diabetes mellitus and diabetes insipidus.

What are the other significant lower urinary tract symptoms that need to be assessed?

Lower urinary tract symptoms can be categorised into (i) storage symptoms and (ii) voiding symptoms.

Storage Symptoms

- Increased daytime urinary frequency: Voiding ≥8 times per day.
- Decreased daytime urinary frequency: Voiding ≤3 times per day.
- Incontinence: Involuntary leakage of urine, which can be continuous or intermittent. Continuous incontinence may suggest congenital anomalies such as ectopic ureter.
- Urgency: A sudden, compelling need to void, commonly associated with bladder overactivity.
- Nocturia: Waking up at night to void. The condition is not necessarily pathological.

Voiding Symptoms

- Hesitancy: Difficulty in initiating urination.
- Straining: The need for exerting abdominal pressure to initiate and maintain voiding.
- Weak stream: Reduced force of urinary flow.
- Intermittency: Interrupted flow of urine, with discrete stops and starts during a single voiding episode.
- Dysuria: Pain or discomfort during voiding.

The presence of any of these symptoms indicates non-monosymptomatic enuresis. In such cases, further evaluation may be warranted to investigate underlying bladder dysfunction.

What are the red flags that should prompt further evaluation or specialist referral?

Referral to a specialist should be considered if any of the following are present:

- Polyuria and/or polydipsia
- Recurrent urinary tract infections
- Elevated blood pressure
- Signs suggestive of spinal cord pathology or lower limb neurological deficits
- Continuous urine leakage or daytime lower urinary tract symptoms
- Secondary nocturnal enuresis (i.e. child who was previously dry >6 months)

Further history revealed that Ryan has no other lower urinary tract symptoms. He did not report excessive thirst, polydipsia or polyuria. The overall assessment is consistent with primary monosymptomatic nocturnal enuresis. You suggest a bladder diary to quantify the fluid intake and urine output for further management.

What is the underlying pathophysiological mechanism for PMNE?
PMNE is postulated to result from a combination of the following three mechanisms:

Nocturnal polyuria	Usually, the body produces less urine at night due to a circadian rise in vasopressin (antidiuretic hormone), which promotes water reabsorption in the kidneys. Patients with reduced circadian secretion or reduced response to vasopressin can experience nocturnal polyuria. Excess fluid intake before bedtime may also contribute.
Bladder factor	Some children with PMNE have a smaller bladder capacity or show signs of uninhibited detrusor contractions during sleep.
Arousal problem	Children with PMNE may have a high arousal threshold or delay in maturation, and thus reduced ability to wake up in response to the sensation of a full bladder.

Genetics also plays a significant role in nocturnal enuresis. The risk of enuresis increases to 44% if one parent has a history of enuresis, and up to 77% if both parents were affected. Studies have shown that monozygotic twins have twice the concordance rate of enuresis compared to dizygotic twins, supporting a genetic basis for the condition.

What is the purpose of a bladder diary?
A bladder diary, also known as a frequency-volume chart, is a tool used to record fluid intake and urine output at home. It provides an objective means of assessing a patient's drinking habits, voiding patterns and any episodes of incontinence. This information is valuable for identifying underlying bladder dysfunction or other contributing pathologies, which help guide effective treatment strategies. When completed at intervals, it can also help monitor the response to therapy. A vessel with 10–20 measurement increments is needed to quantify the urine volume.

A minimum of 3–4 days of record is recommended to provide representative information for the daytime urinary condition. The daytime chart is helpful in assessing.

- Volume and distribution of fluid intake throughout the day.
- Frequency of voiding.
- Voided volume.

The maximum voided volume (MVV) can be compared to the expected bladder capacity (EBC), which is estimated by (age in years + 1) × 30 ml for children under 12 years old, and around 400 ml for those ≥12 years old. A voided volume >150% of EBC is considered significantly excessive, whereas a voided volume <65% of EBC is considered reduced bladder capacity.

Besides, estimation of overnight urine output can be useful to identify any nocturnal polyuria. The amount can be estimated by adding (i) the weight difference of wet diapers or pull-ups before and after bedwetting, (ii) the volume of the first morning void and (iii) any recorded nocturia amount. Nocturnal polyuria is defined as a total nocturnal urine output of >130% of EBC.

What else is important to include in the assessment?

Bowel Symptoms

The presence of any constipation or faecal incontinence should be assessed. Constipation is not uncommon in children with nocturnal enuresis, with some studies showing that up to one-third of affected children have constipation. Chronic constipation and a distended rectum can exert physical pressure on the bladder wall, causing a reduction in functional bladder capacity and possibly triggering bladder overactivity. Faecal incontinence should also be evaluated, as it may be a manifestation of constipation (overflow incontinence) or underlying spinal cord pathologies.

Assessment for Comorbidities

Patients with attention deficit hyperactivity disorder (ADHD) have twice the incidence of enuresis as compared to the general population. The co-existing behavioural conditions may also influence the treatment compliance and response to the standard therapies. However, the use of methylphenidate, a common treatment for ADHD, has shown conflicting evidence, with some case reports suggesting that it may induce enuresis.

There is also an established association between enuresis and sleep-related problems such as snoring and obstructive sleep apnoea. Proposed mechanisms include reduced arousability to a full bladder due to constant arousal stimuli from the airway, and increased negative intrathoracic pressure from inefficient breathing, leading to elevated secretion of atrial natriuretic peptide and increased urine production at night. Some studies have shown that adenotonsillectomy can improve enuresis in children with sleep-disordered breathing.

Family Expectation

Many families have already searched for information online or tried various methods before attending the consultation. It is important to explore these experiences and understand the family's expectations, as this provides valuable context for guiding further treatment planning.

Upon further conversation with Ryan, you understand that he feels unhappy and ashamed about his ongoing bedwetting. He is particularly concerned because he will be attending an overnight school camp in a few months. Ryan is worried about his classmates finding out about his condition. He wants to know how common the condition is and whether there is any way to prevent bedwetting during the school camp.

How common is enuresis in children?

The prevalence of enuresis varies across studies but is commonly reported as 10% to 15% at 6 years of age, approximately 3% to 5% at 10 years, and 1% to 2% in adolescents and young adults. The condition is more common in boys than in girls.

What are the treatment options for PMNE?

Effective treatment begins with an open and supportive discussion with both the child and their family. It is important to reassure them that enuresis is a relatively common condition that they should not be ashamed of, and that effective treatment options are available. Misconceptions are not uncommon; some parents may believe the bedwetting is due to laziness, a lack of motivation to wake up or even blame themselves for poor toilet training. This highlights the importance of understanding the parents' perceptions and addressing any misconceptions they may have. Punishment is ineffective and only adds unnecessary stress and tension for both the child and the family.

General Advice

- Drink adequately during the daytime, but avoid large amounts of fluid intake 1 to 2 hours before bedtime.
- Regular voiding during the day, and void before sleep.
- Identify and treat constipation.
- Avoid caffeine-containing food or drinks which can irritate the bladder, such as tea, coffee and chocolate.

Simple Behavioural Interventions (e.g. Star Charts or Reward Systems)

These strategies are most suitable for children who are developmentally able to cooperate and understand the goals of treatment. They involve positive reinforcement to encourage desired behaviours. Gradual and realistic goals should be set between the child and their parents, based on the child's current status. Rewards can be offered not only for dry nights but also for other signs of progress, such as helping to change the bedding, thereby reinforcing effort and involvement. While the resolution rate with behavioural interventions is relatively modest (estimated at around 25%), this approach remains a reasonable first-line option, particularly in younger children.

Enuresis Alarm

An enuresis alarm is a device that detects moisture in the child's underwear or bedding and triggers an arousal stimulus, most commonly a ringing sound to wake the child. The goal is to interrupt bedwetting, prompt the child to wake and to void in the toilet. Success with alarm therapy relies heavily on parental involvement and consistency, as children often need assistance waking up or may otherwise just switch off the alarm. The device should be used every night without interruption. The success rate is around 50% to 70%, with a significant proportion of children achieving long-term resolution. However, poor compliance and early discontinuation are common, likely due to disrupted sleep for the child and family.

Follow-up support, such as a scheduled phone call, is recommended to improve adherence and outcomes. The therapy should be stopped, and the condition re-evaluated if there is no progress after 6 to 8 weeks of enuresis alarm treatment.

Desmopressin Therapy

Desmopressin is an antidiuretic vasopressin analogue which reduces nocturnal urine production when taken before bedtime. It is most effective in children with nocturnal polyuria, defined as nighttime urine output exceeding 130% of expected bladder capacity for age, as aforementioned. Desmopressin should be administered one hour before bedtime. Fluid intake should be restricted starting one hour before medication and for the subsequent 8 hours to optimise treatment efficacy and reduce the risk of hyponatraemia.

Desmopressin acts immediately to prevent wet nights, making it particularly useful for short-term needs, such as attending a school overnight camp, as in Ryan's case. Since its effect is limited to the night it is taken, daily use is required if the goal is ongoing symptom control. If there is no clinical response after several weeks, treatment should be discontinued. Reports show that up to 70% of children experience dry nights during treatment; however, relapse occurs in about half after stopping the medication.

What are the treatment options for therapy-resistant patients?

In patients who are resistant to standard therapies such as desmopressin and enuresis alarm, a thorough reassessment is essential. This should include a detailed review of treatment compliance, evaluation of any comorbid conditions and assessment of voiding patterns and bowel habits. In such cases, uroflowmetry is recommended to exclude other underlying conditions such as anatomical obstruction or neurogenic bladder. Additionally, post-void residual urine should ideally be measured before initiating anticholinergic therapy. Referral to a specialist is advised for further evaluation and management.

Anticholinergic medications, such as oxybutynin and tolterodine, work by relaxing the detrusor muscle and increasing bladder capacity. These medications are commonly used to treat bladder overactivity and may be particularly helpful in children with non-monosymptomatic nocturnal enuresis or those who do not respond to desmopressin. Since detrusor overactivity is a contributing mechanism in some cases of enuresis, anticholinergics can be an effective part of the treatment strategy. However, side effects include constipation and post-void residual urine, which may predispose the child to urinary tract infections. Therefore, families should be educated about healthy voiding habits and the warning signs of urinary infection. Other therapies that have been reported or studied include imipramine (a tricyclic antidepressant), acupuncture and urotherapy, but their efficacy and safety profiles may need further evaluation.

35.3 Case Illustrations

Primary monosymptomatic nocturnal enuresis (PMNE) is defined as nighttime bedwetting in children aged ≥5 years who have never achieved consistent nighttime dryness for ≥6 months and have no daytime urinary symptoms. It must be distinguished from secondary and non-monosymptomatic forms, which may indicate underlying pathology. Assessment includes ruling out red flags and evaluating bowel habits and comorbidities. Treatment options include behavioural strategies, enuresis alarms and desmopressin, with specialist referral warranted in resistant cases.

Suggested Further Readings

1. Nevéus T, Fonseca E, Franco I, Kawauchi A, Kovacevic L, Nieuwhof-Leppink A, et al. Management and treatment of nocturnal enuresis-an updated standardisation document from the International Children's Continence Society. J Pediatr Urol. 2020;16(1):10–9.
2. Vande Walle J, Rittig S, Bauer S, Eggert P, Marschall-Kehrel D, Tekgul S. Practical consensus guidelines for the management of enuresis. Eur J Pediatr. 2012;171(6):971–83.
3. Kuwertz-Bröking E, von Gontard A. Clinical management of nocturnal enuresis. Pediatr Nephrol. 2018;33(7):1145–54.

A Boy Who Can't Wait

36

36.1 Case Description

You saw James, an 8-year-old boy, in your clinic who was referred for nocturnal enuresis. He had previously achieved daytime and nighttime continence at 3 years old. However, over the past 2 months, he had five episodes of bedwetting. During this time, he had also been experiencing sudden, strong needs to pass urine, having to rush to the toilet. Besides, he had been voiding more than 12 times per day, sometimes only 30 to 45 minutes after his last urination, with only small amounts each time. There was no associated fever, dysuria or haematuria.

36.2 Interactive Case Discussion

What urinary conditions were James presenting with?
From history, James was having the following:

- Secondary nocturnal enuresis: Recurrence of nocturnal enuresis after >6 months of dryness.
- Daytime urinary frequency: Eight or more times of urination during the daytime.
- Urgency: A sudden, strong need to void. Other behaviours suggestive of urgency include rushing to the bathroom, crossing of legs, grabbing the penis, squatting or sitting on heels.

What are the possible causes of James' urinary symptoms?
The combination of urinary frequency, urgency and secondary nocturnal enuresis is characteristic of overactive bladder, supported by the observation of small voided volumes. Other differential causes or contributing factors include the following:

W. K. Y. Chan, M. C. I. Kuok, *Paediatric Nephrology*,
https://doi.org/10.1007/978-981-95-5060-9_36

- Urinary tract infection: Should be considered in children presented with frequency and urgency. However, the absence of fever and dysuria, with the long-standing history, makes this less likely.
- Constipation: Can lead to urinary frequency and urgency, and contribute to bladder overactivity, or may indicate bladder-bowel dysfunction.
- Causes of polyuria: These include diabetes mellitus and diabetes insipidus, which typically present with increased urine volumes and polydipsia.
- Psychological stressors: Particularly relevant in secondary nocturnal enuresis, and stress may also worsen urgency.
- Structural or neurological causes: Less likely given the sudden onset of symptoms at 8 years in a previously continent child. Nonetheless, assessment for spinal dysraphism and lower limb neurology, including gait, remains important.

What investigations can help identify the cause of the symptoms?

- Urine dipstick: A simple test to detect the presence of leukocytes and nitrites for urinary tract infection, and glycosuria which may indicate diabetes mellitus.
- Bladder diary: Records patient's drinking habits and voiding patterns. Typical findings in overactive bladder include urinary frequency with small voided volumes. Episodes of urge incontinence and nocturnal enuresis can also be recorded in the diary. The total urine volume per day helps exclude polyuria.
- Uroflowmetry: An objective assessment to screen for voiding dysfunction or bladder outlet obstruction.

What is uroflowmetry?

Uroflowmetry is a simple and non-invasive test that measures the speed, duration and volume of urine flow during voiding. The child is instructed to drink enough water to achieve a comfortably full bladder, with the voided volume ideally at least 50% of the expected bladder capacity. The child then voids into a toilet or a funnel connected to an electronic flowmeter, which collects the voiding parameters. The test is often followed by a bladder scan to assess the post-void residual volume. The sum of voided volume and post-void residual represents the bladder capacity.

Uroflowmetry provides data on the urine flow rate, which is dependent on bladder contraction, relaxation of the bladder outlet sphincters and a patent urethral outflow tract. Abdominal straining, which is sometimes used as a compensatory mechanism to empty the bladder, can also be reflected. Analysis of different uroflow curve patterns, which plot urinary flow rate against time, provides further clues on the underlying voiding problems (Fig. 36.1).

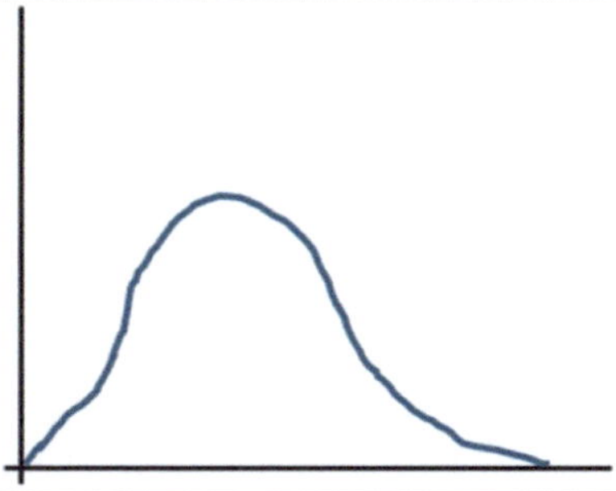	Shape: Bell-shaped curve Appearance: Smooth and single-peaked curve Interpretation: Suggests normal detrusor contraction and no obstruction of urinary flow
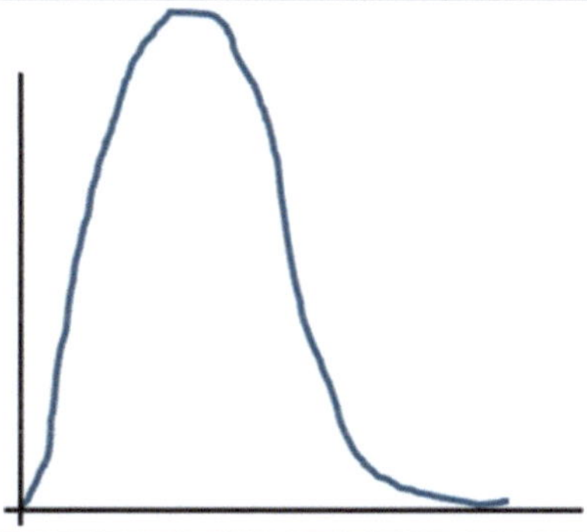	Shape: Tower-shaped curve Appearance: Sharp peak with high flow rate and shorter duration Interpretation: Suggests overactive bladder with forceful detrusor contraction and small voided volume
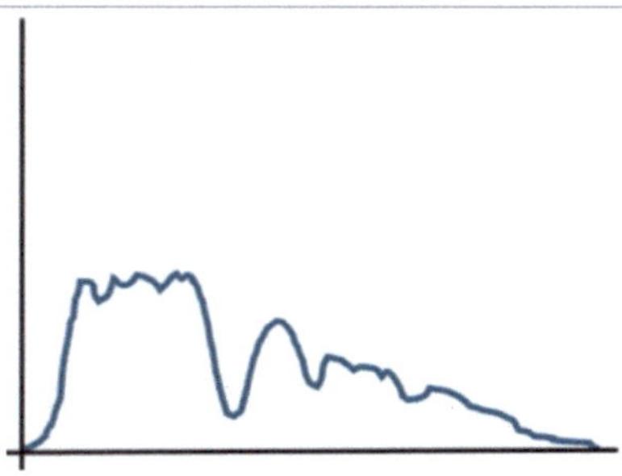	Shape: Staccato curve Appearance: Fluctuating flow pattern with multiple peaks, but the urine flow does not stop completely. Interpretation: Suggests dysfunctional voiding, with uncoordinated sphincter activities during voiding.
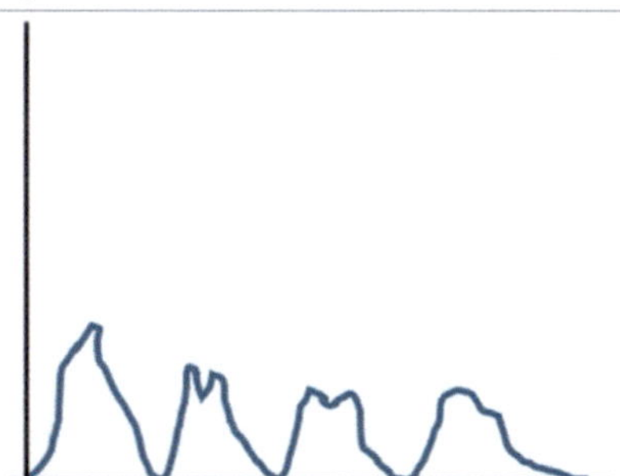	Shape: Interrupted curve Appearance: Non-continuous voiding with starts and stops Interpretation: Suggests an underactive detrusor muscle, with voluntary abdominal straining to empty the bladder
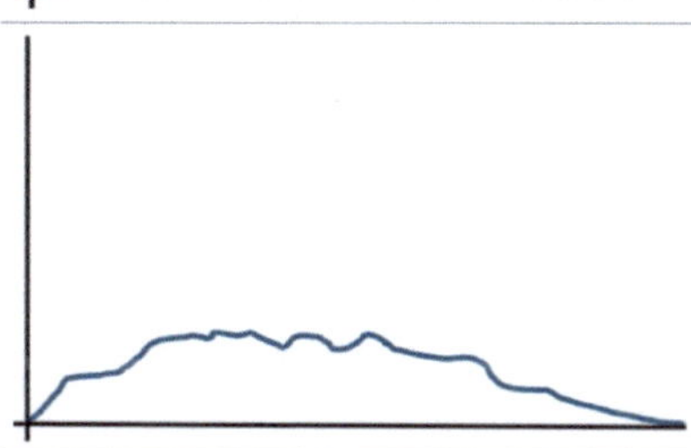	Shape: Plateau curve Appearance: Low flow rate over a prolonged period without a clear peak Interpretation: Suggests outlet obstruction, unable to generate high flow due to resistance

Fig. 36.1 Different uroflow curve patterns

The addition of pelvic floor electromyography (EMG) applied to the skin around the anus can provide further diagnostic information on pelvic floor activity during voiding. Normally, the pelvic floor muscles should be relaxed to allow uninterrupted urine flow; therefore, any activity in the pelvic floor during voiding can be considered abnormal. Furthermore, a time delay between pelvic floor relaxation from EMG and actual urinary flow may suggest bladder neck dysfunction.

James' urine dipstick was unremarkable, showing no leukocytes, nitrites or glucose. His bladder diary confirmed urinary frequency during daytime with voided volume ranging from 30 ml to 100 ml, and there were episodes of leaking before reaching the toilet. His uroflowmetry showed a tower-shaped curve with total void volume of 120 ml and a peak flow rate (Qmax) of 36 ml/s, without significant post-void residual volume. The overall findings were consistent with a diagnosis of overactive bladder.

What is the normal neurological control of bladder function in children?
Bladder function consists of two phases: the storage and voiding phases.

- Storage phase: Bladder filling is facilitated by stimulation of the hypogastric plexus (T10-L2), leading to sympathetic relaxation of the detrusor muscle and bladder neck contraction.
- Voiding phase: As the bladder stretches, signals are transmitted to the pontine micturition centre in the brainstem, and a descending signal through the spinal cord leads to parasympathetic stimulation from the sacral micturition centre (S2–S4) via pelvic splanchnic nerves and results in detrusor contraction and bladder neck relaxation. With age, children become increasingly aware of bladder distension and, through maturation of cortical control, learn to inhibit and delay voiding until it is socially acceptable.

Smooth coordination of these processes via intact neural pathways involving autonomic and somatic nerves is essential for normal bladder function and for achieving reliable continence in toilet-trained children.

What is an overactive bladder?
Overactive bladder (OAB) is a clinical syndrome defined by the presence of urinary urgency, usually accompanied by increased daytime frequency and/or nocturia. Based on symptoms, it is categorised as OAB-wet (with incontinence) or OAB-dry (without incontinence). The diagnosis is made in the absence of urinary tract infection or other identifiable pathology. OAB represents a form of storage-phase dysfunction, commonly observed in school-aged children, with a prevalence of 5–12% of children aged 5–10 years old.

The exact pathophysiology of OAB is not fully understood, but it is thought to involve delayed cortical maturation, abnormal urothelial-afferent signalling and neural pathways, and possible myogenic elements contributing to involuntary contractions. Detrusor instability is a urodynamic finding seen in some patients with OAB, characterised by involuntary detrusor contractions during the bladder filling phase.

What are the treatment approaches for overactive bladder in children?

Urotherapy is the first-line, non-surgical, non-pharmacological approach in the treatment of children with OAB. The key initial element is patient and family education, helping them understand the child's bladder dysfunction and how it relates to the presenting symptoms, which is important to improve treatment adherence and outcome. Constipation should always be identified and appropriately managed. Timed voiding, typically six times per day, along with adequate hydration, is encouraged, and positive reinforcement is used to sustain these behavioural changes. For children with significant post-void residual urine, double voiding is recommended to ensure bladder emptying.

Biofeedback is a behavioural therapy that teaches children to relax the pelvic floor muscles through interactive visual or auditory cues, often presented in a game-like format. This enhances the children's awareness of pelvic floor activity and improves muscle coordination, achieving better bladder control. While most effective in children with dysfunctional voiding, studies have also demonstrated that biofeedback can significantly improve symptoms of OAB.

Pharmacological treatment mainly includes anti-cholinergic agents and, more recently, beta-3 adrenoceptor agonists.

Anti-cholinergic Agents

These agents, such as oxybutynin, tolterodine and solifenacin, act by blocking muscarinic receptors on the bladder smooth muscle, thereby reducing the frequency of uninhibited detrusor contractions during the bladder filling phase and increasing bladder capacity. This class of medication remains the mainstay of pharmacological treatment in the majority of patients.

Beta-3 Adrenoceptor Agonists

Beta-3 adrenoceptor agonists promote relaxation of bladder smooth muscle during the storage phase, thus increasing bladder capacity without increasing voiding pressure or post-void residual volume. Mirabegron is an established treatment for OAB in adults and was approved by the FDA for use in children with neurogenic detrusor overactivity in 2021. Studies have demonstrated its effectiveness in treating paediatric OAB refractory to anti-cholinergic therapies.

What are the treatment options if the condition is refractory to conventional treatment?

Intravesical injection of botulinum toxin A has been used in children with OAB who are refractory to, or cannot tolerate, medical treatment. The toxin works by blocking acetylcholine release at the parasympathetic presynaptic neuromuscular junction, leading to reduced detrusor muscle contractility and improved urinary urgency in OAB. The clinical effect typically begins around 5–7 days, with the maximum effect achieved after 4–6 weeks. However, the effect only lasts around 6 months; therefore, re-injection is often required if symptoms recur.

Neuromodulation is another emerging therapeutic option with growing evidence of benefit in paediatric OAB. Electrostimulation of the parasacral or posterior tibial nerves, delivered via surface electrodes or fine needles, is postulated to suppress bladder overactivity by inhibiting excessive parasympathetic signalling that drives detrusor contractions. The posterior tibial nerve, a distal branch of the sciatic nerve (L5–S3 roots), provides a retrograde pathway to the sacral plexus, enabling modulation of bladder control pathways. Reported success rates of neuromodulation in OAB vary from 30% to 80%, likely due to differences in baseline symptom severity and neurostimulation protocols. The treatment is generally well tolerated in children, particularly when using transcutaneous electrode pads, and the increasing availability of home-based therapy further enhances the practicability. Neuromodulation is therefore considered a promising option for children with OAB unresponsive to behavioural and pharmacological treatment.

36.3 Case Illustrations

Careful history-taking, with the help of a bladder diary, can provide important clues to the underlying diagnosis in children presented with urinary symptoms. Uroflowmetry offers additional information and helps distinguish different pathologies, including overactive bladder. The first-line management of overactive bladder includes urotherapy and medical treatments such as anti-cholinergics and beta-3 adrenoceptor agonists. Botulinum toxin A injections and neuromodulation are promising options in refractory cases.

Suggested Further Readings

1. Franco I. Overactive bladder in children. Nat Rev Urol. 2016;13(9):520–32.
2. Shim J, Oh MM. Updates of overactive bladder in pediatrics. Int Neurourol J. 2023;27(1):3.
3. Clothier JC, Wright AJ. Dysfunctional voiding: the importance of non-invasive urodynamics in diagnosis and treatment. Pediatr Nephrol. 2018;33(3):381–94.

The Silent Progression

37

37.1 Case Description

Cindy was born at full term by caesarean section for a maternal history of previous uterine surgery. The antenatal history and ultrasound scan were unremarkable. She was born with a birth weight of 3.2 kg. We were consulted to assess Cindy, as a sacral dimple was noted after birth. Upon physical examination, Cindy's body weight and height were at the 50th centile. Her head circumference was at the 75th centile. The neurological examination was normal. There was a left buttock mass, located 1 cm above the anal opening. It is soft in consistency and measured around 8 cm in diameter. The overlying skin was intact. There was a sacral dimple. The lower limbs examination showed normal muscle tone and reflexes, but there was a right postural clubfoot. The anal tone was not decreased.

37.2 Interactive Case Discussion

How would you investigate Cindy's sacral mass?

Cindy has a subcutaneous soft buttock mass, which could be a lipoma. With the sacral dimple, one has to look for other features that may suggest an occult spinal dysraphism. Cutaneous midline back lesions such as a subcutaneous mass, a dermal vascular malformation, a tuft of hair, a midline dimple, a sinus tract, a skin tag or an asymmetric gluteal cleft may signify an underlying bony or spinal cord malformation. An X-ray, early ultrasound and MRI examination will help to make the diagnosis. Most infants with these occult spinal dysraphisms have normal lower limb neurology at birth. These lesions, however, are sometimes only detected when the child develops urinary problems, faecal incontinence or when there is asymmetry in the lower limb size and physical function, especially as the child grows older.

An X-ray of Cindy's lumbosacral spine showed partly fused S2 and S3 vertebral bodies (Fig. 37.1). An urgent ultrasound of the spine revealed a low-lying cord with

W. K. Y. Chan, M. C. I. Kuok, *Paediatric Nephrology*, https://doi.org/10.1007/978-981-95-5060-9_37

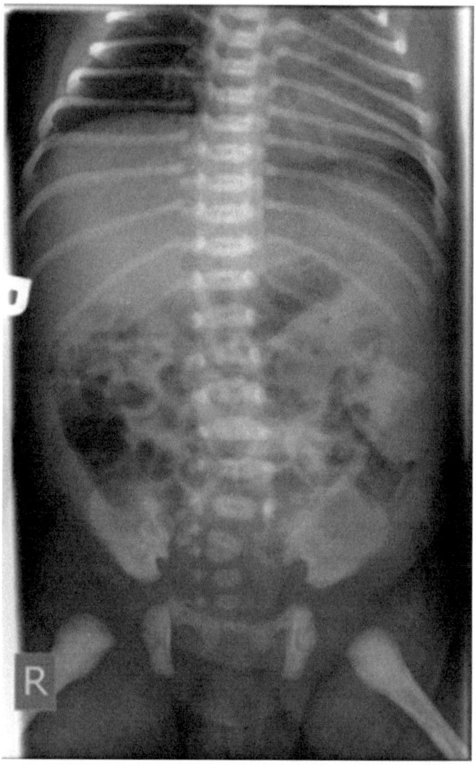

Fig. 37.1 The anteroposterior X-ray of the spine. Sacral vertebrae S2 and S3 were abnormal and appeared fused at the left osteal zones with angulation

lipomyelomeningocele and a nonspecific hyperechoic mass with hypoechoic rim over the left buttock (Fig. 37.2a, b). MRI of the lumbosacral region confirmed the diagnosis of lipomyelomeningocele with cord tethering. The left buttock lesion was contiguous with the subcutaneous lipomatous tissue and was part of the lipomyelomeningocele.

How would you assess Cindy's urological system?

The most urgent assessment was to decide whether Cindy can empty the bladder at low pressure and evaluate any impact on the upper urinary tract. Hence, the initial evaluation would involve an ultrasound of the bladder and the kidneys, a measurement of residual urine after voiding and a blood test for the serum urea and creatinine levels. An early urodynamic study and voiding cystogram would support the early evaluation of the lower urinary tract function.

Cindy's blood test was normal. The ultrasound of the kidneys showed a prominent left renal pelvis. The right kidney was normal, and the bladder outline was smooth. A baseline micturition cystourethrogram (MCUG) performed at 2 months of age showed a smooth bladder with a left-sided grade 3 vesicoureteric reflux (Fig. 37.3). The first urodynamic study performed at 3 months old showed a normal bladder compliance without bladder overactivity, and the residual urine was 14–15 ml. A Tc99m-DMSA renal scan was also performed at 3 months old and was normal.

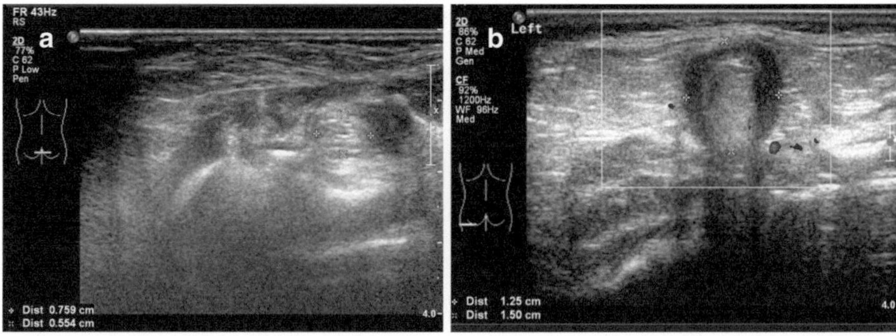

Fig. 37.2 (**a**) Ultrasound of the spine showed a low-lying spinal cord with distal end at the lumbosacral region, where it was continuous with an irregular soft tissue mass measuring about 0.76 cm × 0.56 cm in size. The intraspinal mass was, in turn, continuous and joined with the subcutaneous region of the lower back. (**b**) The ultrasound of the left buttock showed a hyperechoic mass with a hypoechoic rim, measuring 1.25 cm × 1.5 cm at the left buttock

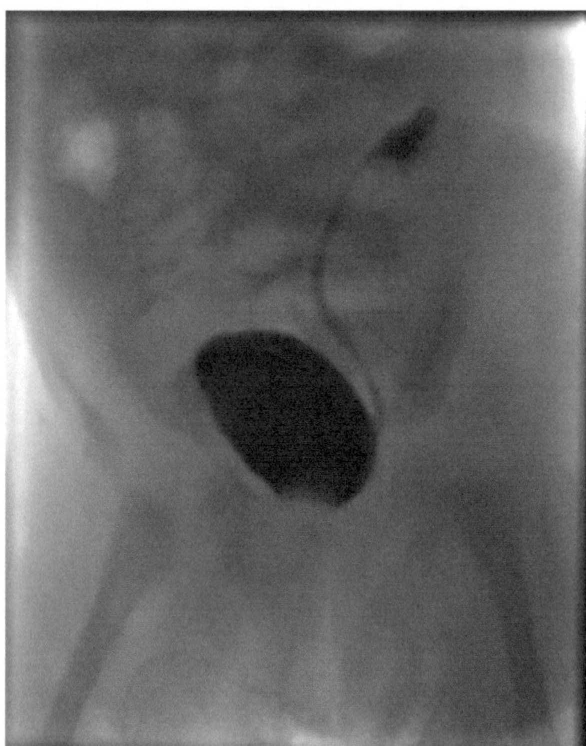

Fig. 37.3 Micturating cystourethrogram performed at 2 months of age showed a smooth bladder outline with left side grade 3 vesicoureteric reflux. The bladder emptying was prompt and normal

Would you start prophylactic antibiotics for Cindy in view of the grade 3 VUR?

For isolated vesicoureteric reflux without risk factors, a VUR of grade 3 severity is not routinely recommended for long-term antibiotic prophylaxis. However, in view of the underlying lipomyelomeningocele, Cindy has a high probability of having a neurogenic bladder despite her first urodynamic study being normal. There was no substantial evidence to suggest a routine antibiotic prophylaxis, and the practice depends on the preference of the centres.

Suppose Cindy was advised to take a nocturnal antibiotic for prophylaxis of urinary tract infection. To ensure compliance with treatment, the parents must be thoroughly counselled on the pros and cons of taking antibiotics and educated on the symptoms of urinary tract infections. An alternative recommendation is to keep observation and close surveillance of any urinary tract infection. Prompt administration of an antibiotic when there is a symptomatic or febrile urinary tract infection. In our centre, Cindy was advised to take regular antibiotics at night and monitored for any urinary tract infection.

What are the choices of prophylactic antibiotics?

The first-choice options of prophylactic antibiotics are usually either nitrofurantoin or trimethoprim-sulfamethoxazole (TMP-SMX). These antibiotics are inexpensive and well-tolerated, with effectiveness for long-term use. Neither oral cephalosporins nor amoxicillin-clavulanic acid is recommended as the initial therapy due to the risk of antibiotic resistance. There is no evidence to suggest a specific dose of the prophylactic antibiotics. In general, doses from one-quarter to one-third of the standard treatment dosage are recommended.

What is a neurogenic bladder, and how would you classify it?

The brain and spinal cord control the bladder and sphincter function through the autonomic nervous system and the somatic pudendal nerve.

- The sacral parasympathetic nerves (S2–S4) stimulate bladder contraction and relax the urethra.
- The lumbar sympathetic nerves (T11-L2) inhibit bladder contraction and stimulate bladder neck and urethral contraction.
- The pudendal nerve excites the external urethral sphincter.

Any lesions affecting the brain, spinal cord and autonomic nervous system will impact normal bladder function, resulting in neurogenic bladder or neurogenic bladder-sphincter dysfunction.

A normal bladder stores urine at a low pressure and empties without significant residual urine. A high-pressure, small and noncompliant bladder or a ‘flaccid bladder’ will fail to perform these functions. A normal sphincter function is the cornerstone to control urinary continence; an abnormal muscle tone of the sphincter will cause either urinary retention or urinary incontinence (Table 37.1).

Table 37.1 The different types of neurogenic bladder-sphincter dysfunction and the resultant medical problems

Dysfunction types	Sphincter muscle	Bladder (detrusor)	Clinical problems
Type A	Overactive	Underactive	– Urinary retention with high filling pressure and urinary leakage
Type B	Overactive	Overactive	– High filling pressure and high voiding pressure (DSD) – Very unsafe bladder since birth
Type C	Underactive	Underactive	– Bladder pressure is not high, but continuous urinary leakage (safe but wet)
Type D	Underactive	Overactive	– High filling pressure with continuous leakage

DSD detrusor sphincter dyssynergia

What is a urodynamic study?

In normal children, the detrusor, bladder neck and external urethral sphincter coordinate to allow adequate storage, voiding and secure urinary continence.

- The Koff Formula can estimate normal bladder capacity.
  - Bladder volume = [age (in years) + 2] × 30 ml.
- Urine storage with a low bladder pressure <10–15 cmH_2O.
- Effective voiding pressure is 50–80 cmH_2O in males and 40–65 cmH_2O in females.
- Post-void residual urine (PVRU) is minimal, and abnormal PVRU is defined.
  - For children aged 4–6 years, a single PVRU >30 ml or >21% bladder capacity or dual PVRU >20 ml or >10% bladder capacity is considered elevated.
  - For children aged 7–12 years, a single PVRU >20 ml or 15% bladder capacity, or dual PVRU >10 ml or 6% bladder capacity is considered elevated.

Urodynamic study is an invasive method, and it involves inserting catheters and electrodes to study the dynamic function of the bladder-sphincter function and coordination.

1. A triple-lumen urodynamic catheter was put into the bladder either transurethraly or suprapubically. It aims to measure the relationship between bladder pressure and volume during the filling, storage and emptying phases.
2. A catheter is inserted into the rectum to measure the intra-abdominal pressure during the cystometrogram to identify artefacts of motion, monitor abdominal pressure and determine the leak point pressure.
3. An electrode is inserted in the perineum to measure the electrical activity of the external urethral sphincter (electromyography).

A urodynamic study, hence, helps to assess the bladder and sphincter functions and provide information on the following:

- Bladder storage capacity.
- Bladder compliance.
- Leakage pressure.
- Detrusor overactivity (DO).
  - Defined as any short-lived pressure rise of >15 cm H_2O from baseline before the capacity is reached.
  - It is considered an abnormal finding at any time point.
- Voiding efficiency.
- Residual urine.
- Detrusor sphincter dyssynergia (DSD).

What are the risk factors for kidney damage and long-term renal function in a child with neurogenic bladder?
The risk factors for secondary kidney damage are related to factors that cause an 'unsafe bladder'. The clinical course of the patient, imaging results, urodynamic studies and renal function test help to predict the long-term outcome. These factors include the following:

- Any recurrent urinary tract infection and pyelonephritis.
- Significant Imaging results such as the following:
  - Any hydronephrosis detected in the ultrasound examination.
  - Any vesicoureteric reflux or abnormal bladder shape ± bladder trabeculations in the MCUG.
  - Abnormal Tc99m-DMSA renal scan that indicates kidney scars.
- Unfavourable urodynamic study.
  - Poor bladder compliance.
  - Detrusor filling pressure >40 cm H_2O.
  - Intermittent elevation of bladder pressure (means bladder hyperreflexia).
  - Persistent elevation of bladder pressure (detrusor hypertonia) results from a hypertrophic small-capacity bladder secondary to outflow tract obstruction.
  - Bladder outflow tract obstruction caused by DSD.
- Renal function test.
  - Abnormal serum creatinine or cystatin C in young age.

The initial assessment of Cindy before 3 months old did not have any unfavourable factors for subsequent renal damage except the presence of a left grade 3 VUR. Excision of the lipoma with laminectomy and lysis of adhesion of the spinal cord was performed when she was one year old. She remained stable without any history of urinary tract infection, and her renal function test was normal all along. After the laminectomy surgery, the parents decided to stop the prophylactic antibiotic, as apparently, Cindy was doing well. They also defaulted on the clinic follow-up, as the various appointments had exhausted the family, and travelling was a big issue during the COVID-19 pandemic. Cindy returned to the clinic at 3 years old as she was noticed to have an abnormal posture of her left foot. Reassessment revealed that Cindy still wore a diaper during the day and at night. Toilet training was not successful. Physical examination showed muscle wasting below the left knee with pes cavus of the left foot. Follow-up urodynamic study, MCUG and Tc99m-DMSA scan were repeated. It showed a drastic worsening in the bladder function, and Tc99m-DMSA scan showed scarring over the left kidney (Figs. 37.4 and 37.5). Cystoscopy showed turbid urine and severe bladder trabeculation. The urine culture showed overgrowth of mixed organisms. Urodynamic study showed an end-fill detrusor pressure up to 50 cmH_2O, a voided volume of 70 ml and a post-void residual urine of 165 ml. Electromyography of the sphincter at rest and during voiding was normal. With a high-pressure and incomplete voiding picture, clean intermittent catheterisation and oral oxybutynin were commenced. Subsequently, Cindy received an intravesical injection of botulinum toxin (Botox) to treat the bladder overactivity (Fig. 37.6). Her renal function test remained stable, and she was free from symptomatic urinary tract infections.

What is clean intermittent catheterisation (CIC)?

Before the widespread use of CIC in the management of neurogenic bladder, urinary tract infection and renal scarring were common in children with neurogenic bladder. Incomplete bladder emptying is a significant factor for recurrent urinary

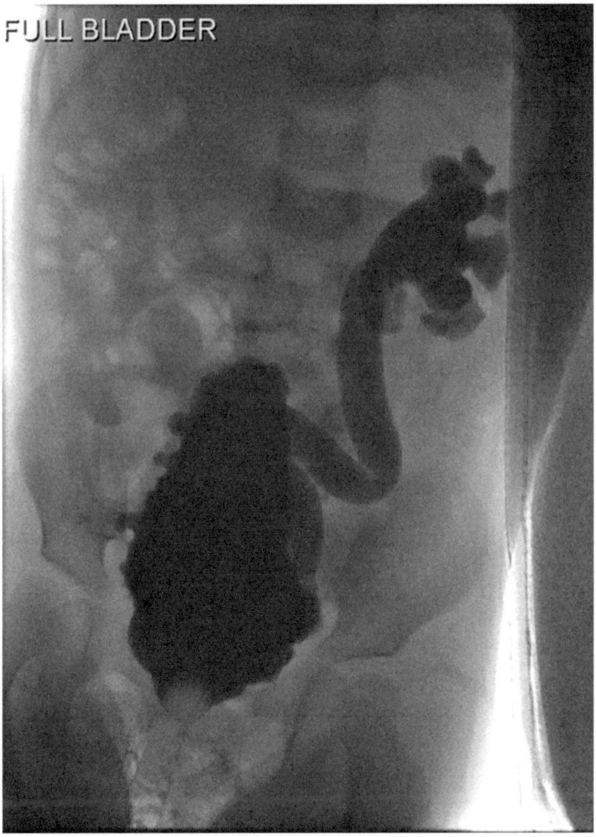

Fig. 37.4 Micturating cystourethrogram (MCUG) was performed at 3 years old. It showed an elongated urinary bladder with a pine cone appearance and sacculations. There was a grade 4 vesicoureteric reflux on the left side. Large post-void residual urine was noted after the examination

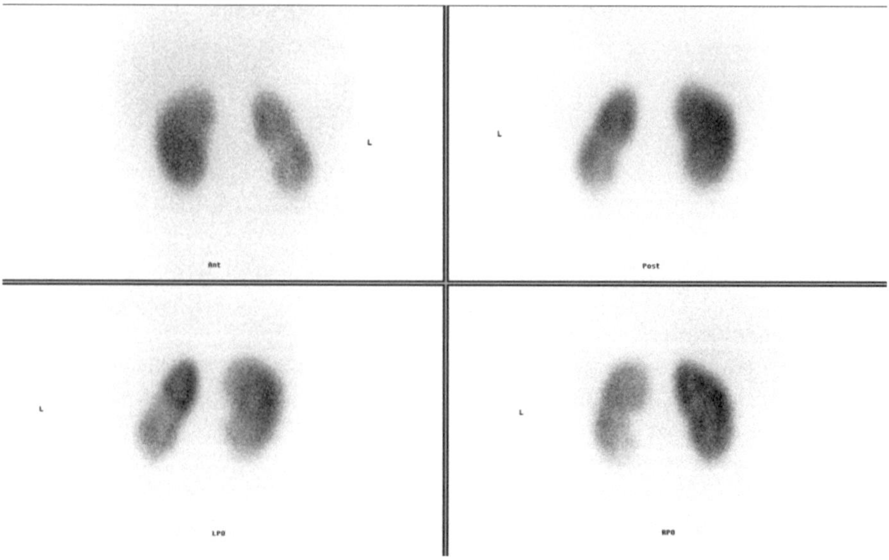

Fig. 37.5 Tc99m-DMSA scan performed at 3 years old showed moderately decreased DMSA uptake in the lower 2/3 of the left kidney, representing cortical scarring. The differential left-to-right function was 36%:64% as compared to 54%:46% at 3 months old, indicating progressive scarring of the left kidney

tract infection. CIC is the technique of intermittent catheterisation of the bladder using a single-use or a reused catheter. The procedure is performed in a clean technique, and it is not a sterile procedure.

It had been postulated that regular bladder emptying would prevent the bladder from overdistension, reduce intravesical bladder pressure and improve blood circulation in the bladder mucosa, making it more resistant to infection. Patients on CIC commonly have bacterial colonisation, but they are less prone to urinary tract infection compared to those with an indwelling catheter. Maybe during each emptying process, bacteria are 'drained' with the urine. However, the adherence to CIC treatment is always tricky. The reasons for nonadherence to CIC include the following:

- Lack of caregivers, especially when the child is placed in a nursery.
- Physical barriers of the child that affect adherence, like hypospadias in males or excessive adduction of the hips in females, make CIC not an easy procedure.
- Misconception, embarrassment and stigma of using a catheter to empty the bladder.
- Unacceptance by parents.
- Refusal by the child, especially if there are behaviour problems.
- Fear of injury or trauma to the urethra.
- Fear of introducing infection while putting in a catheter.
- Lack of public clean space for CIC.
- Lack of a proper training program and not being confident in performing the procedure.

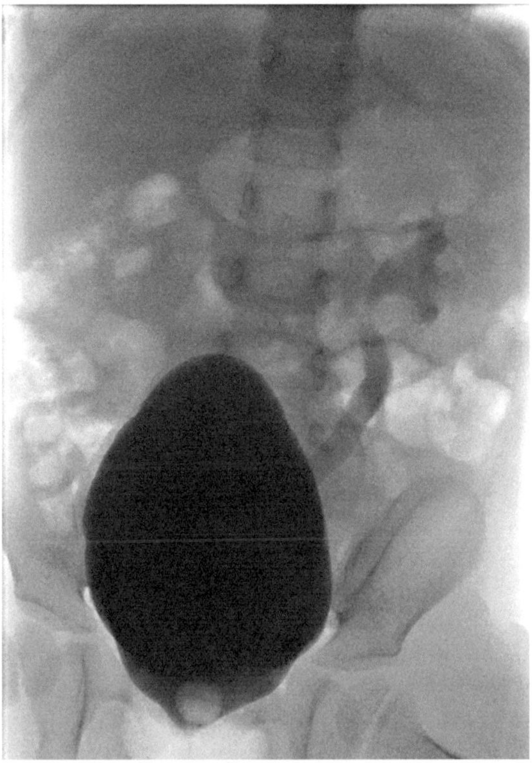

Fig. 37.6 Micturating cystourethrogram (MCUG) after intravesical injection of botulinum toxin (Botox). It still showed an elongated bladder with a pine cone shape, and the grade 4 vesicoureteric reflux persisted. Compared to the previous MCUG, the bladder volume increased and the abnormal sacculation was not observed

Some of the reasons for nonadherence are due to the physical health of the child, and most of the reasons are psychosocial-related and misconceptions. CIC has been used in the treatment of neurogenic bladder for more than 50 years; advancements in catheters and surgical procedures help enhance the acceptance of the treatment by the family and the child.

- CIC can be performed via the urethra or a continent catheterisable channel, such as a Mitrofanoff conduit, which facilitates self-catheterisation through a self-sealing opening in the abdomen.
- Pre-lubricated or low-friction hydrophilic-coated catheters help decrease pain and trauma during catheterisation.
- 'Touchless' or 'no-touch' catheters offer a good alternative when toilet facilities are not readily available.

How would you manage Cindy's medical problem?

Cindy is a child with a congenital lipomeningocele. Her urological problem is complex and not an isolated issue. A multidisciplinary approach is needed to address each medical problem. Apart from the kidney and urological problems, there are many other aspects the team needs to address, including neurogenic bowel, unequal limb length, pes cavus, retethering of the spinal cord, abnormal neurology of the lower limbs, psychosocial issues within the family and the child's overall well-being. Education issue, growth, pubertal impact and even future sexual function of the child need to be addressed as the child grows. Adherence to treatment recommendations is also essential.

Focusing on the nephron-urological issue, the treatment strategy and the goals of our treatment are the following:

Two Different Treatment Strategies
The proactive strategy recommends frequent laboratory, imaging and urodynamic studies, as well as early initiation of clean intermittent catheterisation, pharmacotherapy or surgery. The expectant strategy is a selective or reactive approach which suggests surveillance and reacting to abnormalities detected (Table 37.2).

The Goal of Treatment

1. To preserve kidney function.
   - Maintain a low bladder filling pressure.
2. Avoid urinary tract infection.
   - Avoid urinary retention.
   - Good bladder emptying (minimise excessive residual urine after void).
3. To be continent.
   - Able to keep dry in between voiding (social continence).

What is the prognosis of Cindy?
Cindy is at risk of developing chronic kidney disease (CKD), especially when her urodynamic study showed a high detrusor pressure with a noncompliant bladder. She has an abnormal renal cortical function at an early age. Hence, even though her serum creatinine is normal at this juncture, she is at risk of progression to

Table 37.2 The medical and surgical treatment of the neurogenic bladder-sphincter dysfunction

Site of the urological problem	Treatment options (medical and surgical)
The bladder	
Improve bladder emptying	– Intermittent bladder catheterisation, CIC
Improve bladder compliance and increase the bladder capacity	– Anticholinergic drugs (oxybutynin and tolterodine) – Injection of botulinum toxin into the bladder – Augmentation cystoplasty
The sphincter	
Augment the sphincter control to maintain urinary continence	– Endoscopic injection of bulking agents to the sphincter muscle – Surgical bladder neck reconstruction – Urethral lengthening procedure – Bladder neck suspension – Artificial urinary sphincter – Continent cystostomy with closure of the bladder neck
Bypass sphincter resistant	– Bladder catheterisation, CIC

CKD. Aggressive management of the neurogenic bladder, prompt treatment of any urinary tract infection, frequent monitoring of the bladder-kidney function, early detection and treatment of hypertension and proteinuria are all important in managing her nephron-urological problem.

37.3 Case Illustrations

Children with lipomyelomeningocele may have normal urological studies at presentation, which may mislead and give a false sense of security to parents and the managing doctors. The urological condition may deteriorate silently as the child grows. A proactive approach involving frequent assessments and early intervention before any abnormalities are detected may be a better option to prevent kidney damage.

The multifaceted management requires a multidisciplinary team approach. Parents must be educated on the life-long management plan, along with adequate social support, as adherence to treatment is of utmost importance. Early commencement of CIC, anticholinergic therapy, intravesical injection of botulinum toxin (Botox) and surgical augmentation to maintain a low bladder filling pressure are the cornerstones to protect the kidneys and avoid renal scarring. Cindy's case, 'The Silent Progression,' concludes the book's case series and serves as a reminder that kidney disease can develop without warning. Despite normal initial findings, Cindy developed renal scarring, underscoring the importance of vigilance in paediatric care.

Suggested Further Readings

1. Chua ME, Yadav P, Wang PZT, Mau EE, Keefe DT, De los Reyes TJ, et al. 2023 Canadian Urological Association/Pediatric Urologists of Canada guideline: Pediatric patients with neurogenic lower urinary tract dysfunction: full-text version. Can Urol Assoc J. 2023;17(10):E338.
2. Fairchild RJ, Aksenov LI, Hobbs KT, Krischak MK, Kaplan SJ, Purves JT, et al. Medical management of neurogenic bladder in patients with spina bifida: a scoping review. J Pediatr Urol. 2023;19(1):55–63.
3. Bauer SB, Austin PF, Rawashdeh YF, de Jong TP, Franco I, Siggard C, Jorgensen TM. International children's continence society's recommendations for initial diagnostic evaluation and follow-up in congenital neuropathic bladder and bowel dysfunction in children. Neurourol Urodyn. 2012;31(5):610–4.
4. Stein R, Bogaert G, Dogan HS, Hoen L, Kocvara R, Nijman RJ, et al. EAU/ESPU guidelines on the management of neurogenic bladder in children and adolescent part I diagnostics and conservative treatment. Neurourol Urodyn. 2020;39(1):45–57.

MIX
Papier aus verantwortungsvollen Quellen
Paper from responsible sources
FSC® C105338

If you have any concerns about our products,
you can contact us on
ProductSafety@springernature.com

In case Publisher is established outside the EU,
the EU authorized representative is:
Springer Nature Customer Service Center GmbH
Europaplatz 3, 69115 Heidelberg, Germany

Printed by Libri Plureos GmbH
in Hamburg, Germany